Sociobiology: Beyond Nature/Nurture?

Reports, Definitions and Debate

AAAS Selected Symposia Series

Published by Westview Press, Inc.
5500 Central Avenue, Boulder, Colorado

for the

American Association for the Advancement of Science
1776 Massachusetts Avenue, N.W., Washington, D.C.

Sociobiology: Beyond Nature/Nurture?

Reports, Definitions and Debate

Edited by George W. Barlow and James Silverberg

AAAS Selected Symposium **35**

AAAS Selected Symposia Series

This book is based on a symposium which was held at the 1978 AAAS National Annual Meeting in Washington, D.C., February 12-17. The symposium was sponsored by AAAS Sections G (Biological Sciences), H (Anthropology), J (Psychology), K (Social and Economic Sciences), L (History and Philosophy of Science), Q (Education), and X (General).

Published in 1980 in the United States of America by
Westview Press, Inc.
5500 Central Avenue
Boulder, Colorado 80301
Frederick A. Praeger, Publisher

Library of Congress Cataloging in Publication Data
Main entry under title:
Sociobiology:beyond nature/nurture?
(AAAS selected symposium ; 35)
"Based on a symposium ... held at the 1978 AAAS national annual meeting in Washington, D.C., February 12-17."
Includes bibliographical references and index.
1. Sociobiology. I. Barlow, George W. II. Silverberg, James. III. American Association for the Advancement of Science. IV. Series: American Association for the Advancement of Science. AAAS selected symposium ; 35.
GN365.9.S6155 306'4 80-10256
ISBN 0-89158-372-6
ISBN 0-89158-960-0 pbk.

Printed and bound in the United States of America

About the Book

To most biologists, sociobiology represents the concept of strict Darwinian individual selection married to an analytical application of ecological principles and brought to bear on social behavior in an unusually exciting and productive way. Joining the biologists are a small number of social scientists. But there are radically divergent views as to how the field should be delimited, and sociobiology is one of the most widely discussed fields in biology and anthropology today.

The symposium on which this book is based was arranged by a biologist and an anthropologist. The participants, leaders in their fields, ably present contrasting and responsible views on current issues. This is the first collection of essays on sociobiology in which opposing views are aired. It is an exciting, timely book and an important historical document.

About the Series

The *AAAS Selected Symposia Series* was begun in 1977 to provide a means for more permanently recording and more widely disseminating some of the valuable material which is discussed at the AAAS Annual National Meetings. The volumes in this *Series* are based on symposia held at the Meetings which address topics of current and continuing significance, both within and among the sciences, and in the areas in which science and technology impact on public policy. The *Series* format is designed to provide for rapid dissemination of information, so the papers are not typeset but are reproduced directly from the camera-copy submitted by the authors. The papers are organized and edited by the symposium arrangers who then become the editors of the various volumes. Most papers published in this *Series* are original contributions which have not been previously published, although in some cases additional papers from other sources have been added by an editor to provide a more comprehensive view of a particular topic. Symposia may be reports of new research or reviews of established work, particularly work of an interdisciplinary nature, since the AAAS Annual Meetings typically embrace the full range of the sciences and their societal implications.

WILLIAM D. CAREY
Executive Officer
American Association for the Advancement of Science

Contents

About the Editors and Authors................xvii

Preface.....................................xxiii

PART 1. INTRODUCTION

1 The Development of Sociobiology: A Biologist's Perspective--*George W. Barlow*.......3

Biological Roots 3
Evolutionary Genetics, 4; Ecology, 8; Ethology, 10
Sociobiology and the Social Sciences 11
Epigenesis 12
Relevance of Animal Behavior 14
Adaptiveness, 15; Posing Questions, 16; Inaccessible Questions, 16; Resistance to Comparisons, 16; Ideas and Their Implementation, 17
Scope of This Book 18
Summary 18
Acknowledgements 19
Literature Cited 19

2 Sociobiology, the New Synthesis? An Anthropologist's Perspective--*James Silverberg*.................................25

Anthropology: A Science of Human Adaptation 25
A Discipline That Is Both Biological and Cultural, 26; Language, Linguistics

and Anthropology,27; How Anthropologists Study Human Behavior,28; "Primatology,"32; The Continuity of Life vs. Human Uniqueness,33; Synthesis Through a Focus on Human Adaptation,33

Sociobiology: Neither Sin-Thesis Nor the Great Beyond 35

Reductionism: The Synthesis of Teeth and Tasty Morsel,36; "Beyond Nature/Nurture" ≠ Beyond Inherited vs. Learned,38

Some Fallacies and Cautions in the Study of Human Behavioral Data 41

Don't Attribute What Is Learned to the Genes for a Learning Capacity, 41; Some Cautions in Using Adaptation and Selection as Explanatory Concepts,44; Downplaying Behavioral Diversity in General,50; Downplaying Human Behavioral Diversity,53; Inferring Biological Significance from Culture Trait Distributions,57; The Early Pleistocene Behavioral Fixation, 59; Interpreting by Labelling,60

Conclusions 62

Summary 63

Acknowledgements 66

Literature Cited 66

PART 2. VIEWED FROM AFAR

3 Sociobiology: Another New Synthesis--*David L. Hull* 77

The Sociology of Science 79

The Essence of Sociobiology 84

Conclusion 90

Summary 91

Acknowledgements 93

Literature Cited 93

4 A Critical Examination of Current Sociobiological Theory: Adequacy and Implications--*Arthur L. Caplan* 97

Values and Sociobiology 97

Determinism 98

Nature/Nurture 100

Evolutionary Theory and Sociobiology 100
Methodological Difficulties 101
Causation,101; Comparison,104; Adaptation,108
Ethics, Politics and Values 111
Summary 113
Literature Cited 113

PART 3. THE ORGANISM IN ITS ENVIRONMENT

5 Ecological Determinism and Sociobiology--*Stephen T. Emlen*....125

Basic Principles of Ecological Sociobiology 129
To Be or Not to Be Social,129; Costs and Benefits of Territoriality,131; Ecological Determinants of Mating Systems,135
Relevance to Human Sociobiology 137
Summary 143
Acknowledgements 144
Literature Cited 144

6 The Coevolution of Behavioral and Life-History Characteristics--*Robert R. Warner*.....151

The Nature of Adaptations 153
Environmental Parameters 155
Primary Adaptations 159
Primary Adaptations in Life History, 159; Primary Adaptations in Social/Mating Systems, 163
Secondary Adaptations 167
Secondary Adaptations in Life History,167; Secondary Adaptations in Social and Mating Systems,170
Discussion 172
Phylogenetic Constraints,172; Short-Term Adaptive Responses,174; Testing Hypotheses,174
Summary 177
Acknowledgements 179
Literature Cited 180

7 Foraging, Social Dispersion and Mating Systems--*Jack W. Bradbury*....189

Introduction 189

Embballonurid Bats 191
Greater Spear-Nosed Bats 196
Epomophorine Bats and Lek Behaviors 199
Closing Comments 203
Summary 203
Acknowledgements 204
Literature Cited 204

8 Predictive Sociobiology: Mate Selection in Damselfishes and Brood Defense in White-Crowned Sparrows--*David P. Barash* 209

Two Predictions and Their Tests 213
Mate Selection Among Damselfishes, 213; Brood Defense Among White-Crowned Sparrows, 219
Summary 224
Acknowledgements 224
Literature Cited 225

9 Tradition and the Social Transmission of Behavior in Animals--*Danilo Mainardi*..........227

Nongenetic Transmission of Information Can Be Conservative or Innovative 230
Situations and Behaviors Linked to Social Transmission 236
Evolutionary Aspects of Social Transmission 241
Summary 244
Acknowledgements 245
Literature Cited 245

10 Sociobiology and the Theory of Natural Selection-- *Stephen Jay Gould*.................257

Natural Selection as Storytelling 257
Sociobiological Stories 259
Special Problems for Human Sociobiology 262
Limited Evidence and Political Clout, 262; Adaptation in Humans Need Not Be Genetic and Darwinian, 264
Failure of the Research Program for Human Sociobiology 264

Summary 267
Literature Cited 268

PART 4. GENES AND THE GAMES THEY PLAY

11 Genetics of Animal and Human Behavior-- *John C. DeFries* 273

Introduction 273
Open-Field Behavior 273
Social Dominance 281
Specific Cognitive Abilities 287
Conclusion 289
Summary 290
Acknowledgements 291
Literature Cited 291

12 A Consideration of the Genetic Foundation of Human Social Behavior-- *Edward O. Wilson*...295

Summary 303
Literature Cited 304

13 Cultural Causes of Genetic Change--*Frank B. Livingstone*....................................307

Models of Evolutionary Change 308
Genetic and Behavioral Variation 309
Drinking Habits and Genetic Change 313
Cultural Adaptation and Genetic Change 315
Cultural and Genetic Causes of the Incest Taboo 316
Ongoing Genetic Evolution and Its Cultural Causes 319
The Problem of Population Control and Its Cultural Causes 322
Summary 325
Literature Cited 325

14 Good Strategy or Evolutionarily Stable Strategy?-- *Richard Dawkins*..................331

Genes and Strategies 331
Good, Bad and Stable 332
Fishers and Pirates--A Hypothetical Example 333

Diggers and Enterers--A Real Example 334
An ESS Is Not Necessarily Optimal, but It Is Uncheatable 335
Dying Gasp Retaliation 336
The Strategy Set 337
Discrete Strategies or Continuum? 338
The Cowpat War 340
A Mixed Strategy Can Be Mixed Within an Individual or Can Be a Polymorphism 341
Frequency-Dependent Behavior 343
Conditional Versus Mixed Strategies 343
Making the Best of a Bad Job 344
One Generation's Conditional Strategy as the Previous Generation's Mixed Strategy 346
Sons Versus Daughters as Parental Strategy 347
Broad Applicability of the ESS Concept 348
Cooperative ESSs 352
The Individual Phenotype as a Genetic Strategy 353
Developmentally Stable Strategy and Culturally Stable Strategy 354
Is Anything Not an ESS? 356
Summary 358
Acknowledgements 361
Literature Cited 361

PART 5. SEX AND REPRODUCTIVE STRATEGIES

15 Kin Selection and the Paradox of Sexuality--*George C. Williams* 371

History of the Concept of a Cost of Sexuality 372
Meiosis as a Problem for Kin Selection and Outbreeding 372
Recent Models of the Cost of Meiosis 375
Isogamy and Anisogamy 377
Paternal Investment 380

The Paradox of Sexuality 381
Summary 382
Acknowledgements 383
Literature Cited 383

16 Genes, Hormones, Sex and Gender--
Elizabeth Kocher Adkins........................385

Sex Differences and Psychosexual Differentiation in Nonhuman Mammals 385
Sex Differences and Psychosexual Differentiation in Humans 387
Sex Differences in Human Behavior, 387; Psychosexual Differentiation in Humans: Gender Identity in Cases with Incongruous Sex or Absent Gonads, 390; Psychosexual Differentiation in Humans: Subjects with Abnormal Prenatal Hormone Exposure Compared with Controls,393
Comparison of Human and Nonhuman Data 399
Homosexuality 401
Conclusions 403
Summary 406
Acknowledgements 407
Literature Cited 407

17 Is Yomut Social Behavior Adaptive?--
William Irons 417

Some Alternative Working Hypotheses: Group Versus Individual Selection 418
The Data 423
The Population Under Study 424
The Group-Selection Hypothesis 424
The Individual-Selection Hypothesis 436
The Null Hypothesis 456
Conclusion 457
Summary 457
Acknowledgements 459
Literature Cited 459

18 Social Behavior, Biology and the Double Standard--*Eleanor Leacock* 465

Evolutionary Levels and Sociobiological Theory 465
Sociobiological Conjectures and Ethnographic Data 469
Social Behavior in Egalitarian Societies, 472; Male Dominance and the Double Standard, 476
Sociobiology and Social Considerations 479
Summary 483
Acknowledgements 484
Literature Cited 484

19 Nineteenth-Century Evolutionary Theory and Male Scientific Bias--*Stephanie A. Shields* 489

Assumptions Regarding Gender Differences 490
The Traits of Women 493
Gentility, 494; Perceptiveness, 495; Emotional Lability, 495
Values and Science 496
Implications for Sociobiology 498
Summary 499
Literature Cited 500

PART 6. NEPOTISM AND CONFLICT

20 The Limits of Ground Squirrel Nepotism--*Paul W. Sherman* 505

Introduction 505
Study Animal and Techniques 507
Sexual Dimorphism in Dispersal 509
Nepotism Does Not Occur Among Males 511
Nepotism Among Females 512
Alarm Calls and Nest Burrow Defense are Nepotistic, 512; Close Relatives Seldom Fight When Establishing Nest Burrows, 513; Close Relatives are Permitted Access to Defended Areas, 515; Close Relatives Codefend Areas, 519; Close Relatives Cooperate Directly to Defend Their Young, 519; Close

Relatives Warn Each Other When Predatory Mammals Approach, 521
Mechanism by Which Close Relatives Are Favored 524
Recognition "Errors" and the Ontogeny of Recognition 526
The Limits of Nepotism 529
Summary 535
Acknowledgements 536
Literature Cited 537

21 Kin-Selection Theory, Kinship, Marriage and Fitness Among the Yąnomamö Indians--*Napoleon A. Chagnon* 545

Introduction 545
Favoring Kin 549
Differences in Reproductive Success 551
Possible Adaptiveness of Yąnomamö Marriages 558
Fitness and Cross-Cousin Marriage in One Descent Group 560
Summary 568
Acknowledgements 569
Literature Cited 569

22 Kin Selection, Fitness and Cultural Evolution--*B. J. Williams*.....................573

Kin Selection 573
Group Selection and Cultural Evolution 580
Summary 584
Acknowledgements 585
Literature Cited 585

23 Parent-Offspring Conflict--*Judy A. Stamps and Robert A. Metcalf* 589

Theoretical Models of Parent-Offspring Conflict 590
Parent-Offspring Conflict and Reproductive Success, 590; Conditions for the Spread of Selfish Alleles, 593; Coefficient of Relationship and Parent-Offspring Conflict, 598

Empirical Tests of Parent-Offspring Conflict 600
Does Conflict Exist in Nature? 600; Control of Egg Laying in Social Hymenoptera,601; Control Over Sex Ratios in Social Hymenoptera,603; Brood Reduction in Birds,605
Parent-Offspring Conflict Versus Altruism 611
Summary 613
Literature Cited 614

Index....................................619

About the Editors and Authors

George W. Barlow *is professor of zoology at the University of California-Berkeley. His most recent work has focused on the social and mating behavior of Cichlid fishes, and on life-history strategies of coral-reef fishes. He has published more than 80 articles in his field. He is president of the Animal Behavior Society of North America, a former chairman of the Ecology Division of the American Society of Zoologists, and a former member of the National Science Foundation's Panel on Psychobiology. He currently serves on the editorial boards of* Behavioral Ecology and Sociobiology *and* Behavior and Brain Sciences.

James Silverberg *is professor of anthropology at the University of Wisconsin-Milwaukee. He has done field research in India, Mexico, Colombia, and Venezuela. He has written many papers in his field; has written or edited three films; and is the editor of and a contributor to several books, including* The Mode of Production: Method and Theory *(Queen's College Press, in press). He has served on the executive board of the Society for Applied Anthropology, and has been a representative to Section H and a member of Council, American Association for the Advancement of Science.*

Elizabeth Kocher Adkins *is assistant professor of psychology at Cornell University. She has published numerous articles on the hormonal bases of sexual and aggressive behavior in birds, reptiles and fish, with emphasis on the role of sex hormones in the psychosexual differentiation on non-mammalian vertebrates.*

David P. Barash, *a former fellow at the Center for Advanced Study in the Behavioral Sciences, is associate professor of psychology and zoology at the University of Washington-Seattle. A specialist in sociobiology, he has emphasized the link between evolutionary biology and the social behavior* *of insects, fish, birds and mammals. His many publications include two books,* The Whisperings Within *(Harper & Row, 1979) and* Sociobiology and Behavior *(Elsevier North-Holland, 1977).*

Jack W. Bradbury *is an associate professor of biology at the University of California-San Diego. Since 1969 he has been studying social evolution in vertebrates, particularly bats, with primary focus on the role of foraging in social evolution. Much of his extensive field work in Central America and in West Africa has emphasized the role of foraging in determining group size and spacing, mating systems, and parental investment patterns in various bats. His recent work has been concerned with the genetic consequences of harem mating.*

Arthur L. Caplan, *a philosopher of science, is an associate for the humanities at the Hastings Center and an associate for social medicine at the College of Physicians and Surgeons, Columbia University. He has published widely on sociobiology, ethics and science, and is the author of* The Sociobiology Debate *(Harper & Row, 1978).*

Napoleon A. Chagnon *is professor of anthropology at Pennsylvania State University. He has specialized in the social organization of tribal peoples; emphasizing quantitative and demographic aspects of social life; marriage systems as mating systems; tribal politics; economics and warfare; and population expansion, dispersal and settlement patterns. His extensive field research, particularly among the Yanomamö Indians, has yielded 21 documentary films, numerous articles and several books, most recently,* Evolutionary Biology and Human Social Behavior: An Anthropological Perspective *(coedited with W. Irons; Duxbury Press, 1979).*

Richard Dawkins *is University Lecturer in Animal Behaviour at Oxford University, and a Fellow of New College. His earlier research focused on the development and experimental testing of theoretical models in ethology, especially stochastic and hierarchical models of animal decision-making. Recently he has become more interested in functional and evolutionary models of decision-making in animals. He is the author of* The Selfish Gene *(Oxford University Press, 1976), and is now working on a book about the levels at which natural selection acts.*

John C. DeFries *is a professor of behavioral genetics and psychology at the Institute of Behavioral Genetics and Psychology, University of Colorado-Boulder. He is the author of* Introduction to Behavioral Genetics *(with*

G.E. McClearn; Freeman, 1973). He was the editor of Behavior Genetics *from 1970 to 1978 and is a former secretary of the Behavior Genetics Association.*

Stephen T. Emlen, *a professor of animal behavior at Cornell University, has done extensive field research, primarily in East Africa, and has written numerous articles dealing with the mating systems of birds and amphibians; adaptiveness of colonial or gregarious living, cooperative breeding social systems, and communication in birds; and orientation and navigation systems in vertebrates. He is a member of the National Research Council (National Academy of Sciences) and of the NSF Psychobiology Review Panel.*

Stephen Jay Gould, *professor of geology at Harvard University and curator of invertebrate paleontology, Museum of Comparative Zoology, is a specialist in evolutionary theory and its history. A member or former member of the editorial boards of* Systematic Zoology, Paleobiology, *and* American Naturalist, *he is also the author of* Ever Since Darwin: Reflections in Natural History *(W.W. Norton, 1977) and* Ontogeny and Phylogeny *(Harvard University Press, 1977). In 1975 he received the Schuchert Award for excellence in paleontological research.*

David L. Hull *is a professor in the Department of Philosophy at the University of Wisconsin-Milwaukee. His specific interest is the philosophy of biology, and he is the author of* Darwin and His Critics *(Harvard University Press, 1974) and* Philosophy of Biological Science *(Prentice-Hall, 1974). He is a member of the editorial boards of* Systematic Zoology *and* Philosophy of Science.

William Irons, *a specialist in human ecology, sociobiology and anthropology in the Middle East, is associate professor of anthropology at Northwestern University. Coeditor of* Evolutionary Biology and Human Social Behavior: An Anthropological Perspective *(with N.A. Chagnon; Duxbury Press, 1979), he is also the author of articles on the implications of natural selection theory for human behavior, human kinship and kin selection, and economic behavior and reproductive success.*

Eleanor Leacock, *professor and chair, Department of Anthropology, City College of New York, is a social anthropologist and a specialist in studies of urban and gatherer-hunter societies, North American Indians, women cross-culturally, and education. She is coeditor of* Women and Colonization: Anthropological Perspectives *(with M. Etienne; J.F. Bergin, in press) and* North American Indians in Historical

Perspective *(with N.O. Lurie; Random House, 1971). She is the author of various articles on sociobiology, social evolution and male-female cross-cultural relations. Now president of the Council of Anthropology and Education, she has also served on the executive boards of the American Anthropological Association and the Society for Applied Anthropology.*

Frank B. Livingstone, *a specialist in biological anthropology, human population genetics, and human evolution, is professor of anthropology at the University of Michigan-Ann Arbor. He has published on the topics of natural selection in man, simulation of human population genetic change, abnormal hemoglobins in human populations, and the sickle cell gene, and is the author of* **Abnormal Hemoglobins in Human Populations** *(Aldine, 1967).*

Danilo Mainardi, *a specialist in the evolution of behavior, is professor of general biology in the Faculty of Medicine, University of Parma, and director of the School of Ethology of the Ettore Majorana Centre for Scientific Culture. A researcher in the field of biological evolution, his interests include phylogenetic relationships in groups of vertebrates, the influence of early learning on sexual selection, and the relationship between cultural and biological evolution. He is the author of* **L'animale culturale** *(Milan: Rizzoli, 1974) and* **La scelta sessuale** *(Turin: Boringhieri, 1975).*

Robert A. Metcalf *is assistant professor of zoology at the University of California-Davis. His specific area of specialization is behavior and genetics of the social insects.*

Paul W. Sherman, *assistant professor of psychology at the University of California-Berkeley, is primarily interested in behavioral ecology and evolutionary psychobiology. He has published on the topics of coloniality and mating systems in birds; sex ratios and chromosome numbers in insects; and mating systems, territoriality, sex ratios, and nepotism in ground squirrels. He received the Jackson Award (American Society of Mammalogists) in 1977 and the Howell Award (Cooper Ornithological Society) in 1974.*

Stephanie A. Shields, *a developmental psychologist, is an assistant professor of psychology at the University of California-Davis. Her research and publications have been in the area of the history of sex differences and the psychology of women.*

Judy A. Stamps *is an associate professor of zoology at the University of California-Davis. Her specialty is in* *ecological determinates of animal behavior, the evolution of behavior, and in behavioral ontogeny. She has a special interest in parent/offspring conflicts and has developed mathematical models of such conflicts. She has also published on the development of aggressive behavior and the relationship between resources and aggression in lizards.*

Robert R. Warner *is an assistant professor in the Department of Biological Sciences at the University of California-Santa Barbara and is a specialist in evolutionary ecology. He has studied sex change, sexual selection, and mating systems, particularly in coral-reef fishes.*

B. J. Williams, *professor of anthropology at the University of California-Los Angeles, is specifically concerned with the population genetics of human groups. He is the author of* A Model of Band Society *(Memoirs of the Society for American Archaeology #29, 1974) and is a member of the Executive Board of the American Anthropological Association.*

George C. Williams *is professor of ecology and evolution, State University of New York-Stony Brook. He is the author of* Sex and Evolution *(1974) and* Adaptation and Natural Selection *(1966), both published by Princeton University Press. A former vice president of the Society for the Study of Evolution, he is currently editor of* American Naturalist *and assistant editor of the* Quarterly Review of Biology.

Edward O. Wilson *is Baird Professor of Science at Harvard University and is a specialist in the field of social insects, sociobiology, and biogeography. He is the author of* On Human Nature *(1978),* Sociobiology: The New Synthesis *(1975), and* The Insect Societies *(1971), all published by Harvard University Press. He has received numerous honors and awards for his work, including the Pulitzer Prize for General Non-Fiction (1978) and the National Medal of Science (1976). He is a member of the National Academy of Sciences and a fellow of the American Philosophical Society and the American Academy of Arts and Sciences.*

Preface

In 1975 E.O. Wilson's book appeared, bearing the ambitious title of Sociobiology: The New Synthesis. Until then, sociobiology was an unnamed and loosely defined field of study. Wilson drew it together around the idea that natural selection favors the individual that maximizes the chances that it and its close relatives will leave descendents. To this he added his considerable knowledge in population ecology and blended in a large body of information about animal behavior.

The book propelled sociobiology to center stage, and with incredible speed. There seem to have been three reasons for this. One, it was superbly written and was an impressive survey of biological literature. Two, the last chapter was a widely ranging and imaginative attempt to interpret human behavior in the context of individual and kin selection. Three, it caught the attention of the mass media and thereby of an audience far larger than is usual for scholarly work.

Had Wilson's book not been a scholarly work, or had the last chapter not been provocative, the field probably would not have become such a burning public issue. The two together, however, resulted in a burst of interest among biologists while among some biologists and in other quarters it evoked outright rejection. The most strenuous objectors allege that sociobiology is politically motivated and that its findings are therefore suspect.

A major function of the American Association for the Advancement of Science (AAAS) is to air controversial issues at its annual meetings. Doing so is often a delicate undertaking. This is particularly true when the issues border on the political, or have political implications. The aim, then, is to keep the controversy above the purely political fray, insofar as possible. While a sharp distinction is never realistic, one can at least try to be sure that there is discussion directed to the scientific aspects.

Sociobiology is a case in point. AAAS appreciated the need for a symposium in this field while recognizing its potentially political overtones. Thus AAAS had the task of deciding how to arrange the symposium. That translates into whom to trust to make the arrangements. After consultation, they sought out a biologist working on problems considered to fall within sociobiology (the first editor). Later it became obvious that to present a broader perspective of this emerging field an anthropologist would also be needed; that led to the addition of the second arranger.

That collaboration proved so harmonious that it evolved into a partnership of editors. That was all the more remarkable since we often found that our sympathies point in opposite directions, even when we reached a good level of agreement on substantive issues. Perhaps it is due to our dissimilar scientific backgrounds and predispositions that we were able to assemble and agree upon a panel of speakers with such divergent positions and, in most instances, to get them to express themselves so as to be understood outside their own disciplines.

There have been a number of symposia and seminars recently on sociobiology. They have been predominantly of two types. In one, sociobiologists have spoken to one another. In the other, sociobiology's critics have spoken to one another. Seldom have the two sides got together.

Given that background, we set out to put together a symposium that would examine as simply and clearly as possible the conceptual issues in sociobiology. Issues vulnerable to distorted extension to humans were to be stressed. It was the hope of the biological editor that the debate could be moved off what he sees as a sterile dichotomy of genetic versus environmental determinism; he feels that it is a dead issue in biology. It was the view of the anthropological editor that much of the orientation and publicity concerning sociobiological work re-evokes or perhaps perpetuates the nature-nurture debate. He argued that our symposium should have a question mark after its title, "Sociobiology: Beyond Nature/Nurture." And, indeed, the papers we received and the tone of the discussions and the Washington Symposium persuaded us to insert the question mark in the title of this volume.

It soon became apparent that a tight focus on sociobiology would not fulfill the larger needs of the annual meetings of AAAS. There had to be more, and that more meant considering the actual extension of sociobiology to humans, and a consideration of the views of those who oppose such extensions.

We would like to believe that this is the first symposium in which competent advocates and critics of sociobiology have come together and spoken responsibly. This was not easy to carry out. Some of our participants were at first reluctant to appear, fearing harassment. In fact, when E.O. Wilson started to speak he was actually assaulted by a small mob screaming epithets (surely, AAAS must take reasonable precautions against the occurrence of such unscholarly and unproductive forms of confrontation). We also received unsolicited, late-arriving but forcefully stated advice from some individuals who sought to restructure the symposium to their liking.

We have some practical difficulties, as well, one of them of tragic proportions. Marcia Guttentag was to have spoken on sexual selection in humans, but shortly before the symposium she died suddenly. Similarly, the late Margaret Mead was to have chaired the final session of the symposium, but was kept away by illness (our thanks to Alex Alland for filling in, and to Jane B. Lancaster for chairing the other session). Another problem was that we wanted a paper on the acquisition and transmission of tradition in animals, as a counterpoint to considering the genetics of human behavior. Unfortunately, that speaker had to withdraw her paper. However, Danilo Mainardi agreed to prepare an article on that subject for the book, even though it was too late to bring him to Washington, D.C., to present a paper.

There is a general difficulty inherent in the arrangement of an occasion such as our symposium. It is the degree to which the organizers can, or should, control the participants. We sought speakers to cover particular points. That was to give structure to the symposium. And, we urged the participants to try to avoid the dilemma of opposing nature and nurture, or at least to go beyond that issue. We also wrote to each person that "one may develop exciting ideas so long as (1) they are clearly identified as such, (2) they are not contradicted by the existing body of evidence, and (3) they can be shown to flow logically from that which has been established. You should not be inhibited from developing stimulating testable hypotheses."

Not all the speakers covered their topics in the way we wished, though often this was to the improvement of a paper. Nonetheless, that blurred the overall organization. We had tried to arrange our four sessions with distinctive topics in mind, but also to encourage representation in each session from our panelists' several different disciplines. In this way we hoped to overcome the past talk-only-and-repeatedly-to-each-other character of many symposia. Frankly, we also sought to promote the widest audience attendance and participation at each session, rather than to fragment the audience by designing each session in terms of a restricted disciplinary appeal. For all of these reasons, we have organized this book differently from the original symposium.

As editors of this volume, we resolved from the outset not to restrict the authors, nor to impose on them our views, no matter how much we disagreed with what they wrote. We have, however, offered suggestions for improvement: We have stated contrary arguments, suggested additions or deletions or a tempering of the tone in the article, and so on. Each author was reminded that s/he could ignore our advice if s/he so wished, and a number did. Each author is ultimately responsible for the content of his/her article.

We leave it to you to judge the extent to which each author has transcended the nature/nurture question or has implicitly if not explicitly perpetuated it as an issue. We also leave it to you to judge the extent to which each paper flows logically from the available evidence. On these matters even we two editors find points of disagreement.

We hope you will read this book in the spirit of a historical document, and that the somber print conveys some of the excitement of the symposium. We also hope you will find enough information to appreciate the nature of the issues and to evaluate their implications. The skepticism voiced by the critics here, finally, should serve to remind us all of the controversy that surrounds sociobiology.

George W. Barlow
University of California - Berkeley

James Silverberg
University of Wisconsin - Milwaukee

August 1979

Sociobiology: Beyond Nature/Nurture?

Reports, Definitions and Debate

Part 1

Introduction

George W. Barlow

1. The Development of Sociobiology: A Biologist's Perspective

Seldom has a field of science excited so much enthusiasm in recent years as has sociobiology while at the same time inspiring such vituperation. Part of the difficulty lies in a misconception about the very nature of the field. When critics or advocates use the word sociobiology they often mean different things. At best, there is only partial overlap in their cognitive maps of sociobiology. As we learn from Hull (this volume) such misunderstandings are common in science and are no need for alarm.

To biologists working in sociobiology the term signifies a strict application of evolutionary theory to the social behavior of animals. To its critics, however, sociobiology is just another attempt to invoke genetic determinism to explain human behavior. The most vociferous critics lump writers in sociobiology together with authors such as Ardrey (1970) and Coon (1962). Individuals from these two camps have difficulty talking to one another. They speak different scientific languages, are concerned with different research problems and therefore have no literature in common; they view one another's positions with suspicion.

Biological Roots

The situation might be illuminated by delimiting sociobiology as a biologist regards it, that is, in the narrow sense. That can be best accomplished through an historical treatment, illustrating how certain fields of study have converged to produce sociobiology. It will necessarily reflect my own perceptions; others might well write a different account. It will also be highly selective and therefore a disservice to many who should be mentioned. Wilson (this volume) reviews the history of the term sociobiology. Sketching the development within biology will help you to appreciate the connections between the papers in this book.

There are three historical themes that have come together to produce sociobiology. The most visible of these originated in Charles Darwin's evolutionary theory, a theory conceived in ignorance of genetic mechanisms. That theory was given a genetic algebra by Sewell Wright, J. B. S. Haldane and R. A. Fisher, though it is usually Fisher who is cited in sociobiology. I will call this population or evolutionary genetics; it provides the rules of the game. The second theme is that of ecology; it is the arena that constrains or stimulates the players. The third theme is ethology; it answers the behavioral questions of how animals cope.

Evolutionary Genetics

Fisher's contribution (e.g., 1930) was to develop the logic of a genetic basis for natural selection. His most cited example in sociobiology is probably the explanation of the one-to-one sex ratio that characterizes so many species. He deduced that fitness is optimized by producing male and female offspring in equal numbers, assuming the general case of equal investment in each sex. (Fitness can be defined as "the contributions to the next generation of one genotype in a population relative to the contributions of other genotypes. By definition, this process of natural selection leads eventually to the prevalence of the genotype with the highest fitness" (Wilson 1975:585).)

The sex-ratio argument goes as follows: Since males can inseminate many females, while each female can produce only one (set of) young at a time, one might conclude that an animal could increase its number of grandchildren by producing only sons. The strategy's success, however, is its own downfall. As it spreads through the population more and more males will be produced, thus making females scarcer and scarcer. Therefore, the probability of an individual's daughter having offspring approaches one, while the probability of an individual's son having offspring plummets. Thus the production of daughters becomes a better strategy than the production of sons, and the sex ratio will again revert to 50:50. This argument applies with equal force in the opposite direction as females become numerous and males scarce. The proposition is still being refined as more is learned about short-term and also persistent departures from a one-to-one sex ratio (e.g., Hamilton 1967; Leigh 1970; Trivers & Willard 1973).

W. D. Hamilton (1964, 1966, 1967, 1970, 1971a, b, 1972) is considered by most to be Fisher's intellectual descendant. Indeed, some consider his papers the founding stones of sociobiology. In Hull's lexicon (this volume) these works are exemplars of the early stages of sociobiology. It does Hamilton an injustice just to cite his key articles because he contributed so many ideas in each article.

The most pivotal of Hamilton's (e.g., 1964) contributions was the concept of inclusive fitness, which can be summarized as "The sum of an individual's own fitness plus all its influence on fitness in its relatives other than direct descendants; hence the total effect of kin selection with reference to an individual" (Wilson 1975:586). The corollary concept, which has gained so much attention, is that of altruism; it is said to occur when an animal behaves in such a way that it decreases its own fitness in the process of increasing the fitness of another individual. It does a "favor" for another animal but at some cost to its own well being. Hamilton argued that apparent altruism should therefore be shown only toward kin, and the less so as the relationship becomes more remote (in this volume see Sherman on kin selection, but also see Bradbury).

Hamilton came to ideas such as these while considering the paradox of sterile worker insects, which are so characteristic of the highly social wasps, ants, and bees (hymenopterous insects). Why should the worker increase the queen's reproductive success while reducing her own to zero? That would seem to be the ultimate in altruism.

The solution lies in kin selection and inclusive fitness, all tied into the peculiar reproductive biology of these insects, haplodiploidy. In haplodiploidy, males develop from unfertilized eggs and are thus derived from one set of chromosomes (haploidy), as contrasted to females; the latter develop from fertilized eggs and therefore have two different sets of chromosomes (diploidy). Males are consequently totally homozygous.

In diploid animals each parent has 50% of its genes in common with its offspring, as do <u>on average</u> brothers and sisters; they are said to be related by a factor of 1/2. This results from sexual reproduction, which entails a halving of the chromosomes during the production of the male and female gametes (the ova and sperm).

In a colony of hymenopterous insects, because the haploid father is homozygous, sisters have on average a whopping 75% of genes in common, but if they reproduced they would share only the usual 50% with their daughters. Thus producing sisters, through the queen, results in a higher number of their own genes in the population than would producing their own daughters. Theory predicts that the daughters' interests would therefore best be served by helping to produce and rear more sisters. The situation, as so often happens, is actually more complicated than this and has many ramifications (see Wilson 1975).

One has to be cautioned, however, against overextending the concept of kin selection (see also Sherman, this volume). It is probably applicable to but a small portion of animals since most species don't live in kin groups. Those that do are most notably the social species among the hymenopterous insects, termites, birds, and mammals; humans are a good example (see Chagnon, Irons, B. J. Williams, this volume).

About the same time as Hamilton, G. C. Williams was stating remarkably similar ideas (Williams 1966; Williams and Williams 1957). Williams's book (1966) was stimulated in part by a provocative essay of Wynne-Edwards (1962). Wynne-Edwards had put forth and amply documented the thesis that gregarious animals regulate their population density through social feedback. They assess their density during behavioral interactions. If their density is too great in relation to the carrying capacity of their environment, they behave altruistically by refraining from breeding. Williams took it upon himself to refute that "group selectionist" doctrine. He did that by demonstrating that individual selection could account for all the phenomena, and that group selection logically could not (but see B. J. Williams, this volume).

Another key concept, in whose development G. C. Williams (1966, 1975) has played a major role, is that of sexual asymmetry. It stems from the prevailing situation in higher animals that males turn out nearly limitless numbers of small sperm, whereas females either lay large eggs or gestate small ones. Thus males are said to invest little in each gamete while females invest heavily.

Gordon Orians (1969) and Robert Trivers (1972) carried the idea forward by showing how this asymmetry could explain the conflicting objectives of males and females when mating: males should favor polygyny (having many female mates), females monogamy. A further extension is that a male should try to desert the female. That leaves her to care for the offspring while he seeks new mates. This line of thought has experienced considerable modification and refinement of late (Maynard Smith 1977).

Maynard Smith (1971) and Williams (1975) have written extensively about another concept, the cost of sex. It is a tricky argument, so the reader is advised to consult Williams's article on this subject in this book. The question behind this term is, why did sex evolve? Many species, not generally known to nonbiologists, and usually in relatively "primitive" groups, reproduce asexually. That is, they don't produce gametes that require another gamete to make a new individual. Rather, each reproductive cell is competent to make a new individual. A parent and all its offspring are therefore genetically the same, barring the rare mutation. Williams then contrasts the advantages and disadvantages of avoiding the cost of sex through asexuality, and of increased genetic variation through sexual reproduction. Each individual produced sexually is, of course, genetically unique, though it has many genes in common with its kin.

One question that flows from this will be of interest to many readers. It concerns the extent to which natural selection works for or against inbreeding in sexually reproducing forms (see Livingstone on the incest taboo, this volume).

Related to these concepts, especially to that of parental investment, is the one of parent-offspring conflict. Trivers (1974) reasoned that caretakers and their progeny should come into conflict over the time when caretaking should cease. Weaning is an example. The parent will want the young to cease nursing before the young would like to stop. That is because, it is argued, further nursing would reduce the parent's ability to invest in subsequent offspring.

The young's interest comes into conflict because getting still more milk increases its individual fitness, though at some cost to its mother and to its siblings. Consequently the young has to consider, as it were, how far it should go in competing with its siblings, present and future, by diminishing its mother's capacity to care for them. The young's selfish interests therefore have to be weighed in relation to its inclusive fitness; the point of balance will differ from the one favored by the caretaker (see Stamps and Metcalf, this volume). Richard Alexander (1974) has treated this from a different perspective, that of parental manipulation of its own young (see Dawkins 1976b for a contrary position).

No coverage of the development of the evolutionary theory of sociobiology would be complete without mention of John Maynard Smith. His earlier writings (compilations: 1958, 1972) on the genetic basis of evolution spread across a number of topics ranging from the species problem, fossil history, the origin of sex, polymorphism, altruism, and aggression, to a sober critique of eugenics. But his most obvious contribution to sociobiology was the blending of game theory with genetic evolutionary theory. This led him first, and with the important collaboration of G. R. Price (Maynard Smith and Price 1973) to simulate postulated strategies of fighting. And that flowered into the concept of Evolutionarily Stable Strategies (see Dawkins, this volume).

The evolutionary genetic approach to explaining the social behavior of animals is growing with remarkable speed and extends well beyond the foregoing. Richard Dawkins (1976b) has recently summarized the state of this field in a succinctly written book, The Selfish Gene. As a cautionary note, however, there is the danger of circularity in arguments about fitness that derive from population genetics (MacArthur 1971). The genetic models need testing within the framework of models coming from ecology (Gould, this volume, points to a number of shortcomings commonly encountered in evolutionary theorizing).

Ecology

The ecological scene is more difficult to treat with an even hand in a few pages than was population genetics. I will, nonetheless, touch upon the central issues relevant to contemporary sociobiology and the the more restricted scope of this book.

One major line is that of demography, a subdiscipline of natural history (Stearns 1976; Warner, this volume); it is the study of the dynamics and structures of populations and how they come to be that way. A pioneering paper here was one by Robert MacArthur (1962) in which he applied the reasoning of natural selection to stable populations of animals that fully occupy their habitats. Such animals are termed K-selected. Later articles (e.g. MacArthur and Wilson 1967) treated the subject in a larger framework, contrasting K- and r-selected populations (r-selected refers to opportunistic species that disperse to exploitable but fluctuating habitats, breed there with great speed and fecundity and disperse again). It is now recognized that r- and K-selection were useful concepts in developing further theories, but that the concepts are overly simple and encounter difficulties as our knowledge grows (see Warner, this volume).

This type of thinking led to explanations of breeding schedules in terms of costs and benefits, in relation to age and frequency of breeding (Gadgil and Bossert 1970; Williams 1966). Repeated breeding, or iteroparity, is favored if either or both of the following gradual changes occur as the animal gets older: the costs of reproducing slowly rise, or the benefits slowly sink (costs and benefits are measured in fitness). With iteroparity different schedules may occur, reflecting the ecological setting. At one extreme are many coral-reef fishes that spawn almost daily, year around (references in Warner, this volume). At the opposite extreme is semelparity, or the big-bang phenomenon: reproduction occurs in one massive effort at the end of the animal's life, as in the well-known Pacific salmon.

Another important line of research centers around competition for limiting resources (MacArthur 1972). The behavior of animals is related to the availability of resources such as food, breeding site, and place of refuge. These are seen to be limiting in many instances, both within and between species. Resources can be abundant or scarce, continuously distributed or patchy. And competition can be indirect or direct. How these factors interact bears on what the animals do, and relates directly to behavior (see Emlen, Warner, this volume).

David Lack (1954, 1968) was instrumental in showing how life-history phenomena can be adaptive. He was interested in the way birds adjust their reproductive output to the realities of their environment. He was especially concerned with the role of nutrition as a key limiting factor. Consequently, Lack reduced the argument to one of bioenergetics, but still within the framework of individual selection.

The exemplar for Lack's work is embodied in the question of why birds lay so few eggs when they could lay so many. That is, how does having fewer young maximize fitness? He reasoned that if too few young were raised, relative to available food, the reproductive success of the parents would decrease relative to those who raised more. If they laid too many, on the other hand, all of the brood would be undernourished and thus too weak to compete. Each bird, therefore, has to "predict" the best number of eggs to lay in its particular environment. The prediction is accomplished retrospectively by natural selection removing those who lay too many or too few eggs.

The significance of this line of research lay in illustrating how the reproductive output of an animal can be tuned to the ecological demands of its environment. This approach was nicely carried forward to social behavior by the insightful work of John Crook (1964). From comparative field studies on weaver finches, he constructed a plausible argument to account for their social organization, and even the forms of their displays, as consequences of being adapted to a prevailing set of circumstances. Those ecological variables were analyzed into type and distribution of food, physical environment, and predation. The continuing growth of that approach is reflected in the chapters by Jack Bradbury and Steve Emlen in this book; they stress the importance of patterns of distribution of resources.

Ethology

While population genetics and ecology were evolving, ethology was coming into being. The writings of Konrad Lorenz (1935, 1937, 1939) had a galvanic effect on the field of animal behavior, rather like that of E. O. Wilson's Sociobiology. Niko Tinbergen's (1951) The Study of Instinct was the first comprehensive treatment of ethology in English, and it moved ethology to the center of the stage.

Lorenz's training had been in comparative anatomy. It was only natural, then, that he applied this approach to animal behavior. The stereotyped movements and vocalizations of animals were treated as traits in the same way as morphology, and with the same problems of homology and analogy (see Caplan, this volume). Using these behavioral traits in comparative studies of ducks, he diagrammed phyletic relationships in the then prevailing style of taxonomists (Lorenz 1941).

At that time, however, the adaptiveness of behavior was assumed or argued post hoc. The focus was on the population as the evolutionarily significant unit. Behavior was viewed as being species typical. While genetic differences between individuals were recognized, they were regarded as natural variation and were not central to ethological theorizing. In contrast, individual differences are pivotal to sociobiological theorizing; and the differences are presumed to have a genetic basis, though the presumption is seldom tested.

Lorenz was also concerned with behavioral models of physiological substrates, and with behavior as an organized system. This concern with processes such as communication and species recognition, pair bonding, eliciting and inhibiting aggression, and socialization, all have import for current issues in sociobiology. They provide answers or methodologies for questions now being posed.

Lorenz took the initiative in ethology through his broad view, creative insights, and writing skill. Tinbergen then moved the field in the direction of evolutionary theory and ecology. Even before his contact with Lorenz, he was asking questions about the adaptiveness of learning in the nesting behavior of a solitary wasp (e.g., Tinbergen 1932). His close association with Lack probably spurred him later to ask more directly, how is the behavior adaptive? This is a different question than how did the behavior evolve. Questions about adaptation are evolutionary ones; they make predictions, so they are explicitly testable and are not post hoc.

Typical are the field experiments on egg-shell removal in the black-headed gull as an antipredator adaptation (Tinbergen et al. 1962). His students Kruuk (1964) and Patterson (1965) explored through careful field studies the adaptiveness of colonial nesting in gulls. It bears mentioning here, too, that Crook (1964) is an ethologist, though his work was cited above in the context of ecology.

Thus at the time E. O. Wilson (1975) was preparing his opus, Sociobiology, three major lines were converging. Reflecting this, his book has as its central theme evolutionary theory, in particular inclusive fitness. The ecological dimension gets considerable attention initially, but serves more as a backdrop than as a structure. Ethology is used extensively to provide explanations in the form of underlying behavioral mechanisms.

Sociobiology and the Social Sciences

Most biologists in these areas would accept the three themes, evolutionary theory, ecology, and ethology, as roughly defining sociobiology. I think they would also agree that it is the stressing of an evolutionary genetic logic, as epitomized by Fisher and Hamilton, that sets the field apart. That is important to keep in mind when talking about sociobiology with regard to humans.

Social scientists have concerned themselves with the ecological basis of human behavior, and human ethology is a growing field. Moreover anthropologists have long been schooled in traditional evolutionary theory. Relatively few social scientists, however, have examined human behavior in the light of those evolutionary hypotheses emanating from sociobiology (e.g., Chagnon, Irons, also references in Wilson, this volume).

Wilson, however, intended the compass of sociobiology to be larger than I have delimited it here. He defined it "as the systematic study of the biological basis of all social behavior" (1975:4). He went on to suggest, with reservations, that the social sciences, and even the humanities, might come to be embraced by sociobiology.

That larger view of sociobiology disturbed many social scientists. They resented having their fields expropriated by a spokesman whom they regarded as uninformed. For many years anthropologists have been studying social organization as an ecological adaptation in humans (see Harris 1977). They have made clear that they feel no need to respond to the visionary appeal of the sociobiologists on this score.

Still other critics were emerging. These took umbrage (see especially Gould, this volume) over the speculation of a few sociobiologists (e.g., Alexander 1971; Barash 1977; Wilson 1975) about the biological bases of human behavior. Any attempt to interpret human behavior in a biological context is anathema to many in our society, and the objections found voice in organized opposition.

The major irritant turns around the heart of evolutionary theory, the necessity that the behaviors in question have genetic correlates (see the section on genetics, this volume). This has been taken to mean genetic determinism; and some of the writings of the sociobiologists could be so construed, in large part because they were writing about simple models, or were using a convenient shorthand. The reason for the opposition to genetic determinism is clear enough, for in its worst form it is seen as a justification for racism.

Another major irritant derives from the biological reality that males and females invest disproportionately in their offspring. Extended to humans it is seen, again, as a kind of determinism, dictating that the roles that men and women have traditionally held in some societies are natural. Interestingly, another issue is emerging, that of dominance through aggression. Increasingly, dissident groups are calling for a re-assessment, or re-examination, of the animal data showing that males are generally more aggressive than are females; their contention is that male scientists have merely read into animal behavior the conclusion of male dominance (see Shields, this volume, for an historical account of male bias in science).

Epigenesis

Much of this strife, if not all of it, is needless. A large measure of it stems from a persistent misunderstanding of the gene-environment relationship that results in the phenotype, here the behavior. This is puzzling because morphogenesis, including neurogenesis, has always been viewed as a complex gene-environment transaction.

As early as 1828 the embryologist von Baer described the necessarily interactive nature of development. Even though genetics had not yet been discovered, he enunciated an essentially modern statement of epigenesis. And that interactive view of development has prevailed among biologists ever since Oppenheim, 1980). Likewise, all behavior results from a developmental interaction between the genome and its environment. Thus it is inaccurate to call one trait genetic and another acquired, whether we are speaking about a rooster crowing or human speech, respectively (see Lehrman 1970; Marler 1975; also Barash, this valume).

It is just as misleading to ascribe a certain percent of a trait of an individual to the genome, and another percent to the environment. This is a common misconception arising from estimates of heritability. Those estimates derive from differences between, not within, individuals; and they are only relevant to specified environments (Waddington 1975). It is furthermore unsound to speak of a gene causing a particular trait, though one can analyze correlations between genes and traits, as has been so elegantly demonstrated by DeFries (this volume) and his co-workers.

The genetics of behavior is in fact a prospering field (Broadhurst et al. 1974; Frank 1974; Manning 1975). And the genetics of human behavior is a growing discipline, though it is still struggling with the frustration of not having access to the more powerful experimental approaches of traditional genetics (DeFries & Plomin 1978; DeFries, Livingstone, Wilson, this volume).

When behavior is left out, there is no voiced objection to the field of human genetics, which is a direct extension of animal and plant genetics. Consider the well known cases of sex-linked hemophilia and color blindness. Recall the studies of the ancestry of polydactyly, hair patterns and sickle-cell anemia. Population geneticists have found that the distribution among humans of phenythiocarbamate tasters follows a well known principle (while this is a behavioral trait, strictly speaking, it is of little apparent sociological consequence). Thus the genetics of human nonbehavioral traits finds general acceptance.

It is easy to confuse a cultural lineage with a genetic one. Higher vertebrate animals show that which we can call protoculture, the acquisition and transmission of tradition, which is a form of inheritance (Mainardi, this volume). As Livingstone points out in this book, any normal person should be able to learn the traditional roles of any society, though with varying competence, if raised in that society. That speaks to an enormous adaptability (see also Leacock, this volume).

Following up on that theme, another frequently employed term can be, hopefully, clarified. That is the use of biology in expressions such as biological basis, biological roots, and so on. "Biological" should never be used as synonymous with "genetical." Further, to speak of biological determinism is internally contradictory. Biology, in this sense, should be taken as shorthand for the epigenetic point of view. Given the latitude of expression of the phenotype in humans, it is anything but a deterministic notion (contra Washburn 1978:405). Implicit, however, is that behavior is, or once was, adaptive in the evolutionary sense.

Relevance of Animal Behavior

Now to another controversial topic, that of the relevance of animal behavior to humans. We had hoped to have this topic in the body of the symposium, but events conspired against us. The topic should be considered, however briefly, because some people deeply resent the use of animal findings, while others feel just as strongly that such information is helpful. The position taken here is that we cannot ignore the information about animal behavior, its ecological setting, and its evolution.

One never explains human behavior, or proves something about it, by reference to animals' behavior, no matter how general the observation. It is difficult enough to explain animal behavior itself. And absolute proof of anything is unattainable. Nonetheless, an understanding of animal behavior, that is, of the principles we can derive from it, can be useful.

Animal behavior is instructive in two interrelated ways. For one, its comparative study allows us to abstract principles, by analogy, as to how the behavioral system of an organism is adaptive. For another, and following from the first, it stimulates us to pose questions about ourselves that would not otherwise be asked.

There is, of course, a danger in making facile comparisons between animals and humans (Klopfer 1977). As Margaret Mead put it, if there is any particular point you want to make about human behavior, you can always find at least one species of animal that behaves in just the way you need to substantiate your position. Here is Barlow's corollary: For all but the most general conclusions, across animal species and humans, you can always find some obscure human society that negates the generality. So where does that leave us?

Adaptiveness

It leaves us with one of the major precepts of sociobiology. The essential point is to understand how behavior is adaptive. And that means favoring the method of analogy over the older preoccupation with homology. Homology means different things to different people (e.g., Cranach 1976; Caplan, this volume), though the meaning most often invoked in the present setting is common ancestry, i.e., shared genetic basis. Homology also suggests the need for proof, which is always difficult. In contrast, analogy refers to a functional similarity and thus an analogy is a model (Mason & Lott 1976). The objective of reasoning by analogy is to understand how systems work. What are their underlying processes, their principles, irrespective of their constituents (see Dawkins 1976a; Emlen, this volume)?

If comparisons are to be made, one must seek patterns in systems that are integrated in similar ways and that cope with the environmental exigencies in an analogous fashion. The systems need not map isomorphically one on the other. Indeed, they probably never will. It is precisely the discrepancies between them that will be the most informative. They constitute natural experiments that will lead to a better comprehension of environment-behavior correlations, and therefore to tighter predictions. One should then be able not only to extrapolate soberly from animals to humans, and vice versa (e.g., Chevalier-Skolnikoff 1977), but to be in a position to predict the exceptional environmental differences correlated with those peculiar human societies that break the general rules. Differences are thus as meaningful as similarities (Mason & Lott 1976); this caveat must be kept in mind in the current reconsideration of the literature on animal behavior.

As an especially clear case I refer to arguments about dominance. It would be easy to select examples to document the position that in general males dominate females, the reverse, or that they do not differ. One has to ask instead about the patterns of dominance relations and the conditions under which they arise. How does dominance relate to mating systems, dimorphism and general gregariousness, and how do these relate to the environment of the organism? How does the very expression of dominance vary? How do dominance interactions change within a species, and why? Failure to seek the underlying principles will nullify any attempt to generalize from the findings on dominance relationships.

Posing Questions

Employed properly, the principles derived from studying animals can help us to understand ourselves. We need to be able to step back, to take a more distant and objective view of ourselves. One way to do that is to formulate new questions about our behavior. And sociobiology offers the opportunity to do that. That may mean simply observing humans in a different way, gathering new data to test the new hypotheses, as Chagnon and Irons (this volume) have been attempting in analyzing "altruism" in relation to kinship.

Inaccessible Questions

There is another reason for studying animals when we really want to know about humans. Often important hypotheses are brought forth that can only be tested experimentally. But by their nature such experiments should not and, fortunately, cannot be performed on humans. In that event, animals sometimes provide useful information.

Having done the animal experiments, confirming evidence can often be obtained from humans in benign ways (but see Adkins, this volume). One need think only of the research in physiology that has lead to powerfully useful knowledge in medicine. No one would dream of doing such research on humans, nor of rejecting the information obtained from animals. Such research, incidentally is not limited to mammals. The basic properties of the nerve impulse and its chemical mechanisms, for example, were illustrated by the study of giant axons in a squid.

More relevant to behavioral research, much of modern learning theory is based on studies done on animals such as rats and pigeons (e.g., Hilgard & Bower 1966). And advances in and recasting of theory continue to take place (Garcia et al. 1973). The principles derived here have had a great influence on our thinking about learning in humans.

Resistance to Comparisons

One has to wonder why there is such an emotional response to comparisons of animal and human behavior. There is, after all, widespread acceptance of the continuity of our evolution from animals. Our close affinity to chimpanzees and gorillas has been persuasively documented (e.g., Miller 1977). And, as John Searle said in his paper at the AAAS Symposium on Sociobiology in San Francisco, "We love to be told we are animals"; the warm chuckle from the audience indicated substantial agreement.

This feeling of affinity with animals has been around a long time, and found voguish expression during the sixties when the USA experienced a wide-scale rejection of materialism. Eastern religions enjoyed a measure of popularity. A central theme was our oneness with nature, a blurring of the lines between humans and animals, even plants. The conservation movement has added immensely to this identification with nature. It has also stirred a feeling of fear, and of a distrust of the forces that drive animals to extinction.

The spirit of naturalism has embedded in it a powerful countercurrent. It is a resentment of the disruptive, even destructive, impact that our materialistic society has had on its environment and on its members. Such destruction is facilitated by advancing technology. And scientists provide the knowledge that feeds technology. It is understandable, then, that laypersons, nonbiological scientists, and even some biologists, become suspicious when biological scientists interpret human behavior.

Ideas and Their Implementation

There is an important distinction to be made between ideas and their implementation. It is easier to be clear about the overt application of ideas or information, particularly in the extreme case. Thus arguments about nuclear powerplants and bombs, dams, contraceptive pills, and psychosurgery differ from those about nuclear physics, hydrodynamics, endocrinology, and psychiatry, respectively. Yet is has been proposed that some types of research should not be done because the findings or the research itself sow the seeds of human destruction. Nuclear physics and molecular biology (e.g., May 1977) have experienced such debates. I find it a thorny issue, and not one to dismiss.

Sociobiology has been attacked for producing a doctrine that is susceptible to exploitation by powerful forces within our society. It has been argued that its precepts might be used to support repressive or sexist practices or legislation. I don't believe the danger is real, but I could be wrong. So I welcome responsible criticism from the skeptics. I am reassured by the thought that in a free society the public will be exposed to a broad range of views from a number of scientists, and that the subsequent prevailing view will reflect both a synthesis and a large measure of common sense.

Scope of This Book

The chapters that follow will only now and then reflect the underlying stresses and strains reflected in the foregoing. Most of the chapters deal dispassionately with the issues in sociobiology that have the most import for humans, even when the subjects are as remote as wasps, fishes and bats. The divisions of the book treat environmental and related factors, genetics, sex, kin selection and criticisms. While by no means comprehensive coverage, it should suffice to communicate a feeling for sociobiology here and now.

Summary

Sociobiology has attracted considerable attention in the last few years and has become a center of controversy. Much of the controversy turns around a failure to understand the field. The field of sociobiology is actually older than the term itself, as it has been applied recently by Wilson (1975), and the field is still developing.

The nature of the discipline can best be understood in the context of its biological roots. It has had three major sources. The most important has been evolutionary genetics; it provides the cohesive theoretical basis. Ecology has also played a significant role, contributing both to the theoretical framework and to the testing of hypotheses. Since the phenomenon of behavior is central, it was inevitable that ethology became involved, furnishing the proximal mechanisms.

Resistance to sociobiology has been vigorous in the social sciences, particularly within anthropology: Sociobiology is held to be old wine in new bottles. Some social scientists, however, have begun research on questions raised by sociobiological theory. Sociobiology has also been attacked on the grounds that it implies genetic determinism; critics have argued that sociobiological thinking leads to racism and sexism.

Biologists have long been schooled in embryology, which has as a central precept epigenesis, that the phenotype results from a complex gene-environment interaction. Epigenesis applies to behavior as well as to morphology. Having a genetic basis does not therefore necessarily conflict with a wide range of possible outcomes in the phenotype. To speak of a "biological basis" means the epigenetic point of view, not genetic determinism.

Animal behavior is relevant to humans, but not in the sense of explaining human behavior. From comparative studies, we learn how the behavior of animals forms a system that is adapted to the environment. This provides models for comparison by analogy in which differences are as revealing as similarities. The single most important consequence of such research is the posing of questions about humans that otherwise might not be thought of. Experiments with animals can also be helpful when such experiments cannot be done on humans. When behavior is not considered, we readily accept information obtained from animals, physiology being an excellent example.

Why is there so much resistance to comparisons with animals when in so many ways the Zeitgeist favors a feeling of affinity to animals? It comes partly from a fear of the misuse of such information to further racist and sexist doctrines. It also stems from a feeling of unease that the technology that emanates from science brings harm as well as good, as in nuclear radiation, persistent pesticides, and carcinogens. That unease, when aroused, makes people suspicious of biologists if they apply their findings to humans.

It is crucial that we distinguish here between the implementation of scientific findings as contrasted to the research or theorizing. That is not to say that the research or theorizing itself should be above scrutiny or debate. However, it is an issue that requires dispassionate discussion, free of emotional posturing, because the risks are real in both directions.

Acknowledgements

The article was prepared while I was on special leave of absence to participate in a project on the development of behavior in humans and animals at the Zentrum für interdisziplinäre Forschung of Bielefeld Universität; I am grateful to Professor Klaus Immelmann for providing that opportunity. I am also grateful to Gerta O. Barlow, Colin G. Barnett, Eric A. Fischer, Stephen E. Glickman, Mary Main, Lewis Petrinovich, and James Silverberg for their helpful suggestions and to the AAAS for supporting my participation in the symposium.

Literature Cited

Alexander, R. D. 1971. The search for an evolutionary philosophy of man. Proceedings of the Royal Society of Victoria 84:99-120.

_______. 1974. The evolution of social behavior. Annual Review of Ecology and Systematics 5:325-383.

Ardrey, R. 1970. The social contract. Atheneum, New York.

Baer, K. E. von. 1828. Entwickelungsgeschichte der Thiere: Beobachtung und Reflexion, Part 1. Borntrager, Konigsberg.

Barash, D. P. 1977. Sociobiology and behavior. Elsevier, New York.

Broadhurst, P. L., D. W. Fulker & J. Wilcock. 1974. Behavioral genetics. Annual Review of Psychology 25:389-415.

Chevalier-Skolnikoff, S. 1977. A Piagetian model for describing and comparing socialization in monkey, ape, and human infants. In S. Chevalier-Skolnikoff & F. E. Poirier (eds.), Primate biosocial development: Biological, social, and ecological determinants. Garland, New York, pp. 159-187.

Coon, C. S. 1962. The origin of races. Knopf, New York.

Cranach, M. von (ed.). 1976. Methods of inference from animals to human behavior. Aldine, Chicago.

Crook, J. H. 1964. The evolution of social organization and visual communication in the weaver birds (Ploceinae). Behaviour Supplement 10:1-178.

Dawkins, R. 1976a. Hierarchical organisation: A candidate principle for ethology. In P. P. G. Bateson & R. A. Hinde (eds.), Growing points in ethology. Cambridge University Press, Cambridge, pp. 7-54.

_______. 1976b. The selfish gene. Oxford University Press, Oxford.

DeFries, J. C. & R. Plomin. 1978. Behavioral genetics. Annual Review of Psychology 29:473-515.

Fisher, R.A. 1930. The genetical theory of natural selection. Clarendon, Oxford.

Frank, D. 1974. The genetic basis of evolutionary changes in behaviour patterns. In J. H. F. van Abeelen (ed.), The genetics of behaviour. North-Holland, Amsterdam, pp. 119-140.

Gadgil, M. & W. H. Bossert. 1970. Life history consequences of natural selection. American Naturalist 104:1-24.

Garcia, J., J. C. Clarke & W. G. Hankins. 1973. Natural responses to scheduled rewards. In P. P. G. Bateson & P. H. Klopfer (eds.), Perspectives in ethology. Plenum, New York, 1:1-41.

Hamilton, W. D. 1964. The genetical theory of social behaviour. I & II. Journal of Theoretical Biology 7:1-52.

______. 1966. The moulding of senescence by natural selection. Journal of Theoretical Biology 12:12-45.

______. 1967. Extraordinary sex ratios. Science 156:477-488.

______. 1970. Selfish and spiteful behaviour in an evolutionary model. Nature 228:1218-1220.

______. 1971a. Geometry for the selfish herd. Journal of Theoretical Biology 31:295-311.

______. 1971b. Selection of selfish and altruistic behaviour in some extreme models. In J. F. Eisenberg & W. S. Dillon (eds.), Man and beast: Comparative and social behavior. Smithsonian Press, Washington, D. C., pp. 57-91.

______. 1972. Altruism and related phenomena, mainly in social insects. Annual Review of Ecology and Systematics 3:193-232.

Harris, M. 1977. Cannibals and kings. The origins of culture. Random House, New York.

Hilgard, E. R. & G. H. Bower. 1966. Theories of learning. Third edition. Appleton-Century-Crofts, New York.

Klopfer, P. H. 1977. Social Darwinism lives! (Should it?). Yale Journal of Biology and Medicine 50:77-84.

Kruuk, H. 1964. Predators and anti-predator behavior of the black-headed gull (Larus ridibundus). Behaviour, Supplement 11:1-129.

Lack, D. 1954. The natural regulation of animal numbers. Oxford University Press, Oxford.

______. 1968. Ecological adaptations for breeding in birds. Methuen, London.

Lehrman, D. S. 1970. Semantic and conceptual issues in the nature-nurture problem. In L. R. Aronson, E. Tobach, D. S. Lehrman & J. S. Rosenblatt (eds.), Development and evolution of behavior. Freeman, San Francisco, pp. 17-52.

Leigh, E. G. 1970. Sex ratio and differential mortality between the sexes. American Naturalist 104:205-210.

Lorenz, K. 1935. Der Kumpan in der Umwelt des Vogels. Journal für Ornithologie 83:137-213, 289-413.

______. 1937. Uber die Bildung des Instinkbegriffes. Die Naturwissenschaften 25:289-300, 307-318, 324-331.

______. 1939. Vergleichende Verhaltensforschung. Zoologische Anzeiger, Supplement 12:69-102.

______. 1941. Vergleichende Bewegungsstudien an Anatinen. Journal für Ornithologie, Supplement 89:194-294.

MacArthur, R. H. 1962. Some generalized theorems of natural selection. Proceedings of the National Academy of Sciences, U. S. A. 48:1893-1897.

______. 1971. Patterns of terrestrial bird communities. In D. S. Farner, J. R. King & K. C. Parkes (eds.), Avian Biology. Academic Press, New York, 1:189-221.

______. 1972. Geographical ecology: Patterns in the distribution of species. Harper & Row, New York.

______ & E. O. Wilson. 1967. The theory of island biogeography. Princeton University Press, Princeton.

Manning, A. 1975. Behaviour genetics and the study of behavioural evolution. In G. Baerends, C. Beer & A. Manning (eds.), Function and evolution in behaviour. Clarendon, Oxford, pp. 71-91.

Marler, P. 1975. On strategies of behavioral development. In G. Baerends, C. Beer, & A. Manning (eds.), Function and evolution in behaviour. Clarendon, Oxford, pp. 254-275.

Mason, W. A. & D. F. Lott. 1976. Ethology and comparative psychology. Annual Review of Psychology 27:129-154.

May, R. M. 1977. The recombinant DNA debate. Science 198:1144-1146.

Maynard Smith, J. 1958. The theory of evolution. Penguin, Baltimore.

______. 1971. What use is sex? Journal of Theoretical Biology 30:319-335.

______. 1972. On evolution. Edinburgh University Press, Edinburgh.

______. 1977. Parental investment: A prospective analysis. Animal Behaviour 25:1-9.

______ & G. R. Price. 1973. The logic of animal conflict. Nature 246:15-18.

Miller, D. A. 1977. Evolution of primate chromosomes. Science 198:1116-1124.

Oppenheim, R. W. 1980. Preformation and epigenesis in the origins of the nervous system and behavior: Issues, concepts and their history. In K. Immelmann, G. W. Barlow, M. Main & L. Petrinovich (eds.), Behavioral development: The Bielefeld interdisciplinary project. Cambridge University Press, New York (in press).

Orians, G. H. 1969. On the evolution of mating systems in birds and mammals. American Naturalist 103:589-603.

Patterson, I. J. 1965. Timing and spacing of broods in the black-headed gull Larus ridibundus. Ibis 107:433-459.

Stearns, S. C. 1976. Life-history tactics; a review of the ideas. Quarterly Review of Biology 51:3-47.

Tinbergen, N. 1932. Über die Orientierung des Bienenwolfes, Philanthus triangulum. Zeitschrift für vergleichende Physiologie 16:305-335.

______. 1951. The study of instinct. Clarendon, Oxford.

______, G. J. Broekhuysen, F. Feekes, J. C. W. Houghton, H. Kruuk & E. Szulc. 1962. Egg shell removal by the black-headed gull Larus ridibundus; a behaviour component of camouflage. Behaviour 19:74-117.

Trivers, R. L. 1972. Parental investment and sexual selection. In B. Campbell (ed.), Sexual selection and the descent of man, 1871-1971. Aldine, Chicago, pp. 136-179.

_____. 1974. Parent-offspring conflict. American Zoologist 14:249-264.

______ & D. E. Willard. 1973. Natural selection of parental ability to vary the sex ratio of offspring. Science 179:90-92.

Waddington, C. H. 1975. The evolution of an evolutionist. Edinburgh University Press, Edinburgh.

Washburn, S. L. 1978. Human behavior and the behavior of other animals. American Psychologist 33:405-418.

Williams, G. C. 1966. Adaptation and natural selection. A critique of some current evolutionary thought. Princeton University Press, Princeton.

______. 1975. Sex and evolution. Princeton University Press, Princeton.

______ & D. C. Williams. 1957. Natural selection of individually harmful social adaptations among sibs with special reference to social insects. Evolution 11:32-39.

Wilson, E. O. 1975. Sociobiology. The new synthesis. Belknap, Cambridge, Massachusetts.

Wynne-Edwards, V. C. 1962. Animal dispersion in relation to social behaviour. Oliver & Boyd, Edinburgh.

James Silverberg

2. Sociobiology, the New Synthesis? An Anthropologist's Perspective

Sociobiology has been proclaimed "The New Synthesis" (Wilson 1975). I cannot speak for all anthropologists, but many of us question whether for our discipline sociobiology is a new synthesis. If sociobiology seeks "the biological basis for social behavior" or its "genetic foundation" (Wilson, this volume), some of us must even question whether it provides a true synthesis. We would question this even though Wilson (this volume) painstakingly adds a potential disclaimer in the case of human behavior: Sociobiology

> in no way depends on a demonstration that human social behavior has a genetic basis . . . [T]he genetic evolution of human behavior . . . is one possibility that can be derived from sociobiology, but it is not identical with it.

Let me first ask, then, whether an effort to synthesize biological and sociological study is new. To answer this I give a brief review of anthropology, especially American anthropology, in the first major part of this chapter. In a second section, I examine whether sociobiology entails a reduction of sociological concerns to biological ones instead of a synthesis. In the third part, under seven general headings, I discuss eleven specific cautions and potential fallacies that should be kept in mind when we deal with behavioral data, particularly human behavior.

Anthropology: A Science of Human Adaptation

Anthropologists have long been concerned with the evolution of humans as biological organisms and with the evolution of culture. They deal with the ecology of human populations and use an essentially ethological approach to human behavior. They describe human biological and behavioral variation through space and time. The many anthropologists whose orientation is similar to my own explain such variations in terms of evolutionary adaptation.

Humans are not the only animals with traditions that are innovated and transmitted socially (intelligently) rather than genetically (sexually) (Mainardi, this volume). Social transmission is variously termed learning, socialization, or enculturation in the literature. But this is so extensively true for humans that we anthropologists--devoting ourselves so largely to the study of humans--must take into account such "cultural behavior."

A Discipline That Is Both Biological and Cultural

Because human adaptation takes place in two highly interdependent but nevertheless distinguishable ways, we anthropologists divide our science into two subdisciplines, both having an evolutionary perspective. The biological/physical subdiscipline is primarily concerned with morphological and physiological adaptation; the sociocultural subdiscipline, which includes archeology, deals mainly with cultural adaptation. But this is a division of labor. To conceptualize anthropology overall as a science of human adaptation unites our wide-ranging, perhaps presumptuous, discipline.

Biological Anthropologists. Biological/physical anthropologists explain human variation in bodily form and function in terms of the interaction of hereditary and environmental factors. In recent decades, population genetics has provided a valuable corrective to the typological approach that had characterized earlier work on human biological variation. It does so by emphasizing the limited distinctiveness of "breeding populations" and their internal heterogeneity. The hallmark of biological anthropologists as anthropologists, even when they are housed in medical schools, is their concern with human (and general primate) evolution. Almost all of them have had some training in sociocultural anthropology. Also, they pursue their work with the knowledge that the major mechanism of human adaptation is culture--i.e., the innovated and learned patterns of behavior, material items and ideas that largely characterize the ways different human populations survive.

Sociocultural Anthropologists. I shall use the term "sociocultural" for both social and cultural anthropologists to avoid distinctions that are not germane here. Sociocultural anthropologists explain cultural variation by the way cultural innovation and subsequent social transmission interact with three general variables: environment, demography and already existing cultural phenomena. Despite the narrower focus on particular aspects of culture that characterizes specific studies, sociocultural anthropologists regard any culture as a more or a less integrated system. They consider such systems from all times and places as well as observed occasions of culture change when they formulate and test generalizations about culture and its evolutionary significance. Almost all of them get some training in biological anthropology, for they must be aware of the culture building capacities of the human animal, the extent to which those capacities are shared with other animals (especially other primates), and the extent to which human biological variation is pertinent to explaining cultural differences and developments. For example, much work was done early to demonstrate how the distributions of cultural and biological phenomena were usually not correlated among humans (e.g., Boas 1911).

This volume is concerned with social behavior and this chapter with that of humans. Thus, my discussion will focus on behavior as it varies culturally rather than on other cultural traits. Correspondingly, I shall not devote much attention to studies of morphological and physiological variation in humans.

Language, Linguistics and Anthropology

The universal occurrence of language in human populations is and has long been of vital importance to anthropologists. Much of modern descriptive linguistics, especially that outside the Indo-European domain, was born and nourished within cultural anthropology. In the 19th and early 20th centuries, when anthropologists went into the field--even where their primary commitment was to the gathering of behavioral and other cultural data--they also had to learn, transcribe, analyze, and prepare dictionaries and grammars for hitherto unrecorded languages. (Some gathered biometrical and other biological data as well.)

In method and theory there has been continual interplay between linguistics and anthropology. In recent decades this interplay has been enriched with findings from studies of nonhuman primates in laboratories and in the field (e.g., Peng 1978).

The significance of language for human behavior or for culture in general has generated some disagreement among anthropologists in their theoretical orientation and even in the way they collect field data. I shall refer to both disagreements, the fieldwork implication almost immediately and the theoretical implication later in this chapter.

How Anthropologists Study Human Behavior

An Ethological Approach. Most sociocultural anthropologists are concerned to obtain information about the actual, in situ social behavior of the populations studied. Thus, as opposed to experimental work (in its narrower sense, see Kaplan 1964:163), the overwhelming mass of our field studies is ethological in approach.

Like other students of ethology (Sherman, this volume), we try to control for the effect of our presence on the behavior we study. Unobtrusive measures of data-collecting (Webb et al. 1966) are frequently used. Cross-checking of findings from different data-collecting procedures is also practiced.

When we collect data on a dead population from the remote past, unless we can rely exclusively on written historical accounts, our fieldwork is archeology. We "detect" the social behavior that was once present from indirect evidence. We use the inventory and layout of material culture items, including the settlement patterns, and the evidence of accompanying habitat conditions.

As ethnographers we do fieldwork on a living culture. A wide panoply of data-collecting procedures is available. In addition to doing detective work like that of archeologists, we obtain the evidence on social behavior directly by eyewitnessing (and earwitnessing)--sometimes unobtrusively, sometimes not--or by probing, mostly in the form of interviewing.

It is here that language enters in. Some ethnographers emphasize verbal elicitation of information. The "cognitive" ethnographers analyze a culture exclusively in terms of the folk classifications and behavioral rules that are implicit (if not explicit) in the very words used by local informants (e.g., Tyler 1969). "Actonic" ethnographers, on the other hand, emphasize techniques for recording and processing eyewitness data (Harris 1964; Hutt & Hutt 1970; Silverberg 1976).

Unfortunately, many cultural descriptions mix data from these two data-collecting procedures: the verbal or cognitively-oriented approach, so greatly influenced by linguistics, and the behavioral or actonic approach. Consequently, such ethnographers are not always careful to lay bare the all-important distinction between modal tendencies in actual behavior from the idealizations (rules) and putative versions of behavior verbalized by local informants.

The actonic approach is more ethological (Hutt & Hutt 1970) in the sense that it explicitly seeks to analyze actual behavior patterns rather than verbalizations. Some of us regard the parallel between this approach to human behavior and the approach used in field studies of nonhuman animals as a useful contribution to interspecies comparison and evolutionary study (Silverberg 1976). After all, actual behavior--not idealized or putative behavior--is what has to be adaptive in the long run.

My colleagues who emphasize interview data, however, correctly argue that such findings also constitute a behavioral reality present in the population studied. They claim further that the rules which they learn or infer from what informants tell them, prescribe "appropriate" behavior in the society studied (Conklin 1964; Frake 1964; Goodenough 1965, 1970: 98-112; for counterarguments see Burling 1964; Harris 1974a).

All of us emphasize the necessity of being able to check what we are told by informants against the behavior we see taking place. This is significant in terms of what I am addressing here as the fundamentally ethological orientation of fieldwork in sociocultural anthropology.

Cultural Ecology in Evolutionary Perspective. The literature reveals the great extent to which biological and cultural studies in anthropology are committed to cultural ecology in an evolutionary theoretical perspective (Harris 1968:654-687).

Nineteenth century monographs would start with "the natural setting" ("habitat"), but usually little connection was explicitly drawn between that habitat and the culture described in the succeeding pages. Around the turn of the century, much effort was devoted to combatting a one-sided "geographical determinism," an approach whereby factors of topography and climate "caused" psychological "predispositions" (e.g., "hardy mountaineers," "invigorated" temperate zone inhabitants) which in turn "explained" human behaviors. Nevertheless, a concern with the mutual interrelation between culture and environment is a longstanding one in anthropology (e.g., Mason 1894, 1895). It has been a feature of some important studies in the history of the discipline (chronologically, Wissler 1917, 1926; Forde 1934; Kroeber 1939; Steward 1936, 1937, 1938, 1955; Helm 1962).

Since World War II the emphasis on cultural-ecological analysis has been especially marked. Efforts to delineate the mutual effects of the two variables, environment and culture, have been noteworthy (Steward 1955). The concept "environment," earlier used exclusively for the geographical habitat, now includes the impingement of other human populations on the particular population being analyzed (Barth 1956; Sahlins 1961). Much work with ethnographic and archeological data in recent decades has taken the same approach as that taken by students of animal ecology (Barash, Bradbury, Emlen, Sherman, Warner, this volume).

For well over a century, anthropologists have been concerned with studying the possibly deleterious impact of Western, industrialized societies on the cultures of simpler societies and of ways to mitigate that impact in specific instances (Emlen, this volume). This was once treated as "culture contact." However, to explain the behavioral forms of one population in terms of the full ecological system of which it is a part--including its relationship with other societies--has been a more recent interest.

The cultural-ecological approach has sometimes been identified as "specific evolution": the way a particular culture changes in response to environmental pressures, demographic variables, and internal tensions, concerns shared by "ecological sociobiologists" (Emlen, Warner, this volume). It is useful to identify the parallels and the differences in the specific processes, rapidity and scope of cultural as compared with biological evolution, as do Gould, Livingstone, Mainardi, and B.J. Williams (this volume).

As biological anthropologists, when we know an anatomical or physiological trait varies genetically among humans, we are enjoined to study its distribution in space and time in terms of mutations, gene flow, genetic drift, selective stresses, genetic fitness, reproductive success, etc. But when we have to explain the occurrence in a population of some behavioral trait that can readily be acquired through social transmission (Mainardi, this volume), we are dealing with a phenomenon that at one time had to be innovated in that population.

For the process of innovation we find an adequate set of explanatory factors: (1) the psychic (= inference-using) unity of the human species (Silverberg 1978b), discussed later; (2) the presence of cultural antecedents (whether informational, technological, sociological, or some combination of these) which must be present for the innovation to take place; and (3) an adaptive problem to be coped with, which must be present for the innovation to catch hold and become historically noticeable. The requisite antecedents must be available for any type of innovation to occur: an <u>invention</u> synthesizes them into some new cultural item; a <u>discovery</u>

brings them to bear on something in the natural environment that also has to be "available" although it was not hitherto perceived and incorporated into the culture; an importation takes the trait or the idea for it from another sociocultural system through the process of diffusion. In accounting for the occurrence, the three explanatory factors are each necessary. Perhaps together they are sufficient for explaining where and when an innovation takes place.

An important contribution of the ecological approach to specific evolution is that, other things being equal, different populations, when faced with similar adaptive problems and given similar cultural antecedents, will come up with similar or at least comparable adaptative solutions. The "other things being equal" relate to specific cautions about using adaptation and selection as explanatory concepts, to be discussed later.

This explanatory paradigm gives sociocultural anthropologists the possibility of explaining the recurrence of particular behavioral forms in different cultures. We welcome the prospect of sharing this perspective with "ecological sociobiologists" (Emlen, this volume).

The approach explains parallel but independent developments in cultural evolution such as the strikingly similar change that followed the acquisition of horses by Indians of the North American Great Plains and of the South American Pampas (Steward 1949a:764) or the development of irrigation agriculture and state formation in five independent semiarid regions of the world (Steward 1949b). The same paradigm explains the innumerable instances we can document for simultaneous, independent innovations within the same widespread civilization (e.g., Ogburn 1950[1922]). In this regard, zoologists have before them the well-known cases of Darwin and Wallace on natural selection and of De Vries, Correns and Tschermak in rediscovering Mendelian inheritance.

The same three explanatory factors help to account for the cumulative nature of culture growth and for the relatively sudden fluctuations within and between populations in the rate at which innovations appear, something impossible to expect in terms of genetic shifts (White 1949:168-171,190-232). Finally, the explanatory power of these factors is documented by the fact that more productive cultural techniques and cultural systems tend to spread at the expense of less productive ones throughout a common ecological system (Kaplan 1960).

Specific evolution explains how a particular culture becomes simpler or more complex through invention, discovery or importation. A "general evolutionary perspective" abstracts from specific evolutionary data the broad directional trends that have characterized human social traditions from their earliest and simplest forms to their most recent and complex forms. It is concerned with their initial invention and discovery in each case. Even so, the focus in general evolution is on the kind of ecological situation that generated such an innovation.

"Primatology"

Anthropologists have long devoted considerable attention to the nearest relatives of humans with whom we share so much anatomically, physiologically, immunologically, and in other ways biochemically.

In recent decades, some anthropologists have passed beyond the limitations suggested by our disciplinary label to do research among nonhuman primates. This work, at least when carried on by anthropologists and when done in the field, is usually but inaccurately called "primatology," as if humans were not themselves primates. In an early period, such fieldwork was dominated by comparative psychologists and zoologists.

Earnest A. Hooton (1942:xxxii) grumbled about "the students of animal behavior, who sometimes regrettably call themselves psychobiologists." Hooton himself labelled the field research far more accurately as "primate ethnography" or "primate sociology," a perspective unfortunately ignored by those who persist in regarding such studies as "physical" rather than sociocultural anthropology.

Aside from the "primatologists," however, a much larger body of anthropologists tries to incorporate the results of laboratory and field research on nonhuman primates into their teaching and writing. I was first struck as a graduate student in 1948 by what seemed an inconsistency in the work of the comparative psychologists on nonhuman primate behavior. In one paragraph they would insist that the behavior they were describing was learned, a result of socialization. In other paragraphs (or, indeed, in the very titles of their monographs) they would label or implicitly treat the behavior as if it were universal and invariant throughout the species even though they gave no evidence of having checked for this (see also Hull, this volume). The behavior-through-socialization theme gained full recognition with the research on intraspecies variation in behavior through innovation and social transmission among Japanese rhesus monkeys (Itani 1961; Miyadi 1967; see also Mainardi, this volume). My participation in the symposium leading to this volume and in the others I helped organize for AAAS (see Bishop 1976; Teleki in press) evidence my sustained interest in primate sociology.

The Continuity of Life vs. Human Uniqueness

Human language is sometimes distinguished from other forms of communication in terms of the making and using of symbols rather than signals (White 1949). Most anthropologists relate the concept "culture" to the effect of language on the content, transmission and cumulative character of human social traditions. They part company with each other to some extent in their willingness or unwillingness to see a qualitative as well as quantitative difference between language-related culture and the social traditions of nonhuman animals (Mainardi, this volume). Many emphasize the verbal and in other respects symbolic level on which cultural data can be treated (e.g., Sahlins 1976:esp. pp. 61-67). Caplan (this volume), though not an anthropologist, expresses the views of a large number of my colleagues, when he describes human behavior as "categorically different from other varieties of social behavior normally found in the animal kingdom."

The tendency to affirm an unbridgeable gulf between human and nonhuman animals has never been universal among anthropologists. In the light of recent experimental work on the symbol-using capacities of other primates, particularly chimpanzees, the fullest acceptance of biological continuity and its extension to continuity in social behavior has been gaining ground (Peng 1978). We shall see later how this continuity is reflected in the difficulty of knowing how far down the phylogenetic "tree" we must go to find places where innovating and social transmission begins to supersede sexual reproduction in the determination of behavioral forms.

Synthesis Through a Focus on Human Adaptation

The anthropological synthesis of biological and sociocultural investigation stems from a common concern with selection and adaptation as explanatory or at least interpretive concepts. Ideally, we would like to predict biological and cultural attributes in terms of the selective pressures of an ecological context (cf. Caplan, this volume).

For present purposes, selection is measured by the perpetuation (including spread) of a given biological or cultural trait. Such selection is governed by a set of ecological conditions. These are the selective pressures imposed by environment, demography and a system of already existing biological and cultural traits. They include what Caplan (this volume) calls interspecific and conspecific selectional demands.

The perpetuation of biological traits takes place through sexual reproduction (G.C. Williams, this volume); that of cultural traits through social transmission (Mainardi, this volume). In this context, we may speak of selection as short-run adaptation. It is "short-run," because a long time-span and, for example, rapid environmental change, may make an "adaptive" trait maladaptive; the population could even become extinct. An adaptation, in the short-run sense, is a modification or a response whose fitness, success or advantage is measured by the biological or the cultural selection process (but see Caplan, this volume). From this point of view, morphological and physiological traits can be considered adaptive in terms of "reproductive success" (Chagnon, this volume; Hamilton 1964; Irons, this volume; Williams 1966) or, as Warner (this volume) puts it, "the number of copies of a gene passed on." A cultural trait can be considered adaptive in terms of cultural diffusion--how widely does it spread (Sahlins & Service 1960, especially Kaplan 1960)--for such traits follow "the Lamarckian mode . . . of cultural transmission" (Gould, this volume).

We should consider separately any assumption holding all existing biological and cultural traits to be adaptive; Caplan (this volume) considers this notion "Panglossian panselectionism." We should also consider separately whether the unit making a biological or cultural response to selective pressures is a gene (Dawkins and Stamps & Metcalf, this volume), an individual (Hamilton 1964; Irons, this volume: Williams 1966), or some social aggregate or population (Harris 1968, 1974b; Livingstone, this volume; Merton 1949; Sahlins & Service 1960; B.J. Williams, this volume).

Most anthropologists recognize culture as the major mechanism of adaptation for human populations. We see its sources as lying in the processes of innovation and social transmission. We understand that the capacity of the human animal to develop and transmit culture is a product of biological evolution. Nevertheless, in keeping with Dawkins (this volume), the fact that a specific behavioral form is an adaptive "strategy" does not warrant the inference that it is genetically determined or sexually transmitted (see also Gould, Mainardi, this volume).

The anthropological synthesis is reflected in the way the two modes of adaptation, biological and cultural, can be interdependent. There is "feedback" between them. For example, innovation in culture--more effective hygiene and sanitation measures as well as improved medical technology and health care delivery--may be regarded as adaptive because they spread throughout a society or whole set of societies. These cultural innovations may also have biological consequences that many biologists would regard as adaptive: more people survive to reproduce, but also to reach old age. The population, faced with this change in its demographic structure, will respond culturally. There will be pressure for cultural innovations on behalf of senior citizens in the form of pensions, social security, special housing facilities, geriatric medical care, and reduced transportation and recreation fees.

Furthermore, cultural behavior can generate changes in gene frequencies as Livingstone and B.J. Williams indicate (this volume; see also Reid 1973; Ward 1973:388). Had the Bushmen of Namibia or the Australian aborigines been located where the domestication of plants and animals, "the food-producing revolution," took place and had they experienced the accompanying population explosion how prevalent would their genotypes have been today?

Biological and cultural adaptation, therefore, are interdependent processes. They show "coevolution," as Warner says (this volume). The primacy of either one depends on the particular investigative situation.

In their day-to-day work, sociocultural and biological anthropologists do not always consciously and consistently manifest the anthropological synthesis. Subdisciplinary specialization and the need to limit the scope of a research problem means that we usually study cultural adaptation and biological adaptation separately. However, we are committed to bringing out an interrelationship where one can be shown. Studies which do demonstrate the feedback between biological and cultural adaptation are among the best and most widely cited in the discipline (e.g., Livingstone 1958, relating the spread of horticulture and malarial infestation to Allison's [1954] work on the adaptive contribution of the sickling allele).

Sociobiology: Neither Sin-Thesis Nor the Great Beyond

The previous section should have made one thing clear: the idea and utility of uniting biological and sociological understandings--of using one to illuminate the other, in both directions--is and has long been the anthropological synthesis. That synthesis employs a theoretical perspective of ecological evolution, ethological fieldwork (and laboratory study), population genetics for analyzing the distribution of hereditary traits, and study of innovation and social transmission as adaptive processes where heredity is not helpful in explaining behavioral variation. In some respects our synthesis resembles the 1950 vision of John Paul Scott (cited by Wilson, this volume):

> an interdisciplinary science which lies between the fields of biology (particularly ecology and physiology) and psychology and sociology [emphasis added--JS].

Anthropologists have periodically come up with neologisms such as "biosocial perspective" or "bioculturology" to describe the synthesis that unites our division of labor. It is not surprising that the term, "Sociobiology," was first used by a scholar with anthropological commitments, the linguist Charles F. Hockett (Wilson, this volume). Accordingly, as anthropologists, we have no reason to overreact to "Sociobiology" as a term. Its use should not plunge us into a Hell of Oversimplified Determinism. Unfortunately, its adoption does not automatically lift us into a Promised Land of Fruitful Syntheses.

Reductionism: The Synthesis of Teeth and Tasty Morsel

Few anthropologists would welcome a sociobiological synthesis that makes the subject matter sociological and the mode of analysis biological. Not all definitions of sociobiology do suggest such reductionism. As a discipline, sociobiology is not itself fully synthesized. Hull (this volume) adverts to its competing "invisible colleges" and we must be cautious in selecting a "type specimen."

Anthropologists would have little quarrel with the "basic premise" of sociobiology given by Emlen (this volume): "given certain ecological constraints ('problems') there exist a limited subset of adaptive social organizations ('solutions')." However, other definitions of sociobiology have been offered: it seeks "the genetic foundation of . . . social behavior" (Wilson, this volume); its "Central Theorem . . . [is] that organisms can be expected to behave so as to maximize their inclusive fitness" (Barash, this volume); its explanatory synthesis necessarily includes population genetics (Barlow, personal communication). And with regard to its future, Wilson (1975:4) has said:

> Sociology and the other social sciences as well as the humanities, are the last branches of biology waiting to be included in the Modern Synthesis. One of the functions of sociobiology, then, is to reformulate the foundations of the social sciences in a way that draws

> these subjects into the Modern Synthesis. Whether the social sciences can be truly biologicized in this fashion remains to be seen.

Levels of Analysis. "Social facts in terms of social facts" was the slogan of the sociologist, Emile Durkheim (1895). The "Father of Sociology," Auguste Comte (1830) had argued earlier against the tendency to reduce sociological phenomena to a biological level of analysis. Analysis at a level appropriate to behavioral traits that arise from innovation and spread by social transmission is the basis of the division of labor in anthropology.

We cannot reduce all explanation of social behavior to a biological base, nor even do so by stages, first to phenotypic "predispositions" and then to underlying genes (Sahlins 1976). It is just as inappropriate as it would be to reduce all explanation of biological phenomena to a chemical base. The latter reduction might be tempting as we learn more about the biochemical nature of the genetic molecular materials and what they do. And, in fact, Hull (this volume) tells us that

> as the sociobiologists tuck in their napkins in preparation for their feast on philosophy and the social sciences, physicists and chemists are busily gnawing away at the flanks of biology

(see also Gould, this volume). But we also know that the structure and physiology of organic matter is not simply or adequately to be approached at the level of molecular chemistry.

Claims to the privilege of a distinctive level of analysis carry with them a responsibility. That is, we are obliged to make our approach at that level consistent with the findings at other levels of analysis. For example, generalizations that account for phenomena at a social behavioral level of analysis cannot contradict generalizations at a physiological or biological level of analysis. No more can generalizations in biology contradict generalizations at a physical/ chemical level of analysis. G.C. Williams (1966:5-6) took the responsible stand: he warned against reducing biological processes (e.g., natural selection) to physics while citing the simultaneous need to retain physical laws when treating biological objects as physical objects.

We may also enrich our understandings with findings made at another level of analysis. As I understand it, the proposition being tested by anthropologists Chagnon and Irons (this volume) may be of this nature: to what extent are learned behaviors perpetuated socially because they also confer reproductive success upon their performers?

The perspective that phenomena must be dealt with at their own level of organization for adequate understanding, is a long respected one within the sciences (Kaplan 1964). Thus, while there is nothing wrong (or new) in the desire to synthesize sociological and biological study, anthropologists do not see reductionism as a form of synthesis. Unless the strategy of sociobiology is carefully planned with regard to the reductionist/synthesis distinction, we cannot expect our discussions to advance beyond the nature/nurture dispute.

"Beyond Nature/Nurture" ≠ Beyond Inherited vs. Learned

I known of no anthropologists, biological or sociocultural, who reject epigenesis. Any hereditary trait is expressed phenotypically through an interaction between genotype and environment (but see Barash, this volume). The interaction varies: Some hereditary features develop almost identically in the individuals that share the genotypes, responding with little sensitivity to environmental differences. Other hereditary features are so malleable as to develop in different ways under the influence of differing environmental conditions; an underlying genotype is still detectable or we could not speak meaningfully of them as hereditary features. Adkins (this volume) argues that human gender identity and gender behavior are surprisingly malleable in view of the role of genes and hormones in determining morphological sex.

Thus, we want no false antithesis of heredity versus environment (Caplan, this volume). They are not mutually exclusive determinants. If the symbol "nature/nurture" is a shorthand way of representing that fallacious dichotomy, then we can say that our discussions should be "beyond nature/nurture."

Controversy arises when the perspective "beyond nature/nurture" is taken to mean that we are also beyond considering the way specific behavioral forms originate and get transmitted. If the phrase "nature versus nurture" means sexual reproduction versus social transmission in what sense can we say we are "beyond nature/nurture"?

A given behavioral variant arises either through the occurrence of some new genotype or through innovation; it spreads either genetically through sexual reproduction or it is socially transmitted. One behavioral form (e.g., PTC tasting) can result from a biochemical reaction triggered by the genotype; its phenotypic variability is then determined by interaction between those genetic conditioners and the nourishing quality of the particular environment in which it develops. Another behavioral form (e.g., spouse-selecting behavior) can be invented by some actor and, once invented, learned by other actors. And the form of that behavior will also reflect the attributes of the environment in which the learning and subsequent behaving takes place. I am describing the same contrast made by vertebrate paleontologist George Gaylord Simpson (1971:307-308) when he wrote: "Cultural evolution proceeds only by interthinking, as organic evolution does only by interbreeding."

When some of us mutter "beyond nature/nurture" we mean that "of course there's a genetic component underlying capacities and predispositions." But we go on to discuss innovations of behavioral forms which occur without genotype change; we discuss their perpetuation through socialization or learning; we analyze their distributions ecologically; we talk of social traditions and culture.

When others of us mutter the same incantation, we mean that "of course behaviors can be learned." But we go on as if the term "environment" subsumes the learning process. In such usages, behaviors are coded in terms of genotypes; we discuss their perpetuation as a result of sexual reproduction, as an expression of fitness and gene replication; we talk of genomes and fitness strategies in relation to ecology. With Barash (this volume), we speak of "all behavior deriv[ing] from both genotype and environment" and of behavior "represent[ing] some component of genotype."

In other words, the catechistic question is asked: "Are we beyond nature/nurture"? And the answer is "Yes. We believe in epigenesis. We believe in the interaction of genome and environment." But the lurking question of the social vs. epigenetic source and transmission of specific behaviors goes unnoticed and unanswered.

We cannot be beyond controversy if some of us treat the same specific behavioral form as a hereditary trait whose variation is primarily genetic variation (ultimately mutation), while others treat it as a social tradition--a cultural trait in the case of humans if not for other animals as well--which varies from one population to another as a result of learning (and ultimately innovation). Those who will ask, "But, doesn't the learning process itself have a genetic component?" will find that question discussed in the next major section of this chapter.

At What Level Phylogenetically Should Social Transmission be Treated in Terms of Social Transmission? I have decried the tendency to emphasize human uniqueness at the expense of the evolutionary continuity of life forms. But, of course, in evolution something is always new and yet not new; the new is always a modification of something already present.

Some junctures in the phylogenetic tree seem critical for particular purposes of analysis. Most social scientists and many biologists regard culture as a major emergent phenomenon, one that requires its own mode of analysis (Dobzhansky 1962; Harris 1968; Huxley 1963; Mainardi, this volume; Rensch 1978; Sahlins & Service 1960; Simpson 1971; Steward 1955; White 1949). Leacock (this volume) cites that juncture and two others (plant/animal; invertebrate/vertebrate). Two contributors to this volume apparently see comparable junction points at which their sociobiological predictions encounter difficulties: these entail the emergence of "modern, industrialized societies" (Emlen) and "populations which have . . . experienced the reduction in fertility by means of contraception which is associated with the demographic transition" (Irons).

The contrast between social (communicative) and genetic (sexual) transmission requires us to answer the question where in the phylogenetic tree should our ecological explanation of the occurrence of behavioral forms emphasize one as against the other of these two processes by which specific behavioral forms emerge and spread.

I believe it is safest to leave open the question of social versus sexual transmission for all vertebrates and even higher invertebrates (Rensch 1978). I would do so especially in the case of those "evolutionarily stable strategies . . . [between which] . . . individuals switch back and forth throughout their lives" (Dawkins, this volume).

In his meticulous study of "nepotism" among Belding's ground squirrels, Sherman (this volume) indicates that an inclusive fitness explanation has to be modified by demographically conditioned differences in their experienced interactions. Although Dawkins (this volume) in some passages speaks of evolutionarily stable strategies as "genetically determined behavioral alternatives," elsewhere he allows for other determinants of behavior and recognizes "developmentally and culturally stable strategies" that are determined by experience, innovation and learning. However, what of the cases where insects display a "conditional strategy" or a "monomorphic mixed strategy (each individual follows the same probabilistic rule)," particularly if there is a "continuous quantative variation" to that behavior? If their strategies are of this nature and insects are capable of learning (Rensch 1978), can we be sure that those strategies are "genetically determined behavioral alternatives"?

Accordingly, even though it complicates the task of unifying the study of social behavior and its adaptation, I would argue that we must welcome the work of scientists who study the social transmission and adaptation of innovated behavioral forms as well as that of scientists who study the sexual reproduction of epigenetic behavioral forms.

The two concept contrasts--heredity/environment and sexual transmission/social transmission--seem to have been fused conceptually. Perhaps the distinction between them is blurred by the use of the phrase "nature/nurture." Most anthropologists might wonder how to measure behavioral adaptations so as to say that "human behavior is more influenced by environment than the behavior of other species" (but see Barash, this volume); it is an interesting idea. Without hesitation, however, we would say that "human behavior is more extensively a result of social transmission--of innovation and learning--than the behavior of other species."

The label "nature/nurture" has been used for the interplay of heredity and environment; confusingly, it is invoked for the contrast between sexual and communicative transmission. The confusion is bound to provoke controversy. The question "Beyond Nature/Nurture?" in the title of this volume expresses that; it is at the heart of my doubt that sociobiology represents a synthesis.

Some Fallacies and Cautions in the Study of Human Behavioral Data

Certain questions arise when we want to understand, interpret, explain, or predict the behavioral forms that vary culturally between human populations (and even some that do not vary significantly). These questions are not new; most anthropologists have long been familiar with them. We need to be reminded of them from time to time in anthropology; but also if we are to develop a synthesis where biologists and social scientists in general will benefit from a mutual exchange of their experience in decades of separate work.

Don't Attribute What Is Learned to the Genes for a Learning Capacity

The distinction of genetic from innovated, of sexual transmission from social, already discussed, had to do with the source and perpetuation of particular behavioral forms. While discussing the distinction I acknowledged that the learning process is itself a Nature X Nurture one. Now I want to clarify the distinction between learning as a process and the content of what is learned--e.g. specific behavioral forms.

The learning process and the content of what is learned are not completely unrelated, of course. There are behaviors, clearly part of our organic heritage as vertebrates, mammals, primates, etc., which are nevertheless subject to some modification by innovation and learning. Within some limits, we can learn to alter the duration of inhaling air into our lungs, our metabolic rate, the pulsation of our heartbeats, the flow of our tears, etc. On the other hand, and even more important when we want to study behavior, the learning process of which we humans are capable has a hereditary component. The learning process and its genetic component are related to the behavioral content, to that which is learned. However, they are not identical.

<u>The How of Learning: The Social Transmission Process.</u> To assert that the ability to learn has a genetic component is acceptable to all anthropologists, I am sure. The human capacity for learning (and for innovation) results from a long series of evolutionary changes in the genes of animal organisms.

We must immediately add that there has been no convincing demonstration of significant differences between human populations in the distribution of "the hereditary component" of learning. Environment and heredity are inextricably interwoven; it is a Nature X Nurture process par excellence. We are unable to identify such a component in terms of unit characteristics of heredity; the genetic components are apparently complex.

First, despite impressive work in neurolinguistics and the ingenuity of behavioral geneticists using identical twins reared apart and foster siblings reared together, no scientist has successfully isolated and measured the genetic component of a human learning capacity. To attempt computation of particular percentages of responsibility to be assigned to heredity on the one hand and to environment on the other (DeFries, Livingstone, this volume) has been an extremely difficult pursuit, given the limitations of research on human subjects. It may be an impossible one given the complexity of epigenic interaction and the fact that environments, at least, are not constant. In the study of human "intelligence" and other aptitudes, there have even been instances of apparent chicanery (Gillie 1979).

Second, the only tests we have measure performance rather than a "genetic component." The greater our control over environmental conditions--factors that affect, for example, the equality of experience, motivation, energy level and general metabolism--the more similar are the frequency distribution curves of test scores for different human populations.

Finally, we may ask why we should expect significant differences between human populations in attributes that are critical to survival everywhere. To account for significant differences in learning capacities from population to population, the selective stresses would have to differ. I don't believe that a satisfactory case has been made even for variation in the flexibility of reaction that varying degrees of resource stability might promote.

The "psychic unity of humanity" is evident in the similar range of variation in learning capacity for all human populations and in the universality of logic (= inference-making, see Silverberg 1978b). At one time an assumption or, perhaps, a testable hypothesis (Wilson, this volume), it has become a tested and retained hypothesis (Silverberg 1978b). I cited its importance for explaining the distribution of behavioral and other cultural forms. It underlies the proposition that populations with similar cultural antecedents, faced with similar adaptive problems, will come up with similar cultural solutions.

Thus, genes are involved in the capacity for learning. To what extent and in what way we do not as yet know. How does this help us explain why one behavioral form rather than an alternative one is learned and perpetuated in one human population rather than another?

<u>What is Learned: The Content of Social Traditions</u>. If the learning process has a genetic component, we can say that humans have an "innate predisposition to learn," or perhaps, even, that humans follow "genetically determined learning rules" (Wilson, this volume). But do we risk the "fallacy of misplaced concreteness" when we tie that acceptable proposition to specific behavioral forms? Is that not what happens if we say that humans have an "innate predisposition to learn one thing and not another" (Wilson, this volume).

The problem lies in the vagueness and the inductive specification of that "one thing and not another." To confuse the learning of behavioral forms with the learning process is a Heads-I-Win-Tails-You-Lose invitation to formulating unfalsifiable hypotheses about the occurrence of behavioral forms. When behavior <u>A</u> fails to be manifest in a population, we must deem the underlying genotype to have conditioned only "learning rules" or "a predisposition to learn." When behavior A does occur, then we can affirm "the predisposition will out," it is a predisposition to learn one thing rather than another, and thus the behavioral form is genetically based after all. When behavior A' occurs for the first time, then we must reformulate the range of the "predisposition" in much the way we have had to reformulate the "ultimate" capabilities of humans as the hitherto existing track and field "limits" are surpassed.

A specific form of learned behavior occurs among (some) humans--e.g. cross-cousin marriage, birth control, headhunting, polygyny, pollution, writing. It can be innovated or acquired by any healthy member of our species regardless of genotype (Adkins, Emlen, Leacock, Livingstone, Mainardi, B.J. Williams, all this volume). (Sometimes it can be acquired even by members of other animal species as in chimpanzee use of sign language.) How can a genetic component to the learning capacity help us explain the varying distribution of that behavioral form in our species?

To explain the distribution of a particular behavioral form in terms of its cultural-ecological adaptiveness (discussed elsewhere in this chapter) is not equivalent to identifying a genetic component nor even an invitation to look for one. Learned behavior can be adaptive, nonadaptive, or maladaptive just as anatomical or physiological traits can be. Explaining the occurrence of human behavior in terms of ecological adaptation is an important scientific finding, not to be disregarded or downplayed just because it does not entail a search for some "responsible" genotype.

A synthesizing discipline of comparative animal ecology, concerned with the adaptation and evolution of behavior, will have to analyze behavior genetic in source and sexually perpetuated. It will also have to analyze behavior that results from innovation and social transmission. It will be obliged to avoid the fallacy of mistaking learned behavior for the learning process. It will not be well served by proclaiming that genes are responsible for learning one thing rather than another.

Some Cautions in Using Adaptation and Selection as Explanatory Concepts

Many anthropologists are aware of a need to exercise caution in using the related concepts "adaptation" and "selection" (see also Caplan, this volume).

<u>Does "Adaptation" Explain?</u> My discussion here is couched largely in terms of cultural adaptation; it owes a great deal to the discussion of "functionalism" by the sociologist Robert Merton (1949). Similar considerations apply to biological adaptation.

(1) As is widely recognized, a post factum inference about adaptiveness has only its plausibility as a support. A first step only, it requires testing. In sociocultural anthropology, cross-cultural analysis may reveal the extent to which specified adaptive conditions correlate with specified cultural phenomena. This is in keeping with the analysis of cultural ecology in an evolutionary perspective. Selected cases may help convert a correlation to a probable causal sequence. Sometimes an experimental test of causation can be executed. Without such testing, the interpretation of plausible adaptive consequences is indeed a "Just-So Story" (Gould, this volume). Empirical tests and imaginative game-playing models pertaining to the adaptation of traits and "strategies" are found in many chapters of this volume (Barash, Bradbury, Chagnon, Dawkins, Emlen, Irons, Livingstone, Sherman, Stamps & Metcalf, Warner, B.J. Williams, and G.C. Williams).

(2) Just because some trait exists, its adaptiveness is not established. We know that biological traits (Livingstone 1958) and cultural traits (Harris 1974b) can be nonadaptive or even maladaptive for some of their carriers, perhaps for all. And we also know of populations that could not adapt to changed circumstances; they became extinct (e.g. the Tasmanians).

The selective pressures of adaptation may operate at cross purposes. For example, workers may choose to continue on a job that endangers their health, lives and reproductive potential because they are convinced that the given job is essential in the bread-and-butter sense--it addresses other "felt needs," which they also see as crucial to survival. This choice sometimes induces workers to join their employers in resisting public measures to ameliorate the health- or life-threatening characteristics of their working conditions rather than risk shutdown or flight by the enterprise. It is obvious that adaptation in one sense is being promoted at the expense of adaptation in another. How "reproductive success" is being promoted by their behavior is by no means clear.

A behavioral trait (e.g. contraceptive practice) can manifest its adaptiveness culturally by spreading throughout a population or a whole set of populations. It does not enhance and in some cases it even lowers the "Darwinian fitness" of its performers (Livingstone, B.J. Williams, both this volume)--that is, if fitness is defined only in terms of maximizing gene self-replication.

A biological or cultural trait is likely to be adaptive if it has existed for a considerable period of time. Were it in all respects maladaptive, its carriers would perish and so would the trait unless it left archeological or paleontological evidence of having existed. Perhaps it is scientifically responsible to regard adaptiveness not as an a priori assumption but as an empirical question. Then we can focus attention on how and for whom a given biological or cultural trait is adaptive, nonadaptive or maladaptive.

(3) To demonstrate that some trait is adaptive does not eliminate a need to seek possible alternative traits that have comparable if not identical adaptive consequences. This is particularly true in the case of cultural traits and their "functional equivalents" (Merton 1949). Sahlins (1976:81-83) illustrates the applicability of this caution as against "the fallacy of an a priori fitness course" in biology.

Chagnon (this volume), in an exemplary application of computerized analysis to quantitative genealogical data, persuasively argues for the adaptiveness of reproductive success in terms of cross-cousin marriage in certain Yąnomamö descent lines. He indicates the significance of cross-cousin marriage for inclusive fitness. I anticipate that his future research will explore in fitness terms the question of why parallel-cousin marriage (defined later) is not an adaptive equivalent among the Yąnomamö or why cross-cousin marriage is replaced by other marriage forms for many Yąnomamö as, of course, for many other peoples around the world.

(4) It is necessary to specify the unit for which a trait is being interpreted as adaptive. Just as in the case of a biological form (e.g. the sickling allele, Allison 1954; Livingstone 1958), so a cultural behavior (e.g. witchcraft, Harris 1974b) may promote the survival of the society as a whole or some segment(s) of a society while at the same time its occurrence is unadaptive or even maladaptive for some other segment(s) of the same society.

To specify the unit is a must when analyzing selection through social transmission. Behavioral forms are retained in a society through persuasion or coercion because they serve the adaptive interests of an influential or powerful segment. With regard to biological traits the case for and against group-selection is still being argued (Dawkins, Irons, Livingstone, B.J. Williams, all this volume). Also, there is some support for gene- rather than individual-selection

(Dawkins and Stamps & Metcalf, this volume).

(5) We do not expect the adaptive significance of a trait to be in the consciousness of its bearers. People may display a biological or cultural trait that promotes their adaptation in ways they do not perceive or appreciate. Merton identified such adaptation as the "latent" social function of behavior (Merton 1949). It is similar to Abraham Kaplan's (1964) "action meaning" and in some ways to Harris' (1964) "etic analysis." It is not the same as trying to extricate some conscious motivation from among the many that may induce individual humans to act, a point Sahlins recently restated (1976:xii).

<u>The Intelligent Gene's Guide to Adaptation</u>. So far, I have been discussing problems in the study of cultural adaptation. Now I come to some questions of concern to anthropologists when our attention is directed to biological adaptation, particularly to the role genes play. I shall discuss (1) genes and their "strategies," (2) genes and selection, and (3) genes and evolutionary change.

As a student of human behavior I am fascinated but also troubled by the recent history of the language used to describe genetic phenomena. After World War II, with the rise of transistor radios, television, and computer technology, emphasis on information and on communication theory increased. This transcended the scientific world. Personal tragedies were ascribed to an "inability to communicate." Conflicts, domestic and international, were spoken of as "breakdowns in communication." The medium was the message and vice versa.

At about this time we began to hear of the "genetic code," "carrying the information of heredity." Organisms were "wired to" and "programmed by" their genes. Finally, as the double-helix model of chromosome molecules gained popularity, the identification of "messenger RNA" took its place in this terminological set.

More recently, as lineal descendents of such mentalistic chemicals, genes became decision-makers pursuing strategies. Perhaps the strategist model reflected a world of "brinksmanship," "defense postures," and a "balance of terror"; "Game-Theory" was being invoked in Board Rooms, Command Post Shelters and Think Tanks to analyze the alternative consequences of pursuing belligerent or pacific action (see Dawkins & Krebs in press). In any case we began to hear of the "strategies" by which genes, sometimes "selfish" and sometimes acting through maximization of inclusive fitness by their phenotypic agents, pursue their own replication (Caplan, this volume).

A game-theory approach is not restricted to sociobiologists (Lewontin 1961), nor is it ubiquitous among them, but scattered throughout this volume we have a roster of colorful gene-manipulated phenotypic strategists: retaliators, intruder responders, brood defenders (Barash); pirates, honest fishers, "hawks" and "doves" (figuratively), bullies, philanderers (Dawkins); generational and sibling rivals (Stamps & Metcalf); exploiters, cooperators and hypothetical cheater breeders (G.C. Williams). These organisms (or their genes) "choose" among alternative strategies, even deceit, for they may develop masking strategies that hide their real ones (Barash, Dawkins, both this volume). Strategies are carefully weighed in terms of "cost/benefit analysis," "investments, measured in terms of pay-offs," "economic outcomes," "profit" (e.g. G.C. Williams, this volume).

Most proponents of such terminology would correctly state that they are indulging in graphic and useful metaphor. But is there not also a danger that we will mistake the metaphors for reality, that we will see the reproductive strategies of "informed" genes as an actual evolutionary process? If so, will not the direction of the relation between organism and environment reverse that of the classical Darwinian paradigm? A terminological preference for "kin selection" over "natural selection" may reflect this. What Warner (this volume) calls "the force of natural selection" was for Darwin simply the relative advantage or disadvantage conferred on particular phenotypic traits by a given impersonal environment. Seen thus, selection helped to explain evolutionary change in a population (e.g. a species) and merely indicated the direction of that change. But with kin selection, gene and organism strategists are in the driver's seat. They command the process as they pursue a final outcome: the replication of an existing genotype (see also Sahlins 1976: 74-77).

We may be victims of our own culture in this change; perhaps we are not being sufficiently wary about the way the terminology and perspective of our own society influence our view of the evolutionary process. In being "a means of the organism's ends," says Sahlins (1976:xv):

> 'natural selection' has been progressively assimilated to the theory of social action characteristic of the competitive marketplace, . . . a late and historically specific development of Euro-American culture (p. xiv). . . . Darwinism, at first appropriated to society as 'social Darwinism,' has returned to biology as genetic capitalism (p. 72).

We should be cautious about taking our metaphors for reality; this is particularly true when we seek to explain the evolution of cultural behavior in terms of a selection process. Of course, we must also be prepared for our current terminological fashions and conceptual models to pass from the scene. As Gould (this volume) shows, earlier models for conceptualizing biological forms and their functions have enjoyed enthusiastic and widespread use only to be replaced by others.

Genetic Diversity and Selection. What follows is not at all new. Nevertheless, it bears repeating in the light of wariness about genes that not only carry "information" but do so as reproductive strategists.

Most anthropologists have been trained in a Darwinian-Mendelian tradition whereby (1) selection operates on the hereditary variation present in any population; (2) a hereditarily heterogeneous population--i.e. a gene pool characterized by diversity--has the evolutionary advantage of flexibility as the environment changes; and (3) genetic diversity is guaranteed by particulate inheritance in sexual reproduction, given alternative alleles at some gene loci (approximately 30% in humans). (Of course, discussion of the comparative advantage of different modes of reproduction must hold constant or must cope with variables such as average duration of fertility, average length of gestation, average litter size, and factors affecting fertility. See G.C. Williams, this volume.)

We understand that selection operates through the differential survival and, in the final analysis, the differential reproduction of individuals. For anthropologists and many biologists, the development of population genetics contributes to this Darwinian understanding in evolutionary terms: In the differential survival of populations; in the changed frequency distribution of their phenotypes and, by implication, their genotypes through time; in speciation and the like. On the other hand, the same focus on reproduction by individuals has induced many sociobiologists and their predecessors to emphasize the continual replication of existing genes by the reproductive strategies of inclusive fitness or kin selection pursued by organisms if not genes. Can it be the latter view that leads G.C. Williams (this volume) to say:

> The near universality of sexual reproduction remains a major unsolved mystery. It is explicitly a mystery in relation to kin selection, on which so much of sociobiological thought depends.

Our understanding leads us to emphasize the factors that retain genetic heterogeneity in a population despite selective stresses. (1) The selective neutrality of much genetic variation. (2) The operation of selection directly on the phenotype and only indirectly on the genotype (Caplan, this volume; but see Dawkins and Stamps & Metcalf, this volume). This factor has particular consequences for traits that are polygenic or those affected by alleles with differential expressivity and differential penetrance. (3) The nature of selection in operating on the total organism rather than single features, a factor further complicated by pleiotropy. (4) Variation in selective stresses as environment changes, so that what was adaptive yesterday may not be today. (5) The effect of germinal mutations and recombination. (6) The effect of gene flow and genetic drift. (7) Balanced polymorphism as in the already cited case of the sickling allele or in thalassemia and other hemoglobin variants. (See Lewontin 1974.)

The Protozoan Perspective: Fitness vs. Evolutionary Change. Anthropologists have a longstanding concern with the evolutionary background of our own species and thus with evolutionary change. We favor as instructive those biological models which, like the study of industrial melanism among English moths (Kettlewell 1958; Cook & Askew 1970) emphasize hereditary variation, changing environments with changing selective stresses, and change in phenotype frequencies and implicitly in genotype frequencies.

To most anthropologists, those fitness studies that focus only on reproductive strategies to replicate existing genes do not help in explaining the history of successive changes and the fascinating diversity that mark the evolutionary record (Leacock, this volume). Such a static version of Darwinism would seem to be a "Protozoan Perspective," best suited to explaining why all forms of life should continue today to be unchanging single-celled organisms.

Downplaying Behavioral Diversity in General

Anthropologists should approach the question of behavioral comparison within the primate order and even within broader taxonomic categories bearing in mind at least three caveats. These are not always observed by anthropologists and may be partially or wholly overlooked in sociobiological writings on catarrhine or Old World high primate "properties" (e.g. Wilson, this volume).

Don't Violate Phylogenetic Relationships. Leacock (this volume) argues that we must "deal with evolution in its full sense." Our analysis must recognize "qualitative differences [that have] emerged in the course of organic evolution . . . when analyzing relations among reproductive strategies, social interaction patterns, and environmental influences." She asks why we should ignore such differences while implicitly recognizing the differences between animals and plants: "After all, plants rather more easily than animals can be described as the means DNA uses to replicate itself."

There is a related terminological problem. We need a better scientific taxonomy for the higher primates than that which still seems to prevail in anthropology and zoology textbooks; we certainly need a better one than our folk usages. The common phrase "monkeys and apes" is a case in point (cf. "Affen" in German or "mono" in Spanish). Such folk taxonomies, widely used in scientific writings, distort the phylogenetic picture that rests on anatomical, physiological, parasitological, immunological and other biochemical evidence. The folk term "monkey" classes together certain catarrhines (the cercopithecoids) and all platyrrhines. It does so on the basis of analogies rather than homologies (Caplan, this volume). Even the phrasing "Old World monkeys, great apes and humans" ignores data that, within the catarrhines, would put chimpanzees and gorillas closer to humans than any of those three is to orang-utans and even more so than they are to gibbons and siamangs. The data would also put all apes closer to humans than they are to the cercopithecoids or "Old World monkeys" (Buettner-Janusch 1966; Goodman & Tashian 1976; Lancaster 1973).

The relations given reflect the present biochemical evidence. Probably on anatomical and neurological grounds relating to bipedal locomotion and language and the related nonorganic or "superorganic" (White 1949) factor of culture, most anthropologists would separate humans from the closely related African apes (Buettner-Janusch 1966:165). In my discussion below I shall loosely use "hominoid" to cover humans and all apes, including hylobatids.

Don't Minimize Intraspecies Behavioral Variation. The impression that a behavioral form has an obvious genetic component is strengthened by the assumption that such behavior is universal among the members of a species or higher taxon. We must remember the recency of good information on intraspecies behavioral variation for nonhuman primates in relation to differing ecological circumstances--e.g. the Japanese macaque research (Miyadi 1967), varying baboon aggression, dominance gradients and group sizes (DeVore & Hall 1965). Intraspecies behavioral variation is the name of the game with humans. To analyze and explain such variation has been the driving force of sociocultural anthropology; that experience should contribute usefully to its study among other animals.

Don't Overgeneralize the Findings. The evidence on mating behavior and social group size among hominoids is a case in point. Hominoid behaviors do not support widely circulated generalizations about the prevalence of primate polygyny nor about an association between polygyny and sexual dimorphism. In my discussion of this I shall follow the anthropomorphizing practice of those who use the terms for marriage to describe mating patterns. I have misgivings about doing so. Marriage has the social function of replicating a system of social statuses and roles; mating has the function of reproducing organisms and some of their genes. The etymology of "gamous" is related to Sanskrit terms for "in-laws," it should be said, and I don't believe any nonhuman animals perform "in-law" roles (Lowie 1948:79-84).

The most dimorphic apes, orang-utans, are not exclusively polygynous (MacKinnon 1974:55), nor are the quite dimorphic and closer-to-human gorillas (Harcourt et al. 1976; Schaller 1963). Since females in both species can copulate with more than one male, matings might as easily be described as "polyandrous," or rather "promiscuous" to cover the gamut of encounters, as among Belding's ground squirrels (Sherman, this volume). (By "promiscuity," I do not mean that matings occur at random nor that they necessarily include copulations between siblings or between parents and offspring.)

Chimpanzees are somewhat dimorphic but not polygynous (Sugiyama 1973). They, too, seem to display promiscuity. The nondimorphic siamangs and gibbons seem to be almost universally monogamous (Carpenter 1941; Chivers 1972). Among humans, marriage and other mating patterns are diverse, responding to local ecological circumstances and subject to rapid change (within a single generation). Polygyny is widely permitted among humans; indeed, it is an idealized form of marriage in many societies. However, its actual occurrence is far less frequent and, I repeat, selection has to do with actual behavior rather than privileges or wishes. It is also not permitted in many societies. These data are not cited to test the possibility of a dimorphism-polygyny correlation, necessarily, but to correct the notion that either of these traits are universal properties among hominoids.

The size of what Wilson (this volume) calls the "intimate social grouping," also seems to depend on the ecological situation more than on the taxon (e.g. Sugiyama 1973:404). If we wish to generalize for the various species of hominoids, gibbons and siamangs are almost always limited to two adults plus two or three young; orangs seem to be confined to small mother-offspring groups and may often be solitary. It is difficult to demarcate boundaries, much less to assess an average size, for the loosely-bonded, accordion-like chimpanzee groups. Depending on local ecology, chimpanzees can be organized into groups or communities as large as 60 individuals, but they generally travel about their home range in small temporary parties, quite fluid in membership (Goodall 1977:260). Although gorilla groups are relatively more stable than those of chimpanzees, gorillas also exhibit a loose form of social organization (Harcourt et al. 1976). And human settlement patterns, of course, range in diversity from the megalopolis to the seasonally solitary family of hunter or trapper.

The danger of overgeneralizing is compounded by using anthropomorphic labels for behavioral forms and structures across phylogenetic lines where similarities are meaningless (see "Interpretation by Labelling" below). Sharply cutting terms, of course, enhance interobserver reliability. Having done research on South Asian caste (Silverberg 1959, 1961, 1968, 1978a, in press), I am uncomfortable with the use of "caste" for both human and ant social organization and I shall use it as an example.

Ant "castes" have little in common with the source, form, function, or the culturally flexible and socially transmitted behavior of human castes. There is a superficial resemblance in form and function in two respects only; this resemblance breaks down under careful analysis. The distinction between ant "castes" is marked by a sharp division of productive labor and by social ranking, perhaps (how do we know?). Human castes are only sometimes characterized by such a division of labor; frequently, they are not. Human castes jockey with each other for relative rank. "Castes" among ants are not endogamous social units; members of different ant "castes" share the same, often "polyandrous," mother. Human castes are endogamous; ideally there can be no reproduction through mating outside their boundaries (though actually this does occur). Individual members of the same human caste have differing genomes. Those of ant "castes" do not. Finally, each significant action or interaction that can be described as caste behavior for humans, is a role that has to be learned by the human actor. None is determined in any way that resembles the epigenetic determination of behavior for the members of ant "castes."

Downplaying Human Behavioral Diversity

Anthropological data and an anthropological perspective have often been useful for correcting erroneous folk beliefs as well as scholarly generalizations based on an overly narrow and unrepresentative sample of human cultures. Anthropologists, some psychologists, and more recently, other social scientists, have provided extensive documentation on the malleability of humans and the great diversity of roles they are capable of learning (Adkins, Leacock, Livingstone, Shields, all this volume).

It is possible to be impatient with anthropologists when they seem to regard their responsibility as that of constantly turning up "negative instances." It is appropriate to remind them of the probabilistic nature of scientific laws and to ask them to measure the extent and significance of their "exceptions" to such laws. However, if we are to test "the particular hypothesis of the genetic evolution of human nature" (Wilson, this volume), anthropologists have a responsibility to make known the actual distribution of the specific behavioral forms hypothesized as having genetic correlates. Does their actual distribution support any assumption that they are universal in our species or even an assumption that actual behavior corresponds to idealized or putative behavior?

<u>Taking What's Familiar or Widespread as Universal</u>. Nonanthropologists will sometimes take as a universal trait of humans, that behavior with which they are familiar because it is characteristic of their own and related societies (Leacock, Shields, this volume). If parent-offspring, sibling, and first cousin mating is forbidden as incestuous in all societies known to them, such individuals assume it to be a species-wide behavioral form. They then go on to speculate as to why human beings "universally have incest tabus." Undefined, the behavioral form is assumed by such a label to be the same, single, familiar phenomenon, "universally."

However, incest is not a single phenomenon for our species. Almost any introductory sociology or anthropology text will document the following assertions: Mother-son copulation is apparently prohibited as incestuous universally. Nonetheless many societies permit, some prefer and some even prescribe marriage between the very categories of individuals whose casual mating (much less marriage) is regarded as incestuous and prohibited by other societies. "One man's taboo 'sibling' is the same man's wife elsewhere" (Slater 1959:1046). On the other hand, "in no human society is the incest taboo limited to the nuclear family, whatever its range of variation may be" (Aberle et al. 1963:261). (See also Mead 1968; Middleton 1962; White 1949:303-329.)

The equivalent of generalizing our concept of incest would be for people from other cultures to see their special behaviors as species-wide, human universals: for the pre-British Todas of South Asia, infanticide; for the Yąnomamö, "Yąnomamö-type aggression" (Wilson, this volume); for the Rajput, clan and lineage hypergamy; for the Tibetan, polyandry;

for the Dobuan of Melanesia, sorcery; for the Melanesian in general, sister-exchange; and, to return home once more, for the U.S. American, spouse-selection by romantic love and getting what the market will permit through cost-benefit calculation.

If we speak of deliberate reproductive strategies, of inclusive fitness via kin selection, and the like, the caveat is clear. We come to the study of another culture armed with understandings whose logical calculus uses a familiar premise of our culture, namely, the "diploid process discovered by twentieth-century biologists" (Sahlins 1976:39). We assume those understandings are universally relevant. However, local understandings of kin connection, perhaps even of reproduction, in the culture studied may not coincide with ours. They are derived, also by logical calculus, from locally accepted premises that are not familiar to us (Silverberg 1978b).

The question of mistaking the familiar as "human" transcends the unfamiliarity of particular, local cultural understandings. If anthropologists are going to make use of challenging biological concepts like inclusive fitness or kin selection, sociobiologists should be more receptive to information about the ways human reproduction is actually organized in different cultures. For example, Sahlins (1976:30) harbors doubts that there is a correlation between "the cultural organization of reproductive success" and "inclusive fitness calculated on biological connections." He presents some 28 pages of coefficient of relationship-modeling and data to support his assertion (p. 26) that:

> there is not a single system of marriage, postmarital residence, family organization, interpersonal kinship, or common descent in human societies that does not set up a different calculus of relationship and social action than is indicated by the principles of kin selection.

I believe that most anthropologists could add examples from their own field experience also indicating that

> the members of the kinship groups which organize human reproduction are more closely related genealogically to persons outside the group than to certain others within it (Sahlins 1976:40).

However, the overall conclusion about the relative relatedness of coresidents versus noncoresidents is still open to research (Chagnon, this volume) as is its cultural or biological significance.

Taking Ideal Behavior to be Actual Behavior. At our present stage of being able to communicate with chimpanzees and other nonhuman animals, the problem of confusing verbalized accounts with actual behavior does not exist in the study of their performances. To have data on human behavior that can be compared with those from animal ethograms and to interpret them in terms of adaptation, anthropologists must work harder than they have in the past to derive the modal tendencies in actual behavior along with locally reported (putative) behavior tendencies and normative statements of what is permitted, preferred or prescribed. In fact, where several behavioral forms occur as mutually exclusive alternatives, we should obtain and make available the incidence of each--a frequency distribution of the variant actual behaviors.

Relevant to the importance of working with actual behavior rather than idealizations, a considerable amount of anormative (in our society illegal) incestuous behavior does take place in actuality, despite the underestimation in available data (Chagnon, Livingstone, this volume).

Chagnon (this volume) is careful to indicate that he is analyzing the Yąnomamö ideal pattern of bilateral cross-cousin marriage as it is actually practiced by the descendants of particularly prolific, polygynous men. In discussing the failure of many Yąnomamö to follow the cross-cousin marriage prescription and the political usefulness of unprescribed marital ties, especially for those in small villages, he asserted: "It is for this reason that such a large discrepancy exists between the ideal behavior and the actual practice. . . ." (Chagnon 1968:80-81; see also MacCluer 1973:227; Reid 1973:101).

When we anthropologists talk about genealogies and the regulation of behavior in terms of kinship roles, we are referring to sociological identifications whether or not they correspond to biological realities. Most societies go by the Napoleonic Code: the father of any child is the husband of its mother. Furthermore, deliberate adoption, which is institutionalized and widespread in some societies, and an insistence on classificatory kinship terms (if not by an informant then by his or her ancestors) will contribute "relationships" to a genealogy that are not really biological (Lowie 1948:57-59; Reid 1973:85; Rivers 1910; Sahlins 1976:48-52; Schneider 1968; Weinstein 1968).

If we wish to interpret in terms of "coefficients of relationship," great care must be exercised lest we erroneously take the putative sociological identifications as actual biological relationships. Chagnon (this volume) affirms that he observed just such precautions.

Finally, there is the questionable reliability of putative (informant-estimated) behavioral information. As I indicated earlier, this may be different from the ideal and the actual. When infant mortality figures, for example, are derived from reports by mothers of their miscarried, stillborn, and early dying infants, one must allow for the unreliability of such reports as memory loss increases with age and with poverty and work preoccupation (see Irons, this volume).

Inferring Biological Significance from Culture Trait Distributions

Species-Specific + Universal ≠ Part of Our Genetic Base. The controlled use of fire is a universal trait among humans, though the knowledge of how to make fire is not and, where it isn't present, a fire must be kept smoldering or borrowed from another person. Does the universality of fire-use and its restriction to our species mean that we must attribute the origin and spread of this highly adaptive behavior to some allele(s) that arose through mutation and have been perpetuated through sexual reproduction? Fire-use, of course, was a cultural innovation which made human "adaptations for food intake" less "invariant" (see Warner, this volume).

A behavioral form may be restricted to our species (= species-specific); it may be universal to humans, or assumed to be. Those conditions do not warrant the conclusion that the trait tells us anything we didn't already know about the genetic basis for human behavior. Nor does that universal genetic base, the capacity for human culture-building, tell us anything useful for predicting what item of culture will come next, nor where, when and why any particular innovation occurred in the past. Whether we are concerned with a universal trait or one whose distribution varies, to inquire about its genetic component simply postpones a serious effort to explain its origin and spread in cultural-ecological terms.

Fitness and Behavioral Variants. A number of human behavioral forms, however, do seem at first glance to be suitable for consideration in terms of "inclusive fitness" (defined as the transmission of gene sets as similar as possible to those of the parents). Marriage regulations and incest prohibitions exemplify such behavioral forms. They are pertinent to the transmission of gene sets; rather, they are if we give due consideration to and have sufficient research control over the difference between socially recognized and biologically exact genealogies, as discussed earlier.

Most societies in the world do not leave spouse selection to the potential spouses. If the model of "strategies" pursued by individuals who are mating on behalf of the replication of their genes (Barash, Dawkins, this volume) is being used, such surrogate strategists as parents, other kinfolk, perhaps even matchmakers must somehow be incorporated into the model. There may of course be strong cultural constraints --e.g. prescriptions to marry persons of a proper "genealogical connection" or a proper lineage or clan. But frequently, these requirements (or corresponding prohibitions) are defined in terms so general as to make other factors primary for the parties who actually arrange the marriage. Those factors--economic success, political alliance, and such personal attributes as dutifulness, hard work, freedom from scandal, demureness, attractiveness--may have no intrinsic connection with the degree to which gene sets are shared, and thus with the workings of inclusive fitness.

Chagnon (this volume) analyzes intricate genealogical data to support the hypothesis that Yąnomamö preferential marriage with cross-cousins is characterized by reproductive success in terms of both fertility and inclusive fitness. Such a finding will have to be replicated in many cultural-ecological situations and alternative hypotheses tested before conclusions can be generalized to a wider universe.

For example, the coefficient of relationship, r, that applies to cross-cousins is "identical" to the r for parallel-cousins. The only difference between cross- and parallel-cousins is in the sex of the sibling in their parents' generation that connect them as cousins: if those connecting parents are of different sexes, their respective offspring are cross-cousins; if of the same sex, the offspring are parallel-cousins. The "identity" between cross- and parallel-cousin r's is so even if we adopt the definition of r as

> the probability that a certain gene is shared with a relative through common descent, rather than as the proportion of genes shared between relatives through common descent

as is usefully suggested by Stamps and Metcalf (this volume).

If the potential inclusive fitness is "identical" for parallel-cousin marriage, we must investigate why parallel-cousins are tabued from marrying or even casual mating with each other among the Yąnomamö. Such marriages are tabued, although incestuous marriages may have an actual incidence as high as eight percent among the Yąnomamö, according to Chagnon's data reported earlier (1968:73). I put their r's as "identical" in quotation marks because there is one biological difference between the two kinds of cousin: the connecting parents of parallel-cousins must of course share an identical sex chromosome by descent; the connecting parents of cross-cousins cannot. This would, on balance, suggest a slightly higher r for parallel-cousins than cross-cousins. But the higher r for parallel-cousins refers to sex-linked traits only and, for them, it depends on the sex chromosome in question (present knowledge emphasizing the X chromosome), the sex of the parents, and, in the case of cross-cousins, sex agreement between parent and offspring (Levitan 1977:490; Neel & Schull 1954:64).

If there is the slightest r advantage, the inclusive fitness measurement should call for parallel-cousin marriage with a much higher incidence in the world than its rare occurrence suggests. I hasten to add that it does occur (e.g. among Arabs and some other Moslems, Murphy & Kasdan 1959; in Bechuanaland, I. Schapera cited in Lerner & Libby 1976:366), lest greater approximation toward sibling incest be argued as the reason for its relative infrequency as a preferential marriage form. The problem requires further research before it can be asserted that particular behavioral variants are favored in terms of inclusive fitness. And it would still be advisable to analyze the distribution of such behavioral variants in terms of cultural ecology.

The Early Pleistocene Behavioral Fixation

Anthropologists are almost universally critical of popularizations that "explain" some familiar forms of human behavior today in terms of their alleged adaptiveness for our ancestors of the late Pliocene or early Pleistocene (Ardrey 1961, 1966, 1970, 1976; Lorenz 1966; Morris 1967; Tiger 1969; Tiger & Fox 1972). Sahlins (1976) shows how this argument often takes the form of an early adaptiveness of phenotypical drives and dispositions; these are then viewed as underlying a variety of specific behavioral forms today and in human history.

In such accounts, "aggressiveness," "avarice," "proprietariness" (often treated as "territoriality"), etc. became fixed at least four million years ago, when our ancestors were small-brained, nomadic, tropical or semitropical, savanna-dwelling foragers. In a comparable exposition, "nest-fouling" millions of years earlier, when our ancestors were arboreal, became a trait that helps "explain" our polluting of the environment today (Barash 1977:323).

With regard to this "Early Pleistocene Fixation," first, evidence for the occurrence of the alleged "drives" in those early periods is not secure. Second, their adaptiveness for the early Pleistocene is often an untested post factum assertion, though in the best of cases it is perhaps plausible. Third, the assumption that the behavioral traits which exemplify such "drives" arose genetically rather than through innovation is also untested. Fourth, such "drives" are manifest only in situational behaviors today--i.e., "aggression" is displayed in particular personal encounters or is culturally stimulated (in wartime, for example), and it often alternates with traits that exemplify diametrically opposed "drives."

However, even if the "drives" were Pleistocene adaptations, attributable to some genotypic factors inherited from earlier hominoid ancestors or to some mutations among early humans, why should we expect evolutionary processes to have ceased in the Pleistocene (Livingstone, this volume)? Data from contemporary foragers (e.g. Leacock, this volume) do not indicate that such "drives" were perpetuated throughout the millions of years that preceded the domestication of plants and animals and the abandonment of gathering-hunting as a primary mode of subsistence. Thus, such drives should have been subjected to contrary selective pressures in the intervening millions of years. Environmental selection always threatens the alleles of a gene pool (through the phenotypic organism) with the question: "Well, what have you done for me lately?"

Indeed, if our species is to avoid thermonuclear suicide, if any fitness or reproductive success for humans is to be maintained, the selective stress will have to be on eliminating aggressive behavior and eliminating an ideology that rationalizes aggression as inevitable. Perhaps the vast majority of our genes, as strategists safeguarding their own future reproduction, will somehow succeed in linking up with "cooperative," "generous," "pacific" dispositional "alleles" to eliminate "aggressive," "selfish," "competitive" ones. (Oops. We've just invented a new game. We can call it "Evolutionary Mobile Strategy (EMS) modeling.")

Interpreting by Labelling

Anthropologists are still struggling to overcome a series of difficulties that have to do with formulating and using labels for specific behavioral forms.

Using Overly General Labels. We must beware of the fallacy of creating the checklist type label that subsumes an array of diverse behavioral traits. It may imply a more specific and deliberate behavioral form than is actually present in some populations. The error lies in interpreting the category label as a behavioral trait and regarding it as universal or even specific for some species (or broader taxon). "Funeral rites" would be an example (Murdock 1945:124). Perhaps that category cell has to be filled for some societies by an entry such as "leave bodies where they fall." We would be misled and misleading if we went on to say that funeral rites "occur in every culture known to history or ethnography" (Ibid.). Emlen (this volume) indicates that "territoriality" is of this nature. "Dominance" may also be, especially if "dominance" is taken to mean "control over women's sexuality" (Leacock, this volume).

Using Overly Simple Labels. We take an interpretive step of comparable riskiness when we put complex behavior under an overly simple label. The risk is compounded when our findings become part of the evidence in a sample for a wider universe whose other cases employ the label more precisely. The label "polygyny" or "male dominance polygyny" is sometimes used to designate a situation where several females mate with a single male but where each such female can herself mate with more than one male (i.e. polyandry in those instances), as among Belding's ground squirrels (Sherman, this volume). Similarly, the characterization "dominant" must be used with care. It cannot be used without some adjective if it refers, say, to mating behavior only, in a population where there is differential dominance in other, nonmating kinds of interaction as well and where the ordinal rankings are not consistent with "mating dominance."

Using Evaluative Labels. I have mentioned the wariness anthropologists have had to develop about ethnocentrism. They try, through their training, to overcome the tendency to judge behavior in another culture by what is familiar or normative in their own.

There seems to be a comparable risk in research on nonhuman animals. Some labels for behavioral "strategies," for example, read motivation into behavior: impressing females; preferring aggressive males; deceit; mere bravado; dying gasp retaliation; sneaking; making the best of a bad job; honesty; philandering; bullying. Other labels seem to explain away nonconfirming behavior: "misdirected chases."

I do not say that the behaviors cannot or should not be described in this fashion. However, we should exercise caution as well as ingenuity. We want to satisfy the desirability of vivid exposition, but also the necessity of specifying empirical indicators so that we can test and if necessary reject hypothesized motivations.

Conclusions

Anthropologists are students of human behavior. As such, they have reason to explore the linkages between science and society, linkages that are of concern to the American Association for the Advancement of Science. Anthropologists should carry out and be receptive to research in the sociology of science (Caplan, Gould, Hull, Leacock, Shields, all this volume; Sahlins 1976). Science develops in a broader society, subject to the pulls and pressures of its contending forces; it does not develop in a vacuum. To propose biologizing the social sciences has political and ethical implications even if the proponent is not conscious of them. These implications are legitimately explored as part of the sociology of science.

However, to assess the behavior-conditioning role that genes may have is not solely a matter of politics or ethics. It is a scientific one as well. To speak of a genetic component, or even to identify one if that were possible, will not explain behavioral variation where such variation responds to the processes of innovation and social transmission.

Anthropology represents a synthesis, but also a division of labor between those studying morphology and physiology and those studying cultural behavior. For intraspecies variation in behavior has long been recognized for human animals. Perhaps decades of work on human behavior at its own level of analysis by sociocultural anthropologists can provide some useful insights, techniques, and modes of analysis to scientists who are concerned with the comparative study of animal behavior. Since the processes of learning and social transmission are by no means restricted to the human animal, even though they may be present to a unique degree among humans, we have something to offer zoologists, just as they can contribute to our understanding of population genetics for humans at a biological level of analysis. (After drafting this chapter I received an excellent statement of substantially the same viewpoint about "a biologically and socially based behavioral science" from the eminent physical anthropologist, Sherwood L. Washburn, 1978).

We have accumulated a great amount of data on human behavioral variation, both within and between societies and during the life-cycles of individuals. These data on the malleability of humans enable us to assert the importance of innovation and social transmission as efficient causes of such varying behavior and to seek cultural-ecological explanations for the occurrence of variant behavioral traits. Our explanations relate a particular behavior form to particular adaptive conditions--those of environment, demography and the rest of the behavioral system (culture). As explained in the discussion on cultural ecology in evolutionary perspective, we test hypotheses of correlation and causal sequence between these variables.

There is room for a comparative approach something like the anthropological synthesis that uses evolutionary ecology in both sociological and biological explanation, extending it beyond its present focus on primates. However, it cannot use a reductionist approach that attempts to explain sociocultural phenomena only in terms of biological structures and mechanisms. We continue to recognize the difference between the social (communicative) and genetic (sexual) transmission of traits even though both kinds are subject to adaptational analysis. Such a synthesis would be the best way to make intraspecies behavioral study and phylogenetic comparisons productive.

Summary

Anthropology seeks and sometimes demonstrates a synthesis in the study of human biological and sociocultural adaptation. We deal with an animal whose primary mechanism of adaptation is culture. We have reason to feel that our decades of work on behavioral variation in the human species may provide insights, techniques, and modes of analysis useful to scientists who are concerned with the comparative study of animal behavior.

The fieldwork we do in sociocultural anthropology is essentially ethological. We get behavioral data by indirectly "detecting" it, by witnessing it, or by asking about it. We try to check what we hear by what we see or can detect. However, we should probably do more than we now do to emphasize actual behavior over ideal or putative versions of behavior. After all, selection works on actual behavior.

Our perspective is generally an evolutionarily ecological one, much of it "specific evolution." When we analyze hereditary features we use population genetics. In sociocultural analysis, often called "cultural ecology," we explain the occurrence (and recurrence) of innovations and thus the distribution of behavioral variants. Given the psychic unity (= inference-making) of humanity, similar adaptive problems and similar cultural antecedents, different populations will come up with similar (or comparable) sociocultural solutions. Some anthropologists extend our ethological, ecological, evolutionary perspective to work on nonhuman primates ("primatology").

Given this background on what anthropologists do, it is clear that the concept "sociobiological synthesis," cannot be rejected. Is it not new to us. However, we cannot accept it in a reductionist form whereby the subject matter is sociological while the analytical approach is purely genetical. The phrasing, "genetic foundations of social behavior," suggests such reductionism.

We agree that we should go beyond nature/nurture; we accept an epigenetic interaction of heredity and environment in producing phenotypes. This does not eliminate a distinction between the genetic (sexual) and the social (communicative) transmission and perpetuation of behavioral traits on the part of phenotypic organisms.

Our division of labor in anthropology reflects the distinction just made: we have to deal with both biological and sociocultural adaptations. We feel it should be at the heart of a comparative approach to social behavior throughout the animal kindgom provided the approach encompasses evolutionary change, phylogenetic differences, and the emergence and development of social transmission. While humans and other animals may differ qualitatively, may exemplify what Simpson (1971:212) labelled "quantum evolution," we all accept the evolutionary continuity of life. For now, however, it seems reasonable to leave open the question of which branches in the phylogenetic tree require us to work with these two kinds of adaptation.

Work with human behavioral data, at least, requires attention to some cautions and potential fallacies. (1) It is misleading to speak of a "genetic component" in the learning <u>process</u> as helping us to predict or explain specific, learned, behavioral variations in genetic terms. Different behavioral forms are present and get adopted and dropped readily by individual humans and human populations. In that sense, it is misleading and unproductive to talk of a genetically-based predisposition to learn one thing rather than another.

(2) We should observe cautions about the concept "adaptation": (a) It should not be left without further testing for correlations and causal sequences as an unfalsifiable, albeit plausible, post factum "Just-So Story"; (b) We should not be blind to non- and maladaptive consequences of traits nor to traits that alternatively meet the same adaptive problem; (c) We should be aware that the same trait may have different consequences for units at different levels of analysis --e.g. individuals, segments, whole populations; (d) We should not confuse adaptation with conscious motivations; (e) We should be sensitive lest imaginative models and terms--e.g.

"intelligent" genes pursuing their "strategies"--distort our understanding; (f) We must keep in mind that if genes are busy replicating themselves, they do so in a real world where selective stresses act directly on whole, phenotypic organisms and only indirectly affect the genes, and we should not lose sight of the fact that those stresses are subject to change quite apart from what the gene's "strategies" are.

(3) Certain fallacies obscure behavioral diversity in general: (a) to violate phylogenetic relationships either by ignoring significant evolutionary changes or by using inappropriate terminology; (b) to minimize intraspecies variation; and (c) to overgeneralize the findings--e.g., speaking of <u>all</u> primates as dimorphic and polygynous, or underrepresenting the diversity in the size and composition of their social groups. (4) In the case of human behavior, where diversity is what we expect and find, there are two common dangers: (a) to take the culturally familiar or widespread as if it were universal and species-specific, and (b) to take norms (rules) as if they were actual behaviors. (5) The further fallacy of prematurely attributing genetic significance to behavioral phenomena is seen to operate in two ways: (a) to assume that some behavioral form is genetically transmitted only because it is restricted to and universal within a species and (b) to affirm the reproductive fitness of a specific behavioral form prior to assessing the extent to which its demonstration is substantiated elsewhere (in an adequate and representative sample of the populations that possess the trait) or prior to demonstrating the nonfitness of alternative traits. (6) A fallacy of popularizations uses the alleged "drives" of early humans to "explain" human behavioral traits today. Such exposition assumes knowledge of prehistoric emotions, their adaptiveness at that time, their genetic basis, their perpetuation unchanged for millions of years without establishing a concomitant continuation of the alleged early selective stresses, and it fails to encompass the range of behavioral variation in ethnographically known cultures. (7) A final fallacy unintentionally presents an interpretation of behavioral data by its use of overly general labels, overly simple labels, and evaluative labels that imply motivations.

We do need a comparative discipline having to do with social behavior throughout the animal kingdom. It should deal appropriately with biological and cultural adaptation, with genetic and social transmission. It should not be entirely reductionist. The prospects for such a synthesis are good. Our experience in sociocultural anthropology may be just as useful for zoologists studying intraspecies behavioral variation, as a greater sophistication in genetics should prove for us. But the precautions discussed in this chapter will have to be observed.

Acknowledgements

Had there been time to do so, I would have liked to submit the draft of this chapter to all contributors to this volume. They all suffered my editorial questions and turnabout would have been fair play. As it is, I wish to thank them all for the learning experience entailed in reading their papers. All of the questions I have raised in my chapter were raised individually with them; others were raised and disposed of by their patient efforts to clarify my understandings. In this regard I particularly want to thank Richard Dawkins, John DeFries, Steven Emlen, William Irons, Danilo Mainardi, Paul Sherman, Robert Warner, and George C. Williams. I am most grateful to the following for their sometimes detailed but always helpful comments and suggestions on earlier drafts of this paper: George W. Barlow, Victor Barnouw, Napoleon A. Chagnon, John Dowling, Millicent Ficken, Greysolynne J. Fox, Stephen Gould, Sidney Greenfield, Robert Harrison, David Hull, Jane B. Lancaster, Eleanor Leacock, Frank Livingstone, Gene Muehlbauer, Ruth B. Phillips, Steve Rudman, Marshall Sahlins, Conrad Silverberg, Neil C. Tappen, William Washabaugh, and Edward Wellin. All of us owe a great debt, but only I am fully cognizant of its extent, to the intelligent resourcefulness and technical skill of my typist, Linda Dobrushken. In every chapter she deftly made corrections on the camera-ready pages. Last, but not least, I thank Joellen Fritsche, Kathryn Wolff and the AAAS Publications Office staff for their forebearance and cooperation as deadline after deadline went by and yet the work went on in readying the entire volume.

Literature Cited

Aberle, D.F., U. Bronfenbrenner, E.H. Hess, D.R. Miller, D.M. Schneider & J.N. Spuhler. 1963. The incest taboo and the mating patterns of animals. American Anthropologist 65: 253-265.

Allison, A.C. 1954. Protection afforded by sickle-cell trait against subtertion malarial infection. British Medical Journal 1:290-294.

Ardrey, R. 1961. African genesis. Atheneum, New York.

______. 1966. The territorial imperative. Atheneum, New York.

_______. 1970. The social contract. Atheneum, New York.

_______. 1976. The hunting hypothesis. Atheneum, New York.

Barash, D.P. 1977. Sociobiology and behavior. Elsevier, New York.

Barth, F. 1956. Ecological relationship of ethnic groups in Swat, North Pakistan. American Anthropologist 58:1079-1089.

Bishop, N.H. 1976. Intraspecies variability in behavior: A problem of reconstruction in nonhuman primate studies. Paper presented at the 142nd annual meeting of the American Association for the Advancement of Science, Boston. (Not published.)

Boas, F. 1911. The mind of primitive man. Revised edition. Macmillan, New York.

Buettner-Janusch, J.J. 1966. Origins of man: Physical anthropology. John Wiley, New York.

Burling, R. 1964. Cognition and componential analysis: God's truth or hocus-pocus? American Anthropologist 66: 20-28.

Carpenter, C.R. 1941. A field study in Siam of the behavior and social relations of the gibbon (Hylobates lar). Johns Hopkins Press, Baltimore.

Chagnon, N.A. 1968. Yąnomamö: The fierce people. Holt, Rinehart and Winston, New York.

Chivers, D.J. 1972. The siamang and the gibbon in the Malay Peninsula. In D. Rumbaugh (ed.), Gibbon and siamang, Vol. 1. Karger, Basel, pp. 103-135.

Comte, A. 1830. Cours de philosophie positive. Vol. 1. Bachelier, Paris.

Conklin, H.C. 1964. Ethnogenealogical method. In W.H. Goodenough (ed.), Explorations in cultural anthropology. McGraw-Hill, New York, pp. 25-55.

Cook, L.M. & R.R. Askew. 1970. Increasing frequency of typical form of the peppered moth in Manchester. Nature 227:1155.

Dawkins, R. & J.D. Krebs. In press. Arms races between and within species. Proceedings of the Royal Society of London.

DeVore, I. & K.R.L. Hall. 1965. Baboon ecology. In I. DeVore (ed.), Primate behavior. Holt, Rinehart and Winston, New York, pp. 20-52.

Dobzhansky, T. 1962. Mankind evolving. Yale University Press, New Haven, Connecticut.

Durkheim, E. 1895. Les règles de la méthode sociologique. F. Alcan, Paris.

Forde, C.D. 1934. Habitat, economy and society. Metheun, London.

Frake, C. 1964. A structural description of Subanum 'religious behavior.' In W.H. Goodenough (ed.), Explorations in cultural anthropology. McGraw-Hill, New York, pp. 111-129.

Gillie, O. 1979. Burt's missing ladies. Science 204:1035-1039.

Goodall, J. 1977. Infant killing and cannibalism in free living chimpanzees. Folia Primatologica 28:259-282.

Goodenough, W.H. 1965. Yankee kinship terminology: A problem in componential analysis. American Anthropologist 67: 2:259-287.

_______. 1970. Description and comparison in cultural anthropology. Aldine, Chicago.

Goodman, M. & R.E. Tashian. 1976. Molecular anthropology. Plenum, New York.

Hamilton, W.D. 1964. The genetical theory of social behavior. I & II. Journal of Theoretical Biology 7:1-52.

Harcourt, A.H., K.S. Stewart & D. Fossey. 1976. Male emigration and female transfer in wild mountain gorillas. Nature 263:226-227.

Harris, M. 1964. The nature of cultural things. Random House, New York.

_______. 1968. The rise of anthropological theory. Thomas Y. Crowell, New York.

______. 1974a. Why a perfect knowledge of all the rules one must know to act like a native cannot lead to the knowledge of how natives act. Journal of Anthropological Research 30:242-251.

______. 1974b. Cows, pigs, wars, and witches. The riddle of culture. Vintage Books, Random House, New York.

Helm, J. 1962. The ecological approach in anthropology. American Journal of Sociology 67:630-639.

Hooton, E.A. 1942. Man's poor relations. Doubleday Doran, Garden City, New York.

Hutt, S.J. & Corinne Hutt. 1970. Direct observation and measurement of behavior. Charles C. Thomas, Springfield, Illinois.

Huxley, J.S. 1963. Evolution, the modern synthesis. Allen and Unwin, London.

Itani, J. 1961. The society of Japanese monkeys. Japan Quarterly 8:421-430.

Kaplan, A. 1964. The conduct of inquiry: Methodology for behavioral Science. Chandler, Scranton, Pennsylvania.

Kaplan, D. 1960. The law of cultural dominance. In M.D. Sahlins & E.R. Service (eds.), Evolution and culture. University of Michigan Press, Ann Arbor, pp. 69-92.

Kettlewell, H.B.D. 1958. A survey of the frequencies of Biston betulara (L.) (Lep.) and its melanistic forms in Great Britain. Heredity 12:51-72.

Kroeber, A.L. 1939. Cultural and natural areas of native North America. University of California Press, Berkeley and Los Angeles.

Lancaster, J.B. 1973. On the evolution of tool-using behavior. In C.L. Brace & J. Metress (eds.), Man in evolutionary perspective. John Wiley, New York, pp. 79-90.

Lerner, I.M. & W.J. Libby. 1976. Heredity, evolution, and society. Second edition. W.H. Freeman, San Francisco.

Levitan, M. 1977. Textbook of human genetics. Second edition. Oxford University Press, New York.

Lewontin, R. 1961. Evolution and the theory of games. Journal of Theoretical Biology 1:382-403.

_______. 1974. The genetic basis of evolutionary change. Columbia University Press, New York.

Livingstone, F.B. 1958. Anthropological implications of sickle cell gene distribution in West Africa. American Anthropologist 60:533-562.

Lorenz, K. 1966. On aggression. Bantam, New York.

Lowie, R.H. 1948. Social organization. Rinehart, New York.

MacCluer, J.W. 1973. Computer simulation in anthropology and human genetics. In M.H. Crawford & P.C. Workman (eds.), Methods and theory of anthropological genetics. University of New Mexico Press, Albuquerque, pp. 219-248.

Mason, O.T. 1894. Technogeography, or the relation of the earth to the industries of mankind. American Anthropologist 7:137-161.

_______. 1895. Influence of environment upon human industries or arts. Annual Report of the Smithsonian Institution, pp. 639-665.

McKinnon, J. 1974. The behaviour and ecology of wild orangutans (Pongo pygmaeus). Animal Behaviour 22:3-74.

Mead, M. 1968. Incest. In D.L. Sills (ed.), International encyclopedia of the social sciences. Macmillan and The Free Press, New York, 7:115-122.

Merton, R.K. 1949. Social theory and social structure. Free Press, Glencoe, Illinois.

Middleton, R. 1962. Brother-sister and father-daughter marriage in ancient Egypt. American Sociological Review 27: 603-611.

Miyadi, D. 1967. Differences in social behavior among Japanese macaque troops. In D. Starck, R. Schneider & H. Kuhn (eds.), Progress in primatology. Gustav Fischer, Stuttgart, pp. 228-231.

Morris, D. 1967. The naked ape. Jonathan Cape, London.

Murdock, G.P. 1945. The common denominator of cultures. In R. Linton (ed.), The science of man in the world crisis. Columbia University Press, New York, pp. 123-142.

Murphy, R.F. & L. Kasdan. 1959. The structure of parallel cousin marriage. American Anthropologist 61:17-29.

Neel, J.V. & W.J. Schull. 1954. Human heredity. University of Chicago Press, Chicago.

Ogburn, W.F. 1950[1922]. Social change, with respect to culture and original nature. Viking, New York.

Peng, F.C.C. (ed.). 1978. Sign-language and language acquisition in man and ape: New dimensions in comparative pedolinguistics. AAAS Selected Symposium 16. Westview, Boulder, Colorado.

Reid, R.M. 1973. Inbreeding in human populations. In M.H. Crawford & P.C. Workman (eds.), Methods and theory of anthropological genetics. University of New Mexico Press, Albuquerque, pp. 83-116.

Rensch, B. 1978. Psychogenesis from lowest organisms to man. In M.D. Loflin & J. Silverberg (eds.), Discourse and inference in cognitive anthropology: An approach to psychic unity and enculturation. Mouton, The Hague, pp. 259-280.

Rivers, W.H.R. 1910. The genealogical method of anthropological inquiry. The Sociological Review 3:2-12.

Sahlins, M.D. 1961. The segmentary lineage: An organization of predatory expansion. American Anthropologist 63:322-345.

_______. 1976. The use and abuse of biology: An anthropological critique of sociobiology. University of Michigan Press, Ann Arbor.

_______ & E.R. Service (eds.). 1960. Evolution and culture. University of Michigan Press, Ann Arbor.

Schaller, G.B. 1963. The mountain gorilla: Ecology and behavior. University of Chicago Press, Chicago.

Schneider, D.M. 1968. American kinship: A cultural account. Prentice-Hall, Englewood Cliffs, New Jersey.

Silverberg, J. 1959. Caste-ascribed 'status' vs. caste-irrelevant roles. Man in India 39:148-162.

_______. 1961. Peasant behavior and its caste-relevancy: The Kolis of Kasandra. Ph.D. Thesis, University of Wisconsin, Madison.

_______ (ed.). 1968. Social mobility in the caste system in India: An interdisciplinary symposium. Mouton, The Hague.

_______. 1976. A culture as a system of witnessed behavior. Paper presented at the 142nd annual meeting of the American Association for the Advancement of Science, Boston. (Not published.)

_______. 1978a. Social categories vs. organizations: Class conflict in a caste-structured system. In G.B. Gupta (ed.), Cohesion and conflict in modern India, Vol. 3, Main Curents in Indian sociology series. Vikas, Delhi & London and Carolina Academic Press, Durham, North Carolina, pp. 3-32.

_______. 1978b. The scientific discovery of logic: The anthropological significance of empirical research on psychic unity (inference-making). In M.D. Loflin & J. Silverberg (eds.), Discourse and inference in cognitive anthropology: An approach to psychic unity and enculturation. Mouton, The Hague, pp. 281-295.

_______. In press. Exchange in the mode of production: 'The Hindu jajmani system' as a custodial (feudal) group. With D.C. Silverberg. In J. Silverberg (ed.), Modes of Production. Queens College Publications in Anthropology, Queens College Press, Flushing, New York.

Simpson, G.G. 1971[1949]. The meaning of evolution. Bantum Books, New York.

Slater, M.K. 1959. Ecological factors in the origin of incest. American Anthropologist 61:1042-1059.

Steward, J.H. 1936. The economic and social basis of primitive bands. In R. Lowie (ed.), Essays in anthropology presented to A.L. Kroeber. University of California Press, Berkeley, pp. 331-345.

_______. 1937. Ecological aspects of southwestern society. Anthropos 32:87-104.

_______. 1938 Basin-Plateau aboriginal sociopolitical groups. Bureau of American Ethnology, Bulletin 20. Government Printing Office, Washington, D.C.

_______. 1949a. South American cultures: An interpretive summary. In J.H. Steward (ed.), Handbook of South American Indians. Bureau of American Ethnology, Bulletin 143. Government Printing Office, Washington, D.C., 5:669-772.

_______. 1949b. Cultural causality and law: A trial formulation of early civilization. American Anthropologist 51: 1-27.

_______. 1955. Theory of culture change. University of Illinois Press, Urbana.

Sugiyama, Y. 1973. The social structure of wild chimpanzees. In R.P. Michael & J.H. Crook (eds.), Comparative ecology and behaviour of primates. Academic Press, London, pp. 395-410.

Teleki, G. In press. The organized utilization of natural resources by primate societies. In J. Silverberg (ed.), Modes of Production. Queens College Publications in Anthropology, Queens College Press, Flushing, New York.

Tiger, L. 1969. Men in groups. Random House, New York.

_______ & R.Fox. 1972. The imperial animal. Delta Books, New York.

Tyler, S.A. (ed.). 1969. Cognitive anthropology. Holt, Rinehart and Winston, New York.

Ward, R.H. 1973. Some aspects of genetic structure in Yanomama and Makiritare: Two tribes of southern Venezuela. In M.H. Crawford & P.C. Workman (eds.), Methods and theory of anthropological genetics. University of New Mexico Press, Albuquerque, pp. 367-388.

Washburn, S.L. 1978. Human behavior and the behavior of other animals. American Psychologist 33:405-418.

Webb, E.J., D.T. Campbell, R.D. Schwartz & L. Sechrest. 1966. Unobtrusive measures: Nonreactive research in the social sciences. Rand McNally, Chicago.

Weinstein, E.A. 1968. Adoption. In D.L. Sills (ed.), International Encyclopedia of the Social Sciences. Macmillan and The Free Press, New York, 1:96-99.

White, L.A. 1949. The science of culture: A study of man and civilization. Grove Press, New York.

Williams, G.C. 1966. Adaptation and natural selection. A critique of some current evolutionary thought. Princeton University Press, Princeton, New Jersey.

Wilson, E.O. 1975. Sociobiology: The new synthesis. Belknap Press of Harvard University Press, Cambridge, Massachusetts.

Wissler, C. 1917. The American Indian: An introduction to the anthropology of the New World. D.C. McMurtie, New York.

______. 1926. The relation of nature to man in aboriginal America. Oxford University Press, New York.

Part 2

Viewed from Afar

David L. Hull

3. Sociobiology: Another New Synthesis

In the heat of battle we tend to forget that sociobiology is just one more scientific dispute out of many, just one more attempt by one group of scientists to convert the larger scientific community. Sociobiologists are trying to expand the frontiers of biology to include territory which has traditionally been part of the domain of the social sciences. They are also attempting to some extent to redefine the very notion of empirical science to include considerations normally treated by philosophers and theologians.

Neither activity is unusual. From the point of view of the combatants, the controversy may well look like a battle between the forces of good and evil, between unwitting dupes of a capitalist, sexist conspiracy and the new inquisitors bent on suppressing truth for ideological reasons. Although no one connected with the dispute is likely to be in the least interested, the history of science presents a continuous showing of such scientific morality plays (Hull 1978b). Time and again one group of scientists attempts to appropriate the territory of another. Time and again new research programs are judged on the basis of "extra-scientific" considerations. The success or failure of these research programs in turn redefines both the internal and the external borders of science.

In the early part of the nineteenth century, for instance, philosophers such as William Whewell (1840) argued that questions concerning first beginnings were not an appropriate subject for scientific investigation. However, before the century was over, cosmologists, geologists and evolutionists had not only delineated their own subject matters but also made them a legitimate part of science.

Today sociobiologists are engaged in similar, time-honored expansionary activities. They are attempting to explain behavioral and social phenomena biologically and possibly to include issues of morals and ethics within the domain of empirical science. That the intended victims are uneasy should occasion no surprise. Slight as it may be, philosophers and social scientists may gain some consolation from the knowledge that, as the sociobiologists tuck in their napkins in preparation for their feast on philosophy and the social sciences, physicists and chemists are busily gnawing away at the flanks of biology. Reduction in science gives every appearance of a many-headed hydra attempting to consume itself.

A lack of historical perspective is not the only impediment to understanding the current controversy over sociobiology. Another is the tendency of both sides to accept a hypocritical view of science engendered by generations of scientific propaganda. For example, Sir Peter Medawar (1972:87), in one of his mellower moods, remarks:

> Scientists, on the whole, are amiable and well-meaning creatures. There must be very few wicked scientists. There are, however, plenty of wicked philosophers, wicked priests, and wicked politicians.

That Nicholas Wade (1976:1153) shares Medawar's high opinion of scientists is revealed by his dismay over the treatment of Wilson's work by the Sociobiology Study Group:

> In short, the Sociobiology Study Group has systematically distorted Wilson's statements to fit the position it wishes to attack, namely that human social behavior is wholly or almost wholly determined by the genes. Such a degree of distortion, though routine enough in political life, is perhaps surprising from a group composed largely of professional scholars.

One scientist distorting the views of another? Incredible. I see no point in the continuation of such hypocrisy. Perhaps the openly political motivation of the Sociobiology Study Group is somewhat unusual in scientific controversies; the reliance on distortion is not. Distortion is not only routine in science, it is a hallowed method of debate. Darwin's opponents consistently castigated him for claiming that natural selection was all-sufficient when he never did. Darwin in turn argued in the Origin (1859) as if the only alternative to his theory was miraculous special creation when it was not.

If scientists throughout history have consistently caricatured the views they oppose and show not the slightest inclination of doing otherwise today, it is about time we admitted it. Of course, the sociobiologists have been misrepresented. Some of the opponents of sociobiology reveal only the haziest understanding of its basic principles. For example, Sahlins (1976) happily cites mother's brother/sister's son forms of social inheritance as refuting sociobiology when Alexander (1977) presents such phenomena as its strongest confirmation. In their turn, sociobiologists propose to reduce sociology to biology while freely admitting that they do not know very much sociology. They plan to read up on it. Such interdisciplinary arrogance is common in science. Molecular biologists were just as ignorant of the Mendelian genetics which they planned to reduce to physics and chemistry.

A common practice in ethics is to compare the behavior of real people to some abstract ideal. People always come up wanting, but that is all right. After all, people are only human, and feelings of guilt are good for the soul. What I find disconcerting is that in many cases it is not just human weakness which keeps us from behaving the way we should. Even if we could, we would not because we have too much sense.

I find myself reaching similar conclusions with respect to traditional ideal standards of proper scientific method. The net effect of the scientific enterprise may well be an increase in objective knowledge. A common goal of individual scientists may well be truth for its own sake. But that does not mean that scientists are selfless, dispassionate calculating machines or that science would be improved if they were.

The emotional character of the dispute over sociobiology is not in the least unusual. Scientists, like all of us, find objectivity harder to maintain in areas which touch them personally. The point that needs emphasizing is that, to scientists, their subject matter is always personal. As difficult as it is to believe, the mating habits of *Escherichia coli* are as important to a bacteriologist as those of her husband, maybe more so.

At the very least, we need to distinguish between real scientists and the Ideal Platonic Scientist. But more importantly, we need to scrutinize this ideal type to find out if possibly the reason that scientists fail even to approach it, let alone attain it, is that they have too much sense. The ideal standard is not only ideal, it is mistaken.

The Sociology of Science

The controversy over sociobiology has taken on the character it has for several reasons. First, the participants do not view themselves from an historical perspective, as just one more episode in a continuing saga. As far as they are concerned, this is the first time that scientists have criticized science on the basis of extra-scientific considerations. Second, everyone concerned judges the behavior of their opponents by extremely unrealistic standards. They are adhering to the best scientific standards, while their opponents have all but invented the art of scientific parody. Finally, no one is paying the slightest attention to the social dimension of science -- as it applies to themselves.

One of the chief goals of science is to discover as much as possible about the world in which we live. For most research scientists, research is not just an occupation, it is a compulsion. But one area in which scientists have shown surprisingly little curiosity is in their own social organization. When the issue is raised, scientists are quick to admit that science is a social institution like any other, but they are sure that such social considerations have no direct effects on the content of science. Truth will out. More than that, when scientists chance to read something written about themselves by a sociologist of science, they react with all the irate indignation characteristic of other human beings who find themselves under scientific scrutiny. Nor are sociologists of science themselves exempt from these generalizations. For years the Merton group studied a variety of research communities. Not until quite recently have members of the Merton group got around to studying the Merton group itself, and then only with utmost gentleness (Cole & Zuckerman 1975). If the same sort of intra-group competition so characteristic of other research communities also characterizes the Society for Social Studies of Science, we do not hear about it.

One would think that sociobiologists, a group of scientists devoted to discovering the biological bases of social organization, might be interested in their own social organization and would be quick to apply their own principles to themselves. People in general, so the sociobiologists claim, are basically selfish. Genuine altruism is a myth. All creatures are devoted almost exclusively to the pursuit of their own selfish gains, all creatures except scientists. They are selflessly devoting their lives to the search for truth. Then why the rush for priority? Why arguments over who thought of what first? Truth is truth regardless of who discovers it. But if scientific disputes are just one more example of competition between totally selfish groups, how can sociobiologists possibly justify their righteous indignation over the vigilantism of some of their opponents (Wilson 1976)? Is it just one more instance of the hypocrisy which the sociobiologists find so characteristic of societies or does it have some genuine moral foundation?

Conversely, if all the views set forth by scientists are basically a product of their socio-economic background, then the same observations should apply equally to the opponents of sociobiology. Strangely enough, the sociobiologists come from the same variety of socio-economic backgrounds as their opponents. In the case of the sociobiologists, the fact that they live in a highly competitive, elitist, male-dominated society has forced them to produce a biological theory possessing these same characteristics. Their opponents, however, have somehow freed themselves from these same influences.

Clearly, both sides are presented with difficulties. The paradoxes of vulgar social determinism are no less intransigent than those of vulgar genetic determinism. The Marxists' claim that my living in a capitalist society makes me hold capitalist beliefs is no more palatable than the sociobiologists' claim that my being male makes me hold male beliefs. Although neither side is likely to admit it, they have narrowed their dispute to the time-honored problem of free will, and any scientist worth his salt knows better than to introduce such a topic into a scientific debate. Although I have serious doubts about the direct connections which Marxists see between socio-economic causes and the content of scientific theories, I also find it impossible to believe that scientists are exempt from the same social determinants which they attribute to everyone else. Perhaps the sociobiologists realize that they are as self-serving as bankers and politicians and that their protestations about the unfair treatment which they have received at the hands of their opponents are to be viewed as sheer hypocrisy, but they have yet to say so in print. Of course, given their views on the role of hypocrisy in society, they should not.

In any case, a sociobiological analysis of the sociobiologists themselves might prove to be not only instructive but also entertaining (Hull 1978a). What is good for the goose and all that. How did Wilson become the head honcho? What sorts of submissive behavior do others lower in the sociobiological dominance hierarchy exhibit to deflect his aggressive behavior? Do others in Wilson's research group behave like juveniles, or like females in estrus? What strategies are they employing to depose him?

Wilson is popularly considered to be the father of sociobiology, his term "sociobiology" the appropriate name for the movement, and his book Sociobiology: The New Synthesis (1975) its official bible. No matter who presents a paper on sociobiology, the main topic of discussion is inevitably Wilson and his book, or more accurately the first and last chapters of his book. How come Wilson, his term, and his book?

If one wants to understand sociobiology as a scientific research program, one fact must be kept in the forefront: the sociobiologists do not form a homogeneous group, either conceptually or socially. Sociobiologists in a broad sense all want to extend biological modes of explanation to behavior, including human behavior. They cooperate to the extent necessary to oppose their joint enemies. However, not all sociobiologists belong to the Wilson group.

A year before Wilson's book appeared, Michael Ghiselin published his The Economy of Nature and the Evolution of Sex (1974a), a work as ambitious as Wilson's and even more provocative. Who can resist quoting Ghiselin's description of his book as a "cross between the Kama Sutra and the Wealth of Nations," his Copulatory Imperative, or his departing quip, "Scratch an 'altruist,' and watch a 'hypocrite' bleed"? Yet Ghiselin's book has played almost no role in the controversy. Similarly, Ghiselin (1974a), R.D. Alexander (1974) and Robert Trivers (1974) all produced an analysis of parent-offspring conflict at roughly the same time, yet priority is almost always given to Trivers.

Perhaps these and other features of the sociobiological research program can be explained entirely in terms of the inherent worth of the ideas contributed. Perhaps Wilson's book has received the attention it has because it is so vastly superior to all its competitors. Perhaps Trivers receives all the credit for parent-offspring conflict because he actually thought of it first and his development is scientifically superior to that of Ghiselin and Alexander. Or possibly, sociological factors may have played a role.

Sociologists claim that scientists are organized into small, ephemeral groups which they term "invisible colleges." The scientists in these groups cooperate with each other to push new views, treating each other differently from the members of competing research communities. Within-group competition can be even more brutal than between-group competition, but it is different in kind. Although sociologists call these research groups "invisible colleges," they are anything but invisible. References to the work of sociobiologists outside the Wilson group by the Wilsonians are rarer than within-group citation and a good deal less positive. Correspondingly, sociobiologists outside the Wilson camp tend to cite members of their own research community more frequently than the Wilsonians and avoid using Wilson's term to characterize the movement.

I hasten to add that the preceding observations are not intended to be critical of the Wilson group, other sociobiology research communities, or their anti-sociobiology opponents. The formation of such research communities is highly efficacious, if not absolutely necessary in science. For example, initially Darwin formulated his ideas on evolution in relative isolation. Later, as he developed them, he solicited the aid of numerous other workers, usually without letting them in on his heresy. He also established his reputation firmly among other scientists so that when he announced his theory, he would have to be taken more seriously than Lamarck and Chambers before him. Finally, when it came time to disseminate his views, Darwin carefully and consciously formed a small band of scientists to help him push his theory. Charles Lyell and J.D. Hooker read the joint Darwin-Wallace papers at the Linnaean Society, and both T.H. Huxley and Hooker did battle with Bishop Wilberforce at the famous meeting of the British Association for the Advancement of Science in 1860. As Darwin (1899:101) remarked in a letter to Hooker,

> One thing I see most plainly, that without Lyell's yours, Huxley's, and Carpenter's aid, my book would have been a mere flash in the pan,

and later to Asa Gray,

> I can now very plainly see from many later Reviews, that I should have been fairly annihilated, had it not been for 4 or 5 men, including yourself.

Other evolutionists attempted to preempt the Darwinians, but with no great success. Few scientists accepted Darwin's theory, but everyone agreed that the Darwinians had won. The opponents of Darwinism were no more successful. Behind nearly all the most effective critiques of evolutionary theory can be found the specter of one man -- Lord Kelvin. Although Kelvin himself attacked Darwin only indirectly, others in his invisible college were more open in their opposition (Haughton 1860, Hopkins 1860, Jenkin 1867, Tait 1869). The Kelvin conspiracy, of course, failed, but if Darwin could legitimately form a group to promote his brainchild, he could hardly complain of Kelvin doing the same in opposition.

Scientific discovery and even development can often be carried on in relative isolation, but conversion of the larger scientific community is a social process. If truth were all that mattered in science, there would be no unsung scientific heroes and heroines. There are plenty, from Mendel to Sister Kenny.

In this paper I cannot present a detailed analysis of the sociobiologists as an emerging research community. I do not have the necessary empirical data, and proper scientific etiquette precludes my mentioning that which I do have. However, I can make a few general observations about scientific research communities as such. I cannot explain with any justification why Wilson, his book and his term have become so central to the sociobiological research program, but I can explain why some scientist, some book, and some term had to materialize.

The Essence of Sociobiology

Thus far I have mentioned three factors which tend to frustrate an adequate understanding of the emergence of sociobiology: our failure to view it in its historical context, the unreal standards we use to evaluate science, and inattention to the sociology of science. One final feature of the way in which we conceptualize scientific change which all but precludes coherent discussion is the assumption that sociobiology has an "essence."

Throughout the controversy, people constantly ask, What _is_ sociobiology? That this question is answered exclusively in terms of the substantive content of sociobiology is bad enough. Worse yet, everyone concerned also assumes that one set of substantive claims can be found to characterize sociobiology if only we look hard enough. For example, Dawkins (1976:210) asserts that, in spite of all the change which has taken place in evolutionary theory since Darwin, "there is something, some essence of Darwinism, which is present in the head of every individual who understands the theory."

If evolutionary theory has anything to teach us about evolutionary processes, it is that the entities which evolve have no eternal, immutable essences. Whether evolution takes place as gradually as Darwin and modern gradualists think, or in terms of punctuated equilibria as modern proponents of "saltative" evolution maintain (Eldredge and Gould 1972), heterogeneity in the makeup of the units which are evolving (as distinct from those being selected) is necessary for the evolutionary process. (Incidentally, modern advocates of saltative evolution are playing the same sort of game all scientists play, and central to it is systematic equivocation over the term "gradualism.") The general absence of universal covariation of morphological traits is well known, but the demise of species specificity for behavioral traits has been slow in coming. For example, Emlin and Oring (1977:222) remark that:

> Until recently, many field biologists have worked under a preconception that species specificity was a

characteristic not only of courtship behavior but of mating systems as well. We are now coming to realize that variability in social organization, including mating systems, is widespread.

In spite of the implications of evolutionary theory, scientists consistently treat species as if they were distinguishable by sets of traits which are severally necessary and jointly sufficient for membership, as if evolving species formed unchangeable discrete entities. This tendency results from our need to identify and individuate species. If everything about a species can change through time, how can we possibly pick it out? Biologists have developed a method of individuating species which does not presuppose the existence of a trait (or set of traits) which all and only the members of a particular species possess -- the type specimen method. Regardless of the connotations of the term (left over from pre-evolutionary biology), type specimens need not be typical.

Given the existence of extensive metamorphosis in certain species, sexual dimorphism in others, polymorphic species, etc., the notion of a "typical" specimen verges on being nonsense. For example, Linnaeus designated himself the type specimen for Homo sapiens, but in what biologically significant sense are males more typical than females, Caucasians more typical than other races, Swedes more typical than other nationalities, and so on? The point is not that Linnaeus is the wrong type specimen but that the notion of a single organism embodying the essence of any species is nonsense (Mayr 1976). According to present-day taxonomic practice, type specimens need not be typical. Instead they are one node in the genealogical nexus. The type specimen merely facilitates attaching the right name to the right chunk of the genealogical nexus (Ghiselin 1974b, Hull 1976, 1978c).

One increasingly popular way to view scientific development is from an evolutionary perspective (Burian 1977; Hooker 1975; Laudan 1977; McMullin 1976; Popper 1972; Toulmin 1972). If evolving species are not counterintuitive enough, evolving concepts, theories and research programs are even more mystifying. The urge to find something changeless in the midst of scientific change is all but irresistible. Dawkins makes his claim about what is present in the head of every individual who understands evolutionary theory, not on the basis of any empirical research, but because of a philosophical conviction concerning the necessary prerequisites of human understanding. If everything can change, including the very meanings of the words which we are using, then rational discussion seems impossible.

Thomas Kuhn (1970:176) is popularly interpreted as distinguishing between scientific communities and paradigms. "A paradigm is what the members of a scientific community share, <u>and</u>, conversely, a scientific community consists of men who share a paradigm." As important as this distinction is, neither communities nor paradigms form discrete natural units. At best, they form temporary clusters. At any one time, the boundaries of research groups seem to be surprisingly sharp, but not all members are equally important, nor does their relative status remain unchanged. New members join the group, old members drop out until eventually the make-up of the group is completely changed. For example, J.S. Henslow was one of the earliest Darwinians. He died soon after Huxley joined. Obviously, none of the earliest Darwinians has survived to the present, yet many biologists still consider themselves "Darwinians."

Similar observations apply to units of conceptual evolution. Not all the elements which comprise a scientific paradigm are equally important. Certain ideas which start off as central become demoted as the paradigm develops. Conceptual evolution can be just as drastic as, and frequently more rapid than, the evolution of research communities. Contrary to the intuitive response of famous scientists from Darwin to Max Planck, new scientific truths do not triumph simply by means of their opponents eventually dying off and being replaced by a new generation raised in the new orthodoxy (Hull, et al. 1978). For example, within five years after the rediscovery of the principles of Mendelian genetics, all but one of these principles had been abandoned or modified extensively. The exception, the law of segregation, has been modified since. Yet Mendelian genetics remains "Mendelian genetics" in the face of all this change.

Similar observations hold for every other scientific paradigm I have ever studied. To make matters worse, contrary to Kuhn, the boundaries of scientific communities and paradigms do not always coincide perfectly. A scientist can be sociologically part of a research group even though he does not share its paradigm, and many scientists who share the same paradigm are not part of the same scientific community. In the case of the Darwinians and Darwinism, Henslow is an example of the first sort, St. George Jackson Mivart is an example of the second.

In the midst of all this diversity and change, how can we possibly talk about particular scientific communities and paradigms? The technique which taxonomists have developed for dealing with evolving species turns out to be just as effective in dealing with social and conceptual change. A type specimen need not be "typical" to perform its role. It is merely one node in the genealogical nexus and designates its species accordingly. In his original exposition, Kuhn used the term "paradigm" in a multiply ambiguous fashion. He (1970:175) has since distinguished between two senses of the term:

> On the one hand, it stands for the entire constellation of beliefs, values, techniques, and so on shared by the members of a given community. On the other hand, it denotes one sort of element in that constellation, the concrete puzzle-solutions which, employed as models or examples, can replace explicit rules as a basis for the solution of the remaining puzzles of normal science.

Kuhn recognizes the need for type specimens, or exemplars as he terms them, in conceptual evolution. However, he does not acknowledge the need for type specimens to individuate scientific communities, and he takes for granted that conceptual exemplars must be in some sense "typical" (Kuhn 1977:308-318).

Both conceptual and social evolution are extremely variable and at times amorphous. The habit of picking a particular work as an exemplar for a conceptual system and a particular scientist as the focus for a scientific community facilitates the individuation of both sorts of evolutionary units. What I wish to emphasize is that neither needs to be typical in order to perform its assigned function.

Wilson can serve as the focus for the sociobiologists and his book as the exemplar for sociobiology without either being especially exemplary. Usually the scientist who emerges as the leader of a research group does so because of his ability and contributions, but he need not. Darwin, for instance, was justly the focus for the Darwinians, but T.H. Morgan was just as effective as a focus for the Morganians even though he seems to have been mistaken on every particular of his research program and had to be persuaded slowly and painfully by his students (Bowler 1977).

Similarly, conceptual type specimens usually are extremely important works, possessing all the virtues of major contributions, but they need not. Once again, Darwin's _Origin of Species_ (1859) is justly treated as the exemplar for Darwinism, while Erwin Schroedinger's _What is Life?_ (1947) was just as efficacious in catalyzing the molecular biology research program even though in retrospect its content is minimal (Olby 1971).

As attractive as the use of exemplars in designating both scientific communities and their conceptual correlates may appear, it also brings with it accompanying dangers. Both scientific communities and paradigms encompass considerable internal diversity. Sociobiologists agree that there is an essence to sociobiology, but when they get down to details, no two can agree what this essence is. Each is busily trying to get his version of sociobiology accepted as standard, while not openly breaking with his fellow sociobiologists. Because Wilson has emerged as the type specimen, he has some edge, but it does not follow that his views will necessarily prevail. For example, as central to the Darwinian revolution as Darwin was, his ideas were not the ones that swept across the Western world like the tide. Certainly scientists came to accept the evolution of species but not the sort of gradual, undirected evolution favored by Darwin. Instead the evolution which was widely accepted at the time was directed, saltative and progressive. Darwin did not triumph in this respect until this century.

Both scientific communities and their conceptual correlates change through time, sometimes changing so extensively that later stages have little in common with earlier stages. That research communities can undergo total change while remaining the "same" community occasions no surprise. We are used to conceptualizing social groups in this way. But comparable observations about conceptual evolution are likely to produce dismay. The possibility that Darwinism in Darwin's day, at the turn of the century, soon after World War II and today might have no claims in common seems extremely counterintuitive. But if one attempts to view scientific development from an evolutionary perspective, this conclusion follows necessarily.

Regardless of which version of sociobiology becomes standard, later sociobiologists, if there are any, may hold radically different views from those which they hold today. In fact, future sociobiologists may end up holding views indistinguishable from present-day critics of sociobiology. Conversely, the sociobiologists may lose. In a generation or so, people may see sociobiology as being as mistaken and pseudoscientific as nineteenth-century phrenology. That will not preclude all scientists of the day accepting ideas indistinguishable from those currently being enunciated by the sociobiologists.

The insistence of political groups and religious cults that their beliefs are really descended from some great figure, such as Marx, Jesus or Alexander Hamilton, strikes the unconverted as irrelevant, if not downright irrational. What difference does it make whether Marx in Das Kapital anticipated all possible future socio-economic development? Why should it matter today that the authors of the Bible viewed homosexuality as an abomination? Who in his right mind should care what the original version of the Constitution of the United States of America actually said?

But scientists spend just as much time arguing over the views of scientists long dead. Everyone, it seems, needs patron saints. Opponents of present-day Darwinism not only argue against the views of contemporary Darwinians but also feel obligated to denigrate Darwin's contributions. Diverse Darwinians in their turn are adamant that their ideas are really those intended by Darwin all along. For example, a half dozen or so papers published recently have attempted to show that Darwin had anticipated cladism, a newly emerging view of the proper methods of biological classification. Just as many argue that he had not. He really held the current majority position (Ghiselin & Jaffe 1973; Nelson 1971, 1974).

Historians of science hold only scorn for the "histories" written by practicing scientists in which they argue that all truth converges on them. But there is a legitimate point to such undertakings. In their discussions of earlier scientists, contemporary scientists are not attempting to describe history as it actually occurred but to define their own research program, showing it to be a natural outgrowth of previous work.

Defining a research program is in part a creative process. Scientists are not only engaged in adding to the cutting edge of science but also in reinterpreting past science in the light of later achievements. If the recognition of biological taxa is in part a retrospective exercise, no one should be surprised that comparable observations apply to the units of social and conceptual evolution. In evolution, continuity, integration and causal influence are what matter, not atemporal, acausal abstract similarity (Hull 1975, 1976, 1978c, 1979).

Both the opponents of sociobiology and those sociobiologists outside the Wilson camp have objected to the term "sociobiology." It means too many different things to too many different people, but such elasticity of meaning is one of the most important properties of terms like "sociobiology." In advance, there is no way of knowing what sociobiology is going to turn out to be, anymore than one could know at the turn of the century what people's republics were going to be.

The meaning of "sociobiology" will certainly expand and contract as the occasion demands the way that terms like "gene," "atom" and "species" have. Requiring that key terms in newly emerging research programs be given fixed meanings at the outset would frustrate the growth of knowledge. Socrates called for us to define our terms! Most people have the good sense to know when to ignore him. What then <u>is</u> sociobiology? Although this question is legitimate, one of the purposes of this paper has been to show why an adequate answer to it cannot be given in terms of a fixed set of characteristics.

Conclusion

In this paper I have tried to set out some of the reasons why scientific development does not always appear to be totally a matter of reason, argument and evidence. Part of the problem is that we concentrate on the substantive content of science to the exclusion of all else, and when we do turn our attention to the sociological side of science, we tend to view it hypocritically.

Of course, the substantive content of science is of fundamental importance to scientists and non-scientists alike. Scientists themselves are so fixated on it that they can hardly be brought to think of anything else. And if scientists did not make substantive advances, the rest of us would lose the slight interest we have in their efforts and would certainly be less anxious to support them financially.

I can understand why certain professions insist on keeping a wall of hypocrisy between themselves and the outside world, but if any group can afford to be honest, research scientists can. Perhaps they investigate things which the general public might find silly, perhaps they use the funds obtained to work on one project to investigate something else, but research scientists really do spend most of their time, money and energy doing what they claim to be doing -- research (Shapley 1977:804).

Scientists do not have a corner on the use of reason, argument and evidence in making decisions. Nor are these the only factors that matter in the course of scientific development. But they play as great a role in science as in any other endeavor, usually greater. Once the sociological development of science and its use of particular scientists as reference points in individuating scientific communities is distinguished clearly from conceptual development and the use of certain exemplars as reference points for the individuation of paradigms, the "irrational" aspects of science which recent commentators have emphasized appear more, rather than less rational (Ghiselin 1971).

In this paper I have also been concerned to emphasize those features of the controversy over sociobiology which are common to such disputes. It would not be fair to conclude without mentioning two features which are relatively uncommon. In most cases, scientists are able to carry on their disputes in obscure scientific journals rather than in the glare of popular attention. Sociobiology has had the misfortune to capture the popular imagination the way that phrenology, Darwinism, Freudianism, behaviorism and a few other research programs before it have. Scientists are not used to conducting their business under the public eye and are not very good at it. And, as far as I know, the leaders of these other research programs did not suffer physical abuse at the hands of their opponents the way that Wilson has at the hands of some of his more extreme opponents (Walsh 1978). To quote a short piece sent to me by Mary Jane West-Eberhard:

> Watching scientists come under the Public Eye, watching the effect of a wave of publicity as it sweeps across a quiet field of science, watching the heads bob in its wake, some gasping, sputtering and bewildered in their dumb fixity on science, others struggling up into the public light, grabbing at the chance for attention and power (were they always so desperate for it?) ..., watching this glorious dunking, so chilling to some and exhilirating to others, one sees the careful clothing washed away and then the painful comic spectacle of the unwittingly naked, blinking, smiling, bowing to the crowds, forgetting in the glory of the spotlight that it has caught them with their pants down.

Summary

Many people on both sides of the controversy over sociobiology treat it as if it were especially unusual in science when in most respects it is not. The attempt by sociobiologists to invade the traditional territory of other scientists and their less than hospitable reception from the indigenous natives, the emotional character of the controversy, the prevalence of methodological objections and the extensive caricature of the positions on both sides, and even the introduction of such "extra-scientific" considerations as the ethical implications of the principles of sociobiology are far from unusual. Increased attention to the history of science and an attempt to penetrate the hypocritical image of science currently so popular would help us to see the controversy over sociobiology more clearly.

The self-referential character of the sociobiological research program and the position of their Marxist critics pose parallel problems for both sides. If no widespread behavior can be genuinely altruistic, hypocritical protestations to the contrary notwithstanding, then scientific activity must be interpreted in this same light. Claims made by scientists that they are interested in truth for its own sake have to be viewed as sheer hypocrisy. Similarly, if all beliefs are largely a function of prevalent socio-economic conditions, then this belief itself is a function of these same conditions. Any reference to reason, argument, and evidence must be put down as empty show. Both sorts of self-referential dilemmas can be avoided but only with great care.

Many philosophers are currently attempting to explicate the plausible position that science is an "evolutionary" phenomenon. If so, then neither the sociological nor the conceptual development of science can be conceptualized the way that it has been in the past. Neither research groups nor the scientific positions which they are attempting to promulgate can be interpreted as having immutable, internally homogeneous "essences," any more than biological species can. All three must be viewed as internally heterogeneous historical entities capable of indefinite change through time. As such, they must be individuated but not in terms of sets of necessary and sufficient conditions. The method which biologists have devised to designate biological species can profitably be extended to social groups and conceptual schemata. Biologists pick a single organism as the type specimen for a species. Type specimens need not be "typical," but they must be part of the historical entity for which they serve as a focus.

Those of us who study science are frequently dismayed by the prevalence of certain seemingly irrational and intellectually suspect tendencies among scientists: the prevalence of scientific patron saints which scientists invest with superhuman prescience, the tenacity with which scientists cling to certain terms and methods of solving scientific problems, and the rewriting of history in extremely ahistorical ways. Instead of being signs of a lack of intellectual integrity, these practices are merely the techniques which scientists have developed to individuate scientific groups and their conceptual correlates in the absence of any essential defining criteria for either.

In this connection, the seemingly undue importance placed on E.O. Wilson, his book, and the term "sociobiology" make sense. Wilson serves as the focus for both the larger community of scientists attempting to explain behavior and social organization completely in biological terms and his own more localized research group. Sociobiology: The New Synthesis, regardless of its particular strengths and weaknesses, serves as an exemplar for the sociobiologists, and the term "sociobiology," as much as it is condemned by Wilson's opponents and sociobiologist competitors alike, has become the recognized name for both the research group and its program. That Wilson, his book, and his term serve the functions which they do is highly contingent; that some scientist, some book, and some term emerged is not. Such devices are necessary to designate such internally heterogeneous, continuously changing historical entities as research groups and their programs.

Acknowledgements

The research for this paper was supported in part by NSF grant Soc 75 03535.

Literature Cited

Alexander, R.D. 1974. The evolution of social behavior. Annual Review of Ecology and Systematics 5:325-383.

______ 1977. Evolution, human behavior, and determinism. In F. Suppe and P.D. Asquith (eds.), PSA 1976. Philosophy of Science Association, East Lansing, Michigan, 2:3-21.

Barash, D. 1977. Sociobiology and behavior. Elsevier, New York.

Bowler, P.J. 1977. Hugo DeVries and Thomas Hunt Morgan. The mutation theory and the spirit of Darwinism. Annals of Science 33:55-73.

Burian, R.M. 1977. More than a marriage of convenience: On the inextricability of history and philosophy of science. Philosophy of Science 44:1-42.

Cole, J.R. & H. Zuckerman. 1975. The emergence of a scientific specialty: The self-exemplifying case of the sociology of science. In L.A. Coser (ed.), The idea of social science. Harcourt Brace Jovanovich, New York, pp. 139-174.

Darwin, C. 1859. On the origin of species, a facsimile of the first edition (1859) with an introduction by Ernst Mayr (1966). Harvard University Press, Cambridge, Massachusetts.

Darwin, F. (ed.). 1899. The life and letters of Charles Darwin. D. Appleton, New York.

Dawkins, R. 1976. *The selfish gene*. Oxford University Press, New York and Oxford.

Eldredge, N. & S.J. Gould. 1972. Punctuated equilibria: An alternative to phyletic gradualism. *In* T.J.M. Schopf (ed.), *Models of paleobiology*. Freeman, Cooper, and Company, San Francisco, pp. 82-115.

Emlin, S.T. & L.W. Oring. 1977. Ecology, sexual selection, and the evolution of mating systems. *Science* 197:215-223.

Ghiselin, M.T. 1971. The individual in the Darwinian revolution. *New Literary History* 3:113-134.

——— 1974a. *The economy of nature and the evolution of sex*. University of California Press, Berkeley.

——— 1974b. A radical solution to the species problem. *Systematic Zoology* 23:536-544.

——— & L. Jaffe. 1973. Phylogenetic classification in Darwin's *Monograph on the sub-class Cirripedia*. *Systematic Zoology* 22:132-140.

Haughton, S. 1860. Bíoyéveois. *Natural History Review* 7:23-32.

Hooker, C.A. 1975. Philosophy and meta-philosophy of science: Empiricism, Popperianism and realism. *Synthese* 32:177-231.

Hopkins, W. 1860. Physical theories of the phenomena of life. *Fraser's Magazine* 61:739-752; 62:74-90.

Hull, D.L. 1975. Central subjects and historical narratives. *History and Theory* 14:253-274.

——— 1976. Are species really individuals? *Systematic Zoology* 25:174-191.

——— 1978a. Altruism in science: A sociobiological model of cooperative behavior among scientists. *Animal Behaviour* 26:685-697.

——— 1978b. Sociobiology: A scientific bandwagon or a traveling medicine show? *Society* 15:50-59; also *in* M.S. Gregory, A. Silvers & D. Sutch (eds.). *Sociobiology and human nature*. Jossey-Bass Inc., San Francisco (in press).

_______ 1978c. A matter of individuality. Philosophy of Science 45:335-360.

_______ 1979a. In defense of presentism. History and Theory 18:1-15.

_______, P. Tessner & A. Diamond. 1978. Planck's principle. Science 202:717-723.

Jenkin, F. 1867. The origin of species. North British Review 46:149-171.

Kuhn, T. 1970. The structure of scientific revolutions (first ed. 1962). The University of Chicago Press, Chicago.

_______ 1977. The essential tension. The University of Chicago Press, Chicago.

Laudan, L. 1977. Progress and its problems. The University of California Press, Berkeley.

Mayr, E. 1976. Evolution and the diversity of life. Harvard University Press, Cambridge, Massachusetts.

McMullin, E. 1976. The fertility of theory and the unit for appraisal in science. In R.S. Cohen, et. al. (eds.), Essays in memory of Imre Lakatos. D. Reidel Publishing Company, Dordrecht-Holland, pp. 395-432.

Medawar, P.B. 1972. The hope of progress. Methuen, London.

Nelson, G. 1971. "Cladism" as a philosophy of classification. Systematic Zoology 20:373-376.

_______ 1974. Darwin-Hennig classification: A reply to Ernst Mayr. Systematic Zoology 23:452-458.

Olby, R. 1971. Schrödinger's problem: What is life? Journal of the History of Biology 4:119-148.

Popper, K.R. 1972. Objective knowledge. Oxford University Press, Oxford.

Sahlins, M. 1976. The use and abuse of biology. The University of Michigan Press, Ann Arbor.

Schroedinger, E. 1947. What is life? The physical aspect of the cell. Doubleday, New York.

Shapley, D. 1977. Research management scandals provoke queries in Washington. Science 198:804-806.

Tait, P. 1869. Geological time. North British Review 50: 215-233.

Toulmin, S. 1972. Human understanding. Princeton University Press, Princeton.

Trivers, R.L. 1974. Parent-offspring conflict. American Zoologist 14:249-264.

Wade, N. 1976. Sociobiology: Troubled birth for a new discipline. Science 191:1151-1155.

Walsh, J. 1978. Sociobiology baptized as issue by activists. Science 199:955.

Whewell, W. 1840. The philosophy of the inductive sciences, founded upon their history. John Parker, London.

Wilson, E.O. 1975. Sociobiology: The new synthesis. The Belknap Press, Cambridge, Massachusetts.

_______ 1976. Academic vigilantism and the political significance of sociobiology. Bio Science 26:183-190.

Arthur L. Caplan

4. A Critical Examination of Current Sociobiological Theory: Adequacy and Implications

Values and Sociobiology

Questions of values and ideology have taken on increasing prominence in discussions concerning the adequacy of various scientific explanations of behavior during the past two decades. Discussions and criticisms of sociobiology prove no exception to this observation: charges of potential abuse, bias, prejudice, distortion, demogogery and vigilantism have filled a considerable number of pages in many books and journals (Allen et al. 1975; Alper et al. 1976, 1978; Chorover 1979; Lewontin 1977; Miller 1976; Sociobiology Study Group 1977; Wilson 1976).

There has been a discernable pattern among a number of the controversies occasioned by recent scientific speculation concerning the biological causes of human behavior. Arguments about criminality and chromosomes, IQ tests and hereditary racial differences, the genetic basis of gender differences, genetic engineering, the biological basis of human aggression, and most recently and emphatically, sociobiology (Block & Dworkin 1976; Caplan 1978b; Tobach 1974), have manifested a distinctive and somewhat peculiar ontogeny. First, claims are advanced about the possible hereditary sources of some behavioral feature. Objections are then raised that such claims violate central human values, such as equity, dignity, autonomy or equality and ought not be advanced. Counter-claims are made which deny these allegations, and, argue that, at any event, the 'truth' is requisite for any meaningful value determination. Objections are then raised against present scientific methodologies and, occasionally, against the overall feasability of inquiring into the biological sources of human behavior. These claims are inevitably countered with pleas for time to conduct further research, along with disquisitions about the freedom of inquiry in science.

The irony of this evolutionary sequence should be obvious. Critics of biological research into the etiology of behavior often begin with valuational objections, but, often end up invoking methodological reasons why such research is unsound. Advocates, in contrast, often begin by making scientific pronouncements about human behavior and end up by invoking values of one sort or another to defend their right to conduct their work (Davis 1976; Hull 1978; Ruse 1978; Suppe 1977). It would be rash to baptize this historical trend as a law, but it, like all evolutionary trends, is a phenomenon which merits an explanation.

Unfortunately, I have no explanation for this trend. However, I will return to the subject of values and sociobiology at the end of this paper. For now it will suffice to note the way in which values are used as a kind of club with which disputants in the public arena batter each other from time to time when it seems politically or rhetorically expedient.

Determinism

There are other features familiar from recent disputes concerning the possible etiologies of various human behaviors which also appear in debates about sociobiology. Central among these is the problem of determinism.

Critics of theorizing about the biological sources of human behavior have maintained that such theorizing is dangerously deterministic in orientation and intent (Alper et al. 1976, 1978; Burian 1978, Chorover 1979; Gould 1977a; Lewontin 1977; Sociobiology Study Group 1976, 1977). Defenders of such theorizing often presume that it is genetic determinism that the critics of scientific research on behavior find offensive. And they have gone to great lengths to show (a) that such fears are misplaced because there is no such view as 'genetic determinism' concerning human behavior since all such views necessarily involve cultural and environmental variables and, (b) that environmentalist accounts of human behavior are just as deterministic as genetically oriented accounts (Davis 1976; Morison 1975).

The common presupposition underlying both the general disputes and the special case of sociobiology is that biologically deterministic theories demean and belittle humankind, and provide grist for the mill of conservative defenders of existing social policies (Allen 1975; Klopfer 1977; Lewontin 1977; Sociobiology Study Group 1976, 1977). This is so because if biological determinism were true, it would be pointless to try and modify society and social institutions since the behavior observed among people would constitute the rigid, unmodifiable outcome of their hidden and fixed biological natures.

For the most part, these worries about the implications of allegedly deterministic theories of human behavior seem overblown. There are three main reasons for this view.

First, the truth of scientific determinisms of any sort --be they in biology, physics, social science, or political theory--leads to no logical consequences or implications about the desirability of any particular social, political, or economic arrangement. Deterministic theses may tell us how we might go about altering or reforming society in order to get to a particular goal, but they say nothing about the acceptability or defensibility of any given goal. The only way theories of human behavior could narrow the range of possible and accessible social goals would be if they claimed explanatory power over <u>all</u> contingent historical events, and, over the entire range of contemporary factors and variables that affect or contribute to human action (Gardiner 1974; Nagel 1961). I know of no theory in any discipline which claims or has such power.

Second, some sort of crude determinism--a thesis about the specifiable causes of human behavior being subsumable under a law or set of laws--is usually <u>presumed</u> as true at the outset of any scientific inquiry. This assumption closely resembles a metaphysical belief or programmatic research guideline. If some belief in determinism is an assumption requisite for theoretical scientific inquiry into human behavior, there would seem to be little hope of proving the validity of such a thesis from the results of that inquiry. Such a proof of determinism would, at best, be quite circular.

Third, one does not need an extravagant theory such as sociobiology to worry about the problem of reconciling free will and determinism. Observation of a few billiard balls interacting, or the quandries raised by the possibility of an omnipotent deity, will suffice to get the problem going. It matters little whether determinism is advanced on the basis of a belief in a simple or complex scientific theory, or on some other grounds--the problem (and the solutions, Caplan 1978a; Dworkin 1970) remain the same. The puzzle of determinism will not rise or fall with the fate of scientific speculations about the biological causes of human behavior.

Nature/Nurture

Yet another issue typically plagues discussions of the biological explanation of behavior. It merits some attempt at clarification. Despite all the pleas and disclaimers that have been issued by various scientists, scientific discussions of human behavior manifest an uncanny resistance to moving beyond polarized debates about the role of nature vs. nurture, heredity vs. environment, or, to cite a more recent version of the same theme, biology vs. culture. The remarkable persistence of these categorizations bodes ill for those well-intentioned thinkers of various persuasions who hope to abandon these sterile labels once and for all.

Part of the confusion surrounding these bifurcating labels may arise from a simple conceptual mistake. Care must be exercised in using terms like 'genetic,' 'environmental,' 'biological' or 'cultural' to label scientific explanations of behavior. It is relatively easy to confuse a kind of scientific explanation (e.g., genetic), with the set of factors that can act as causes in such an explanation--hereditary factors, developmental factors, environmental factors, etc. While the explanatory labels may lack some utility, their use need not result in the exclusion of specific factors or causes from different kinds of explanations. Different kinds of explanations of behavior may vary in emphasis, focus, shape, or attention. But it is simply wrong to assume that 'cultural' explanations of behavior allow no room for biological factors, or that 'genetic' explanations exclude any type of environmental factors.

Evolutionary Theory and Sociobiology

There is one final point worth making about the general course of arguments concerning sociobiology. Sometimes critics of human sociobiological theorizing are depicted as anti-Darwinian obscurantists, sentimentally defending the bastions of human morals, culture, and politics against onrushing hordes of sociobiological "realists" (Davis 1976; Eckberg 1977; Wilson 1976). The notion that a critic of sociobiology bears a resemblance to Bishop Wilberforce is rather hard to swallow. In fact, the critics may see themselves as the biological realists.

Those who hope to use the insights of an amended modern synthetic theory of evolution to shed light on social behavior (Wilson 1975, 1978) must bear in mind the fact that many of those who have critically assessed neo-Darwinian theory find it still to be clouded by serious doubts and difficulties (Barker 1969; Eckland 1976; Flew 1967; Lewontin

1968, 1978, Lovtrup 1976, 1977; Peters 1976). For better or worse, the sorts of methodological worries that have long plagued evolutionary theory will reappear with a vengeance when such a theory is applied to human behavior.

It is not always clear whether objections to sociobiological explanations of behavior are explicitly directed to sociobiological theory or to neo-Darwinian theory in general. For example, when critics claim that sociobiological accounts of behavioral evolution are untestable and ad hoc, it is not clear whether these alleged failings are a consequence of sociobiological models or of neo-Darwinian theory. Since sociobiological accounts do, to a great extent, depend upon the validity of evolutionary theory (Ruse 1978), methodological problems concerning evolutionary theory ought not be confused with methodological problems that are specific to sociobiological accounts.

Methodological Difficulties

The primary area in which methodological worries about evolutionary theory have come to a head is in the application of sociobiological insights to human behavior. While many of these same problems are relevant to the sociobiological analysis of other organisms, it is human sociality that provides the most compelling case for assessing the conceptual adequacy of current sociobiological analysis.

There are a number of areas in which the conceptual apparatus of sociobiology appears to leave a great deal to be desired. Moreover, the fact that the problems are primarily conceptual makes their analysis and clarification extraordinarily compelling. For no amount of empirical evidence, modeling or testing will suffice to bolster the validity of sociobiological theorizing, if the theory suffers from conceptual ambiguity and confusion. There are three key subject matters where the presumptions and conceptual apparatus of current sociobiological theorizing appear to be in dire need of critical analysis and explication: causation, comparison and adaptation.

Causation

It should surprise no one that the concept of causation, as it is utilized in biology and the social sciences, is fraught with murkiness and ambiguity. Sociobiological models of social behavior, be they models of kin selection, individual selection, group selection, or parental reproductive strategies, prove no exception to this observation.

Advocates and critics of sociobiology seem to agree on a number of points concerning the causes of social behavior. For one, it is commonly agreed that many factors contribute to the overt manifestation of a particular behavior (Alcock 1975; Barash 1977; Ehrman et al. 1972; Ehrman & Parsons 1976). For another, all seem to agree that any particular kind of causal factor or variable is flexible in the range of its outcomes (Dobzhansky 1937; Ehrman & Parsons 1976; Hirsch 1967, Mayr 1955). Thus, in speaking about genes, sociobiologists and their critics will note the wide range of reactions or effects potentially consequent from such factors. And most social scientists will carefully hedge the causal powers legitimately assignable to cultural or environmental factors by speaking of complexity, interactionism, or the reciprocal feedback that exists between these and other kinds of variables.

Yet, despite this obeisance to the complex etiological story underlying overt behavior, there is a frustrating tendency on the part of some sociobiologists to lay these qualifications aside in analyzing human social behavior. Rather than utilizing the important notions of genotypic unity, gene complex, or even phenotypic feature (Carson 1959; Dobzhansky 1937; Mayr 1955) when they analyze the power of selective forces on human social evolution, these sociobiologists talk about single genes as controlling behaviors, or about the effects of selection upon a single genetic variant in a population (Dawkins 1976; Trivers 1971; Wilson 1975)--situations that simply do not square with known biological reality. It may be true that genetic commonality and coefficients of genetic relationship play key roles in understanding the evolution and persistence of various forms of social behavior. But it is wrong to portray natural selection as consisting of forces that can 'see through' phenotypes to act directly upon the genotypic variants present in a population (Dawkins 1976; Hamilton 1964).

Nor is it acceptable to treat the relationship that exists between various causal factors that affect behavior in an additive fashion. It is not the case that one can parse out the contributions of genes, developmental environments, phenotypic properties, selectional environments and culture into a kind of seriatim list and then sum the results to generate the observed social behavior of a population. Factors from all of these classes of causes can be and often are present at all levels of organic organization. The notion that social behavior is the calculable sum of genes plus environment plus culture unduly restricts the wide range of complex relationships possible between factors of these types. Such views contribute to the unfortunate notion that the causal analysis of behavior is something akin to peeling an onion--with layers upon layers of causally efficacious factors to be uncovered by the inquiring scientist. Such an onion-layered model of causation fosters the sort of simplistic, either/or, dichotomous thinking that seems to pervade a good deal of biological thinking about the causes of behavior (Feldman & Lewontin 1976; Hawkins 1978; Lewontin 1974a).

The primary stumbling block confronting those engaged in the causal analysis of social behavior would seem to be the complex, dynamic, processual nature of the phenomena which require causal analysis. It is one thing to espouse the platitude that human behavior is the end-product of a series of complex interactions between genes, environments, and culture. It is a different matter to translate this notion into an illuminating causal analysis. Serious difficulties confront those who would like to fit the complicated processes of ontogenetic development and phylogenetic behavioral evolution into the traditional Humean picture of causation (Beauchamp 1974; Hart & Honore 1958; Mackie 1974).

According to the Humean view, causation can be understood in terms of specifiable, static events or states that are linked via universal or probabilistic laws or generalizations. But there are many familiar difficulties for this view, not the least of which is the question of how one goes about correctly distinguishing and labelling the causes, conditions, contributing factors and circumstantial requirements for the occurrence of a particular instance of behavior (Hart & Honore 1958; Shope 1967). Moreover, it is difficult to see how complex processes at various levels of biological organization can be adequately analyzed in terms of individualizable event-event relationships of a single kind at a particular level of organization. Multiple types of factors are involved at any given stage or phase of the generation of social behaviors.

Most biologists and social scientists seem to agree that a bewildering array of discernible etiologies intersect to produce a particular instance of behavior. It is doubtful that this ornate causal picture can be adequately captured by any law or laws that attribute <u>the</u> cause of behavior simply to the presence or absence or a particular gene, genetic activity, selectional force, functional demand, cultural pattern or occurrent mental state. The simplifications and abstractions essential to analyzing complex phenomena scientifically, ought not distort our overall understanding of the complex causal underpinnings of human behavior.

There are three further facts about human social behavior which deserve note. They may pose special problems for understanding the causal genesis of such behavior from an evolutionary perspective. First, human social behavior can have a powerful influence over environmental and selectional forces: the behavior can result in the alteration, negation or amplification of these forces (Barash 1977; Tobach 1974). Thus, it is necessary to think in terms of reciprocal feedback loops rather than unidirectional causal chains in formulating a causal analysis of this type of behavior. Second, human social behavior permits rapid and immediate responses, via innovation, language, learning, and communication, to the demands of the environment. Third, and most important, human social behavior is often conducted with a conscious eye toward rules, norms, motives, and purposes. Given this fact, social scientists and sociobiologists are likely to disagree (Eckberg 1977; Eckland 1976; Harris 1977; Montagu 1976; Sahlins 1976) about the efficacy of the sociobiologist's mechanistic causal account.

One need not resort to the invocation of any mystical variety of vitalism, teleology, or emergentism to defend the claim that because human behavior is often intentional rule-following behavior rather than rule-governed behavior, it is categorically different from other varieties of social behavior normally found in the animal kingdom.

Many social scientists are skeptical of human sociobiology, not because they fear unemployment, but because they feel biologists commit a serious methodological gaffe in trying to explain intentional, volitional, or traditional social behaviors in terms of mechanistic causal laws of one sort or another (Peters 1958; Rudner 1966; Thorpe 1974; Winch 1958). If human social behavior gives some ground for doubting the validity of a univocal sense of causality in interpreting the behavior of organisms, then further philosophical argumentation will be requisite before social scientists permit sociobiologists to cross the conceptual gulf that has long been thought to divide human and animal behavior (Care & Landesman 1968; Kaplan 1964; Kroeber 1962; Nickles 1976; Sahlins 1976).

Comparison

Despite the importance of comparative studies in the biological and behavioral sciences, the techniques and methods involved in such activities have received relatively little analytical attention (Bock 1977, 1978; Hodos & Campbell 1969; Masterson et al. 1976; Tobach et al. 1973). Yet the question of when an inference about the behavior of one species can be drawn from studying the behavior of another species is of central importance for sociobiology. Comparison is especially important in constructing generalizations about behavior which are meant to apply to many species.

Certain important, if simple, qualifications can be made concerning comparisons. Enough has been written already about the dangers of facile anthropomorphization and zoomorphization and about the use of distorting metaphors in describing animal behavior, so that these points need not be repeated here in any great detail (Allen et al. 1975; Montagu 1968; Tinbergen 1968; Wilson 1975). And those involved in the study of behavior are well aware of the difficulties facing the researcher in inferring and reconstructing the behavior of living or ancestral organisms.

A casual glance at any textbook of evolutionary biology will reveal the further problems posed for behavioral comparisons by the phenomena of reticulate evolution, pleiotropy, gender differences, racial variations, seasonal fluctuations, parallelism, convergence, mimicry, and imitation. Further problems are posed for attempts to construct behavioral laws and to reconstruct the phylogenetic evolution of behavior by the scanty sample of available fossil materials and by the difficulties of determining polarity, primitiveness, or direction in a series of fossil remains. While it is generally true that simplicity can be used as a guide to the primitiveness or ancestry of a feature, the number of exceptions to this rule from morphology alone must give pause to anyone who is trying to compare the behavioral attributes of ancient and contemporary creatures. Comparison is made even murkier by the fact that what is primitive or ancestral in one lineage may be complex and derived in another, and by the fact that similarities between traits in form, structure, development, or pattern do not always prove reliable as evidence for imputing similarities in their function, role, or purpose (Atz 1970; Cranach 1976; Masterson et al. 1976; Montagu 1968; Tinbergen 1951).

What is more difficult to find in textbooks on evolutionary biology is any discussion of the two central concepts of comparative inquiry in biology--homology and analogy. Nor do these terms receive much discussion in anthropological or sociobiological texts concerned with applying evolutionary insights to animal and human behavior. Such lacunae are most unfortunate since these notions play a prominent role both in licensing cross-species inferences drawn from behavior based on observations of one species, and in assigning causal significance to observed similarities in behavior between species. These two concepts, homology and analogy, form key elements in the meager armementarium available to those interested in the formulation, weighting, and evaluation of comparative judgments and laws concerning social behavior (Bock 1969, 1977; Cranach 1976; Lorenz 1971).

Homology, as the term is commonly used by systematists, morphologists, and paleontologists, refers to particular traits or features of two organisms that can be traced phylogentically to a feature in a common ancestor of both organisms. Thus, the humerus of a gorilla and the humerus of a human being are homologous traits since they are traceable, phylogentically, to a similar bone in a common primate ancestor.

Analogy is used to refer to those traits of organisms which perform similar functions or biological roles in the life history of the organisms, Thus, despite their obvious structural differences, the wings of a bird and a butterfly are analogous as tetrapod airfoils since both enable their possessors to fly.

In defining these terms particular stress has been placed on 'descent from a common ancestor' and 'similarity of function or biological role' as the defining characteristics of homology and analogy. Regrettably, not all definitions of these terms are this circumspect. Many show a tendency to build the notion of similarity in trait form or trait appearance into both of these definitions. It is often said (Alcock 1975; Bock 1969; Eibl-Eibesfeldt 1975; Gould 1970; Lorenz 1971, 1974; Masters 1973; Nelson 1970; Simpson 1963) that homologous features are features whose similarities are due to descent or inheritance from a similarly endowed common ancester, while analogous traits are traits whose similarities are due to functional or environmental demands. This subtle emendation to the definition of these concepts has left a legacy of confusion and misunderstanding in its wake, particularly for those concerned with the interspeciational study of behavior.

Debates about the significance of observed commonalities of form and pattern between human and animal behavior are rife with claims and counter-claims of the following sort: 'behavioral similarities between primates and humans are trivial since they are merely analogies,' 'only homologies and not analogies are of theoretical biological significance,' 'differences between human and animal behavior are so great as to make homology or analogy impossible,' or, 'behavior, unlike other traits, cannot be homologized' (Allen et al. 1975; Alper et al. 1976, 1978; Atz 1970; Montagu 1976).

These kinds of claims, like the explications they are based upon, have fallen prey to a confusion between the definitions of homology and analogy and the criteria to be used to judge the homologous or analogous status of features (Bock 1969; Ghiselin 1966). Similarity, commonality, and identity in the form of traits are the primary means for determining homology and analogy. But, as criteria they must be used for the determination of <u>both</u> homology and analogy.

The conflation of one of the key criteria for homology and analogy with the definition of these terms has totally muddled the assessment of behavioral traits and the generalizations built upon such assessments. It is simply wrong to assume that if behavioral features are different in form or appearance in animals and man that they then cannot be homologous, or that if they appear similar it can only be as the result of homology. And the same points hold true for analogy. Analogical determinations rest upon the demonstration of common functions of behaviors, not dissimilarities or similarities in their form or appearance. And, while it may be true that homologous behavioral features are likely to be similar to one another in their observable manifestations, this in great measure depends upon the recency with which populations of organisms have diverged from a common ancestor (Simpson 1953, 1958, 1963). Thus, the building of dams by human and beaver may be both homologous and analogous, despite the overt differences in the manifestations of these behaviors. The vocalizations of primates, birds, and whales may be homologous if it is possible to trace these features back to a very distant, but nonetheless common, ancestor. Similarity does play a role in the determination of homology and analogy. But the similarities and dissimilarities of form, appearance, and pattern among the traits of contemporary organisms constitute only empirical evidence for determining homology and analogy--not proofs.

The conflation of the definition of these concepts with their criterial evidence has led to a further serious misunderstanding in arguments between sociobiologists and their critics. It is commonly argued by evolutionary biologists that behavioral traits which are homologous are similar as a result of common ancestry and, thus, that such similarity is a result of genetic inheritance from a common ancestor. This is interpreted to mean that homologous traits are similar solely as a consequence of genetic commonalities in the organisms possessing the traits at issue (Alcock 1975; Allen et al. 1975; Caplan 1978b; Dawkins 1976; Gould 1970, 1977a, 1977b; Lorenz 1971, 1974; Oster & Wilson 1978; Wilson 1975, 1978). Similarly, analogous features are viewed as similar as a result of serving common functional roles, environmental demands or meeting the same selection pressures. It is a small (although confused) step from such a claim to the interpretation that analogous traits are similar solely because of nongenetic, environmental factors (Harris 1977; Masters 1974; Montagu 1976). Both interpretations are, quite simply, wrong.

A homologous feature may be homologous as a result of its traceability up a phylogentic lineage to a common ancestor, but this fact says nothing about the etiology involved in producing the trait or behavior in any given organism. As was argued earlier, the etiology of behavior always involves a large number of complex variables of all sorts--genetic, developmental, environmental, cultural, etc. Thus, even when homologous behaviors in the organisms of distinct species do closely resemble one another in appearance, this resemblance cannot be used to show, and, is not indicative of, a common and exclusively genetic cause for both behaviors. Likewise, dissimilarities in analogous behaviors are not assignable solely to nongenetic environmental causes.

Homology and analogy are not antonyms. Homology cannot be equated with genetic causation and analogy with an environmental etiology. All traits involve factors of both kinds. Consequently, even if war, dominance, territoriality, aggression, xenophobia, competitive zeal, and altruism can be shown to be homologous in humans and lower primates, such a demonstration does not thereby prove the exclusive genetic source of such behavior. And, if the ability to mimic behavior proves analogous among birds, chimps, and human babies, such a functional demonstration would not thereby show mimicry to be a nongenetic, environmentally or culturally caused behavior. The assessment of the homologous or analogous status of social behavior, while requisite for the formulation of generalizations about behavior, does not, in itself, explain the etiological origins of such behavior.

Adaptation

One final source of conceptual confusion and ambiguity in sociobiological thinking revolves around the concept of adaptation. Critics of sociobiological analyses of social behavior are prone to accuse sociobiologists of a kind of Panglossion panselectionism in conducting their analyses (Allen et al. 1975; Burian 1978; Chase 1977; Eckland 1976; Gould 1977a; Hirsch 1976; Klopfer 1977; Lewontin 1977, 1978; Miller 1976; Ruse 1978). All behaviors are presumed, prima facie, to be adaptive and, thus, explainable by means of the contribution made toward the maximization of reproductive success or inclusive genetic fitness. An apparent readiness to generate plausible accounts for the evolution of any and all social behavior in terms of the maximization of genetic fitness is held to make sociobiological accounts ad hoc, plastic, and untestable (Alper et al. 1976; Burian 1978; Caplan 1978a, 1978b; Lewontin 1977, 1978; Ruse 1977, 1978; Sociobiology Study Group 1976, 1977).

Indeed, there is good reason to think that sociobiologists do initiate the analysis of behavior by presupposing that every existing, manifest behavior must somehow be adaptive. For example, one approach to analyzing social behavior which is prominent in the literature is to compute the optimal reproductive advantage conferable by a behavior on an individual, and to explain observed adaptive deviations from this hypothetical optimum in terms of conflicting environmental demands (Barash 1977; Cody 1974; McFarland 1977; Oster & Wilson 1978; Slobodkin 1964; Slobodkin & Rapoport 1974; Trivers 1971; Wilson 1975).

As is the case with causation and comparison, much of the problem with this use of the concept of adaptation seems to derive from conceptual confusions that surround the use of this notion in contemporary evolutionary biology in general. A few conceptual points seem especially salient in this regard.

Adaptation has traditionally been defined by biologists in terms of the adaptiveness, benefits, reproductive success, increased fitness, or advantage of some sort that is conferred on an organism by the possession of a certain trait or behavior. Such definitions usually restrict these advantages to a particular environmental context in which the major determinants are imposed by the physical environment and interspeciational competitive pressures. Unfortunately, despite the prominence and frequency of definitions of this sort, this conception of adaptation is seriously flawed.

First, this type of definition, by focusing on the physical environment of the organism, tends to downplay or obscure the role mates, offspring, parents and other kin can play in directing or influencing the adaptational efforts of organisms. Indeed, a concept of adaptation which focuses on benefits in a particular physical environment obscures one of the most fascinating aspects of adaptation--the phenomena of what might be termed 'adaptational load.' Anyone who has ever seen the ornate courtship bowers of a bowerbird, or the horn of a hercules beetle, is instantly made aware of the price all organisms must pay in trying to adjust their phenotypic and behavioral repetoires to the conflicting demands of the environment and conspecific organisms. The 'compromising' role played by social behavior in mediating between conflicting selectional demands which sociobiologists emphasize in their analyses cannot be elucidated using traditional conceptions of adaptation. The textbook definition of adaptation is lagging behind current research on the subject.

Moreover, building the notions of advantage or success into the definition of adaptation is both unnecessary and confusing. If we are to believe the fossil record, and genetic theory, there is no reason to assume that advantageous or successful genetic variants will necessarily appear that will allow populations to maximize their chances of reproductive success. If they do appear, they will usually be selected, but such variations need not occur. Adaptation in evolutionary biology and sociobiology refers to nothing more than the phenotypic and behavioral accommodations or responses made by the members of populations to persistent selectional demands of all kinds--environmental, biotic, interspecific, and conspecific.

Indeed, if the notions of fitness, success and advantage are kept distinct from adaptation, it becomes possible to use the former concepts as means to evaluate the adaptational 'efforts' of various populations of organisms. For example, social behaviors of a given type may conceivably increase the likelihood of survival by increasing energy efficiency or aiding in predator avoidance; but they may simultaneously decrease reproductive success by lowering fertility, decreasing longevity or decreasing male/female encounters. Moreover, random events, such as mutation, drift, recombination, natural catastrophies and fluctuating environments play major roles in determining adaptational responses. There are even cases in human culture of environmental abundance where there is good reason to doubt whether the existing social behavior is adaptive at all. Given a prolonged abundance of resources, it is fallacious to assume that each behavior exists because it guarantees an optimal likelihood of individual survival, or even because it confers a relative immediate advantage upon one population over and against another.

While there is a powerful design component to evolution, there is also a powerful stochastic element as well (Hull 1974; Jacob 1977; Kitts 1976; Lewontin 1974b; Mayr 1965). Given this fact, the assessment of the adaptational status of any observed behavior must follow and not precede functional and comparative assessments. If it is true that selection forces can change rapidly and randomly, that behavior is highly plastic, that social behavior can be transmitted by nongenetic means, and that social behavior can reciprocally influence environments, then idealized optimization models cannot be substituted for functional assessments of specific behaviors in real world settings. Multiple solutions to environmental contingencies are possible. Under the appropriate circumstances, they can viably coexist without selection toward an optimum occurring at all. Some of the apparent unfalsifiability and ad hoc flexibility of sociobiological, and, indeed, of all evolutionary accounts, may arise from the unnecessary theoretical presupposition that a behavior which persists always does so as a result of the fact that it is optimally advantageous or beneficial (Dawkins 1976; Hamilton 1964; Lewontin 1974b, 1977, 1978; Lorenz 1971; Stern 1970; Trivers 1971; Wilson 1975).

Ethics, Politics and Values

At the beginning of this paper, the claim was advanced that values had played a key role in determining the content and nature of the ongoing debate about sociobiology. I hope it is now clear that the role of purely ideological and political values in this debate may have been overblown or at least misunderstood. For sociobiological theory in particular, and, evolutionary biological accounts in general, do seem to be beset by methodological and conceptual confusions and problems. These criticisms ought not be confused with external valuational and ideological criteria in weighing the merits of such theories.

There is one value, however, which appears to be of central importance to understanding the sociobiological enterprise, although it has received relatively little press. It is the philosophical commitment on the part of many scientists (Wilson 1978) to the unity of science--that is, the possibility of explaining, describing and predicting all phenomena in the physical, biological and social domains by means of a single type of explanatory methodology and analysis. One need not be a fascist or a social Darwinist to be committed to the view that if the methodology of evolutionary biology is valid for analyzing bones, muscles, and morphology, it should also be true for analyzing brains, minds, cultures, and language. However, an a priori value commitment to such an explanatory enterprise should not blind one to the serious conceptual pitfalls that lie in wait. Problems concerning causation, comparison, adaptation and determinism cannot be resolved by professions of faith in the utility of evolutionary analysis.

Even if many sociobiologists suffer from this type of valuational bias, one might still wonder about the nature, content, and intent of the various political and ideological pronouncements that have been made with regard to sociobiology (Allen et al. 1975; Alper et al. 1976; Barash 1977;

Caplan 1978a; Davis 1976; Somit 1977). It has been said that conservative, bourgeois, discriminatory views have led certain proponents of sociobiology to make dubious claims about the acceptability, naturalness, and desirability of particular forms of human social behavior. It must be noted that this claim is neither meaningless nor metaphysical. It is a testable proposal about the sociology of scientists and in keeping with current research on the origin and evolution of theories in the history of science (Hull 1978; Laudan 1977; Mitroff 1974; Nelkin 1977; Suppe 1977). My intuition is to say that such a view is overly simplistic. We know enough already about science and the historical evolution of scientific theories to know that the story is richer than this. Whether this is true or not, there is no need to do what so many persons insist on doing, dismissing this empirical claim as liberal or Marxist claptrap. Let's go to the cases and find out.

It does seem fair to claim that, while the solutions suggested in this discussion may miss the mark, the conceptual problems cited are real ones. Accordingly, sociobiologists should exercize caution in evaluating their theoretical solutions to the puzzles of social behavior. They should be wary of those who insist on forcing ideological and political conclusions out of speculative theories. I remain doubtful about the degree to which the social sciences of man or the humanities can profit from biologization. But I have no doubt that sociobiology could profit greatly from the philosophicalization of its methods, concepts, and ideas.

One final comment is in order concerning the relevance of scientific findings for ethics and politics. It is sometimes claimed that any effort to derive a valuational conclusion from empirical premises is an instance of what G. E. Moore termed the naturalistic fallacy (Moore 1903). At least fifty years of ethical philosophy subsequent to Moore have been devoted to refutations of Moore's arguments for this claim and to suggesting ways to bridge the apparent gap between facts and values (Caplan 1978a; Frankena 1939; Flew 1967; Hancock 1974; Harman 1977; Hudson 1969; Taylor 1975). It would be fair to state that this disciplinary effort has at least resulted in the conclusion that the naturalistic fallacy is a label in need of argumentation, rather than a logical prohibition.

What seems less controversial and more germane for assessing the relevance of science for ethics is that, however one links propositions from these domains, it is impossible to assess an ethical argument without some sort of criteria.

And the criteria for the assessment of ethical arguments clearly seem to stand beyond the derivational or reductive grasp of science (Caplan 1978a, 1978b; Flew 1967; Hudson 1969). Human nature may possess limits and constraints, but decisions as to what ought to be done about such facts must come from and be confirmed by sources other than science.

Summary

Ideological and political criticisms have dominated much of the debate about sociobiological theorizing. Much of the debate has centered around issues concerning biological determinism and the alleged biases of various scientists toward genetic or environmental explanations of human social behavior. However, both of these issues appear to have less to do with ideology than they do with philosophical confusions concerning the nature of determinism and causation.

There is a danger in the attempt to base criticism of sociobiological theory solely on political grounds. Some of the serious methodological problems confronting the theory may become obscured by all the talk about values. Biologists have not done an exemplary job of explicating the concepts of causation, comparison and adaptation. This makes for difficulties in trying to assess the validity of the theoretical speculations of sociobiologists concerning the evolution and function of social behavior. A commitment to the utility and efficacy of evolutionary explanations should not blind sociobiologists to the fact that theoretical sophistication and elegant modeling do not, in themselves, provide answers about the legitimacy of optimality assumptions or cross-species generalizations. The methodology and conclusions of sociobiology are only as sound as the concepts from which sociobiological theories are constructed. And there is reason to think that much philosophical work remains to be done in clarifying some of the key concepts of sociobiological theory.

Literature Cited

Alcock, J. 1975. Animal behavior: An evolutionary approach. Sinnauer, Sunderland, Massachusetts.

Allen, E., Beckwith, B., Beckwith, J., Chorover, S., Culver, D., Duncan M., Gould, S., Hubbard, R., Inouye, H., Leeds, A., Lewontin, R., Madansky, C., Miller, L., Pyeritz, R., Rosenthal, M., & Schreier, H. 1975. Against sociobiology. New York Review of Books, November:43-44.

Alper, J., Beckwith, J., Chorover, S. L., Hunt, J., Inouye, H., Judd, T., Lange, R. V., & Sternberg, P. 1976. The implications of sociobiology. Science 192:424-427.

_______, J. Beckwith & L. Miller. 1978. Sociobiology is a political issue. In A. Caplan (ed.), The sociobiology debate. Harper & Row, New York, pp. 476-488.

Atz, J. W. 1970. The application of the idea of homology to behavior. In L. R. Aronson, E. Tobach, D. S. Lehrman & J. S. Rosenblatt (eds.), Development and evolution of behavior. Freeman, San Francisco, pp. 53-74.

Barash, D. P. 1977. Sociobiology and behavior. Elsevier, New York.

Barker, A. D. 1969. An approach to the theory of natural selection. Philosophy 44:271-290.

Beauchamp, T. L. (ed.). 1974. Philosophical problems of causation. Dickenson, Encino, California.

Block, N. J. & G. Dworkin (eds.). 1976. The IQ controversy. Random House, New York.

Bock, W. J. 1969. The concept of homology. Annals of the New York Academy of Sciences 167:71-73.

_______. 1977. Adaptation and the comparative method. In M. Hecht (ed.), Major patterns in vertebrate evolution. Plenum, New York, pp. 57-82.

_______. 1978. Principles and methods of comparative analyses in sociobiology. In A. Caplan (ed.), The sociobiology debate. Harper & Row, New York, pp. 396-410.

Burian, R. 1978. A methodological critique of sociobiology. In A. Caplan (ed.), The sociobiology debate. Harper & Row, New York, pp. 376-395.

Caplan, A. 1978a. In what ways are recent developments in biology and sociobiology relevant to ethics? Perspectives in Biology and Medicine 22:536-550.

_______ (ed.). 1978b. The sociobiology debate. Harper & Row, New York.

Care, N. W. & C. Landesman (eds.). 1968. Readings in the theory of action. Indiana University Press, Indianapolis.

Carson, H. L. 1959. Genetic conditions which promote or retard the formation of species. Cold Spring Harbor Symposium in Quantitative Biology 24:87-105.

Chase, A. 1977. The legacy of Malthus. Knopf, New York.

Chorover, S. L. 1979. From Genesis to genocide. MIT Press, Cambridge.

Cody, M. L. 1974. Optimalization in ecology. Science 183: 1156-64.

Cranach, M. von (ed.). 1976. Methods of inference from animal to human behaviour. Mouton, The Hague.

Davis, B. 1976. Sociobiology: The debate continues. Hastings Center Report 6:19, 44.

Dawkins, R. 1976. The selfish gene. Oxford University Press, Oxford.

Dobzhansky, T. 1937. Genetics and the origin of species. Columbia University Press, New York.

Dworkin, G. (ed.). 1970. Determinism, free will and moral responsibility. Prentice-Hall, Engelwood Cliffs.

Eckberg, D. L. 1977. Sociobiology and the death of sociology. American Sociologist 12:191-196.

Eckland, B. 1976. Darwin rides again. American Journal of Sociology 82:692-697.

Ehrman, L., G. S. Omenn & E. Caspari (eds.). 1972. Genetics, environment and behavior. Academic Press, New York.

_______ & P. A. Parsons. 1976. The genetics of behavior. Sinnauer, Sunderland, Massachusetts.

Eibl-Eibesfeldt, I. 1975. Ethology, the biology of behavior. Holt, Rinehart & Winston, New York.

Feldman, M. W. & R. C. Lewontin. 1976. Heritability of IQ. Science 194:12-14.

Flew, A. G. N. 1967. Evolutionary ethics. St. Martin's, New York.

Frankena, W. 1939. The naturalistic fallacy. Mind 48:103-14.

Gardiner, P. (ed.). 1974. The philosophy of history. Oxford University Press, Oxford.

Ghiselin, M. T. 1966. On physchologism in the logic of taxonomic controversies. Systematic Zoology 15:207-215.

Gould, S. J. 1970. Evolutionary paleontology and the science of form. Earth Science Review 6:77-119.

_______. 1977a. Ever since Darwin. Norton, New York.

_______. 1977b. Ontogeny and phylogeny. Harvard University Press, Cambridge, Massachusetts.

Hamilton, W. D. 1964. The genetical evolution of social behavior. Journal of Theoretical Biology 7:1-51.

Hancock, R. 1974. Twentieth century ethics. Columbia University Press, New York.

Harman, G. 1977. The nature of morality. Oxford University Press, New York.

Harris, M. 1977. Cannibals and kings. Random House, New York.

Hart, H. L. A. & A. M. Honore. 1958. Causation in the law. Clarendon, Oxford.

Hawkins, D. 1978. The science and ethics of equality. Basic, New York.

Hirsch, J. (ed.). 1967. Behavior-genetic analysis. McGraw-Hill, New York.

_______. 1976. Review of Wilson's sociobiology. Animal Behaviour 24:707-709.

Hodos, W. & C. B. G. Campbell. 1969. Scala Natura: Why there is no theory in comparative psychology. Psychological Review 76:337-350.

Hudson, W. D. (ed.). 1969. The is/ought question. St. Martin's, New York.

Hull, D. 1974. Philosophy of biological science. Prentice-Hall, Englewood Cliffs, New Jersey.

_______. 1978. Altruism in science: A sociobiological explanation of altruistic behavior among scientists. Animal Behaviour 26:685-697.

Jacob, F. 1977. Evolution and tinkering. Science 196: 1161-1166.

Kaplan, A. 1964. The conduct of inquiry. San Francisco, Chandler.

Kitts, D. B. 1976. Certainty and uncertainty in geology. American Journal of Science 276:29-46.

Klopfer, P. H. 1977. Social Darwinism lives! (Should it?). Yale Journal of Biology and Medicine 50:77-84.

Kroeber, A. 1962. The nature of culture. University of Chicago Press, Chicago.

Laudan, L. 1977. Progress and its problems. University of California Press, Berkeley.

Lewontin, R. C. 1968. The concept of evolution. In D. L. Siles (ed.), International Encyclopedia of Social Sciences 5:202-210. Macmillan, New York.

_______. 1974a. The analysis of variance and the analysis of cause. American Journal of Human Genetics 26:400-411.

_______. 1974b. The genetic basis of evolutionary change. Columbia University Press, New York.

_______. 1977. Biological determinism as a social weapon. In Ann Arbor Science for the People Editorial Collective (eds.), Biology as a social weapon. Burgess, Minneapolis, pp. 6-20.

_______. 1978. Adaptation. Scientific American 239:212-230.

Lorenz, K. 1971. Studies in animal and human behavior, Volume 2, Methuen, London.

_______. 1974. Analogy as a source of knowledge. Science 185:229-234.

Lovtrup, S. 1976. On the falsifiability of neo-Darwinism. Evolutionary Theory 1:267-283.

_______. 1977. Variation, selection, isolation, environment: An analysis of Darwin's theory. Theoria 43:65-83.

Mackie, J. L. 1974. The cement of the universe: A study of causation. Clarendon, Oxford.

Masters, R. D. 1973. Functional approaches to analogical comparison between species. Social Science Information 12:7-28.

Masterton, R. B., W. Hodos & H. J. Jerison (eds.). 1976. Evolution, brain and behavior. Earlbaum, Hillsdale, New Jersey.

Mayr, E. 1955. Integration of genotypes: Synthesis. Cold Spring Harbor Symposia in Quantitative Biology 20:327-333.

_______. 1965. Cause and effect in biology. In D. Lerner (ed.), Cause and effect. M.I.T. Press, Cambridge, Massachusetts, pp. 33-50.

McFarland, D. J. 1977. Decision-making in animals. Nature 269:15-21.

Miller, L. 1976. Fated genes. Journal of the History of the Behavioral Sciences April, pp. 183-190.

Mitroff, I. I. 1974. The subjective side of science. Elsevier, Amsterdam.

Montagu, M. F. A. (ed.). 1968. The concept of the primitive. The Free Press, New York.

_______. 1976. The nature of human aggression. Oxford University Press, New York.

Moore, G. E. 1903. Principia ethica. Cambridge University Press, Cambridge.

Morison, R. 1975. The biology of behavior. Natural History 84:25-29.

Nagel, E. 1961. The structure of science. Harcourt Brace & World, New York.

Nelson, G. J. 1970. Outline of a theory of comparative biology. Systematic Zoology 19:373-384.

Nelkin, D. 1977. Science textbook controversies and the politics of equal time. M.I.T. Press, Cambridge, Massachusetts.

Nickles, T. 1976. On autonomy arguments in social science. In F. Suppe & P. Asquith (eds.), PSA 1976. Volume 1. Philosophy of Science Association, East Lansing, pp. 12-25.

Oster, G. F. & E. O. Wilson. 1978. Caste and ecology in the social insects. Princeton University Press, Princeton.

Peters, R. H. 1976. Tautology in evolution and ecology. American Naturalist 110:1-12.

Peters, R. S. 1958. The concept of motivation. Routledge & Kegan Paul, London.

Rudner, R. S. 1966. The philosophy of social science. Prentice-Hall, Englewood Cliffs, New Jersey.

Ruse, M. 1977. Is biology different from physics? In R. Colodny (ed.), Logic, laws, and life. University of Pittsburgh Press, Pittsburgh, pp. 89-127.

_______. 1978. Sociobiology: Sound science or muddled metaphysics? In F. Suppe & P. Asquith (eds.), PSA 1976. Volume 2. Philosophy of Science Association, East Lansing, pp. 48-76.

Sahlins, M. 1976. The use and abuse of biology. University of Michigan Press, Ann Arbor.

Shope, R. K. 1967. Explanation in terms of 'the cause.' Journal of Philosophy 64:312-20.

Simpson, G. G. 1953. The major features of evolution. Simon & Schuster, New York.

_______. 1958. Behavior and evolution. In A. Roe & G. G. Simpson (eds.), Behavior and evolution. Yale, New Haven, pp. 373-384.

_______. 1963. The meaning of taxonomic statements. In S. L. Washburn (ed.), Classification and human evolution. Aldine, Chicago, pp. 1-31.

Slobodkin, L. B. 1964. The strategy of evolution. American Scientist 52:342-357.

_______ & A. Rapoport. 1974. An optimal strategy of evolution. The Quarterly Review of Biology 49:181-200.

Sociobiology Study Group of Science for the People. 1976. Sociobiology--another biological determinism. Bioscience 26:184-186.

_______. 1977. Sociobiology: A new scientific determinism. In The Ann Arbor Science for the People Editorial Collective (eds.). Biology as a social weapon. Burgess, Minneapolis, pp. 133-151.

Somit, A. (ed.). 1977. Biology and politics. Mouton, The Hague.

Stern, J. T. 1970. The meaning of 'adaptation' and its relation to the phenomenon of natural selection. Evolutionary Biology 4:39-65.

Suppe, F. (ed.). 1977. The structure of scientific theories, 2nd ed. University of Illinois Press, Urbana.

Taylor, P. W. 1975. Principles of ethics. Dickenson, Encino, California.

Thorpe, W. H. 1974. Reductionism in biology. In F. J. Ayala & T. Dobzhansky (eds.), Studies in the philosophy of biology. Macmillan, New York.

Tinbergen, N. 1951. The study of instinct. Clarendon, Oxford.

_______. 1968. On war and peace in animals and man. Science 160:1411-1418.

Tobach, E. 1974. Social Darwinism rides again. In E. Tobach (ed.), The four horsemen: Racism, sexism, militarism and social Darwinism. Behavioral, New York.

_______, H. E. Adler & L. L. Adler (eds.). 1973. Comparative psychology at issue. Annals of the New York Academy of Sciences 223:3-193.

Trivers, R. L. 1971. The evolution of reciprocal altruism. The Quarterly Review of Biology 46:35-47.

Wilson, E. O. 1975. Sociobiology: The new synthesis. Harvard University Press, Cambridge, Massachusetts.

_______. 1976. Academic vigilantism and the political significance of sociobiology. Bioscience 26:183-190.

_______. 1978. On human nature. Harvard University Press, Cambridge, Massachusetts.

Winch, P. 1958. The idea of a social science. Prentice-Hall, Englewood Cliffs, New Jersey.

Part 3

The Organism in Its Environment

Stephen T. Emlen

5. Ecological Determinism and Sociobiology

The field of sociobiology has made major advances and attracted widespread attention during its short decade of existence as a theoretical and predictive science. When one steps back and examines the field, it becomes apparent that research is progressing along two separate, but interrelated, frontiers (Fig. 1).

The first is concerned primarily with describing the types of behavioral interactions that occur between organisms living within the confines of a particular society. Building upon the evolutionary tenet of natural selection, this frontier attempts to better understand such aspects of social behavior as dominance and submissive interactions, male and female strategies of parental investment and mate selection, parent-offspring interactions and conflict, differential behavior toward members versus "outsiders" of a group, preferential interactions with kin as opposed to non-kin (nepotism), etc. (Fig. 2). Some of the recent developments on this frontier have included interpretations of current human behavior in terms of its probable adaptiveness during our recent evolutionary past, and predictions of behavioral interactions based upon the recent expansion of the theory of individual natural selection to encompass kin (Hamilton 1964a, 1964b; Trivers 1974; West-Eberhard 1975).

It is this frontier of sociobiology that has attracted wide attention and become the focus of heated debate (Allen et al. 1975; Allen et al. 1976; Wade 1976; Wilson 1976).

Evolution is basically a selfish doctrine, preaching that the individual that maximizes its own welfare and reproduction relative to others will gain the selective edge --- by leaving more descendants who, themselves, carry the same behavioral traits. If the basis of a particular human behavior is considered to be largely genetically deter-

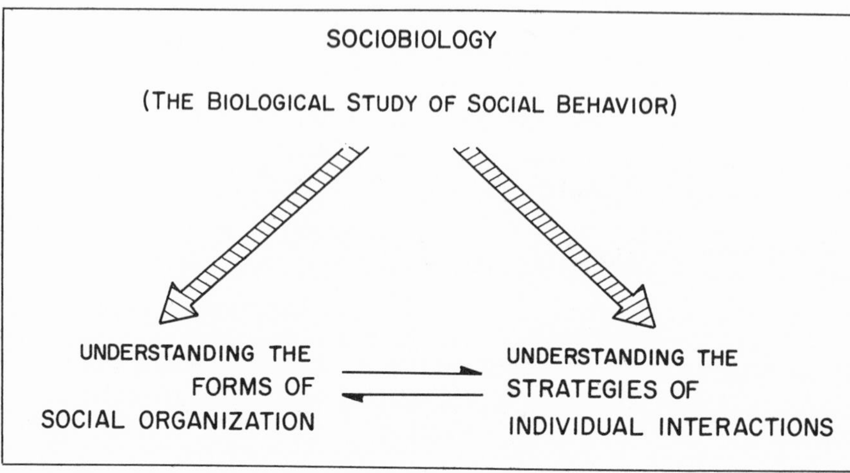

Figure 1.

STRATEGIES OF INDIVIDUAL INTERACTIONS

TOPICS

Types of Dominance Interactions
Patterns of Parental Investment
Strategies of Mate Selection
Parent-Offspring Interactions
Member / Stranger Tolerance
Kin / Nonkin favoritism (Nepotism)

GOAL

To better understand why an organism behaves the way it does when living in a particular society.

Figure 2.

mined, this can lead to a somewhat fatalistic acceptance of the behavior as being unavoidable, or even desirable. Since behaviors predicted to convey selective advantages to the actors are frequently at variance with culturally promoted ideals (of unselfish altruism, or generosity towards strangers, etc.), the value of sociobiology has been viewed with skepticism by many. What is often overlooked is that the slow time scale of genetic change compared with cultural change creates an evolutionary time lag. Thus the "adaptiveness" of a particular behavior we observe today may relate to a past ecological setting or social milieu that is very different from present day conditions.

Sociobiology can <u>not</u> be used to make value judgments on what an organism "<u>should</u>" do. But sociobiology <u>can</u> provide a theoretical framework that may help us understand <u>why</u> an organism behaves the way it does (Barash 1977).

It is the misapplication of theory from this frontier of sociobiology that can lead (and has led) to attempts to justify unjust status quo tactics or to maintain politically oppressive policies. As a consequence of these potentially dangerous misuses, interest in this aspect of sociobiology has spread far beyond the realm of biology, into the areas of philosophy, ethics, and the entire range of the social sciences.

There is a second major research frontier in sociobiology --- one whose primary concern is understanding the <u>forms of social organization</u> that are found in nature. Why does one form of society exist under one set of ecological conditions, and another form exist in another?

Building on over a century's accumulation of natural history studies, workers in the last decade have begun developing models that allow a better understanding of the type and structure of animal societies. By integrating behavioral and ecological theory, it has become possible to begin to predict various aspects of social organization on the basis of a small number of ecological variables. The types of questions being asked include: When do we expect an animal to live socially as opposed to solitarily? Under what conditions will an animal be territorial and defend an area or a resource rather than be nomadic or share the resource? If social, what determines the optimal group size, and does this vary for different activities (foraging versus breeding, etc.)? What are the methods of resource acquisition and how are resources divided among members of the population? What is the form of the mating system, and what are the options for the accumulation of multiple mates? How and

FORMS OF SOCIAL ORGANIZATION

TOPICS

DEGREE OF SOCIALITY (SOLITARY OR GREGARIOUS)
IF GREGARIOUS: OPTIMAL GROUP SIZE
EXISTENCE OF TERRITORIALITY
METHODS OF RESOURCE ACQUISITION
PATTERN OF RESOURCE DIVISION
FORM OF MATING SYSTEM
PATTERN OF DISPERSAL (BY AGE AND SEX)
FAMILY AND KIN-STRUCTURE OF THE POPULATION

GOAL

TO UNDERSTAND AND, ULTIMATELY, TO PREDICT THE BASIC FORM AND STRUCTURE OF A PARTICULAR SOCIETY.

Figure 3.

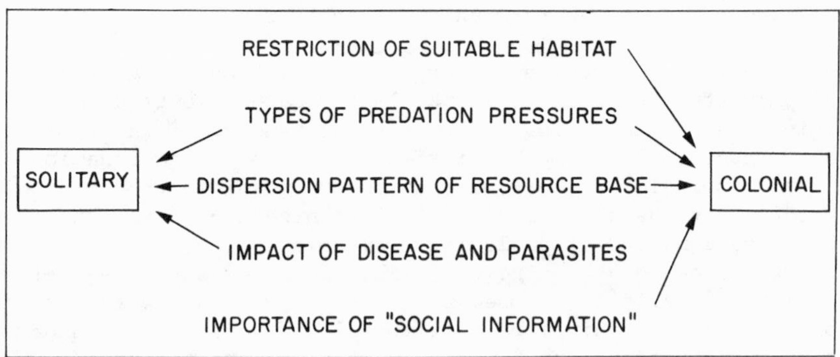

Figure 4. General schema of major factors influencing tendencies to live gregariously.

when do animals disperse, and what is the effect of this upon the kin structure of the population? (Fig. 3.)

In essence, this side of sociobiology attempts to predict the basic elements of the form of animal societies. The generalizability of these ecological predictions is impressive, as attested to by their broad applicability across phylogenetic lines. Similar ecological determinants seem to apply when we examine such diverse groups as dragonflies (Campanella and Wolf 1974; Jacobs 1955; Pajunen 1966; Waage 1973) or frogs (Emlen 1976a; Wells 1977a, 1977b); coral reef fish (Barlow 1974; Reese 1975; Robertson and Warner 1978; Warner and Robertson 1978) or marine birds (Lack 1967; Nelson 1970); tropical bats (Bradbury 1977; Bradbury and Vehrencamp 1976, 1977a, 1977b) or weaverbirds (Crook 1964); African ungulates (Estes 1974; Jarman 1974) or primates (Clutton-Brock 1974; Crook and Gartlan 1966; Crook 1970, 1972; Denham 1971; Eisenberg et al. 1972; Jolly 1970). Animals faced with similar ecological "problems" exhibit a predictable convergence in their "solutions" as shown in their social organizations (Emlen 1976b).

As the accuracy of such predictions increases in the decade ahead, so will their importance to other areas of science. The potential use and misuse of such information is fraught with some of the same dangers that have been discussed concerning sociobiology's first frontier. But, ironically, the importance and the impact of this ecological side of sociobiology has been largely overlooked to date.

It is this ecological frontier, and its implications both to sociobiology and to the issues raised in the sociobiology "debates" that I wish to address in this paper.

Basic Principles of Ecological Sociobiology

To Be or Not to Be Social

What determines whether an animal will be solitary or gregarious? As correctly pointed out by Alexander (1974), there are a number of inescapable costs associated with group living. These include 1) an increased conspicuousness to predators, 2) an increase in competition for, and exploitation of, resources near the aggregation, and 3) an increased probability of disease and parasite transmission. Group living is expected only under circumstances where advantages accrued through sociality more than offset these potential liabilities.

At least five factors affect the costs and benefits of social living (Fig. 4).

1) Restriction of suitable habitat or resources to a small number of discrete spatial areas can lead to a passive accumulation of individuals at those areas. This, in turn, can lead to the development of specialized behavioral adaptations to minimize the liabilities mentioned above and to maximize the individual gains accruing from social advantages listed below.

2) Predator pressure, depending upon its form and intensity, can promote either widely dispersed, asocial living or dense, gregarious coloniality. Fixed aggregations of breeding animals are not only more conspicuous to predators but provide a reliable, long-term source of prey. Consequently, many predators might be expected to return frequently to a breeding colony and come to specialize upon colonial species as a source of food. Counteracting this, organisms residing in close proximity to one another can benefit from the increased surveillance and alertness of the group. This increases the likelihood of early detection and thus avoidance of approaching predators. Social living also makes possible different forms of group mobbing, harassment, or attack on would-be predators. Finally, being part of a large aggregation decreases the probability that any given individual will be the specific one preyed upon when a predator does attack the group. The security afforded by this "selfish herd" principle (Hamilton 1971) is greatest for individuals that cluster in the dense, central areas of the flock or colony, or which breed during the peak of synchrony with other members of their group (Emlen and Demong 1975; Feare 1976; Patterson 1965; Williams 1975; Yom-Tov 1975). The relative weighting of these costs and benefits of sociality will depend upon the types and abundance of potential predators, the effectiveness of the anti-predator group responses, the number of animals in the social group, etc.

3) The pattern of dispersion of critical food resources (in terms of both spatial and temporal availability) is another important determinant of social organization. When food resources are distributed sparsely but uniformly over a large area, the consumer species generally will be widely dispersed as well. If food is locally clumped and abundant, individual consumers may also clump their distribution without danger of over-exploitation. But under conditions when the food resource occurs patchily, but the spatial locations or temporal outbreaks are unpredictable, individual organisms can actually localize and exploit the resource <u>more</u> efficiently by living gregariously. The increased number of

foragers increases the likelihood of rapid discovery of hard-to-locate or ephemeral concentrations of food. By following successful foragers to areas of temporary resource abundance, individuals can take advantage of the pooled resource localizing capabilities of the larger group (Brown 1964; Emlen and Demong 1975; Horn 1968; Krebs 1974; Lack 1968; Ward 1965; Ward and Zahavi 1973).

4) In dense aggregations of animals, the chances for build up and transmission of parasites and/or communicable diseases increase. Such detrimental effects of crowded living can promote a more dispersed form of spatial organization.

5) The last factor listed as favoring gregariousness is the importance of "social information." Gregarious living provides a social milieu that allows observational learning and cultural transmission of adaptive solutions to ecological problems. Such social learning provides a mechanism allowing for rapid changes in behavior patterns; in turn these changes enable individuals to adjust adaptively to short-term changes in ecological conditions. The studies of the social acquisition of new feeding habits among Japanese macaque monkeys provides a good example of the advantages of this phenomenon (Kawai 1965).

The task of the ecological sociobiologist is to evaluate the importance of these types of factors to the biology of the particular species in question. From this, he attempts to estimate the costs and benefits of group living and then to predict the most adaptive form of spatial social organization.

Costs and Benefits of Territoriality

Under what ecological conditions should we expect an organism to exclude most conspecifics from a given area, e.g. to be territorial? Viewed in cost/benefit terms, this question can be answered with the following two statements: 1) When some resource in the area is worth defending (the benefits are high), and 2) when the area or resource is energetically defendable (the costs are low) (Brown 1964) (Fig. 5). Whether or not the conditions for the first statement being true are met depends in large part on the quantity, quality, and reliability of the specific resource.

If a food source is unpredictable in space, and either unpredictable or ephemeral through time, its lack of reliability might render it not worth defending. Alternatively, a food resource that is uniformly dispersed in space and long-lasting through time generally would be worth defending.

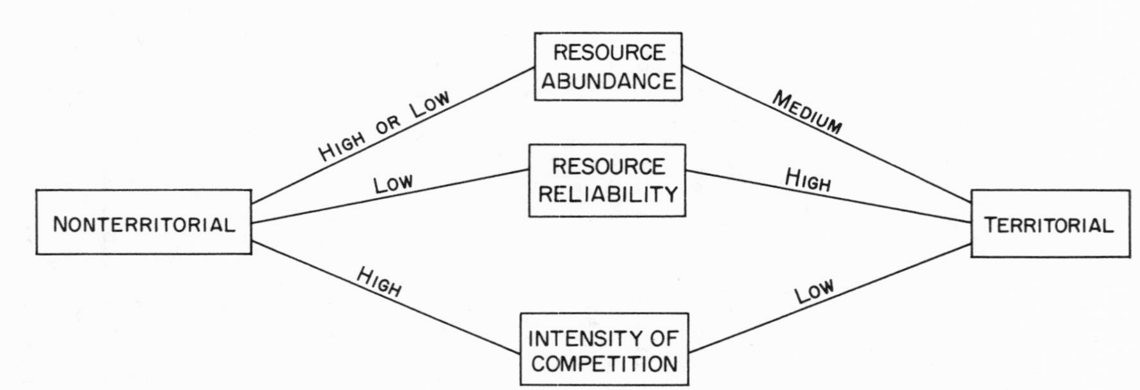

Figure 5. General schema of cost/benefit considerations affecting the expression of territorial behavior.

The abundance of a resource, as well as its pattern of dispersion, is an important determinant of territorial behavior. This point is best exemplified by recent studies of Hawaiian and African nectar-feeding birds (Carpenter and MacMillan 1976; Gill and Wolf 1975). Several workers have demonstrated (by calculating time and energy budgets) that when flowers are scarce and/or sugar concentrations of nectar are low, the resource base is insufficient to permit territorial behavior. At intermediate abundances of nectar, the benefits of aggressively excluding conspecifics from a given patch of flowers exceeds the costs of such aggression. Specifically, the energy saved by not having to forage over flowers that have already been depleted through the foraging activities of other individuals exceeds the costs of the aggressive behavior necessary to maintain exclusive foraging use of the patch. Thus territorial behavior is energetically adaptive. At still higher levels of nectar abundance, sufficient undepleted flowers are available that little benefit is gained by excluding other individuals. Although the costs of territorial behavior would remain the same, the benefit of exclusive use decreases until territorial behavior is no longer energetically practicable. Field observations show that individuals can shift from a territorial to a nonterritorial mode of behavior, and that these changes occur where predicted by the cost-benefit model.

Note that an increase in the number of competitors and/or a decrease in the abundance level of the resource could lead to an increase in the intensity of competition (Fig. 5). This would lead to an increase in the cost of territorial defense. As this cost rises, so too must the gain realized by exclusive control of the resource if territorial behavior is to be favored. Hence the second statement, that the resource must be energetically defendable.

Resource abundance, resource dispersion, and resource reliability are proving to be excellent predictors of the occurrence of territorial behavior among a wide range of species belonging to taxonomic groups as divergent as insects, fishes, birds, and mammals.

Recently, several experimenters have tested the economic defendability model of territoriality by artificially manipulating the abundance and/or the spatial distribution of food resources. Territorial behavior has been shown to be quite plastic, being expressed with certain manipulations and not with others, in accord with the principles discussed above (Magnuson 1962; Zahavi 1971).

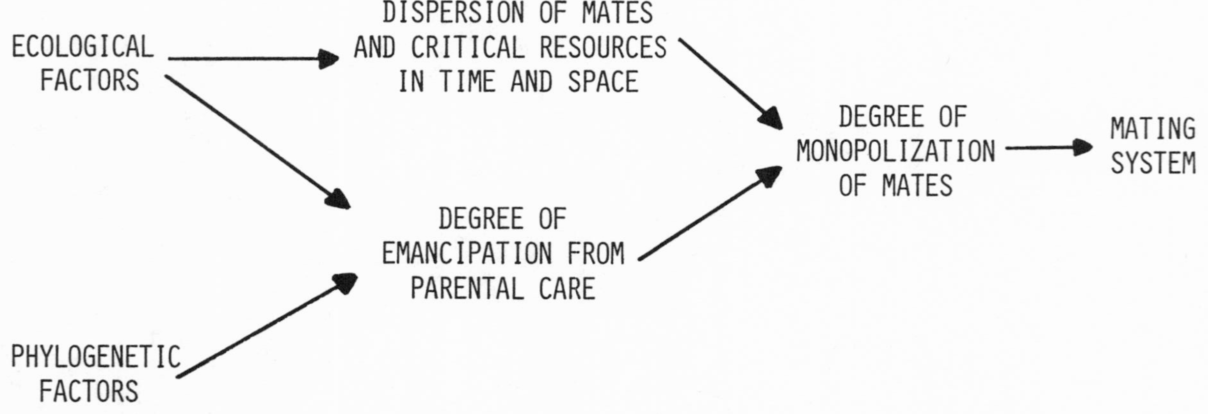

Figure 6. General schema of the determinants of a mating system.

Ecological Determinants of Mating Systems

The same principle of energetic defendability is important in understanding the different types of mating systems found in animal societies. Under certain conditions, a portion of the male (or female) population may be able to control the access of others to potential mates. This control can be direct, as in the physical herding of potential mates and the physical exclusion of other members of the same sex from these mates, or indirect, by controlling resources that are critical either for mate attraction or for successful reproduction. The greater the degree of control or monopolization of multiple mates, the greater the intensity of sexual selection and the greater the tendency for some form of polygamous mating system.

L.W. Oring and I recently proposed that certain environmental factors determine the degree to which mates can be defended or monopolized (Emlen and Oring 1977). This Environmental Potential for Polygamy, as we termed it, is strongly influenced by both the spatial distribution of key resources and the temporal availability of receptive mates (Fig. 6). When mates or resources essential for attracting mates are highly clumped in space, successful individuals can monopolize matings through the control of these resources. The benefits derived from such resource defense are presumed to lie in an increased probability of mate attraction and acquisition. Obviously, the magnitude of this benefit depends upon the temporal pattern of availability of sexually receptive partners. These two factors interact in determining the environmental potential for polygamy (Fig. 7).

Note that not all species will be able to take full advantage of the EPP. Polygamy should be less common whenever the efforts of both parents are crucial for the successful rearing of young. Both ecological factors (e.g. resource abundance) and phylogenetic considerations (e.g. stage of development of young at hatching/birth; growth rate and dependency period of young, etc.) influence the ability to capitalize on the EPP (Fig. 6).

By extending these ideas, it is possible to develop an ecological categorization of mating systems (Emlen and Oring 1977). The precise form of the mating system will depend upon which sex is limiting and on the manner and the degree to which the limited sex controls the critical resource base or monopolizes mates (or both).

These three brief discussions have, of necessity, been

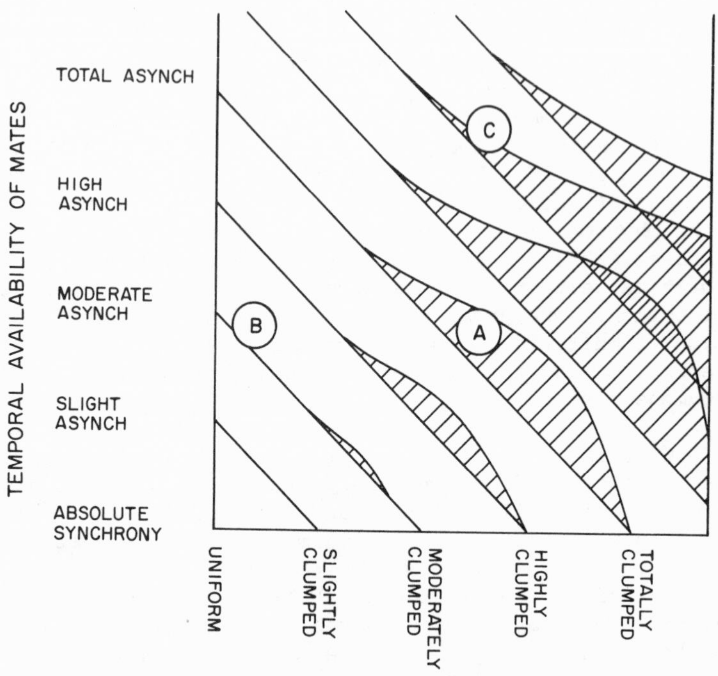

Figure 7. Schematic representation of the environmental potential for polygamy (indicated by the perpendicular height of the shaded area) and its relation to the spatial distribution of resources and the temporal availability of receptive mates.

Consider the following simplified example: Females of a hypothetical species of ungulate have a seasonal period of estrus and live in herds containing 10 to 15 individuals. This combination of spatial and temporal clumping of females should allow certain, dominant, males to directly monopolize access to mates by forcibly excluding other males from the herd. We would speak of a high EPP, shown by point A on the figure.

Suppose that, rather than living in small herds, females were solitary and widely dispersed. The system would shift along the X-axis to point B and the expected degree of polygamy would be much lower.

Alternatively, if females remained in herds, but showed no seasonality in times of estrus, the cost to the male of prolonged defense of the herd could become excessive. Tendencies to defend herds might decrease, or turnover rates of defending males might increase. In either case, the result is a lower EPP as shown by point C.

oversimplified. But they should serve to illustrate the approaches being used by ecological sociobiologists to understand and predict different details of social organization.

Relevance to Human Sociobiology

Homo sapiens exhibits the greatest amount of behavioral plasticity and potential for cultural change of any species. Consequently, many critics of sociobiology prefer to exclude humans from considerations such as those described above. But it is my belief that the resulting form of a social organization will converge upon that which is most energetically efficient and predation-secure (adaptive) to its individual members, regardless of the degree of genetic determinism or cultural plasticity of the behaviors.

Different species are expected to be differentially flexible with respect to the need and the ability of making rapid changes in social organization to meet environmental changes. The more stable and predictable the long-term environment for a species, the more we may expect genetic determinism of behavior. Wilson (1975) describes this in terms of the "phylogenetic inertia" that an animal carries with it. In species whose environments are highly variable or unpredictable, and in species that show tremendous cultural plasticity (including, but not exclusive to, humans), we expect this phylogenetic inertia to be less pronounced and the potential for rapid behavioral change to be greater. But this does not mean that human societies are fundamentally different from all other species and are free from ecological constraints. Most human societies that retain a close connection to their environment are still faced with ecological "problems," and we still should expect a limited range of resulting "solutions." Knowing whether the social organization is arrived at through long-term genetic change by natural selection, through individual trial-and-error learning, or through the cultural transmission of optimal strategies of resource utilization is not the crux to understanding the potential importance of ecological sociobiology. An organism that has the cultural flexibility to adapt its social organization to changing ecological pressures merely has the capability of arriving at a more optimal social organization more rapidly than one that is locked into the slower process of evolutionary change in gene frequencies dictating changes in its behavior.

As anthropologists and sociobiologists are converging in their use of these ecological approaches, parallels between animal and human social organizations are becoming

TRIBE	ECOLOGICAL ASPECTS OF RESOURCE BASE	ENERGETIC CONSIDERATIONS OF RESOURCE BASE	SOCIAL STRUCTURE
WESTERN SHOSHONE (SUMMER)	GRASS SEEDS: SPARSE / PATCHY / UNPREDICTABLE / EPHEMERAL / HENCE UNRELIABLE	NEITHER WORTH DEFENDING NOR ENERGETICALLY DEFENDABLE	NOMADIC INDIVIDUAL FAMILY UNITS NONTERRITORIAL
PAIUTE (SUMMER)	GRASS SEEDS: ABUNDANT / PREDICTABLE / LONG-LASTING / RELIABILITY INCREASED VIA IRRIGATION	BOTH WORTH DEFENDING AND ENERGETICALLY DEFENDABLE	SEDENTARY SMALL VILLAGES TERRITORIAL

Figure 8. An example of an ecological analysis of simple social organization in two human societies. Data from Steward, 1938, and Dyson-Hudson and Smith, 1978.

apparent. To cite one example, R. Dyson-Hudson and E. Smith recently reanalyzed the information available on the social structure and ecology of several groups of Basin-Plateau Indians (Dyson-Hudson and Smith 1978).

The Western Shoshone inhabited the short-grass prairies of the Central Great Basin. They subsisted primarily on plant foods, principally grass seeds in the summer and piñon nuts in the winter. The short-grass prairies are well known for their low productivity, and their patchy and unpredictable rains. Steward (1938), in his early analyses of the Western Shoshone, noted that most plant foods and all game were extremely scarce. He further commented that the locations of patches of seed plants were unpredictable and unreliable (as a direct result of the unequal and unpredictable distribution of rainfall), and that grass seeds were only available for harvesting for a short period of days or weeks after ripening since they fell from the plant and became unavailable thereafter. Sparce, ephemeral and unreliable resources are neither worth defending nor energetically defendable. The social organization of the Western Shoshone during the summer months consisted of small, nomadic, family groups that moved from location to location following the rains. No areas were defended as stable territories. Rather, the individual family units remained in any given area for only a short period, moving on as the food was depleted (Fig. 8).

The Paiute Indians lived on the eastern foothills of the Sierra Nevada Mountains, on the edge of the Great Basin. Their summer staple also was grass seeds, but the more abundant and predictable rainfall in this region gave it a high productivity. The Paiute settled primarily along the rivers, where a permanent supply of water made systematic irrigation of wild seed patches possible. Not only was the abundance of the resource increased, but it became reliable in time and space. The Paiute lived in permanent villages along the rivers and defended linear stretches of land along the river banks as territories (Fig. 8).

During the winter, new supplies of grass seeds became unavailable and both tribes shifted to a staple of piñon nuts that grew in the nearby mountains. For the Western Shoshone, this entailed additional traveling, to the Piñon-Juniper belt at an elevation of 1700 to 2400 meters. For the Paiute, piñon-pine was available within a 15 kilometer radius of most settlements.

Piñon-pine have an interesting biology of their own, with each individual tree producing mast (nuts) only every third to fifth year, but with stands of pine in any given area producing nuts synchronously. Thus the location of a good piñon nut crop is unpredictable from year to year, but the supply is often super-abundant once discovered.

The social structure of the Western Shoshone shifted greatly between summer and winter months. Family groups would converge and form temporary "villages" at the sites of productive piñon groves. The erratic nature of both the abundance and the location of the piñon crop brought different families together at different places each fall. Lack of territorial defense, and cooperation via information-sharing are predicted under these circumstances, and both were characteristic of the Western Shoshone.

The unpredictable but super-abundant nature of the piñon crop also applied in the lands of the Paiute. The piñon-pine areas were located at higher elevations in the mountain valleys, but close to the permanent villages along the rivers. Maintenance of territoriality in the piñon areas was greatly reduced, and other persons were often invited to share the harvest.

A large number of other anthropological studies of human societies that are still closely linked with their environment have reached conclusions similar to those predicted from ecological sociobiology. It appears that understanding human resource bases in ecological terms can increase our understanding of such features of human social organization as foraging strategies, group size, interactions between groups (territoriality), and possibly even mating systems (Blurton-Jones 1976; Damas 1969a, 1969b; Durham 1976a, 1976b; Harris 1968, 1975; Lee 1969, 1972; Vayda 1969; Wilmsen 1973; Winterhalder 1977).

Cultural, as well as genetic, changes can lead to adaptive forms of social organization. In a society that is closely linked with its environment, alterations in group size, foraging patterns, territorial defense, etc., that are maladaptive (in terms of efficient resource use and predator defense) initiate negative feedback in the form of decreased energetic intake, deterioration of physiological condition and, ultimately, reduced fecundity and survival. Such ecological feedback is a stabilizing influence, shaping certain features of the society to cope most efficiently with the constraints imposed by the abundance and dispersion pattern of critical resources.

The problems and challenges of ecological sociobiology come in attempting to apply it to modern, industrialized societies. Here man no longer lives in harmony with his environment. Western man is buffered from the ecological consequences of his actions. Technology and industrialization, exploitation and colonization, and mobile transportation of resources, all complicate the picture to the point where feedback mechanisms (whether genetic or cultural) no longer operate efficiently, and stabilizing and adaptive responses of society are obscured. In the absence of such feedback, we construct our own artificial environments. The process of shaping a social organization in an "environment" devoid of its real ecological base is a totally new experience --- one that, to my knowledge, has never occurred before in the evolutionary history of any species. It is as though western society is floating on a sea of endless possibilities, but without a rational, biologically-based, means of charting its course. The greatest danger of sociobiology might lie not so much with the possible misapplications of the doctrine of genetic determinism to human behavior, but with our frequent inability to apply the principles of ecological sociobiology in attempting to understand the complexities of modern society.

What is the future value of sociobiology in terms of modern western society? One possibility is that the principles of behavioral ecology could be "applied in reverse." Suppose that the advances of the next decade allow us to become increasingly precise in predicting the fine structure of certain aspects of the social organizations of animals on the basis of ecological variables. Might we then be in a position to alter or manipulate resource bases or distributions in such a way as to favor or shape a particular "desired" form of social organization? Such an idea might sound like science fiction. But, at a simplistic level, tendencies towards gregariousness versus nongregariousness, territoriality versus nonterritoriality, and changes in group size have all been artificially "produced" in avian species as a result of field manipulations of resources.

Even the possibility of such manipulations among human societies raises fundamental ethical questions. Should conscious manipulation of resources to promote particular social structures be permitted? What makes one form of social organization more "desirable" than another, and who should make such decisions?

These are not hollow questions. On a small scale, we are performing such manipulations currently, whenever we export technology to countries whose people are still living in close harmony with their environment. As these nations attempt to rapidly enter the world of 20th century technology, many industrial and agricultural reforms are initiated. These frequently result in the introduction of new resource bases, or changes in the distribution of existing resource bases for the country and lead to significant changes in the potential for monopolization of these resources by certain individuals or groups. This, in turn, frequently causes disruptive changes in the cultures of the recipient nations and often leads to increasingly stratified and nonegalitarian societies. Such changes are occurring constantly, in all corners of the world.

As our knowledge of ecological sociobiology and anthropology increases, we should become able to predict more of these changes in advance and, if necessary or desirable, to minimize their disruptive nature. In my classes at Cornell, I frequently discuss the notion of "sociobiological impact statements." Their function would be to evaluate the probable shifts in social structure of the recipient group that would result from the implementation of a particular program of agricultural or technological development. As with ecological impact statements, the predictions would be devoid of value judgments. But they could provide a beginning basis for predicting the types and magnitudes of social changes to be expected, as well as evaluating different options for achieving the developmental goal while minimizing changes in social organization (if that is a desired goal).

To many, these ideas may smack of scientific conceit. I am the first to admit that the predictive powers of ecological sociobiology are still in an embryonic state. But we are currently exporting technology and altering the cultures of recipient nations without giving sufficient consideration to the sociobiological implications of our actions.

Many will say that these ideas are not new; that political scientists and international economists do consider such implications and make such value judgments regularly. But it was only three years ago that AID began requiring a social assessment as well as an economic statement of the impact of its projects. And it was only last year that the first conference was held on "The Role of Anthropology in AID." The proceedings from this conference (AID Workshop 1977) represent a commendable start toward the realization of the importance of anthropological and sociobiological input in such social assessment.

If biology is now converging on problems normally asked by social scientists, it is doing so from a different starting point and building upon a different set of underlying theories. Hopefully, these different disciplines will complement one another and lead to a better understanding of human social organizations.

In closing, let me return to the question of the possible misuses of sociobiology, a topic of current debate. Neither the potential benefits nor the political dangers of sociobiology rest solely with the issue of genetic determinism of behavior. If human social behavior is tremendously plastic, we must ask, what are the goals that one should strive for if it does become possible to manipulate resource bases in such a way as to cause predictable changes in certain aspects of the social organizations of peoples relying on those resources? These are questions that start to shift from the scientific arena into the political arena. And to the degree that such manipulation becomes possible, the potential for political misuse becomes great.

But so, too, does the potential for constructive good. The best formula for increasing our understanding of sociobiology, while at the same time safeguarding against political misuse of information, lies in promoting basic research in this new field, and in disseminating the findings to as broad an audience as possible. In this way, when important decisions must be made, they can be made by an informed and educated public.

Summary

The ecological frontier of sociobiology is concerned with understanding and predicting the forms of social organization that are found in nature. Its principles are based on behavioral and ecological models of predator-prey interaction, optimal foraging strategy, and resource defendability and accumulation. Its basic premise is that given certain ecological constraints ("problems"), there exist a limited subset of adaptive social organizations ("solutions"). This is because alterations in group size, foraging patterns, territorial defense, etc. that are maladaptive (e.g., in terms of effective predator defense or efficient resource use) initiate negative feedback in the form of decreased energetic intake, deterioration of physiological condition, and, ultimately, reduced fecundity and survival. Such ecological feedback is a stabilizing influence, shaping certain features of society structure to maximize the ability of the participants to cope efficiently with the constraints imposed by the environment.

When applied to human societies, anthropologists are

finding the ecological approach valuable provided the society in question is closely linked with its environment. Predictions become more difficult in discussing modern, industrialized societies since technology provides man with a temporary buffer from the ecological consequences of his actions. Feedback mechanisms no longer operate efficiently, and stabilizing and adaptive responses of society are obscured.

What are the practical applications of ecological sociobiology? Recently biologists have been able to alter several major features of animal social organizations (tendencies toward gregariousness, territoriality, and monogamous versus polygamous mating) by experimentally manipulating the abundance and distribution patterns of critical resources. The principles emerging from such studies should prove invaluable in programs of wildlife management and land use modification. And we must ask whether analogous "manipulations" might be feasible (or justifiable) in human societies. When we export technology to a people who live in close harmony with their environment, we often are introducing new resource bases or altering the distribution of existing ones. Frequently, a side result of such "manipulations" is a major disruption in the social structure of the recipient group. In the future, ecological sociobiologists and anthropologists should become increasingly able to predict many of these changes in advance, and to suggest means of keeping their disruptive nature to a minimum.

Acknowledgements

The author's work on sociobiology has been supported by the John Simon Guggenheim Foundation, the Chapman Fund of the American Museum of Natural History, the National Geographic Society, and the National Science Foundation (through grant BMS-76-81921).

Literature Cited

AID Workshop. 1977. The role of anthropology in AID. Agency for International Development, Washington, D.C.

Alexander, R.D. 1974. The evolution of social behavior. Annual Review of Ecology and Systematics. 5:325-383.

Allen, E., et al. 1975. Against "sociobiology". New York Review of Books 22:43-44.

Allen, L., et al. 1976. Sociobiology --- Another biological determinism. BioScience 26:182, 184-186.

Barash, D.P. 1977. Sociobiology and behavior. Elsevier Press, New York.

Barlow, G.W. 1974. Contrasts in social behavior between Central American cichlid fishes and coral-reef surgeon fishes. American Zoologist 14:9-34.

Blurton-Jones, N.G. 1976. Growing points in human ethology: Another link between ethology and the social sciences? In P.P.G. Bateson and R.A. Hinde (eds.), Growing points in ethology. Cambridge University Press, England, pp. 427-450.

Bradbury, J. 1977. Social organization and communication. In W. Wimsatt (ed.), Biology of bats. Academic Press, New York, Vol. 3, pp. 1-73.

Bradbury, J. and S. Vehrencamp. 1976. Social organization and foraging in emballonurid bats II: A model for the determination of group size. Behavioral Ecology and Sociobiology 1:383-404.

_______. 1977a. Social organization and foraging in emballonurid bats III: Mating systems. Behavioral Ecology and Sociobiology 2:1-17.

_______. 1977b. Social organization and foraging in emballonurid bats IV: Parental investment patterns. Behavioral Ecology and Sociobiology 2:19-29.

Brown, J.L. 1964. The evolution of diversity in avian territorial systems. Wilson Bulletin 76:160-169.

Campanella, P.J. and L.L. Wolf. 1974. Temporal leks as a mating system in a temperate zone dragonfly I: Plathemis lydia. Behaviour 51:49-87.

Carpenter, F.L. and R.E. MacMillan. 1976. Threshold model of feeding territoriality and test with a Hawaiian Honeycreeper. Science 194:639-642.

Clutton-Brock, T.H. 1974. Primate social organization and ecology. Nature (London) 250:539-542.

Crook, J.H. 1964. The evolution of social organization and visual communication in the weaver birds (Ploceinae). Behavior Supplement 10:1-178.

_______. 1970. The socio-ecology of primates. In J.H. Crook (ed.), Social behavior in birds and mammals:

Essays on the social ethology of animals and man. Academic Press, New York, pp. 103-166.

_______. 1972. Sexual selection, dimorphism, and social organization in the primates. *In* B. Campbell (ed.), *Sexual selection and the descent of man, 1871-1971.* Aldine Publishing Company, Chicago, pp. 231-281.

Crook, J.H. and J.S. Gartlan. 1966. Evolution of primate societies. *Nature* (London) 210:1200-1203.

Damas, D. (ed.). 1969a. *Contributions to anthropology: Ecological essays.* National Museum of Canada, Bulletin No. 230.

_______. 1969b. Environment, history, and Central Eskimo society. *In* D. Damas (ed.), *Contributions to anthropology: Ecological Essays.* National Museum of Canada, Bulletin No. 230, pp. 40-64.

Denham, W.W. 1971. Energy relations and some basic properties of primate social organization. *American Anthropologist* 73:77-95.

Durham, W.H. 1976a. The adaptive significance of cultural behavior. *Human Ecology* 4:89-121.

_______. 1976b. Resource competition and human aggression Part I: A review of primate war. *Quarterly Review of Biology* 51:383-415.

Dyson-Hudson, R. and E.A. Smith. 1978. Human territoriality: An ecological reassessment. *American Anthropologist* 80:21-41.

Eisenberg, J.F., N.A. Muchenhirn and R. Rudran: 1972. The relation between ecology and social structure in primates. *Science* 176:863-874.

Emlen, S.T. 1976a. Lek organization and mating strategies in the bullfrog. *Behavioral Ecology and Sociobiology* 1:283-313.

_______. 1976b. An alternative case for sociobiology. *Science* 192:736-738.

Emlen, S.T. and N.J. Demong. 1975. Adaptive significance of synchronized breeding in a colonial bird: A new hypothesis. *Science* 188:1029-1031.

Emlen, S.T. and L.W. Oring. 1977. Ecology, sexual selection, and the evolution of mating systems. Science 197:215-223.

Estes, R.D. 1974. Social organization of the African Bovidae. In V. Geist and F. Walther (eds.), The behavior of ungulates and its relation to management. International Union for the Conservation of Nature Publication (New Series) 1:166-205.

Feare, C.J. 1976. The breeding of the Sooty Tern Sterna fuscata in the Seychelles and the effects of experimental removal of its eggs. Journal of Zoology (London) 179: 317-360.

Gill, F.B. and L.L. Wolf. 1975. Economics of feeding territoriality in the Golden-winged Sunbird. Ecology 56:333-345.

Hamilton, W.D. 1964a. The genetical theory of social behaviour I. Journal of Theoretical Biology 7:1-16.

_______. 1964b. The genetical theory of social behaviour II. Journal of Theoretical Biology 7:17-52.

_______. 1971. Geometry for the selfish herd. Journal of Theoretical Biology 31:295-311.

Harris, M. 1968. The rise of anthropological theory. A history of theories of culture. Crowell Press, New York.

_______. 1975. Cows, pigs, wars and witches. The riddles of culture. Random House (Vintage Books), New York.

Horn, H.S. 1968. The adaptive significance of colonial nesting in the Brewer's Blackbird (Euphagus cyanocephalus). Ecology 49:682-694.

Jacobs, M.E. 1955. Studies on territorialism and sexual selection in dragonflies. Ecology 36:566-586.

Jarman, P.J. 1974. The social organization of antelope in relation to their ecology. Behaviour 58:215-267.

Jolly, A. 1970. The evolution of primate behavior. MacMillan Publishers, New York.

Kawai, M. 1965. Newly acquired precultural behavior of the natural troop of Japanese monkeys on Koshimi Isled. Primates 6:1-30.

Krebs, J.R. 1974. Colonial nesting and social feeding as strategies for exploiting food resources in the Great Blue Heron (*Ardea herodias*). *Behaviour* 51:99-131.

Lack, D. 1967. Inter-relationships in breeding adaptations as shown by marine birds. *In* D.W. Snow (ed.), *Proceedings of the XIV International Ornithological Congress (Oxford).* Blackwell Scientific Publications, Oxford, pp. 3-42.

_______. 1968. *Ecological adaptations for breeding in birds.* Methuen and Company, London.

Lee, R.B. 1969. !Kung Bushman subsistence: An input-output analysis. *In* A.P. Vayda (ed.), *Environment and cultural behavior: Ecological studies in cultural anthropology.* Natural History Press, New York, pp. 47-79.

_______. 1972. !Kung spatial organization: An ecological and historical perspective. *Human Ecology* 1:125-147.

Magnuson, J.J. 1962. An analysis of aggressive behavior, growth, and competition for food and space in Medaka. *Canadian Journal of Zoology* 40:313-363.

Nelson, J.B. 1970. The relationship between behaviour and ecology in the Sulidae with reference to other seabirds. *Oceanography and Marine Biology; an Annual Review* 8:501-574.

Pajunen, V.I. 1966. The influence of population density on the territorial behaviour of *Leucorrhinia rubicunda*. *Annales Zoologici Fennici* 3:40-52.

Patterson, I.J. 1965. Timing and spacing of broods in the Black-headed Gull, *Larus ridibundus.* *Ibis* 107:433-459.

Reese, E.S. 1975. A comparative field study of the social behavior and related ecology of reef fishes of the family *Chaetodontidae.* *Zeitschrift Tierpsychologie* 37:37-61.

Robertson, D.R. and R.R. Warner. 1978. Sexual patterns in the Labroid fishes of the Western Caribbean, II: The parrotfishes (Scaridae). *Smithsonian Contributions to Zoology* 255:1-26.

Steward, J.H. 1938. Basin-plateau aboriginal socio-political groups. U.S. Bureau of American Ethnology. Bulletin 120.

Trivers, R.L. 1974. Parent-offspring conflict. American Zoologist 14:249-264.

Vayda, A.P. (ed.). 1969. Environment and cultural behavior: Ecological studies in cultural anthropology. Natural History Press, New York.

Waage, J.K. 1973. Reproductive behavior and its relation to territoriality in Calopteryx maculata. Behaviour 47:240-256.

Wade, N. 1976. Sociobiology: Troubled birth for new discipline. Science 191:1151-1155.

Ward, P. 1965. Feeding ecology of the Black-faced Dioch, Quelea quelea, in Nigeria. Ibis 107:173-214.

Ward, P. and A. Zahavi. 1973. The importance of certain assemblages of birds as "information-centres" for food-finding. Ibis 115:517-534.

Warner, R.R. and D.R. Robertson. 1978. Sexual patterns in the Labroid fishes of the Western Caribbean, I: The wrasses (Labridae). Smithsonian Contributions to Zoology 254:1-27.

Wells, K.D. 1977a. Territoriality and male mating success in the Green Frog (Rana clamitans). Ecology 58:750-762.

_______. 1977b. The social behaviour of anuran amphibians. Animal Behavior 25:666-693.

West-Eberhard, M.J. 1975. The evolution of social behavior by kin selection. Quarterly Review of Biology 50:1-33.

Williams, A.J. 1975. Guillemot fledging and predation on Bear Island. Ornis Scandinavia 6:117-124.

Wilmsen, E.N. 1973. Interaction, spacing behavior, and organization of hunting bands. Journal of Anthropological Research 29:1-31.

Wilson, E.O. 1975. Sociobiology: The new synthesis. Harvard University Press, Cambridge, Massachusetts.

______. 1976. Academic vigilantism and the political significance of sociobiology. BioScience 26:183, 187-190.

Winterhalder, B.P. 1977. Foraging strategy adaptations of the Boreal Forest Cree: An evaluation of theory and models from evolutionary ecology. Unpublished Ph.D. thesis, Cornell University.

Yom-Tov, Y. 1975. Synchronization of breeding and intra-specific interference in the Carrion crow. Auk 92: 778-785.

Zahavi, A. 1971. The social behaviour of the White Wagtail, *Motacilla alba alba* wintering in Israel. Ibis 113: 203-211.

Robert R. Warner

6. The Coevolution of Behavioral and Life-History Characteristics

Two rather independent schools of thought have developed over the past forty years, both of which deal with the evolution of nonmorphological traits. One deals in part with the adaptiveness of the demographic variables that biologists call "life histories"; it seeks an evolutionary explanation of the variability seen among organisms in longevity, fecundity, sex ratio, and sexual expression (unisexuality, dioecism, or some form of hermaphroditism). Sociobiology, on the other hand, deals with the evolution of behavior, particularly mating and other social systems.

These two approaches have been relatively isolated from one another. Often, sociobiologists treat life-history traits as a set of conservative genetic characteristics which act as constraints upon, or causes for, the evolution of the supposedly more flexible and responsive behavioral traits (e.g., Crook et al. 1976; Wilson 1975). On the other hand, other authors have discussed how life history patterns might evolve given a particular social/mating system (e.g., Selander 1972; Trivers 1972; Warner 1975). If evolutionary biology in general hopes to be a predictive science, there is clearly a need to determine which traits are direct adaptations to the environment (here called primary adaptations) and which are accommodations to other less flexible traits (secondary adaptations).

Traits which are secondary adaptations are truly coevolved characteristics, where the expression of one evolved trait is due, wholly or in part, to a particular expression of another. For example, the life-history trait of changing sex from female to male, which occurs commonly in many species of fishes, appears to be a secondary adaptation to a mating system in which a few males mate with most of the available females (Warner 1975; Warner et al. 1975). That mating system, in contrast, appears to be a primary adaptation to certain resource distributions in time and space (Emlen & Oring 1977). As a step toward making other such distinctions, this paper explores some of the interrelationships between adaptations in social systems and life-history traits.

To do this, I first identify those environmental parameters which have been suggested to be important selective forces. Second, I describe the life-history traits and social/mating systems of an animal in terms of a series of variables, relatively independent of each other. Most of these variables have a large range of possible values, ensuring a wide applicability to many species. The primary adaptations are then identified, detailing how each environmental parameter might (or might not) select for a particular expression of each adaptation. I then indicate what have been suggested as likely secondary adaptations to pre-existent life-history traits or social/mating systems. Deductions based on the selective forces produced by the environmental parameters lead to a more objective set of hypotheses about nonmorphological adaptation.

In the discussion, I point out which characteristics appear to lead to secondary adaptations in other traits, and consider why this is so in terms of fitness. I then discuss some other factors that can have a profound effect on selection for nonmorphological traits, namely sex, body size, the site of fertilization, and aquatic versus terrestrial life. Finally, the different schemes for testing hypotheses about adaptation are reviewed, with particular attention paid to the considerable problems they all share.

Throughout this paper I avoid distinguishing any syndromes of traits when the employment of such a syndrome implies that certain environmental parameters necessarily co-occur. Because there are often so many exceptions to these syndromes, I have treated environmental parameters for each trait independently. Often, of course, a particular environmental condition (e.g., low resource density) may lead to simultaneous selection for several nonmorphological traits (e.g., small group size and parental care).

I have also avoided terms like polybrachygamy (Selander 1972) or male dominance polygyny (Emlen & Oring 1977) which imply a set of associated behavioral and/or life-historical traits. These associations may be due to separate primary adaptations to the same environmental parameter, primary adaptations to different parameters, or a set of primary and secondary adaptations. By initially considering each behavioral and life-history trait in turn, we can avoid some of the pitfalls of overgeneralization.

Other pitfalls are not so easily avoided. I have had to ride roughshod over finer distinctions, and predictive power has certainly been lost in the process. Also, almost all of my sources of empirical information deal strictly with vertebrates.

Any attempt at a synthesis inevitably commits sins of omission. I do not intend this paper to be a comprehensive review of either life-history traits or sociobiology. Readers are referred to Stearns (1976, 1977) and Ricklefs (1977) for the former and to Wilson (1975) for the latter. I also do not claim to have uncovered all examples of secondary adaptations. Due to space limitations, many of the interrelationships among the characteristics can only be outlined, with no discussion of the quantity and quality of the supporting evidence. I hope this paper will serve to point out the responsive nature of nonmorphological adaptation in general, and so to alert evolutionary ecologists to the danger of assuming any such characteristic to be an inflexible constraint.

The Nature of Adaptations

One of the goals of evolutionary biology is to explain various characteristics shown by organisms as adaptations to the environment. Adaptations are those traits that convey the highest fitness (measured in terms of numbers of descendants or numbers of copies of a gene passed on) out of an array of possible alternative traits. "Environment", for the purpose of this paper, is characterized by the distribution of resources in space and time, and by the sources of mortality acting on adults and juveniles. Ideally, we would like to predict the attributes of an organism on the basis of the environment.

The problems of this approach are immediate and numerous. Aside from the difficulty of measuring fitness and of accurately describing the array of possible trait expressions (for a discussion, see Lewontin 1978; Maynard Smith 1978; Stearns 1977), it is often impossible to specify where the environment ends and adaptations begin. It is important to keep in mind that although resource distribution and sources of mortality will be treated as part of the environment, they, too, are ultimately under the control of natural selection. For example, the perceived distribution of food resources for any species is affected strongly by the feeding adaptations it possesses, which, of course, are modifiable over time.

As Emlen (1973:157) and Wilson (1975:143) suggest, it is usually assumed that adaptations for food intake and avoidance of mortality are critical in terms of fitness. These adaptations, which involve anatomy and physiology as well as behavior, can form a class of characteristics that are often termed "conservative." They tend to be inherited and relatively invariant; deviations from the norm in these traits often result in extreme losses of fitness. Therefore "environment," in the sense of this paper, is a combination of the external environment and conservative traits in the organism for feeding and avoidance of mortality. Together these create the selective pressures for other adaptations and set the limits on the array of possibilities. For example, there may be physical limitations on age at first maturity (Emlen 1970), sexual expression (Warner 1978), or minimum energy investment per young (Smith & Fretwell 1974).

Note that I am assuming that adaptations for feeding and avoidance of mortality tend to take precedence over other adaptations, not that they are any less flexible or responsive to selection than traits in life history or social behavior. Once they are determined, we may then specify the resource distributions and age-specific mortality risks that a particular organism faces. The question that this paper addresses is the interaction of traits in life history and social behavior: whether a particular trait is an independent adaptation to the environment as defined (and therefore a primary adaptation), or whether its expression depends strongly on the expression of other life-history or social traits (and therefore a secondary adaptation).

The expression of a particular nonmorphological trait may be relatively constant between individuals, or show some degree of variability. This variation can be the result of a number of different processes. Individuals may display one of a fixed set of alternative adaptations (short-term adaptive responses) depending upon the environment in which they find themselves. At the extreme, organisms may have only general tendencies provided by their genes, the actual expression being determined by previous experiences with the environment. Extremely variable or unpredictable environments should place a selective premium on flexible adaptive responses (Emlen 1976).

Variability in a specific trait can also arise in other ways. Spatial or temporal heterogeneity may lead to the evolution of different types suited to different environments (Giesel 1976). Some forms of frequency-dependent selection can result in a stable mixture of types within a population (for examples see Gadgil 1972; Maynard Smith 1974).

In general, evolutionary hypotheses about both life-history traits and sociobiology predict invariant adaptations given the environmental parameters. Invariant organisms can be used in tests of these hypotheses through interspecies comparisons, and those showing alternative short-term responses can be used in tests by analogy (see below). When the adaptation rests primarily on directed or generalized learning (Wilson 1975), however, testing evolutionary hypotheses becomes less feasible.

Environmental Parameters

To clarify the predictions arising from hypotheses about the evolution of life-history traits and social behavior, it is first necessary to specify the environmental parameters which one or both approaches cosider to have important selective effects. I have simplified the parameters to an extreme degree, and therefore stand in danger of ignoring significant interactions. Drawing the parameters as distinctly as possible may, however, facilitate independent tests for their effects.

The list of environmental parameters below was taken mainly from the sociobiological literature, because sociobiologists tend to be more concerned with the direct effects of the environment. A resource refers to food, breeding or shelter sites, or other requisites.

Under each parameter I have included a suggestion of how it might be measured. Making such measurements objectively presents a major problem. As mentioned above, an animal's own adaptations affect what can be identified as resources or sources of mortality. In addition, organisms differ in such things as size, nutritional needs, and generation time. Although the ideal situation would be to predict an organism's adaptations in life history and social behavior based on an a priori measurement of the environment, at this point the predictions must depend on prior knowledge of the organism and properly scaled measurements of the environmental parameters. For these same reasons, predictions should be limited to comparisons between closely related species or different populations of the same species in different environments.

A. Resource density in space. This is the mean amount of resource per unit area. This is what most researchers refer to when they describe resources as "sparse" or "abundant."

B. Resource variability in space. This can be measured as the variance in resource density per unit area. When compared with the mean, this describes the amount of patchiness or degree of aggregation of the resource, ranging from evenly distributed to highly aggregated. In the terminology of Colwell (1974), this would measure the constancy of resource distribution in space.

C. Resource predictability in space. This describes the degree to which there are dependable concentrations of resource abundance in certain areas. One way of estimating this parameter is to rank different areas in terms of relative resource density, and measure the correlation between this ranking and those in successive time units. A high degree of correlation indicates that some areas have dependably higher resource densities than others. In the terminology of Colwell (1974), this would estimate the contingency of relative resource distribution in space.

The following three parameters reflect the opinion of the many authors who suggest that the length, variability, and predictability of periods of relative resource abundance have a strong effect on the evolution of social systems and life-history traits (see below). This is particularly true if periods of resource abundance also designate breeding periods. Unfortunately, "resource abundance" is a subjective term, and must be set at some arbitrary density value or denoted by the level which is associated with the onset of breeding activity.

D. Resource density in time. This parameter would be estimated by the mean length of time that resource density remains at a high level. If the breeding season parallels the period of high resource density, this measure is related to the length of the breeding season.

E. Resource variability in time. This could be measured by the variance in the length of time that resources are at high density. Again, if the resources are used for breeding, this could estimate the variability of the length of the breeding season.

F. Resource predictability in time. This describes whether there are dependable times of higher resource density. One way of measuring it is to determine to what degree the periods of higher resource density occur cyclically. Alternatively, one could rank different months in terms of relative resource density, and measure the correlation between this ranking and those in successive years. A high degree of correlation indicates predictable seasonality. In Colwell's (1974) terminology, this would estimate the contingency of relative resource distribution in time.

The following parameters tend to decrease fitness by increasing the probability of death. As mentioned above, the avoidance of predators, parasites, or harsh weather is not beyond the bounds of natural selection. However, I assume here that the mortality or loss of fitness due to these factors is unavoidable in the sense that further reductions in mortality would result only at a relatively greater cost in loss of present or future reproduction.

G. Adult mortality rate. Many hypotheses (especially those in sociobiology) refer directly to predation rates, but in general this refers to the mean adult mortality per unit time due to factors not associated with reproduction. When one of the following predictions strictly involves predation, it will be stated as such. Determining the proportion of mortality due to reproduction can be a nearly insurmountable task (Hirschfield & Tinkle 1975; Pianka & Parker 1975), but it may be possible to estimate it by comparing mortality rates inside and outside of the breeding season (Ricklefs 1977).

H. Variability in adult mortality rate. This is estimated by the variance in adult mortality rates over time, on a year-to-year or breeding period-to-breeding period basis.

I. Juvenile mortality rate. This is estimated by the mean juvenile mortality per unit time.

J. Variability in juvenile mortality rate. Similar to the measure for adults, this is estimated by the

Table 1. Suggested primary adaptations in life history characteristics. +, level of characteristic increases with increasing level of environmental parameter; –, level of characteristic decreases with increasing level of environmental parameter; a, short-term adaptive response. References in text.

Environmental Parameters	Life History Characteristics			
	Reproductive Effort (Female)	Investment/Young	Sex Allocation: Simultaneous Hermaphroditism	Sex Allocation: Parthenogenesis
Resource density in space	–(+[a])		–	+
Resource variability in space		–	–	
Resource predictability in space	–	+		–
Resource density in time				–
Resource variability in time				+
Resource predictability in time	–			–
Adult mortality	+			
Variability in adult mortality	+			
Juvenile mortality	–			
Variability in juvenile mortality	–			

variance in juvenile mortality rates over time, on a year-to-year or breeding season-to-breeding season basis.

Primary Adaptations

Primary Adaptations in Life History

Most of the hypotheses dealing with life-history traits have sprung from analyses of Lotka's (1907) equation, which relates the intrinsic rate of increase of a genotype to its schedule of births and expected mortality. The pitfalls involved in such a procedure have been discussed in detail by Stearns (1977). Of primary interest here is that this approach stresses the importance of mortality factors in selection for life-history traits.

There has been little discussion on how the distribution of resources in time and space might affect life-history traits, except in the context of r- and K-selection (e.g., MacArthur & Wilson 1967; Pianka 1970) and clutch size (e.g., Cody 1966; Lack 1968). However, r- and K-selection equate selection for low reproductive effort with selection for high energy investment per young. The environmental parameters affecting these traits do not necessarily covary, and this has led to many "contradictions" to the proposed scheme (e.g., Menge 1975; Wilbur et al. 1974). Stearns (1977) mentioned other objections to the r- and K-selection concept.

By the same token, clutch size is the result of a combination of life-history and behavioral characteristics (see below). As I explained earlier, I shall keep the various life-history traits separate, reserving for later discussion how certain combinations of life-history traits might result from the co-occurrence of some environmental parameters.

For each of the following life-history characteristics I discuss problems of measurement and their interpretation as primary adaptations to various environmental parameters (summarized in Table 1).

1. Pattern of reproductive effort. Reproductive effort (RE) is defined here as the proportion of available energy that is devoted to reproduction (Williams 1966). The concept is intuitively appealing, in that an organism with no RE suffers only from the unavoidable mortality factors, while an organism with an RE of one dies; animals with such a single "suicidal" burst of reproductive effort are called semelparous. Age of first reproduction is the

first age at which RE is not zero. Reproductive efforts of less than one imply iteroparity (repetitive reproduction), perhaps surviving to reproduce again.

The measurement of RE is difficult because it is often impossible to know how much energy is available to an organism in any particular year. Additionally, RE may include an element of risk-taking that cannot be measured energetically. Hirschfield and Tinkle (1975) discussed these and other problems.

Reproductive effort should be considered separately for the sexes, because the predicted adaptations and associated variables are often different for males and females. For example, in females low RE and iteroparity are usually associated with a late age of first reproduction, both theoretically (Cole 1954; Schaffer 1974a), and in nature (e.g., Amadon 1964). There is virtually no information on RE in males, mainly because RE in males often involves more risk than in females; but it is obvious that a late age of first reproduction is often associated with high RE in males of polygynous species (e.g., Carrick et al. 1962; Selander 1972; and see below).

Hypotheses about life-history traits suggest that a low level of RE is an adaptation to high adult survival and/or low juvenile survival (Charnov & Schaffer 1973; Schaffer 1974a). Alternatively, constant adult survival and/or variable juvenile survival have also been suggested as causes for low RE (Murphy 1968; Schaffer 1974b).

The reasoning behind these hypotheses is that if mortality factors make it likely that an adult will survive from one year to the next, but juvenile survival is low and variable, it should be best to hedge one's bet and spread reproduction over several seasons (low RE). On the other hand, if adult survival is unlikely and variable, and/or the young have a good chance of survival in any year, it would be maladaptive to hold back any energy from current reproduction (high RE).

We can relate these factors to the other environmental parameters in the following manner. When resources for adults are abundant and predictable in space and time, this should result in a lower reproductive effort to the extent that it raises the mean and lowers the variance of adult survival (Brown 1974; Geist 1974; Ricklefs 1977). In situations where resource density is unpredictable in time, reproductive effort may be one of the most flexible of nonmorphological traits, with the level of RE closely tied to the level of resources as a short-term adaptive response (Hirschfield & Tinkle 1975; Nichols et al. 1976; Orians 1969; Ricklefs 1977; and others). A change in RE at any point should be reflected in changes in fecundity patterns and mortality probabilities in later portions of the life-span.

2. Energy investment per young (I_y). This is defined here as the energy invested by the female per egg or young before birth. It does not include parental care. A female with the same total energy investment can produce a few large eggs (high I_y) or many small ones (low I_y).

Although this quantity is often associated with reproductive effort, its level depends upon whether size conveys an advantage in the competition that young individuals will have to face, and upon the size-specific mortality patterns of the young (Brockelman 1975; Janzen 1969; Smith & Fretwell 1974). Where competition is exploitative, and dispersal is necessary, natural selection should favor low I_y. Under more stable conditions, where contest competition is likely and dispersal is unimportant or unproductive, there should be a large investment per young.

These relations have led to the predictions that where resource distribution is not extremely patchy, and/or where resources are predictable in space, I_y should be high. Predictable resources supposedly also select for low reproductive effort, hence the hypothesized connection in K-selection between low reproductive effort and high investment per young.

Actual clutch size, or progeny number, is the result of four factors, the first three being intrinsic and the fourth one environmental: the reproductive effort, the investment per young, the amount of parental care (to be discussed below), and the total energy available. Mortality patterns in species result from unavoidable mortality factors and mortality due to reproduction, the latter being a function of reproductive effort (Pianka & Parker 1975; Williams 1966).

3. Sex ratio of progeny. In general, sex ratio of progeny is in frequency-dependent evolutionary equilibrium (Fisher 1930; MacArthur 1965; and others), with equal energy supplied to males and females. Resource distribution and mortality appear to have little direct effect on this trait.

However, Howe (1976, 1978) has shown that females of the common grackle facultatively adjust sex ratios within a brood at conception and later through differences in I_y and parental care. Early in the season, when food is generally scarce, more females are born than males. Later in the season, the males starve first if food resources become reduced. In this case, sex ratio represents a short term response to the environment.

4. Sex allocation. This is the sexual expression of an individual over its lifetime, and involves morphological as well as nonmorphological adaptations. Individuals within a species can be (a) purely male or female (gonochorism), (b) all female (parthenogenesis), (c) both male and female at the same time (simultaneous hermaphroditism), or (d) change sex at some point in the life history (sequential hermaphroditism). Often, sexual expression is under severe constraints, especially in the terrestrial environment, and it can be both a primary and a secondary adaptation (Warner 1978; and see below).

Parthenogenesis can be adaptive in situations that place a premium on high rates of production of offspring. In contrast, genetic recombination (sexuality) may be of advantage in contest competition situations where slight differences in genotypes can lead to extreme differences in fitness (Williams 1975). So environments of high resource density, but unpredictable in time and space, should cause selection for the superior colonizing ability of unisexuals, especially when the resources are available for short and variable periods of time. Sexuality should be favored when available resources are sparce, but occur over longer periods at predictable times and places.

There have also been suggestions that when resource density is low and distributed evenly, the resulting low population density makes finding mates difficult. Thus simultaneous hermaphroditism or parthenogenesis is adaptive in that it increases the chance of encountering a suitable mate (Ghiselin 1969; Tomlinson 1966) or eliminates the necessity entirely (Williams 1975). Much of the variety in sexual expression may also be an adaptation to the mating system (see below).

Sex determination may also be a short-term adaptive response to the environment. Where fecundity of females varies directly with size, it may be of advantage to be a female in situations where resources are abundant and growth is possible, but to be a male if resources are less available. The individuals of several species of echiuroids, gastropods, and isopods will develop as females if they settle into unoccupied habitats, but as males if other individuals are already there (e.g., Reinhard 1949).

Primary Adaptations in Social/Mating Systems

The mating and other social behaviors of organisms have been characterized in numerous ways (e.g., Crook et al. 1976; Eisenberg et al. 1972; Emlen & Oring 1977; Pitelka et al. 1974; Wilson 1975). In the spirit of describing adaptations as independently as possible, I have drawn up a series of traits which together describe in general fashion the social/mating system of a particular species (Table 2).

1. Group size and composition. Do the organisms characteristically spend their time as solitary individuals, in sexually segregated groups, or in mixed groups? This is actually three measures: (i) the distribution of group size, and (ii) the distribution of sex ratio between groups, and (iii) the distribution of age classes of each sex between groups. Generally "group size" will refer to the mean of the first measure. This is perhaps the most variable of all the behavioral traits, and may defy classification for many species.

Many authors have suggested that the threat of mortality from predation is the major environmental factor affecting group size (Altmann 1974; Brown 1972; Elliot 1975; Geist 1974; Goss-Custard 1970; Hamilton 1971; Kaufman 1974; Treisman 1975a,b; Wilson 1975). In open habitats larger groups may provide a higher degree of safety from predators (Barlow 1974; Brock & Riffenburgh 1960; Cushing & Harden-Jones 1968; Hamilton 1971; Neill & Cullen 1974; Pulliam 1973; Vine 1971; Williams 1964). Increased predation may lead to a higher proportion of males in a group if these individuals provide defense capability (Eisenberg et al. 1972; Elliot 1975). However, there is often a cost for larger groups in terms of inefficient utilization of resources; low resource density in space may place a limit on group size (Altmann 1974; Crook 1972; Crook et al. 1976; Kaufman 1974; but see Cody 1971; Pulliam 1973; Thompson et al. 1974; Ward & Zahavi 1974). Finally, groups are more likely to form when resources are undefendable by individuals, that is, when they are distributed uniformly or in very dense aggregations in space (Altmann 1974; Crook 1972; Crook et al. 1976).

Table 2. Suggested primary adaptations in behavioral characteristics. +, level of characteristic increases with increasing level of environmental parameter; –, level of characteristic decreases with increasing level of environmental parameter; +–+, characteristic highest at intermediate levels of the parameter; +–+, characteristic lowest at intermediate levels of the parameter. References in text.

Environmental Parameters	Behavioral Characteristics						
	Group Size	Individual Movement	Exclusivity of Range	Polygyny	Polyandry	Total Parental Care	Male Parental Care
Resource density in space	+	–	–+–	+		–	–
Resource variability in space	+–+	–+–	–+–	–+–			
Resource predictability in space		–	+	+		+	
Resource density in time				–+–		–	–
Resource variability in time				–	+		
Resource predictability in time			+	+	–	+	
Adult mortality	+		–				
Juvenile mortality					+	+	+
Variability in juvenile mortality					+		

2. Individual movement. This describes the home range of the individual, varying from zero in strictly sedentary animals to large values in those which range widely. It should be scaled to the size of the organism, perhaps measured in body lengths. Obviously, animals should stay put when there is little reason to move, as when resource density in space is high (Altmann 1974; Geist 1974), resources are evenly dispersed or highly aggregated (Altmann 1974) or predictable in space (Brown 1972; Geist 1974).

3. Exclusivity of range. This can be measured in terms of how many other conspecific individuals are tolerated within the normal movement area of the organism, and serves as an indicator of territoriality. Environmental factors that tend to select for increased exclusivity are those that enhance the defendability of the territory (Brown 1964; Brown & Orians 1970), namely moderate resource density in space (Barash 1974; Crook 1972; Gill & Wolf 1975), resources neither completely uniform nor extremely aggregated (Barlow 1974; Crook et al. 1976; Horn 1968), resources predictable in space and in time (Brown 1974; Geist 1974; Horn 1968), and low predation pressure (Geist 1974; Heller 1971).

4. Degree of polygamy. This is the average number of mates an individual has in a breeding season. It is best considered separately for males and females.

Because of the nature of anisogamy, Trivers (1972) suggested that males are generally in competition for females, and a male's fitness often depends on the number of mates he acquires. Thus we may assume that polygyny (male polygamy) is maximized against the constraints of the ability to monopolize resources or mates and the requirements of male parental care (Emlen & Oring 1977).

We can relate these factors to the environmental parameters in the following way: the degree of polygyny should be higher if the resource density in space is high (Armstrong 1955; Downhower & Armitage 1971; Emlen 1968; Orians 1969; Verner & Willson 1966), is distributed in a moderately patchy fashion (Brown 1974; Elliot 1975; Haartman 1969; Orians 1969), and is predictable in space (Brown 1974). Mates are not monopolizable if the breeding season is very short (no time for a second courtship) or very long (energetically inefficient to guard nonreproductive females). Thus polygyny is increased when resources are available for a moderate length of time (Emlen & Oring 1977; Orians 1969) which is not highly variable (Emlen & Oring 1977), and if resources are available on a predictable schedule.

Emlen and Oring (1977) suggested that polyandry (female polygamy) will be more likely when the ability to produce multiple clutches in rapid succession is important. This occurs when replacement clutches are necessary, such as when density is variable and unpredictable in time (Emlen & Oring 1977), or juvenile mortality is high and variable (Emlen & Oring 1977; Jenni 1974).

5. Amount of parental care. This is the total energy expended by either parent on the eggs after laying or on the young after birth. It is extensive when the young cannot survive without it. This can occur under conditions of low resource density in both time and space (Emlen & Oring 1977; Haartman 1969; Pitelka et al. 1974) and high mortality of juveniles (Barlow 1974; Eisenberg et al. 1972; Millar 1977; Pitelka et al. 1974). Alternatively, parental care can be extensive under the same conditions that lead to high energy investment in young prior to birth, namely when dispersal is unimportant and the young face intense competition as adults. This can occur when resources are predictable in space and time (Brown 1972; Geist 1974).

6. Degree of male participation in parental care. This can be measured by the proportion of total care that is provided by the male to all his offspring. While the degree of parental care often depends on the survival probabilities of the young in its absence, the question still remains of whether one or two parents are needed. Furthermore, if only one is needed, should it be the male or the female?

High levels of the factors which cause selection for parental care in the first place can necessitate care by both parents, thus increasing male participation. These conditions are low resource density in space or time (Emlen & Oring 1977; Haartman 1969; Maynard Smith 1977; Pitelka et al. 1974) or high juvenile mortality (Barlow 1974; Eisenberg et al. 1972; Millar 1977; Pitelka et al. 1974). The question of whether the male or the female should undertake sole parental care depends on secondary adaptations and on whether fertilization is external or internal. Both of these topics are discussed below.

Secondary Adaptations

Secondary Adaptations in Life History

Secondary adaptations refer to the interactions of behavioral and life-history traits. My aim here is to make more clear the distinction between proximate and ultimate causation for a particular characteristic. A trait which is often a secondary adaptation to other characteristics is an unlikely candidate for a conservative character. Secondary adaptations are summarized in Table 3.

The pattern of reproductive effort in males appears to be strongly affected by the mating system (Trivers 1972). This does not appear to be as true of females. A female's reproductive success is often directly related to the amount of energy she can supply to the eggs and developing young. The more energy she can supply, the higher her reproductive success, up to some limit where the cost in mortality outweighs the benefit gained. This would produce a concave shape in the curve representing reproductive success versus RE, and is probably common. It can lead to selection for an RE of less than one and repeated reproduction (Schaffer 1974a).

In organisms where there is a large amount of male parental care and a low degree of polygyny, we might expect the male pattern of RE to be much like the female's, since the same sort of relationship between energy allocation and reproductive success should hold. But as the degree of polygyny increases, males increasingly come into competition with each other for females, and relatively few are reproductively successful. This type of competition leads to a situation in which there is little reproductive return for energy expenditure until very high levels are reached (Schaffer & Gadgil 1975; Trivers 1972). When such a convex or sigmoid relationship between RE and reproductive success exists, the optimal life-history tactic is not to attempt to reproduce until a high probability exists of doing so successfully, and then putting a high proportion of available energy into reproduction (Pianka & Parker 1975; Schaffer 1974a).

If the attainable reproductive success is very high and correlated with size rather than age, energy may be channeled by males into growth, even at the cost of higher mortality (Caughley 1966; Selander 1972; Trivers 1972; Warner & Downs 1977). Alternatively, as in elephant seals (Carrick et al. 1962; LeBoeuf 1974), males may delay

Table 3. Suggested secondary adaptations in life history and behavioral characteristics. The level of the characteristics listed on the left has an effect on the level of the expression of the characteristics listed along the top. -, negative effect; +, positive effect, x, complex effect, see text. References in text.

Proximate Causes	Secondary Adaptations								
	Reproductive Effort (male)	Investment/ Young	Sex Ratio (% male)	Simultaneous Hermaphroditism	Sex Change	Polygyny	Polyandry	Total Parental Care	Male Parental Care
Reproductive Effort (Female)									+
Investment/ Young								+	+
Group Size			x						
Individual Movement		+		-					
Polygyny	+		x		+				-
Total Parental Care						-			
Male Parental Care						-	+		

maturity far longer than females, grow over a longer time, and eventually engage in a large amount of reproduction over a relatively short period of time. In these extreme cases, females may be iteroparous and males essentially semelparous.

Notice that in species where a few males garner most of the reproduction, the success of a particular male life-history pattern depends on the number and condition of other males around him. In the absence of other males, even a small, early-maturing individual would have a high degree of reproductive success. This has led to the development of short-term adaptive responses in some species. For example, in _Xiphophorus variatus_, a poeciliid fish, the males mature early when no other mature male is present. In small mixed experimental groups, young males mature only when they are larger than the other mature males in the group (Borowsky 1973).

Female RE appears to be less affected by the behavioral characteristics of the species. Under conditions of increased polygyny and decreased male parental care, females can shift their energy allocation within a particular RE, having fewer young and providing them with more care. For example, female bobolinks can adjust their clutch size downward and their time spent feeding young upward when they are the second mate of a previously mated male (Martin 1974). However, it is not clear whether the actual level of RE changes.

The _investment of energy per young_ has not been suggested as a secondary adaptation to other characteristics, except by Geist (1977). He argued that as individual movement increases in ungulates, the young must be born at a relatively large size in order to keep pace with the group soon after birth. Females may also vary I_y to adjust within-progeny sex ratios (see below).

Sex ratio, originally thought to be fixed at unity, may be surprisingly labile. This variability may be controlled by social processes. Trivers and Willard (1973) proposed that in species with extensive polygyny and sexual selection, females in good condition should bias their progeny toward males. They argue that healthy females can produce large, robust offspring that stand a better chance of being highly successful as large adult males. Some evidence was offered that this may be the case in some polygynous species (Trivers & Willard 1973; but see Myers 1978).

Another characteristic which could affect selection for sex ratio is group size and composition (Hamilton 1967; Trivers & Willard 1973). In large groups with the overall sex ratio at unity, any sex ratio of progeny yields equal fitness for the parent. As groups get smaller, the number of possible matings are increased by within-progeny sex ratio at unity. Finally, if groups consist totally of siblings and inbreeding cannot be avoided, it is adaptive to produce only enough males to fertilize all the females and thus maximize production.

Sex allocation was first dealt with as a secondary adaptation by Ghiselin (1969), who suggested several socially-related proximal causes for the evolution of hermaphroditism. Low individual movement, like low population density, can lower the probability of encountering suitable mates and thus make simultaneous hermaphroditism adaptive. Also, if mating is restricted to small groups, simultaneous hermaphroditism maximizes the number of possible matings and lessens the danger of inbreeding.

Sex change (sequential hermaphroditism) appears to be strongly controlled by the mating system (Ghiselin 1969; Leigh et al. 1976; Warner 1975; Warner et al. 1975). Polygyny and the resultant sexual selection can lead to differences in age-specific fecundities between males and females, with small males having lower fecundities than small females, and vice versa. Sex change at some point from female to male is an adaptation to being the right sex at the right size or age. On the other hand, if sexual selection is not operating, and females increase in fecundity with age, it may be of advantage to function first as a male and later change to female (Charnov et al. 1978; Warner 1975). Short-term adaptive responses in sex allocation have been documented in two sex-changing fishes (Robertson 1972; Warner et al. 1975). In both cases, removal of a dominant, highly polygynous male can induce a female to change sex and take his place.

Secondary Adaptations in Social and Mating Systems

Behavioral secondary adaptations generally have been related to other behavioral characteristics rather than to life history. Most involve the interaction of polygamy with parental care.

Emlen and Oring (1977) suggested that as the amount of parental care decreases, selection can increase the degree of polygyny if the environmental parameters are at appropriate levels (resources patchy and predictable in space, and available for a moderate and predictable period of time; see above). This is especially true if females assume most of the parental care. Alternatively, if resources are variable and unpredictable in time, male parental care may increase due to the necessity for the female to prepare for a replacement or second clutch (Emlen & Oring 1977). As mentioned above, polyandry may develop in this case.

On the other hand, high parental care can also result from a shift in male energy allocation when the environmental parameters reduce the opportunity for polygyny. Energy is then better spent on the young (Emlen & Oring 1977; Trivers & Willard 1973).

One suggested behavioral secondary adaptation to a life-history characteristic is the relationship of investment per young to parental care. When I_y is small, as in most fishes, the parent is usually unable to provide food to the young after birth and the sole function of parental care would be in guarding (Perrone & Zaret 1979). Under such circumstances dual parental care is unlikely (Maynard Smith 1977; Williams 1975; but see Barlow 1974; Perrone & Zaret 1979).

It has also been suggested that male parental care can be extensive when female reproductive effort is high (Maynard Smith 1977; Orians 1969). However, the predictions in this case are equivocal. Reproductive effort includes parental care, and therefore RE sets an upper limit to the amount of parental care a male or a female can administer. What is important, however, is the allocation of energy by the female with a given RE to either I_y or parental care. For example, low juvenile survival relative to adults should select for a low level of reproductive effort in females (Charnov & Schaffer 1973), but a high amount of parental care. In this case, male parental care may also be necessary to ensure any survival of young at all. Some pelagic sea birds may be examples of this case (e.g., Amadon 1964). On the other hand, if RE in females is high, and the energy is expended in I_y, then extensive male parental care may result because the female cannot contribute more toward the care of the young (Emlen & Oring 1977; Maynard Smith 1977).

Discussion

The preceding sections suggest that interactions between traits in life history and behavior are common. Why should some characteristics tend to be primary adaptations and others secondary? I suggest that primary adaptations have the same property as those conservative characteristics, feeding and avoidance of mortality, that were discussed earlier: given a constant environment, deviations from certain values tend to cause extreme losses in fitness. When a characteristic has this property, it tends to induce secondary adaptations in other traits which can be altered with less disastrous consequences.

The best example of such a conservative nonmorphological trait is behavioral: a high level of polygyny and the resultant sexual selection. In a highly competitive mating system, males that win have high reproductive success, but losers suffer extreme reductions in fitness. This uncompromising situation can lead to secondary adaptations in reproductive effort, investment per young, sex ratio, and sex allocation, as detailed above, as well as the more familiar adaptations in morphology (e.g., horns and other defensive structures) and behavior (aggressiveness, territoriality, etc.).

Rather than labelling a particular characteristic as conservative or inflexible a priori, we need to consider how fitness might be altered by variation in that characteristic relative to changes in other traits. If the certain expression of a particular trait is critical in terms of fitness, it should tend to be a primary adaptation, while other traits will exist at levels which are compromises between the demands of the environment and the demands of the critical characteristics.

Phylogenetic Constraints

There are several characteristics, however, that do appear to act as important constraints on the expression of adaptations in both life history and behavior because their own expression is so stable in the face of different environmental conditions. Four such constraints will be mentioned here: sex, body size, the site of fertilization, and aquatic versus terrestrial life.

The influence of sex on nonmorphological adaptation is so pervasive that separate predictions usually must be made for males and females. As mentioned above, males generally should be in competition for females, while females are attempting to maximize their energy intake. The time and energy budgets of the two sexes should thus be different, with males spending the minimum amount of time feeding in order to spend more time in reproductive activities, while females maximize their time spent feeding (Schoener 1971). So female behavior and life history should often represent a primary adaptation to the environment, while male behavior should often be a secondary adaptation to female activity. Thus males may defend areas favored by females for feeding or reproduction (Geist 1974). In another example, male parental care and polygyny may depend on female energy allocation and grouping tendencies, as mentioned above.

Body size can alter the effect of mortality. Larger animals may be able more effectively to flee predators or defend themselves (Geist 1974). Also, their individual movements may be disproportionately larger, thus ensuring a more constant food supply (Crook et al. 1976; Geist 1974; Southwood et al. 1974). It has been suggested that because of decreased predation and a more defendable food supply, larger animals may have a longer life and thus lower reproductive effort, and have a higher level of parental care as well (Southwood et al. 1974; Wilson 1975).

Another constraint to consider is the site of fertilization. External fertilization should increase a male's confidence in parentage (Barlow 1976; Perrone & Zaret 1979; Trivers 1972), and at the same time it may leave him in possession of the eggs after fertilization (Dawkins & Carlisle 1976). Thus, in the fishes, where parental care occurs it is usually done by the male. Since many males can easily fertilize the eggs of a single female, alternative male mating behaviors involving spawning interference can develop, simultaneously promoting both male and female polygamy (Leigh et al. 1976).

Finally, relative to aquatic forms, terrestrial vertebrates produce their young in relatively large packages. This is probably due to the danger of dessication and the relative lack of small primary producers, which eliminates the food supply for a small planktonic larva (Dawkins & Carlisle 1976; Warner 1978). Thus, the young are either raised internally or are provided with a large food source in an egg. Either of these conditions tend to commit the female to a large amount of time and energy investment for young, and this can lead to polygyny (Emlen & Oring 1977). An additional effect is that the anatomical differences between males and females are accentuated, which can place a constraint on certain forms of sex allocation. Thus sex change and simultaneous hermaphroditism are common in fishes and marine invertebrates, but absent in terrestrial vertebrates (Warner 1978).

Short-Term Adaptive Responses

Mating and other social systems have been shown to change in predicted directions with changes in the environment (for example, see references on territoriality and polygamy in Emlen (1976), and on other traits in Wilson (1975:19-21)). On the other hand, life histories have been considered rather invariant in this respect, supposedly changing only over the course of generations (Wilson 1975:145).

As reviewed above, however, it is possible for reproductive effort, age or size at first maturity, sex ratio of offspring, and sexual expression to vary as an individual adaptive response in some species. Changes in these characteristics can affect the fecundity and expectations of survival throughout the remaining lifespan. Populations polymorphic in life history appear especially common in the aquatic environment, where sexual expression and adult size appear to be under fewer constraints (Charnov et al. 1978; Robertson & Warner 1978; Warner & Downs 1977; Warner & Robertson 1978).

Testing Hypotheses

Testing hypotheses about nonmorphological adaptation presents enormous difficulties. Virtually none of the primary or secondary adaptations reviewed above have been substantiated to any large degree, and some remain purely hypothetical. Altmann (1974) reviewed some of the ways that the relationship between environment and adaptation might be explored. By comparing closely related species in different habitats, differences in characteristics may be interpreted as adaptations. Conversely, similar characteristics shared by unrelated species in similar habitats may also represent adaptations to the environment. Procedures such as these help in formulating hypotheses, but we need to make falsifiable predictions in order to test them. Otherwise we are left with post-hoc explanations that may be of little value.

The problems of an experimental approach to testing evolutionary hypotheses have recently been discussed by

Stearns (1977). They include the necessity of using organisms with short generation times, the difficulty of relating laboratory results to field situations, and the near impossibility of performing realistic manipulations. These problems tend to restrict testing to static predictions about the co-occurrence of a particular environment with a particular trait, or testing by analogy, using short-term responses (see below).

Although a reasonable goal of evolutionary biology is to predict a set of adaptations on the basis of the environment, this is often an impossible task. D. L. Kramer (personal communication) has pointed out that some adaptations optimize a process in relation to a selection pressure that cannot be changed (as when iteroparity is interpreted as a response to variability in juvenile survival); others have a feedback effect which alters the selection pressure itself (as in reduction of the threat of predation by grouping). In these latter circumstances, it is difficult to specify what the environment was like before the adaptation occurred.

In addition, evolution is to a certain extent a chance affair, and traits that depend on special structures or complex behaviors may simply not arise. Also, unsuspected opposing selection pressures may prevent any adaptation from expressing itself in the expected fashion. For example, sex change may be adaptive for sexually-selected terrestrial species, but the differences between males and females may be so great as to prevent its evolution (Warner 1978).

One way around this problem is to consider traits which all animals possess to some degree or another, and predict how an environmental parameter will evoke a certain level of expression for such a trait. Most of the characteristics mentioned above have such a quality: for example, all animals have some amount of energy investment per young; group size can range from one to many thousands. However, since trait expressions are probably always the result of compromises between opposing selection pressures, one should consider the level of as many of the possible influences as is feasible. Since we rarely know the relative importance of multiple influences, their existence makes testing extremely difficult (Stearns 1977).

An additional problem is posed by alternative stable states, or multiple possible responses to a particular environmental parameter. These can occur in life histories

(Schaffer 1974a; Schaffer & Rosensweig 1977) as well as behavior (Emlen 1976). For example, extremely low resource density and the associated problem of finding mates may be solved by hermaphroditism or attached dwarf males (Ghiselin 1969), and high predation may lead to increased group size or decreased individual movement.

In some cases, a limited but more feasible test could consist of predicting the existence of a particular influence on the basis of an existing trait or set of traits. This avoids the difficulties imposed by the chance nature of evolution and the existence of alternative stable states. For example, one can make a falsifiable prediction that sex change from female to male should only be found in animals with a high degree of polygyny and strong sexual selection (Robertson & Warner 1978; Warner 1975; Warner & Robertson 1978).

While the problems of multiple causation cannot be eliminated when this process is applied to a single trait, at times it is possible to narrow down the possible environmental parameters through an inspection of a series of associated traits. Only certain combinations of characteristics should co-occur in particular environments, and we can use these combinations to make predictions. By using both life-historical and behavioral traits, we have a broader base of coevolved and co-occurring characters with which to work, and thus a higher probability of eliminating some prospective environmental causes. However, caution should be used in this approach, because in the process of testing one hypothesized relationship, it assumes that other, usually untested, relationships are true.

One example of this multiple approach will be given. Parental care may increase in response to low resource density, high juvenile mortality, or when food resources are predictable in space (see above). The latter parameter also selects for increased polygyny, while the other two do not. A high level of reproductive effort associated with large amounts of parental care could occur under low resource density situations, but should not occur under conditions of high juvenile mortality or predictable resources.

Perhaps the most feasible test of these hypotheses is one using organisms with variable expression of the trait in question. If the variability is in the form of a short-term adaptive response, it may be possible to predict that a particular environment will evoke a particular response in an individual, or that all individuals showing a certain trait will be found in a specific environment. The test in this case is by analogy, since most theory has developed as a description of long-term genetic response. But as Emlen (1976) stressed, the predictions are based on the same premise: adaptive shifts in behavior or life history result in increases in fitness due to better foraging efficiency, increased protection from predators, higher reproductive rates, etc. For testing, it matters little whether the response is in terms of changes in gene frequencies or changes in phenotype due to a flexible genotype. Again, multiple possible causes may lead to an a priori prediction involving the "wrong" environmental parameter, especially if several parameters covary. Also, the variability may be due to factors other than short-term adaptive response, as mentioned above.

As the above review indicates, there now exist many hypotheses about the selective forces acting to shape social behavior and life history. However, it is not clear that we are yet in a position to proceed with speculation about how they may apply to an organism as complex as the human being. Instead, I think it is imperative that we investigate more closely the validity of the hypotheses themselves. Part of this process involves clarifying our assumptions and distinguishing proximate from ultimate causation, dealt with in part by this paper. Most important, we need to turn our attention to rigorously testing the hypotheses in the field and laboratory.

Summary

Evolutionary hypotheses about life-history traits suggest how certain environmental conditions would lead to selection for a particular set of demographic characteristics. A parallel set of hypotheses has emerged in sociobiology, predicting what sorts of behaviors (especially in social/mating systems) are adaptive in certain environments.

These two approaches have been somewhat isolated from one another in the past. Often, researchers in one field view a set of characteristics in another field as rather inflexible constraints on the evolution of the traits in which they are interested. To clarify our predictions, we need to distinguish traits that are independent adaptations to the environment (here termed primary adaptations) from those which are accommodations to other traits (secondary adaptations). As a step toward making such a distinction, this paper explores some of the interrelationships between behavioral and life-historical adaptations. I emphasize the responsive nature of nonmorphological adaptations in general, and the danger of assuming any such adaptation to be an inflexible constraint.

The environment can be characterized by the mean level, variance, and predictability of resources in time and space, and by the rate and variability of adult and juvenile mortality. Resources are usually food, but may also be such things as breeding sites or shelter from predators.

The basic life history of an animal can be described by its pattern of reproductive effort, its investment of energy per young, the sex ratio of its offspring, and the sexual identity that it adopts through its lifetime (male, female, sex-changer, hermaphrodite). Characterizing the social system of an organism is more problematical, but the major categories are reduced here to group size, individual movement, exclusivity of range, degree of polygamy, amount of parental care, and the degree of male participation in parental care.

While the list of primary adaptations suggests the basic traits we might expect to see in organisms in particular environments, the secondary adaptations point out the interactions of social system and life history. These interactions are often complex. For example, under the influence of a polygynous mating system, males can show patterns of reproductive effort vastly different from females; these differences are reflected in growth and mortality. Both the sex ratio and the expression of some forms of hermaphroditism can also depend on the mating system and group size. On the other hand, the level of polygamy appears to be constrained by the demands of parental care.

If deviations from particular values in a characteristic cause extreme losses in fitness, that characteristic will tend to induce secondary adaptations in other traits. For example, for males in a polygynous mating system the rewards for winning and the penalties for losing are extreme, and this has led to many secondary adaptations in morphology, life history, and behavior. Therefore, rather than labelling a particular characteristic as inflexible a priori, we need to consider how fitness might be altered by variation in that characteristic relative to changes in other traits. However, there do appear to be certain characteristics which act as important general constraints on the expression of adaptations in both behavior and life history. These include sex, body size, the site of fertilization, and aquatic versus terrestrial life.

Testing hypotheses about nonmorphological adaptation presents many difficulties. Because of the chance nature of evolution, or due to unsuspected opposing selection pressures, it is often nearly impossible to predict a particular trait on the basis of the environment. Also tending to make testing difficult are the existence of (i) multiple possible causes for a single trait and (ii) alternative stable states as possible results from a single cause. In certain cases a limited but more feasible test could consist of predicting a particular environmental condition on the basis of an existing trait or set of traits. Although multiple causation cannot be eliminated by this process, it may be possible to narrow down the possibilities by using both behavioral and life-history traits in the analysis.

Organisms that demonstrate flexible adaptive responses are, of course, impossible to characterize as to specific traits. Although most theory assumes a long-term genetic response of the population, we may be able to use these flexible organisms in a test by analogy, predicting that a particular environment will evoke a particular response, or predicting that individuals demonstrating a certain trait will be found in a specific environment.

Acknowledgements

I am grateful to P. Abrams, G. Barlow, A. Blaustein, T. Carlisle, J. Collins, R. Day, M. Hixon, S. Hoffman, A. Kuris, R. Panza, R. Peters, and A. Sih for their extremely helpful comments on this manuscript. D. Kramer, J. Silverberg, and S. Rothstein provided me with particularly insightful and detailed advice. I have also profited from discussions with G. Bell, E. Brothers, S. Emlen, and S. Levin. Financial aid was provided by the Committee on Research, University of California, Santa Barbara, and the Smithsonian Tropical Research Institute. The American Association for the Advancement of Science generously provided funds for my participation in the symposium which provided the basis of this book.

Literature Cited

Altmann, S. A. 1974. Baboons, space, time, and energy. *American Zoologist* 14:221-248.

Amadon, D. 1964. The evolution of low reproductive rates in birds. *Evolution* 18:105-110.

Armstrong, E. A. 1955. *The wren*. Collins, London.

Barash, D. P. 1974. The evolution of marmot societies: A general theory. *Science* 185:415-420.

Barlow, G. W. 1974. Contrasts in social behavior between Central American cichliid fishes and coral-reef surgeon fishes. *American Zoologist* 14:9-34.

———. 1976. Introduction. *In* G. W. Barlow (ed.), *A Scientific American reader in ichthyology*. Freeman, San Francisco, pp. 3-8.

Borowsky, R. L. 1973. Social control of adult size in male *Xiphophorus variatus*. *Nature* 245:332-335.

Brock, V. E. & R. H. Riffenburgh. 1960. Fish schooling: A possible factor in reducing predation. *Journal du Conseil, Conseil Permanent International pour l'Exploration de la Mer* 25:307-317.

Brockelman, W. Y. 1975. Competition, the fitness of offspring, and optimal clutch size. *American Naturalist* 109:677-699.

Brown, J. L. 1964. The evolution of diversity in avian territorial systems. *Wilson Bulletin* 76:160-169.

———. 1972. Communal feeding of nestlings in the Mexican jay (*Aphelocomia ultramarina*): Interflock comparisons. *Animal Behaviour* 20:395-403.

———. 1974. Alternate routes to sociality in jays - with a theory for the evolution of altruism and communal breeding. *American Zoologist* 14:63-80.

——— and G. H. Orians. 1970. Spacing patterns in mobile animals. *Annual Review of Ecology and Systematics* 1:239-262.

Carrick, R., S. E. Csordas, S. E. Ingham, & K. Keith. 1962. Studies on the southern elephant seal, Mirounga leonina L. III, IV. C.S.I.R.O. Wildlife Research, Canberra, Australia 7:119-197.

Caughley, G. 1966. Mortality patterns in mammals. Ecology 47:906-918.

Charnov, E. L., D. W. Gotshall, & J. G. Robinson. 1978. Sex ratio: Adaptive response to population fluctuations in pandalid shrimp. Science 200:204-206.

——— & W. M. Schaffer. 1973. Life history consequences of natural selection: Cole's result revisited. American Naturalist 107:791-793.

Cody, M. L. 1966. A general theory of clutch size. Evolution 20:174-184.

———. 1971. Finch flocks in the Mojave Desert. Theoretical Population Biology 2:142-158.

Cole, L. C. 1954. The population consequences of life history phenomena. Quarterly Review of Biology 29:103-137.

Colwell, R. E. 1974. Predictability, constancy, and contingency of periodic phenomena. Ecology 55:1148-1153.

Crook, J. H. 1972. Sexual selection, dimorphism, and social organization in the primates. In B. C. Campbell (ed.), Sexual selection and the descent of man, 1871-1971. Aldine, Chicago, pp. 231-281.

———, J. Ellis, & J. D. Goss-Custard. 1976. Mammalian social systems: Structure and function. Animal Behaviour 24:261-274.

Cushing, D. H. & F. R. Harden-Jones. 1968. Why do fish school? Nature 218:918-920.

Dawkins, R. & T. R. Carlisle. 1976. Parental investment and mate desertion: A fallacy. Nature 262:131-133.

Downhower, J. F. & K. B. Armitage. 1971. The yellow-bellied marmot and the evolution of polygamy. American Naturalist 195:355-370.

Eisenberg, J. F., N. A. Muckenhirn, & R. Rudran. 1972. The relation between ecology and social structure in primates. Science 176:863-874.

Elliot, P. F. 1975. Longevity and the evolution of polygamy. American Naturalist 109:281-287.

Emlen, J. M. 1970. Age specificity and ecological theory. Ecology 51:588-601.

———. 1973. Ecology: An evolutionary approach. Addison-Wesley, Reading, Massachusetts.

Emlen, S. T. 1968. Territoriality in the bullfrog, Rana catesbiana. Copeia 1968:240-243.

———. 1976. An alternative case for sociobiology. Science 192:736-738.

——— & L. W. Oring. 1977. Ecology, sexual selection, and the evolution of mating systems. Science 197:215-223.

Fisher, R. A. 1930. The genetical theory of natural selection. Clarendon, Oxford.

Gadgil, M. 1972. Male dimorphism as a consequence of sexual selection. American Naturalist 106:574-576.

Geist, V. 1974. On the relationship of social evolution and ecology in ungulates. American Zoologist 14:205-220.

———. 1977. A comparison of social adaptations in relation to ecology in gallinaceous bird and ungulate societies. Annual Review of Ecology and Systematics 8:193-207.

Ghiselin, M. T. 1969. The evolution of hermaphroditism among animals. Quarterly Review of Biology 44:189-208.

Giesel, J. T. 1976. Reproductive strategies as adaptations to life in temporally heterogeneous environments. Annual Review of Ecology and Systematics 7:57-79.

Gill, F. B. & L. L. Wolf. 1975. Economics of feeding territoriality in the golden-winged sunbird. Ecology 56:333-345.

Goss-Custard, J. D. 1970. Feeding dispersion in some over-wintering wading birds. In J. H. Crook (ed.), Social behavior in birds and mammals: Essays on the social ethology of animals and man. Academic Press, New York.

Haartman, L. von. 1969. Nest-site and evolution of polygamy in European passerine birds. Ornis Fennica 46:1-12.

Hamilton, W. D. 1967. Extraordinary sex ratios. Science 156:477-488.

———. 1971. Geometry for the selfish herd. Journal of Theoretical Biology 31:295-311.

Heller, H. C. 1971. Altitudinal zonation of chipmunks (Eutamias): Interspecific aggression. Ecology 52:312-329.

Hirschfield, M. F. & D. W. Tinkle. 1975. Natural selection and the evolution of reproductive effort. Proceedings of the National Academy of Sciences, U.S.A. 72:2227-2231.

Horn, H. S. 1968. The adaptive significance of colonial nesting in the Brewer's blackbird (Euphagus cyanocephalus). Ecology 49:682-694.

Howe, H. F. 1976. Egg size, hatching asynchrony, sex, and brood reduction in the common grackle. Ecology 57:1195-1207.

———. 1978. Sex-ratio adjustment in the common grackle. Science 198:744-746.

Janzen, D. H. 1969. Seed eaters versus seed size, number, toxicity, and dispersal. Evolution 23:1-27.

Jenni, D. A. 1974. Evolution of polyandry in birds. American Zoologist 14:129-144.

Kaufman, J. H. 1974. The ecology and evolution of social organization in the kangaroo family (Macropodidae). American Zoologist 14:51-62.

Lack, D. 1968. Ecological adaptations for breeding in birds. Methuen, London.

LeBouef, B. J. 1974. Male-male competition and reproductive success in elephant seals. American Zoologist 14:163-176.

Leigh, E. G., Jr., E. L. Charnov & R. R. Warner. 1976. Sex ratio, sex change, and natural selection. Proceedings of the National Academy of Sciences U.S.A. 73:3656-3660.

Lewontin, R. C. 1978. Adaptation. Scientific American 239:212-230.

Lotka, A. J. 1907. Studies on the mode of growth of material aggregates. American Journal of Science 24:199-216.

MacArthur, R. H. 1965. Ecological consequences of natural selection. In T. Waterman and H. Morowitz (eds.), Theoretical and mathematical biology. Blaisdell, New York, pp. 388-397.

——— & E. O. Wilson. 1967. The theory of island biogeography. Princeton University Press, Princeton, New Jersey.

Martin, S. G. 1974. Adaptations for polygynous breeding in the bobolink, Dolichonyx oryzivorus. American Zoologist 14:109-119.

Maynard Smith, J. 1974. The theory of games and the evolution of animal conflicts. Journal of Theoretical Biology 47:209-221.

———. 1977. Parental investment: A prospective analysis. Animal Behaviour 25:1-9.

———. 1978. Optimization theory in evolution. Annual Review of Ecology and Systematics 9:31-56.

Menge, B. A. 1975. Brood or broadcast? The adaptive significance of different reproductive strategies in two intertidal sea stars Leptasterias hexactis and Pisaster ochraceus. Marine Biology 37:87-100.

Millar, J. S. 1977. Adaptive features of mammalian reproduction. Evolution 31:370-386.

Murphy, G. I. 1968. Pattern in life history and the environment. American Naturalist 102:390-404.

Myers, J. H. 1978. Sex ratio adjustment under food stress: Maximization of quality or numbers of offspring? American Naturalist 112:381-388.

Neill, S. R. St. J. & J. M. Cullen. 1974. Experiments on whether schooling by their prey affects the hunting behaviour of cephalopods and fish predators. Journal of Zoology 172:549-569.

Nichols, J. D., W. Conley, B. Batt, & A. R. Tipton. 1976. Temporally dynamic reproductive strategies and the concept of r- and K-selection. American Naturalist 110:995-1005.

Orians, G. H. 1969. On the evolution of mating systems in birds and mammals. American Naturalist 103:589-603.

Perrone, M., Jr. & T. M. Zaret. 1979. Parental care patterns in fishes. American Naturalist 113:351-361.

Pianka, E. R. 1970. On r- and K-selection. American Naturalist 104:592-597.

——— & W. S. Parker. 1975. Age specific reproductive tactics. American Naturalist 109:453-464.

Pitelka, F. A., R. T. Holmes, & S. F. MacLean, Jr. 1974. Ecology and evolution of social organization in arctic sandpipers. American Zoologist 14:185-204.

Pulliam, H. R. 1973. On the advantages of flocking. Journal of Theoretical Biology 38:419-422.

Reinhard, E. G. 1949. Experiments on the determination and differentiation of sex in the bopyrid Stegophryxius hyptius Thompson. Biological Bulletin 96:17-31.

Ricklefs, R. E. 1977. On the evolution of reproductive strategies in birds: Reproductive effort. American Naturalist 111:453-478.

Robertson, D. R. 1972. Social control of sex reversal in a coral-reef fish. Science 177:1007-1009.

——— & R. R. Warner. 1978. Sexual patterns in the labroid fishes of the western Caribbean, II: The parrotfishes (Scaridae). Smithsonian Contributions to Zoology 255:1-26.

Schaffer, W. M. 1974a. Selection for optimal life histories: The effects of age structure. Ecology 55:291-303.

———. 1974b. Optimal reproductive effort in fluctuating environments. American Naturalist 108:783-790.

——— & M. Gadgil. 1975. Selection for optimal life histories of plants. In M. L. Cody and J. Diamond (eds.), The ecology and evolution of communities. Harvard University Press, Cambridge, pp. 142-157.

——— & M. L. Rosenzweig. 1977. Selection for life histories: II. Multiple equilibria and the evolution of alternative reproductive strategies. Ecology 58:60-72.

Schoener, T. W. 1971. Theory of feeding strategies. Annual Review of Ecology and Systematics 2:369-404.

Selander, R. K. 1972. Sexual selection and dimorphism in birds. In B. Campbell (ed.), Sexual selection and the descent of man, 1871-1971. Aldine, Chicago, pp. 180-230.

Smith, C. C. & S. D. Fretwell. 1974. The optimal balance between size and number of offspring. American Naturalist 708:499-506.

Southwood, T. R. E., R. M. May, M. P. Hassel, & G. R. Conway. 1974. Ecological strategies and population parameters. American Naturalist 108:791-804.

Stearns, S. C. 1976. Life history tactics: A review of the ideas. Quarterly Review of Biology 51:3-47.

———. 1977. The evolution of life history traits: A critique of the theory and a review of the data. Annual Review of Ecology and Systematics 8:145-171.

Thompson, W. A., I. Vertinsky, & J. R. Krebs. 1974. The survival value of flocking in birds: A simulation model. Journal of Animal Ecology 43:785-820.

Tomlinson, J. T. 1966. The advantages of hermaphroditism and parthenogenesis. Journal of Theoretical Biology 11:34-58.

Treisman, M. 1975a. Predation and the evolution of gregariousness. I. Models for concealment and evasion. Animal Behaviour 23:779-800.

———. 1975b. Predation and the evolution of gregariousness. II. An economic model for predator-prey interaction. Animal Behaviour 23:801-825.

Trivers, R. L. 1972. Parental investment and sexual selection. In B. Campbell (ed.), Sexual selection and the descent of man, 1871-1971. Aldine, Chicago, pp. 136-179.

——— & D. E. Willard. 1973. Natural selection of parental ability to vary the sex ratio of offspring. Science 179:90-92.

Verner, J. & M. F. Willson. 1966. The influence of habitats on mating systems of North American passerine birds. Ecology 47:143-147.

Vine, I. 1971. Risk of visual detection and pursuit by a predator and the selective advantage of flocking behavior. Journal of Theoretical Biology 30:405-422.

Ward, P. & A. Zahavi. 1973. The importance of certain assemblages of birds as "information centers" for food finding. Ibis 115:517-534.

Warner, R. R. 1975. The adaptive significance of sequential hermaphroditism in animals. American Naturalist 109:61-82.

———. 1978. The evolution of hermaphroditism and unisexuality in aquatic and terrestrial vertebrates. In E. Reese & F. Lighter (eds.), Contrasts in behavior. Wiley Interscience, New York, pp. 77-101.

——— & I. F. Downs. 1977. Comparative life histories: Growth vs. reproduction in normal males and sex-changing hermaphrodites of the striped parrotfish, Scarus croicensis. Proceedings of the 3rd International Coral Reef Symposium 1. Biology:275-281.

——— & D. R. Robertson. 1978. Sexual patterns in the labroid fishes of the western Caribbean. I: The wrasses (Labridae). Smithsonian Contributions to Zoology 254:1-27.

———, D. R. Robertson, & E. G. Leigh. 1975. Sex change and sexual selection. Science 190:633-638.

Wilbur, H. M., D. W. Tinkle & J. P. Collins. 1974. Environmental certainty, trophic level, and resource availability in life history evolution. *American Naturalist* 108:805-817.

Williams, G. C. 1964. Measurement of consociation among fishes and comments on the evolution of schooling. *Publications of the Museum, Michigan State University, East Lansing, Biological Series* 2:349-384.

———. 1966. *Adaptation and natural selection: A critique of some current evolutionary thought.* Princeton University Press, Princeton, New Jersey.

———. 1975. *Sex and evolution.* Princeton University Press, Princeton, New Jersey.

Wilson, E. O. 1975. *Sociobiology: The new synthesis.* Belknap Press, Cambridge, Massachusetts.

Jack W. Bradbury

7. Foraging, Social Dispersion and Mating Systems

Introduction

One of the more widely accepted concepts in sociobiology is the notion that social systems are determined by, or at least limited by, the distribution of crucial resources (Cf. Wilson 1975). As Emlen has argued in an earlier chapter (this volume), analogous resource bases often lead to similar social configurations, and the resulting convergences frequently cut across both phylogenetic lines and the mechanisms, e.g., behavioral vs. genetic polymorphisms, by which these adaptive solutions are reached. There are clearly sufficient data to support the contention that social convergence or divergence is directly correlated with habitat type or habitat usage (Crook 1964; Denham 1971; Geist 1977; Jarman 1974). The challenge is now to identify the specific causal links between resource and social variables and to determine which links have the greatest generality.

I shall limit my discussion to the potential links between resource distributions and mating systems. I shall deal primarily with mammals for which, with the exception of a few primates, male parental care is not an important component in mate choice. Mating systems can be broadly classified into three general categories (Bradbury & Vehrencamp 1977; Cronin & Sherman 1976; Emlen 1976). The first is called "resource defense" and is characterized by the establishment of territories by males over patches of resources required by females. Typical resources include food, roosting sites, parturition sites, and water. By excluding other males from these areas, the territorial owners gain a biased access to any females coming to use the resources. A second system, "female defense," arises when females form groups, usually for reasons extrinsic to males, and subsets of the male population join each group and prevent other males from gaining access to the females. Here the defending males follow the moving female group, whereas in resource defense, males are static within a defined area and await visitation by females. In the third system, males defend neither resources nor females, but instead aggregate in traditional sites and are visited by females solely for the purpose of mating. In the more evolved systems, each male has its own "display territory" within the aggregation and females are free to make choices of mates without interference by other males. These latter aggregations are called "leks."

The usefulness of these general categories arises from the fact that we can ask more rigorous evolutionary questions about mating systems. Specifically, one is not obliged to explain why a given population shows system A, but alternatively, one asks why system A is found instead of the known alternatives B and C. The latter question is more amenable to field study in part because we can often find close taxonomic relatives or even different populations of the same species showing different mating systems. The African antelope, the topi, is a case in point. In one part of its range in Rwanda it exhibits classical resource defense while in another nearby area, it exhibits lek behavior (Montfort-Braham 1975). By looking to see which ecological variables shift in parallel with these social differences and which do not, the potential number of links between environmental and social factors can be drastically reduced.

There are two types of links which one might expect to find between resource distributions and mating systems. Indirect links operate through the spatial dispersion of the animals. Specifically, particular spatial and seasonal patterns of food, water, and refuge availability will determine the number of animals per group, the compositional stability of groups, and the size of each group's home range. Because group size, compositional stability, and home range size are important determinants of the mating strategy options for both sexes, an indirect line of causation is established between resource distributions and mating systems. This presumes, and has generally been shown to be justified, that the basic social parameters such as group size and stability constitute limits within which mating system evolution occurs, as opposed to the alternative hypothesis that mating system evolution results in particular patterns of group size and stability. Resource distributions can also affect mating options directly by imposing time and energy constraints on either sex. Thus a male can defend a territory containing females only if there is sufficient time and energy to do so: a more locally concentrated food source may be more easily and economically defended than a dispersed one (Carpenter & MacMillen 1976; Gill & Wolf 1975). Any given mating system will thus be the net result of both indirect and direct influences of the resources used by the animals.

In the following discussion, I shall outline our recent studies on three groups of tropical bats in which we have tried to identify and weigh the links between resource distributions and mating systems. Bats have proved to be an excellent group for asking general questions because they exhibit such wide diversities of social systems and patterns of habitat use. In addition, large samples can be obtained in reasonable time and within bounded study sites. As a rule, my colleagues and I (see Acknowledgements) have tried to select species to answer specific questions as opposed to letting general descriptive work generate questions a posteriori. I shall leave to the reader the final judgement as to whether these choices have been judicious or not.

Emballonurid Bats

This widespread family of bats occurs in both the New and Old World tropics. They are all insectivorous and prefer to roost in well illuminated situations during the day. By marking each animal with individually recognizable plastic arm bands, direct observation in ambient light is sufficient to tease apart their diurnal social organizations. By using reflecting colored materials on the bands, we have also been able to locate and identify the same animals on their foraging grounds at night and thus to see if their social structure at the roost bears any relation to that when feeding.

The best studied species in this group is the white-lined bat, *Saccopteryx bilineata* (Bradbury & Emmons 1974; Bradbury & Vehrencamp 1976a). This small animal roosts in colonies of 2-50 bats within the large buttresses of forest trees. Within each colony, adult males partition the available roosting surface into contiguous territories. Females return from foraging each morning and distribute themselves, usually unequally, among the roosting territories of the males. During this morning period of settling, males exhibit a diverse array of vocalizations, visual displays, and olfactory displays. While females may visit a number of male territories at the dawn return, most females remain resident in the same male's territory for weeks or months at a time. One factor leading to this discrepancy between dawn visits and daytime residency is the aggressiveness of other females. Most visitors are quickly chased out of a male's territory by his other females at the same time that he is displaying to them. Residency per se must have some adaptive significance for females since actual mating only occurs during a two-week period in December, whereas the harem social structure with its associated displays is maintained throughout the year.

The adaptive value to females of residing in a particular harem was made more clear by comparing the dispersion of the bats on the foraging grounds to their social affilitations at the day roost (Bradbury & Vehrencap 1976a). Using the light-reflecting bands, we were able to show that the entire social organization at the roost is mapped directly onto the foraging sites. Thus members of the same colony feed in the same area, although the locations of these feeding sites changes every 5-10 weeks. Within the current colony feeding area, each male patrols and defends a portion of air space. The females currently roosting with that male are found in individual feeding territories within the defended portion of that male. When females change residency to a roost territory of a new male, they also change foraging territories. This is true for relocation both within and between colonies.

Nearly all adult males defend day roost territories and most defend nocturnal feeding territories. At any one time, however, only a few of the males have females within their territories and which males are so honored changes seasonally. This is particularly striking in seasonally variable habitats where females may shift male territories as often as every month. There seems to be some consensus among females, even if from different colonies, as to which male territories are most desirable at any given time. Thus solitary males may suddenly find themselves with a group of females from various colonies at certain times of year, and then be abandoned again at a later season. This situation is clearly one of male resource defense as we have defined it. It is not immediately obvious whether the day roost or the foraging site is the critical defended resource. All of the available evidence, however, favors the latter alternative.

Careful mapping of roost areas indicates that acceptable roost sites (as evidenced by their occasional use by harems or by solitary males), are much more common than colonies. More importantly, whenever there are massive relocations of females between harems, there are contemporaneous changes in the densities and distributions of aerial insect prey. If roosts were the critical resource, it is hard to see why males would defend feeding territories at all since copulations occur at the day roost (Tannenbaum 1975). Certainly in other bats for which roosts are known to be limiting, only the roost is defended and males do not attend females on the foraging grounds (Morrison 1975). Saccopteryx bilineata is thus interpreted as a resource-defense species in which the critical resource is the foraging site.

Wherever S. bilineata are common, we typically find two closely related species roosting in the same habitats. One of these is the congener, S. leptura. This little bat also roosts on tree exteriors, but it prefers clear tree boles to enclosed buttresses. S. leptura colonies are smaller with a typical range of 2-9 animals per colony. While colonies consist of equal numbers of males and females, there is no partitioning of the roost site as in S. bilineata. In small groups, this may be because the colony consists of only a single adult pair and recent young. In larger roosting groups, however, several adult pairs are present and no territorial behaviors have been observed. At night, the members of the same colony will defend their foraging grounds from members of other colonies with aerial chases and loud vocalizations. These bats do not partition the foraging grounds into individual territories, and group foraging at a single site is not unusual. S. leptura thus appear to live in monogamous pairs, have smaller colony sizes, and do not partition the roost or foraging sites into individual territories (Bradbury & Emmons 1974; Bradbury & Vehrencamp 1976a). Because the male of a pair always accompanies his female as she shifts between day roosts and foraging sites within their territory, this is best characterized as a female-defense system.

A third species is also sympatric with the previous two. Rhynchonycteris naso shares with S. leptura a predilection for clear tree boles. In fact, the two species may even use the same tree roosts. In contrast to S. leptura, R. naso groups consist of from 2-50 individuals with a mean value about 2-3 times that of the former species. Colonies contain equal numbers of adult males and females. Like S. leptura, but unlike S. bilineata, R. naso males do not partition either the day roost surface or the foraging areas. Instead, the adult females forage in groups at varying sites within the colony-specific territory, and all but one of the adult males forage singly at more peripheral locations. In groups where most members are individualy identifiable, we have found that one male is more likely to forage with the females and to patrol territorial boundaries. This same male is most often found roosting with the females during the day, while other males may roost on adjacent trees. However, this male follows the females instead of defending a site and waiting for them to appear. This appears to be an example of female defense as we have defined it.

The appeal of these animals arises from the fact that, within a single roosting habitat, we can find three closely related species showing quite diverse social configurations. As noted earlier, contrasts between these species allow us to reduce the nubmer of potential variables which might be postulated to affect the structure of the mating system. For example, we might hypothesize that roost site, working indirectly through group size, was an important determinant of the number of mates a male could obtain. The fact that *R. naso* and *S. leptura* used identical roosts in the same habitat, but have different group sizes, argues that roost site is not a major determinant of this aspect of social dispersion. Access by predators to the day roost can also be ruled out as a major factor leading to different social structures in these two species.

The one set of variables which produces a good across-the-board fit to mating-system structures are those which describe the food dispersion (Bradbury & Vehrencamp 1976b, 1977). While all three species roost in the same habitat, they differ considerably in where and how they feed. *S. bilineata* is a seasonal opportunist that moves from site to site at 5-10 week intervals. The location and size of the areas over which a colony will forage correlate well with the areas of forest which are currently producing new leaves, flowers, or fruit. *S. leptura* forages only within the wet and high-species diversity forests in which it roosts. *R. naso* specializes in foraging on the dense swarms of Diptera, mayflies and caddisflies which form at most times of the year over running water.

The spatial parameters describing the distributions of insect prey, and the underlying plant or aquatic structures leading to these distributions, are different for these three foraging habitats. In particular, the seasonal forests favored by *S. bilineata* tend to releaf or fruit synchronously in large patches. Local insect densities are not as high as we have measured over running water, but they are significantly higher than over adjacent, less active vegetation. The large size of the patch and the moderate insect densities enable a large colony to feed in such a site. Because these seasonal sites are often far apart, the annual foraging range for an *S. bilineata* colony is 10-20 ha.

In contrast, the wet forests used by *S. leptura* show much lower levels of releafing, flowering, or fruiting synchrony. Often only a single tree is active at a given time, and hence patch size is much smaller than for *S. bilineata*. Since over-patch densities of insects are not substantially different in these sites, the number of bats which can feed on a single patch is much smaller than for the congener. Because successively active trees are not far apart, again due to the plant activity asynchrony, annual foraging ranges for S. leptura can be as small as 1 ha.

R. naso food supplies have an interestingly hybrid nature when compared to the other two species. Insect patches are small but dense. This apparently facilitates the cooperative foraging of as many as 5-10 bats in the same location at the same time. Because patches are not far apart, annual foraging ranges of these bats are also about 1 ha.

In short, if we assume that colony size is determined by the numbers of insects in a given patch, and that colony home range size is determined by the distance between patches, then there is an excellent fit between the spatial parameters of the food distribution and the social dispersion, e.g., group size and spacing, of the emballonurids we have studied. These conclusions have been further substantiated with data on two other emballonurids and by intraspecific correlations between social dispersion and forest structure in S. leptura (Bradbury & Vehrencamp 1976a, 1976b).

These relationships point up the probable route by which food dispersion, acting through social dispersion, can indirectly modify such aspects of mating system as number of accessible mates. They presumably explain the apparent monogamy of S. leptura over much of their range. They do not immediately explain the different male strategies in S. bilineata and R. naso which have similar group sizes but different mating systems. To explain these differences we must turn to the direct effects of resource distributions (Bradbury & Vehrencamp 1977).

There are two immediate hypotheses. To be worth establishing a territory, a patch of resources must be available in a given location for a long enough period. Patches of insects used by S. bilineata are available for 5-10 weeks at a time in the same location. By contrast, the swarms of insects used by R. naso for food may move 10-50 m. on successive nights as the subtle sign cues which trigger the aggregations are changed by rising and falling river levels and by amount and angle of moonlight (Downes 1969). We might therefore predict that S. bilineata would be more likely to engage in resource defense than would R. naso. Clearly, this is what occurs.

Alternatively, we might expect female defense to be a viable strategy only when female groups were sufficiently stable in size to justify the costs of defending them. If, as we have postulated, group size is determined by the richness of current food patches, any variations in the richness of successively used patches would decrease the value of female defense. Our estimates indicate that insect prey densities over the river are significantly less variable than are the prey densities over the seasonal vegetation used by *S. bilineata*. This should lead to greater fluctuations in group size with *S. bilineata* than with *R. naso* and bias the latter species more toward female defense. This is again the case. At this point, we cannot distinguish between the duration of patches or the predictability of patches as the critical variable determining the mating systems of these two species. It may be true that both are playing a role. Subsequent field work should clarify these relationships.

Greater Spear-Nosed Bats

A second widespread Neotropical family of bats is the Phyllostomatidae. The third largest member of this family is the greater spear-nosed bat, *Phyllostomos hastatus*. *P. hastatus* is a cave roosting form which lives in colonies of from several hundred to several thousand animals. The bats are omnivorous. On a single night they may feed on large beetles, pollen and ripe fruit. They appear to have few enemies either within or outside of the cave once they are adult, and they can give a field worker a nasty bite.

Each colony of *P. hastatus* is divided up into contact clusters of from 10 to 100 individuals. Most of these clusters consist of adult females, recent young, and one adult male. Other clusters consist of many males and a few juvenile females. The former clusters are clearly harems. Although mating is highly seasonal, each harem male actively defends his roosting females from other adult males throughout the year.

Female compositional stability within harems is high and the same harem male may maintain control of his group for several years. By removing males in both wild and captive colonies, it is possible to demonstrate that males are effectively appendages to a female-based system. That is, female groups are stable regardless of which male defends them and even in the absence of any male. Dr. Gary McCracken, working in Trinidad, has been able to show that once a male does gain control of a female group, he may account for 80-100% of the offspring born into that harem. This system is thus one of female defense as defined above (Bradbury 1977a; McCracken & Bradbury 1977).

In many mammalian species, the central core of the social structure is a matrilineal kin group (Bertram 1976; Sherman 1977). Several of the reasons that have been advanced to explain why female groups should consist of close relatives could easily apply to populations of _P. hastatus_: e.g., chances for cooperative brood care, chances for cooperative suckling, and guaranteed sanctuary for juveniles unable to disperse. Accordingly, McCracken used patterns of enzyme variability (an accepted index of genetic variability), to determine whether females in the same harem showed greater homogeneity for five enzymes than when they were pooled with other harems in the same cave or with other cave populations. The results were unequivocal: even with large sample sizes and two successive years' data, there was no tendency for females in the same harem to be more genetically alike than each was to the population as a whole (McCracken & Bradbury 1977; G. McCracken, personal communication). This result was indeed surprising, given the correlation between degrees of relatedness and the stability of female groups in most other mammals.

McCracken has since attempted to find other correlates of harem membership which could explain the stable female groups. The results are still being analyzed, but a fascinating picture is beginning to emerge from this study. He first looked to see what happened to the female offspring which were _not_ being preferentially recruited into maternal groups. Each year, just prior to parturition, the yearling females which have to date remained in their maternal social clusters, move out to untenanted portions of the cave and form loose aggregations of virgin females or migrate singly to other caves and join aggregations there. By the time parturition has occurred, all yearling females have left the parental harem. At the same time, groups of yearling females have appeared from other caves and attempted to establish residence.

It is clear from the dispersion of marked juveniles that the formation of juvenile groups is accomplished with nearly random mixing of all juveniles from different harems and even from different caves. This explains the lack of genetic homogeneity within harems when compared to the population as a whole. As soon as a juvenile group has established residence in a cave, males begin to fight over them and eventually new harems are generated.

This method of harem formation leads to a great disparity in the age structures of adjacent harems in the same cave. Using five classes of age, based on tooth wear, McCracken has found a highly significant ($p < .005$) heterogeneity in the age distributions of the four study harems in his Lopinot Cave site. This was still the case when the single juvenile harem was deleted from the analysis. The stable female groups in *P. hastatus* are thus age cohorts formed as yearlings and retained, with some replacement of mortalities from the population as a whole, for the rest of their lives.

The problem of why females should form such stable groups still remains. In searching for an answer, McCracken has radio-tracked 37 *P. hastatus* on 188 nightly foraging flights out of the colony at Guanapo Cave. Nine of these were females resident in Harem X, 10 were from Harem C, and six were from Harem D. All nine of the Harem X females, some of them radio-tracked for three successive seasons during the year, always foraged within a common 500 ha. tract of forest north of the cave. All 16 of the females in Harems C and D foraged south of the cave. Because of difficulties in triangulating south of the cave, the degree of foraging overlap between the C and D Harems was not ascertained.

Each female tracked tended to forage on successive nights in her own area within the harem foraging tract. Foraging ranges for two females in the X Harem were 28 and 57 ha. However, on several occasions, females in the same harem converged and foraged in a common location. One female was originally marked in another cave 8 km. away. Several months after establishing residence in the C Harem, she too was foraging in the same tract as her current harem mates.

Females in the same harem do *not* leave the cave as a group; instead, there is a relatively asynchronous departure with at most twos and threes leaving together. The females are often vocal in flight. These vocalizations begin as they leave the cave, may continue when they are foraging singly, and are most pronounced when several bats are feeding at the same site.

We suspect that *P. hastatus* females may have evolved a system of reciprocal altruism involving the sharing of information about foraging sites. Reciprocal altruism, as defined by Trivers (1971), involves the contribution of aid to another at some personal cost to the donor but with the expectation that the roles will be reversed at some future time.

Reciprocal altruism can only evolve if the costs of contributing aid are less than the benefits of being helped devalued by the probability that such aid is forthcoming. Two necessary conditions are thus that groups be stable enough in time for costs to be evenly distributed among group members, and that some mechanisms for identification and expulsion of "cheaters" be developed.

Reciprocal altruism does seem to be a possibility in Phyllostomus hastatus. First, many of their food sources occur in unpredictable patches, and information sharing by following or through advertising vocalizations is certainly feasible. Secondly, the stable age cohorts are exactly what is required to ensure equitable distributions of costs among all group members. Finally, the ability to at least recognize other group members has been demonstrated by marking wild harems, mixing them, and releasing them in new captive enclosures. Such units always segregate out into the original groups if left undisturbed.

In short, the female-defense mating system of P. hastatus arises because of the partitioning of the female population into stable groups. These groups are not matrilineal kin, as in most mammals, but age cohorts of unrelated animals formed at dispersal. The correlation between harem membership and contiguity of foraging area suggests that the advantages of stable groups are related to behavior on the foraging grounds. Since the bats neither group forage nor defend foraging territories, we suspect that this advantage is reciprocal sharing of information about better feeding sites among group members. Again, we have returned to an indirect determination of the mating system as a result of resource patterning.

Epomophorine Bats and Lek Behaviors

I would now like to turn to some bat species in which neither females nor resources are defended by males, but instead males form leks for mating. All are members of the African subfamily Epomophorinae. In most groups of animals in which leks have been described, there are related species which exhibit a more loose clustering of males on larger territories (called "exploded leks"), and even some with resource defense (Gilliard 1969; Hjorth 1970). As I shall show below, this is also true of epomophorine bats.

One mechanism which has been advanced to explain a shift from resource defense to exploded leks, or from exploded leks to "classical" leks, is an increase in population density (Emlen & Oring 1977; Snow 1973). At low male population densities, we expect male territories to be large and thus to contain substantial resources, and we expect female choice of mates to rely heavily on the quality of a male's territory. As male density increases, each male will have a smaller territory, control fewer resources, and female choice may include both the characteristics of a given territory and phenotypic characters of the males themselves. As male characteristics become more important, males should evolve various signals to advertise these traits. At high enough densities, males can control so few resources individually that they abandon resource defense entirely and rely on "self-advertisement." Thus classical leks are established in sites which include no substantial resources required by females. Given this density hypothesis, we might expect "exploded leks" to show a range of emphases on self-advertisement relative to the amount of resources contained in a male's territory. Specifically, as density increases, the amount of resources should decrease and the emphasis on self-advertisement should increase.

We have attempted to test these predictions by monitoring two sympatric species of epomophorine bats. The hammer-headed bat, _Hypsignathus monstrosus_, shows classical lek behavior (Bradbury 1977b). Twice each year, during the two dry seasons, 30-135 males of this species aggregate at traditional sites and spend the first three to four hours of each night calling. Each male has a calling territory about 10 m. in diameter to which it returns night after night. Females visit these sites singly, hover before a series of males, and eventually select one for mating. Extensive mapping of the preferred fruit trees of these bats and their diurnal sleeping sites have shown that there are no resources within the aggregation area required by females. The latter visit the displaying aggregations solely for mating.

During the day, many of the bats of both sexes roost solitarily in the forest canopy. A few roost in small groups, but these are unstable in composition, and there are no interactions between group members during the day. Males thus do not defend females at day roosts. In short, male _Hypsignathus_ defend neither females nor resources, but instead rely on self-advertisement at lek aggregation sites.

A second species, the epauletted bat, _Epomops franqueti_, has a more exploded lek system. Again, males aggregate on display territories during the two dry seasons and return to the same sites night after night. However, the display territories of male _Epomops_ are 100 times larger than those of sympatric _Hypsignathus_.

As with the latter species, we have been able to identify and map the main food plants for _Epomops_. To our surprise, these large territories are never placed over either food or roosting sites for Epomops females. Instead, these bats have already shifted completely to self-advertisement as a mating strategy. It also appears that in certain grouse and bird-of-paradise species, although male territories are large enough to contain significant resources, males again do not attempt to defend resources. As with Epomops, a shift to self-advertisement has occurred long before territorial compression models would predict (Gullion 1967; Schodde & McKean 1973). The fact that in a number of exploded lek species, male territories are large but contain no resource, suggests that the density hypothesis of lek evolution has little generality.

This finding led us, during a recent study in Gabon, to turn to size of female home range as a critical intervening variable between resource dispersion and mating system. Consider a uniform field of resource-defending males on contiguous territories. Suppose the diet of the females is modified by selection to favor larger and more overlapping home ranges. This could arise if the patches of food were harder to find, could not be used at one time due to allelochemicals, or varied sufficiently in quality so that what was suitable for one animal was not suitable for another.

It should be obvious that as female home ranges increase, holding density constant, each territorial male encounters more females but each female remains within a given territory for a shorter time. This may not change the access of the average male to females, but it dramatically changes the options open to females. Specifically, the greater numbers of males encountered by each female, and the fact that each male has less "leverage" over a female, are exactly the conditions which are most likely to lead to mate choice by phenotypic cues and to intense sexual selection (Fisher 1958). This model therefore allows males to shift completely to self-advertisement even when male territory sizes are still large enough to contain significant resources. It should be noted that either an increase in density or an increase in female home range can produce this shift. However, it is the latter possibility which best explains the systems we have studied.

We have attempted to explore the effects of female home-range size further by asking which parameters determine the final dispersion of displaying males. We have developed a simple model which assumes that lek size and dispersion are dynamic variables (Bradbury 1979). In particular, the model predicts that a) clusters of displaying males (leks) should be no closer together in space than the diameter of one female home range, and b) that male territory size should be inversely related to female home-range size.

To date, the predictions of this model appear to be supported by the available data. In terms of the epomophorine bats, we have discovered substantial differences in sizes of the home ranges of female *Hypsignathus* and female *Epomops*. The average home range for *Hypsignathus* over a 30-day period is 10^4 ha., or a range with a diameter of about 12 km. Equivalent values for *Epomops* females are 10^2 ha. or a diameter of about 1.4 km.

This 100-fold difference in home-range size of females is easily related to differences in the foraging of the two species. The diets of the two species are remarkably analogous. Each consists of a "staple" component (*Anthocleista spp.* for *Hypsignathus* and *Solanum torvum* for *Epomops*) which occurs in conspicuous patches of plants which bear fruit at all times of year. However, little fruit is ripe at any one time, and a typical female will visit one plant after another in a patch, often returning to the first plants as she feeds on the ripest fruit first. Clearly this type of behavior leads to large and overlapping home ranges since fruit rejected as not ripe enough by one female may be suitable for another.

Each diet also contains opportunistic components which are primarily fruit of species of the genus *Ficus* for both species. Nearly all *Ficus* in Gabon are strangler figs with small-crop biomasses. They are hard to find (as shown by radio-tracking females in areas where all known fruiting trees were mapped), and they are available for only 6-10 days. Again this leads to large and overlapping foraging ranges. The differences between the home ranges of the two species can be attributed to:

1. The smaller body size of *Epomops*, which, all other things being equal, should lead to smaller home ranges as found.

2. Higher local densities of the staple component of *Epomops* when compared to that of *Hypsignathus* which should lead to smaller home ranges in *Epomops*.

3. Greater use of the more widely dispersed opportunistic component in *Hypsignathus* (36% of the total diet vs. only 21% in *Epomops*) thereby leading to larger home ranges in *Hypsignathus*.

4. Greater range of additional opportunistic components in the diet of *Epomops* (43% of diet as opposed to only

12% in *Hypsignathus*), thus leading to smaller home ranges in *Epomops*.

Given these differences in female home range size of 100 times, we would predict with our model that male territories should be 100 times smaller in *Hypsignathus* than in *Epomops*, and that the distances between leks should be equal to the diameters of each female home range size. The average distance between 10 leks of *Hypsignathus* in Gabon was 14 km. (range 5-18 km.) which is reasonably close to our estimate of female home range diameter of 12 km. Gaps between clusters of calling male *Epomops* in Gabon range from 1-4 km which is in reasonable agreement with the predicted value of 1.4 km. Male territory size in *Hypsignathus* is about .008 ha., while that in *Epomops* is about 0.8 ha. Again the predictions are reasonably well met.

Closing Comments

It would be unreasonable (indeed, wrong) to conclude from our studies on bats that food dispersion is the *only* variable affecting mating system structure. In fact, we have to some degree selected species in which pilot studies showed a low level of predation pressure either at the roosts or on the foraging grounds. On the other hand, it has been surprising to us how far we have been able to relate food dispersion to mating systems given the diversity of bats studied. It *is* clear that one must look both at the direct effects of resources on mating strategies and at the indirect effects working through social dispersion. In spite of those complexities, I am optimistic that we shall eventually arrive at a relatively simple set of rules for the evolution of mating systems. We are currently at the point where field studies can discriminate between alternative hypotheses for the same social system, reject the poorer fits, and refine the better ones. In the case of the bats, there are still over 800 species to choose from, and we expect to keep busy for some time.

Summary

Resource distributions appear to be an important determinant of animal mating systems. This determination can be effected directly by limiting the time and energy options available to either sex, or indirectly by modulating the size, stability, and home ranges of groups and thus setting constraints on the mating strategies available. Examples of the relations between resource distribution and mating systems are given using three families of tropical bats.

The emballonurid bats show a good correlation between

the patterns of group size, group stability, and group home ranges on the one hand and the size, distribution, and predictability of seasonally varying patches of food on the other. Differences in mating strategies between species are clearly related to both the direct and indirect constraints imposed by these food distributions.

The greater spear-nosed bat (family Phyllostomatidae) has stable harems as its basic social unit. The harems are generated by the females themselves which form age cohorts of unrelated individuals after leaving their parental harems at 10-11 months of age. Available data suggest that these groups are highly stable in composition throughout the lives of the animals. Again, the social structure appears to be related to foraging in that females which roost together as a harem during the day have adjacent foraging territories at night. While we have not yet identified the adaptive reason for this correlation, we suspect that it involves sharing of unpredictable and locally rich food resources within the harem foraging areas when they appear.

Finally, epomophorine bats are introduced because of their use of "lek" (male communal display) mating behaviors. A correlation is noted between the sizes of female foraging ranges in these bats and the dispersion of displaying males in related species. The model has yet to be tested on other taxa, but appears to have internal consistency in specifying the conditions that might lead animals to evolve leks instead of alternative mating systems and in predicting the actual dispersion of males in a particular species.

Acknowledgements

In addition to the author, this work represents the combined efforts of Sandra Vehrencamp, Louise Emmons, Bernice Tannenbaum, Douglas Morrison, William Lopez-Forment, Kurt Fristrup, Amasa Miller, Gary McCracken, and Ivan Lieberburg. The work reported here was supported by the Bache Fund of the National Academy of Sciences and NSF grants GB-30478 and BNS 76-04400 to the author. The American Association for the Advancement of Science helped make possible my participation in the symposium "Sociobiology: Beyond Nature/Nurture" where the materials of this paper were first presented.

Literature Cited

Bertram, B.C.R. 1976. Kin selection in lions and in evolution. In P.P.G. Bateson & R.A. Hinde (eds.), Growing points in ethology. Cambridge University Press, Cambridge, pp. 281-301.

Bradbury, J.W. 1977a. Social organization and communication. In W. Wimsatt (ed.), Biology of bats. Academic Press, New York, 3:1-72.

_______. 1977b. Lek mating behavior in the hammer-headed bat. Zeitschrift für Tierpsychologie 5:225-255.

_______. 1979. The evolution of leks. In R.D. Alexander & D. Tinkle (eds.), Natural selection and social behavior. Chiron Press, New York (in press).

_______ & L. Emmons. 1974. Social organization of some Trinidad bats. I. Emballonuridae. Zeitschrift für Tierpsychologie 36:137-183.

_______ & S.L. Vehrencamp. 1976a. Social organization and foraging in emballonurid bats. I. Field studies. Behavioral Ecology and Sociobiology 1:337-381.

_______. 1976b. Social organization and foraging in emballonurid bats. II. A model for the determination of group size. Behavioral Ecology and Sociobiology 1:383-404.

_______. 1977. Social organization and foraging in emballonurid bats. III. Mating systems. Behavioral Ecology and Sociobiology 2:1-17.

Carpenter, F.L. & R.E. MacMillen. 1976. Threshold model of feeding territoriality and test with a Hawaiian honeycreeper. Science 194:639-642.

Cronin, W.E. & P.W. Sherman. 1976. A resource-based mating system: The orange-rumped honeyguide. The Living Bird 15:5-32.

Crook, J.H. 1964. The evolution of social organization and visual communication in the weaver birds (Ploceinae). Behaviour Supplement 10:1-178.

Denham, W.W. 1971. Energy relations and some basic properties of primate social organization. American Anthropologist 73:77-95.

Downes, J.A. 1969. The swarming and mating flight of Diptera. Annual Review of Entomology 14:271-298.

Emlen, S.T. 1976. Lek organization and mating strategies in the bullfrog. Behavioral Ecology and Sociobiology 1:283-313.

_______ & L.W. Oring. 1977. Ecology, sexual selection, and the evolution of mating systems. Science 197:215-223.

Fisher, R.A. 1958. The genetical theory of natural selection, 2nd Edition. Dover Publications, New York.

Geist, V. 1977. A comparison of social adaptations in relation to ecology in gallinaceous bird and ungulate societies. Annual Review of Ecology and Systematics 8:193-207.

Gill, F.B. & L.L. Wolf. 1975. Economics of feeding territoriality in the golden-winged sunbird. Ecology 56:333-345.

Gilliard, E.T. 1969. Birds of paradise and bower birds. Weidenfeld & Nicolson, London.

Guillion, G.W. 1967. Selection and use of drumming sites by male ruffed grouse. Auk 84:87-112.

Hjorth, I. 1970. Reproductive behavior in Tetraonidae. Viltrevy 7:183-596.

Jarman, P.J. 1974. The social organization of antelope in relation to their ecology. Behavior 48:215-267.

McCracken, G.J. & J.W. Bradbury. 1977. Paternity and genetic heterogeneity in the polygynous bat, Phyllostomus hastatus. Science 198:303-306.

Montfort-Braham, N. 1975. Variations dans la structure sociale du topi, Damaliscus korrigum Ogilby, au Parc National de l'Akagera, Rwanda. Zeitschrift für Tierpsychologie 39:332-364.

Morrison, D.W. 1975. Foraging behavior and feeding ecology of a neotropical bat, Artibeus jamaicensis. Ph.D. Thesis, Cornell University, Ithaca, New York.

Schodde, R. & J.L. McKean. 1973. The species of the genus Parotia (Paradiseidae) and their relationships. Emu 73:145-156.

Sherman, P.W. 1977. Nepotism and the evolution of alarm calls. Science 197:1246-1253.

Snow, B.K. 1973. The behavior and ecology of hermit hummingbirds in the Kanuku Mountains, Guyana. Wilson Bulletin 85:163-177.

Tannenbaum, B. 1975. Reproductive strategies in the white-lined bat. Ph.D. Thesis, Cornell University, Ithaca, New York.

Trivers, R.L. 1971. The evolution of reciprocal altruism. Quarterly Review of Biology 46:35-57.

Wilson, E.O. 1975. Sociobiology: The new synthesis. Belknap Press, Cambridge, Mass.

David P. Barash

8. Predictive Sociobiology: Mate Selection in Damselfishes and Brood Defense in White-Crowned Sparrows

Ethologists have recently emphasized that the old instinct-learning, nature-nurture controversy is finally dead and buried. A rapprochment has been achieved between ethology and comparative psychology--a new synthesis, in fact, that was impressively displayed in two massive books by Robert Hinde, first in 1966 and then even more convincingly in 1970.

The title of this symposium: Sociobiology: beyond nature/nurture, suggests that the organizers' intent is to emphasize that sociobiology must follow this road and avoid that old dichotomous quagmire, thereby--we all hope--avoiding much argument at the same time. This is all well and good, and I daresay it probably *is* the organizers' intent, and as such I have no real quarrel with it. However, I would like to suggest a different interpretation: the opportunity that I see provided in sociobiology is not simply that it reflects a synthesis of internal and external factors in influencing the behavior of living things--after all, that is really a rather old synthesis by this time--but rather that it enables us to go beyond the old synthesis itself. In going "beyond nature/nurture," sociobiology shows us not only how to go beyond that old and troublesome dichotomy, but also beyond that rather tired synthesis as well. As far as I can see, the much ballyhooed recognition that behavior derives from an interaction between internal and external factors was appropriate and indeed, long overdue. Certainly, it was not wrong. Rather, it was not very interesting.

We learned that since behavior is caused in all cases by an interaction between organisms and their environments, it is most appropriate to ask ontogenetic questions--that is, how does the behavior in question develop over time, via these great and universal combined forces: genotype and experience (e.g., Aronson et al. 1970). This is fine;

indeed, it may be the only viable way to study the pecking response of gulls, migratory orientation or even the establishment of social hierarchies. However, this synthesis lacked a wider view--it was almost totally immersed in the trees and treatened to keep us there, without vision of the forest. It was empirically correct but conceptually claustrophobic and philosophically tedious.

The real promise of sociobiology then, as I see it, is that it truly does offer the opportunity of moving beyond nature/nurture--that is, beyond the narrowly-defined analysis of how a behavior develops. This is not to say that carefully fashioned empirical research is not important to sociobiology. Indeed, it is the cornerstone of all science. Rather, sociobiology enables us to raise our heads--albeit perhaps only occasionally--above the detail of behaviors deriving from the interaction of organism and environment, to ask a bigger question, namely: Why? And sociobiology permits us to ask that question intelligently because it suggests a plausible theory with which to operate: insofar as the behavior in question reflects some component of genotype, we can expect that behavior to maximize the inclusive fitness of the individual. In this way we can go beyond the accurate but rather uninspiring recognition of nature/nurture interactions to deal with the question: why do nature and nurture interact the way they do?

I think it is important at this point that we distinguish between scientific models and theories, and I would like to show how both relate to sociobiology. As I see it, a model is a scientific construct, intended to represent reality in some manner. It may be physical or purely conceptual but in any event it is essentially a metaphor, a representation, and its hope is to aid us in understanding reality. And this is where theory comes in. It is all too easy to get lost in the beauty of our model until, as some model builders are inclined to do, we lose track of what we are doing, and why.

Theory, then, is the idea that our model relates in a particular way to part of what we hopefully call the "real world." For example, in the early nineteen fifties, Linus Pauling was working on a model of nucleic acids that depicted them as a triple helix--his theory was that this was the way genetic substance was put together. Had his triple helix model and theory been correct, he probably would have been our only triple Nobel Prize winner. But it was not; the Watson-Crick double-helix model came closer to reality, as we all know today.

There are two models, each with its associated theory, that are especially relevant to sociobiology. The first was initially identified clearly by Darwin, inspired by his reading of Malthus, and is the model of natural selection--differential reproduction plus hereditary variation, in a situation of interindividual competition, produce evolutionary change. Darwin's theory was that this model applied to and explained the evolution and adaptation of all living things. That theory has turned out to be correct. As George Gaylord Simpson (1949) first pointed out, there are theories of evolution and there is the theory of evolution: although biologists may argue about the fine points of mechanism, the general theory is as secure as atomic theory or the theory of relativity. In fact, it is the closest thing that we have to a single concept unifying the biological sciences.

The second model is less easily associated with a particular individual, and yet is is no less important than the first. It derives in large part from developmental genetics, applied initially to embryogenesis: it states that phenotypes--all phenotypes--derive from an interaction between the organism's genotype and its environment. The theory, recently espoused by students of animals and perhaps to a lesser extent, humans, is that this model applies to behavior as well (Ehrman and Parsons 1976).

Now, enter sociobiology. Its novelty and its promise is that it provides a new, synthetic theory and, let me emphasize, one that is testable as well. Essentially, the theory is that the two models described above, relate to each other. In other words, the process of natural selection (model one) applies to behavior (model two). Elsewhere (Barash 1977), I have referred to the consequence of this as the Central Theorem of Sociobiology: insofar as a behavior in question represents at least some component of the individual's genotype, then that behavior should act to maximize the inclusive fitness of the individual concerned. Note that this new theory differs in an important way from ethology. Although ethology anticipated sociobiology in recognizing that evolution applies to behavior, it was essentially static and, occasionally, historical in its approach. Accordingly, sociobiology's roots in ethology come much more from the tradition of Tinbergen, who concerned himself with the adaptive significance of behavior, than from Lorenz, for example, who was primarily concerned with the construction of behavioral phylogenies and motivational models for specific behaviors.

Now, although the Central Theorem is testable, the

actual testing is not easy. There are numerous difficulties. Not the least of these involves the concept of inclusive fitness, which may be defined as the sum of individual fitness (reproductive success) and the reproductive success of an individual's relatives, with each relative devalued in proportion as it is more distantly related (Hamilton 1964; West-Eberhard 1975). A major difficulty is the practical one of actually measuring inclusive fitness; indeed, I know of few studies that have even measured individual fitness (e.g., Tinkle 1967).

In most cases, we must be content for now with measures that we intuit as being related to fitness (inclusive or individual)--such as, efficiency in foraging, avoiding predators, success in acquiring a mate, or, often, simple copulation frequencies. Furthermore, it is not even clear at what point we should measure fitness: offspring born (or hatched), the number successfully dispersed (or fledged), or the number surviving to reproductive age themselves, or successfully breeding, or perhaps the success of their offspring in producing offspring in turn, or their's after that, and so on.

Finally, as difficult as it is to conduct field studies in sociobiology, it is even more difficult to do field work in behavior genetics. Yet, the Central Theorem that I stated began with the caveat "insofar as a behavior in question represents some component of genotype." Of course, to some extent this issue was answered by the resolution of the nature/nurture dichotomy. If indeed all behavior derives from both genotype and environment, then we can safely go on our sociobiological way, confident that evolution has relevance to behavior--all behavior.

However, many students of behavior are likely to balk at the notion of any genetic influence on certain complex social behaviors, especially for certain species. And, indeed, there are few empirical data, either supporting or refuting this idea at present.

For sociobiologists, then, I suggest that one useful way to proceed is to employ the Central Theorem in a predictive mode--after all, many claim that prediction, made before the facts are in, is an important test of science. In sociobiology, as in other science, it is all too easy to fall prey to post hoc explanations, after which the data and interpretations are then turned around and used as support for the legitimacy of the paradigm in the first place. Anything can be made to seem adaptive, if we are ingenious enough. One possible approach then is to use the

Central Theorem to predict the behavior of animals, ideally in a free-living state. Insofar as these predictions are verified and alternative interpretations can be ruled out, such research supports the appropriateness of sociobiology's paradigm. What is more important, it provides us with enormous and, until recently, unavailable intellectual leverage for understanding the behavior of living things.

Two Predictions and Their Tests

Having completed this rather hurried excursion into sociobiologic empistemology, I would like now to consider briefly two field studies that I have recently conducted. Both use sociobiology's Central Theorem in a predictive manner, focusing on considerations of individual Darwinian fitness.

Mate Selection Among Damselfishes

Gordon Orians (1969) among others, has pointed out that when it comes to choosing a mate, we can expect females in particular to be influenced by evolutionary considerations, such that they select males who contribute maximally to their reproductive success. The Pomacentrids, or damselfishes, provide some especially good test cases. This is a family of coral-reef inhabitants in which males typically establish, prepare and defend a territory on the reef floor. They court females, one of whom spawns with each. The female typically then leaves, and the male alone has sole responsibility for parental care.

The paternal activities of the male are largely two-fold: for one, he tends the eggs, probably removing any that have been infected by fungus. Most important, however, he defends the eggs against predators. Coral reefs teem with an incredible number of fishes, many of which will eagerly eat damselfish eggs. I experimentally removed three males, each of which was tending a clutch of eggs: predators began eating the undefended eggs with a latency of 17, 44 and 49 seconds. It therefore seems reasonable to conclude that predators are a major source of mortality for damselfish eggs. Accordingly, paternal damselfish are constantly vigilant, defending their territories against intruders. They do this by making quick, darting, aggressive forays against other fishes that come too close, occasionally as often as several times per minute. Intruders generally depart after a single foray by a defending male.

What sort of male will a female damselfish choose?

Table 1. <u>Observation Regime and Raw Data</u>

	Observation hours		Observation hours	Number of intrusions	Number of male responses	Number of male "no responses"
No eggs in nest	61.2	Females within 2 m.	5.1	311	282	29
		No Females within 2 m.	56.1	3297	2014	1283
Eggs in nest	30.1	Females within 2 m.	1.9	153	143	10
		No Females within 2 m.	28.2	2023	1814	209

From the female's viewpoint, we can predict that an appropriate mate with whom to entrust her precious store of eggs is one that will contribute maximally to the eventual success of those eggs--and hence, to the fitness of the female making the choice. In view of the obvious importance of egg-predation to most damselfishes, I predicted that females would spawn preferentially with males that were highly aggressive in defense of their territories. Furthermore, if vigorously defending males enjoy a reproductive advantage over their more lethargic counterparts, then males might be selected to put on a "show" for the females. In other words, they should predictably be more vigorous in defending their territories when females are watching than when they aren't.

The subjects were damselfishes of the species Dascyllus albisella, a common species endemic to Hawaii. My observations were made at a coral reef off the southeast coast of the Island of Maui, an area known as Kihei. All observations were made while scuba-diving, at depths of eight to ten meters. I made the observations between April 1 and July 1, 1977, based on 91 hours of underwater observation, with a total of 27 territorial males of which at least 13 were different individuals.

After locating a male damselfish that had cleared the sediment from the center of his territory, thereby indicating that he was ready to court females, I established a circle with a radius of 1.5 meters from the center of the male's territory. I then recorded any intrusions by another fish into the cylinder of water with radius 1.5 meters, height two meters (the observational cylinder, OC), as well as whether these intrusions elicited a defensive charge by the resident male, so that males could be scored for the frequency of responses per intrusion.

Females and nonbreeding males of this species typically swim in relatively compact schools, feeding off suspended particles. When such a school passes over a territorial male, he may begin courting, after which a female may or may not detach herself from the school and spawn with the male on his territory. Thus, it is possible to divide observations of the defensive charges by territorial males into two categories: those occurring when a school is within the OC (I arbitrarily define this as "females are watching"), and those when there is no school present ("females not watching").

The observation regime and raw data are presented in Table 1; the results are shown in Figure 1. When not

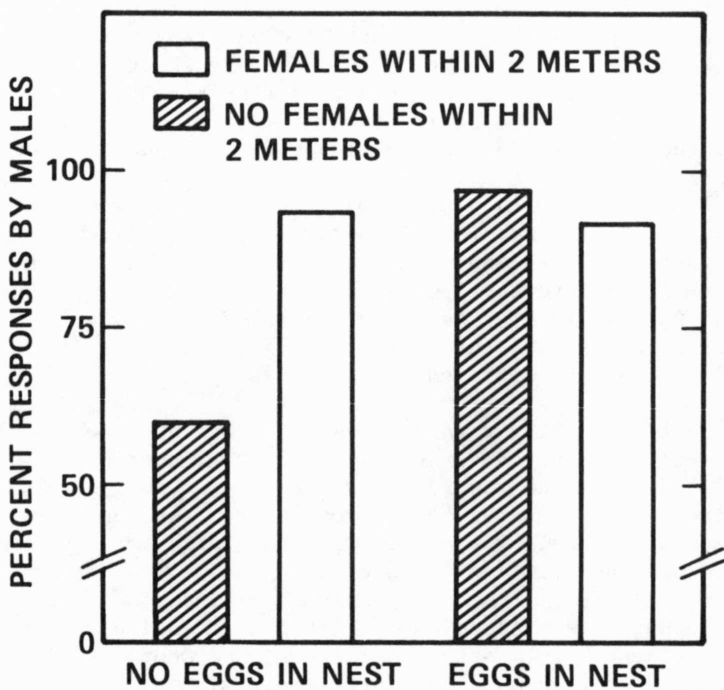

Figure 1. Percent responses of territorial males to intruders as a function of whether or not females are within a two-meter cylinder of the male's territory, both before and after eggs have been deposited in the territory.

maintaining eggs, males are significantly more likely to respond with defensive charges to the intrusion of other fish when a school of damselfishes is within the OC than when there is no such school (x^2 = 106, corrected for continuity, α = .01, P < .01 one-tailed test). I might add that there is no significant differences in intrusion rates when a school is or is not within the OC, although there is a slight tendency for more intrusions during the former situation. In addition, when a school is within the OC, males often initiate courtship--hence, their time is likely to be occupied a great deal, thereby making this higher rate of defensive charges toward intruders all the more striking.

If, as I assume, increased male response to intruders as a function of female observers is itself adaptive as a means of increasing the males' attractiveness to females, then the presence or absence of females should have less influence on response rate once the male is already guarding eggs. To the extent that male response to intruders is an evolved strategy serving to impress females, rather than simply to defend his territory, this strategy should disappear, or at least it should be greatly reduced, once the males have already attained their end. This is also apparent from Figure 1. There is no significant difference between male response rates in the presence and absence of females, once the males are already guarding eggs (x^2 = 1.86 corrected for continuity, one-tailed test).

This study assumed not only that males will vary their behavior as a function of presence or absence of females, but also that the inclination of females to spawn with different males will vary, as a function of the response rate of males to intruders. Here my sample is unfortunately rather small, as I only observed 13 cases of females actually spawning. However, a strong trend is nonetheless apparent, and it favors the sociobiologic prediction: if we divide males into two categories, "high responders" versus "low responders," with high responders being males that respond to more than 75% of intrusions when females are watching, and low responders being males that respond to less than 75% of intrusions under the same circumstances, ten of 13 cases of spawning I observed were with high responder males and only three with low responders.

I also predicted that territorial males would respond more to intruders that are potential egg-predators than to nonegg-predators. I am currently attempting to classify Hawaiian coral reef inhabitants in this manner. But once again, at a superficial level at least, the data support the prediction: for example, squirrel-fishes (Holocentridae) and tangs (Acanthuridae) do not eat eggs, and their intrusions did not elicit response by territorial males, whereas wrasses (Labridae), angelfishes (Pomocanthidae) and other damselfishes do eat eggs, and were charged vigorously.

In studies of this sort one must also consider alternative interpretations of the data. At this preliminary stage, they are not all easy to rule out. Thus, male damselfishes mght be defending their territories against food competitors--although this does not explain defense against wrasses for example, which eat eggs and do not compete with damselfishes for food. On the other hand, perhaps males are responding to the presence of females by simply developing a higher level of behavioral activation, one result of which is greater responsiveness to intruders. This might approximate a possible interpretation from classical ethology, wherein "action specific energy," has been released in the resident males, perhaps because of frustration from a lack of female responsiveness. This "energy" is discharged via attacks on intruders. The weaknesses of this approach are already apparent to most ethologists today. Furthermore, such concerns are orthogonal to sociobiology--they represent another level of interpretation; namely, proximal (or immediate) rather than distal (or evolutionary). From a sociobiologic perspective, the question remains: what is the adaptive significance of such behavior, regardless of its proximal (immediate) causes?

There are, however, other possibilities, that are more difficult to rule out at present: perhaps males step up their responses to intruders because females are simply "turned off" by the presence of potential egg-predators near the nest, and/or perhaps such intruders must be kept at an especially far distance in order for spawning to be successful. These issues can be addressed, but it will take a good deal of ingenuity, time, and effort.

One of the real strengths of sociobiology, as I see it, is that it enables us to ask an enormous number of novel questions--that is, it is a great deal of fun. Let me conclude this brief case study with some of the more intriguing questions that it raises. For one, if females prefer aggressive males, what prevents all males from evolving into super-defenders? That is, what sets an upper limit to their responsiveness to intruders? One possibility is that the eggs of hyper-responders might suffer from "aggressive neglect" (Ripley 1961); males who are too responsive to intruders may spend too much time chasing one intruder, while another eats the eggs. Accordingly, females may actually discriminate against such hyper-responders. In fact, there may be a more immediate mechanism for this discrimination, since a male who responds excessively to intruders while females are watching may literally have insufficient time to court successfully. And selection would operate against those who would rather fight than mate.

This mate-selection system also provides interesting opportunities for evolutionary strategies of deceit by males. That is, what is to stop a male from defending his nest vigorously when females are watching but more lethargically once he has obtained her eggs? In general, individuals who scored high in the absence of females also scored high when females were present, but in at least one case, a discrepancy appeared--one of the males who scored highest when females were watching scored low when they weren't. Of course, a possible female counter-strategy is to watch males at a greater distance--that is, when they don't think they are being watched. Females might also simply devalue a certain amount of the behavior of all males, as mere bravado put on for the benefit of the ladies. However, this would penalize the "honest" males as well as the "dishonest," and would therefore have the intriguing consequence of selecting for dishonesty in all males.

Brood Defense Among White-Crowned Sparrows

My other example is from a brief, preliminary study of nest defense by white-crowned sparrows, *Zonotrichia leucophrys*. This species is represented in the State of Washington by two subspecies. *Z. l. gambelli* is at its southern limit in the North Cascades. It breeds north into the Yukon and Alaska and is adapted to short breeding seasons, producing only one clutch per year. It does not renest if that clutch is destroyed. By contrast, the other subspecies, *Z. l. pugetensis*, is at its northern limit in the Seattle area; it breeds south into Oregon and northern California. It produces at least two and sometimes three clutches per year and will re-nest.

Given that *gambelli* has "all its eggs in one basket," I predicted that it would demonstrate greater vigor in defense of its nest than would *pugetensis*, which could lose a clutch and still have an opportunity to reproduce that same year. To test this, I attached a clothesline pulley one meter from nests of both subspecies, and affixed a plastic model of a great horned own to the cord going through the pulley. I then slowly advanced the owl model toward the

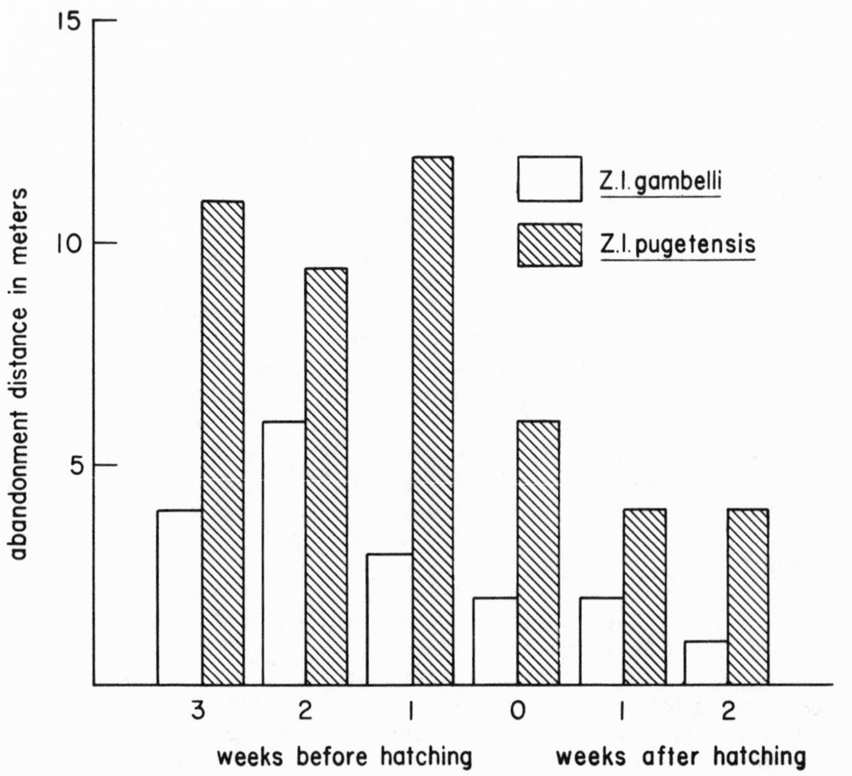

Figure 2. Abandonment distance (see text) of Z. l. gambelli and Z. l. pugetensis as a function of stage of the nesting cycle.

nests, stopping for two minutes each 15, ten, five and one-meter distance.

I arbitrarily defined the "abandonment distance" for the two subspecies as the distance of the owl from the nest at which both parents went more than five meters away from the owl and the nest, and stayed away for at least ten minutes (Fig. 2). The *pugetensis* parents consistently showed a greater abandonment distance than did the *gambelli*--in other words, they left the nest sooner, and with much less "fight," defined as the time, out of two minutes, spent by either parent within two meters of the owl dummy when it was five meters from the nest (Fig. 3). Much of this time was spent swooping and diving at the owl. Again, *gambelli* parents were substantially more active in defending their nests than were *pugetensis* parents. The owl dummy was actually struck by a defending white-crown on seven occasions; in all seven it was a *gambelli* who did it.

Both figures also reveal an interesting trend which supports another prediction which I had evaluated several years ago in a study of another small bird, the alpine accentor (Barash 1975). This prediction states that parents should defend their young more strongly in proportion as the young get older but are not yet capable of independence, insofar as the chances of replacing them decline as the breeding season progresses. This trend should be especially prominent in species adapted to short breeding seasons, such as alpine accentors or *gambelli* white-crowns vis-a-vis *pugetensis*.

As with the damselfish project, this also is a preliminary study, and one that isn't altogether "clean," in that alternative interpretations cannot be ruled out so far. For example, it is possible that great horned owls are not equally appropriate predators for both the alpine environment of *gambelli* and the lowland environment of *pugetensis*. I was also unable to gather data on mobbing by individuals other than the parents. Quite a bit of mobbing took place, however, and although my impression is that the two areas did not differ appreciably, I may be wrong. Furthermore, and most seriously, the sample size is small--at this time, only three *gambelli* nests and five *pugetensis*, thereby precluding statistical analysis. Nonetheless, I believe the trends are real, and the approach is certainly worth pursuing. Indeed, it suggests the rudiments of a general theory relating parental defense to multiple brooding, such that single-brooded species might be expected to show more defense against predators than multi-brooded species.

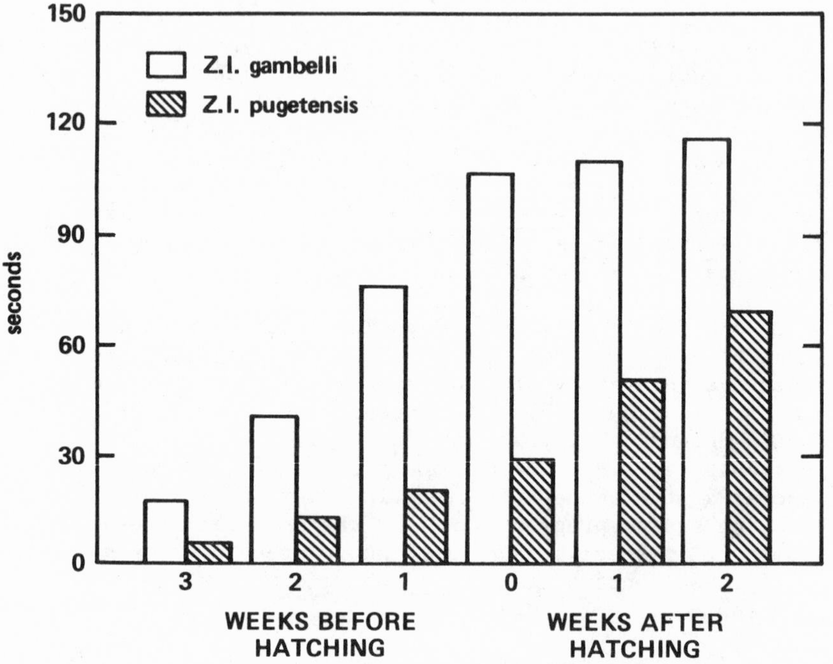

Figure 3. The number of seconds (out of two minutes) spent by Z. l. gambelli and Z. l. pugetensis parents within two meters of the owl model when it was five meters from the nest.

In conclusion, none of these studies can be said either to prove or refute the underlying paradigm of sociobiology: that evolution has something useful to say about behavior. Specifically, neither one proves or refutes what I have called the Central Theorem of Sociobiology. Indeed, it may be that fitness maximization cannot truly be "proved," in which case perhaps "Central Postulate of Sociobiology" would be preferable terminology. But similarly, as far as I know, there are no studies that have "proven" the law of gravity; we simply accumulate an increasing number of studies that either increase or decrease our confidence in the approach. In fact, some deviations from fitness maximization may be anticipated, since Fisher's Central Theorem of Natural Selection (Fisher 1958) is not absolutely valid. Population geneticists recognize that mutational equilibrium will cause persistent deviations from "true" optimality, a situation which is further exacerbated by difficulties in multi-locus models (e.g., Karlin 1975), linkage disequilibrium, etc. The degree and even the direction of these expected deviations are unknown at present, although they are anticipated to be small. As a consequence, sociobiology indicates a suggested trajectory toward which we can expect behavioral systems to move. It may not describe exactly what happens, but it provides a very useful approximation.

I am not interested in proving or disproving sociobiology--whatever proof means in this context--but rather, in using its insights insofar as they allow me to ask and answer interesting questions about behavior. In this respect, it seems that we have more and more reason to take heed of sociobiology and of the value in creatively uniting the models of natural selection and of nature/nurture interaction. Furthermore, thus far I have not treated the application of predictive sociobiology to human behavior, an obviously controversial area and one that is considered from diverse perspectives in this volume, as well as in a separate treatment of my own (Barash 1978). It seems clear that we are animals but also very special animals. It also seems clear that human behavior, like that of all animals, derives from the interaction of genotype and environment, although I freely grant that human behavior is almost certainly less influenced by the former than is the behavior of any other species. Furthermore, it seems likely that human behavior is more influenced by learning than by relatively automatic, "instinctive" behavior. (It also warrents emphasizing, however, that whereas both avowed opponents and most proponents of sociobiology give lip service to both those notions, there are no clear data supporting them.) In any event, the application of predictive sociobiology to human behavior appears to me a logical next step, and one that can be carried out with an open, scientific attitude.

No claim need be made that sociobiology will provide "the" answer to human behavior--there is probably no single answer in any event. To quote Gertrude Stein: "What is the question?" Rather than worry about absolutism, it seems reasonable to inquire "How much intellectual leverage does sociobiology provide in any attempted understanding of the human condition?" Certainly, not even the most incurable Pollyanna would claim that social science, as currently practiced, has "understood" human behavior. Therefore, the prospects, although uncertain, appear good enough to warrant further effort, much of which will doubtless focus on predictions relative to fitness maximization. Indeed, the excitement and the promise, and even, perhaps, the controversy that we now see, provide at least for me much of the real reason for doing science in the first place.

Summary

The application of evolutionary biology to social behavior (i.e., sociobiology) provides a new general theory: organisms can be expected to behave so as to maximize their inclusive fitness. This permits a predictive approach to the study of behavior, exemplified here by two studies--mate selection in Hawaiian damselfishes and brood defense in white-crowned sparrows. The first case reveals a complex of adaptations concerning female choice of males who appear to be successful defenders of eggs, whereas the second involved predicted differences between two subspecies, as a function of the probability of renesting.

Acknowledgements

This manuscript was written while I was a Fellow at the Center for Advanced Study in the Behavioral Sciences, Stanford, California. I also thank the psychology department of the University of Washington and particularly Earl B. Hunt, for permitting the leave time necessary for conducting the Hawaii research.

Literature Cited

Aronson, L. R., E. Tobach, D. S. Lehrman, & J. S. Rosenblatt, (eds.) 1970. Development and evolution of behavior: essays in memory of T. C. Schneirla. W. H. Freeman, San Francisco.

Barash, D. P. 1975. Evolutionary aspects of parental behavior: The distraction behavior of the alpine accentor, *Prunella collaris*. Wilson Bulletin 87: 367-373.

_______. 1977. Sociobiology and behavior. Elsevier, New York.

_______. 1978. The whisperings within: Explorations of human sociobiology. Harper & Row, New York.

Ehrman, L., & P. Parsons. Behavior Genetics. Sinnauer, Sunderland, Mass.

Fisher, R. A. 1954. The genetical theory of natural selection. Clarendon Press, Oxford.

Hamilton, W. D. 1964. The genetical theory of social behaviour, I. and II. Journal of Theoretical Biology 7: 1-52.

Hinde, R. A. 1966. Animal behaviour: a synthesis of ethology and comparative psychology. McGraw-Hill, New York.

_______. 1970. Animal behaviour: a synthesis of ethology and comparative psychology. McGraw-Hill, New York.

Karlin, S. 1975. General two-locus selection models: Some objectives, results and interpretations. Theoretical Population Biology 7: 364-398.

Orians, G. H. 1969. On the evolution of mating systems in birds and mammals. The American Naturalist 103: 589-603.

Ripley, S. D. 1961. Aggressive neglect as a factor in interspecific competition in birds. Auk 78: 366-371.

Simpson, G. G. 1949. The meaning of evolution. Yale University Press, New Haven.

Tinkle, D. W. 1967. The life history and demography of the side-blotched lizard, Uta stansburiana. Miscellaneous Publications, Museum of Zoology, University of Michigan, Ann Arbor, 132. 182 pp.

West-Eberhard, M. J. 1975. The evolution of social behavior by kin selection. Quarterly Review of Biology 50: 1-33.

Danilo Mainardi

9. Tradition and the Social Transmission of Behavior in Animals

Most of the theorizing in sociobiology has centered on differences in behavior between individuals that are taken as genetic and the differential survival of the genotypes presumed responsible for those differences. In extending these models to humans, those aspects of behavior that are so well exemplified in humans are overlooked. I refer explicitly to the acquisition of information through experience, and the transmission of that information to other individuals such that traditions are formed and evolve. This is a simplified definition of culture, but one that permits an enquiry into the nature of tradition among animals.

Recent years have seen the accumulation of knowledge about the ability of some kinds of animals to transmit information or new patterns of behavior, acquired through experience, from one individual to another. This is the capacity for social learning. It requires at least two individuals, the one that has the information (or new pattern of behavior) and the one that receives it. It has been possible to follow the rapid spread of new habits by this process through entire populations as well as the transmission of these new habits from one generation to another. Thus one can observe the formation of traditions among animals.

The social transmission of acquired habits is a phenomenon apart and one with precise adaptive meanings: it is qualitatively different from other adaptive behavioral mechanisms. This can best be appreciated by considering species without the capacity for social transmission. Here we find that their response to the environment consists either in (1) relatively unmodifiable behavior, limited and transmitted genetically, and "preprogrammed" as seemingly automatic responses to phyletically predictable situations, or in

(2) the capacity of the individual to adjust through individual learning. I know I overstate the dichotomy, and that all behavior is the outcome of a gene-environment interaction. The essential point, however, is that many if not most species lack the capacity to manifest social learning.

When present, social learning offers a different and novel adaptive solution. Then a solution that is discovered by an individual, i.e. new information, can be transmitted within the same generation. If it has survival value it can spread through the population much more rapidly than if it were a response narrowly constrained by genetics. Thus social transmission can be an efficient mechanism for rapid adaptation and hence the differentiation of populations.

However, this is not always the case. There are processes of social transmission of information that instead of producing a rapid spread of adaptive novelties act, on the whole, as conservative mechanisms. Within the field of social transmission it is therefore necessary to analyze the differences between various processes as well as their adaptive significance.

The social transmission of information emerged late in the history of life and it probably depends on certain social characteristics of the populations. It also appears sporadically in the phylogenetic tree. Take imprinting, for example, which has been reported in certain insects (Eoff 1973; Jaisson 1975; Le Moli & M. Mainardi 1972; Le Moli & Passetti 1977; D. Mainardi et al. 1966; Thorpe 1938, 1939), in some fishes (Destexhe-Gomez & Ruwet 1968; Fernö & Sjölander 1973; Kop & Heuts 1973; Myrberg 1964, 1975), and in a few reptiles (Arnold 1978; Burghardt & Hess 1966; Fuchs & Burghardt 1971). In certain birds and mammals, in addition to imprinting, social transmission is found that is neither limited to a sensitive period nor irreversible. This type of social transmission may also occur in some fishes (Beyer 1976; Mochek 1972, 1974) and reptiles (Greenberg 1976).

Despite gaps in our knowledge of the distribution of this phenomenon, there is little room for doubt that social transmission appeared independently various times in the course of evolution (see also Galef's (1976) recent review and the complementary ones by Gandolfi (1975) and Menzel (1973)); it is thus not a single phenomenon but a series of analogous ones that have developed through evolutionary convergence. Consequently, it is likely that different types of learning underlie social transmission. It is also likely that the terminological confusion, particularly in the field of social learning that is not limited to sensitive periods (e.g. allelomimetic behavior, social facilitation, local enhancement, matched dependent behavior, following, imitation, mimesis, copying, emphatic learning, observational learning, etc.), derives in part from trying to treat and define as a single phenomenon an assemblage of phenomena that are comparable only in certain respects.

I find that, at least from an operational standpoint, Thorpe's classification (1963) provides a welcome simplification. It distinguishes three levels of imitation: (1) social facilitation, (2) local enhancement and (3) true imitation. Social facilitation is the elicitation by a model of a response already in the observer's (the subject's) repertoire. Local enhancement refers to the power of a social model to direct the attention of an observer to some salient feature of the environment and consequently to accelerate trial-and-error learning. True imitation is distinguished by the sudden acquisition of a novel response by the observer, as through insight learning. Obviously, this classification doesn't take vocal imitation into consideration.

I shall not try to unravel here either the problem of the means by which animals as diverse as insects and primates learn socially, or the related terminological question. I could do no more than reiterate Galef's (1976) and Pallaud's (1977) recent analyses. Instead, starting from the assumption that social transmission of acquired behavior (or information) is an assemblage of phenomena that are analogous through evolutionary convergence, I shall first elaborate on the selective pressures that have determined such a convergence. The further aim of this paper relates to the likelihood that once a species acquires the capacity for social transmission there is an increase in selective pressures favoring the development or reinforcement of certain collateral capacities that facilitate such transmission. These would be the capacity for making discoveries (curiosity, play, exploration), that for teaching, a greater overlapping of the generations in time (lengthening of the period of parental care), a differentiation of social roles related to social transmission, or a particular development of systems of communication.

Thus the final objective of this paper is to try to understand the effects, past and present, of social transmission on the species endowed with this capacity. In so doing, it will be impossible to ignore our own species, though this paper does not aim to explain human behavior. Nonetheless, our species is the only one that has really specialized in social transmission. Perhaps this is the reason for its being the only one with all of the "collateral capacities" mentioned above.

Nongenetic Transmission of Information Can Be Conservative or Innovative

Even though they are often included under the heading of social transmission, I have excluded from this paper those mechanisms that serve to synchronize the behavior of members of a social group, e.g. social facilitation (Thorpe 1963). Instead I shall concentrate on the social transmission of information or behavior that is neither restricted to sensitive periods nor irreversible. However a brief discussion of the imprinting type of social transmission will contribute to a general understanding of the other sort of social transmission since the one shades gradually into the other.

The broad and discontinuous distribution of learning phenomena with sensitive periods and irreversibility suggests that here again similar phenomena are lumped because of their converging functions. In a variety of species it is sometimes useful for a particular bit of environmental information to become relatively fixed. This is particularly so when the information is provided during a well defined period of life, and the probability of error is low. Often such information concerns characteristics of the species, but imprinting having to do with food or the characteristics of the habitat also occurs (Hess 1973; Immelmann 1975). As a rule, the animal forms an association through imprinting rather than learning a new pattern of behavior. However, there are exceptions. For example, in many bird species there is vocal imprinting: vocal imitation is limited in time and later crystallized (Konishi 1965; Marler 1970).

The case of those birds (*Carduelis spinus*, *C. tristis*, *C. pinus*) that exhibit both vocal imprinting and vocal imitation, free of critical periods and song crystallization, sheds light on the function of imprinting. Through imprinting these birds learn the territorial song, a specific characteristic worth learning, when the possibility of error is minimal. Learning takes place in the nest with close contact with the parents. That explains the temporal limits of the sensitive period. The fact that the behavior learned is the one characteristic of the species and does not change during the individual's life time, explains the function of irreversibility. On other hand, it is possible for a bird to change its social companions or even its mate. Thus we come to certain functions of vocal imitation.

The same Carduelinae discussed so far emit brief calls during flight. When pairs are formed, the male and female gradually acquire the same flight call through reciprocal imitation. The signal so developed works excellently for their mutual recognition. The following experiment makes the point. The flight calls of numerous males were recorded and played near nests where females were incubating their eggs. The females remained indifferent to all the calls except those of their mates, to which they responded with the characteristic behavior for requesting food. In the same species, the same mechanism of reciprocal imitation tends to unify the flight calls of winter groups. In other words, the function of this mechanism is to foster individual recognition and social cohesion in groups (Mundinger 1970). An analogous situation has been reported for the function of vocal imitation in Gracula religiosa (Bertram 1970) and for the imitation that gives rise to antiphonal singing (Thorpe et al. 1972).

Imprinting and analogous forms of learning are thus means of transmitting information or behavior that then identify the species or is at any rate likely to be useful for an entire lifetime. Thus even though the transmission of information through imprinting is not genetically specified it turns out to be conservative and in certain respects similar to genetic transmission. It is, however, not altogether conservative. According to Nottebohm (1972), the recent burgeoning of new species in the suborder Passeres of the Passeriformes has been favored by the sexual-isolation effect of dialects that arise as a byproduct of transmission via vocal imprinting.

Nevertheless, when information can be cancelled and replaced, or new information added, social learning can obviously be a means of producing extremely rapid behavioral changes in a population. This requires that the social learning not be restricted to sensitive periods nor subject to crystallization. In such cases we can expect the new information or behavior to have a shorter-lived survival value for the individuals acquiring it in relation to changing environmental conditions.

We now know of numerous examples of this new and different phenomenon, usually evidenced by the formation of local traditions. The most famous instances are those of the tits, small parid birds that learned to open milk bottles, and of the Japanese macaques on the island of Koshima. Because these cases are so well known, I shall restrict myself to but a few remarks.

The tits provide us with a spendid record of the rapid spread of a new habit throughout England, and from only a few starting points. According to Hinde and Fisher (1951), this is an example of local enhancement.

The macaques also provide an instance of the rapid development of new habits (feeding techniques and others) by invention. The spread of the new behavior, at least in some instances, occurred by means of imitation. Here, however, the monkeys were stimulated by the researchers changing the environment, offering new problems to be solved. The experiment demonstrated a real capacity for progress, with the social accumulation of new knowledge over a period of time (Kawai 1965; Kawamura 1963; Tsumori 1967). Even without interference by humans, Japanese macaques differ from one population to another in certain feeding (Itani 1959) and social habits (Miyadi 1967).

Other examples of the spread of new feeding habits are known in birds, as in the greenfinch, *Chloris chloris* (Petterson 1956), in the redpoll *Carduelis flammea* (Stenhouse 1962), and in the oystercatcher *Haematopus ostralegus* (Norton-Griffith 1969). The case of *Geospiza difficilis*, a Darwin finch from the Galapagos, is particularly interesting because it has acquired the habit of feeding on blood. Bowman and Billeb (1965) suggested that certain individuals on the island of Wenman, in the course of their usual behavior of gleaning insect parasites from two species of booby (*Sula sula* and *S. dactylatra*), discovered the possibility of feeding on the birds' blood, probably by accidentally breaking a superficial blood vessel in the wing. The new habit would then have spread by social transmission. Thus a mutualistic way of life may have evolved into a parasitic one.

These traditions, and other ones involving birds and the use of tools (*Sitta pusilla* described by Morse (1968); *Neophron percnopterus* described by Van Lawick-Goodall and Van Lawick (1966) and subsequently by Alcock (1970), and that of *Haemirostra melanosternon* described by Chisholm (1954) have all been studied only in nature: the type of learning involved is consequently unclear. In most of these cases the fact that these traditions are limited to single populations suggests the operation, nonetheless, of social transmission. Also, much laboratory research has been done, attesting to social transmission in birds (Alcock 1969a, 1969b; Bullock & Neuringer 1977; Cronhelm 1970; Dawson & Foss 1965; Klopfer 1961; Zentall & Hogan 1976). Particularly interesting is a recent experiment with captive blackbirds (*Turdus merula*), which has shown that enemy recognition can also be socially transmitted (Curio et al. 1978).

The capacity for social transmission, often revealed by local tradition, exists among mammals. Examples are found in many species of primates (reviews by Galef 1976; D. Mainardi 1974a; Menzel 1973), ungulates (Darling 1937; Edwards 1976; Geist 1971; Schloeth & Burckardt 1961), carnivores (Ewer 1968), cetaceans (Bondarchuk et al. 1976; Tayler & Saayman 1973), and rodents (reviews by Galef 1976; Gandolfi 1975; Pallaud 1977).

Primates and cetaceans are unquestionably the most skilled at learning new behavior patterns by means of true imitation. In primates this sometimes gives rise to local traditions. The function of imitation in porpoises appears to be different and more analogous to free vocal imitation in birds. In ungulates and carnivores the traditions seem to deal essentially with knowledge about food, routes, or territorial boundaries.

Among rodents, the rat (*Rattus norvegicus*) and mouse (*Mus musculus*) have received the most attention. In these species social transmission is important in the adaptation to changing and difficult environmental situations. Social transmission among rats has been widely studied both in the laboratory and in nature and amply summarized by Galef (1976), Gandolfi (1975), Lore & Flannelly (1977) and Pallaud (1977). This species can adapt rapidly to new situations by learning socially to avoid dangers and by socially transmitting information about new sources of food and even new feeding techniques. Numerous laboratory studies prove the capacity for observational learning (true imitation) in the rat (Benel 1975; Galef 1976; Gandolfi 1975; Pallaud 1977). Ewer (1971) has studied *Rattus rattus* in seminatural conditions and she maintains that the establishment of traditions in this species is attributable to local enhancement.

The house mouse is also an instructive species. Even though traditions among mice have not been observed in nature, the mouse has amply demonstrated its capacity for social transmission in the laboratory (Destrade & Cardo 1977; D. Mainardi & Pasquali 1968; Manusia & Pasquali 1969; Pallaud 1969). An experiment by Manusia and Pasquali (1969) illuminated how this mechanism might work in nature. They showed that among a group of mice the presence of a few demonstrators who know an escape technique leads to the rapid acquisition of this technique with the consequent escape, by a high percentage of the mice, in a short time (33.9% in 24 hr). In the control group furnished with pseudodemonstrators (that is, mice of the same age, strain and sex as the demonstrators but ignorant of the technique), only a few mice escaped (3.6% in 24 hr). Furthermore, 12 out of 56 mice in the experimental group escaped during the first hour, whereas none of the 56 controls did so.

An analogous case has been described by Valzelli (1973). He observed that when mice are housed in groups of eight in cages where water is supplied by an automatic device constructed so that the animals have to press lightly with their tongues on a lever inserted into the water duct in order to drink, they easily learn such a simple task. In contrast, more than 30% of mice housed singly in such cages, without any previous experience, are absolutely unable to learn how to obtain water and die within a few days. According to Valzelli, in every group of mice there is at least one individual who discovers the solution, that is socially learned by the other mice.

Even though the preceding two experiments were "artificial" they simulated likely natural events. It is easy to understand from these studies how rapid social transmission of information can be invaluable for the survival of a population.

That which makes the mouse a particularly instructive species in this context is its overall sociosexual behavior. It seems to be organized to produce individuals who can take advantage of the capacity for rapid behavioral modification afforded by social transmission. The mouse is a nearly cosmopolitan species, one that is able to live in extremely different environments. Consequently, behavioral flexibility has a high selective advantage.

The resulting sociosexual behavior of the mouse is such that it works against the subdivision and specialization of the species. For one, the mouse tends toward heterogamy at the level of sexual choice, and that is based on early learning (D. Mainardi, Marsan & Pasquall 1965; Yanai & McClearn 1972a, 1972b).

After insemination has occurred an element of sexual "choice" is still possible. If a female, inseminated by a male of the same social group, meets a male from another group she undergoes an exteroceptive block of pregnancy, and shortly thereafter she goes back into estrus. This block is brought about by a male pheromone, and may occur during the first five days after mating, that is, until the fertilized eggs have attached themselves to the uterine wall (Bruce 1960; Bruce & Parrot 1960; Dominic 1969).

Another relevant finding is that mice make communal nests in which they bring up their pups (Sayler & Salmon

1971). Age of pups being equal, the parents show no retrieving preferences; any pup that is found is gathered into the communal nest. This behavior may afford an alternative to heterogamic sexual choice for bringing outside genes into the population (Favoriti & D. Mainardi 1976).

Taken together, these behaviors promote crossbreeding that might otherwise be prevented by the mouse's territorial habits. These behaviors thus reduce genetic isolation between populations while favoring individual variability within them, as is well known and studied (Berry 1970; Van Oortmerssen 1970).

If we consider _Mus musculus_ as an unspecialized species (although it might be better to say specialized in adapting to different and variable environments by means of the mechanisms of social transmission, among other things) we can understand how, because of the individual variability produced by the above-described sociosexual mechanisms, an individual suited to solving a new problem posed by a new situation is likely to be present in the population. This should also favor colonization. In this context, the mouse is known to be a highly exploratory species. It continues to explore even in the absence of obvious rewards. This suggests that the activity is in itself reinforcing (Brant & Kavanau 1964).

Mus musculus is, as we have seen, a species that illustrates well how social transmission can be a special adaptive route, and one that can be taken even by not particularly "intelligent" species, in contrast with, say primates. The English tits have provided a convincing example of this, probably basing their social transmission on local enhancement only.

So-called social transmission also occurs between species. (I prefer to restrict the term social to phenomena involving only members of the same species.) Cases are known in which a member of one species plays the role of demonstrator while one of another species does the learning. In some of these instances the contact between one species and another is favored by imprinting, or by similar forms of early learning (true imprinting probably does not occur in primates). The learner may have social ties with the demonstrator due to particular experiences during infancy. The examples of chimpanzees imitating humans, proceeding from the early experiment on Viki (Hayes & Hayes 1952) to the recent ones in which chimpanzees have learned American Sign Language from people (Fouts 1973; Gardner & Gardner 1969, 1971), fall into this category. Despite these being laboratory experiments they serve as models for the beginning of a new culture, transplanted interspecifically.

A case that occurs in nature is that of the African widows (Steganura). These birds are nest parasites, like cuckoos. They learn the song of their hosts, different species of estrildids, through vocal imprinting (Nicolai 1964).

Then there are other cases in which the imitation is independent of socialization: hamsters learn from observing demonstrator mice (D. Mainardi et al. 1972), and rats from gerbil demonstrators (Benel 1975). Lastly, porpoises spontaneously imitate the movements of a wide variety of animals, such as seals, sea turtles, fish and penguins (Tayler & Saayman 1973), while wild Gracula religiosa imitate the voices of primates (Tenaza 1976).

Situations and Behaviors Linked to Social Transmission

Certain species of insects and of birds are able "socially" to pass information to their offspring without coming into contact with them. This is achieved by oviposition in particular sites. Thus the moth Ephestia küniella transmits information about "what substrate to lay on" (D. Mainardi et al. 1966). In the same fashion the wasp Idechthis canescens transmits information about "what host to parasitize" by laying its eggs on a particular larva (Thorpe 1938, 1939). The same sort of information is passed on to the offspring of the parasitic birds of the genus Steganura (Nicolai 1964) and Cuculus canorus (Jensen 1966; Wickler 1968) by preferential oviposition, i.e. by selecting which nest to lay their eggs in. In all these species, early learning directs later oviposition.

The above instances have been mentioned to show that without contact between generations social transmission can occur, and traditions can be maintained through time. As a rule, however, temporal overlapping and contact between generations seem to be essential. And the longer the period of contact the greater the amount of information that can be passed on. At least this was suggested by MacKinnon to explain the short period of parental care in the orang-utan, which he considers to be a "desocialized" species. MacKinnon stated (1974:66): "Advantages from a cultural environment would be only slight as the way of life of these apes is very simple and there is little that need be learned apart from feeding and nesting techniques and locomotor patterns. These can be learned by individual experience or from the mother in the absence of other animals, and young orang-utan are sufficiently independent to leave their mothers at a relatively earlier age than the young of other ape species."

When social transmission occurs through imprinting, the differentiation of roles (learner, demonstrator) is clear and easily shown. The learners are the young during their sensitive period, and the demonstrator is usually a parent. But it is precisely this distinct definition of roles, tied to certain ages, with the accompanying irreversibility of that which is learned, that makes imprinting somewhat resemble genetically specified transmission; it does not normally allow the spread of a new habit (or information) within the same generation. Sometimes during parental care true teachint does occur and that is the social transmission of information.

The term teacher is meant to differ from that of demonstrator. A demonstrator merely performs an action (and thus presents the information) in the presence of the learners. A teacher displays behavior tending specifically to stimulate the behavior of the learner and it gears its own behavior to that of the learner (Barnett 1968).

Examples of teaching are found among carnivores. In the domestic cat, for instance, the female at first merely brings her prey and eats it in the presence of her young. Later she permits them to attack the prey which she has killed. Finally, she brings in live prey and liberates it in the presence of the young, and she may summon them by a special call. In the last phase, adjustment to the performance of the young is often seen (Leyhausen 1956).

This teaching process consists of a progressive inhibition of predatory behavior, working from the terminal stages forward. The female cat first delays her eating until the food has been brought back to the young. Later, she kills but fails to eat. Finally, she captures but fails to kill. If the prey eludes the young, it at once evokes in the cat the only part of the sequence that has not been inhibited: She responds to the escaping prey by recapturing it (Ewer 1969). The information transmitted seems to relate exclusively to the characteristics of prey. The teaching has primarily the function of organizing the chain of acts (the capture, the kill, the feeding) that make up predatory behavior. In fact if cats do not make a kill during a sensitive period in their youth, they grow up as nonkillers who fail to attack a mouse (Ewer 1968; Roberts & Kiess 1964).

Teaching also occurs among chickens (Hogan 1966), and has even been described for the fish *Aequidens latifrons*

(Mochek 1972, 1974). Even though it is not always clear whether the learning involved is like imprinting (Galef 1976) the observation that it is normally the parent who teaches an offspring implies the emergence of a new generation before information can be transmitted. Thus, in the cases considered up to now, there is a tendency for the times and roles to be pre-established, predictably in the case of imprinting and the likes, and still rather predictably where there is teaching.

Even in other cases, there is evidence that information does not spread haphazardly through populations, but that it follows "pathways of least resistence." For example, kittens quickly learn to press a lever to obtain food by observing their own mother, while learning occurs much more slowly when they observe strange cats, and then only when the latter have adopted the kittens (Chesler 1969). In *Lemur fulvus* observational learning passes more easily from the mother to her children than vice versa (Feldman & Klopfer 1972). In the porpoise *Tursiops truncatus* it is the young who imitate the movements of adults (Bondarchuk et al. 1976).

There is also some evidence that information does not spread haphazardly in primates, but follows "channels" depending on sex, age, kinship, affiliative bonds and dominance status (Frisch 1968; Jolly 1972; Menzel et al. 1972; Kawamura 1959, 1963; Kawai 1963, 1965; Strayer 1976). Using information on the "precultural" evolution of the Koshima macaques, Masali (1966) described the channels through which information spreads. The young are particularly suited both to making discoveries and to assimilating them. In contrast, the adults tend to render acquired traditions stable. The qualities that distinguish the young are a marked tendency to explore (great curiosity) and the capacity for easily modifying their behavior, both through individual learning and imitation. Exploration is further facilitated by play, which is widely practiced.

Transmission of new habits is also influenced by factors related to social status. These factors have, among other things, an effect on the localization of the individuals in the group. That, in turn, contributes to the formation of the pathways of least resistence for the transmission of new habits. Adult male macaques of low social status, for example, are usually found at the periphery of the group. They therefore have little chance to come into contact with the young, who occupy a more central position near the females and the males of higher social status.

The pathways of least resistance can be described by following the spread of a discovery in a population of Macaca fuscata. A juvenile makes the discovery and incorporates it into his behavioral repertory. Shortly thereafter his playmates acquire the new habit. The habit also spreads upward in terms of social status, to certain older individuals through the affective bonds of kinship. Thus the mother, brothers and older sisters of the juveniles, who were the first to adopt the new habit, are the first macaques to whom the new behavior is transmitted.

In most cases, however, it is not until the inventor and his contemporaries have grown in age and rank that they can transmit their discovery, as one of many normal habits, to the new young; then it really spreads through the population. In 1962 Kawai (1965) took a census of all the individuals that had adopted the habit of washing sweet potatoes started by the macaque Imo in 1953, when she was a year and a half old. Almost all the macaques of her age or younger had the new habit in their repertory, but only a tiny percentage of individuals older than Imo had changed their behavior.

Among the many functions of playing and exploring, the boundaries of which are sometimes hard to distinguish (Weisler & McCall 1976), one appears to be that of facilitating the emergence of new behavior. This has been observed in young chimpanzees (McGrew et al. 1975; Savage & Malick 1977), and in young porpoises, who produce new patterns of behavior not only through play but also by observing adults (Bondarchuk et al. 1976). Young lions (and many other felines) learn hunting techniques through play and from their mother's teaching (Barnett 1968; Schenkel 1966). The relationship between play and learning, with particular reference to the rhesus macaque, has recently been discussed by Simpson (1976).

A revealing example of this relationship can be seen in the transmission of the habit of "fishing" for termites with a stick among the chimpanzees of the Gombe Stream Reserve (Van Lawick-Goodall 1968). This habit requires some skill and patience because the stick must be inserted into the opening of the termite hill slowly and removed in the same way. Otherwise the termites will not cling to the tool with their jaws and thus will not be captured. Juveniles over two years old begin to practice in play, using tools discarded by adults and sticking them into the termite hill. But their early efforts are rarely crowned with success. It takes as long as two years for the young chimpanzees to master the new technique. And it is only upon approaching mastery that the activity becomes rewarding from an alimentary point of view.

Thus in this case play gives the young chimpanzees the impetus to continue practicing during the early phases of their learning, when there is no obvious reinforcement.

The use of tools, which has been reported in very different groups of animals (mammals, birds, fishes, insects and crustaceans) does not always involve social transmission (Alcock 1972; Beck 1974; D. Mainardi 1974a). Sometimes, even among birds and mammals, it remains an individual event. In other cases, even though the habit occurs only among individuals within a certain geographical area, it is not possible to ascertain whether it is a local tradition or not.

There are sometimes alternative interpretations, as in the case of the sea otter Enhydra lutris. As it swims on its back the otter carries on its chest a stone and a food object, such as clams or crustaceans. The otter holds the hard food object between its forepaws and hits the object against the stone until the object breaks and the animal within can be eaten. This habit is widespread within the Californian population (Hall & Schaller 1964), but has been observed in only one wild individual of the Aleutian population (Hall 1963). An Aleutian otter, captured as an adult, was immediately able to use rocks as anvils on which to pound clams, like its Californian counterparts (Kenyon 1959). According to Hall (1963), all members of the species have the habit in their repertory, but opening Aleutian molluscs usually does not require tools. On the other hand, as Hall (1963) himself pointed out, this species has the important requisite for the social transmission of the habit in the close and lengthy relationship between parent and offspring.

The study of the use of tools has provided some information about the ways new habits are discovered. This may happen in play (Lethmate 1976a; McGrew et al. 1975), in the wake of frustration (Hall 1963; Alcock 1970; Van Lawick-Goodall 1968), and also through insight while animals (always primates in this case) are in what seems to be a contemplative and inquisitive frame of mind (Chance 1960; Köhler 1927; Kortlandt 1966; Lethmate 1976b). Naturally there are also instances in which the use of tools is narrowly constrained by genetics: this appears to be universal when invertebrates or lower vertebrates are involved (Alcock 1972; D. Mainardi 1974a).

The examples cited up to this point, though largely derived from anecdotal information that is fragmentary, hard to compare and in need of critical testing, suggest that various factors influence the discovery and spread of information in a population. The greater or lesser rigidity of roles (the discoverer, the demonstrator or teacher, the learner), along with the type of learning involved, tend to determine the way animal traditions are founded and how conservative they will be.

Given our present state of knowledge, a tentative list of animal traditions can be made and in order of decreasing conservatism: (1) Traditions transmitted by imprinting or the likes, with or without teaching. (2) Traditions transmitted by local enhancement or true imitation, with teaching. (3) Traditions transmitted by local enhancement or true imitation and without teaching, but with differentiation of roles creating special pathways of least resistance for the passage of information. (4) Traditions transmitted through local enhancement or true imitation, but without differentiation of roles.

Examples of the first three categories have already been given. As for the fourth, a good example derives from the one mentioned in the preceding section, that of free vocal imitation among the Carduelinae (Mundinger 1970). Within each winter flock of these birds a traditional flight call is developed through reciprocal imitation, which becomes almost an identification badge. Among mice, too, according to a recent study by Renzi et al. (1978), information can be socially transmitted as easily from submissive individuals to dominant ones as vice versa. Obviously those species belonging to the fourth category are those in which social transmission can spread with the greatest speed within a generation. Thus those species will show the greatest behavioral flexibility.

Evolutionary Aspects of Social Transmission

Generally speaking we have a clear idea of what a tradition is. It is a habit transmitted socially from one generation to another within a population, and it distinguishes that population from others. However, the consideration of natural cases makes us dissatisfied with this definition, both with regard to distribution within the species and in time. The following questions arise.

If a tradition is adopted by an entire species, due either to its ubiquitous diffusion or to the extinction of those populations lacking it, does it cease to be a tradition? Bird dialects, for example, would fall within the definition of tradition, but not the normal acquisition of song through imprinting if there is no geographical differentiation (Galef 1976). And can we consider the flight calls of winter flocks of Carduelinae (Mundinger 1970) to be traditions if, as is likely, they last only a season? And what about the flight calls during the mating season of Carduelinae?

Consider, too, the rapid adaptation to a new problem, posed by the environment, through social transmission within a population of mice; the habit may last many generations or hardly at all according to how long the problem to be solved persists. The English tits opened milk bottles as long as those special bottles lasted; the habit could last much longer, possibly forever; but it also could be cut short.

What, then, are the temporal limits of a tradition? Can a tradition "belong" to an entire species, or at the other extreme, can it be shared by only two individuals?

Such doubts lead me to set aside the term "tradition" for the moment and to reason in terms of social transmission of information or habits, I would like to understand the reasons for the differences within the phenomenon in terms of adaptation. (a) Extension in time: This depends on the greater or lesser stability in time of the survival value of the habit or information. Where the survival value is most stable (e.g. information regarding the species), mechanisms that make the transmission particularly conservative develop (i.e. irreversibility of learning). (b) Extension in space: This depends on whether the habit or information has greater or lesser survival value in different environments. If it has the same survival value everywhere, and if the distribution of the species is discontinuous, the new habit or information will have to be independently discovered in various places. In certain cases the survival value of a new habit consists of its facilitating recognition between individuals or cohesion within groups (as in the often mentioned case of vocal imitation among the Carduelinae). In such cases, the size of the group, which is ultimately a species characteristic, sets the limits to the spread of the tradition.

Thus, the heading "social transmission of information or habits" covers various phenomena that probably have arisen through evolutionary convergence. Consequently, they probably involve different types of learning and, at least in part, different adaptive functions. What they have in common is their dependence on nongenetic information. In certain social species, part of the behavioral phenotype therefore depends on this nongenetic form of heredity.

A comparison between the mechanism of biological evolution and those of cultural evolution (the term "cultural" is used in its broadest sense) has shown (D. Mainardi 1973,

1974a) how certain factors play the same role in both types of evolution: natural selection (the maintenance and diffusion of both cultural and genetic mutations depends on their survival value), chance, migration. One should recognize, however, that genetic mutation differs from cultural mutation because genetic mutation is always random, while cultural mutation may be, and frequently is, purposeful.

But beyond that, the most important and significant difference between the two may lie in the mode of transmission: constrained and slow in chromosomal evolution but malleable and swift (at least in extreme instances) in cultural evolution. A genetic mutation occurring in an individual must await the next generation before it can start to spread, and then only to the offspring of some of them. Each further step requires waiting another generation, and then it can occur only along the lines of kinship. Instead, the spread of cultural mutations, when not limited by sensitive periods, irreversibility or an excessive rigidity in social roles, resembles the spread of an epidemic. Thus the nongenetic evolution of behavior can be an efficacious means for populations to adapt rapidly to changing situations or to conquer new and different environments.

We have already seen how certain types of behavior (play, exploration, teaching and other behavior involving parents and offspring) can facilitate the origin and maintenance of social transmission. From an evolutionary point of view, it is likely that such behavior favored an increase in the capacity for social transmission, while at the same time it was selectively reinforced by it. Thus such behavior is in part cause and in part effect of social transmission in a synergistic action.

Mention has not yet been made of communication. If we consider the enormous development of social transmission in the evolutionary line leading to humans we are compelled to appreciate that it is largely due to the communication, both symbolic and plastic, that is typical of our species. The capacity for abstraction and for dealing in symbols in our language has allowed human cultural evolution to detach itself from objects and to rest preponderantly on symbols (Dobzhansky 1962; Huxley 1963; Lorenz 1973; Rensch 1967). Even though human cultural evolution is beyond the scope of this paper, it should be mentioned that during the evolution of man the adaptive advantages deriving from social transmission must have placed strong selective pressure on this capacity for abstraction and symbolic communication, which was already present in a primitive form in the apes (Bronowski & Bellugi 1970).

What is peculiar to our species, at least when compared to the apes, is the capacity for vocal imitation. The independent appearance of this capacity in various animals is, as a rule, related to individual recognition or the maintenance of socio-affective bonds within a group. It has been suggested that analogous selective pressures were involved in the rise of this capacity in humans (D. Mainardi 1974b).

It has already been mentioned that dialects transmitted by vocal imprinting have possibly accelerated speciation among birds of the order Passeres (Nottebohm 1972). In certain situations imprinting may also promote particular forms of sexual selection and thus influence the genetic structure of populations (Kalmus & Maynard Smith 1966; Karlin 1968; D. Mainardi 1964, 1967; D. Mainardi, Scudo & Barbieri 1965; Matessi & Scudo 1975; Seiger 1967). Recently, Feldmann and Cavalli-Sforza (1975, 1976) have developed theoretical models to study the spread of characters transmitted by an interaction of genetic and cultural heredity. Even though these models refer to human beings, they are of general interest.

Summary

The capacity for socially transmitting habits and information has appeared independently in different animal groups, indicating evolutionary convergence. Such transmission is a nongenetic form of behavioral heredity, which differs in its adaptive significance and which is linked to genetic heredity in ways that largely remain to be discovered.

The formation of animal traditions is a noticeable and central subphenomenon in the general field of social transmission. It is characterized by not being conservative, as opposed to imprinting, so that traditions, as a rule, characterize populations rather than species. The lower degree of conservatism, in contrast to imprinting, can be explained by the different quality of the habits and information transmitted: their survival value relates to contingencies (i.e.: the solution of an actual problem) rather than to near certainties (i.e.: learning of a species signal characteristic). Traditions (and more generally, social transmission) are based on different types of learning. These different types of learning can sometimes be found together in the same species, though with different functions, and are used to transmit different kinds of information.

The degree of conservatism of social transmission depends on the type of learning involved (with or without sensitive periods and irreversibility) and the presence or lack of differentiation of roles within the population (teaching, dependency due to age or social status). Nonetheless, in comparison with the slow pace of biological evolution, social transmission in all its forms affords swift adaptation and rapid behavioral evolution.

Acknowledgements

I wish to thank Professors George W. Barlow, Eberhard Curio and James Silverberg who were extremely helpful in improving the original manuscript. I am also grateful to Dr. Anna Lisa Cavaggioni, who helped me at various stages in the preparation of the paper, and to Mrs. Anna Renzoni, who translated it into English.

Literature Cited

Alcock, J. 1969a. Observational learning in three species of birds. *Ibis* 111:308-321.

_______ 1969b. Observational learning by fork-tailed fly-catchers (*Muscivora tyrannus*). *Animal Behaviour* 17: 652-657.

_______ 1970. The origin of tool-using by Egyptian vultures *Neophron percnopterus*. *Ibis* 112:542.

_______ 1972. Evolution of the use of tools by feeding animals. *Evolution* 26:464-473.

Arnold, S.J. 1978. Some effects of early experience on feeding responses in the common garter snake, *Thamnophis sirtalis*. *Animal Behaviour* 26:455-462.

Barnett, S.A. 1968. The "instinct to teach." *Nature* 222: 747-749.

Beck, B.B. 1974. Baboons, chimpanzees, and tools. *Journal of Human Evolution* 3: 509-516.

Benel, R.A. 1975. Intra- and interspecific observational learning in rats. *Psychological Reports* 37:241-242.

Berry, R.J. 1970. Covert and overt variation, as exemplified by British mouse populations. *Symposia of the Zoological Society of London* (26):3-26.

Bertram, B. 1970. The vocal behavior of the Indian hill mynah, *Gracula religiosa*. *Animal Behaviour Monographs* 3:81-192.

Beyer, I. 1976. Gruppenlernen and Einzellernen bei Schwarmfischen (Rotfeder: Scardinius erythrophthalmus L.) Behavioural Ecology and Sociobiology 1:245-263.

Bondarchuk, L.S., S.K. Matisheva & R.N. Skibnevsky. 1976. Development of behaviour in young Tursiops truncatus. Zoologichesky Zhurnal 55:276-281.

Bowman, R.I. & S.L. Billeb. 1965. Blood-eating in a Galapagos finch. Living Bird 4:29-44.

Brant, D.H. & J.L. Kavanau. 1964. "Unrewarded" exploration and learning of complex mazes by wild and domestic mice. Nature 204:267-269.

Bronowski, J. & U. Bellugi. 1970. Language, name and concept. Science 168:669-673.

Bruce, H.M. 1960. Further observations on pregnancy block in mice caused by the proximity of strange males. Journal of Reproduction and Fertility 1:311-312.

_______ & D.M.V. Parrot. 1960. Role of olfactory sense in pregnancy block by strange males. Science 131:1526.

Bullock, D. & A. Neuringer. 1977. Social learning by following: An analysis. Journal of the Experimental Analysis of Behavior 25:103-117.

Burghardt, G.M. & E.H. Hess. 1966. Food imprinting in the snapping turtle, Chelydra serpentina. Science 151:108-109.

Chance, M.R.A. 1960. Köhler's chimpanzees - how did they perform? Man 60:130-135.

Chesler, P. 1969. Maternal influence in learning by observation in kittens. Science 166:901-903.

Chisholm, A.H. 1954. The use by birds of "tools" or "instruments." Ibis 96:380-383.

Cronhelm, E. 1970. Perceptual factors and observational learning in the behavioural development of young chicks. In J.H. Crook (ed.), Social Behaviour in birds and mammals. Academic Press, New York, pp. 393-440.

Curio, E., U. Ernst & W. Vieth. 1978. Cultural transmission of enemy recognition: One function of mobbing. Science, in press.

Darling, F.F. 1937. A herd of red deer. Oxford University Press, London.

Dawson, B.W. & B.M. Foss. 1965. Observational learning in bugderigars. Animal Behaviour 13:470-474.

Destexhe-Gomez, F. & J.C. Ruwet. 1968. Impregnation et cohésion familiale chez les Tilapia (Poisson cichlides). Annales de al Société Royale Zoologique de Belgique 97:161-173.

Destrade, C. & B. Cardo. 1977. Apprentissage par observation ches la souris. Effects a long terme de l'observation et influence de la privation alimentaire. Biology of Behaviour 2:83-91.

Dobzhansky, T. 1962. Mankind evolving. Yale University Press, New Haven and London.

Dominic, C.J. 1969. Pheromonal regulation of mammalian reproduction. Indian Biologist 1:1-18.

Edwards, J. 1976. Learning to eat by following the mother in moose calves. American Midland Naturalist 96:229-232.

Eoff, M. 1973. The influence of being cultured together on hybridization between Drosophilia melanogaster and Drosophilia simulans. American Naturalist 107:247-255.

Ewer, R.F. 1968. Ethology of mammals. Logos, London.

_______ 1969. The "instinct to teach." Nature 222:698.

_______ 1971. The biology and behaviour of a free-living population of black rats (Rattus rattus). Animal Behaviour Monographs 4:127-174.

Favoriti, M.P. & D. Mainardi. 1976. Assenza di discriminazione tra figli ed estranei nell'ambito dell'adozione nel topo. Ateneo Parmense, acta naturalia 12:259-269.

Feldman, D.W. & P.H. Klopfer. 1972. A study of observational learning in lemurs. Zeitschrift für Tierpsychologie 30:297-304.

Feldman, M.W. & L.L. Cavalli-Sforze. 1975. Models for cultural inheritance. A general linear model. Annals of Human Biology 2:215-236.

_______ 1976. Cultural and Biological evolutionary processes. Selection for a trait under complex transmission. Theoretical Population Biology 9:238-259.

Fernö, A. & S. Sjölander. 1973. Some imprinting experiments on sexual preferences for color variants in the platyfish (Xiphophorus maculatus). Zeitschrift für Tierpsychologie 33:417-423.

Fouts, R.S. 1973. Use of guidance in teaching sign language to a chimpanzee (Pan troglodytes). Journal of Comparative and Physiological Psychology 80:515-522.

Frisch, J.E. 1968. Individual behaviour and intertroop variability in Japanese macaques. In P. Jay (ed.), Primates: Studies in adaptation and variability. Holt, Rinehart & Winston, New York, pp. 243-252.

Fuchs, J.L. & G.M. Burghardt. 1971. Effects of early feeding experience on the responses of garter snakes to food chemicals. Learning and Motivation 2:271-279.

Galef, B.G., Jr. 1976. Social transmission of acquired behavior: A discussion of tradition and social learning in vertebrates. Advances in the Study of Behavior 6: 77-99.

Gandolfi, G. 1975. Social learning in non-primate animals. Bollettino di Zoologia 42:311-329.

Gardner, B.T. & R.A. Gardner. 1971. Two-way communication with an infant chimpanzee. Behavior of Nonhuman Primates 4:117-184.

Gardner, R.A. & B.T. Gardner. 1969. Teaching sign language to a chimpanzee. Science 165:664-672.

Geist, V. 1971. Mountain sheep. University of Chicago Press, Chicago.

Greenberg, N. 1976. Observations of social feeding in lizards. Herpetologica 32:348-352.

Hall, K.R.L. 1963. Tool-using performances as indicators of behavioral adaptability. Current Anthropology 4:479-494.

_______ & G.B. Schaller. 1964. Tool-using behavior of the California sea otter. Journal of Mammology 45:287-298.

Hayes, K.C. & C. Hayes. 1952. Imitation in a home-raised chimpanzee. Journal of Comparative and Physiological Psychology 45:450-459.

Hess, E.H. 1973. Imprinting. Van Nostrand Reinhold, New York.

Hinde, R.A. & J. Fisher. 1951. Further observations on the opening of milk bottles by birds. British Birds 44: 393-396.

Hogan, J.A. 1966. An experimental study of conflict and fear: An analysis of behaviour of young chicks toward a mealworm. Part II. The behaviour of chicks which eat the mealworm. Behaviour 27:273-289.

Huxley, J.S. 1963. Evolution, the modern synthesis. Allen and Unwin, London.

Immelman, K. 1975. Ecological significance of imprinting and early learning. Annual Review of Ecology and Systematics 6:15-37.

Itani, J. 1959. On the acquisition and propagation of a new food habit in the troops of Japanese monkeys at Takasakijama. Primates 1:84-98.

Jaisson, P. 1975. L'impregnation dans l'ontogenèse des comportements de soins aux cocons chez la jeune fourmi rousse (Formica polyctena). Behaviour 52:1-37.

Jensen, R.A.C. 1966. Genetics of cuckoo egg polymorphism. Nature 209:827.

Jolly, A. 1972. The evolution of primate behaviour. Collier-MacMillan, London.

Kalmus, H. & S. Maynard Smith. 1966. Some evolutionary consequences of pegmatypic mating systems (imprinting). American Naturalist 100:619-635.

Karlin, S. 1968. Equilibrium behavior of population genetic models with non-random mating. Gordon & Breach, New York.

Kawai, M. 1963. On newly acquired behaviours of the natural troop of Japanese monkeys on Koshima island. Primates 4:113-114.

_______ 1965. Newly acquired pre-cultural behaviour of the natural troop of Japanese monkeys of Koshima islet. Primates 6:1-30.

Kawamura, S. 1959. The process of sub-cultural propagation among Japanese monkeys. Primates 3:45-60.

_______ 1963. The process of sub-cultural propagation among Japanese macaques. In C. Southwick (ed.) Primate social behavior. Van Nostrand, Toronto.

Kenyon, K.W. 1959. The sea-otter. Annual Reports of the Smithsonian Institute pp. 399-407.

Klopfer, P.H. 1961. Observational learning in birds. Behaviour 17:71-80.

Köhler, W. 1927. Mentality of apes. Methuen, London.

Konishi, M. 1965. The role of auditory feedback in the control of vocalization in the white-crowned sparrow. Zeitschrift für Tierpsychologie 22:770-783.

Kop, P. & B. Heuts. 1973. An experiment on sibling imprinting in the jewel fish (Hemichromis bimaculatus). Revue de Comportement Animal 7:63-76.

Kortland, A. 1966. On tool-use among primates. Current Anthropology 7:215-216.

LeMoli, F. & M. Mainardi. 1972. Effetto di esperienze recenti sull'isolamento riproduttivo tra Drosophila melanogaster e Drosophila simulans. Istituto Lombardo (Rendiconti Scientifici) B 106:29-35.

_______ & M. Passetti. 1977. The effect of early learning on recognition, acceptance and care of cocoons in the ant Formica rufa L. Atti della Società Italiana di Scienze Naturali 118:49-64.

Lethmate, J. 1976a. Gebrauch und Herstellung von Trinkwerkzeugen bei Orang-Utans. Zoologischer Anzeiger 197:251-263.

_______ 1976b. Versuche zur Doppelstockhandlung mit einen jungen Orang-Utan. Zoologischer Anzeiger 197:264-271.

Leyhausen, P. 1956. Verhaltensstudien an Katzen. Parey, Berlin.

Lore, R. & K. Flannelly. 1977. Rat societies. Scientific American 236:106-116.

Lorenz, K. 1973. Die Rückseite des Spiegels. Piper, München.

MacKinnon, J. 1974. The behaviour and ecology of wild orang-utans (Pongo pygmaeus). Animal Behaviour 22:3-74.

Mainardi, D. 1964. Effetto evolutivo della selezione sessuale basata su imprinting in Columba livia. Rivista Italiana di Ornitologia 34:213-216.

_______ 1967. Commento ad un recente studio sugli effetti evolutivi dell'accoppiamento preferenziale basato sull' imprinting. Rivista Italiana di Ornitologia 37:51-60.

_______ 1973. Biological bases of cultural evolution. Accademia Nazionale dei Lincei, Quaderno No. 182:175-188.

_______ 1974a. L'animale culturale. Rizzoli, Milano.

_______ 1974b. Origine della communicazione verbale umana: il punto di vista etologico. Italian Journal of Psychology 2:131-146.

_______ M. Mainardi & A. Pasquali. 1972. Interspecific observational learning: From house mice to golden hamsters. Bollettino di Zoologia 39:634-635.

_______ M. Marsan & A. Pasquali. 1965. Causation of sexual preferences in the house mouse. The behaviour of mice reared by parents whose odour was artificially altered. Atti della Società Italiana di Scienze Naturali 104: 325-338.

_______ L. Ottaviani & A. Pasquali. 1966. Apprendimento e fattori genetici nel determinismo dell'oviposizione preferenziale in Ephestia kühniella. Rendiconti dell' Accademia Nazionale dei Lincei 41:134-138.

_______ & A. Pasquali. 1968. Cultural transmission in the house mouse. Atti della Società Italiana di Scienze Naturali 107:147-152.

_______ F.M. Scudo & D. Barbieri. 1965. Assortative mating based on early learning: Population genetics. Ateneo Parmense, acta biomedica 34:584-605.

Manusia, M. & A. Pasquali. 1969. A new case of imitation in the house mouse. Atti della Società Italiana di Scienze Naturali 109:457-462.

Marler, P. 1970. A comparative approach to vocal learning: Song development in white-crowned sparrows. Journal of Comparative and Physiological Psychology 71:1-25.

Masali, M. 1966. Nuove acquisizioni sulla etologia dei primati: Il comportamento "preculturale" della *Macaca fuscata*. Natura 57:207-221.

Matessi, C. & F.M. Scudo. 1975. The population genetics of assortive mating based on imprinting. Theoretical Population Biology 7:306-337.

McGrew, W.C., C.E.G. Tutin & S. Midgett, Jr. 1975. Tool use in a group of captive chimpanzees. I. Escape. Zeitschrift für Tierpsychologie 37:145-162.

Menzel, E.W., Jr. (ed.) 1973. Precultural primate behavior. Karger, Basel.

_______ R.K. Davenport & C.M. Rodgers. 1972. Protocultural aspects of chimpanzees' responsiveness to novel objects. Folia Primatologica 17:161-170.

Miyadi, D. 1967. Differences in social behaviour among Japanese macaque troops. 1st Congress of the International Society of Primatology, Stuttgart, pp. 228-231.

Mochek, A.D. 1972. Interrelationships of parents and progeny in family groups of *Aequidens latifrons*. Zoologichesky Zhurnal 51:1353-1360.

_______ 1974. Training of fry of *Aqueidens latifrons* in familial groups. Zoologichesky Zhurnal 53:594-598.

Morse, D.H. 1968. The use of tools by brown-headed nuthatches. Wilson Bulletin 80:220-224.

Mundinger, P.C. 1970. Vocal imitation and individual recognition of finch calls. Science 168:480-482.

Myrberg, A.A., Jr. 1964. An analysis of the perferential care of eggs and young by adult cichlid fishes. Zeitschrift für Tierpsychologie 21:53-98.

_______ 1975. The role of chemical and visual stimuli in the preferential discrimination of young by the cichlid fish *Cichlasoma nigrofasciatum*. Zeitschrift für Tierpsychologie 37:274-297.

Nicolai, J. 1964. Der Brutparasitismus der Viduinae als ethologische Problem. Prägung-phänomene als Faktoren der Rassen und Artbildung. Zeitschrift für Tierpsychologie 21:129-204.

Norton-Griffith, M. 1969. The organization, control and development of parental feeding in the oystercatcher (Haemotopus ostralegus). Behaviour 34:57-114.

Nottebohm, F. 1972. The origins of vocal learning. American Naturalist 106:116-170.

Pallaud, B. 1969. Mise en évidence d'un comportement d'imitation chez la souris. Revue de Comportement Animal 3:28-36.

_______ 1977. L'apprentissage par observation chez la souris et le rat. These presentée a l'Universite Pasteur de Strasbourg, pp. 1-286.

Pettersson, M. 1956. Diffusion of a new habit among greenfinches. Nature 177:709-710.

Rensch, B. 1967. The evolution of brain achievements. Evolutionary Biology 1:26-68.

Renzi, P., B. Volpe and M. Galli. 1978. Observational learning in the mouse and social dominance in avoidance behavior. Behavioural Processes (submitted).

Roberts, W.W. & H.O. Kiess. 1964. Motivational properties of hypothalamic aggression in cats. Journal of Comparative and Physiological Psychology 58:187-193.

Savage, E.S. & C. Malik. 1977. Play and socio-sexual behaviour in a captive chimpanzee (Pan troglodytes) group. Behaviour 60:179-194.

Sayler, A. & M. Salmon. 1971. An ethological analysis of communal nursing in the house mouse (Mus musculus). Behaviour 40:62-85.

Schenkel, R. 1966. Play, exploration and territoriality in the wild lion. Symposia of the Zoological Society of London 18:11-22.

Schloeth, R. & D. Burckhardt. 1961. Die Wanderungen des Ratwildes Cervus elaphus L. im Gebeit des Schweizerischen National-parkes. Revue Suisse de Zoologie 68: 75-77.

Seiger, M.B. 1967. A computer simulation study of the influence of imprinting on population structure. American Naturalist 101:47-57.

Simpson, M.J.A. 1976. The study of animal play. In P.P.G. Bateson & R.A. Hinde (eds.), Growing points in ethology. Cambridge University Press, London, pp. 385-400.

Stenhouse, D. 1962. A new habit of the redpoll Carduelis flammea in New Zealand. Ibis 104:250-252.

Strayer, F.F. 1976. Learning and imitation as a function of social status in macaque monkeys (Macaca nemestrina). Animal Behaviour 24:835-848.

Tayler, C.K. & G.S. Saayman. 1973. Imitative behaviour by Indian Ocean bottlenose dolphins (Tursiops aduncus) in captivity. Behaviour 44:286-298.

Tenaza, R.R. 1976. Wild mynahs mimic wild primates. Nature 259:561.

Thorpe, W.H. 1938. Further experiments on olfactory conditioning in a parasitic insect. The nature of the conditioning process. Proceedings of the Royal Society of London, Series B 126:370-397.

_______ 1939. Further experiments on pre-imaginal conditioning in insects. Proceedings of the Royal Society of London, Series B 127:424-433.

_______ 1963. Learning and instinct in animals. (3rd edition), Methuen, London.

_______ J. Hall-Craggs, B. Hooker & T. Hutchinson. 1972. Duetting and antiphonal song in birds. Its extent and significance. Behaviour Supplement 18.

Tsumori, A. 1967. Newly acquired behaviour and social interactions of Japanese monkeys. In S. Altman (ed.), Social communication among primates. University of Chicago Press, Chicago, pp. 207-220.

Valzelli, L. 1973. The "isolation syndrome" in mice. Psychopharmacologia 31:305-320.

Van Lawick-Goodall, J. 1968. The behaviour of free-living chimpanzees in the Gombe Stream reserve. Animal Behaviour Monographs 1:165-311.

_______ & H. Van Lawick. 1966. Use of tools by the Egyptian vulture Neophron percnopterus. Nature 212:1468-1469.

Van Oortmerssen, G.A. 1970. Biological significance, genetics and evolutionary origin of variability in behaviour within and between inbred strains of mice (Mus musculus). Behaviour 38:1-92.

Weisler, A. & R.B. McCall. 1976. Exploration and play: Résumé and redirection. American Psychologist 31:492-508.

Wickler, W. 1968. Mimetismo animale e vegetale. Il Saggiatore, Milano.

Yanai, J. & G.E. McClearn. 1972a. Assortative mating in mice and the incest taboo. Nature 238:281-282.

_______ 1972b. Assorative mating in mice. I. Female mating preference. Behavior Genetics 2:173-183.

Zentall, T.R. & D.E. Hogan. 1976. Imitation and social facilitation in the pigeon. Animal Learning and Behavior 4:427-430.

Stephen Jay Gould

10. Sociobiology and the Theory of Natural Selection

Natural Selection as Storytelling

Ludwig von Bertalanffy, a founder of general systems theory and a holdout against the neo-Darwinian tide, often argued that natural selection must fail as a comprehensive theory because it explains _too_ much--a paradoxical, but perceptive statement. He wrote (1969:24, 11):

> If selection is taken as an axiomatic and _a priori_ principle, it is always possible to imagine auxiliary hypotheses--unproved and by nature unprovable--to make it work in any special case... Some adaptive value... can always be construed or imagined.
>
> I think the fact that a theory so vague, so insufficiently verifiable and so far from the criteria otherwise applied in "hard" science, has become a dogma, can only be explained on sociological grounds. Society and science have been so steeped in the ideas of mechanism, utilitarianism, and the economic concept of free competition, that instead of God, Selection was enthroned as ultimate reality.

Similarly, the arguments of Christian fundamentalism used to frustrate me until I realized that there are, in principle, no counter cases and that, on this ground alone, literal bibliolatry is bankrupt. The theory of natural selection is, fortunately, in much better straits. It could be invalidated as a general cause of evolutionary change. (If, for example, Lamarckian inheritance were true and general, then adaptation would arise so rapidly in the Lamarckian mode that natural selection would be powerless to create and would operate only to eliminate.) Moreover, its action and efficacy have been demonstrated experimentally by 60 years of manipulation within Drosophila bottles--not to mention several thousand years of success by plant and animal breeders.

Yet in one area, unfortunately a very large part of evolutionary theory and practice, natural selection has operated like the fundamentalist's God--he who maketh all things. Rudyard Kipling asked how the leopard got its spots, the rhino its wrinkled skin. He called his answers "just-so stories." When evolutionists try to explain form and behavior, they also tell just-so stories--and the agent is natural selection. Virtuosity in invention replaces testability as the criterion for acceptance. This is the procedure that inspired von Bertalanffy's complaint. It is also the practice that has given evolutionary biology a bad name among many experimental scientists in other disciplines. We should heed their disquiet, not dismiss it with a claim that they understand neither natural selection nor the special procedures of historical science.

This style of storytelling might yield acceptable answers if we could be sure of two things: 1) that all bits of morphology and behavior arise as direct results of natural selection, and 2) that only one selective explanation exists for each bit. But, as Darwin insisted vociferously, and contrary to the mythology about him, there is much more to evolution than natural selection. (Darwin was a consistent pluralist who viewed natural selection as the most important agent of evolutionary change, but who accepted a range of other agents and specified the conditions of their presumed effectiveness. In Chapter 7 of the Origin (6th ed.), for example, he attributed the cryptic coloration of a flat fish's upper surface to natural selection and the migration of its eyes to inheritance of acquired characters. He continually insisted that he wrote his 2-volume Variation of Animals and Plants Under Domestication (1868), with its Lamarckian hypothesis of pangenesis, primarily to illustrate the effect of evolutionary factors other than natural selection. In a letter to Nature in 1880, he used the sharpest and most waspish language of his life to castigate Sir Wyville Thomson for caricaturing his theory by ascribing all evolutionary change to natural selection.)

Since God can be bent to support all theories, and since Darwin ranks closest to deification among evolutionary biologists, panselectionists of the modern synthesis tended to remake Darwin in their image. But we now reject this rigid version of natural selection and grant a major role to other evolutionary agents--genetic drift, fixation of neutral mutations, for example. We must also recognize that many features arise indirectly as developmental consequences of other features subject to natural selection--see classic (Huxley 1932) and modern (Gould 1966 and 1975; Cock 1966) work on allometry and the developmental consequences of size increase. Moreover, and perhaps most importantly, there are a multitude of potential selective explanations for each feature. There is no such thing in nature as a self-evident and unambiguous story.

When we examine the history of favored stories for any particular adaptation, we do not trace a tale of increasing truth as one story replaces the last, but rather a chronicle of shifting fads and fashions. When Newtonian mechanical explanations were riding high, G.G. Simpson wrote (1961:1686):

> The problem of the pelycosaur dorsal fin...seems essentially solved by Romer's demonstration that the regression relationship of fin area to body volume is appropriate to the functioning of the fin as a temperature regulating mechanism.

Simpson's firmness seems almost amusing since now--a mere 15 years later with behavioral stories in vogue--most paleontologists feel equally sure that the sail was primarily a device for sexual display. (Yes, I know the litany: It might have performed both functions. But this too is a story.)

On the other side of the same shift in fashion, a recent article on functional endothermy in some large beetles had this to say about the why of it all (Bartholomew and Casey 1977: 883):

> It is possible that the increased power and speed of terrestrial locomotion associated with a modest elevation of body temperatures may offer reproductive advantages by increasing the effectiveness of intraspecific aggressive behavior, particularly between males.

This conjecture reflects no evidence drawn from the beetles themselves, only the current fashion in selective stories. We may be confident that the same data, collected 15 years ago, would have inspired a speculation about improved design and mechanical advantage.

Sociobiological Stories

Most work in sociobiology has been done in the mode of adaptive storytelling based upon the optimizing character and pervasive power of natural selection. As such, its weaknesses of methodology are those that have plagued so much of evolutionary theory for more than a century. Sociobiologists have anchored their stories in the basic Darwinian notion of selection as individual reproductive success. Though previously underemphasized by students of behavior, this insistence on selection as individual success is fundamental to Darwinism. It arises directly from Darwin's construction of natural selection as a conscious analog to the laissez-faire economics of Adam Smith with its central notion that order and harmony arise from the natural interaction of individuals pursuing their own advantages (see Schweber 1977).

Sociobiologists have broadened their range of selective stories by invoking concepts of inclusive fitness and kin selection to solve (successfully I think) the vexatious problem of altruism--previously the greatest stumbling block to a Darwinian theory of social behavior. Altruistic acts are the cement of stable societies. Until we could explain apparent acts of self-sacrifice as potentially beneficial to the genetic fitness of sacrificers themselves--propagation of genes through enhanced survival of kin, for example--the prevalence of altruism blocked any Darwinian theory of social behavior.

Thus, kin selection has broadened the range of permissible stories, but it has not alleviated any methodological difficulties in the process of storytelling itself. Von Bertalanffy's objections still apply, if anything with greater force because behavior is generally more plastic and more difficult to specify and homologize than morphology. Sociobiologists are still telling speculative stories, still hitching without evidence to one potential star among many, still using mere consistency with natural selection as a criterion of acceptance.

David Barash (1976), for example, tells the following story about mountain bluebirds. (It is, by the way, a perfectly plausible story that may well be true. I only wish to criticize its assertion without evidence or test, using consistency with natural selection as the sole criterion for useful speculation.) Barash reasoned that a male bird might be more sensitive to intrusion of other males before eggs are laid than after (when he can be certain that his genes are inside). So Barash studied two nests, making three observations at 10-day intervals, the first before the eggs were laid, the last two after. For each period of observation, he mounted a stuffed male near the nest while the male occupant was out foraging. When the male returned he counted aggressive encounters with both model and female. At time one, males in both nests were aggressive toward the model and less, but still substantially, aggressive toward the female as well. At time two, after eggs had been laid, males were less aggressive to models and scarcely aggressive to females at all. At time three, males were still less aggressive toward models, and not aggressive at all toward females. Barash concludes that he has established consistency with natural selection and need do no more (1976: 1099-1100):

> These results are consistent with the expectations of evolutionary theory. Thus aggression toward an intruding male (the model) would clearly be especially advantageous early in the breeding season, when territories and nests are normally defended... The initial, aggressive response to the mated female is also adaptive in that, given a situation suggesting a high probability of adultery (i.e., the presence of the model near the female) and assuming that replacement females are available, obtaining a new mate would enhance the fitness of males... The decline in male-female aggressiveness during incubation and fledgling stages could be attributed to the impossibility of being cuckolded after the eggs have been laid... The results are consistent with an evolutionary interpretation. In addition, the term "adultery" is unblushingly employed in this letter without quotation marks, as I believe it reflects a true analogy to the human concept, in the sense of Lorenz. It may also be prophesied that continued application of a similar evolutionary approach will eventually shed considerable light on various human foibles as well.

Consistent, yes. But what about the obvious alternative, dismissed without test in a line by Barash: male returns at times two and three, approaches the model a few times, encounters no reaction, mutters to himself the avian equivalent of "it's that damned stuffed bird again," and ceases to bother. And why not the evident test: expose a male to the model for the <u>first</u> time <u>after</u> the eggs are laid.

We have been deluged in recent years with sociobiological stories. Some, like Barash's are plausible, if unsupported. For many others, I can only confess my intuition of extreme unlikeliness, to say the least--for adaptive and genetic arguments about why fellatio and cunnilingus are more common among the upper classes (Weinrich 1977), or why male panhandlers are more successful with females and people who are eating than with males and people who are not eating (Lockard et al. 1976).

Not all of sociobiology proceeds in the mode of storytelling for individual cases. It rests on firmer methodological ground when it seeks broad correlations across taxonomic lines, as between reproductive strategy and distribution of resources, for example (Wilson 1975), or when it can make testable, quantitative predictions as in Trivers and Hare's work on haplodiploidy and eusociality in Hymenoptera (Trivers and Hare 1976). Here sociobiology has had and will continue to have success. And here I wish it well. For it represents an extension of basic Darwinism to a realm where it should apply.

Special Problems for Human Sociobiology

Sociobiological explanations of human behavior encounter two major difficulties, suggesting that a Darwinian model may be generally inapplicable in this case.

Limited Evidence and Political Clout

We have little direct evidence about the genetics of behavior in humans; and we do not know how to obtain it for the specific behaviors that figure most prominently in sociobiological speculation--aggression, conformity, etc. With our long generations, it is difficult to amass much data on heritability. More important, we cannot (ethically, that is) perform the kind of breeding experiments, in standardized environments, that would yield the required information. Thus, in dealing with humans, sociobiologists rely even more heavily than usual upon speculative storytelling.

At this point, the political debate engendered by sociobiology comes appropriately to the fore. For these speculative stories about human behavior have broad implications and proscriptions for social policy--and this is true quite apart from the intent or personal politics of the storyteller. Intent and usage are different things; the latter marks political and social influence, the former is gossip or, at best, sociology.

The common political character and effect of these stories lies in the direction historically taken by innatist arguments about human behavior and capabilities--a defense of existing social arrangements as part of our biology.

In raising this point, I do not act to suppress truth for fear of its political consequences. Truth, as we understand it, must always be our primary criterion. We live, because we must, with all manner of unpleasant biological truth--death being the most pervasive and ineluctable. I complain because sociobiological stories are not truth but unsupported speculations with political clout (again, I must emphasize, quite apart from the intent of the storyteller). All science is embedded in cultural contexts, and the lower the ratio of data to social importance, the more science reflects the context.

In stating that there is politics in sociobiology, I do not criticize the scientists involved in it by claiming that an unconscious politics has intruded into a supposedly objective enterprise. For they are behaving like all good scientists--as human beings in a cultural context. I only ask for a more explicit recognition of the context and, specifically, for more attention to the evident impact of speculative sociobiological stories. For example, when the New York Times runs a weeklong front page series on women and their rising achievements and expectations, spends the first four days documenting progress toward social equality, devotes the last day to potential limits upon this progress, and advances sociobiological stories as the only argument for potential limits--then we know that these are stories with consequences:

> Sociologists believe that women will continue for some years to achieve greater parity with men, both in the work place and in the home. But an uneasy sense of frustration and pessimism is growing among some advocates of full female equality in the face of mounting conservative opposition. Moreover, even some staunch feminists are reluctantly reaching the conclusion that women's aspirations may ultimately be limited by inherent biological differences that will forever leave men the dominant sex (New York Times, Nov. 30, 1977).

The article then quotes two social scientists, each with a story.

> If you define dominance as who occupies formal roles of responsibility, then there is no society where males are not dominant. When something is so universal, the probability is--as reluctant as I am to say it--that there is some quality of the organism that leads to this condition.
>
> It may mean that there never will be full parity in jobs, that women will always predominate in the caring tasks like teaching and social work and in the life sciences, while men will prevail in those requiring more aggression--business and politics, for

example--and in the 'dead' sciences like physics.

Adaptation in Humans Need Not Be Genetic and Darwinian

The standard foundation of Darwinian just-so stories does not apply to humans. That foundation is the implication: if adaptive, then genetic--for the inference of adaptation is usually the only basis of a genetic story, and Darwinism is a theory of genetic change and variation in populations.

Much of human behavior is clearly adaptive, but the problem for sociobiology is that humans have so far surpassed all other species in developing an alternative, nongenetic system to support and transmit adaptive behavior--cultural evolution. An adaptive behavior does not require genetic input and Darwinian selection for its origin and maintenance in humans; it may arise by trial and error in a few individuals that do not differ genetically from their groupmates, spread by learning and imitation, and stabilize across generations by value, custom and tradition. Moreover, cultural transmission is far more powerful in potential speed and spread than natural selection--for cultural evolution operates in the "Lamarckian" mode by inheritance through custom, writing and technology of characteristics acquired by human activity in each generation.

Thus, the existence of adaptive behavior in humans says nothing about the probability of a genetic basis for it, or about the operation of natural selection. Take, for example, Trivers' (1971) concept of "reciprocal altruism." The phenomenon exists, to be sure, and it is clearly adaptive. In honest moments, we all acknowledge that many of our "altruistic" acts are performed in the hope and expectation of future reward. Can anyone imagine a stable society without bonds of reciprocal obligation? But structural necessities do not imply direct genetic coding. (All human behaviors are, of course, part of the potential range permitted by our genotype--but sociobiological speculations posit direct natural selection for specific behavioral traits.) As Benjamin Franklin said: "We must all hang together, or assuredly we shall all hang separately."

Failure of the Research Program for Human Sociobiology

The grandest goal--I do not say the only goal--of human sociobiology must fail in the face of these difficulties. That goal is no less than the reduction of the behavioral (indeed most of the social) sciences to Darwinian theory.

Wilson (1975) presents a vision of the human sciences shrinking in their independent domain, absorbed on one side by neurobiology and on the other by sociobiology.

But this vision cannot be fulfilled, for the reason cited above. Although we can identify adaptive behavior in humans, we cannot tell thereby if it is genetically based (while much of it must arise by fairly pure cultural evolution). Yet the reduction of the human sciences to Darwinism requires the genetic argument, for Darwinism is a theory about genetic change in populations. All else is analogy and metaphor.

My crystal ball shows the human sociobiologists retreating to a fallback position--indeed it is happening already. They will argue that this fallback is as powerful as their original position, though it actually represents the unravelling of their fondest hopes. They will argue: yes, indeed, we cannot tell whether an adaptive behavior is genetically coded or not. But it doesn't matter. The same adaptive constraints apply whether the behavior evolved by cultural or Darwinian routes, and biologists have identified and explicated the adaptive constraints. (Steve Emlen (this volume) reports, for example, that some Indian peoples gather food in accordance with predictions of optimal foraging strategy, a theory developed by ecologists. This is an exciting and promising result within an anthropological domain--for it establishes a fruitful path of analogical illumination between biological theory and non-genetic cultural adaptation. But it prevents the assimilation of one discipline by the other and frustrates any hope of incorporating the human sciences under the Darwinian paradigm.)

But it does matter. It makes all the difference in the world whether human behaviors develop and stabilize by cultural evolution or by direct Darwinian selection for genes influencing specific adaptive actions. Cultural and Darwinian evolution differ profoundly in the three major areas that embody what evolution, at least as a quantitative science, is all about:

1. Rate. Cultural evolution, as a "Lamarckian" process, can proceed orders of magnitude more rapidly than Darwinian evolution. Natural selection continues its work within *Homo sapiens*, probably at characteristic rates for change in large, fairly stable populations, but the power of cultural evolution has dwarfed its influence (alteration in frequency of the sickling gene vs. changes in modes of communication and transportation). Consider what we have done with ourselves in the past 3000 years, all without the slightest evidence

for any biological change in the size or power of the human brain.

2. Modifiability. Complex traits of cultural evolution can be altered profoundly all at once (social revolution, for example). Darwinian change is much slower and more piecemeal.

3. Diffusibility. Since traits of cultural evolution can be transmitted by imitation and inculcation, evolutionary patterns include frequent and complex anastomosis among branches. Darwinian evolution in sexually reproducing animals is a process of continuous divergence and ramification with few opportunities for coming together (hybridization or parallel modification of the same genes in independent groups).

I believe that the future will bring mutual illumination between two vigorous, independent disciplines--Darwinian theory and cultural history. This is a good thing, joyously to be welcomed. But there will be no reduction of the human sciences to Darwinian theory and the research program of human sociobiology will fail. The name, of course, may survive. It is an irony of history that movements are judged successful if their label sticks, even though the emerging content of a discipline may lie closer to what opponents originally advocated. Modern geology, for example, is an even blend of Lyell's strict uniformitarianism and the claims of catastrophists (Rudwick 1972; Gould 1977). But we call the hybrid doctrine by Lyell's name and he has become the conventional hero of geology.

I welcome the coming failure of reductionistic hopes because it will lead us to recognize human complexity at its proper level. For consumption by _Time_'s millions, my colleague Bob Trivers maintained: "Sooner or later, political science, law, economics, psychology, psychiatry, and anthropology will all be branches of sociobiology" (_Time_, Aug. 1, 1977:54). It is one thing to conjecture, as I would allow, that common features among independently developed legal systems might reflect adaptive constraints and might be explicated usefully with some biological analogies. It is quite another to state, as Trivers did, that the mores of the entire legal profession will be subsumed, along with a motley group of other disciplines, as mere epiphenomena of Darwinian processes.

I read Trivers' statement the day after I had sung in a full production of Berlioz' _Requiem_. And I remembered the visceral reaction I had experienced upon hearing the 4 brass choirs, finally amalgamated with the 10 tympani in the massive din preceding the great *Tuba mirum*--the spine tingling and the involuntary tears that almost prevented me from singing. I tried to analyze it in the terms of Wilson's conjecture--reduction of behavior to neurobiology on the one hand and sociobiology on the other. And I realized that this conjecture might apply to my experience. My reaction had been physiological and, as a good mechanist, I do not doubt that its neurological foundation can be ascertained. I will also not be surprised to learn that the reaction has something to do with adaptation (emotional overwhelming to cement group coherence in the face of danger, to tell a story). But I also realized that these explanations, however "true," could never capture anything of importance about the meaning of that experience.

And I say this not to espouse mysticism or incomprehensibility, but merely to assert that the world of human behavior is too complex and multifarious to be unlocked by any simple key. I say this to maintain that this richness--if anything--is both our hope and our essense.

Summary

Even since Darwin proposed it, the theory of natural selection has been marred by an uncritical style of speculative application to the study of individual adaptations: one simply constructs a story to explain how a shape, function, or behavior might benefit its possessor. Virtuosity in invention replaces testability and mere consistency with evolutionary theory becomes the primary criterion of acceptance. Although this dubious procedure has been used throughout evolutionary biology, it has recently become the primary style of explanation in sociobiology.

Human sociobiology presents two major problems related to this tradition. First, evidence is so poor or lacking that speculative storytelling assumes even greater importance than usual. Secondly, the existence of behavioral adaptation does not imply the operation of Darwinian processes at all--for non-genetic cultural evolution, working in the Lamarckian mode, dwarfs by its rapidity the importance of slower Darwinian change. The sociobiological vision of a reduction of the human sciences to biology via Darwinism and natural selection will fail. Instead, I anticipate fruitful, mutual illumination by analogy between independent theories of the human and biological sciences.

Literature Cited

Barash, D. 1976. Male response to apparent female adultery in the mountain bluebird (*Sialia currucoides*): An evolutionary interpretation. *American Naturalist* 110:1097-1101.

Bartholomew, G.A. and T.M. Casey. 1977. Endothermy during terrestrial activity in large beetles. *Science* 195:882-883.

Bertalanffy, L. von. 1969. Chance or law. *In* A. Koestler (ed.). *Beyond reductionism*. Hutchinson, London.

Cock, A.G. 1966. Genetical aspects of metrical growth and form in animals. *Quarterly Review of Biology* 41:131-190.

Darwin, C. 1868. *The variation of animals and plants under domestication*. John Murray, London.

_______, 1880. Sir Wyville Thomson and natural selection. *Nature* 23:32.

Gould, S.J. 1966. Allometry and size in ontogeny and phylogeny. *Biological Reviews* 41:587-640.

_______, 1975. Allometry in primates, with emphasis on scaling and the evolution of the brain. *In* Approaches to primate paleobiology. *Contributions to Primatology* 5: 244-292.

_______, 1977. Eternal metaphors of paleontology. *In* A. Hallam (ed.). *Patterns of evolution*. Elsevier, Amsterdam, pp. 1-26.

Huxley, J. 1932. *Problems of relative growth.* MacVeagh, London.

Lockard, J.S., L.L. McDonald, D.A. Clifford, and R.Martinez. 1976. Panhandling: Sharing of resources. *Science* 191: 406-408.

Rudwick, M.J.S. 1972. *The meaning of fossils*. Macdonald, London.

Schweber, S.S. 1977. The origin of the *Origin* revisited. *Journal of the History of Biology* 10:229-316.

Simpson, G.G. 1961. Some problems of vertebrate paleontology. *Science* 133:1679-1689.

Trivers, R. 1971. The evolution of reciprocal altruism. Quarterly Review of Biology 46:35-57

Trivers, R. and H. Hare. 1976. Haplodiploidy and the evolution of the social insects. Science 191:249-263.

Weinrich, J.D. 1977. Human sociobiology: Pair-bonding and resource predictability (effects of social class and race). Behavioral Ecology and Sociobiology 2:91-118.

Wilson, E.O. 1975. Sociobiology: The New Synthesis. Harvard University Press, Cambridge, Massachusetts.

Part 4

Genes and the Games They Play

John C. DeFries

11. Genetics of Animal and Human Behavior

Introduction

Sociobiology has been defined as the "systematic study of the biological basis of all social behavior" (Wilson 1975: 595). Therefore, studies of the genetic basis of social behavior are of obvious relevance to sociobiology. Behavioral genetics, however, is concerned with the inheritance of all behavioral characters, both individual and social (McClearn & DeFries 1973a). Thus, although the two disciplines are overlapping (i.e., they are not mutually exclusive), behavioral genetics is not a subset of sociobiology. Nevertheless, a full understanding of the biological basis of social behavior will be possible only after its genetic basis has been elucidated.

One of the first goals of behavioral genetics is to assess the heritable nature of individual differences in behavior. This goal has been achieved, to varying degrees, for numerous behavioral characters (for a recent review, see DeFries & Plomin 1978). However, the type of analysis used and the level of understanding achieved have depended greatly upon the nature of the character and species under investigation. In order to illustrate these differences, three separate studies which my colleagues and I have conducted during the last several years will be reviewed. The first is a genetic analysis of open-field behavior in laboratory mice (*Mus musculus*); the second concerns a measure of social behavior in the same species; the third is a study of specific cognitive abilities in human populations.

Open-Field Behavior

The open-field test was devised by the psychologist, Calvin S. Hall, to provide an objective measure of emotionality (Hall 1934). The test consists of placing a subject in

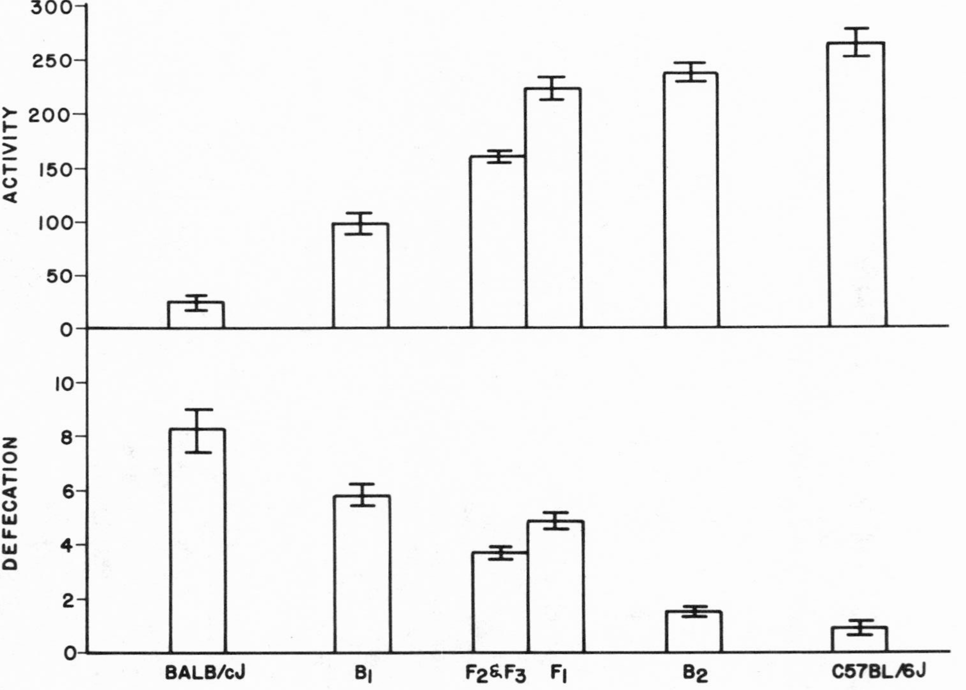

Fig. 1. Mean open-field activity and defecation scores (± twice the standard error) of BALB/cJ and C57BL/6J mice and their derived F1, backcross (B1 and B2), F2 and F3 generations. Sample sizes were as follows: BALB = 64; B1 = 257; F2 and F3 = 1478; F1 = 415; B2 = 315; C57BL = 112. (From DeFries, Gervais and Thomas 1978; reprinted with permission from Behavior Genetics with permission from Plenum

a brightly illuminated enclosure and scoring its behavior. When placed in this novel situation, the animal may "freeze," defecate and urinate, or it may actively explore its surroundings. Subjects which obtain relatively low activity and high elimination scores are regarded as being "emotional" or "reactive," whereas those with relatively high activity and low elimination scores are termed "nonemotional" or "nonreactive."

Although the validity of the open-field test as an index of emotionality is controversial (see Archer 1973, 1975; Broadhurst 1975, 1976), open-field behavior of laboratory rats and mice has been widely used as a prototype for the genetic analysis of complex behavioral characters (Broadhurst 1960; DeFries, Gervais & Thomas 1978; DeFries & Hegmann 1970; DeFries, Hegmann & Halcomb 1974; Halcomb et al. 1975; Henderson 1967). I shall describe one large-scale genetic analysis of open-field behavior which utilized laboratory mice as experimental animals.

Data were obtained initially on 2,641 mice which were members of two highly inbred strains (BALB/cJ and C57BL/6J) and their derived F1, backcross, F2 and F3 generations. Each mouse was tested individually for three minutes on each of two successive days at 40±5 days of age in a square (three-foot by three-foot) open field (DeFries & Hegmann 1970). The floor of the field was brightly illuminated (incident light levels of about 48 foot-candles) and partitioned by a grid of photobeams, interruption of which activated counters. At the conclusion of each test, the mouse was removed and the numbers of light beams interrupted and fecal boluses deposited in the field were recorded. The floor was then washed with tap water and wiped dry with a paper towel.

For all practical purposes, individual members of a given inbred strain (such as BALB/c or C57BL/6) are genetically identical, whereas members of different inbred strains may differ at many gene loci. Thus, a comparison of different inbred strains reared in the same laboratory environment provides a direct test of the importance of gene differences. There was about a ten-fold difference between the mean activity scores of the two highly inbred strains (Fig. 1). Moreover, among the derived generations, there was a monotonic increasing relationship between activity level and percent of genes obtained from the C57BL/6J progenitor strain. The fact that the mean of the F1 generation was significantly higher than that of the F2 and F3 generations provided evidence of some directional dominance for open-field activity. In the case of the defecation scores (Fig. 1), there was about an eight-fold difference between the means of

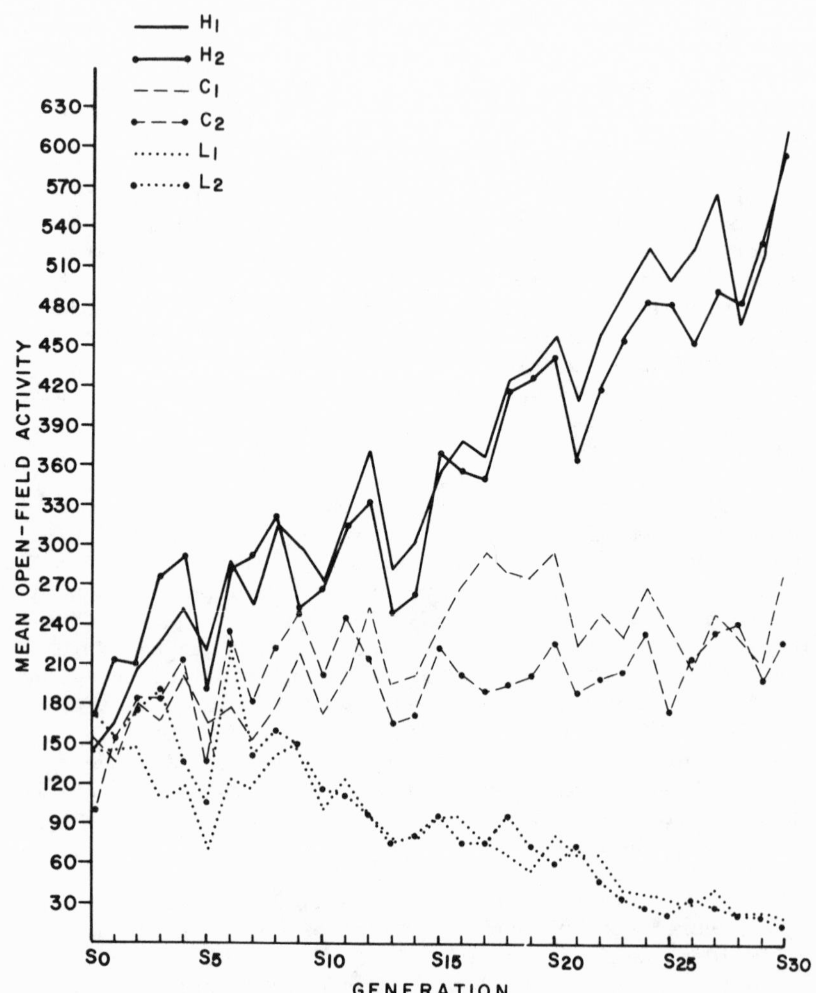

Fig. 2. Mean open-field activity scores of six lines of mice--two selected for high open-field activity (H1 and H2), two selected for low open-field activity (L1 and L2), and two randomly mated within line to serve as controls (C1 and C2). (From DeFries, Gervais & Thomas 1978; reprinted from Behavior Genetics with the permission of Plenum Publishing Corporation.

the two inbred strains and a pronounced negative correlation with mean activity level across the derived generations.

Quantitative genetic analyses of these data have been reported (DeFries & Hegmann 1970). The proportions of observed variance due to average, or "additive," gene effects for open-field activity and defecation scores were found to be moderately low--about .25 and .10, respectively. [As explained by McClearn and DeFries (1973a), heritability = V_A/V_P, where V_A is the additive genetic variance and V_P is the phenotypic variance.] In contrast, evidence was obtained for a large, negative genetic correlation (about -.80) between the two measures, suggesting that individual differences in open-field activity and defecation scores are influenced by many of the same genes.

Minimum estimates of the number of loci responsible for differences between the two inbred strains were 3.2 and 7.4 for activity and defecation, respectively. Since these are minimum estimates, it was concluded that both characters are probably polygenic, i.e., influenced by genes at many loci. Nevertheless, evidence for a major-gene effect was obtained: Albino mice, on the average, were found to have lower activity and higher defecation scores than pigmented animals (DeFries 1969; DeFries et al. 1966; Hegmann et al. 1974).

Members of the heterogeneous F3 generation were used as the foundation population for a selection experiment in which six closed lines were formed--two selected for high open-field activity (H1 and H2), two selected for low activity (L1 and L2), and two maintained as unselected controls (C1 and C2). Within-litter selection was practiced, and the number of mating pairs per line was ten or less each generation. Thirty generations of selection were completed between June, 1966, and November, 1976. The number of mice tested in the individual lines each generation varied from 44 to 108 (total N = 14,184).

Examination of Figure 2 shows that a marked and highly reliable (as indicated by the similarity of the replicated lines) response to selection was achieved. After 30 generations of selection, the high-activity lines had mean activity scores more than 30 times higher than those of the low-activity lines. This difference is almost three times greater than that observed between the two inbred parental strains (see Fig. 1). If C57BL/6J mice had been homozygous for all of the genes which result in high open-field activity ("increasing" alleles), and if members of the BALB/cJ inbred strain had been homozygous for all of the "decreasing" alleles, the difference between the selected lines could not

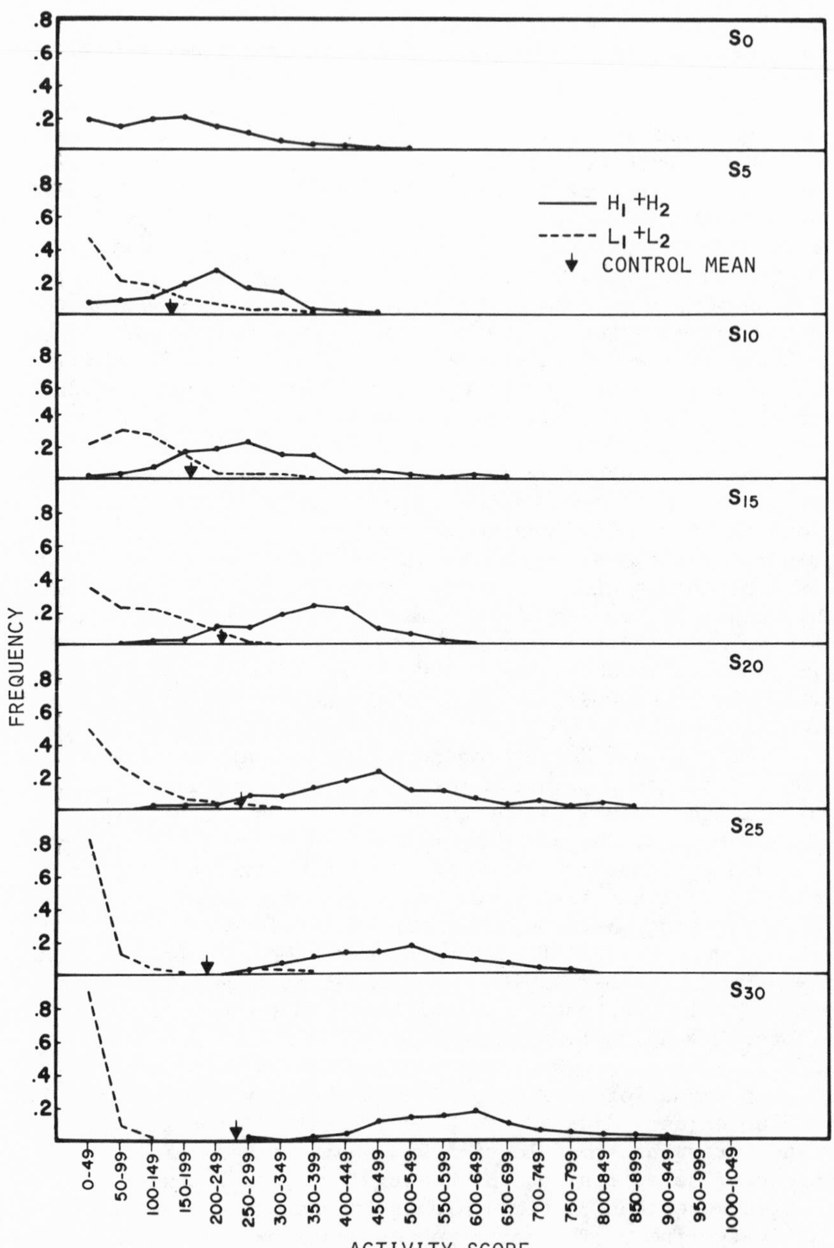

Fig. 3. Distributions of activity scores of lines selected for high and low open-field activity. Average activity of controls each generation is indicated by an arrow. (From DeFries, Gervais & Thomas 1978; reprinted from Behavior Genetics with the permission of Plenum Publishing Corporation.

have exceeded that between the inbred progenitor strains in the absence of intracistronic recombination. A difference of the size observed in this experiment indicates that members of the low-active inbred strain (BALB/cJ) must be homozygous for some "increasing" alleles, while members of the high-active (C57BL/6J) strain must be homozygous for some "decreasing" alleles. This finding, plus the observation that the response to selection continued over a period of 30 generations, supports the previous evidence for the polygenic nature of open-field activity.

The response to selection for open-field activity was relatively symmetrical through the 20th generation (S20), i.e., the high and low lines were about equally different from the controls. During the last ten generations, however, the response to selection became asymmetrical. This asymmetrical response was apparently due to a "floor effect," the existence of which is obvious in Figure 3. The distributions of the high and low lines are presented at five-generation intervals in this figure, and the unweighted means of the control lines are indicated by arrows. A marked "piling up" of scores at the lower end of the distribution of the low lines, which became progressively more pronounced during the course of selection, may be noted. By the 30th generation, the distributions were completely nonoverlapping; in other words, the most active mouse in the low-activity lines exhibited lower activity than the least active mouse in the high-activity lines. This result demonstrates the power of selection to modify behavior, even for a character with only a moderately low heritability.

Distributions of the defecation scores are summarized in Figure 4. Note again the existence of a "floor effect," as well as a gradual divergence between the lines as a function of selection for open-field activity. After 30 generations of selection, open-field defecation scores of the low-activity lines were approximately seven times higher than those of the high-activity lines, and there was little overlap of their distributions. This correlated response to selection for open-field activity substantiates previous evidence for a large, negative correlation between these two characters.

It was previously noted that albino mice, on the average, have lower open-field activity scores than pigmented animals. If there is a major-gene effect due to albinism, the frequency of albinism, which is about .25 in generation S0, should increase in the low-activity lines and decrease in the high-activity lines as a function of selection for open-field activity. In our experiment, the frequency of albinism

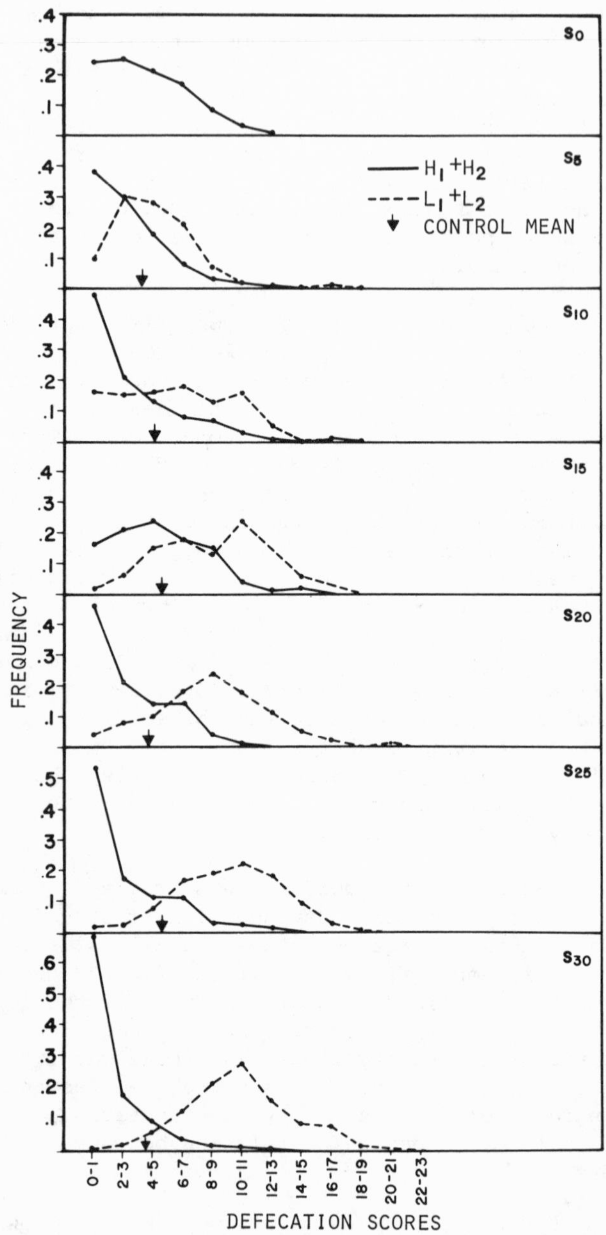

Fig. 4. Distributions of defecation scores of lines selected for high and low open-field activity. Average defecation score of controls each generation is indicated by an arrow. (From DeFries, Gervais & Thomas 1978; reprinted from Behavior Genetics with permission from Plenum Publishing Corporation.

did diverge rapidly between the high- and low-activity lines in the expected direction (Fig. 5). In fact, the allele for albinism became fixed in L2 during generation S8 and in L1 during S23. In contrast, selection apparently eliminated this allele from H2 and greatly reduced its frequency in H1.

A marked divergence in the frequency of albinism may also be noted between the two control lines, C1 and C2. Since no selection was applied to the control lines, these changes must be attributed to stochastic processes. The magnitude of the divergence between C1 and C2 illustrates the fact that chance changes in gene frequency may have marked effects on small populations over a time span of many generations.

As stated previously, quantitative genetic analyses of the data in this study made it possible to estimate the additive genetic variance for open-field activity and defecation scores. It was also possible to estimate that 12 percent of the additive genetic variance for open-field activity level and 26 percent of the additive genetic variance for defecation scores was due to segregation of alleles at the albino locus (DeFries & Hegmann 1970). Thus, although a major-gene effect was found, a relatively large proportion of the genetic variance in these characters is due to segregation of genes at unidentified loci.

Selection studies were undertaken early in the history of behavioral genetics (for a review, see DeFries 1967) and continue to serve as a powerful tool for the genetic analysis of complex behavioral characters. Recently reported responses to selection for diverse behavioral traits (reviewed by DeFries & Plomin 1978) include the following: agonistic behavior in female wild mice; nesting behavior, caudal nerve conduction velocity and seizure susceptibility in laboratory mice; mating ability in quail; and mating reluctance, geotaxis and phototaxis in *Drosophila*. Collectively, these studies demonstrate the ubiquity of genetic variance for behavioral characters and provide valuable subjects to be used in mechanism-related research.

Social Dominance

Numerous experiments have demonstrated that differences in male aggressiveness are, at least to some degree, a function of differences in genotype (see McClearn & DeFries 1973b). Such experiments, however, have usually employed only brief encounters (e.g., 20-minute "bouts") between matched pairs of animals. In order to circumvent to some extent the artificiality of such a paradigm, we developed

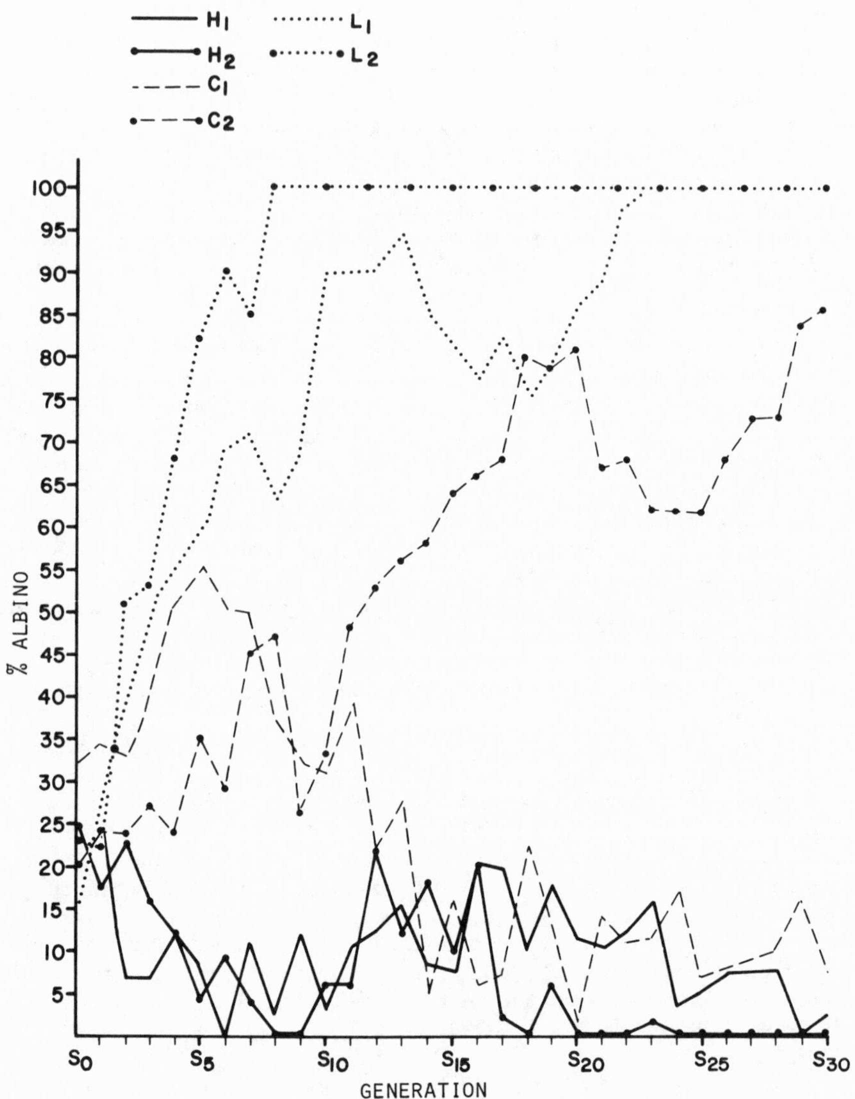

Fig. 5. Frequency of albinism in six lines of mice--two selected for high open-field activity (H1 and H2), two selected for low open-field activity (L1 and L2), and two randomly mated within line to serve as controls (C1 and C2). (From DeFries, Gervais & Thomas 1978; reprinted from <u>Behavior Genetics</u> with permission from Plenum Publishing Corporation.

standardized social living units ("triads") in which the behavior of mice could be observed over extended periods of time. Each triad (Fig. 6) is constructed from three standard mouse cages interconnected by a Y-shaped plastic manifold so that subjects within the triad are free to move from one cage to another. Adequate food, water and bedding are available in each cage.

Results of three experiments employing the triad units were summarized by DeFries and McClearn (1972). In the first experiment, three males, each from a different inbred strain, and three inbred females were placed in each of 22 triads. In the second, each of 20 triads contained inbred males and HS females (a heterogeneous stock derived from an eight-way cross of inbred strains). In the third, 41 triads were assembled which contained F1 males paired with either HS or inbred males, plus either inbred or outbred females. Combination of males placed in a given triad was dictated by the possibility of ascertaining paternity of resulting offspring from their coat colors. Males were examined daily for number of tail wounds (skin punctures) over a two-week period and then removed. Females were retained until any litters conceived in the triad were old enough to be classified for coat color.

In general, strain differences in social dominance were observed. When placed in triads with males from other inbred strains, A and BALB/c males were usually dominant, whereas DBA/2 males were often subordinate. Of even greater interest, however, was the observed relationship between social dominance and reproductive success: In each of the three experiments, over 90 percent of the litters were sired by the dominant males. These results suggest that social dominance among males may be a major component of Darwinian fitness in house mice (*Mus musculus*).

As Bruell (1964) and Roberts (1967) have discussed, characters which are closely (and linearly) related to fitness manifest relatively little additive genetic variance. In other words, most of the genetic variance of fitness characters which have been subjected to directional selection should be nonadditive. Since heterosis, or hybrid vigor, is due to nonadditive gene effects, such characters should be highly heterotic.

When two inbred strains are crossed to produce an F1 generation, all F1 individuals will be heterozygous at each of the loci for which the two inbred strains differ. In a subsequently derived F2 generation, each individual will be heterozygous at half of these loci on the average. Thus, if

Fig. 6. Triad unit used in studies of social behavior of laboratory mice: Interior view. (From DeFries & McClearn 1972; reprinted from _Evolutionary Biology_ with permission from Plenum Publishing Corporation.

social dominance has been a major component of fitness during the evolution of house mice, the predicted rank order of male dominance would be F1 > F2 > inbred, when members of each generation are tested simultaneously.

In order to test this hypothesis, Kuse and DeFries (1976) assembled 30 triads, each containing males (66±5 days of age) from two of three inbred strains (BALB/c, C57BL/6 and DBA/2; symbolized B, C and D, respectively) and corresponding F1 and F2 hybrids. For example, the four males in each of ten BC triads were: a BALB, a C57BL, an F1 obtained from a cross of these two strains, and an F2. BD and CD triads (ten of each) were similarly constituted. In order to investigate the influence of female presence on male aggression, three HS females were placed in half of the triads. Males were examined daily for tail wounds over a seven-day period. The average number of tail wounds for an individual was used as a measure of its social dominance, and the average number of tail wounds for all males in a triad was employed as an index of the intensity of aggressive interactions.

F1 males ranked first (least number of tail wounds) and F2 males ranked second for both BC and CD triad types (Table 1). In the BD triads, however, F1 males ranked third. Nevertheless, when the data were pooled across the three triad types, the comparison of outbred vs. inbred was highly significant ($P < .001$). In addition, significantly more aggression ($P < .001$) was observed to occur in triads which contained females than in those which did not (mean numbers of tail wounds were 6.6 and 3.5, respectively). These

Table 1. Dominance order within triad types.*

BC triads		BD triads		CD triads	
Strain	Mean number of tail wounds	Strain	Mean number of tail wounds	Strain	Mean number of tail wounds
F1	0.63	F2	3.87	F1	0.27
F2	3.89	DBA	6.73	F2	0.44
BALB	5.16	F1	7.47	C57BL	2.67
C57BL	5.86	BALB	10.10	DBA	13.14

*From Kuse and DeFries (1976). BC triads each contained four males: a BALB, a C57BL, an F1 obtained from a cross of these two inbred strains, and an F2. BD and CD triads were constituted in a corresponding manner (see text). (Reprinted from Behavioral Biology with permission from Academic Press, Inc.

Table 2. Names and times of cognitive tests used in the Hawaii Family Study of Cognition.

Test	Test time
Vocabulary, Primary Mental Abilities (PMA) or Korean version	3 minutes
Visual Memory (immediate)	1-minute exposure/ 1-minute recall
Things (a fluency test)	2 parts/3 minutes each
Shepard-Metzler Mental Rotations (modified for group testing by Vandenberg)	10 minutes
Subtraction and Multiplication	2 parts/2 minutes each
Elithorn Mazes ("lines and dots"), shortened form	5 minutes
Word Beginnings and Endings, Educational Testing Servide (ETS) or Korean version	2 parts/3 minutes each
ETS Card Rotations	2 parts/3 minutes each
Visual Memory (delayed recall)	1 minute
PMA Pedigrees (a reasoning test)	4 minutes
ETS Hidden Patterns	2 parts/2 minutes each
Paper Form Board	3 minutes
ETS Number Comparisons	2 parts/1.5 minutes each
Whiteman Test of Social Perception	10 minutes
Raven's Progressive Matrices, modified form	20 minutes

findings of heterosis for social dominance among males and increased intermale aggression in the presence of females support the hypothesis that social dominance is a major component of Darwinian fitness in house mice. Results of a recent selection experiment (Banker 1977) are consistent with this interpretation.

Specific Cognitive Abilities

Inbred strain comparisons and selective breeding studies readily demonstrate that behavioral characters of laboratory animals have a heritable basis. Because such experiments with humans are out of the question, the genetic bases of complex human behavioral characters are necessarily more difficult to ascertain. In order to illustrate some of the complexities inherent in human behavioral genetic investigations, preliminary results of the Hawaii Family Study of Cognition will be briefly reviewed. In this large-scale study, data have been collected on 15 cognitive measures (Table 2), various environmental indices, and blood group and enzyme systems.

Two major ethnic groups, Americans of Japanese ancestry (AJA) and Americans of European ancestry (AEA), were tested in Hawaii, and a cross-cultural sample was tested in the Republic of Korea (ROK). Multivariate analyses have revealed that the cognitive structures of the two ethnic groups tested in Hawaii are nearly identical (DeFries, Vandenberg et al. 1974). Four readily interpretable factors emerged from these analyses: spatial visualization, verbal, perceptual speed, and visual memory. Corresponding analysis of the ROK data (Park 1975) revealed a similar, but not identical, factor structure.

Age-adjusted spouse correlations were calculated for factor scores (linear composites of the 15 cognitive measures which correspond to the four factors). The data in Table 3 show that the spouse correlations of couples tested in Korea are significantly higher than those of couples tested in Hawaii. Tests in Korea were administered to individual family units, whereas tests in Hawaii were administered to large groups under highly standardized conditions. This difference in method of test administration may account for some of the observed differences in the spouse correlations. However, when tests were given to nuclear family units on the United States mainland, resulting AEA spouse correlations were considerably lower than those of ROK couples (Zonderman et al. 1977). Therefore, method of test administration cannot entirely account for the observed differences. It has been suggested (Johnson et al. 1976) that at least some of the

Table 3. Age-adjusted spouse correlations for factor scores in three ethnic groups.*

	Hawaiian AEA	Hawaiian AJA	Korean (ROK)
Factors			
Spatial	.16	.01	.43†
Verbal	.21	.22	.46†
Perceptual Speed	.13	.00	.78†
Visual Memory	.00	.13	.30‡
Number of couples	555	148	200

*From Johnson et al. (1976). AEA = Americans of European ancestry; AJA = Americans of Japanese ancestry. †Significantly greater ($P \leq .05$) than corresponding Hawaiian AEA and AJA correlations. ‡Significantly greater ($P \leq .05$) than corresponding Hawaiian AEA correlation. 1976 Social Biology 23:311-316. Reprinted with permission.

difference between the Hawaiian and the ROK spouse correlations may be due to cultural factors, such as the Korean practice of arranged marriages.

If members of human families were not reared in more similar environments than individuals chosen at random from the population, then the regression of a child's score on the average score of its parents (mid-parent value) could be used as a direct estimate of heritability (see DeFries, Ashton et al. 1978). However, children are likely to be reared in environments which, at least to some extent, are similar to those experienced by their parents. If these common environmental experiences influence the character under study, and if they differ among families, they will contribute to the observed resemblance between children and their parents. Consequently, measures of parent-child resemblance, such as the regression of offspring on mid-parent value, should be regarded only as indices of phenotypic (genetic and/or environmental) similarity. To the extent that common (between-family) environmental effects are important, such measures will yield overestimates of heritability.

Regressions of offspring (children were 13 years of age or older) on mid-parent values for the four factor scores were calculated (Table 4). It may be seen that the coefficients again are higher for families tested in Korea. As was the case with the spouse correlations, some of the difference

Table 4. Regressions of mid-child on mid-parent (± standard error) for factor scores in three ethnic groups.*

	Hawaiian AEA	Hawaiian AJA	Korean (ROK)
Factors			
Verbal	.65±.04	.58±.07	.73±.06
Spatial	.61±.04	.44±.08	.67±.07†
Perceptual Speed	.45±.04	.32±.09	.74±.05‡
Visual Memory	.44±.05	.31±.09	.55±.08†
Number of families	739	244	198

*From Park et al. (1978). AEA = Americans of European ancestry; AJA = Americans of Japanese ancestry. †Significantly greater (P ≤ .05) than corresponding Hawaiian AJA regression coefficient. ‡Significantly greater (P ≤ .05) than corresponding Hawaiian AEA and AJA regression coefficients. Reprinted from Behavior Genetics with permission from Plenum Publishing Corporation.

may be due to the use of different methods of test administration. However, it has been pointed out (Park et al. 1978) that differences in assortative mating (as indexed by the different spouse correlations) may also be a factor. It is well known that assortative mating increases additive genetic variance in a population. An increased additive genetic variance would yield a higher heritability and, hence, a higher regression of offspring on mid-parent value. Thus, differences in spouse correlations may account, at least in part, for the observed differences in parent-child resemblance. On the other hand, since parent-offspring regressions are also influenced by environmental experiences common to members of the same family, the data in Table 4 do not provide unambiguous evidence for differential heritability. (For a more detailed discussion of the relationship between spouse correlations and various measures of parent-child resemblance, see DeFries, Ashton et al. 1978.)

Conclusion

As explained above, measures of resemblance between parents and children in human families should be considered only as measures of phenotypic similarity. Significant familial resemblance is a necessary, but not sufficient, condition for demonstrating the presence of genetic variance. In order to circumvent the problem of shared environmental effects in human families, various methods of analysis have been employed. These include twin studies (Gottesman & Shields 1972; Loehlin & Nichols 1976; Vandenberg 1976), path analysis (Rao et al. 1974, 1976), linkage analysis (Haseman & Elston 1972), and adoption studies (Crowe 1975; Munsinger 1975).

In a recent review of the field, Robert Plomin and I (1978) concluded that the adoption method is the most powerful tool for studying complex human behavioral characters. In adoption studies, the resemblance of genetically related individuals reared apart may be compared to that of genetically unrelated individuals living together. Although all of the adoption studies which we reviewed suffer from some methodological shortcomings, they provide the most compelling evidence for the importance of genetic factors in psychopathology and mental ability.

It is our opinion that definitive adoption studies are both possible and necessary to disentangle unambiguously genetic and environmental contributions to human family resemblance. In addition to providing estimates of genetic and common (between-family) environmental variance, such studies could yield evidence concerning the influence of genotype-environment interactions and correlations (Plomin et al. 1977), which critics of human behavioral genetics have asserted are so important (Feldman & Lewontin 1975; Kamin 1978; Layzer 1974).

In his seminal work, <u>Sociobiology: The New Synthesis</u>, E. O. Wilson states that: "Behavioral genetics is still at a relatively elementary level of analysis . . ." (1975: 349). From the studies reviewed above, it should be obvious that Wilson is absolutely correct. At the same time, it should be recalled that, although behavioral genetics may still be in its infancy, sociobiology has only recently been conceived. It remains to be seen whether or not implantation will occur.

Summary

The polygenic nature of complex behavioral characters is exemplified by genetic analyses of open-field behavior in laboratory mice. Quantitative genetic analyses of data from two inbred mouse strains and their derived F1, backcross, F2 and F3 generations indicate that open-field activity is only moderately heritable. Nevertheless, high and low lines resulting from 30 generations of bidirectional selection for this character have nonoverlapping distributions and more than a 30-fold difference in mean activity. Open-field defecation scores of the low-activity lines are approximately seven times higher than those of the high-activity lines, substantiating previous evidence for a large, negative genetic correlation between these two characters. Although open-field behavior is undoubtedly influenced by genes at many loci, a major gene effect has been found. Albino mice, on the average, have lower activity and higher defecation scores than pigmented animals.

Numerous experiments with laboratory mice have demonstrated that individual differences in male aggressiveness are also heritable. When male mice of various genotypes were placed with females in standardized social living units (triads), one male usually became clearly dominant within one or two days. In each of three experiments, over 90 percent of the litters conceived in such triads were sired by dominant animals. In a subsequent study, considerable heterosis for social dominance was observed, and more aggression was found to occur among males in triads that contained females than in triads containing only males. These results are consistent with the hypothesis that social dominance among male mice is a major component of Darwinian fitness.

With regard to complex human behavioral characters, familial resemblance is a necessary, but not sufficient, condition for demonstrating the presence of genetic variance. Adoption studies are required to disentangle genetic and environmental contributions to human family resemblance. In addition to providing estimates of genetic and environmental variance, such studies could yield evidence concerning the importance of genotype-environment interactions and correlations.

Acknowledgements

I wish to acknowledge the support of NICHD research grant HD-10333. I thank Rebecca G. Miles for typing this manuscript and for her superb editorial assistance.

Literature Cited

Archer, J. 1973. Tests for emotionality in rats and mice: A review. Animal Behaviour 21:205-235.

_______. 1975. The Maudsley reactive and nonreactive strains of rats: The need for an objective evaluation of differences. Behavior Genetics 5:411-413.

Banker, D.E. 1977. Selection for a presumed fitness character: Dominance aggression in mice. Masters Thesis, Univeristy of Colorado.

Broadhurst, P.L. 1960. Experiments in psychogenetics. Applications of biometrical genetics to the inheritance of behaviour. In H.J. Eysenck (ed.), Experiments in personality. Vol. 1. Psychogenetics and psychopharmacology. Routledge & Kegan Paul, London, pp. 1-102.

_______. 1975. The Maudsley reactive and nonreactive strains of rats: A survey. Behavior Genetics 5:299-319.

_______. 1976. The Maudsley reactive and nonreactive strains of rats: A clarification. Behavior Genetics 6:363-365.

Bruell, J.H. 1964. Inheritance of behavioral and physiological characters of mice and the problem of heterosis. American Zoologist 4:125-138.

Crowe, R.R. 1975. Adoption studies in psychiatry. Biological Psychiatry 10:353-371.

DeFries, J.C. 1967. Quantitative genetics and behavior: Overview and perspective. In J. Hirsch (ed.), Behavior-genetic analysis. McGraw-Hill, New York, pp. 322-339.

_______. 1969. Pleiotropic effects of albinism on open-field behaviour in mice. Nature (London) 221:65-66.

_______, G.C. Ashton, R.C. Johnson, A.R. Kuse, G.E. McClearn, M.P. Mi, M.N. Rashad, S.G. Vandenberg & J.R. Wilson. 1978. The Hawaii Family Study of Cognition: A reply. Behavior Genetics 8:281-288.

_______, M.C. Gervais & E.A. Thomas. 1978. Response to 30 generations of selection for open-field activity in laboratory mice. Behavior Genetics 8:3-13.

_______ and J.P. Hegmann. 1970. Genetic analysis of open-field behavior. In G. Lindzey & D.D. Thiessen (eds.), Contributions to behavior-genetic analysis: The mouse as a prototype. Appleton-Century-Crofts, New York, pp. 23-56.

_______, J.P. Hegmann & R.A. Halcomb. 1974. Response to 20 generations of selection for open-field activity in mice. Behavioral Biology 11:481-495.

_______, J.P. Hegmann & M.W. Weir. 1966. Open-field behavior in mice: Evidence for a major gene effect mediated by the visual system. Science 154:1577-1579.

_______ & G. E. McClearn. 1972. Behavioral Genetics and the fine structure of mouse populations: A study in microevolution. In Th. Dobzhansky, M.K. Hecht & W.C. Steere (eds.), Evolutionary biology, Vol. 5. Appleton-Century-Crofts, New York, pp. 279-291.

_______ & R. Plomin. 1978. Behavioral genetics. Annual Review of Psychology 29:473-515.

_______, S.G. Vandenberg, G.C. McClearn, A.R. Kuse, J.R. Wilson, G.C. Ashton & R.C. Johnson. 1974. Near identity of cognitive structure in two ethnic groups. Science 183:338-339.

Feldman, M.W. & R.C. Lewontin. 1975. The heritability hang-up. Science 190:1163-1168.

Gottesman, I.I. & J. Shields. 1972. Schizophrenia and genetics: A twin study vantage point. Academic Press, New York.

Halcomb, R.A., J.P. Hegmann & J.C. DeFries. 1975. Open-field behavior in mice: A diallel analysis of selected lines. Behavior Genetics 5:217-231.

Hall, C.S. 1934. Emotional behavior in the rat. I. Defecation and urination as measures of individual differences in emotionality. Journal of Comparative Psychology 18:385-403.

Haseman, J.K. & R.C. Elston. 1972. The investigation of linkage between a quantitative trait and a marker locus. Behavior Genetics 2:3-19.

Hegmann, J.P., R.A. Kieso & H.B. Hartman. 1974. Gene differences influencing visual system function and behavior. Behavior Genetics 4:165-170.

Henderson, N.D. 1967. Prior treatment effects on open-field behaviour of mice--a genetic analysis. Animal Behaviour 15:364-376.

Johnson, R.C., J. Park, J.C. DeFries, G.E. McClearn, M.P. Mi, M.N. Rashad, S.G. Vandenberg & J.R. Wilson. 1976. Assortative marriage for specific cognitive abilities in Korea. Social Biology 23:311-316.

Kamin, L.J. 1978. The Hawaii Family Study of Cognition: A comment. Behavior Genetics 8:275-279.

Kuse, A.R. & J.C. DeFries. 1976. Social dominance and Darwinian fitness in laboratory mice: An alternative test. Behavioral Biology 16:113-116.

Layzer, D. 1974. Heritability analyses of IQ scores: Science or numerology? Science 183:1259-1266.

Loehlin, J.C. & R.C. Nichols. 1976. Heredity, environment, and personality: A study of 850 sets of twins. University of Texas Press, Austin.

McClearn, G.E. & J.C. DeFries. 1973a. Introduction to behavioral genetics. Freeman, San Francisco.

_______. 1973b. Genetics and mouse aggression. In J.F. Knutson (ed.), The control of aggression. Aldine, Chicago.

Munsinger, H. 1975. The adopted child's IQ: A critical review. Psychological Bulletin 82:623-659.

Park, J-Y. 1975. A study of multivariate cognition in Korea in relation to environmental and hereditary influences. Ph.D. Thesis, University of Hawaii.

Park, J., R.C. Johnson, J.C. DeFries, G.E. McClearn, M.P. Mi, M.N. Rashad, S.G. Vandenberg & J.R. Wilson. 1978. Parent-offspring resemblance for specific cognitive abilities in Korea. Behavior Genetics 8:43-52.

Plomin, R., J.C. DeFries & J.C. Loehlin. 1977. Genotype-environment interaction and correlation in the analysis of human behavior. Psychological Bulletin 84:309-322.

Rao, D.C., N.E. Morton & S. Yee. 1974. Analysis of family resemblance. II. A linear model for familiar correlation. American Journal of Human Genetics 26:331-359.

_______. 1976. Resolution of cultural and biological inheritance by path analysis. American Journal of Human Genetics 28:228-242.

Roberts, R.C. 1967. Some evolutionary implications of behavior. Canadian Journal of Genetics and Cytology 9:419-435.

Vandenberg, S.G. 1976. Twin studies. In A.R. Kaplan (ed.), Human behavior genetics. Thomas, Springfield.

Wilson, E.O. 1975. Sociobiology: The new synthesis. Belknap Press, Cambridge.

Zonderman, A.B., S.G. Vandenberg, K.P. Spuhler & P.R. Fain. 1977. Assortative marriage for cognitive abilities. Behavior Genetics 7:261-271.

Edward O. Wilson

12. A Consideration of the Genetic Foundation of Human Social Behavior

Sociobiology is defined as the systematic study of the biological basis of social behavior and the organization of societies in all kinds of organisms, including human beings. Its novelty comes from the current reconsideration of social phenomena with reference to the principles of population ecology and population genetics, many of the most relevant of which are comparatively new. Only within the last several years has this synthesis achieved a large enough aggregate of self-sufficient ideas to qualify as a distinct discipline of biology, but the logic of demarcating such a discipline was apparent many years earlier.

The term sociobiology was used by C. F. Hockett in 1948 in a way that foreshadowed its present usage with special reference to human beings, but this introduction did not appear to influence later authors. In 1950 J. P. Scott, who had been active as the Secretary of the small but influential Committee for the Study of Animal Behavior, suggested sociobiology as the word for the "interdisciplinary science which lies between the fields of biology (particularly ecology and physiology) and psychology and sociology." From 1956 to 1964 Scott and others belonged to a Section on Animal Behavior and Sociobiology of the Ecological Society of America, which became the present Animal Behavior Society. Subsequently "sociobiology" was employed intermittently in technical papers, a usage evidently inspired by this quasiofficial status. But other expressions, such as "biosociology" and "animal sociology," were also employed. When I wrote the final chapter of *The Insect Societies* (1971), which was entitled "The prospect for a unified sociobiology," and *Sociobiology: The New Synthesis* (1975), suggesting that a discrete discipline should now be built with the assistance of population biology, I chose the word sociobiology rather than some other, novel expression because I knew it would already be familiar to most students of animal behavior and hence more likely to be accepted.

It is important to understand that, contrary to the impression given in many popular articles, sociobiology is a discipline and not a particular theory. At the present time it consists of perhaps 90 percent zoology and 10 percent human biology, but of course, inevitably, at least 90 percent of popular writing on the subject concerns the human applications. Nevertheless, not only does human sociobiology comprise only a small part of the discipline, but the validity of the discipline in no way depends on a demonstration that human social behavior has a genetic basis. And contrary to an impression still widespread among social scientists, sociobiology is not the theory that human behavior has a genetic basis.

Indeed, real sociobiological theory allows no less than three possibilities concerning the present status of human social behavior:

(a) During the rapid evolution of the human brain, natural selection exhausted the genetic variability of the species affecting social behavior, so that today virtually all human beings are identical with respect to behavioral potential. In addition, the brain has been "freed" from these genes in the sense that all outcomes are determined by culture. The genes, in other words, merely prescribe the capacity for culture. Or,

(b) Genetic variability has been exhausted, as in (a). But the resulting uniform genotype predisposes psychological development toward certain outcomes as opposed to others. In an ethological sense, species-specific human traits exist and, as in animal repertories, they have a genetic foundation. Or,

(c) Genetic variability still exists, and, as in (b), at least some human behavioral traits have a genetic foundation.

Having identified these alternatives, and stressed the freedom of the discipline of sociobiology from the necessity of any particular outcome, I can now add that the evidence appears to lean heavily in favor of alternative (c). It is well known to students of evolution that all of the general qualities of human social behavior taken together occupy only a tiny envelope in the space of the realized social behaviors. Furthermore, in this respect we most closely resemble the Old World monkeys and apes, which on anatomical and biochemical grounds are generally regarded as the closest living related species. We share the following traits (see, for example, the documentation in Wilson, 1975, 1978):

—— Intimate social groupings contain on the order of 10-100 adults, never just two as in most birds, marmosets, and certain other groups, or thousands as in many species of fish and insects.

—— Males are larger than females, and the size difference is associated with the mild amount of polygyny expected from comparisons with other mammalian species.

—— Male masturbation is commonplace and utilizes distinctive and possibly unique patterns of autostimulation.

—— The young are socialized by a long period of training, first by close association with the mother, then to an increasing degree with children of approximately the same age and sex.

—— Social play is a strongly developed activity, with emphasis on role practice, mock aggression, and exploration.

These and other properties together diagnose the group consisting of the Old World monkeys, the great apes, and human beings. It is inconceivable that human beings could be socialized into the radically different repertories of other phylogenetic groups such as fishes, birds, antelopes, or rodents. Human beings might self-consciously imitate such arrangements, but it would be a fiction played out on a stage, running counter to deep emotional responses and with no chance of persistence through as much as a single generation. To adopt with serious intent even the broad outlines of the social system of a nonprimate species would be insanity in the literal sense. Personalities could be expected to dissolve, relationships disintegrate, and reproduction decline.

Even so, we cannot rest the hypothesis of genetic constraint in human social behavior on the indirect evidences of homology. It is important to use human data in the testing of specific sociobiological hypotheses derived a priori from evolutionary theory. The power of a scientific theory is measured by its ability to transform a small number of axiomatic concepts into detailed predictions of observable phenomena: the Bohr atom, for example, made modern chemistry more valid, and modern chemistry revolutionized cell biology. The validity of a theory is measured by the degree to which its predictions account for the phenomena in competition with other theories: the Copernican universe won over the

Ptolemaic universe after a brief struggle. A theory waxes in influence and esteem among scientists as it assembles an ever larger body of facts into readily remembered and usable explanatory schemes, and as newly discovered facts conform to its demands. Thus Darwinism is preferred to Lamarckism. The crucial facts can be obtained either by experiments designed for the purpose of acquiring them or from the inspired observation of undisturbed natural phenomena. Science has always progressed in approximately this manner.

In the case of the particular hypothesis of the genetic evolution of human nature (which again I stress is one possibility that can be derived from sociobiology but is not identical to it), we should be able to select some of the best principles from ecology and genetics, which are themselves based on evolutionary theory, and adapt them in detail to explanations of human social organization. The hypothesis must then not only account for many of the known facts in a more convincing manner but also identify the need for new kinds of information not previously conceptualized by the social sciences. The behavior thus explained should be the most general and least rational of the human repertory, the furthest removed from the influence of day-to-day deliberation and from the distracting vicissitudes of fashion. It follows that anthropology is the discipline most likely to make immediate use of sociobiology.

There are in fact a substantial number of anthropological studies completed or underway that meet these exacting criteria of postulational-deductive science. Among them can be cited the work of Joseph Shepher (1971) on the incest taboo, Mildred Dickeman (1979) on hypergamy and sex-biased infanticide, William Irons (1979) on the relation between inclusive genetic fitness and the emic criteria of social success in a herding society, Napoleon Chagnon (1974) on aggression and reproductive competition in the Yanomamö, William Durham (1976) on the relation between inclusive fitness and warfare in the Mundurucú and other primitive societies, Robin Fox (1979) on the relation of fitness to kinship rules, Melvin Konner (1976, 1978) and Daniel G. Freedman (1974) on the adaptive significance of infant development, James Weinrich (1977, 1978) on the relationship of genetic fitness and the details of sexual practice, including homosexuality, and others.

It would be entirely premature to draw a general conclusion from the whole of these studies. But I believe it correct to say that to greater or lesser degree each has been designed in a way that can test the particularities of evolutionary theory, and the results thus far are consistent with the hypothesis that the most emotionally controlled forms of human social behavior promote inclusive genetic fitness. It has sometimes been argued by critics that sociobiological theory cannot be tested with human data, or, to put it the other way around, that human sociobiology is untestable. That perception is simply untrue.

Other approaches exist besides the models of population biology. In his study of patients in institutions for the mentally retarded, Richard Wills (1973) found that two distinct types can be identified. "Cultural retardates" have well below normal intelligence, but their behavior retains many uniquely human attributes. They communicate with attendants and one another by speech, and they initiate a variety of relatively sophisticated actions--singing alone and in groups, looking at magazines, working at simple tasks, bathing, grooming themselves, smoking cigarettes, exchanging clothing, and volunteering favors. The second group, the "noncultural retardates," represent a sudden and drastic step downward. They perform none of the actions just listed, and their exchanges with others entail little that can be labeled as distinctively human communication.

Cultural behavior thus appears to be a whole process, invested in the brain or denied in virtually a single step. At the same time the noncultural retardates retain a substantial repertory of more instinctive behavior, the individual actions of which are complex and recognizably mammalian. They communicate with facial expressions and emotion-evoking sounds, examine and manipulate objects, masturbate, watch others, steal, stake out small territories, defend themselves, and play, both as individuals and in groups. They frequently seek physical contact with others, offering and soliciting affection by means of strongly expressed, unmistakable gestures. Virtually none of their responses is abnormal in a mammalian biological sense. Fate appears merely to have denied these patients entry into the cultural world of the brain's outer cortex.

The evidence of genetic variation affecting social behavior is also strong. Many of the more than one thousand loci that have been distinguished in the human genome contain low incidences of alleles that lower intelligence, while most of the chromosomal aberrations have the same effect (McClearn and DeFries 1973). The Lesch-Nyhan syndrome, based on a single gene, and Turner's syndrome, caused by the deletion of a sex chromosome, alter behavior in narrow ways that can be related to specific neuromuscular mechanisms. The closer study of such particularity can provide the means for genetic dissection of the kind successfully used in *Drosophila* behavioral genetics. This method provides new insight into both the details of the organization of behavior and the development of the central nervous system.

As a rule, traits as complex as the attributes of social behavior are influenced by many genes, each of which shares only a small fraction of the total control. In the case of human beings these polygenes can in most instances be evaluated only by twin and adoption studies. Identical and fraternal twins in particular provide a natural controlled experiment with large numbers of replications. The control is the set of identical twins: any differences between the members of a pair must be due to the environment, barring the rare occurrence of a mutation. Differences between the members of pairs of fraternal twins can be due to their heredity, their environment, or some interaction between the two. If identical twins prove to be closer to one another on the average in a given trait than are fraternal twins of the same sex, the difference between the two kinds of twins can be taken as prima facie evidence that the trait is influenced to some degree by heredity. Using this method, geneticists have implicated heredity in the development of a variety of traits that affect social behavior: number ability, word fluency, memory, the timing of language acquisition, sentence construction, perceptual skill, psychomotor skill, extroversion-introversion, homosexuality, and certain forms of neurosis and psychosis, including the manic-depressive syndrome and schizophrenia.

There is a catch in these results that render most of them less than definitive. Identical twins are routinely treated more alike by their parents than are fraternal twins. They are dressed alike more frequently, kept together for longer times, fed the same way, and so forth. In the absence of other information it is possible that the greater similarity of identical twins could, after all, be due to their environment. However, new, more sophisticated studies have begun to take account of this additional factor. For example, Loehlin and Nichols (1976) analyzed the environmental histories and performances of 850 sets of twins who took the National Merit Scholarship test in 1962. The early treatment of the twins by the parents was included in the comparisons. The results showed that the generally more similar treatment of the identical twins cannot account for their greater similarity in general abilities, personality traits, or even ideals, goals, and vocational interests. The conclusion to be drawn is that either the similarities are based in substantial part on genetic identity, or else environmental factors were at work that remained hidden to the investigator.

My overall impression of the existing information is that Homo sapiens is a typical animal species with reference to the quality and magnitude of the genetic diversity affecting its behavior. If this generalization is even approximately correct, the psychic unity of mankind has been reduced from a dogma to a testable hypothesis.

I also believe that it will soon be within the grasp of biologists to identify many of the genes that influence behavior. Thanks largely to advances in techniques that identify minute differences in the chemical products prescribed by genes, our knowledge of the fine details of human heredity has grown exponentially during the past twenty years. In 1977 McKusick and Ruddle reported that no less than 1200 loci had been distinguished. Of these, the position of 210 had been pinpointed to a particular chromosome, and at least one gene had been located on each of the twenty-three pairs. Most of the genes ultimately affect anatomical and biochemical traits with minimal influence on behavior. Yet behavioral mutants do occur in human beings, and at least some are closely linked to biochemical modifications. Also, more subtle behavioral controls are known to incorporate alterations in levels of hormones and transmitter substances that act directly on nerve cells. The recently discovered enkephalins and endorphins are polypeptides of relatively simple composition that can alter mood and temperament. A single mutation changing the structure of one or more of them is easily conceivable, and might influence the personality of the person bearing it.

Thus it is possible, and indeed probable, that the positions of genes affecting even the most complex forms of behavior will soon be mapped on the human chromosomes. These genes are unlikely to prescribe particular patterns of behavior, such as a sexual practice or mode of dress. More probably, they will influence the form and intensity of emotional responses, the readiness to learn certain stimuli, and other general factors that predispose cultural evolution in one direction as opposed to another.

Genetic determinism is a perilous concept in the realm of the social sciences. To those who so earnestly desire to reject sociobiology out of hand, it means that development is insect-like, proceeding down one biochemical pathway, from a given set of genes to the corresponding predestined pattern of behavior. But the development of behavior can be under substantial genetic influence and still be circuitous and difficult to predict. Rather than a single trait, human genes are more likely to prescribe the capacity to develop a certain array of traits. In some categories of behavior, the array is limited and the outcome can be altered only by a strenuous training effort--if at all. In others, the array is vast and the outcome easily influenced.

A simple example of a restricted behavior is handedness. Each person is genetically predisposed to be either left- or right-handed. In present-day Western societies, parents are relatively tolerant of the outcome in their children who therefore follow the direction set by the genes. But in traditional Chinese societies there is still a strong social pressure for right-handed eating and writing. A recent study of Taiwanese children by Evelyn Lee Teng et al. (1976) found that there is a nearly complete conformity in these two activities but little or no effect on handedness in other activities not made the object of special training. Thus the genes have their way unless specifically contravened by conscious choice.

Hence even in the most elementary cases no sharp boundary exists between the inherited and the acquired. We need a new imagery to replace the archaic nature-nurture dichotomy. The most appealing to me is that recommended by the late Conrad Waddington (1957). Waddington said that development is like a landscape that descends from the highlands to the shore. Development of one category of trait--eye color, for example, or handedness--is like a ball that rolls down the slope. Each trait traverses a different part of the landscape, each is guided by a different pattern of ridges and valleys. In the case of eye color, given a starting set of genes for blue or some other iridal pigment, the topography is a single, deep channel. The ball rolls inexorably to one destination: once the egg has been joined by a sperm, only one color is possible. The developmental landscape of the typical insect, such as a mosquito, can also be envisioned as a parallel series of deep, unbranching valleys, one leading to the sexual attraction of the wingbeat's sound, another to the sucking of blood, and so on through a repertory of perhaps twenty or thirty discrete responses. The valleys consist of a precise, unyielding series of biochemical steps that proceed from the DNA in the fertilized egg to the formation of the insect's brain.

The developmental topography of human behavior is enormously broader and more complicated, but it is still a topography. In some cases the valleys divide once or twice. For example, a person can end up either right- or left-handed. If he starts with the genes that predispose him to the use of the left hand, we can view that branch of the developmental channel as cutting more deeply. If no social pressure is exerted, the "ball" will in most cases roll on down into the channel for left-handedness. But if the parents train the child to use the right hand, the ball can be nudged into the shallower channel for right-handedness. The landscape for schizophrenia and other complex phenomena is a broader network of anastomosing channels, more difficult to trace, chancier to predict. The ridges and channels will prove to consist in part of the genetically determined learning rules, the innate predisposition to learn one thing and not another (Seligman and Hager 1972). We are, in the terminology of some psychologists, *prepared* to learn sexual bonding but *counterprepared* to learn it when it is incestuous (at least between brothers and sisters), prepared to learn xenophobia as the general response to the threat of alien human groups, prepared to acquire phobias against snakes, spiders, and heights, the ancient perils of mankind, but unprepared to acquire phobias against most other objects, including such dangerous modern artifacts as knives and electric sockets. This heuristic approach to human behavior is in a very early stage and holds great promise.

The landscape is only a metaphor, but it focuses our attention on an important truth about human behavior. If we are to gain a full understanding of the processes of genetic and cultural determinism, each behavior has to be analyzed separately, and traced mechanistically as a developmental pathway from the gene to the final product. It is not enough to account for behavior as the outcome of cognitive and learning phenomena examined by *ad hoc* psychological hypotheses. In my opinion this broader biological conception should be the starting point of social theory.

Summary

Sociobiology is the systematic study of the biological basis of all forms of social behavior in all kinds of organisms. As such it is a discipline, not a specific hypothesis. Current sociobiological theory envisions three alternative outcomes in the evolution of human social behavior: (1) human populations have exhausted their genetic variability and hence are uniform with respect to the genes affecting social behavior, yet the genes prescribe at least some of the behavior; *or*, (2) genetic uniformity has been reached, and the genes prescribe only the capacity for transmitting culture; *or*, (3) there is still some genetic variability and the genes influence at least some forms of social behavior.

In this article I show that substantial and diverse evidence supports the third alternative. It may first be noted that human social behavior is species-specific in certain traits, such as the remarkable capacity for language and the proneness to invent elaborate kin classifications, and its overall properties most closely resemble the general qualities in other mammals and especially in Old World monkeys and apes, which on anatomical and biochemical grounds are our nearest living phylogenetic relatives. Furthermore, sociobiological theory, which is based primarily on the theory of population genetics and ecology, permits certain complex, specific predictions about human social behavior that cannot easily be reached in any other manner. Current studies are underway to test these predictions in such phenomena as the incest taboo, hypergamy, infanticide, primitive warfare, male dominance, kinship rules, and sexual practice. The results thus far are sufficiently consistent with sociobiological theory to justify their continued pursuit as a complementary mode of analysis in the social sciences. Still another approach to the characterization of innate behavioral constraints is through the study of severely retarded individuals in which most or all forms of ordinary cultural behavior is missing.

The evidence for a genetic basis of variation in behavior within human populations is also strong. In addition to the demonstration of behavioral mutants at the levels of both the genes and chromosomes, the more carefully controlled twin studies indicate some degree of heritability in a wide array of mental and psychomotor abilities and personality traits. *Homo sapiens* appears to be a typical animal species with reference to the quality and magnitude of the genetic diversity affecting its behavior. But the relation of this genetic control to environmental influences can be understood only if each category of behavioral trait is analyzed separately and traced mechanistically as a developmental pathway from the gene to the final product, paying special attention to the inherited rules of prepared and counterprepared behavior.

Literature Cited

Chagnon, N. A. 1974. *Studying the Yanomamö*. Holt, Rinehart and Winston, New York.

Dickeman, Mildred. 1979. Female infanticide and the reproductive strategies of stratified human societies: a preliminary model. In N. A. Chagnon & W. G. Irons (eds.), *Evolutionary biology and human social behavior*. Duxbury Press, North Scituate, Massachusetts. (In press.)

Durham, W. H. 1976. Resource competition and human agression, Part I: A review of primitive war. *Quarterly Review of Biology* 51: 385-415.

Fox, R. 1978. Kinship categories as natural categories. In N. A. Chagnon & W. G. Irons (eds.), Evolutionary biology and human social organization. Duxbury Press, Scituate, Massachusetts. (In press.)

Freedman, D. G. 1974. Human infancy: An evolutionary perspective. Lawrence Erlbaum, Hillsdale, New Jersey.

Hockett, C. P. 1948. Biophysics, linguistics, and the unity of science. American Scientist 36: 558-572.

Irons, W. G. 1978. The criteria of fitness. In N. A. Chagnon & W. G. Irons (eds.), Evolutionary biology and human social organization. Duxbury Press, Scituate, Massachusetts. (In press.)

Konner, M. J. 1976. Maternal care, infant behavior and development among the !Kung. In R. B. Lee & I. DeVore (eds.), Kalahari hunter-gatherers. Harvard University Press, Cambridge, Massachusetts, pp. 219-245.

_______ 1978. Evolution of human behavior development. In H. Leiderman & S. Tulkin (eds.), Cross-culture and social class influences in infancy. Academic Press, New York. (In press.)

Loehlin, J. C. & R. C. Nichols. 1976. Heredity, environment, and personality: A study of 850 sets of twins. University of Texas Press, Austin.

McClearn, G. E. & J. C. DeFries. 1973. Introduction to behavioral genetics. W. H. Freeman, San Francisco.

McKusick, V. A. & F. H. Ruddle. 1977. The status of the gene map of the human chromosome. Science 196: 390-405.

Scott, J. P. 1950. Foreword to methodology and techniques for the study of animal societies. Annals of the New York Academy of Sciences 51: 1003-1005.

Seligman, M. E. P. & Joanne L. Hager (eds.). 1972. Biological boundaries of learning. Prentice-Hall, Englewood Cliffs, New Jersey.

Shepher, J. 1971. Self-imposed incest avoidance and exogamy in second generation kibbutz adults. Ph.D. thesis, Rutgers University, New Brunswick, New Jersey.

Teng, Evelyn Lee, Pen-Hua Lee, K. Yang & P. C. Chang. 1976. Handedness in a Chinese population: Biological, social, and pathological factors. Science 193: 1146-1150.

Waddington, C. H. 1957. The strategy of the genes. Allen & Unwin, London.

Weinrich, J. D. 1977. Human sociobiology: Pair-bonding and resource variability (effects of class and race). Behavioral Ecology and Sociobiology 2: 91-118.

_______ 1978. Non-reproduction and intelligence: an apparent fact and one sociobiological explanation. Archives of Sexual Behavior. [In press.]

Wills, R. H. 1973. The institutionalized severely retarded. C. C. Thomas, Springfield, Illinois.

Wilson, E. O. 1971. The insect societies. Belknap Press of Harvard University Press, Cambridge, Massachusetts.

_______ 1975. Sociobiology: The new synthesis. Belknap Press of Harvard University Press, Cambridge, Massachusetts.

_______ 1978. On human nature. Harvard University Press, Cambridge, Massachusetts.

Frank B. Livingstone

13. Cultural Causes of Genetic Change

The resurgence of interest in the last decade in the biological causes or basis of human behavior has resulted in one of the most exciting and vigorous current controversies in science. It has led to increased communication among biological and social scientists, and the ensuing debate should lead to a more rigorous definition of the issues and surely some advances in our understanding of human behavior.

The controversy has arisen primarily by the efforts of many different kinds of biologists to re-emphasize the biological factors in human behavior. Among them behavior geneticists have developed models to estimate the genetic component of various behavior traits; ethologists have applied the methods of analysis of behavior in other animal species to humans; and sociobiologists have been developing a theoretical model for the evolution of behavior that is based primarily on data from other species but is presumed to be applicable to man (Wilson 1975; Barash 1977).

Although everyone would agree that there are both biological and cultural aspects of human behavior, there is still considerable disagreement as to their specific roles. This is basically the same issue as the nature-nurture controversy of fifty years ago, but then it was debated within an either/or framework. Now it is a question of how much of each. For example, a figure frequently cited in the news media is that 80% of the variation in IQ in the white American population is due to genetic factors. However, such simple percentages are not particularly useful.

A resolution of the issue requires models of how biological and cultural factors interact to produce the resultant behavior. Differences among individuals within a population require growth or developmental models, and some progress has been made in delimiting how genetic and environmental factors interact during an individual's life to produce variation for some human traits. On the other hand, differences in average or normal behavior between human populations require models of how the behavior of a population changes, and this is part of the evolutionary process. These are two different problems but are often confounded in many discussions. Anthropology and other social sciences, because they are concerned with the behavior of human populations, are in great need of models of the evolutionary process, or what is commonly called adaptation.

Recent writings have referred to the biological causes, determinants, aspects, components, or basis of human behavior, and all these terms have been used to some extent synonomously, which they are not. There are obviously biological aspects of human behavior, and of course every human behavior has a biological basis in the sense that it is dependent on the biological abilities of the human species; but the causes or determinants of human behavior are very different from these generalities.

Models of Evolutionary Change

The concept of cause has had a long, tortuous history in science and philosophy; but in my naive view of science as simply mathematical models of processual change, causes are just the parameters of the equation of change. For genetic evolution, gene frequency change is a function of mutation, natural selection, and population structure. The usual parameters of gene flow, gene drift, and inbreeding are included within population structure since they are functions of population dispersal, population size, and mating patterns, respectively.

Natural selection and the other parameters thus "cause" genetic evolution, and for any set of gene frequency differences one can attempt to estimate their effects. But then the question arises as to what causes the causes, or in other words what accounts for variation in the parameters. Wilson (1975) identifies these causes as phylogenetic inertia and ecological pressure, which he calls the prime movers of social evolution, and the latter in his terms is gene frequency change associated with behavior change. Phylogenetic inertia limits the possible new ecological niches that a population can occupy and hence is only a limiting factor. Ecological pressure is thus the major cause, prime mover, or determinant of natural selection and population structure; and this is especially true within a single species such as man where there would not be as much phylogenetic inertia. Wilson's general model outlined above is a concise resume of widely accepted evolutionary theory. The problems with it concern the relationships between gene frequency change and behavior change and which occurs first.

Natural selection results from differential fitnesses of genotypes. Of course, as is frequently stated, natural selection operates on phenotypes, but if there are no fitness differences among genotypes, there will be no selection at that particular locus. Natural selection can also be considered as occurring by differential mortality and fertility of the genotypes. Ecological pressure thus "causes" natural selection by changing the causes of mortality and fertility.

How do the causes of mortality and fertility of a population change? Usually it is by a change in behavior or an altered relationship of the population to other organisms in the community, or in other words, by a change in its ecological niche. The sickle cell gene is the classic example of selection in human populations, and it increased in frequency after malaria became an important cause of death. This change in causes of mortality was apparently due to the increase in human population density after the development of agriculture (Livingstone 1958). Ecological pressure thus precedes gene frequency change.

Wilson (1975) has pointed out that phylogenetic inertia is closely related to the concept of preadaptation, and the process of preadaptation implies that a population is able to change its ecological niche and consequently its behavior with no genetic change. This is comparable to our example of malaria selection due to the invention of agriculture and then subsequent genetic change. On the other hand, it seems to conflict with many theoretical discussions by sociobiologists of behavioral evolution which assume that specific behaviors are due to genetic factors and thus that behavior and gene frequency change occur together or are in fact one process. For example, most sociobiological discussions of altruism assume that this behavior is due to a mutant allele (Barash 1977), and most explanations of the incest taboo in terms of the deleterious effects of inbreeding assume the frequencies of the deleterious genes preceded the taboo.

Genetic and Behavioral Variation

The causes or determinants of human behavior have been the major source of the controversy between the biological and social sciences. Too often the recent work of biologists on human behavior has characterized the social scientists' position or more specifically the tabula rasa model of the behaviorists as assuming that human behavior is "infinitely malleable." This characterization is meaningless and, I will add, usually pejorative. Given the actual range of human behavior, how infinite is it? Or if the statement means that the behaviorists consider humans capable of any conceivable behavior, then it is useless for analyzing actual, existing differences in human behavior. Wilson (1977) has emphasized the narrow range of human behavior when compared to the behavior of all organisms. This certainly demonstrates the existence of genetic differences among species but its significance for the evolution or interpretation of behavioral differences between human populations is still dubious.

As support for a great amount of human malleability, J. B. Watson's famous dictum that he could make any healthy baby into a doctor, lawyer, Indian chief, or even beggar or thief is usually cited as evidence of how unrealistic the tabula rasa position is. But the most reasonable interpretation of his dictum, that any healthy individual can learn the major roles in our society, doesn't seem unrealistic to most anthropologists. In fact, for anthropology this assertion is extended to behaviors in other societies: the behavioral variations that characterize any population in the world are capable of being learned by most individuals from any other population. Evolutionarily the statement implies that the major social roles of any society are limited to those that most humans can perform.

Anyone <u>can</u> be trained to be a doctor, or even president for that matter, but this emphatically does not mean that anyone can be trained to be the best performer in any role. For the abilities required to perform any role, there are surely significant differences among individuals within any population. Environmental factors are important in determining these differences, but genetic factors are also present.

There has been considerable controversy about the genetic component of human behavior, but the most reasonable assessment of the evidence seems to me to indicate that a positive heritability would be found for almost all behaviors for individuals within a single population. There may be disagreement as to whether the average heritability is .2 or .8, but this is unimportant from an evolutionary viewpoint in the sense that it will only change the rate of evolution and not its direction. For this reason the exact value of the heritability of any behavior trait is not of crucial significance.

Heritability has been estimated for many human traits, but the results have been confusing, with great disparity among the various estimates for the same trait. Generally twin and adoption studies have yielded higher heritability estimates than parent-offspring correlations. There have been assertions that heritability is impossible to measure (Moran 1973; Layzer 1974). Feldman and Lewontin (1975) have shown that knowing the heritability for many traits is not useful for several medico-genetic problems or for genetic counseling. This may be true, but nevertheless the heritability of behaviors is the basis of evolution. If no association or correlation between genetic variation and behavior existed, than there wouldn't be any evolution.

Despite the problems with the concept of heritability, and these are present for both the narrow and broad definitions of heritability, there have surely been associations of additive genetic variability with many recent patterns of human behavior. But these are simply associations and not genetic determinants. For example, the debate about the XYY chromosome abnormality seems to suffer from this confusion. Even though there are inconsistencies in the data, the positive associations between XYY and institutionalization reported from Europe, United States, and Japan are significant. However, XYY is not a cause of criminality; most XYY individuals--at least 97%--lead normal lives. Of course, this association has little evolutionary significance, but many comparable ones for genetic loci do. Thus to use the phrase, "the gene for such and such behavior," is meaningless in terms of the causal model advocated here. There is no gene "for" most behaviors when they appear in a society's repertoire due to ecological pressure; rather behavior is associated with some additive genetic variation which then causes a change--usually a very small one--in the fitness values and leads to new evolution.

Organized sports seem to provide many examples of associations that are not causes, and basketball is most striking. There seems to be a clear association between the ability to play basketball and some additive genetic variation, namely stature. In a single breeding population with a normally distributed, uncorrelated environmental component for stature, I am sure there would be a significant heritability associated with this ability. And if the ability to play basketball were to have a measurable effect on fitness, there would be evolution for greater stature. Some years ago, Alice Brues (1959) wrote a provocative essay entitled "The Spearman and the Archer" in which she pointed out that populations whose principal weapon was the spear tended to be tall and linear, while those with the bow and arrow were smaller. The same kind of association of behavior and physical characteristics with some additive genetic variability has caused these differences, and the genetic differences resulted from the adoption of the behavior by the population.

The existence of differences in behavioral abilities is thus not evidence at all of underlying genetic differences, anymore than differences in basketball, spear-throwing or archery ability would be evidence of genetic variation. However, in both the biological and anthropological literature one frequently encounters the statement that populations adopt behaviors or cultures that are compatible with their abilities, which is again inconsistent with our causal model that has ecological pressure as the prime mover. Populations do not make choices according to their genetic predispositions; this is only a reflection of our free-will ideology.

Many of the contributions to this symposium have been concerned with behavior genetics or have stressed the great number of human genetic variants that are associated with behavior differences. Lesch-Nyhan syndrome and phenylketonuria are due to a single gene, while schizophrenia and severe mental deficiency seem to have a polygenic component. That genetic variations can have considerable effects on behavior should not be debatable or one of the issues. On the other hand, the fact that genetic differences can lead to variation in behavior does not mean that any of the behavioral variations between human populations are due to differences in gene frequencies or that the evolution of these differences has occurred by the usual model of gene frequency change.

Both behavioral and physical traits can change rapidly with little genetic change involved. The recent marked increase in stature in many human populations is clear evidence that a trait with a very high heritability can change by as much as two standard deviations due to environmental factors alone. Currently IQ in the Black American population seems to be undergoing the same type of rapid change. Although even today the Black-White difference in IQ is stated to be about 15 points in textbooks(e.g.,Ehrman & Parsons 1976), recent data from Boston, Baltimore, and Philadelphia show the difference to be only four points (Nichols & Anderson 1973). And the differences between cities are as great as or even greater than the race differences. On the whole one would not prefer to be in Philadelphia, in school at least. The marked change in IQ that has accompanied enormous changes in culture and social structure in the last 30 years would seem to be evidence for the environmentalist position and for our causal model. However, this does not mean that there is no heritability for IQ within a single population, or that natural selection is not occurring for the mental abilities associated with IQ tests.

Drinking Habits and Genetic Change

The complexity of the relationship between genetic and behavioral variation among human populations can be further illustrated by the effects of differences in diet. I will consider the two favorite drinks of the human species, booze and milk. Alcoholism is considered to be a disease, but its diagnosis is imprecise. It is known to "run in families," and a recent adoption study seems to indicate a genetic component. Although Goodwin conducted this adoption study, his recent book (1976) is an excellent, impartial account of the problems connected with viewing alcoholism as inherited.

One would presumably expect a genetic component of alcoholism to be associated with the metabolism of alcohol, and there is recent evidence of both group and individual differences in alcohol metabolism. Whether or not American Indian and Oriental populations metabolize ethanol faster or slower than European populations has been controversial, but the most recent evidence (Reed et al. 1976) indicates that they metabolize it faster. This is in accord with studies on the genetic variation of alcohol dehydrogenases, which have shown that 5-20% of European populations have a genetic variant that metabolizes alcohol much faster than the normal variant, while 85% of the Japanese have this fast variant (Stamatoyannopoulos et al. 1975). The high frequencies of this fast variant would seem to account for the much greater incidence of visible red flushing of the skin after ethanol ingestion in Japanese, Taiwanese and Koreans (Wolff 1972) and in American Indians and Chinese (Wolff 1973), although the other groups have not been tested for enzyme variants.

On the other hand, the frequency of alcoholism is apparently much higher in European, American White, and American Indian populations than it is in Orientals, so that this variation in alcoholism does not correlate with the genetic variation in enzyme function. Cultural factors must be involved in alcoholism variation between populations, but the genetic variation in alcohol dehydrogenases between human populations seems to be due to selection that resulted from the extreme use of alcohol.

Despite prohibition and religious sanctions, the populations of Europe and their descendants elsewhere for the last 1000 years have been noted for their prodigious consumption of alcohol. There are several remarkable estimates of alcohol consumption in Europe: one from the 12th century in the Canons of St. Paul's Cathedral is 30 gallons of beer per person per week (Curwen & Hatt 1953). Although drunkenness was severely punished among Puritans in New England, they still consumed great quantities of beer and considered it essential for life. Given this high level of consumption and the fact that acetaldehyde, the metabolite of ethanol, is involved in alcoholism and intoxication, it seems plausible that a slower-acting alcohol dehydrogenase variant would be selected for.

Differences between human populations in the lactase enzyme seem to be due to selection caused by excessive use of another beverage, milk. Most adult humans and also other mammals are unable to digest lactose, but in populations in Northern Europe and in East and West Africa that consume large quantities of milk the majority of the adult population can digest lactose. Although again there are problems with the data, it seems reasonably clear that most of this variation is due to the presence of a dominant gene to continue production of the enzyme lactase into adulthood. This allele has increased in frequency from about .05 or less in hunters and other populations who do not consume milk to .6 in milk-drinking populations. In the 100 to 200 generations that herding and milk drinking have been the economic basis of these cultures such an increase would require approximately 2-4% selection at this locus. Considering that milk is one of the major food sources in these populations this estimate does not seem unreasonable.

The changes in both the alcohol dehydrogenase and lactase enzymes seem to be obvious examples of adaptation to a new food supply or, in terms of our causal model, genetic responses to a change in the fitnesses of the genotypes that in turn was caused by behavioral change. But there is still a question as to how the process began and whether genetic variation had any role in it. For example, in a discussion of lactase evolution, the late Herman Slatis (1973) stated that "it is hard to imagine selection as the factor that caused an increase in the frequency of the genetic constitution for lactose tolerance. Rather, milk consumption probably occurred in lactose tolerant communities and was less common in those communities that were not tolerant." Similarly Barash has stated "Cultural practices may have selected for the presence of lactase among herding peoples; or the fortuitous presence or absence of the relevant genes may have predisposed different societies to different cultural norms" (1977:283). These interpretations advocate the prior existence of genetic differences to which culture has adapted. In addition to denying the efficacy of selection, they provide no explanation of the genetic variation. The usual recourse is to random genetic drift, or as Barash says the differences may be "fortuitous."

Cultural Adaptation and Genetic Change

Although our causal model assumes that changes in cultural practices exist prior to genetic change, there is also the problem of how cultural practices are adopted by a population. By analogy with the roles of mutation and selection in genetic evolution, Campbell (1975) has proposed a "blind-variation-and-selective-retention" model for social and cultural evolution. He sees the selective-retention process as primarily occurring among individuals with no need for "group-selective processes." But the process of the adoption of a new trait is imitation or learning, so that it is usually much faster than genetic change and has been labelled Lamarckian by others.

On the other hand, much of the theorizing of sociobiology implicitly and even at times explicitly assumes that cultural change is concurrent with genetic change or that the adoption of a cultural trait is due to the increase in genotypes predisposed to it. For the lactase enzyme this would seem to be obviously inappropriate. If one assumes that the change in gene frequency with modest selection has taken 200 generations certainly the adoption of milk drinking did not occur at the same slow rate. Similarly, North America north of Mexico was the one major ethnographic area with no alcoholic beverages, but the rapid acceptance of alcohol by the Indians or their relatively high incidence of alcoholism cannot be attributed to genetic variation in the alcohol dehydrogenases.

Campbell's model of cultural change is comparable to the usual gene frequency change model of genetic evolution. Both are concerned with change in a single population, and Campbell's selective retention is based on analogy with natural selection. This factor is considered to be the major cause of change, but like natural selection it cannot explain the differences in cultural practices between populations. We are still faced with the problem of what causes the causes, and again we are back to ecological pressure as the most likely prospect.

I have used the lactase and alcohol dehydrogenase enzyme variations to illustrate what I think is the inadequacy of genetic models of cultural change because they are rather well accepted genetic traits and we have some knowledge of their variation. The thrust of the argument is that most genetic theorizing about other cultural characteristics would run into similar difficulties if we knew the genetic component of these traits. However, the origin of any particular cultural or behavioral trait may have a different cause than the maintence of that trait in a population. For example, the absence of milk in the Chinese diet could be due to a reluctance to drink milk because of the almost complete lactose intolerance of the population. But I would maintain that sufficient ecological pressure could alter their drinking habits.

Cultural and Genetic Causes of the Incest Taboo

Another cultural trait that has similar problems of interpretation is the old favorite, the incest taboo. There is an increasing consensus--not including me--that the deleterious genetic effects of close inbreeding are the cause of the supposed universality of this taboo in human societies. However, there is disagreement as to how natural selection operated on the incest taboo, although it is generally agreed that individuals who inbred had a decreased fitness. Ember (1975) and many other social scientists have argued that the absence of close inbreeding in any population would give it a competitive advantage over other populations with close inbreeding. This argument is based on group selection, and the recent reluctance of biologists to accept any major role for group selection would lead them to reject this interpretation and to stress selection among individuals.

To attribute an increase in fitness to individuals who practice incest avoidance seems to imply that it increased by a change in gene frequency. On the other hand, exactly how the trait spread through the population is still debatable: the practice could be inherited in Lamarckian fashion by learning or imitation, or it could spread through the population by Campbell's (1975) model of culture change. In either case the change in fitness values accompanying this new practice could have led to genetic change. Whatever the specific interpretation, the incest taboo is widely considered to have a biological or genetic basis which both accounts for its universality and maintains it in modern human populations.

The incest taboo is assumed to be universal in human societies and thus is "species-specific" or part of basic human nature. But the evidence for its biological nature consists of the often repeated data from the kibbutzes in Israel (Shepher 1971; Talmon 1964), and Wolf's (1966) study of infant or childhood betrothal in Taiwan, neither of which is convincing given the range of sexual behavior in the human species. The fact that individuals who grow up together in the same kibbutz do not get married is cited as evidence for an aversion to sexual behavior among them; but Kaffman (1977) has shown that there are simpler cultural explanations for the absence of marriage, and that sexual interaction is not only present but increasing.

The incest taboo together with aggression, dominance, pair bonding and many other behavioral traits have been of particular interest to ethologists and animal behaviorists since these traits can be observed in other animal populations, and evidence from other animal species has been used to interpret their presence in human populations. Beginning with Sade's (1968) investigation on the rhesus monkeys of Cayo Santiago, there have been several reports of the incest taboo or incest avoidance in primates and other animals. This has led Bischof (1975:42) to state "*in the whole animal world with very few exceptions no species is known in which under natural conditions inbreeding occurs to any considerable degree*"(his italics).

Frankly, I don't think this is a reasonable interpretation of the data; furthermore, I think there is a strong bias in the literature because incidences of incest avoidance are apparently worth reporting while those of incestuous behavior are not. Missakian (1973) has found much higher frequencies of mother-son and brother-sister mating than Sade originally reported; and although these matings occur with considerable frequency, Bischof asserts that they support his view, presumably because they occur less frequently than "expected." Recent studies of baboons (Packer 1975) and other primates have shown that transfer between groups can occur frequently, and this has been reported in the *New York Times* (Aug. 3, 1975) as showing avoidance of inbreeding and incest. However, the fact that other primate groups, including baboons, are extremely xenophobic and allow no transfer between troops is not reported.

The population size and territoriality of many species would result in a highly inbred population, even if close relatives did not breed, simply due to the very small size of the breeding isolate. For example, the major wolf pack on Isle Royale has consisted of 20 to 30 members for the last 30 years with little or no outside recruitment. This would result in a highly inbred group. Mech's (1977) report on the territoriality and xenophobia of the wolves in northern Minnesota would probably lead to a comparable amount of inbreeding.

There are obviously great differences in the amount of inbreeding in animal populations. Some have in fact close inbreeding, including man. The idea that inbreeding is selected against because of the deleterious effects of increased homozygosity cannot explain these variations in inbreeding. Instead the variations are due primarily to differences in mating structure which are caused by ecological pressure, and these differences in mating patterns have resulted in gene frequency change. It is known that some animals such as wolves and rats can withstand much more inbreeding than others, and this seems to be due to their very inbred natural population structure which has selected more strongly against deleterious mutants and consequently decreased their frequencies.

The same is true of human populations. There are great differences in population structure, some of which include high levels of inbreeding and even prescribed "incestuous" behavior. Some modern and viable populations in South India have a high frequency of uncle-niece marriage (Sanghvi 1966). These differences should lead to differences in the frequencies of deleterious genes in human populations. But the sociobiologists (Wilson 1975:78) and human ethologists (Bischof 1975:38) continue to cite the data from Ann Arbor, Michigan or Czechoslovakia on the deleterious effects of inbreeding in man with the implicit assumption that all human populations can be treated identically. Of course, the inbreeding depression is a well known fact for all animal populations, but the great variation in inbreeding effects must be taken into account. In contrast to the Ann Arbor data, recent data from populations in South India with close inbreeding show that the effects for uncle-niece marriages are minimal (Rao & Inbaraj 1977).

Using a model that Haldane (1940) developed to show that deleterious recessive mutants were increasing in modern societies due to the breakdown of breeding isolates, I have pointed out that inbreeding would lower frequencies of deleterious genes (Livingstone 1969). As population structure changes from small isolated villages to large panmictic nations there will be a considerable increase in deleterious recessives. Recently Spielman et al. (1977) have shown from their work on the Yanomamo Indians of South America how great this change has been. Based on simulations, their estimates of the inbreeding coefficient for villages of Yanomamo are as high as .5, which is much greater than the amount of inbreeding generally considered to be characteristic of human populations. Since the inbreeding coefficient of the offspring of brother-sister matings is only .25, this study is further evidence for the minimal effect of inbreeding in primitive human populations.

I have dealt in detail with incest and inbreeding because this seems to be an issue that clearly distinguishes between causal models of evolution. The view that the genetic causes of behavior are primary sees the deleterious effects of inbreeding causing the incest taboo or in other words determining mating behavior. The view advocated here is that mating behavior as a component of population structure is caused by ecological pressure and that changes in mating behavior result in changes in gene frequency whose effect is to reduce the deleterious consequences of inbreeding. There are enormous variations in the population structure and mating patterns of both human and animal populations, with many practicing close inbreeding. These variations are unexplicable by any gene frequency model. Marrying a close relative, which in some societies is a sibling, would likely have a detrimental effect on individual fitness, so that many mating patterns involve "altruism" as it is defined by sociobiologists. The presence of such behavior implies that individuals do not maximize their individual fitness, and furthermore that the simple models of the evolution of altruism which have been widely discussed in the sociobiological literature (Cohen & Eshel 1976; Barash 1977) do not apply to the evolution of altruism in human societies.

Biosocial anthropologists, ethologists, and others who have applied the methods for the study of animal behavior to the human species have been especially concerned with incest because incest avoidance was considered to be universal and hence a species-specific characteristic and part of basic human nature. But there is a question as to what is universal in all human societies. The incest taboo is commonly present as a rule of the culture, but it now appears to be far from universal. Schneider (1976) discusses the issue and cites several societies which do not seem to have any taboo.

Although sexual intercourse among primary family members is not common, it does occur more than is generally acknowledged (Sarles 1975) and is apparently increasing in modern societies. Estimates of up to one million cases per year in the United States or an occurrence of one in 20 families have appeared in the media. It is thus difficult to see how the concept of basic human nature is useful as an explanation of incest avoidance in man.

Ongoing Genetic Evolution and Its Cultural Causes

Basic human nature or species-specific behaviors in man are assumed to have been adaptations that occurred in the past at the time when all human populations occupied the same ecological niche as hunters and collectors. There is the further assumption that there has been no genetic change since then. For example, Tiger and Fox state that "agricultural and industrial civilization have put nothing in the basic wiring of the human animal" (1971:22, their italics). For the deleterious genes affected by inbreeding, the assumption of no genetic change seems dubious given the great changes in mating patterns and population structure. And for the classic example of selection, the sickle cell gene, all of the genetic change has occurred since agriculture. Thus, for other cultural behaviors that have changed drastically in the past 10,000 years one would also expect considerable adaptation or genetic change. Of course, the pace of cultural evolution has been much more rapid than biological evolution, but this does not mean that genetic change has not occurred. The time since agriculture is only about 400 generations, but with fitness differences of about 5%, one can evolve just about any genetic trait in this time. The lactase and alcohol dehydrogenase cases previously discussed are good examples.

The assumption that there has been no genetic change in the last 10 to 40,000 years for the basis of cultural behavior leads to the conclusion that human cultures "adapt" to human nature or human genetic structure. Thus, Tiger and Fox (1971) argue that formal classroom education, cross-district busing, modern hospitals, and many other aspects of our culture are contrary to our basic primate nature. In their view successful cultures will or should adapt to our basic nature.

The idea that modern culture is maladaptive is now popular due perhaps to the social upheavals of the last ten years or to the counter-culture or to the media. The evidence for this view is the morbidity and mortality associated with our complex, technological, "dehumanized," mass culture. But this is actually evidence for adaptation. Natural selection operates by means of mortality and morbidity, provided that some genetic variability is associated with their causes. The ability to cope with the impersonal nature of mass culture is likely to have some genetic variation associated with it. I think this is demonstrated by the positive heritability for the liability to mental illnesses, particularly schizophrenia. Similarly school busing did result in emotional responses and social upheaval that increased the risk of individuals. But it was adaptive for modern industrial society which does not operate efficiently with a caste social structure. Thus, individuals were forced into school busing behavior against their will by ecological pressure. The breakdown of isolating mechanisms by busing is modern America's version of the incest taboo or exogamy, which in earlier times forced young females to wed unknown males and live in hostile communities.

It is noteworthy that those who emphasize the biological or genetic causes of human behavior also emphasize the emotional determinants of behavior. Wilson (1975) begins his book with a long essay on the limbic system of the brain which contains the emotional centers. However, the most striking trend in human evolution has been the elaboration and increasing dominance of the cerebral cortex. This dominance is undoubtedly associated with the evolution of language and symbolic thought.

There is still considerable disagreement as to the course and time of evolution of language and speech (Steklis et al. 1976), but I am now convinced that the evidence points to a very late development of modern language. It probably began in the Mousterian period with the Neanderthals, and the rapid evolution of modern *Homo sapiens* about 40,000 years ago is the result of this new selective force. This is a short time span, evolutionarily speaking, and the current conflict between rationality and emotional behavior is indicative of the continuing adaptation to symbolic behavior. Of course, this idea is not new; Arthur Koestler (1968) has written a popular account of the evolution of the brain that outlines the conflict between the reptilian limbic system and the neomammalian cortex.

The evolution of symbolic communication has led to enormous changes in the motivation of individual behavior. Our cultures have erected symbolic filters, so that altruism by humans, motivated by communism, fascism, patriotism, or romantic love, is different from the altruism of animals if indeed the latter have any. Language resulted in individuals being "told" what to do, but the evolution of consciousness and rationality are much later. Jaynes (1977) has presented a complicated argument for the evolution of consciousness very recently, in the times of Classical Greece. There are problems with Jaynes' hypothesis, for example, how or when did consciousness evolve in China, the Americas and elsewhere, but his major point as to changes in individual motivation seems to be reasonable although it is highly controversial. In particular, many of the symptoms of schizophrenia seem to have been normal behavior in the past; everyone heard voices, and, as Jaynes points out, major decisions of ancient Greece were based on voices heard by the Delphic oracles. These voices seem to be associated with the right hemisphere of the cerebral cortex which at that time controlled the linguistic abilities of the left hemisphere. The increasing dominance of the left hemisphere that controls language, rationality and quantitative reasoning is the major force of human evolution today.

Of all mental illnesses, schizophrenia has been the most amenable to genetic analysis and seems to have a high heritability. It is found in almost all human populations at rather high frequencies of approximately 1%. This has raised the problem as to how a deleterious genetic condition could attain such high and presumably polymorphic frequencies. Recent attempts to explain the frequencies of schizophrenia assume that they are at equilibrium; and since persons with schizophrenia are assumed to be relatively homozygous for the loci involved and have a fitness lower than normals, there must be some selective advantage associated with heterozygosity for these loci (Kidd 1975; Jarvik & Deckard 1977). But with the changes in mass culture and in the amount of rationality as opposed to emotional bonds involved in interpersonal relations, most human populations would seem to be far from equilibrium--genetic or any other. Instead, schizophrenia as a new cause of mortality and fertility differences has changed the fitness values of the genotypes, so that it is now the cause of directional selection. It is thus a good example of ongoing evolution that is increasing the dominance of the cerebral cortex, and especially the left hemisphere, over the limbic system.

The Problem of Population Control and Its Cultural Causes

The preceding interpretations of cultural and biological evolution can be made to agree with the models of evolution that assume ecological pressure to be the causative factor and behavior change to precede genetic change. However, they seem to have little relevance to the basic assumptions of sociobiology, or what Barash states to be the "Central Theorem of Sociobiology" which is that "When any behavior under study reflects some component of genotypes, animals should behave so as to maximize their inclusive fitness" (1977:63). Certainly human individuals maximize their own behavior--they do what they think is best--at least according to their own rationalizations. But this occurs within the confines of their culture, and in most cases this symbolic maximization does not coincide with their biological fitness.

If all humans are trying to maximize their number of surviving offspring, then this raises problems in explaining the variation in reproduction rates that is so evident between human populations. This, in turn, raises problems of whether and how populations regulate themselves. Since this would be a group-related or functional adaptation in Williams' (1966) terms, Williams initiated the arguments against it, and particularly against Wynne-Edwards' (1962) idea that social behavior evolved by group selection to be the regulator. Although regulation seems to imply intent or purpose, it doesn't. Mathematically it only means that populations maintain relatively constant size, and Bulmer (1975) has shown that many animal populations are regulated by density dependent factors although these are not specified.

The assumption of maximization of individual fitness necessarily implies that the birth rate results in a maximum number of surviving offspring and that human populations are limited by the death rate of extrinsic factors. The view that the human species has only had a problem with population explosion in recent years due primarily to modern medicine is a common belief that was popularized in Ehrlich's (1968) The Population Bomb. This view pictures primitive hunting populations as engaged in a desperate struggle to survive and producing as many offspring as possible to contend with a large death rate from disease, starvation and other extrinsic factors. But all evidence points to the fact that hunting populations have more than adequate diets and little risk of starvation; high rates of infanticide were the major population control (Krzywicki 1934).

Nevertheless, the idea of maximum reproduction persists. With reference to infanticide among the Bushmen, Trivers (1976:29) states that we

> cannot infer that those practices are what controls the population. There is no evidence that they are not trying to reproduce as fast as they are capable; in fact, the birth spacing increases the effective reproductive rate, because healthy infants have a better chance of surviving than infants born close together and less well fed.

This statement implies that the Bushmen have an uncertain and very limited food supply, but there is no evidence for this. And although these cultural practices may maximize the survival of a single child, this has little direct relation to the average number of offspring for any population or its variation between populations. Similarly, most primates have single births while some other animals have large litters. Given their arboreal habitat and long infant dependency on the mother, single births among primates can obviously be interpreted as maximizing the number of surviving offspring per birth. This is similar to Lack's (1968) arguments on clutch size in birds where he showed that the average clutch size had more surviving offspring than smaller or larger ones. However, the fact that litter size is optimized has no direct relevance to the variations in the birth rate or to the total number of offspring per female.

If individuals are maximizing their surviving offspring or presumably even their inclusive fitness, then this has been assumed to mean that the average number of offspring for any population results in a maximum number surviving. But this is obviously not the case for most human populations, which is difficult to reconcile with sociobiological assumptions. The marked decreases in the birth rates in recent years in many industrialized populations are equally difficult to reconcile with them.

There have been attempts to show that condoms and other birth control devices actually increase individual fitness (Colinvaux 1976), or to show that perhaps smaller families have greater survival. For example, Weinrich (1978), replying to a criticism similar to my views by Lande (1978), states that

> Lande concludes his critique in a blaze of unsupported assumptions and premature conclusions. After asserting that 'obviously' the upper classes can 'have more children' he ignores the possibility that we are now seeing the effects of evolved mechanisms operating maladaptively in a new environment. But much more importantly, he confuses fertility with reproductive success. This is analogous to mistaking clutch size for the number of offspring surviving to adulthood--upper-class couples might restrict fertility yet succeed in raising more offspring to the corresponding point in the next generation's life cycle.

Weinrich's reply is equally a blaze of unsupported assertions with the usual mistaken clutch-size analogy. It suggests a will to believe on his part that is more ideological than scientific. That upper class couples who restrict their fertility raise more surviving offspring than those who don't is contradicted by any human demographic data he would chose to examine. And the continual use of "maladaptive" with respect to modern culture is evolutionarily backwards in terms of the causal model of evolution advocated here.

On the other hand the variations in fertility and population growth rates can more easily be interpreted by ecological and cultural pressures. The motivation for breeding among humans is a culturally determined or conditioned behavior that is not primarily emotional but cerebral in origin. Surely symbolic communication in our society has been a major determinant of this recent change in fertility. Since symbolic values are the property of the society, this seems to be a functional or populational adaptation. But we are still a long way from having an adequate model to describe and predict the process of population change.

Although the ideas in this paper may seem to be presented as conclusions, they are certainly not proven or even well-accepted. But I hope they show that there is still room for different interpretations of human biological and cultural evolution, and each may have some useful portions. Perhaps we need a new synthesis.

Summary

The resurgence of interest in the biological causes of human behavior has raised many problems for anthropology and other social sciences that are concerned with differences in behavior between human populations. The major problem is how genetic and environmental factors interact to produce behavioral change. Models of genetic evolution assume that natural selection is one of the major causes of gene frequency change and that natural selection at any individual locus results from different fitnesses among the genotypes.

Cultural behavior is shown to be a primary determinant of fitness differences in human populations. Variations in the use of milk and alcoholic beverages are used as examples of how cultural behavior has led to gene frequency change. This causal model is also shown to contradict the usual assumption that incest taboos have evolved because of the deleterious effects of inbreeding.

The priority of cultural behavior as a determinant of genetic change also has implications for the current controversy on the control of human population growth. If variations in the average number of offspring is determined by cultural factors, then the assumption by most sociobiologists that the average number of offspring for any human population results in a maximum contribution to the next generation, which implies a genetic control of reproduction, is not necessarily true. It is also not supported by any data.

Literature Cited

Barash, D.P. 1977. Sociobiology and behavior. Elsevier, New York.

Bischof, N. 1975. Comparative ethology of incest avoidance. In R. Fox(ed.), Biosocial anthropology. Wiley, New York, pp. 37-68.

Brues, A. 1959. The spearman and the archer. American Anthropologist 61:457-469.

Bulmer, M.G. 1975. The statistical analysis of density dependence. Biometrics 31:901-911.

Campbell, D.T. 1975. On the conflict between biological and social evolution and between psychology and moral tradition. American Psychologist 30:1103-1126.

Cohen, D. & I. Eshel. 1976. On the founder effect and the evolution of altruistic traits. Theoretical Population Biology 10:276-302.

Colinveaux, P.A. 1975. The human breeding strategy. Nature 261:356-357.

Curwen, E.C. & G. Hatt. 1953. Plough and Pasture. Schuman, New York.

Ehrlich, P.R. 1968. The population bomb. Ballantine Books, New York.

Ehrman, L & P.A. Parsons. 1976. The genetics of behavior. Sinauer, Sunderland, Mass.

Ember, M. 1975. On the origin and extension of the incest taboo. Behavior Science Research 10:249-281.

Feldman, M.W. & R.C. Lewontin. 1975. The heritability hang-up. Science 190:1163-1168.

Goodwin, D. 1976. Is alcoholism hereditary? Oxford University Press, New York.

Haldane, J.B.S. 1940. The conflict between selection and mutation of harmful recessive genes. Annals of Eugenics 10:417-422.

Jarvik, L.F. & B.S. Deckard. 1977. The Odyssean personality: A survival advantage for carriers of genes predisposing to schizophrenia. Neuropsychobiology 3:179-191.

Jaynes, J. 1977. The origin of consciousness in the breakdown of the bicameral mind. Houghton-Mifflin, Boston.

Kaffman, M. 1977. Sexual standards and behavior of the kibbutz adolescent. American Journal of Orthopsychiatry 47: 207-217.

Kidd, K.K. 1975. On the possible magnitudes of selective forces maintaining schizophrenia. In R.R. Fieve, D. Rosenthal & H. Brill (eds.), Genetic Research in Psychiatry.

Johns Hopkins Press, Baltimore, pp. 135-145.

Koestler, A. 1968. The ghost in the machine. Macmillan, New York.

Krzywicki, L. 1934. Primitive society and its vital statistics. Macmillan, London.

Lack, D. 1968. Ecological adaptations for breeding in birds. Methuen, London.

Lande, R. 1978. Are humans maximizing reproductive success? Behavioral Ecology and Sociobiology 3:95-96.

Layzer, D. 1974. Heritability analyses of IQ scores. Science 183:1258-1265.

Livingstone, F.B. 1958. Anthropological implications of sickle cell gene distribution in West Africa. American Anthropologist 60:533-562.

_______. 1969. Genetics, ecology, and the origins of incest and exogamy. Current Anthropology 10:45-62.

Mech. L.D. 1977. Wolf-pack buffer zones as prey reservoirs. Science 198:320-321.

Missakian, E.A. 1973. Genealogical mating activity in free-ranging groups of rhesus monkeys(Macaca mulatta) on Cayo Santiago. Behaviour 45:225-241.

Moran, P.A.P. 1973. A note on heritability and the correlation between relatives. Annals of Human Genetics 37:217.

Nichols, P.L. & V.E. Anderson. 1973. Intellectual performance, race, and socioeconomic status. Social Biology 20: 367-374.

Packer, C. 1975. Male transfer in olive baboons. Nature 255:219-220.

Rao, P.S.S. & S.G. Inbaraj. 1977. Inbreeding effects on human reproduction in Tamil Nadu of South India. Annals of Human Genetics 41:87-97.

Reed, T.E., H. Kalant, R.J. Gibbins, B.M. Kapur & J.G. Rankin. 1976. Alcohol and acetaldehyde metabolism in Caucasian, Chinese and Amerinds. Canadian Medical Association Journal 115:851-855.

Sade, D.S. 1968. Inhibition of son-mother mating among free-ranging rhesus monkeys. Science and Psychoanalysis 12:18-37.

Sanghvi, L.D. 1966. Inbreeding in India. Eugenics Quarterly 13:291-301.

Sarles, R.M. 1975. Incest. Pediatrics Clinics of North America 22:633-641.

Schneider, D.M. 1976. The meaning of incest. Journal of the Polynesian Society 85:149-169.

Shepher, J. 1971. Mate selection among second generation kibbutz adolescents and adults: Incest avoidance and negative imprinting. Archives of Sexual Behavior 1:293-307.

Slatis, H. 1973. Comment on V. M. McKusick. Israel Journal of Medical Sciences 9:1308.

Spielman, R.S., J.V. Neel & F.H.F. Li. 1977. Inbreeding estimation from population data: Models, procedures and implications. Genetics 85:355-371.

Stamatoyannopoulos, G., S.-H. Chen & M. Fukui. 1975. Liver alcohol dehydrogenase in Japanese: High population frequency of atypical form and its possible role in alcohol sensitivity. American Journal of Human Genetics 27:789-796.

Steklis, H.B., S.R. Harnad & J. Lancaster (orgs.) 1975. Origin and evolution of language and speech. Annals of the New York Academy of Sciences 280:1-595.

Talmon, Y. 1964. Mate selection in collective settlements. American Sociological Review 29:491-508.

Tiger, L. & R. Fox. 1971. The imperial animal. Holt, Rinehart & Winston, New York.

Trivers, R. 1976. Comment. In B.D. Davis & P. Flaherty (eds.), Human diversity: Its causes and social significance. Ballinger, Cambridge.

Weinrich, J.D. 1978. The author replies. Behavioral Ecology and Sociobiology 3:96-98.

Williams, G.C. 1966. Adaptation and natural selection. Princeton University Press, Princeton.

Wilson, E.O. 1975. Sociobiology: The new synthesis. Harvard University Press, Cambridge.

_______. 1977. Biology and the social sciences. Daedalus Fall Issue, pp. 127-140.

Wolf, A.P. 1966. Childhood association, sexual attraction, and the incest taboo: A Chinese case. American Anthropologist 68:883-898.

Wolff, P.H. 1972. Ethnic differences in alcohol sensitivity. Science 175:449-450.

_______. 1973. Vasomotor sensitivity to alcohol in diverse Mongoloid populations. American Journal of Human Genetics 25:193-199.

Wynne-Edwards, V.C. 1962. Animal dispersion in relation to social behaviour. Oliver & Boyd, Edinburgh.

Richard Dawkins

14. Good Strategy or Evolutionarily Stable Strategy?

Genes and Strategies

Natural selection is differential survival of alleles in gene pools. To explain how a behavior pattern became established in a species we proceed, crudely speaking, as follows. We imagine a time before anyone did the behavior. Then we imagine a rare gene arising which tended to make individuals do it. Then we ask what it was about the behavior that might have contributed to the survival of the gene, so that the behavior ceased to be rare and became common.

We can talk about the Darwinian evolution of behavior only if we are prepared to visualize genetically determined behavioral alternatives in the population. This of course implies no commitment to the belief that any particular behavior difference is genetically determined. I stress this because it has become clear that a logical confusion exists in the minds of some critics. When I say that only genetic differences are subject to Darwinian selection, this is not equivalent to saying that all or most (or even any!) behavior differences are genetic. There are many important differences that are non-genetic, but these are not interesting in the present context because they are not available for Darwinian selection. Even if no studies of behavior genetics had ever been done, the existence of adaptive behavior would imply the existence of genetic differences in behavior (Dawkins 1978a).

In order to fit in with the terminology I shall be using later, I want to refer to each genetically determined behavioral alternative as a strategy. A strategy in this sense can be defined only by contrast with at least one alternative. It emphatically does not have to be something the animal works out in a cognitive or purposive sense. A strategy stands to an animal in the same relation as a program to a computer. It is an unconscious behavior program, a candidate for natural selection in competition with alternative strategies.

Good, Bad and Stable

Of the alternative strategies that we postulate in the population, which will prevail after natural selection? It is tempting to answer that it is the ones that are 'best' for individual survival and reproduction, and this may seem obvious to the point of tautology. But my purpose is to show that this answer is too simple. There may not be such a thing as a straightforwardly 'good' or 'bad' strategy. Instead we should learn to think in terms of evolutionarily stable strategies, a concept that we owe to Maynard Smith (references below). A strategy is said to be evolutionarily stable against a specified list of alternatives if, given that more than a critical proportion of the population adopts it, none of the alternative strategies does better. The key clause is 'given that more than a critical proportion of the population adopts it.' Unstable states, by definition, do not last long. When we look at nature we expect to see populations either sitting in stable states or evolving toward them. This is why evolutionarily stable strategies, henceforward called ESSs, are important.

The idea of the ESS, and methods of setting up ESS models, have been well explained in the literature (Maynard Smith 1972, 1974, 1976a; Maynard Smith & Price 1973; Maynard Smith & Parker 1976; Treisman 1977; Taylor in press), and I have given a simple nonmathematical account (Dawkins 1976) which I will not repeat here. I shall instead develop a number of points that have not been stressed in the literature so far.

The formal affinity of ESS reasoning to the mathematical theory of games has been emphasized often enough. I shall ignore it because, although historically important, I think it is now misleading. It is misleading because it can suggest that the animal is making rational decisions, attempting to outwit an equally rational opponent or, worse, attempting to 'outwit nature.'

Rational decisions do not come into ESS theory. Rather, each animal is assumed to be provided with a nervous system which is wired up in advance so that it performs in a certain way, programmed, in other words. Then we ask which program or combination of programs will be stable against evolutionary invasion by alternative minority programs which might arise in the population by mutation or immigration. In my discussion the game-theoretic roots of ESS theory will show only vestigially in the use of words like 'play' and 'strategy.'

Apart from game theory, the other historical antecedent of ESS theory is the genetical concept of frequency-dependent selection (Fisher 1930; Kojima 1971; Ayala & Campbell 1974; Clarke in press). Maynard Smith's contribution has been one of vision more than invention. He looked at existing concepts in population genetics and game theory, saw the connection between them, and saw that they are not just occasionally relevant to behavioral evolution, they are fundamental to it. In the words of one recent enthusiast quoted by Taylor (in press): "After a while, one sees ESSs everywhere."

Widely relevant as the ESS concept is, it happens to have been discussed largely in the context of intraspecific aggression, and it is in danger of being type-cast in this role. I shall therefore use examples from nonaggressive contexts wherever possible. This means I shall sometimes be forced to abandon familiar and well worked out examples for more tentative cases where the prospects for a future ESS analysis look good, but where no such analysis has yet been done. I begin with one of these.

Fishers and Pirates - A Hypothetical Example

Most common terns catch fish from the sea. This may be called the 'honest fisher' strategy. But there is an alternative strategy practiced by a minority of the population, which may be called the 'pirate' strategy. Pirates, or kleptoparasites (Brockmann & Barnard 1979), do not fish, but wait in the ternery and snatch fish away from others (Hays 1970). Which is the 'best' strategy, honest fisher or pirate? The point I am making is that there does not have to be a simple answer. It may depend on what the rest of the population are doing.

Suppose that most of the population are honest fishers. Now imagine a single pirate. Since there are many honest fishers bringing fish back to the colony, the single pirate makes a good living, better than any honest fisher, who has to spend time and energy catching fish. So, if there is a genetic component to the difference between the two strategies (a big 'if'), we might predict that pirates, being favored by natural selection, would become more numerous in future generations. But now suppose pirates came to form the majority. To go to the extreme, suppose there were almost no honest fishers in the population at all. Why then, obviously everyone would starve, since no fish would be caught. Under these conditions a single honest fisher would do better than a typical pirate. Admittedly he would run a grave risk of losing most of the fish that he caught, but so would any pirate risk losing the few fish that he succeeded in stealing. So, if there were many pirates and few fishers we would expect natural selection to favor the fisher strategy.

There is then no general answer to the question of which is the best strategy, fisher or pirate. The best strategy is the one that happens to be in the minority, whichever that is. Actually the word 'minority' is too simple. There would probably be a critical equilibrium proportion of pirates in the population, which is not particularly likely to be exactly 50%. At the equilibrium proportion an average fisher does exactly as well as an average pirate and there is no selection pressure in favor of either strategy over the other. If the proportion happened to drift in either direction, natural selection would tend to restore it to its equilibrium value.

In Maynard Smith's terminology we would say that neither fisher nor pirate is an ESS, but that there is an evolutionarily stable state of the population which consists of fishers and pirates mixed in such proportion that each fisher does on average as well as each pirate. When evolutionary stability is reached, far from one strategy being 'better' than the other, both strategies are, by definition, equally good.

This should not be misunderstood as meaning that at evolutionary stability all individuals in the population are equally successful. There may be great variance in success among followers of both strategies, but the mean success of followers of the two strategies should be equal.

Our hypothetical tern population seems to behave like a self-regulating system, a homeostat. One is tempted to think of the population as self-regulating for its own, the population's, advantage. It is impossible to overemphasize that this is a misguided idea. We shall see that one of the great virtues of ESS thinking is that it shows us how selection among selfish individuals can create an illusion of unity of function at the group level. I personally would go further. I think it shows us how selection among selfish genes can create an illusion of unity of function at the individual level. I have discussed this elsewhere (Dawkins 1976: 91-93) and I return to it later in this paper.

Diggers and Enterers - A Real Example

Fishers and pirates are hypothetical, as are the 'hawks' and 'doves' of Maynard Smith's papers. So far, the only full studies known to me of mixed ESSs in nature are Parker's on dungflies (Parker 1978 and references cited; Maynard Smith & Parker 1976), and Brockmann's on digger wasps (Brockmann, Grafen & Dawkins 1979; for further developments see Brockmann & Dawkins in press and Dawkins & Brockmann in press). The dungfly work is discussed later. Here I shall briefly tell the digger wasp story, in idealized form for the sake of brevity.

Brockmann's digger wasps (Sphex ichneumoneus) have two alternative ways of getting a nest burrow. They may either dig one, or else enter and take over a burrow that another individual has dug. Enterers save themselves the 'cost of digging', just as pirate terns saved themselves the cost of fishing. The evidence from one study site in New Hampshire suggests that the relative advantages of digging and entering are frequency-dependent: the more digging is going on in the population as a whole, the better off is a wasp who enters; and the more entering is going on in the population, the better off is a digger. If you are an individual wasp, entering becomes less profitable as the frequency of enterers in the population increases, because there is an increasing chance that the burrow you choose has been entered already by somebody else. There is a critical frequency (just over 40% entering) at which digging and entering are exactly equally successful. This is the evolutionarily stable proportion, and it is approximately the porportion actually observed in the New Hampshire population. A mathematical model along these lines yields a series of further predictions which successfully fit the New Hampshire data. The model's assumptions are, however, not met at another study site in Michigan, where a new model is required.

I may have given the impression that there is a polymorphic population of diggers and enterers. This is not so. Individual wasps switch back and forth between digging and entering throughout their lives. It is the success rate of digging itself, when averaged across all wasps, that is equated with the overall success rate of entering, similarly averaged. As we shall see, this kind of within-individual mixed strategy is mathematically equivalent to a polymorphism as far as the present theory is concerned.

An ESS Is Not Necessarily Optimal, but It Is Uncheatable

Returning to hypothetical examples, one of Maynard Smith's best known ones is the aggression game called 'hawks and doves.' Hawks fight viciously until seriously hurt, or until the rival retreats. Doves fight formally, and always surrender to hawks. Like 'fishers and pirates' or 'diggers and enterers', this game can lead to a balanced stable mixture, a mixed ESS. The hawk/dove model can be used (Dawkins 1976: 77-78) to illustrate vividly the discrepancy that may exist between what would be best for all individuals and what is evolutionarily stable. A 'conspiracy of doves', a kind of social contract in which everybody played fair, would be good for every individual. The conspiracy is an equilibrium in that all participants do equally well. But it is not evolutionarily stable: in the absence of some kind of policing, it would be invaded by hawks who would benefit in the short term by exploiting the doves. The inevitable result is evolution toward an ESS in which everybody again does equally well, but much worse than they all would do in the conspiracy of doves.

The defining characteristic of an ESS, then, is not that it is the optimum strategy that could be devised for all individuals. Rather, it is immune to cheating. In this respect it is reminiscent of the alleged Eskimo method of ensuring that food is cut into exactly equal slices before being passed around: the individual who does the cutting gets the last slice!

I now introduce a new version of the hawk/dove game, one with a sting in the tail. I shall call it the scorpion game, and use it to emphasize in another way the difference between simple 'optimality' and evolutionary stability.

Dying Gasp Retaliation

Imagine two alternative fighting strategies in a highly venomous species such as a scorpion. 'Hawk' scorpions go all out for the kill, and use their lethal sting. 'Retaliators' wrestle with their claws, and never sting except in retaliation. A retaliator who has been stung attempts, with his dying gasp, to sting his murderer. If he succeeds, both die.

Calculation shows that the outcome of this simple game depends upon the probability, p, that a mortally wounded scorpion, whether hawk or retaliator, will succeed in stinging his murderer with his dying gasp. Hawk is an ESS only if retaliation is totally ineffective ($p=0$). If p is nonzero but small, a stable mixture of hawks and retaliators evolves. If p is large, retaliator, on its own, is the ESS. Let us make the plausible assumption that p is large, and that the population is therefore dominated by retaliators.

Now we come to the interesting point. As far as his survival or genetic success is concerned, retaliation is pointless for the individual retaliator. Once he has been stung he is doomed. Stinging back does him no good at all. Yet retaliation is the dominant strategy in this model population, because it is the ESS. We are breaking down the idea that animal behavior should necessarily be interpreted in terms of individual benefit. Why do scorpions retaliate? Not because it benefits their inclusive fitness to do so; it does not. Scorpions retaliate because the blind unconscious behavior program called retaliator is the ESS. I must emphasize, by the way, that this is a hypothetical example constructed to make a point. I might just as well have used dragons scorching each other to death.

Moreover, pedants will argue that the retaliator's dying act may in fact benefit his kin, but this is not the point. The point is that, even if an act does not benefit the inclusive fitness of the animal doing it, it can still predominate in the population because it is a manifestation of an ESS.

I shall not leave retaliators without warning the reader that the classic Retaliator in the original model of Maynard Smith & Price (1973) is now known not to be, strictly, an ESS at all (J. Maynard Smith, personal communication). It is an equilibrium, since in a population of retaliators no other postulated strategy would do better. But, like a pencil balanced on its end, it is not stable, for, if the population composition drifted a little from the equilibrium, selection would not tend to restore it. Instead it would push it further away, presumably to the other known equilibrium, a stable mixture of 'hawks' and 'bullies' (Gale & Eaves 1975). It is not difficult to rephrase the model slightly so that retaliator becomes a true ESS. Dawkins & Krebs (1978) incorporate one such improvement in their recent summary of the model.

I made a similar error in a model of sexual strategies (Dawkins 1976). What I thought was an evolutionarily stable balance between 'faithful' and 'philanderer' males, and 'coy' and 'fast' females, turns out to be an unstable equilibrium (H-J. Pohley, personal communication). Like Maynard Smith & Price, I unfortunately omitted to check the stability conditions of my model. It is not enough to find an equilibrium. It is then necessary to check the consequences of slight perturbations away from it. Will selection tend to correct or accentuate them? Only in the former case do we have evolutionary stability.

The Strategy Set

An ESS, then, is not the 'best' strategy, but it is a strategy that is uninvadable by any of a specified list of alternative minority strategies. The list that we specify is important. The ESS that finally emerges in a model depends on the inventiveness of the theorist in dreaming up possible candidates. In the wasp work briefly described above, Brockmann, Grafen & Dawkins (1979) began by postulating two strategies called 'founder' and 'joiner.' It was the decisive failure of this first model that led us to propose our second, successful, model postulating 'diggers' and 'enterers' (the key difference is that 'joiners' positively seek out occupied burrows to join, while 'enterers' enter occupied and abandoned burrows indiscriminately).

A distinguished philosopher has put the following objection

to the whole ESS method. You allow yourself, he said to me, complete freedom in making up imaginary strategies. You could cheerfully invent a strategy called 'fly to the moon.' You are prepared to shoot down the theory of group-selected altruism by saying it would be invaded by an individual selfishness strategy. But how do you know that the necessary mutations would be there to provide the strategy you postulate, any more than a mutation for flying to the moon?

As Davies (in press) remarks in reply to a similar criticism:

> It is a general weakness of game theory models that a strategy can only be said to be an ESS against stated alternatives. It will always be easy to invent an alternative strategy that could invade (e.g. a speckled wood butterfly with a machine gun) and we must rely on biological intuition to define the range of possible strategies in the models.

Davies errs only in singling out game theory models. Exactly the same applies to any models of the evolution of adaptation. The need for biological intuition, indeed biological common sense, is nothing new. An expert on a particular species is in a position to judge whether a proposed mutant strategy, say 'prober-retaliator' (Maynard Smith & Price 1973), is not too far from what seems reasonable. The behavior of related species may be a useful guide, as is a deliberate noting down of unusual, freakish behavior in wild populations (J. Brockmann, personal communication). Occasionally more positive evidence is available. In digger wasps, 'joining' (as opposed to entering) would be a realistic option only if individuals were capable of discriminating occupied from abandoned burrows. There is some evidence that *Sphex ichneumoneus* wasps cannot, or at least do not, perform this discrimination (Brockmann & Dawkins loc. cit.). But this should be regarded as a temporary, not an irrevocable, constraint: mutant individuals capable of the necessary sensory discrimination cannot be ruled out in the future.

In judging whether a postulated mutant strategy is plausible, there is one general distinction that I find helpful. This is the distinction between continuous and discontinuous variation.

Discrete Strategies or Continuum?

So far, all our strategies have been discontinuous. Pirate or fisher, hawk or dove, each is a discrete behavior program and there are no intermediates. But we could easily imagine a continuum of hawkishness, any point along the continuum being linked to any other point by a series of imperceptible steps. Then if any point on the continuum is biologically plausible, or is observed in nature, it is presumably easy to imagine a smooth evolutionary progression to any other point. As the following hypothetical example illustrates, it is usually possible to model a strategy set in either a discontinuous or a continuous way.

As is well known, many small song birds give alarm calls when a hawk approaches. The individual who warns the others subjects himself to some special dangers, and the behavior has therefore been described as altruistic. The taunt of altruism has provoked neo-Darwinians into devising a number of selfish theories. I here make use of one of these, called the 'never break ranks' theory (Charnov & Krebs 1975; Dawkins 1976).

It is assumed that an individual bird is in greater danger from predators when on his own than when in a flock; and also that he would be safer in the air or up a tree than on the ground where he is obliged to feed. Now put yourself in the position of an individual member of a flock feeding on the ground who has seen a hawk. What to do? If you do nothing you remain in the flock, which is good, but you are also on the ground, which is bad. If you fly up by yourself you are off the ground, which is good, but you are also alone, which is bad. But if you give an alarm call, you cause everybody else to fly up and you can fly with them. So now you are off the ground and also in the flock, and both these things are good. This is the 'never break ranks' theory of how alarm calls evolved.

But there is a snag. The individual who gives the alarm puts himself in special danger, because hawks are sometimes attracted by the sound of the call itself--how else could natural selection have shaped the calls into their present ventriloquial tones (Marler 1959)? So the best thing of all for an individual who has seen a hawk might be to wait and 'hope' that one of his companions sees it too and gives the alarm. But of course if everybody played this waiting game all would be in mortal danger. Under these conditions it might pay any given individual to call immediately. Conversely, if most individuals are immediate callers, an individual might benefit by waiting. It seems we may have frequency-dependent selection again: a suitable case for ESS treatment.

We could handle this by postulating discrete strategies, caller and noncaller, and we might even amuse ourselves with more subtle strategies. For instance 'wolf wolf' would give false warnings when there is no hawk, driving his companions needlessly into the air and staying behind to eat their food. But these are discrete, discontinuous strategies. The point I am making is that it may be more realistic to consider a continuum, in this case a continuum of waiting times. Some birds might call as soon as reflexes permit, on seeing a hawk; others wait half a second, others one second, others two, and so on. A strategy, in this example, is a waiting time, and there is no need to break up the continuum of waiting times with discontinuities.

The ESS in such a case would be described by means of a frequency distribution, whose shape a mathematician might enjoy discovering. That is if, indeed, the ESS turns out to be a mixture of waiting times. It could instead be a pure strategy such as 'always call immediately.' It is already clear that this model is not, as it might at first appear, equivalent to a simple 'war of attrition.'

The war of attrition model was proposed by Maynard Smith (1974) and further discussed by Norman, Taylor & Robertson (1977), Bishop & Cannings (1978) and Caryl (1979). It gets its name from the aggressive context in which it was originally proposed: animals threaten each other formally, and the loser is the one who backs down first, the one with the shortest staying time. The model is not confined to aggression, however, and indeed the best data to which the model has been applied (Maynard Smith & Parker 1976) come from Parker's (1978 and references cited) brilliant analysis of courtship in dungflies. I shall introduce the story in terms of the war of attrition model even though, as we shall see, there may be another interpretation.

The Cowpat War

Female dungflies (*Scatophaga stercoraria*) visit cowpats to mate and lay eggs. Males wait for females at cowpats. Females prefer fresh cowpats, and the rate at which they arrive at a dropping falls off as the dropping gets stale. What is the 'best' strategy for a male to adopt? If he were the only male in the world, he would maximize his mating success by leaving each cowpat as soon as it began to get stale and going to a fresh one. That way he would maximize his encounter rate with females. But he is not the only male around, so we must 'think ESS.' If all males adopted the 'fresh pats only' strategy, fresh pats would become overcrowded with males, and competition for females would be acute. In this case a smart male would stay by an older, stale pat. Fewer females would arrive, but he would have them to himself.

We could postulate two male strategies called 'fresh' and

'stale', but it is better to think of a continuum of staying times. A strategy, then, is a staying time. A five minute strategist is a fly who leaves a pat when it is five minutes old; a twenty minute strategist leaves when it is twenty minutes old. The population as a whole contains a continuum of such strategies. Now, remember that we do not ask which of the strategies is 'best.' Instead we seek a mix of strategies such that all do equally well. The theoretical ESS for this game has been calculated mathematically (Maynard Smith & Parker 1976). It turns out to be the same as for the classical war of attrition, a mix in which the frequencies of the various waiting times follow a negative exponential distribution whose mean is adjusted so that the mating success of an early leaver is, on average, equal to the mating success of a late leaver.

The data give an excellent fit to the expected distribution. It should be said, however, that Parker (1978) has recently offered an alternative hypothesis to account for his result. According to this 'input matching theorem', the male staying times simply reflect the exponential distribution of female availabilities at cowpats of different ages. This immediately makes me wonder whether the females may be involved in some kind of war of attrition, but that is a speculation for future research.

A Mixed Strategy Can Be Mixed Within an Individual or Can Be a Polymorphism

A mixed strategy is the opposite of a pure strategy. Hawk, dove and retaliator are all pure strategies. So is 'wait for 5½ minutes' a pure strategy. But 'play hawk with probability p' is a mixed strategy, and so is 'wait for a time t where t is drawn at random from a probability density function.' The diagnostic feature of a mixed strategy is that its specification contains at least one probabilistic statement. 'Stochastic' might be a better label than 'mixed.' To anticipate a later section, a mixed strategy should not be confused with a 'conditional' strategy such as 'retaliate if your opponent attacks you.'

The mathematical equivalent of a mixed strategy can be achieved if each individual plays a pure strategy, the population as a whole containing a mixture of pure strategists. We can thus think of the hawk/dove game as ending in a stable polymorphism, a mixture of pure hawks and pure doves in critical proportion, p. But equivalently the ESS could consist in each individual being a stochastic 'dawk,' choosing to play dove or hawk at random, with a built-in bias corresponding to the critical proportion, p. Any combination of these two extremes would be stable, provided that in the population as a whole the strategy hawk was played p of the time and dove 1-p of the time. Similarly, the war of attrition could lead to a stable polymorphism, the frequencies of the morphs following the predicted negative exponential distribution; alternatively each individual could produce a random sequence of waiting times of different length, drawing them from a negative exponential probability density function.

The two ways of realizing a mixed ESS are mathematically equivalent except in special cases such as when the individuals involved are genetic relatives (Grafen 1979). But, even if mathematically equivalent, they are far from biologically equivalent. The war of attrition could theoretically lead to a stable polymorphism or an individual mixed ESS, but biological common sense in this case argues for the individual mixed ESS. This is because it is extremely hard to imagine a plausible genetic process that could lead to the necessary exponential distribution of morph frequencies, but it is relatively easy to imagine a mechanism in an individual nervous system that would lead to an exponential distribution of waiting times.

A negative exponential distribution is automatically produced by a totally random process, in which there is a fixed probability that the end of the waiting time will occur within the next small interval of time, regardless of how long the individual has waited so far. So if the end of the waiting time depended upon the firing of a single neurone with a randomly fluctuating excitatory potential, an exponential distribution of waiting times would automatically be produced. Natural selection could then easily adjust the mean of the distribution by acting on the threshold of the neurone.

In simple discontinuous games of the hawk/dove type, common sense does not obviously favor either a polymorphism or a within-individual mixture. The only well worked out case, that of Brockmann's digger wasps, happens to be an example of a within-individual mixture. Statistical analysis revealed no tendency for individual wasps to specialize in digging or entering. All individuals seemed to be following the same stochastic rule: 'enter with probability p, dig with probability 1-p' (where p in the New Hampshire population was about 0.41). A runs test uncovered no tendency for individuals to depart from random order in their decisions to dig or enter (Brockmann & Dawkins loc. cit.)

In theory, there is a third way in which something equivalent to a mixed ESS could be realized. This may be called 'frequency-dependent behavior.'

Frequency-Dependent Behavior

Suppose that individuals can use their sense organs to monitor the local population. A dungfly might visually assess the density of male flies at his present cowpat, and leave if the density exceeds some criterion value (G. A. Parker, personal communication). This is quite different from the other two stabilizing mechanisms discussed. There, the stabilization took place over the evolutionary time scale. Here the stabilization occurs in behavioral time, but the end result could be a similar stable equilibrium. Even here we may assume that natural selection acting over evolutionary time would be ultimately involved, in determining the criterion values (<u>Sollwerte</u>) used by individuals.

This idea is akin to Wynne-Edwards's (1962) 'epideictic' behavior and to Fretwell's (1972) 'ideal free distribution.' Notice that there is no need to assume any sophisticated counting mechanism in the nervous system. A wasp, for instance, could in theory achieve the functional equivalent of counting available burrows by following an 'optimal foraging' type of rule of thumb such as: 'search for a burrow to enter; if you fail to find one within a criterion time t, dig your own.' This particular hypothesis, by the way, is decisively rejected by the evidence: searching times culminating in digging are not longer than searching times culminating in entering (Brockmann & Dawkins loc. cit.)

If we apply terminology strictly, 'frequency-dependent behavior' is not a mixed strategy at all. It is a special case of a pure <u>conditional</u> strategy.

Conditional Versus Mixed Strategies

A conditional strategy is like a computer program with an 'IF' statement. Whether pure or mixed, most of the strategies we have so far met have been unconditional. Even 'dig with probability p' is unconditional, since what the animal does on a given occasion is determined by a random process and not by a recognizable event. Retaliator is an example of a conditional strategy, as is 'fish if the weather is fine, steal if it is wet.' Maynard Smith & Parker (1976) have considered the often surprising consequences of postulating strategies conditional upon asymmetries in aggressive contests between two individuals, for instance 'attack if larger, retreat if smaller.' R. Selten (personal communication) has proved that mixed strategies cannot be stable in such asymmetric games.

There is a sense in which, depending upon our philosophical position, we may insist that all mixed (i.e. stochastic) strategies are really conditional if we look at them in enough detail. Even the outcome of tossing a penny is conditional upon a complex set of physical factors. When we hypothesize that animals follow stochastic strategies we may regard this as a temporary cover for our ignorance of what is really going on. But there is the more interesting possibility that animals are selected to adopt quasi-random behavior as an adaptation to deceive others. For instance the erratic zig-zags of a fleeing rabbit may be random in a functionally interesting sense (Humphries & Driver 1967), even if a physiologist eventually uncovers the deterministic conditional rules that underlie them. Game theory tells us that the stable solution to games such as rock/scissors/paper is random play, but in practice this need only mean that the pattern is too complex for the opponent to discern. The rabbit's zig-zags need only be unpredictable enough to avoid being second-guessed by the fox.

Many people find conditional strategies inherently more plausible than mixed strategies. It is therefore of some interest that in the digger wasp study we tried hard but were unable to disprove the hypothesis of a mixed ESS (Brockmann & Dawkins loc. cit.). We failed to find evidence for various conditional strategies that were proposed by skeptics as alternatives to the mixed ESS of Grafen's and our model. A wasp's decision to dig or enter appears not to be based upon her size, nor upon the time of year, nor upon her overall success rate. More interestingly, the wasps are not following a 'win-stay lose-shift' strategy of sticking to whatever paid off last time. Finally, as we have just seen, they are not following a policy of resorting to digging only if they fail to find a burrow to enter within a criterion time.

Making the Best of a Bad Job

Suppose individuals differ from each other in a way that influences their success. Some may happen to be bigger than others, some will be older, some will have lived in the local area longer than others; some may, for one reason or another, be ill-equipped to perform certain tasks. In such cases, less favored individuals may behave in a way that minimizes their inevitable disadvantage: they 'make the best of a bad job.' What appear to be two alternative strategies may therefore turn out to be two different outcomes of the same conditional strategy. There is then no reason to expect the two apparent strategies to be equally successful, as we should if they genuinely were two alternative strategies.

Alcock, Jones & Buchmann (1977) describe two different male mating 'strategies' in the bee Centris pallida. 'Patrollers' search the ground for sites where females are about to emerge, then dig down and mate underground. 'Hoverers' wait for flying females who have been missed by patrollers. Hoverers are always small. Large males always patrol. Patrollers are, on average more successful than hoverers, and large males more successful than small.

It seems, then, that hovering and patrolling should not, strictly, be called 'strategies' at all, for two strategies will not coexist if one is more successful than the other. Instead, it seems that there is but one conditional strategy: 'if large, patrol; if small, hover.' Given that a male is small and therefore unlikely to succeed anyway, he 'makes the best of a bad job' by hovering rather than patrolling. This assumes that a small male would fare even worse if he attempted to patrol, and the authors give some evidence for this.

Cade (1978) discusses two different 'strategies' of mating behavior in male crickets (*Gryllus integer*). 'Callers' stridulate for females but run the risk of attracting parasitic flies too. Silent 'satellite' males station themselves near a calling male and try to intercept approaching females. Satellites are less often attacked by parasitic flies than callers are, but on the other hand they are also less effective at obtaining copulations. Cade clearly sees the necessity for the two strategies to be equally successful if the population is a stable mixture. But, in his discussion of factors which might bring this state of affairs about, he is content to discuss pros and cons of each of the two strategies and show that there are some of each. It is, however, extremely improbable that the net costs and benefits of two strategies would just happen to average out exactly equally. We need to postulate something like frequency-dependent selection in order to maintain the balance: satellites must do especially well when they are rare. This seems not implausible, and Cade may have tacitly assumed it. Alternatively, 'calling' and 'satellite' behavior may not be true strategies at all, but two outcomes of one conditional strategy, in which case there is no reason to expect them to be equally successful: one may be making the best of a bad job.

Great attention is being paid at present to the possible existence of alternative male strategies in vertebrate populations (e.g. Popp & DeVore, in press). For instance, in mammalian species where dominant males hold harems of females, subordinate males sometimes adopt a policy known as kleptogamy (Clutton-Brock, Albon & Guinness 1979; Cox & Le Boeuf 1977). Kleptogamists sneak briefly into harems and steal hurried copulations before being chased away by the harem master. It is just possible that in some species kleptogamy and harem-holding genuinely represent two strategies in a stable mix. In this case the average benefit of the two strategies will be equal. But in most cases it is much more likely that harem masters fare consistently better than kleptogamists, and that the ESS is the pure conditional strategy: 'if possible hold a harem; if you can't, be a kleptogamist.' Then in the stable state all males will be playing this one strategy, and the behavior that an individual actually shows will be conditional on factors like his size or skill in combat.

In general, the hypothesis that there are two or more alternative male mating strategies mixed in a population should perhaps be regarded as a hypothesis of last resort. It is more likely that all individuals are programmed with the same 'best of a bad job' conditional strategy. However, as Dr. J. Brockmann has persuaded me, one generation's conditional strategy may be the previous generation's mixed strategy. This is best illustrated by reference to the patrolling and hovering bees already mentioned (see also Maynard Smith in press).

One Generation's Conditional Strategy as the Previous Generation's Mixed Strategy

Alcock, Jones & Buchmann (loc. cit.) perceptively note that female bees can control the size of their children, for instance by feeding them different amounts. It follows that mothers might be selected to nurture two complementary kinds of sons: expensive, relatively successful, 'close-fielding' patrollers, and cheap, relatively unsuccessful, 'out-fielding' hoverers to catch the few females that the close-fielders miss. Brockmann adds two important points. Firstly, mothers are probably subject to frequency-dependent selection, investment in patrollers being favored when patrollers are relatively rare. Secondly, selection on mothers to manipulate sons may interact with selection on sons to make the best of a bad job, the 'arms race' resulting in a 'mutually compatible stable endpoint' (Dawkins & Krebs in press). To explain this in teleological shorthand, an easy way for a mother to control her sons would be to exploit the fact that the sons themselves will have been selected to 'make the best' of their own size. As far as an individual male is concerned, he would be better off large and patrolling but, given that his mother has forced small size upon him, he makes the best of a bad job, cuts his losses, and hovers. From his point of view he is 'optimizing' within the 'constraint' (Maynard Smith 1978) of his own size. The mother optimizes from her point of view by imposing that constraint. The maternal strategy would then be a mixed one, an evolutionarily stable frequency distribution of amounts of food given to sons. It would work by exploiting a conditional strategy in the next generation.

This kind of thinking has its precedent in the theory of sex ratios, initiated by Fisher (1930).

Sons Versus Daughters as Parental Strategy

In a large outbred population, the ratio of the reproductive success of an average male to that of an average female is a function solely of the sex ratio. Since all children born in the population have one father and one mother, an average member of the rarer sex necessarily has more children than an average member of the commoner sex. When the sex ratio is 1:1, an average male has exactly as many children as an average female. It is therefore theoretically possible, in a species with a 1:1 sex ratio, to regard male and female as two alternative pure strategies in balanced polymorphism maintained by frequency-dependent selection.

But Fisher wisely treated the sex of an individual as, in effect, the outcome of a mixed strategy in the previous, parental generation. This allows for the possibility of unequal sex ratios being evolutionarily stable. If, say, males are more expensive than females for parents to rear, the evolutionarily stable sex ratio will be female-biased: parents will rear more of the cheaper sex. The reproductive success of a typical son will then be higher than that of a typical daughter. From the parents' point of view, a child of the rarer sex promises them more grandchildren than a child of the commoner sex. This precisely compensates them for the extra cost of rearing a child of the rarer sex. If this compensation was not perfect, selection would not rest until it became perfect. In other words, natural selection will tend to equalize the total parental expenditure on male and female offspring, which may or may not be equivalent to equalizing the sex ratio itself.

In ESS language, a parental strategy is a mixed one of the form: 'invest a proportion p of your parental resources in sons and 1-p in daughters.' The evolutionarily stable value of p is ½. If the average p in the population as a whole became greater than ½, selection would favor parents with a p of less than ½, and vice versa. Like any other mixed ESS, this one could be realized at a population level or as a within-individual mixture. As Williams (in press) has emphasized, it is surprisingly not true that individual parents tend to divide their investment equally between sons and daughters. Rather, they show no systematic bias toward either sex, and it is in the population as a whole that parental expenditure on the two sexes is equalized.

If an individual had any choice in the matter, it would

'prefer' to be a member of the rarer sex since it would then have a relatively high chance of being a parent (Trivers 1974). Usually an individual has no control over its own sex. We may surmise that an individual that finds itself a member of the commoner sex, a victim of the parental mixed strategy, will 'make the best of a bad job' in the same kind of way as was suggested for hovering bees.

Those fish species in which sex is determined nongenetically are a special case. In *Labroides dimidiatus* most individuals are female (Robertson 1972). A group of females constitutes a harem for a male, within which the females have a dominance hierarchy. If the male dies or is removed, the dominant female turns into a male and takes over the harem. Here all individuals seem to be programmed with the same pure conditional strategy: 'if dominant, develop male characteristics; otherwise make the best of a bad job and be female.'

Broad Applicability of the ESS Concept

It is my thesis that the ESS concept is more widely relevant in behavioral biology than is commonly recognized. Its virtual omission from *Sociobiology* (Wilson 1975) is one respect in which that valuable work falls short of being truly 'the new synthesis.' The fact that W.D. Hamilton (1977) is of a similar opinion will not lightly be dismissed by anyone acquainted with his prophetic track-record. It happens that most of the published discussions of ESSs have been in the restricted context of intraspecific aggression. In this brief review I concentrate on some of the nonaggressive usages of the concept, beginning, for historical reasons, with nonbehavioral examples.

Maynard Smith (1972, 1974, 1976a) repeatedly mentions his debt to Hamilton's (1967) game-theoretic treatment of abnormal sex ratios, and this in turn stems from Fisher's (1930) original economic analysis of normal sex ratios. As already discussed, this is a clear case of 'minority does best' frequency-dependent selection acting on the parental generation. At least two other applications of essentially the ESS idea are to be found in Fisher's classic book. In his discussion of mimicry he realized that

> A Batesian mimic . . . will receive less protection, the more numerous it is in comparison with the model; a dimorphic Batesian mimic will therefore adjust the numbers of its two forms . . . until they receive equal protection; any increase in the numbers of one form at the expense of the other would diminish the advantage of the former and increase that of the latter, thus

producing a selective action tending to restore the original proportion.

This is another example of a 'minority does best' or 'negative feedback' type of frequency-dependent selection. Fisher also recognized the opposite 'positive feedback' or 'majority does best' kind of frequency-dependent selection. It is the basis of his famous runaway theory of sexual selection. Here the point is that selection favors females whose taste in males conforms to the majority, whatever that majority taste may be. Any female who prefers an unfashionable kind of male will tend to have sons who are unattractive to typical females in the population. Even if these sons have other advantages, for instance they may be relatively unlikely to attract predators, selection still favors modish males because of their attractiveness to females. The startling thing about this notion is that the details of what females find attractive can in theory be arbitrary. Once a consensus emerges among females, even if, to go beyond Fisher, that consensus is originally based upon some frivolous, tradition-determined fashion, the runaway process can take off.

We could seriously waste our time looking for environmental correlates of the fact that, for instance, in one species males are red and in another species they are blue. The difference could stem from an arbitrary, or at least minor, difference in ancestral circumstances, amplified through Fisher's runaway effect.

The general point that given conditions may yield two or even more ESSs (Maynard Smith & Parker 1976) should be borne in mind by field workers. It is yet another illustration of the difference between a 'good' strategy and an ESS. ESS_1 might be markedly better than ESS_2 in terms of payoff to all individuals, yet any population that happened to drift to ESS_2 would tend to stay there. If there were 100 islands, each with an isolated population, we might scratch our heads in vain trying to find some crucial difference in climate or terrain to account for the fact that some island populations behaved according to ESS_1 while others followed ESS_2.

A similar point has been made by Lewontin (1978) using the example of rhinoceros horns, which he asserts 'are an adaptation for protection against predators' (a remark that differs from the 'adaptationist' speculations lampooned by Gould & Lewontin (in press) only in that <u>those</u> 'Just So Stories' might just be so!). However, his real point is that there is no need to seek an adaptive explanation for the fact that Indian rhinoceroses have one horn while African rhinoceroses have two. The difference could reflect an ancient and long vanished difference in evolutionary starting conditions, not a difference in present day ecology. For reasons of his own, Lewontin (1977) chooses to present his view as bitterly inimical to the 'game' approach to evolution, rather than as in perfect harmony with it (Dawkins 1976: 84-87, 91-93).

Ironically, Lewontin (1961) himself is normally credited with being the first to introduce the mathematics of game theory to evolutionary biology (although Dr. P. O'Donald points out to me that Fisher (1958) had proposed the idea three years earlier). Lewontin, however, thought in panglossian terms of species playing games against 'nature' rather than individuals playing against each other. As already noted, it was Hamilton (1967), in his classic revisiting of Fisher's sex ratio theory, who first applied game theory as such to individuals maximizing genetic payoffs. Moving to behavior, Hamilton's (1971) 'equilibrium of parasitism', or EP, was one of several related ideas that cropped up in the literature shortly before the general term ESS was coined. Hamilton introduced his concept in connection with some tentative speculations about nest-stealing in solitary bees and wasps, behavior which, as we have seen, has indeed become the subject of a full ESS analysis using field data on digger wasps (Brockmann, Grafen & Dawkins 1979). Other ESS-like ideas which began to emerge around 1970 include Orians's (1969) 'polygyny threshold', MacArthur's (1972) 'principle of equal opportunity,' and Fretwell's (1972) 'ideal free distribution.'

Gadgil (1972) discussed, in ESS-like terms, the interesting phenomenon, already referred to, of two male mating types coexisting in a population. Charlesworth & Charlesworth's (1975) criticism of Gadgil's paper, and Gadgil & Taylor's (1975) reply, serve to underline the importance of frequency-dependent selection in this case. Rubenstein (in press) has recently developed detailed ESS models of the 'sneaky male' phenomenon.

Since the name ESS was coined (Maynard Smith 1972), it has been applied to a variety of biological situations other than aggression. I used it to clarify Trivers's (1971) model of reciprocal altruism, showing that a strategy called 'grudger', which remembers past favors or the lack of them, is stable against rival strategies called 'sucker' and 'cheat' (Dawkins 1976). To judge from Sahlins (1977), some such clarification was sadly necessary. Following up another paper of Trivers (1972), ESS models of mate desertion and the battle of the sexes are given by Maynard Smith (1977) and, independently, Grafen & Sibly (1978). Parker & Macnair (1978, 1979; Macnair & Parker 1978, 1979) have used ESS theory to provide us with a thorough mathematical counterpart to Trivers's (1974) verbal model of parent/offspring conflict. Parker (in press) has also carried further the theory of sexual ESSs, and has raised the intriguing possibility of evolutionary instability in endlessly recurring limit cycles (see also Dawkins & Krebs, in press).

Lawlor & Maynard Smith (1976) generalized the ESS idea to interpret competition and coevolution in ecosystems, thereby providing an effective theoretical counter to the fallacy, still occasionally found in the ecological literature, that ecological stability implies some kind of 'ecosystem selection', or even 'prudent predation.' Dawkins & Krebs (1978), following Wallace (1973), indicated the relevance of ESS theory to the evolution of deceptive signals or lies. Maynard Smith (in press) weighs up the evolutionary stability of bluff, in the light of Rohwer's (1977) experimental alterations of Harris' sparrows.

Partridge & Krebs (1978) have looked for ESSs of chorusing in tree frogs. Here the 'game' problem arises because each male is assumed to 'want' to be left calling on his own, the better to attract females, while at the same time he wants his rivals to be drowned out in a chorus. An ESS approach seems feasible to the related problems raised by synchronously flashing fireflies, recently rescued by Lloyd (1973) from long-standing group-selectionist interpretation, and to lekking and chorusing generally (Alexander 1975).

Hamilton & May (1977) made powerful use of ESS theory to derive some important and counter-intuitive, yet elegantly simple, results on dispersal in stable habitats. It is natural to suppose that larval dispersion and migration are selectively favored only when the environment is variable. Yet Hamilton & May showed that, even in a wholly uniform model world, a strategy 'have nondispersing children' is unstable against the alternative strategy 'commit many of your offspring to perilous distant dispersion' (not their terms). Of particular interest for the present paper, they emphasized that the ESS "can demand far more migration than is 'best for the population'."

Various authors have joined ESS theory to kin-selection theory in examining the problem of games between genetic relatives. This area turns out to be a minefield for the unwary. As Grafen (1979) shows, no fewer than three recent papers independently converge on the same logical error.

Brockmann & Dawkins (in press) show how ESS theory might be relevant to the reconstruction of phylogenetic history. Evolutionary change comes about when selection pressures change, but there also has to be available variation for the changed selection pressures to work on. If there is an evolutionarily stable minority pattern of behavior, maintained as a constant feature of the population over many generations, that population might be thereby preadapted to respond rapidly to changed selection pressures. Social cooperation in insects presumably evolved from solitary ancestors when selection pressures switched from opposing joint nesting to favoring it. If those solitary ancestors had had, like *Sphex ichneumoneus* today, a steady 40% minority pattern of nest-entering behavior, leading to a steady 20% minority of inadvertently shared nests, new selection in favor of social cooperation would have found a ready-made preadaptation to work on.

Theory is at present running ahead of data. Apart from the field studies already mentioned (Parker's dungflies and Brockmann's digger wasps), ESS theory has been applied by Davies (1978) in elegant field experiments on territorial disputes in butterflies, and by Hyatt, Smith & Ragharan (in press) studying analogous behavior in fiddler crabs. The next few years should see a flowering of such studies.

Cooperative ESSs

Whether concerned with outright aggression or not, most ESS models involve competitive relationships of one kind or another. I therefore want to demonstrate briefly how the idea can be applied to the evolution of more benevolent, cooperative behavior. I will do so using a somewhat fanciful human analogy, since no animal examples have yet been worked out.

Short sighted people need glasses to see distant objects, but without glasses they can see close up objects in more detail than normal people can. Before glasses were invented, myopics might have been superior at certain kinds of fine craftsmanship (Haldane, Muller, quoted in Medawar 1960: 118). From this, a naive group-selectionist might argue as follows about early man. A society needed both short-sighted and normal-sighted individuals to perform complementary skills. Any society that was wholly normal-sighted or wholly short-sighted would be more likely to go extinct than a society with an optimal mix, say 10% myopic.

An analogous group-selection argument was put forward for the sex ratio. Fisher (1930) disposed of that one, and we can follow him here. In a population dominated by normal-sighted individuals, a single short-sighted individual prospers, since he can offer skills complementary to the prevailing skills. Conversely, in a population of myopics an individual with longer sight will be relatively successful. If success means reproductive success, and if there is a genetic component to the difference between the complementary skills, we have a model for the evolution of a stable mix of the two. In this way, selection acting at the individual level can lead to harmony and integration at the group level. This has nothing whatever to do with group selection, which is the differential extinction of whole groups of individuals (Maynard Smith 1976b).

An analogous argument at the level of single genes can be used against the belief (e.g. Gould 1977a) that the unity and integration of the individual implies that the individual is the fundamental unit of natural selection. This is briefly explained in the next section.

The Individual Phenotype as a Genetic Strategy

In Maynard Smith's games the players are individuals. Strategies are programs that individuals obey, and payoffs are reckoned in individual fitness. But the only long-running players on the stage of life are the genes or, more strictly, the replicators (Dawkins 1978b). Individuals are just costumes which they put on for a while and then shuffle off in meiosis. I have already expressed this view at length (Dawkins 1976). I know some people don't like it, often for sensible reasons to which good replies can be made. I have no space here to give a general advocacy of the 'gene is the unit of selection' point of view (Dawkins 1978b). Instead, I will simply apply it to the ESS idea.

Think back to the war of attrition, or the special case of Parker's dungflies. A 'strategy' was simply a waiting time, a number of minutes. This is the time scale which we ordinarily classify as behavioral. But in principle one could regard longer, developmental, times as strategies in the same sense. 'Life-history strategies' (Gadgil & Bossert 1970) are just like dungfly courtship strategies, but on a time scale of months or years rather than minutes. (I suggest, by the way, that we should learn to think about evolutionarily stable life history-strategies — Charlesworth & León, 1976.) The phenotype of an individual is produced by a complicated interplay of rates (at which developmental processes occur) or times (elapsing between various stages of embryonic development). Genes act on phenotypes by controlling these rates and times (Gould 1977b). The genes that survive down the ages are those that are good at controlling developmental rates and intervals, in such a way that bodies are produced which are good at preserving and propagating those same genes.

Now of course the problem with this is that a body is made by a large collection of genes, interacting in a complex environment. I seem to be caught in a contradiction. On the one hand I emphasize the independence and competitiveness of selfish genes, on the other hand the unitariness and functional coherence of the bodies which they collaborate to produce. I believe that something like ESS theory can resolve this apparent paradox.

Recall the example of the myopic and the normal-sighted people. Let's accept for the moment that they do have complementary skills and that a society benefits from the presence of both. We saw two theories of how this could be realized in evolution. One theory, the group-selection theory, concentrated on the welfare of the larger collection of units, the society: societies with both kinds of people were less likely to go extinct than societies with only one or the other kind. The other theory eschewed all ideas of welfare of the larger unit, and concentrated on selection at the lower level. Lower order units of one kind, short-sighted people, prospered in the presence of units of the other kind, and vice versa. The end results of the two theories look similar. Both give rise to a higher order unit, the society, which appears to function as a single harmonious and integrated whole. The message is that, if we find harmonious and integrated units at one level, these do not have to be produced by selection among units at that level. ESS theory shows us how harmony and integration at a high level can be produced by selection among component parts at a lower level.

Let us apply the lesson at the very low level of the genes. Natural selection among genes chooses those that prosper in the presence of certain other genes, just as people skilled in one respect prosper in the presence of other people with complementary skills. Gene pools come to consist of genes that do well in each others' company, and this means genes that tend to interact together to produce well integrated individual bodies (Dawkins 1976: 91-93). A gene pool becomes an evolutionarily stable set of mutually compatible replicators. The integration of the individual body no more implies 'individual selection' than the integration of the ecosystem implies ecosystem selection.

Developmentally Stable Strategy and Culturally Stable Strategy

Baldwin & Meese (in press) trained pigs in Skinner boxes for food reward, but there is an added twist to the tale. The lever which the pigs had to press was at the opposite end of the sty from the food dispenser. A pig had to press the lever, then run over to the other side of the sty to get the reward. Imagine what happens when two pigs are placed together in a Skinner box of this kind. Obviously, if one pig presses the lever, all that the other pig has to do is sit by the food dispenser and get most of the food. Baldwin & Meese found that under some conditions stable patterns of behavior developed in pairs of pigs. Provided that the food, when it came, was sufficiently plentiful that some was left for the bar-pressing pig when he came rushing over, the bar-pressing response was reinforced, and persisted.

Baldwin & Meese noticed an interesting fact. In those pairs of pigs in which such a stable combination of habits developed, the bar-pressing was done by the pig that had shown itself, by other criteria, to be dominant in competitive encounters. So it looks as though the dominant pig is acting as slave and the subordinate pig as master! Apparently a paradoxical result, but the paradox vanishes if we think in terms of stable strategies. All we have to do is adapt the ESS idea to a different time scale. Instead of an evolutionary time scale in which change takes place through differential survival of genes in a gene pool, we shift to a developmental time scale in which change takes place through the differential survival of habits in an animal's repertoire. We seek a developmentally stable strategy, or DSS.

The asymmetric strategy 'if dominant bar-press, if subordinate sit by the food dish' is developmentally stable. This is because once the DSS happens to arise both parties are reinforced for their respective behaviors. The dominant pig presses the bar, then charges over and bullies the subordinate away from the food just in time to prevent the last of it being eaten. The dominant gets less food than the subordinate, but his bar-pressing behavior is still reinforced. Now consider the reverse strategy: 'if subordinate bar-press, if dominant wait by the food dish.' If this combination happened to arise it would not be a DSS. The subordinate would press the bar and rush over to the food, but he would be unable to dislodge the dominant pig, and would therefore never be rewarded for his behavior. The bar-pressing response would extinguish, and neither pig would get any food unless the dominant changed his policy and began to press the bar, in which case the DSS could develop.

Moving now from a developmental to a historical time scale, we look for a culturally stable strategy or CSS. A good candidate seems to be the rule of the road. Why do some nations drive on the right while others keep left? The six historical authorities who have kindly advised me all agree that the answer to the question is today uncertain. The 'sword arm outward' theory is part of the folk wisdom of England, but it founders on the now widely admitted fact that most people in the world drive on the right. It can be rescued only by unparsimoniously invoking the contrariness of Napoleon and the iconoclasm of the American rebels. In the circumstances I feel free to speculate.

Presumably there was a time when vehicles were too slow or too rare for a rule to be needed. I imagine that when two carts met the drivers simply pulled over to whichever side seemed most convenient at the time, much as modern pedestrians do (Collett & Marsh 1974). In later times, when vehicles were fast enough for collisions to be serious, a rule of the road became desirable. But was it formally legislated or did it evolve first as an unofficial convention? If the latter, I suggest that the process may have been analogous to Maynard Smith & Parker's (1976) model for the settling of contests by the use of 'uncorrelated asymmetries.' It differs in that the encounter between two drivers is not in the ordinary sense a contest, and in that the mode of evolution is cultural not genetic.

I suppose that in any particular town forceful personalities among cart drivers would develop a preference for passing on one particular side. Others would imitate them, and in this way a slight majority would arise for one side rather than the other. The majority does not have to be large. However slight, once it had arisen any individual who did not conform to it would be at greater risk of collision than a member of the majority. Thus if just 51% of drivers in the area keep left and 49% keep right, any individual left driver is in danger of collision on 49% of the occasions when he meets another vehicle, while any individual right driver risks collision on 51% of his encounters. Even if a driver is not killed in a crash, the discomfort of a head-on confrontation and near miss might well cause him to reverse his habit in the future.

Thus as soon as a majority emerges, however slight, for driving on any particular side of the road, there will be a tendency for that majority to increase. The strategy 'drive on the left' is stable. So is 'drive on the right.' Whichever happens to attain a slight majority first will become unanimous.

Is Anything Not an ESS?

The question that heads this section was raised, with understandable disquiet, by one of the editors of this volume on reading my first draft. I will take it in two senses. Firstly, is ESS theory intended to supersede conventional optimality theory completely? Secondly, is ESS theory unfalsifiable and therefore trivial?

Is ESS theory going to bury conventional optimality theory?

I will take an example from 'optimal foraging' (Pyke, Pulliam & Charnov 1977; Krebs 1978). If he is to maximize his net rate of energy intake, how long should a predator, working under certain known constraints, stay in one food patch before moving on to another? The theorist calculates the optimum decision rule as 'stay in the present patch until your rate of finding prey drops to the average success rate for the whole habitat.' Is this 'optimum' the same as an ESS? The answer is that it may be, and that if it is not evolutionarily stable it is not a biologically interesting optimum at all.

Our optimal foraging theorist assumes that it does not matter what the other predators are doing. This assumption might indeed be justified: the optimum feeding policy if you are the only redshank in the world might well be identical to the optimum if you are one of twenty competing in a small area. Clearly the presence of competitors will speed up the depletion of a patch, and hence may hasten the departure decision of a given individual; but the decision rule itself could well be optimal both with and without competitors following the same rule. In this case it might seem superfluous to bother to speak of an ESS, something of a sledgehammer to a nut, but it would not be strictly incorrect. If, on the other hand, it turned out that the presence of other individuals, all optimizing from their point of view, affected the optimum rule for any one individual, ESS analysis would become a positive necessity. This is what Parker (1978) found, treating his dungflies as 'foraging' for females in 'patches' of cowdung.

In brief, wherever advantage is frequency-dependent, ESS analysis or its equivalent is necessary. Where advantage is not frequency-dependent, ESS analysis is correct though not strictly necessary: the ESS turns out to be the same pure strategy (the 'optimum') at all frequencies. In the circumstances it seems parsimonious to abandon the phrase 'optimal strategy' altogether, and replace it with ESS. An added advantage of this is that the word optimum is confusing and can lead to the kind of naive perfectionism that has been rightly criticized: it can be taken to mean anything from the most perfect solution conceivable to the best of a specified range of practical alternatives. ESS, since it has no everyday meaning, is less liable to misunderstanding.

As to how often the selective forces bearing upon animal behavior actually are frequency-dependent, that is an empirical question. The intuition of colleagues I have consulted ranges from 'almost never' to 'almost always.' Evidence seems to be scanty, probably because until recently people did not realize it was an important question. This ought to become an active area of field research.

Turning to my second interpretation of the heading to this section, Popperian zealots sometimes upbraid ESS theory (or even neo-Darwinism itself) for being unfalsifiable and therefore trivial. They miss the point. ESS theory as a whole is not intended to be a testable hypothesis which may be true and may be false, empirical evidence to decide the matter. It is a tool which we may use to find out about the selection pressures bearing upon animal behavior. As Maynard Smith (1978) said of optimality theory generally: ". . . we are not testing the general proposition that nature optimizes, but the specific hypotheses about constraints, optimization criteria, and heredity. Usually we test whether we have correctly identified the selective forces responsible . . ."

When a physicist's experiment falsifies predictions of a model that used mathematics, he does not regard his experiment as a test of the laws of mathematics. He assumes the laws of mathematics and uses them in conjunction with his experiments to test the validity of his particular model. When we (Brockmann, Grafen & Dawkins, loc. cit.) disproved the prediction that 'founders' and 'joiners' should be equally successful, we did not thereupon reject the whole ESS principle, any more than we rejected the neo-Darwinian synthesis! Instead, we rejected that particular model and tested a new one that assumed two other strategies, 'digging' and 'entering.' What could be more Popperian?

It may be that all existing ESS models are wrong and too simple (Auslander, Guckenheimer & Oster 1978; Riley 1979). That is an argument for making better ESS models, not for throwing out the basic idea. The basic idea of the ESS is about as falsifiable as the theory of natural selection itself (Maynard Smith 1969). With certain additional assumptions it is, indeed, a logical corollary of natural selection itself, and stands or falls with the whole neo-Darwinian edifice, even though that may not have been realized when the edifice was built. To borrow an analogy from the seer of our subject (Hamilton 1977), ". . . it is like a new interpretation of Shakespeare: it was all in the script but somehow it passed unseen."

Summary

A strategy is an unconscious behavior program, a candidate for natural selection in competition with alternative strategies. It is said to be evolutionarily stable against a specified list of alternatives if, given that more than a critical proportion of the population adopts it, none of the alternatives does better. The term 'evolutionarily stable strategy' (ESS) is the result of Maynard Smith's tailoring of the mathematics of game theory to fit the theory of evolution.

An ESS is not so much a 'good' strategy as a strategy that is immune to cheating, given that policed social contracts cannot occur. The model of 'dying gasp retaliation' shows that it is possible for behavior to be evolutionarily stable even if it does not in any way benefit the individual doing it, or his kin.

ESS theory is relevant whenever the optimum strategy for an individual depends upon the frequencies of strategies in the population. Digger wasps (Sphex ichneumoneus) have two alternative nesting strategies, digging and entering. Entering pays only as long as not too many individuals do it. The painstaking field measurements of Brockmann support a model which assumes that there is an equilibrium frequency of entering in the population at which the two strategies are equally successful. When either strategy drifts below its equilibrium frequency it is favored by natural selection until the equilibrium is restored. The equilibrium is therefore stable (in one of Brockmann's study sites, not in the other).

It is a common misconception that an ESS is defined as uninvadable by any conceivable alternative strategy. On the contrary, the definition refers to a named set of alternatives. The circumscription of the hypothesized strategy-set calls for biological common sense: we cannot postulate a 'flying to the moon' strategy.

It is reasonable to broaden the existing strategy set by postulating continuous quantitative variation. Male dungflies (Scatophaga stercoraria) wait for females at cowpats. Females prefer fresh to stale cowpats. A 'strategy' for a male consists in the age of the cowpat at which he waits: the strategy set is a continuum. The best strategy for a male depends upon the distribution of strategies in the population. Parker's data gave a good fit to the predicted evolutionarily stable distribution, albeit there is an alternative explanation for this result.

In such 'mixed' ESSs, the thing that is stable is the proportionate mix of strategies in the population as a whole. This stable mix can be achieved either by a polymorphism (a mixture of different kinds of individual), or by a monomorphic mixed strategy (each individual follows the same probabilistic rule), or by a combination of the two. The two are mathematically equivalent but not biologically equivalent. For Parker's dungflies an individual mixed strategy is more plausible than a polymorphism. For Brockmann's digger wasps either would be plausible, but the field evidence points to an individual mixed strategy.

Mixed strategies should not be confused with conditional strategies, in which the animal's behavior depends upon some contingency such as the behavior of an opponent. Alleged cases of 'alternative male mating strategies', say 'sneaking' and 'fighting', are often not true alternatives, but outcomes of one conditional strategy such as 'If large, fight; if small, sneak.' Sneaking might then be characterized as 'making the best of a bad job.'

ESS theory has mainly been developed in the context of intraspecific aggression, but it is much more widely applicable. Fisher used essentially the same idea in his treatments of sex ratios, Batesian mimicry, and sexual selection. Much later he was the first to suggest that the formal mathematical theory of games might be valuable in evolutionary biology. Maynard Smith attributes the first actual use of game theory in an ESS-like way to Hamilton. Maynard Smith himself then defined the ESS, and has been mainly responsible for the subsequent development of the idea.

Apart from its application to aggressive behavior, ESS theory has been used to clarify Triver's theories of reciprocal altruism, parent-offspring conflict, and mate desertion. It has also shed light on coevolution and stability in ecosystems, animal deceit, dispersal in stable habitats, and various other examples of conflict and cooperation.

There is a common misconception that cooperation within a group at a given level of organization must come about through selection between groups. If there are two kinds of individual with complementary skills, it might seem that a successful group would be one with an optimal mix: groups without an optimal mix of skills would go extinct. ESS theory provides a more parsimonious alternative: a stable mix is achieved by selection <u>within</u> any one group. Thus in a population dominated by individuals with one skill, selection favors individuals with the complementary skill.

An analogous argument at the level of single genes gives the lie to a common objection to the idea of the selfish gene as the fundamental unit of natural selection. Genes are selected for their capacity to interact 'cooperatively' with the other genes with which they are likely to have to share bodies, the other genes of the gene pool. Individual 'integration' no more implies 'individual selection' than ecosystem integration implies ecosystem selection.

Pigs in Skinner boxes and cars on roads provide possible examples of developmentally stable strategies (DSS) and culturally stable strategies (CSS) respectively.

Should the word 'optimum' be abandoned in favor of 'ESS' in evolutionary writing? If the optimum (e.g. foraging) strategy for an individual is frequency-dependent, ESS theory is necessary. If there is no frequency-dependence, ESS theory is still correct, though it may appear superfluous.

ESS theory, like conventional optimality theory, is sometimes attacked as 'unfalsifiable,' but such an attack misses the point. The existence of ESSs is not a hypothesis which is under test. We assume it and use our assumption to uncover facts about real biological constraints.

Acknowledgements

Understanding something well enough to write about it takes time. My own understanding has grown in countless hours of wrestling over the issues with Alan Grafen and Jane Brockmann. They, together with Mark Ridley and Marian Dawkins, constructively criticized various drafts. In addition to the obvious influence of his published works, I continually benefit from John Maynard Smith's generosity and approachability in pursuance of his listed recreation of talking.

Literature Cited

Alcock, J., C. E. Jones & S. L. Buchmann. 1977. Male mating strategies in the bee *Centris pallida*. *American Naturalist* 111: 145-155.

Alexander, R. D. 1975. Natural selection and specialized chorusing behavior in acoustical insects. *In* D. Pimentel (ed.), *Insects, science and society*. Academic Press, New York, pp. 35-77.

Auslander, D., J. Guckenheimer & G. Oster. 1978. Random evolutionarily stable strategies. *Theoretical Population Biology* 13: 276-293.

Ayala, F. J. & C. A. Campbell. 1974. Frequency-dependent selection. *Annual Review of Ecology and Systematics* 5: 115-138.

Baldwin, B. A. & G. B. Meese. In press. Social behaviour in pigs studied by means of operant conditioning. *Animal Behaviour*.

Bishop, D. T. & C. Cannings. 1978. A generalized war of attrition. Journal of Theoretical Biology 70: 85-124.

Brockmann, H. J. & C. J. Barnard. 1979. The origin of kleptoparasitism in birds. Animal Behaviour 27: in press.

_______ & R. Dawkins. In press. Joint nesting in a digger wasp as an evolutionarily stable preadaptation to social life. Behaviour.

_______, A. Grafen & R. Dawkins. 1979. Evolutionarily stable nesting strategy in a digger wasp. Journal of Theoretical Biology 77:473-496.

Cade, W. 1978. Of cricket song and sex. Natural History 87 (1): 64-72.

Caryl, P. G. 1979. Communication by agonistic displays: what can games theory contribute to ethology? Behaviour 68: 136-169.

Charlesworth, B. & J. A. León. 1976. The relation of reproductive effort to age. American Naturalist 110: 449-459.

Charlesworth, D. & B. Charlesworth. 1975. Sexual selection and polymorphism. American Naturalist 109: 465-470.

Charnov, E. L. & J. R. Krebs. 1975. The evolution of alarm calls: altruism or manipulation? American Naturalist 109: 107-112.

Clarke, B. C. In press. The evolution of genetic diversity. Proceedings of the Royal Society of London.

Clutton-Brock, T. H., S. D. Albon & F. E. Guinness. 1979. The logical stag: adaptive aspects of fighting in red deer (Cervus elaphus L.) Animal Behaviour 27: 211-225.

Collett, P. & P. Marsh. 1974. Patterns of public behaviour: collision avoidance on a pedestrian crossing. Semiotica 12: 281-299.

Cox, C. R. & B. J. LeBoeuf. 1977. Female incitation of male competition: a mechanism of mate selection. American Naturalist 111: 317-335.

Davies, N. B. 1978. Territorial defence in the speckled wood butterfly (Pararge aegeria): the resident always wins. Animal Behaviour 26: 138-147.

_______ In press. Game theory and territorial behaviour in speckled wood butterflies. Animal Behaviour.

Dawkins, R. 1976. The selfish gene. Oxford University Press, Oxford & New York.

_______ 1978a. Reply to Fix and Greene. Contemporary Sociology 7: 709-712.

_______ 1978b. Replicator selection and the extended phenotype. Zeitschrift für Tierpsychologie 47: 61-76.

_______ & H. J. Brockmann. In press. Do digger wasps commit the Concorde fallacy? Animal Behaviour.

_______ & J. R. Krebs. 1978. Animal signals: information or manipulation? In J. R. Krebs & N. B. Davies (eds.), Behavioural ecology: an evolutionary approach. Blackwell Scientific Publications, Oxford, pp. 282-309.

_______ & _______ In press. Arms races between and within species. Proceedings of the Royal Society of London.

Fisher, R. A. 1930. The genetical theory of natural selection. Clarendon Press, Oxford.

_______ 1958. Polymorphism and natural selection. Journal of Ecology 46: 289-293.

Fretwell, S. D. 1972. Populations in a seasonal environment. Princeton University Press, New Jersey.

Gadgil, M. 1972. Male dimorphism as a consequence of sexual selection. American Naturalist 106: 574-580.

_______ & W. H. Bossert. 1970. Life historical consequences of natural selection. American Naturalist 104: 1-24.

_______ & C. E. Taylor. 1975. Plausible models of sexual selection and polymorphism. American Naturalist 109: 470-472.

Gale, J. S. & L. J. Eaves. 1975. Logic of animal conflict. Nature 254: 463-464.

Gould, S. J. 1977a. Caring groups and selfish genes. Natural History 86 (12): 20-24.

_______ 1977b. Ontogeny and phylogeny. Harvard University Press, Cambridge, Massachusetts.

_______ & R. C. Lewontin. In press. A critique of the adaptationist programme. Proceedings of the Royal Society of London.

Grafen, A. 1979. The hawk-dove game played between relatives. Animal Behaviour in press.

_______ & R. M. Sibly. 1978. A model of mate desertion. Animal Behaviour 26: 645-652.

Hamilton, W. D. 1967. Extraordinary sex ratios. Science 156: 477-488.

_______ 1971. Selection of selfish and altruistic behavior in some extreme models. In J. F. Eisenberg & W. S. Dillon (eds.), Man and beast: comparative social behavior. Smithsonian Institution Press, Washington D.C., pp. 57-91.

_______ 1977. The play by nature. Science 196: 757-759.

_______ & R. M. May. 1977. Dispersal in stable habitats. Nature 269: 578-581.

Hays, H. 1970. Common terns pirating fish on Great Gull Island. Wilson Bulletin 82: 99-100.

Humphries, D. A. & P. M. Driver. 1967. Erratic display as a device against predators. Science 156: 1767-1768.

Hyatt, G. W., S. D. Smith & T. E. S. Ragharan. In press. Game theory models of intermale combat in fiddler crabs (Genus Uca). In S. J. Brams, A. Schotter & G. Schwödiauer (eds.), Proceedings of the international conference on applied game theory. Physica Verlag, Vienna.

Kojima, E. 1971. Is there a constant fitness value? No! Evolution 25: 281-285.

Krebs, J. R. 1978. Optimal foraging: decision rules for predators. In J. R. Krebs & N. B. Davies (eds.), Behavioural ecology: an evolutionary approach. Blackwell Scientific Publications, Oxford, pp. 23-63.

Lawlor, L. R. & J. Maynard Smith. 1976. The coevolution and stabilility of competing species. American Naturalist 110: 79-99.

Lewontin, R. C. 1961. Evolution and the theory of games. Journal of Theoretical Biology 1: 382-403.

_______ 1977. Caricature of Darwinism. Nature 266: 283-284.

_______ 1978. Adaptation. Scientific American 239 (3): 156-169.

Lloyd, J. E. 1973. Model for the mating protocol of synchronously flashing fireflies. Nature 245: 268-270.

MacArthur, R. H. 1972. Geographical ecology. Harper & Row, New York.

Macnair, M. R. & G. A. Parker. 1978. Models of parent-offspring conflict. II. Promiscuity. Animal Behaviour 26: 111-122.

_______ & _______ 1979. Models of parent-offspring conflict. III. Intrabrood conflict. Animal Behaviour in press.

Marler, P. 1959. Developments in the study of animal communication. In P. R. Bell (ed.), Darwin's biological work. Some aspects reconsidered. Wiley, New York, pp. 150-206.

Maynard Smith, J. 1969. The status of neo-Darwinism. In C. H. Waddington (ed.), Towards a theoretical biology. 2: Sketches. Edinburgh University Press, Edinburgh.

_______ 1972. Game theory and the evolution of fighting. In J. Maynard Smith On Evolution. Edinburgh University Press, Edinburgh, pp. 8-20.

_______ 1974. The theory of games and the evolution of animal conflict. Journal of Theoretical Biology 47: 209-221.

_______ 1976a. Evolution and the theory of games. American Scientist 64: 41-45.

_______ 1976b. Group selection. Quarterly Review of Biology 51: 277-283.

_______ 1977. Parental investment: a prospective analysis. Animal Behaviour 25: 1-9.

_______ 1978. Optimization theory in evolution. Annual Review of Ecology and Systematics 9: 31-56.

_______ In press. Game theory and the evolution of behaviour. Proceedings of the Royal Society of London.

_______ & G. A. Parker. 1976. The logic of asymmetric contests. Animal Behaviour 24: 159-175.

_______ & G. R. Price. 1973. The logic of animal conflicts. Nature 246: 15-18.

Medawar, P. B. 1960. The future of man. Methuen, London.

Norman, R. F., P. D. Taylor & R. J. Robertson. 1977. Stable equilibrium strategies and penalty functions in a game of attrition. Journal of Theoretical Biology 65: 571-578.

Orians, G. H. 1969. On the origin of mating systems in birds and mammals. American Naturalist 103: 589-603.

Parker, G. A. 1978. Searching for mates. In J. R. Krebs & N. B. Davies (eds.), Behavioural ecology: an evolutionary approach. Blackwell Scientific Publications, Oxford, pp. 214-244.

_______ In press. Sexual selection and sexual conflict. In M. A. & N. A. Blum (eds.), Reproductive competition and sexual selection. Academic Press, New York.

_______ & M. R. Macnair. 1978. Models of parent-offspring conflict. I. Monogamy. Animal Behaviour 26: 97-110.

_______ & _______ 1979. Models of parent-offsrping conflict. IV. Suppression: evolutionary retaliation by the parent. Animal Behaviour in press.

Partridge, B. L. & J. R. Krebs. 1978. Tree frog choruses: a mixed evolutionarily stable strategy? Animal Behaviour 26: 959-963.

Popp, J. L. & I. DeVore. In press. Aggressive competition and social dominance theory. In D. A. Hamburg & J. Goodall (eds.) Perspectives on human evolution. 6: Behavior of great apes. Staples Press, Menlo Park. California.

Pyke, G. H., H. R. Pulliam & E. L. Charnov. 1977. Optimal foraging: a selective view of theory and tests. Quarterly Review of Biology 52: 137-154.

Riley, J. G. 1979. Evolutionary equilibrium strategies. Journal of Theoretical Biology 76: 109-123.

Robertson, D. R. 1972. Social control of sex reversal in a coral reef fish. Science 177: 1007-1009.

Rohwer, S. 1977. Status signaling in Harris sparrows: some experiments in deception. Behaviour 61: 107-129.

Rubenstein, D. I. In press. On the evolution of alternative mating strategies. In J. E. R. Staddon (ed.), Econology: the allocation of individual behavior. Academic Press, New York.

Sahlins, M. 1977. The use and abuse of biology. University of Michigan Press, Ann Arbor.

Taylor, P. D. In press. Game theory as a model of animal behaviour. In M. A. H. Dempster & D. J. McFarland (eds.), Animal economics. Academic Press, London.

Treisman, M. 1977. The evolutionary restriction of aggression within a species: a game theory analysis. Journal of Mathematical Psychology 16: 167-203.

Trivers, R. L. 1971. The evolution of reciprocal altruism. Quarterly Review of Biology 46: 35-57.

_______ 1972. Parental investment and sexual selection. In B. Campbell (ed.), Sexual selection and the descent of man. Aldine, Chicago.

_______ 1974. Parent-offspring conflict. American Zoologist 14: 249-264.

Wallace, B. 1973. Misinformation, fitness, and selection. American Naturalist 107: 1-7.

Williams, G. C. In press. The question of adaptive sex ratio in outbred vertebrates. Proceedings of the Royal Society of London.

Wilson, E. O. Sociobiology: the new synthesis. Harvard University Press, Cambridge, Massachusetts.

Wynne-Edwards, V. C. 1962. Animal dispersion in relation to social behaviour. Oliver and Boyd, Edinburgh.

Part 5

Sex and Reproductive Strategies

George C. Williams

15. Kin Selection and the Paradox of Sexuality*

Whenever an organism normally lives among its relatives, a sociobiologist expects it to be partly benign and cooperative, and partly selfish, in its dealings with those relatives. This is because it is partly identical with them in genetic makeup, but only partly. The theory of kin selection is an attempt to deal with the complex interactions seen among relatives, and the frequent reference to kin selection in this symposium shows its importance to sociobiology. Much of the importance and complexity derives from variation in degrees of relationship arising from sexual reproduction, in which a halving of the chromosome number (meiosis) in eggs and sperm, and subsequent fertilization, are the essential features. Without this chromosome cycle, all coefficients of relationship would be one or zero (complete genetic identity or total independence), and much of the complexity of interactions among organisms would presumably disappear. An understanding of the cycle of meiosis and fertilization, and its genetic, ecological, and social consequences, is basic to an understanding of sociobiology.

It is basic to much else besides. Sociobiology can be defined as the study of social behavior, a set of observable phenomena. Thus its scope would be determined by the phenomena dealt with, not by principles used in ordering these phenomena. The deserved prominence of E.O. Wilson's (1975) work has focused attention on the use of such concepts as kin selection, reciprocal altruism, and parental manipulation in explaining social behavior. These concepts more properly relate to all special interactions among individuals (e.g., between mammalian mother and foetus, or male and female gametophytes in the ovary of a flower), not merely social behavior. In the future I expect them to be applied fruitfully to a

*Contribution number 300 from the Department of Ecology and Evolution, State University of New York, Stony Brook.

broader range of phenomena. R. Warner in this volume shows how they relate to developmental programming, and Janzen (1977) and Willson (1979) have recently emphasized their applicability to plants. In this chapter I suggest applications to cellular processes in microorganisms.

History of the Concept of a Cost of Sexuality

The idea of a quantitative advantage in various forms of uniparental over biparental reproduction dates from at least as early as Weismann (1889:296, 332-335), who proposed that parthenogenesis in cladocerans and other invertebrates is an adaptation to increase the rapidity with which they can occupy temporary habitats. A quantitative statement was given by Maynard Smith (1958:138) who notes that a parthenogenetic lineage consists only of females, all of which contribute resources, at least in the form of yolk reserves, to the next generation. In many sexual populations only the female fraction makes such contributions, and if half the population were male, the sexual line would only have half the reproductive rate of the parthenogenetic. More recently, Maynard Smith (1971) provided a more refined statement of this idea. In discussing what I called the cost of meiosis (Williams, 1975:8-9) I assumed that I was merely providing a Mendelian formulation for an obvious and generally accepted idea. Recent discussions, especially that of Treisman and Dawkins (1976), make it clear that the subject is more complex and confusing than I had thought.

I believe that understanding has been hampered by failure to distinguish the ecological from the evolutionary problem of sexuality. In important ways, insights gained from conceptual or experimental comparisons of sexual populations and competing clones (the ecological problem) may be misleading in relation to sexual and clonal reproduction as alternative processes in a population (the evolutionary question with which I am concerned here). My analysis is based on the assumption that the important evolutionary question is: What would be gained by an individual, in an otherwise sexual population, who cheated by eliminating meiosis and fertilization from its production of an offspring, but remained otherwise the same? Or the question may be put the other way: What is the cost of not cheating?

Meiosis as a Problem for Kin Selection and Outbreeding

In West-Eberhard's (1975) formulation, the benefit from unreciprocated altruism is proportional to (symbolism slightly simplified)

$$\sum_{i=1}^{n}[(r-\bar{r})_i\Delta W_i]$$

where ΔW_i is the resultant increase in fitness of a recipient, r the coefficient of relationship of donor to recipient, and $\bar{r}$ the mean coefficient of relationship between randomly selected individuals. In a large and fluid population, $\bar{r}$ is near zero, and one can say that benefits are proportional to coefficients of relationship with recipients. Any increase in r translates directly into increased fitness for the donor.

Suppose an organism has the option of reproducing asexually, or at least we can imagine it having that option. If instead it invests resources in the production and rearing of sexual offspring, it is devoting these resources to more distant (r = .5) in preference to closer (r = 1) relatives. It seemingly acts to reduce the rate of return on its investment. The loss is 50% of what it would have gained by asexual reproduction, and follows directly from the reduction from two to one of the sets of genes (genomes) that go into gametes. Switching from sexual to asexual reproduction is the most obvious way of increasing genetic relationship with offspring in which resources are being invested.

Another way is by inbreeding. If a female mates with a randomly chosen male, his genes are presumably a random sample of those in the population, and their survival through her progeny in no way affects her own genetic success. But if she mates with a relative, she is assured that a proportion, r, of his genes are identical with her own, and their survival is equivalent to the survival of her own identical copies. If she mates with her brother (r = .5), each offspring will have half its genes like hers because they came from her, and half of the rest will be like hers because they came from her brother. She would relate to each offspring by r = .75, and we can say that the cost of meiosis has been reduced by 50%, or that there has been a 50% increase in her genetic success via the inbred offspring. So inbreeding offers an enormous advantage. If kin selection were the only consideration, outbreeding ought to be unstable in evolution.

I have made some tacit assumptions in this argument that are probably valid for many populations but ought to be made explicit. I assume that males provide no resources for offspring and that a male's mating, with a sister or any other female, has no important influence on the likelihood of subsequent matings. There can be no cost of meiosis for such males, because they make no investments in other individuals. Likewise the increase in reproductive success of a male's sister in no way reduces his own success in reproducing by means of resources invested by other females.

The argument also depends on inbreeding females being rare. If many of the females in the population prefer to mate with their brothers, a male's increased success with his own sisters will be at least partly balanced by decreased success with other individuals sisters. Continued brother-sister mating reduces the cost of meiosis to zero, but such an inbred population need not be reproducing any more efficiently than an otherwise similar outbred population. If parents in both populations continued to spend resources equally on the production of sons and daughters, they would be equally wasteful of resources.

This equal wastefulness would not be equally stable. The waste would continue in the outbred population, because any excess production of females would give males a mating advantage and select for tendencies to produce sons. With brother-sister mating an increased production of daughters is favored, the optimum progeny containing just enough sons to assure fertilization of all daughters. If the sex ratio is free to evolve, the inbred population could reach a reproductive efficiency almost equal to that of an asexual. So we might well expect that, among species that always reproduce sexually, inbreeding and female-biased sex ratios should be the rule.

Obviously it is not the rule. Close inbreeding and heavily female majorities are uncommon in sexual populations. This is explained by a general consensus that close inbreeding, in normally outbred species, exacts a cost that is worse than the cost of meiosis. That cost is the severely depressed fitness of inbred offspring. Individuals produced by brother-sister matings will have only 3/4 as many heterozygous loci as their parents, and some of the homozygous genes may be rare in the population as a whole, kept that way because they are deleterious when homozygous. So perhaps there is no great mystery about why incest is avoided in normally outbred populations.

The question of why outbred populations do not become asexual is another matter entirely. Here the mystery is great indeed, and the rest of this chapter will be devoted to this paradox of sexuality. My discussion will always proceed from the question of what would happen if someone cheated. What happens, for a sexually reproducing individual, when we substitute an equally costly asexual process? With outbreeding this is always equivalent to the question of what happens when the coefficient of relationship between parent and offspring is doubled.

Recent Models of the Cost of Meiosis

Treisman and Dawkins (1976) showed that the cost of meiosis can be analyzed instructively by separate consideration of genes that determine reproductive mode and those that do not. They found that the cost can have different values for these two parts of the genome. In their one-locus example homozygosity for a sexuality allele causes females to reproduce sexually (as opposed to parthenogenetically) so that all crosses can be represented as *aa* x *aa*. It is not required that genes that code for female sexuality also code for male sexuality. A male must be *aa* for geneological reasons. He necessarily had a sexual mother, from whom he got one *a*. The other gene at this locus must also be an *a* from some female ancestor in his paternal line. In Treisman and Dawkins' model a 50% cost of meiosis might be recognized as a formality for genes identical by descent, because a female eliminates one of her *a*'s in meiosis. Such a loss is irrelevant for evolution, because the population is genetically homogeneous at this locus. The lost *a* is replaced by another just like it, and no genetic change takes place. Effects at the *a*-locus are exactly as they would be with self-fertilization.

As developed to this point, the discussion is irrelevant to the evolutionary retention of sexual reproduction, because there is no variability in this character for selection to act upon. The model relates to a Mendelian population (all *aa*) in competition with one or more clones (*AA* or *Aa*). The relevant concepts are ecological (numerical relations between competing species) not evolutionary. Evolutionary relevance was provided in the next step, in which Treisman and Dawkins made genetic determination less than absolute, so that occasionally there is genetic exchange between the Mendelian population and some *AA* or *Aa* individuals. If they had really explored the consequences of this relaxation of initial assumptions, it would have become apparent that their rejection of the cost of meiosis was premature. If an *aa* female can cross with an *AA* or *Aa* male, half her sexuality genes would be replaced by genes from the male, and a 50% cost of meiosis should be recognized. Genes for sexuality in her offspring would be reduced by 50% or 25%, depending on the genotype of the male.

It remains true that any association at all, at any locus, between genotype and mode of reproduction would reduce the cost of meiosis at that locus. The genes provided by a mate would not be a random sample of genes in the population. Unlike inbreeding, this genetically assortative mating would affect only those loci that control the character responsible for mating bias, in this case the tendency to mate.

The cost reduction would be minor if there were any appreciable diversity of genotypes capable of sexual reproduction. Suppose, for instance, that we replace the $\underline{a}$ used so far with a large number of equally numerous a_i's, and replace the $\underline{A}$ by a much larger number of equally numerous A_j's. The sexual individuals will be less diverse genetically than the clones, but an $\underline{a_1a_2}$ female crossing with some $\underline{aa}$ male may be rather unlikely to get either an $\underline{a_1}$ or $\underline{a_2}$ from a sperm, and the cost of meiosis could be nearly 50%. We would expect favorable selection of the $\underline{a}$-alleles with the least tendency to induce sexuality, and the frequency of this character should decline. If sexuality can be caused by variation in other loci, the average genetic similarity between mates would be further reduced and the cost of meiosis brought still closer to 50%.

None of this really relates to the central problem of why so many species continue to propagate themselves exclusively by sexual reproduction. What should be modeled is not a population with a diversity of asexual and restricted range of sexual genotypes, but rather the opposite. Suppose a recessive mutation $\underline{b}$ in a sexual population causes its homozygous bearer, at least occasionally, to reproduce parthenogenetically. Ultimately two $\underline{Bb}$ individuals mate and successfully produce a $\underline{bb}$ daughter, who starts cloning. She will have twice the normal rate of increase if exclusively parthenogenetic, but if so, she is no longer a part of the population under consideration. If $\underline{bb}$ individuals occasionally cross with a $\underline{BB}$ or $\underline{Bb}$, they will, as they become more numerous, release an increasing flood of $\underline{b}$'s into the population. Additional parthenogenetic $\underline{bb}$ lines will be established as the gene rises in frequency. Only as the process nears completion would there be an appreciable degree of genetically assortative mating and consequent reduction in the cost of meiosis. Replacement of sexual reproduction by parthenogenesis would be expected, unless some other process prevents it.

On extending their reasoning to loci that do not affect mode of reproduction, Treisman and Dawkins found that there is always a 50% cost of meiosis, as long as the population is at evolutionary equilibrium with respect to sex ratio (assumed 1:1 for simplicity). As they expressed it, sexual and asexual lines would be equally fit if equally productive of daughters. If sexual genotypes spent half their reproductive resources on sons, and had the same total fecundity, they would be only half as fit as the parthenogenetics.

Comparison of sexual with parthenogenetic reproduction is easy because of the one-to-one correspondence of the two kinds of offspring. This correspondence is lost in comparing sexual with vegetative offspring, but the 50% cost of meiosis is still applicable, because vegetative offspring have twice the value of r as outcrossed sexuals, regardless of physiological details. Resources invested in the production or rearing of sexual offspring would have to have twice the demographic payoff to give the genetic payoff they would have produced if invested in asexual offspring. Here the cost of meiosis would be applicable to both males and females, if males are capable of vegetative forms of reproduction such as budding, as they are in many plant and lower animal groups. The effects of mating bias would be reduced if genes coding for sexual reproduction differed in the two sexes. Treisman and Dawkins dealt only with a comparison of sexual and parthenogenetic reproduction, and did not question the cost of meiosis for sexual as compared with vegetative reproduction. Likewise there seems to be no recent challenge to the applicability of this cost to outbred hermaphrodites (Maynard Smith 1978:40; Williams 1975:119-122).

Isogamy and Anisogamy

It is generally held that there is no cost of meiosis when zygotes are formed by gametes of the same size (isogamy; see Manning 1976; Maynard Smith 1974; Williams 1975). In one sense this is true. When almost the whole supply of resources is provided by a large egg and almost none by a minute sperm (anisogamy), there is a cost of meiosis for the female because the male genes are propagated at her expense instead of half of her own genes. If the fusing gametes are equal, neither parent seems to be subsidizing the reproduction of the other. In a more important sense this conclusion is wrong. Given that one cell fuses with another, we can then ask about the consequences of whether it plays the sexual game (meiosis) in its next cell division, or cheats (mitosis). It then becomes clear that the 50% cost of meiosis is still very much a reality.

A cell may join with another as a gamete in the process of fertilization, or as a parasite or predator to exploit the other cell. If meiosis follows fusion we would label the process sexual reproduction; if mitosis follows we would label it parasitism or predation by the dividing nucleus. To compare mitotic fission to fusion followed by meiotic fission (first two lines of Table 1) is unfair. There is the same payoff, but the sexual reproducer achieves this with resources

Table 1. Summary of the cost of meiosis with outbred sexual reproduction in relation to the evolutionary interests of a female. The relevant comparisons are between sexual ($r = \frac{1}{2}$) and asexual ($r = 1$) uses of the same total resources.

		maternal investment		paternal investment		total investment		r		payoff
	fission	2	+	0	=	2	x	1	=	2
	isogamy	2	+	2	=	4	x	½	=	2
	phagocytosis	2	+	2	=	4	x	1	=	4
no paternal investment	oogamy	2	+	0	=	2	x	½	=	1
	parthenogenesis	2	+	0	=	2	x	1	=	2
with paternal investment	oogamy	2	+	2	=	4	x	½	=	2
	parthenogenesis	2	+	2	=	4	x	1	=	4

provided by the other individual in addition to its own. It is more appropriate to compare the fitness of an isogamete with that of a similar cell that fuses with another like itself and then attacks the other's nucleus with digestive enzymes (second and third lines in Table 1). It could use resources thus released to achieve an extra duplication of its own genotype. Exploitation is twice as rewarding as cooperation.

Maynard Smith (1958:140) suggested that sexual reproduction may have originated as a modification of predatory phagocytosis, but did not elaborate on how natural selection would bring about such a change. A consideration of intensities of selection favoring the ability to exploit and to avoid being exploited might provide a suggestion. To be consumed is to have one's fitness reduced to zero. To consume another merely provides resources for a finite increase in fitness. All else being equal, selection to avoid being exploited should be stronger, and the difference should show most clearly in contests between closely matched pairs. It may occasionally have happened, early in the history of life, that attempted exploitation would produce a stalemate, with neither cell being able to overcome the defenses of the other. There are several conceivable options for a stalemated cell: (1) separate from the other, more or less along the boundaries of the two cytoplasms, and approximately restore the original conditions; (2) form a heterokaryon and try to compete with the other nucleus and its descendents for use of cytoplasmic resources for nuclear proliferation; (3) cooperate with the other nucleus in a meiotic division.

It is reasonable to assume that fitness in a microorganism or zygote is a convex function of size (Bell 1978; Parker 1978; Smith & Fretwell 1974), so that a reduction in mass from 1.0 to 0.9 would lower fitness more than an increase from 1.0 to 1.1 would raise it. Maximum total fitness of daughter cells would be achieved by having them of identical size. The first of the above options could lead to unequal division and a lowered mean expectation of fitness. Perfect cooperation between participants would eliminate this problem, but no cooperation should be expected from an unrelated individual. The second option has the same disadvantage as the first, in multiple form. Increased inequalities could be expected after a period of competition among closely associated nuclei.

Meiosis has no such disadvantage. It assures identity of interest, for all genes in the zygote nucleus, in an exactly equal division of resources for each daughter nucleus. If the fusing cells are exactly the same size, neither participant loses or gains resources. If participants are unequal, the smaller wins and the larger loses. Here the gain for the winner is greater than the loss for the loser, and a small cell's ability to impose meiosis on a larger partner should be greater than a large cell's ability to circumvent meiosis. This is an essential feature of recent ideas on the origin of anisogamy (Bell 1978; Charlesworth 1978; Parker 1978). Exactly equal representation for all participating genes, and nearly equal apportionment of resources, as occurs in meiosis following isogamy, and in cell division generally, certainly has the appearance of compromise and conflict resolution. Meiotic egg production, with whole genomes lost to polar bodies, is the outstanding exception.

Genetic diversification and recombination might thus have evolved as an incidental consequence of self defense, but would then become an important factor in the subsequent evolution of meiosis. The mean economic outcome for participating cells would be the same as with fusion, the cost of meiosis being balanced by the doubling of resources. A genetic outcome would be a recombinational load. This would select against sexual reproduction, especially in a constant environment, in which it is likely that already proven parental genotypes would be superior to most of the new ones generated. There is another important way in which fission would differ from fertilization followed by meiosis. Fission produces two nuclei with similar genomes which, one cycle later, will be represented by 2, 1, or 0 genomes. A cell undertaking fertilization and meiosis will be represented one cycle later by 2, 1½, 1, ½, or 0 genomes. Mean prospects are the same, but the variance for the sexual process is only half as great. It is not at all clear to me whether this variance would be subject to selection.

Paternal Investment

If males contribute in any way to the welfare of their sexual offspring, the population will be making more efficient use of resources than it would if the females bore the entire cost of reproduction. Consider, for instance, a song bird with its reproductive rate limited by its ability to provide food for developing nestlings. A female can, perhaps, do enough foraging to rear two young, and her mate can do the same. We would then expect the female to lay four eggs and the pair jointly to try to raise four young. Such a species would be as reproductively efficient as a species made up of parthenogenetic females that would each produce and attempt to rear two young.

This does not mean that there is no cost of meiosis in a species with equal paternal and maternal investment. Consider the prospects for a cheater female who lays, not four eggs fertilized by her mate, bur four parthenogenetic eggs with her own genotype. Her mate would have no way of responding to this change. He would forage for her young as a male of that species normally would. His genetic payoff would be zero; hers would be doubled. If a pair normally has two successful offspring in its lifetime, such parthenogenetic females would double their number in one generation. Obviously a sexual female pays a 50% cost of meiosis in relation to what she could accomplish by cheating (eliminating meiosis and fertilization).

This reasoning relates to the effects of selection on newly arisen parthenogenetic females in a species with paternal investment. As these asexual females increase in frequency there may be selection on males to reduce their contributions to the young. Other selection pressures could lead to other sorts of changes. Despite these complications, completely parthenogenetic females will always have twice the fitness of outbred sexuals, unless males evolve ways of discriminating between the two kinds of female. If any sort of male contribution or any genetic recombination is ultimately necessary for population survival, the species would rapidly evolve itself to extinction. This final event could in no way influence the process that led to it.

The Paradox of Sexuality

My conclusion is that sexual reproduction, which depends for its completion on meiosis, exacts a cost to fitness that is far greater than the selection differentials usually considered plausible in population genetics. Only by inbreeding, or by a formally possible but rather implausible form of assortative mating, can the cost of meiosis be reduced. Why then is sexual reproduction so prevalent? I can conceive of only two possible answers. Either the cost is payment for benefits that are worth the cost but unattainable without meiosis, or the preadaptations for evolving an asexual alternative are not available.

Only the first possibility is applicable to those forms that already have both sexual and asexual modes of reproduction. In them the sexual mode must be nearly in evolutionary equilibrium with the asexual, even though each gene is only half as likely to be represented in a sexual offspring as in an asexual. The demographic payoff from sexual reproduction must be twice that from asexual, to balance the reduction in kinship.

In earlier work (Williams 1975), I tried to show that this balance is plausible for populations with a great potential for numerical increase over one full cycle from zygote to zygote. This potential proliferation of individuals from a single zygote, whether it resulted from a period of asexual reproduction or merely high fecundity, would make possible a great amplification of physiologically minor differences in fitness. I attempted to show that genetic diversification of sexual progenies would provide advantages that, after acting many times during a life cycle, could double the fitness of a sexual progeny. The cost of meiosis would thereby be repaid. I also argued that selection in some life cycles would favor the complete elimination of asexual reproduction. Then I proposed that asexual reproduction, once lost, might be difficult to regain. In this way I explained the exclusively sexual reproduction of most higher vertebrates and other organisms that do not have high fecundity.

Treisman (1976) criticized some of my proposed advantages of genetic diversification in certain kinds of life cycles. He showed that some of the evolutionary forces that I proposed must be weaker than I represented them, and less plausible as factors capable of balancing the cost of meiosis. Unfortunately, his suggested alternative is unsatisfactory. It requires intensities of selection, and changes in selection coefficients, which would be unsupportable in the low-fecundity populations for which he claims applicability. Rathvon (1977) has recently advanced reasons for doubting that asexual reproduction by higher animals is as difficult to evolve as I claimed. He offered no alternatives to mine or Treisman's on why exclusive reliance on sexual reproduction continues to prevail in these low-fecundity animals.

The near universality of sexual reproduction remains a major unsolved mystery. It is explicitly a mystery in relation to kin selection, on which so much of sociobiological thought depends.

Summary

Females of all species provide for the survival of their offspring, at least in the form of nutrients in the egg. In many species males merely compete for the opportunity to fertilize such eggs and do nothing to benefit the young. Such populations make less efficient use of resources for reproduction than those in which all reproducing adults help to rear offspring. We might expect such less efficient species to be consistently outcompeted by the more efficient. The continued prevalence of species with non-contributing males is a serious ecological problem.

There is an even more serious evolutionary problem. This is easily seen by considering what would result from certain kinds of cheating by individuals in the efficient populations. Suppose that one of two equal-size gametes behaved as a predator or parasite and used all the resources of the other cell for the replication of its own genotype. Or suppose that a normally mated female cheated by producing parthenogenetic eggs that transmitted all her genes, instead of only half of hers and half of her mate's. Any such cheating gives the cheater an enormous advantage. In formal kin-selection terms, we can say that asexual reproduction would double the coefficient of relationship between parent and offspring, and thereby double the profit on parental investments. The only form of sexual reproduction that should not be vulnerable to replacement by asexual would be self-fertilization or other close inbreeding.

Since most species retain sexual reproduction despite its seeming inefficiency, it follows that it must provide advantages great enough to be worth the enormous cost. The search for such powerful evolutionary advantages has yet to produce really convincing results. I conclude that the prevalence of sexual reproduction is a major unresolved mystery.

Acknowledgements

Discussions with Graham Bell clarified my ideas on inbreeding. I was aided greatly by discussions with Robert L. Trivers, who pointed out the implications for male genotypes of there being genes for female sexuality, and with Gerdien de Jong, who pointed out the difference in fitness variance between isogamy and fission.

Literature Cited

Bell, G. 1978. The evolution of anisogamy. Journal of Theoretical Biology 73:247-270.

Charlesworth, B. 1978. The population genetics of anisogamy. Journal of Theoretical Biology 73:347-357.

Janzen, D. H. 1977. A note on optimal mate selection by plants. American Naturalist 111:365-371.

Manning, J. T. 1976. Gamete dimorphism and the cost of sexual reproduction. Are they separate phenomena? Journal of Theoretical Biology 55:393-395.

Maynard Smith, J. 1958. The theory of evolution. Penguin Books A433, Edinburgh.

_______. 1971. The origin and maintenance of sex. In G. C. Williams (ed.), Group selection. Aldine, Atherton, New York, pp. 163-175.

_______. 1974. Recombination and the rate of evolution. Genetics 78:299-304.

Parker, G.A. 1978. Selection on non-random fusion of gametes during the evolution of anisogamy. Journal of Theoretical Biology 73:1-28.

Rathvon, J. P. 1977. Obstacles to the evolution of parthenogenesis: Do they exist? Masters Thesis, State University of New York, Stony Brook.

Smith, C. C. & S. D. Fretwell. 1974. The optimal balance between size and number of offspring. American Naturalist 108:499-506.

Treisman, M. 1976. The evolution of sexual reproduction: A model which assumes individual selection. Journal of Theoretical Biology 60:421-431.

_______ & R. Dawkins. 1976. The "cost of meiosis": Is there any? Journal of Theoretical Biology 63:479-684.

Weismann, A. 1889. The significance of sexual reproduction in the theory of natural selection. In E. B. Poulton, S. Schönland & A. E. Shipley (eds.), Essays upon heredity and kindred biological problems, by Dr. August Weismann. Authorized translation. Clarendon, Oxford, pp. 251-332.

West-Eberhard, M. J. 1975. The evolution of social behavior by kin selection. Quarterly Review of Biology 50:1-33.

Williams, G. C. 1975. Sex and evolution. Princeton University Press, Princeton, N.J.

Willson, M. F. 1979. Sexual selection in plants. American Naturalist 113 (in press).

Wilson, E. O. 1975. Sociobiology: The new synthesis. Belknap, Cambridge, Mass.

Elizabeth Kocher Adkins

16. Genes, Hormones, Sex and Gender

From the moment of birth, when the physician or midwife announces "It's a girl" or "It's a boy," the sex of an individual is a dimension of human life that assumes great importance. By age 5 or 6, most children are firmly aware of their own sex (Money & Ehrhardt 1972) and observe that males and females differ not only physically but also behaviorally.

In this paper I would like to discuss the developmental origin of sex differences in behavior in humans. More specifically, I would like to focus on the question, what is the role of genes or sex hormones in the ontogeny of sex differences in human behavior, a process referred to as psychosexual differentiation? My discussion will be relevant to a related question: should the study of this process, traditionally the province of the social sciences, be incorporated into the biological sciences?

Sex Differences and Psychosexual Differentiation in Nonhuman Mammals

The clearest way to proceed will be to summarize briefly the relevant nonhuman data, and then see if similar data are available for humans. All mammalian species exhibit sex differences in behavior to at least a minor extent and this fact has been particularly well documented for certain laboratory species. For example, female laboratory rats do more exploring than males when placed in a novel environment (Gray et al. 1965), and male laboratory mice are more likely than females to attack an intruder (Edwards 1969). A more obvious example of a sex difference in behavior is that during copulation, males of many species mount, whereas females adopt special postures to solicit and facilitate mounting. These copulatory reflexes are stimulated by gonadal sex hormones.

But even when males and females have been tested under

identical hormonal and stimulus conditions, sex differences in the probability of displaying masculine or feminine sexual patterns have persisted (Young 1961). Numerous experiments have shown that the neural mechanisms for the feminine sexual pattern are more readily activated in females than in males, although males too have these mechanisms. Likewise, the neural mechanisms for the masculine mating pattern are more readily activated in males than in females, although females too have these mechanisms. Thus male rats whose testes are removed and who are treated with the sex hormones estrogen and progesterone and tested with normal male partners occasionally perform the feminine mating pattern. But they do not do so nearly as readily as identically treated females. Similarly, female rats whose ovaries are removed and who are treated with the sex hormone testosterone and tested with receptive female partners exhibit the masculine mating pattern. But their performance is not equal to that of identically treated males. Such a result implies that the nervous system of rats is qualitatively "bisexual"; quantitatively it is sexually dimorphic.

The origin of this apparent neural sexual dimorphism has been traced to the actions of the gonads early in life (Feder & Wade 1974; Lisk 1974), actions remarkably similar to those by which the gonads determine somatic sexual dimorphism. The testes of males secrete sizeable quantities of androgens not only in adulthood, but also during the period of sexual differentiation, i.e., during late fetal or, in some species, late fetal and early postnatal life. It is these androgens that induce not only differentiation of male sex organs, but also development of the male behavioral response pattern.

The female's ovaries are relatively inactive during this neonatal period; ovarian hormones do not seem to make a major contribution to feminine differentiation. Thus female rats deprived of their ovaries before the period of differentiation still look like females, at least externally, and still act like females. In contrast, male rats deprived of their testes before the period of differentiation are feminized physically and behaviorally. When mature they are quite capable of displaying feminine sexual patterns. Females treated with androgens during differentiation are masculinized physically and behaviorally, and when mature are relatively incapable of displaying feminine sexual patterns. Thus, early exposure to androgen masculinizes, early absence of androgen feminizes, and a rat of either genetic sex will develop as a morphological and behavioral female unless androgen is present neonatally.

Additional experiments have provided more direct evidence that androgens from the neonatal testes produce their "organizing" effects on behavior primarily by acting on the brain, specifically on the hypothalamus (Gorski 1971). Furthermore, psychosexual differentiation appears to occur in a similar manner, i.e., early androgen masculinizes behavior, in several other species of mammals, such as mice, guinea pigs, dogs, ferrets, sheep and hamsters (Baum 1976; Beach 1975; Clarke 1977; Clemens 1974; Edwards & Burge 1971; Phoenix et al. 1959).

Differentiation of the gonads responsible for such effects is in turn controlled by the sex chromosomes. As long as at least one Y chromosome is present, testes will develop (Beatty 1964). In fact, recent reports indicate that development of the testes in humans and other mammals may be controlled by a small number of genes on the Y chromosome (Wachtel 1977).

Putting these facts together, one could conclude that at least some behavioral sex differences in mammals are ultimately determined by a very small number of genes. Are human behavioral and physical sex also ultimately determined by a small number of genes on the Y chromosome? Do sex hormones direct human psychosexual differentiation?

Sex Differences and Psychosexual Differentiation in Humans

Sex Differences in Human Behavior

Whether the focus is on humans or other mammals, it is difficult to think about psychosexual differentiation without first identifying the types of behavior in which adult males and females actually do differ. This necessitates a brief look at the literature on sex differences in human behavior.

Significant sex differences have been reported for many categories of behavior. Those that are frequently cited have included sensory thresholds, cognitive abilities (especially verbal and spatial abilities), empathy and nurturance, achievement motivation, activity level, anxiety and emotionality, sociality, aggressiveness and dominance, and sexual arousal (Hoffman 1977; Maccoby & Jacklin 1974; Money & Ehrhardt 1972).

The fact that these reported sex differences are part of our society's cultural stereotypes, embodied in our everyday thinking about the sexes, raises questions about the reliability of the observations made and the validity of the conclusions reached. Moreover, most of our data are based on Europeans or Americans of European descent. Studies in which different cultures were compared have sometimes found that a sex difference in one culture was absent or reversed in another, e.g. Mead's (1935) findings on male-female differences in docility in three New Guinea cultures. The profound importance of cultural variables in human sex-related behavior makes it difficult to conduct a culture-free study of sex differences. It is important to bear this in mind throughout the remainder of this paper.

The serious reader will find many other problems with the data on human sex differences, some of which are nicely articulated by Maccoby and Jacklin (1974). One has to do with the general nature of scientific publication. Studies finding a significant sex difference are more likely to get published than those finding no sex differences. Even if negative results were to be published at the same rate, one could not assume that they were as valuable as positive results. After all, a negative finding could be due to poor methods, especially insensitive measures, rather than to an absence of differences (Hoffman 1977).

Other methodological problems are widespread. Observer bias is frequent, and experiments are seldom blind, since it is usually impossible to disguise the sex of the subjects. Much of the research is based on indirect measures such as self-report pencil-and-paper tests or simulated tasks in laboratory settings, rather than on overt behavior in real-life social environments. Such measurement is frequently of questionable validity. In some cases where data were available from both laboratory experiments and real-life situations, e.g., aggression in adults (Frodi et al. 1977), the results were different.

Also questionable has been the validity of some experimenters' decisions in classifying the behavior they observed (did the experimental task actually measure spatial ability or not, what behaviors were labelled aggression, etc.). Such decisions sometimes have had a self-fulfilling or post hoc air about them. For example, Maccoby and Jacklin (1974) reported that in some studies where the hypothesis was that girls are more social than boys, activities in which boys hit each other or engaged in rough-and-tumble play were not considered social behavior. Other categories have stretched the analysis of behavior to the breaking point. For instance, sex differences in sensory thresholds are widely believed to be responsible for sex differences in many human social behaviors, in spite of the fact that little relevant behavior seems actually to take place at threshold levels of stimulation. Another example of category ambiguity was the claim that sex differences in empathy and imagination are the adult expression of sex differences in touch and pain thresholds in infants (Bardwick 1971).

As described previously, the research on genetic and hormonal bases of sex differences and psychosexual differentiation in nonhumans, which has made significant progress, has focused chiefly on mating behavior per se. Would a similar focus in humans allow us to get around some of the problems just outlined? Unfortunately, the answer is probably no, for, as Money and Ehrhardt (1972:192) put it, "Dimorphism of behavior in the act of sexual intercourse between a man and woman is just about everybody's speciality, and yet there are virtually no experts in this aspect of human behavior..."

Data on sex differences in erotic imagery and arousal showed that women were less responsive than men to visual sexual stimuli (Money & Ehrhardt 1972), but this may have been due to culturally derived sex differences in the willingness to report arousal (Gebhard 1973; Rossi 1973). Furthermore, claims that women are less responsive involve circular logic: the choice of the visual stimuli used as erotic was made by male experimenters, and so of course men found them more arousing (Money 1973; Rossi 1973).

Many studies of sex differences in human behavior have concentrated on children's behavior, especially during play. Some of the observed differences, particularly in physical activity and aggression, may well have been secondary to sex differences in body size and clothing style (pants vs. skirts). Others may have been secondary to observed sex differences in neural and somatic maturation rate (Hutt 1972; Waber 1976).

Even sex differences in behavior found in newborns cannot be safely assumed to be free of social determination. Differential parental treatment of the sexes begins right at birth, as expressed in time spent feeding the infant, talking to it, smiling at it, and handling it (Hoffman 1977; Moss 1974; Thoman et al. 1972). Furthermore, there is evidence that circumcision of males has confounded data obtained from newborns (Korner 1974; Richards et al. 1975). In addition, neonate sex differences cannot be assumed to be ontogenically stable (Korner 1974; Maccoby & Jacklin 1974). Readers who feel that sex differences in newborns are truly significant should consider whether they could accurately identify the sex of diapered infants on the basis of their behavior.

By now it should be apparent that the foundation of information about sex differences in human behavior that is needed in order to investigate genetic and hormonal origins has serious weaknesses. Few unequivocal sex differences have been demonstrated (Maccoby & Jacklin 1974); even these have been questioned on scientific grounds; and some that were demonstrated in previous decades have turned out to be greatly reduced or absent in more recent studies, due to social changes. This has been the fate of the sex differences in sexual arousal to erotic stimuli mentioned earlier. More recent investigations (Gebhard 1973; Schmidt & Sigusch 1973) failed to find much, if any, sex difference in reports of erotic response to sexual films. Finally, it should be emphasized that in all cases where sex differences in behavior were found, they were small and could only be seen by comparing average male and female scores, since the overlap was considerable. In no case is human behavior (or nonhuman, for that matter) dichotomous with respect to sex (Beach 1974; Reinisch 1974). With these caveats in mind, let us turn to the research on the process of human psychosexual differentiation.

Psychosexual Differentiation in Humans: Gender Identity in Cases with Incongruous Sex or Absent Gonads

A rich supply of information on human psychosexual differentiation can be found in publications by John and Joan Hampson (Hampson 1965; Hampson & Hampson 1969) and by John Money and Anke Ehrhardt (Money & Ehrhardt 1972). The following summary draws heavily on this material.

Individuals with clinically recognized syndromes were studied whose gonads had never developed or whose physical sexual characteristics were incongruous or conflicting. In normal individuals, the sex chromosomes, the gonads, the gonadal hormones, the external genitalia, and the internal genitalia are all congruent with respect to sex, and the sex that they indicate agrees with the sex of assignment and rearing. In occasional rare individuals, however, these sex indicators do not agree, and one or more of them contradicts the sex of assignment and rearing.

Some individuals have XY chromosomes and testes, but female external genitals. A cause of this is the androgen-insensitivity or testicular-feminizing syndrome: the testes differentiate properly, but the body tissues lack ability to respond to testicular androgens, and are not masculinized during development. Since the chief criterion that a doctor or midwife uses at delivery to announce the sex of the newborn is the appearance of the external genitalia, babies with testicular-feminizing syndrome are often assigned to the female sex and reared accordingly. At puberty, although they develop feminine secondary sex characteristics in response to the small quantities of estrogen that all testes produce, they fail to menstruate, and the testes are discovered upon internal examination.

To take another example, individuals with XX chromosomes and ovaries are occasionally born that have such masculine external genitalia that they are assigned to the male sex and reared as boys. One cause of this particular incongruity is the adrenogenital syndrome (AGS), a genetic defect that causes the adrenals to secrete excess quantities of androgens, both pre- and postnatally.

Another sexual anomaly that is relevant to the study of human psychosexual differentiation is Turner's syndrome, in which there is only one sex chromosome, an X chromosome, so that they are designated XO. In such people, gonads fail to develop but female external genitalia differentiate.

The morphology of these people with incongruous sex or gonadal agenesis indicates that physical differentiation in humans takes place according to the same rules as were summarized previously for other mammals: the body develops as female unless androgens act on it during development. In humans the period of morphological differentiation is entirely prenatal. Thus, at birth, individuals with Turner's syndrome appear externally to be normal females. Individuals with XX chromosomes who are exposed to androgen prenatally are masculinized. Individuals with the testicular-feminizing syndrome are feminized to the point of appearing externally to be normal females, although internally they lack a developed uterus.

What is the behavior of these people like? Which of the morphological sex indicators, if any, predicts gender identity, the sex that the individual feels himself or herself to belong to?

The conclusion of behavioral analyses was that the only sex indicator that reliably predicted gender identity was the sex of assignment and rearing. Neither chromosomal, gonadal, nor genital sex bore any consistent relationship to gender identity, except insofar as the sex of assignment and rearing often agreed with the sex of the external genitalia. Thus people with one sex chromosome, no gonads, and female external genitalia were regarded and reared as females and had a normal feminine gender identity. People with XY chromosomes and testes, but whose female external genitals caused them to be reared as females, also had a normal feminine gender identity. People with XX chromosomes and ovaries, but whose masculine external genitalia caused them to be reared as males, had a normal masculine gender identity.

Even in those cases where the sex of the external genitalia and the sex of assignment and rearing did not agree, gender identity still conformed to the sex of assignment and rearing. Thus there were cases of individuals reared as girls who possessed large and functional phalluses, or reared as boys who had only rudimentary phalluses. Such people obviously underwent considerable psychological distress, especially at puberty, but nonetheless were apparently firm in their gender identity (female and male, respectively), provided there was no ambiguity about rearing.

The influence of rearing on psychosexual differentiation was seen even more clearly in those studies that compared individuals matched for physical diagnosis and external appearance, but raised as different sexes. Money and Ehrhardt (1972) describe three such matched pairs. One pair, for example, consisted of two unrelated AGS girls that had a similar ambiguous genital appearance at birth. One was raised as a girl after the genetic sex was discovered at age 2 months. The other was pronounced a boy at birth, was found to be a genetic female at age 3 1/2 years, but was allowed to continue living as a boy. As teenagers, they exhibited unremarkable female and male gender identities, respectively.

Thus the studies of people with incongruous sex or gonadal agenesis suggest that the sex chromosomes per se have no major direct effect on gender identity. They also suggest that the primary role of the gonads in human psychosexual differentiation is indirect. During fetal life they determine the form of the genitals that will then determine the sex of assignment and rearing. At puberty they stimulate secondary sexual characteristics that will either confirm or contradict, but not reverse, the gender identity that was established earlier. Evidently the primary mechanism by which biological sex determines behavioral sex is by dictating how other people will behave toward the person during the formative years, and to a lesser extent how the individual views his/her own body.

Clearly this research implies that the social environment is predominant in shaping human sex differences. This conclusion has been criticized by several authors (see, for example, Diamond 1965; Young 1967; Zuger 1970). Some have questioned whether study of these rare and rather bizarre clinical cases can shed much light on the development of normal males and females. A less obvious criticism has been that the data do not entirely rule out the possibility that fetal hormones do have some direct role in psychosexual differentiation, as they do in other mammals. Two examples will make this argument clear.

Consider first the female with Turner's syndrome, who has XO chromosomes and virtually no gonads. Not only does she have female genitalia, which is why she is raised as a girl, but in addition her brain has not been exposed to androgens prenatally. Perhaps it is this lack of androgen exposure that is responsible for her feminine gender identity and behavior. Or consider the AGS individual who is masculinized to the point of being raised as a boy. His nervous system as well as his genitalia have been exposed to androgens prenatally. Perhaps this is why he is so successful as a male in spite of his sex chromosomes.

Clearly if fetal hormones do contribute to psychosexual differentiation, they cannot be the major determinant, or the matched pairs mentioned earlier could not show such divergent gender identity. Nonetheless, it is possible that some less dramatic effects, especially changes in overt behavior as opposed to verbal expressions of gender identity, were overlooked.

Psychosexual Differentiation in Humans: Subjects with Abnormal Prenatal Hormone Exposure Compared with Controls

Inspired by the animal literature on the behavioral effects of early sex hormone treatment, several studies have now been completed that have searched for similar effects in humans. People analogous to the hormone-treated subjects in the experiments with nonhuman animals were compared with normal humans. The investigators expected that genetic females, exposed to excess androgens prenatally but raised as females, would be more masculine than normal female controls. Likewise, they hypothesized that genetic males, deficient in prenatal androgen exposure or else exposed to female sex hormones that would antagonize androgens, would be more feminine than normal male controls, even though they had been reared as males.

The best known study of this kind is one by Ehrhardt, Epstein and Money (1968). They compared 15 girls who had the adrenogenital syndrome with 15 matched controls. The AGS girls were diagnosed in infancy, underwent surgical feminization of the genitals where necessary, and were raised as girls. Their adrenal condition was treated with cortisone from infancy on, so their adrenal androgens had been excessive mainly prior to birth. Controls were roughly comparable in age, intelligence, and family socioeconomic level. Subjects were about 5 to 16 years old (mean 11 years) at the time the data were collected. The girls and their mothers were interviewed and asked about the daughters' interests and behavior.

When compared with the controls, AGS girls showed a behavior profile that, according to U.S. cultural standards at the time the data were collected, was "masculinized": less interest in marriage, greater interest in a career, less interest in infant care and doll play, greater interest in boy's play and boy's clothing, and greater interest in athletics and outdoor activity. The AGS girls were more likely to be regarded as "tomboys" by themselves and their mothers. There were no differences in masturbation, fighting, or desire to be a boy.

It is important to note that these girls were well within the normal range, and appeared no different from thousands of physically normal teenage tomboys. Rather, they were statistically different from the control girls. A similar pattern of results, but with smaller effects, was found when girls exposed to masculinizing progestins prenatally were compared with controls (Ehrhardt & Money 1967).

These findings received considerable attention. The analogy with the nonhuman research quickly led to the popular and uncritical belief that "proof" had been obtained that fetal hormones program the developing brains of humans into male or female and thereby determine sex differences in behavior.

Upon closer examination, however, there are a number of problems with the tomboy experiment, such that its results should be regarded as suggestive rather than conclusive (see, for example, Quadagno et al. 1977). (1) The AGS girls had been treated with cortisone since infancy. Although the dosages were intended to provide normal levels, there is no guarantee that they did. Since cortisone has behavioral effects in humans (Ganong 1973), it would have been preferable to have included a control group of girls treated with cortisone for reasons other than AGS. (2) Conclusions were not based on actual observations of overt behavior. (3) The interviews were not blind, which could produce unreliable measurement. (4) The behaviors and preferences that the results were based on are extremely culturally determined. Their frequencies in normal girls have changed considerably since the study was done and the "tomboyish" behavior of the AGS girls may well now be the norm. (5) Parental treatment may have confounded the results: the parents of the AGS girls may have been more likely to tolerate "tomboyish" behavior. Neither of the investigators felt that this last bias was significant (Ehrhardt 1973; Money & Schwartz 1976), but it is unlikely that it was absent. In some cases, the parents had initially been told that their babies were boys.

Other problems with the tomboy experiment are a bit more subtle, but are probably more serious. They have to do with perceptions and feelings toward the girls' bodies. The AGS subjects were physically masculinized at birth and were expected to have medical problems later on. It is highly likely that they and their mothers were unsure of their physical femininity, and that at least some of the behavioral findings are attributable to this uncertainty. Quadagno et al. have articulated this point (1977:73):

> The condition of the AGS girls required prolonged medical contact, and they were given information about their condition as well as sex education ... It is quite likely they were informed that ... their menses might be a year or so late or perhaps excessively delayed, they might have problems conceiving, they must remain on cortisone therapy during pregnancy, and so forth ... We propose that the AGS girls were unsure of their role as potential mothers due to their biological problems ... Hence, they were less likely to verbalize aspects of maternalism.

Several more recent studies were also interpreted as proving that fetal hormones have behavioral effects that reflect sexual programming of the brain, but none was free of the kinds of serious problems I have been describing. Ehrhardt (1973) and Masica et al. (1971) reported on the sexual arousal and maternalism of adult AGS women age 19 to 48 years. Although their girlhood tomboyism did not preclude marriage and childrearing, interviews indicated an unusually low level of interest in infants, and sexual arousal characteristics seemed slightly "masculinized." In addition to the confounding variables present in the original tomboy experiment, these women were late-treated--their excess adrenal androgens were not corrected until long after birth--so that behavioral findings were not necessarily due to organizing actions of androgens on the fetal brain. And studying the subjects as adults introduces an additional difficulty; AGS females reach puberty at a later than average age, sometimes as late as age 20 or so (Ehrhardt & Baker 1974). This fact alone could account for the reduced interest in children vs. career.

People with Turner's syndrome or with the testicular-feminizing syndrome who were raised as girls impressed their interviewers as being more "feminine", on the average, than normal females, both physically and behaviorally (Ehrhardt et al. 1970; Money et al. 1968). This suggests that when the brain is not affected by prenatal androgen, a female program results. But it is also possible that they were exceedingly feminine because, unlike normal females, they did not experience ovarian androgens at puberty, or because, unlike AGS girls, there was little ambiguity about their sex during childhood since their external genitalia appeared normal.

Yalom et al. (1973) found that boys born to diabetic mothers treated with an estrogen-progesterone regimen during pregnancy were rated lower on several measures of general "masculinity," and specifically on assertiveness and athletic ability, than control boys born to nondiabetic mothers or to diabetic mothers not given hormones during pregnancy. Interviewing and testing were generally, but not always, blind. The reported reliability coefficients were low, however: .64 for aggressivity and .60 for masculine interests. The validity of some of the measures was equally unimpressive. For example, a boy expressing interests in photography, languages, going to a good college, and having Louis Pasteur as a hero, would have been given a <u>low</u> score for masculine interests. Results for aggression and athleticism were confounded by the fact that the experimental subjects were shorter than the controls. In addition,

> A major uncontrolled variable in the study was the state of health of the mothers in the experimental and contrast groups. The mothers of all the experimentals suffered from a chronic illness requiring daily attention. Only 8 of the 37 contrast mothers were also diabetic, and the severity of their diabetes was less. It is possible that chronic illness in the mother induced overprotection of offspring or greater anxiety over health in offspring so as to interfere with aggressive masculine development. It could also be that some endocrine disorder in diabetic women, irrespective of exogenous hormone administration, may have affected the fetal development of the boys (Yalom et al. 1973:559).

Meyer-Bahlburg et al. (1977) found only insignificant differences between boys born to mothers treated with medroxyprogesterone acetate during pregnancy and male controls, whereas Ehrhardt et al. (1977) found that girls born to such mothers were less likely to be tomboys than female controls. They offered two explanations for this discrepancy. One was that male fetuses, unlike female, produce too much androgen for the medroxyprogesterone acetate to overcome. The other was that boys might be under more pressure to conform to a sex stereotype than girls.

Additional investigations of people exposed to hormones during fetal development have focused on personality characteristics or intellectual abilities. Dalton (1968, 1976) and Zussman et al. (1975) compared British children born to mothers treated with progesterone during pregnancy with controls. The progesterone-exposed children got better grades in subjects involving verbal reasoning, English, and arithmetic (an effect which was dose-dependent), had superior numerical ability, were more studious, and were more likely eventually to be admitted to a university. Reinisch and Karow (1977) administered the Cattell personality questionnaire to children born to mothers given estrogen and progesterone during pregnancy, and to control children. Subjects whose mothers had been given a high progesterone-to-estrogen ratio were scored as being more individualistic, independent, self-assured, and self-sufficient than controls, a personality profile that has been related to school achievement and success. Subjects of mothers given a high estrogen-to-progesterone ratio were less individualistic and less self-sufficient. It is unfortunate that this otherwise well-executed study chose to look only at results of a self-report pencil-and-paper test.

I have now described most of the existing investigations of the relationship between fetal hormones and human psychosexual differentiation (the remainder will be mentioned below). What can be concluded from them? Taken together, they suggest that females exposed to androgens or certain progestins prenatally are slightly more "masculine" than controls, and that males and females exposed to lower than normal amounts of androgens prenatally are slightly more "feminine" than controls.

In making such a conclusion, however, it must be remembered that each study had serious defects, many of the measures used were of questionable reliability or validity, and data gathering was seldom blind. There were no controls for effects of the hormones on physical size, maturation rate, or age at puberty, variables which exert profound effects on adolescent behavior (Hamburg & Lunde 1966; Melges & Hamburg 1976). There were also no adequate controls for the mother's health and the incidence of pregnancy complications, the most common reasons for administration of hormones to pregnant women. In fact, it is highly likely that, excepting the work of Reinisch (Reinisch 1977; Reinisch & Karow 1977) and of Meyer-Bahlburg and Ehrhardt (Meyer-Bahlburg et al. 1977; Ehrhardt et al. 1977), none of the studies employed controls that were adequately matched.

The truth of this statement can be seen by looking at the IQ's of the subjects. In those cases where intelligence was measured, girls exposed to androgens or progestins prenatally showed statistically higher IQ's than the "matched" controls or than the expected norm (Ehrhardt et al. 1968; Ehrhardt & Money 1967; Money & Lewis 1966). It is unlikely that this was an effect of the hormone treatment, since there are no sex differences in IQ among normal populations (Baker & Ehrhardt 1974). Furthermore, the only studies that looked for but did not find an IQ effect were those that used the sisters of the hormone exposed girls as controls (Baker & Ehrhardt 1974; Ehrhardt et al. 1977; Reinisch & Karow 1977). Such controls are an excellent way to match for family environment, although controls for birth order and other intrafamily variables are also desirable. This strongly suggests that the IQ effect in other studies may have been an artifact of inadequately matched controls. Even though most of the experiments attempted roughly to match the socioeconomic level of the families, they evidently were not successful enough, and the treated girls came from better educated families.

Obviously much of the difference in "tomboy" behavior could also be a result of improperly matched controls, although not all of it can be explained in this way. Using sisters as controls, Ehrhardt and Baker (1974) still found AGS girls were more tomboyish. This experiment did not, however, avoid the other confounding variables that were described above in connection with the original tomboy experiment (Ehrhardt et al. 1968).

Notwithstanding the methodological problems, the effects obtained in human experiments have been small in magnitude, even in late-treated AGS girls. In no case was a significant increase in transsexualism or decrease in marriage frequency found. Furthermore, none of the studies, not even those including both male and female subjects, provided any data showing that the behavioral measures affected by prenatal hormone exposure actually exhibited sex differences. Yet it is difficult to interpret such studies as having anything to do with normal psychosexual differentiation unless boys and girls can be shown to differ on the measures used. Conversely, abnormal prenatal hormone exposure usually did not affect some behavior patterns that are often assumed to exhibit pronounced sex differences, such as dominance, leadership, aggressiveness, and assertiveness (Money 1976; Money & Schwartz 1976). And what does it mean when girls exposed to greater-than-normal amounts of estrogen prenatally were observed to be "feminized"? Such a finding has interesting implications for the practical management of pregnancy problems, but tells us little about the origins of male-female differences.

Comparison of Human and Nonhuman Data

As summarized earlier, there is evidence that fetal hormones alter brain development with respect to adult performance of sexual behavior in certain mammalian species, and are important in determining sex differences in copulatory pattern. A direct comparison of the human and nonhuman research will make it clear that these results cannot yet be generalized to humans, and that it is premature to conclude that the behavioral sex of humans is also programmed by actions of fetal hormones on the developing brain.

First and foremost, the vast majority of the nonhuman experiments looked solely at copulation, whereas none of the human experiments have done so. The primary effect of early exposure to androgen in the female rat is impairment of the capacity to display lordosis, the receptive posture. Yet there is no human behavior homologous to lordosis. In fact, human female sexual behavior is only weakly, if at all, controlled by sex hormones (Luttge 1971). As Beach (1974:384) stated, "... human sexuality is about as closely related to the mating behavior of other species as human language is related to animal communication, a relationship that is distant indeed."

So far there has been no overlap between the actual behaviors represented in the human and nonhuman studies, even though some of the latter experiments have included effects of early hormones on nonsexual behavior such as open field exploration, fighting, and maternal behavior (see review by Quadagno et al. 1977). Significant effects of early androgen were sometimes obtained, but they were often subtle, and not nearly of the magnitude seen for copulation (Quadagno et al. 1977).

After the first reports of hormone effects on nonhuman psychosexual differentiation appeared, hard data were required to convince the scientific world that the brain itself was actually being affected and was responsible for the behavioral effects of the hormones. Considerable evidence has now been obtained in rats that (1) the brain areas involved in copulation are in fact target organs for sex hormones during the fetal period (Sheridan et al. 1974); (2) these areas are modified structurally and biochemically by early hormones (Dörner and Staudt 1968; Gorski 1971; Pfaff 1966); (3) androgen implanted directly into these areas in neonatal rats masculinizes the behavior of females (Nadler 1973); and

(4) some of these areas are sexually dimorphic (Bubenik & Brown 1973; Dörner & Staudt 1968; Pfaff 1966; Raisman & Field 1971).

We have none of this kind of evidence in humans. Furthermore, much of the human behavior shown to be affected by early hormone exposure--e.g. occupational interest, verbal or spatial skill, self-sufficiency--is probably extensively mediated by the cerebral cortex (Mountcastle 1974; Pincus & Tucker 1974). Yet this brain area is apparently not a target organ for sex hormones (Morrell et al. 1975).

But what about species phylogenetically closer to humans, such as monkeys or apes? Aren't experiments with such animals more analogous to the human research? (Indeed they are, which is why I have delayed discussing them until now.) In experiments with rhesus monkeys, Goy, Phoenix, and co-workers showed that females born to mothers injected with testosterone during pregnancy and observed as juveniles were behaviorally masculinized (Goy 1968, 1970). Compared with control females, they showed increased levels of social behaviors that are normally more frequent in males, such as social threat, play initiation, rough-and-tumble play, juvenile mounting, and pursuit play. Their scores did not always approach those of males, however, and due to variability of the data and the small number of experimental females studied, the effects were sometimes small. When sexually mature, some of these testosterone-exposed females and some control females were ovariectomized and treated with testosterone. The females exposed to androgen prenatally were more aggressive, but did not mount significantly more often (Goy & Resko 1972; Phoenix 1974). The androgenized females had masculinized external genitalia, but there is evidence that physical masculinization was not the cause of the behavioral masculinization: females born to mothers treated with the androgen dihydrotestosterone were masculinized behaviorally but not physically (Goy 1979).

Since feral-reared male rhesus monkeys have been shown to be less aggressive than laboratory-reared males (Harlow 1965), some of the sex differences and prenatal hormone effects just described may have been magnified by the abnormal social and physical environment of the monkeys. Nonetheless, these monkey experiments are valuable because they embody greater control than is possible in experiments with humans.

It is tempting to extrapolate the rhesus monkey findings to humans, but caution should be exercised. The behaviors studied in rhesus monkeys are not homologous with the behaviors studied in the human experiments. Human tomboyism is neither homologous nor analogous to rhesus rough-and-tumble play, and even human rough-and-tumble play might not be homologous (Quadagno et al. 1977). And generalizations from one species to another must take into account species differences in behavioral sex dimorphism. For example, in some mammals males are more aggressive than females (for some types of aggression), while in others the females are more aggressive (Kleiman 1977). If sex differences in aggressiveness are determined by fetal hormones, then in the first kind of mammal, androgenized females should show increased aggression, but in the second kind, androgenized females should show decreased aggression. It is especially risky to use prenatal hormone effects on the juvenile behavior of one species to explain adult sex differences in another species, for some sex differences in the behavior of juveniles disappear or even reverse in adulthood (Wolfheim 1977).

Homosexuality

Before concluding, I would like briefly to discuss male homosexuality, which is often regarded as a disorder of psychosexual differentiation, and which has sometimes been assumed to be primarily biological in origin. Do studies of homosexuality provide any evidence that genes and/or hormones are important determinants of human psychosexual differentiation? The reader is warned that many of the relevant experiments are characterized by a crude level of behavioral analysis, in which different kinds of homosexuals (exclusive, occasional, bisexual, male-role, female-role, etc.) are lumped together into one heterogeneous category.

Genetic theories of the origin of male homosexuality have been tested in several twin studies. Such studies have sometimes found greater concordance for homosexuality in monozygotic twins than in dizygotic twins (e.g., Heston & Shields 1968; Rosenthal 1970), which can be interpreted as indicating a significant genetic component.

In no case, however, have twins reared apart been studied with respect to homosexuality. This procedure, generally regarded as necessary in good twin research, is especially important in this case, since a gender preference in one twin might well be transferred to the other twin for purely social reasons. Kallmann's (1952) often cited data, showing a near 100% concordance for homosexuality in monozygotic twins, were obtained from a population of men defined as mentally ill by criteria other than homosexuality, and in addition are now regarded as a statistical artifact, even by Kallmann himself (Kallmann 1960).

Hormonal theories of homosexuality have been tested in part by looking for evidence that homosexuals have different androgen levels than heterosexuals. So far this approach has been unsuccessful (Barfield 1976; Meyer-Bahlburg 1977). Not only have such differences seldom been discovered, but when homosexuals were found to have lower androgen levels, the most likely explanation has been that the reduced androgens were a consequence of the homosexual life, not the cause of it. Stress, an ever present accompaniment to a statistically deviant lifestyle, has well known depressant effects on sex hormone levels (Mason 1975). Actually, it is not surprising that this approach has not been productive. If the levels of circulating sex hormones were the cause of homosexuality, one would expect to find some physical differences between homosexuals and heterosexuals, however slight. No such differences have been found. In particular, male homosexuals are not necessarily physically effeminate (Ellis 1963; Meyer-Bahlburg 1977).

It has been suggested that male homosexuality is due to insufficient exposure to androgen during prenatal development, but so far there has been no evidence that this is the case (Barfield 1976; Meyer-Bahlburg 1977). In no study described previously, in which humans were exposed to abnormal amounts of sex hormones during development, has there been any effect on the incidence of male (or female) homosexuality. And again, if insufficient prenatal androgen were a factor, one would expect an elevated degree or incidence of physical feminization, at least statistically; yet, as mentioned above, this is not the case.

The major assumption underlying the theory of a prenatal hormone origin of homosexuality is therefore weak. It is based on a false analogy with the nonhuman experiments in which males deprived of early androgen show increased capability for female behavior. To assume that this is a model for human homosexuality is to make a serious error (Beach 1976). The nonhuman experiments look at the type of behavior pattern displayed, e.g. mounting vs. lordosis, not the preference in terms of partners in sex. Yet human homosexuality is defined in terms of partner preference, not in terms of the type of behavior engaged in. Thus a male homosexual who always takes the male role in copulation can be identical to a heterosexual man in his actual behavior patterns, and he is not analogous to the male rat castrated early in life who adopts the lordosis posture in interactions with other males. Nor do male homosexuals (as opposed to transsexuals) have a feminine gender identity.

The fact that homosexual behavior can occur in monkeys

and most other animals under certain conditions (both in the laboratory and in the field), or at certain life stages, suggests that the capacity to display it is probably biological. It does not follow, however, that the major factor determining whether a particular individual human will be a homosexual is a biological one. Yet in spite of the lack of any good evidence, there are still frequent assertions that human homosexuals are made by genes or hormones. As far as I have been able to discern, this opinion seems to result from the following fallacious reasoning: the theory that male homosexuality is caused by a dominant mother and a weak father has not been supported, ergo it must be genetic/hormonal.

Conclusions

On the basis of our knowledge of the development of human sex differences in behavior, it is safe to conclude that heredity and environment interact to produce these differences. This is not a particularly momentous conclusion, however, for this is believed to be true for all behavior in animals. What is interesting is the rather special way that this interaction comes about in human psychosexual differentiation.

The major role of genetic and other constitutional (e.g. hormonal) factors is to determine genital appearance, which in turn determines how the individual will be identified, named, reared, and treated by others, as well as how the individual perceives his/her own body. In the summary diagram proposed by Money and Ehrhardt (Fig. 1), this role is shown as the pathway from "genital appearance" through "juvenile gender identity/role" to "adult gender identity/role." Usually it is reinforced by the pubertal hormonal events also shown in the diagram (the pathway on the right). "Neural pathways" refers to the experiments suggesting that fetal hormones act on the developing brain to have a direct effect on juvenile, and thereby adult, gender identity. Other explanations for the results of these experiments are equally plausible, however, and so this pathway should be considered tentative at this time. The diagram shows "others' behavior," "body image/schema," and "neural pathways" converging on "juvenile gender identity/role." This expresses two intriguing possibilities: first, that there might be some small constitutionally determined sex differences in behavior that are greatly magnified by differential rearing and experience, including social and cultural influences (Beach 1974), and second, as Goy and Resko (1972) suggested, that there might be some sex differences in the reactions individuals show to various kinds of rearing experiences, as have been found in monkeys (Hamburg & Lunde 1966; Sackett 1974).

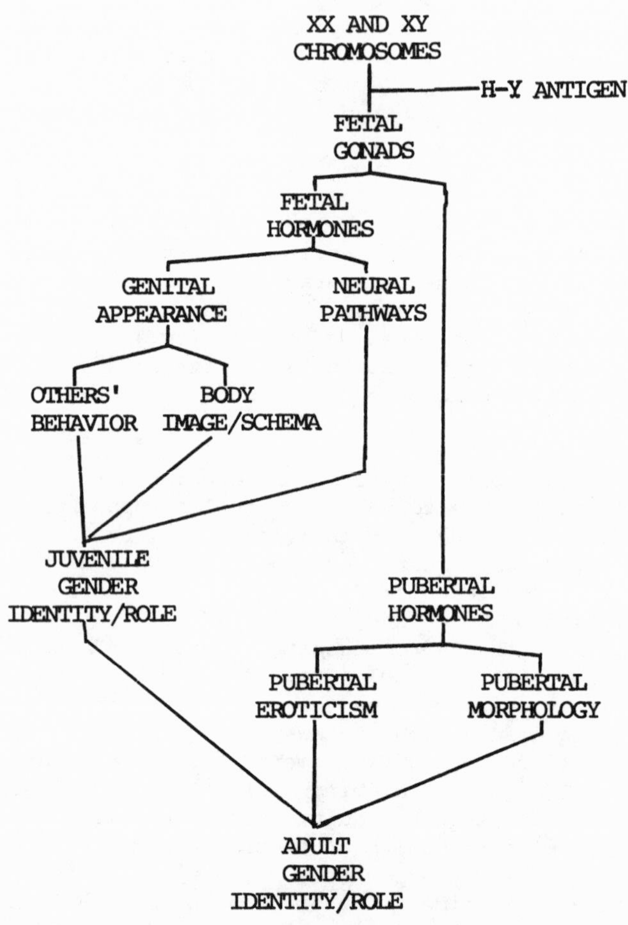

Fig. 1. Diagram to illustrate the sequential and interactional components of gender identity differentiation. From J. Money & A. Ehrhardt, Man and woman: Boy and girl. Copyright © 1972 by The Johns Hopkins University Press. Reproduced by permission.

It is also possible to conclude that humans begin life with a "bisexual" behavioral program and that rearing and experience cause part of the program to be "de-activated" (Money & Ehrhardt 1968), and part to be enhanced. This provides another mechanism by which cultural and social factors could influence psychosexual differentiation.

Consistent with this epigenetic determination of gender is the considerable plasticity in human sex-related behavior that has been shown to occur both within and between cultures (see, for example, Ford & Beach 1951; Martin & Voorhies 1975; Mead 1935). Such plasticity is a highly adaptive product of our evolution, for it allows each culture to arrive at a set of sex roles uniquely suited to its particular ecological demands without having to "wait" thousands of years for genetic changes to provide them.

Readers who still doubt that human gender identity is malleable will find food for thought in a report of a pair of physically normal monozygotic male twins who were raised as different sexes (Money & Ehrhardt 1972). One of the twins accidentally suffered penile ablation during circumcision, and after consultation with doctors, was reassigned as a girl, castrated and surgically reconstructed as a female. At last report, the pair had been followed for six years, and their behavior during this time conformed nicely to the cultural stereotype of proper male and female behavior. The girl preferred dresses to slacks, took pride in her long hair, liked to be neat and clean, liked to help her mother with housework, wanted dolls for Christmas, and planned to get married some day. The boy did not mind being dirty, was not interested in housework, wanted garages with cars and gas pumps for Christmas, and wanted to be a policeman or fireman when he grew up.

It is unlikely that this divergence in psychosexual differentiation is due to the fact that only one twin had testes. The Leydig cells of the testes, the cells that are the source of androgens, are absent from the testes of prepubertal boys and levels of testosterone in the blood of prepubertal boys are low or undetectable (Benson & Migeon 1975; Grumbach et al. 1974). Interviews with the parents indicated that they had tried to shape these behavior patterns by differential treatment. But what is important is that the pressure exerted on these twins was <u>no greater</u> than that exerted on most children at that time. Since the twins were identical both genetically and in their prenatal hormone exposure, this study, in spite of its small sample size, reinforces the idea that genes and fetal hormones are not major determinants of behavioral sex differences in children. The twins are not yet old enough for us to know whether their behavior will remain divergent into adulthood, and so follow-up studies will be important.

It has been pointed out repeatedly in this paper that many studies of human sex differences and psychosexual differentiation have been inadequate methodologically or have used fruitless research strategies. I feel obligated, therefore, to suggest an alternate strategy: this research should take as its model human ethology, rather than differential psychology or psychiatry, as has been the case.

If factors such as hormones do have some kind of effect on brain development or behavior, these effects are most likely to show up in overt behavior, and especially behavior that is universal cross-culturally and at least roughly homologous to behavior seen in other animals. Behavioral measures should be validated in the field and categories of behavior should correspond to those used to describe the naturalistic behavior of nonhuman animals. In collecting the data ethological methods should be used: structured observations of behavior in real-life situations. Results indicating effects of early hormones on behavior should also be supported by data showing that the measures used really do exhibit a significant sex difference in behavior *in the population the subjects are drawn from.*

In summary, human sex related behavior is remarkably flexible. At this time there is little good evidence of significant determination by sex chromosomes or fetal hormones. That this conclusion contradicts many people's beliefs is due in part to questionable assumptions that behavior is dichotomous with respect to sex and in part to certain attitudes about the sexes that reflect cultural stereotypes. It is hoped that this review will motivate those who are interested in the evolution of human sex differences to make sure first that the differences they are trying to explain really exist, and to refrain from assuming that it has already been proven that human sex differences are programmed by fetal hormones. Or, as Barfield (1976:110) puts it, " ... while it need not and cannot be argued that the individual human being is a biological tabula rasa at birth, the slate of a priori assumptions concerning social-biological characteristics should be blank."

Summary

The literature pertaining to genetic and hormonal influences on the development of behavioral sex differences in humans is critically reviewed.

Studies of people with incongruous or conflicting sex indicators (intersexes) indicate that the predominant role of sex chromosomes and fetal hormones is to determine the external genital morphology of the individual at birth. The external appearance in turn determines the sex in terms of which the newborn will be identified and reared. For example, people with XX chromosomes, ovaries, and masculine external genitalia who are raised as males grow up to have a normal male gender identity.

Studies of people exposed to abnormal quantities of sex hormones during fetal development suggest that prenatal hormones may also have some direct, but minor, effects on behavioral differentiation. For example, females exposed to excess adrenal androgens before birth develop a feminine gender identity, but as children or adolescents they are slightly more masculine in interests and preferences than their sisters.

The effects of prenatal hormones on human behavior superficially resemble results of similar studies in nonhuman species, although at a deeper level the results are not entirely comparable. Furthermore, serious methodological problems make the results of the human experiments difficult to interpret. There is little evidence that genetic or hormonal factors are important in the development of male homosexuality.

Thus, the data that are available at this time indicate that genes and sex hormones have a relatively minor role in human psychosexual differentiation, and that human gender identity is surprisingly malleable.

Acknowledgements

I am grateful to R. Bleier, R. Goy, R. Hubbard, H.F.L. Meyer-Bahlburg, J. Money, and F. Salzman for sending preprints and other manuscripts.

Literature Cited

Baker, S. W. & A. A. Ehrhardt. 1974. Prenatal androgen, intelligence, and cognitive sex differences. In R. C. Friedman, R. M. Richart & R. L. Vande Wiele (eds.), Sex differences in behavior. Wiley, New York, pp.53-76.

Bardwick, J. M. 1971. Psychology of women. Harper & Row, New York.

Barfield, A. 1976. Biological influences on sex differences in behavior. In M. S. Teitelbaum (ed.), Sex differences. Anchor, Garden City, New York, pp. 62-121.

Baum, M. J. 1976. Effects of testosterone propionate administered perinatally on sexual behavior of female ferrets. Journal of Comparative and Physiological Psychology 90:399-410.

Beach, F. A. 1974. Human sexuality and evolution, In W. Montagna & W. A. Sadler (eds.), Reproductive behavior. Plenum, New York, pp. 333-366.

_______. 1975. Hormonal modification of sexually dimorphic behavior. Psychoneuroendocrinology 1:3-24.

_______. 1976. Cross-species comparisons and the human heritage. In F. A. Beach (ed.), Human sexuality in four perspectives. Johns Hopkins University Press, Baltimore, pp. 296-316.

Beatty, R. A. 1964. Chromosome deviations and sex in vertebrates. In C. N. Armstrong & A. J. Marshall (eds.), Intersexuality in vertebrates including man. Academic Press, London, pp. 17-144.

Benson, R. M. & C. J. Migeon. 1975. Physiological and pathological puberty and human behavior. In B. E. Eleftheriou & R. L. Sprott (eds.), Hormonal correlates of behavior. Plenum, New York, 1:155-184.

Bubenik, G. A. & G. M. Brown. 1973. Morphologic sex differences in primate brain areas involved in regulation of reproductive activity. Experientia 29:619-620.

Clark, I. J. 1977. The sexual behaviour of prenatally androgenized ewes observed in the field. Journal of Reproduction and Fertility 49:311-315.

Clemens, L. G. 1974. Neurohormonal control of male sexual behavior. In W. Montagna & W. A. Sadler (eds.), Reproductive behavior. Plenum, New York, pp. 23-54.

Dalton, K. 1968. Ante-natal progesterone and intelligence. British Journal of Psychiatry 114:1377-1383.

_______. 1976. Prenatal progesterone and educational attainments. British Journal of Psychiatry 129:438-442.

Diamond, M. 1965. A critical evaluation of the ontogeny of human sexual behavior. Quarterly Review of Biology 40:147-175.

Dörner, G. & J. Staudt. 1968. Structural changes in the preoptic anterior hypothalamic area of the male rat, following neonatal castration and androgen substitution. Neuroendocrinology 3:136-140.

Edwards, D. A. 1969. Early androgen stimulation and aggressive behavior in male and female mice. Physiology and Behavior 4:333-338.

_______ & K. G. Burge. 1971. Early androgen treatment and male and female sexual behavior in mice. Hormones and Behavior 2:49-58.

Ehrhardt, A. A. 1973. Maternalism in fetal hormonal and related syndromes. In J. Zubin & J. Money (eds.), Contemporary sexual behavior: Critical issues in the 1970s. Johns Hopkins University Press, Baltimore, pp. 99-116.

_______ & S. W. Baker. 1974. Fetal androgens, human central nervous system differentiation, and behavior sex differences. In R. C. Friedman, R. M. Richart & R. L. Vande Wiele (eds.), Sex differences in behavior. Wiley, New York, pp. 33-52.

_______ & J. Money. 1967. Progestin-induced hermaphroditism: IQ and psychosexual identity in a study of ten girls. Journal of Sex Research 3:83-100.

_______ , R. Epstein & J. Money. 1968. Fetal androgens and female gender identity in the early-treated adrenogenital syndrome. Johns Hopkins Medical Journal 122:160-167.

_______ , N. Greenberg & J. Money. 1970. Female gender identity and absence of fetal gonadal hormones: Turner's syndrome. Johns Hopkins Medical Journal 126:237-248.

_______ , G. C. Grisanti & H. F. L. Meyer-Bahlburg. 1977. Prenatal exposure to medroxyprogesterone acetate (MPA) in girls. Psychoneuroendocrinology 2:391-398.

Ellis, A. 1963. Constitutional factors in homosexuality: A reexamination of the evidence. In H. G. Beigel (ed.), Advances in sex research. Harper & Row, New York, pp. 161-186.

Feder, H. H. & G. N. Wade. 1974. Integrative actions of perinatal hormones on neural tissues mediating adult sexual behavior. In F. O. Schmitt & F. G. Worden (eds.), The Neurosciences: Third study program. MIT Press, Cambridge, Massachusetts, pp. 583-586.

Ford, C. S. & F. A. Beach. 1951. Patterns of sexual behavior. Harper & Row, New York.

Frodi, A., J. Macaulay & P. R. Thome. 1977. Are women always less aggressive than men? Psychological Bulletin 84:634-660.

Ganong, W. F. 1973. Review of Medical Physiology. Sixth edition. Lange Medical Publications, Los Altos, California.

Gebhard, P. H. 1973. Sex differences in sexual response. Archives of Sexual Behavior 2:201-203.

Gorski, R. A. 1971. Gonadal hormones and the perinatal development of neuroendocrine function. In W. F. Ganong & L. Martini (eds.), Frontiers in neuroendocrinology. Oxford University Press, New York, pp. 237-290.

Goy, R. W. 1968. Organizing effects of androgen on the behaviour of rhesus monkeys. In R. P. Michael (ed.), Endocrinology and human behaviour. Oxford University Press, London, pp. 12-31.

_______ . 1970. Experimental control of psychosexuality. Philosophical Transactions of the Royal Society of London B 259:149-162.

_______ . 1979. Development of play and mounting behaviour in female rhesus virilized prenatally with esters of testosterone or dihydrotestosterone. Proceedings of the Sixth International Congress of Primatology. In Press.

_______ & J. A. Resko. 1972. Gonadal hormones and behavior of normal and pseudohermaphroditic nonhuman female primates. Recent Progress in Hormone Research 28:707-733.

Gray J. A., S. Levine & P. L. Broadhurst. 1965. Gonadal hormone injections in infancy and adult emotional behaviour. Animal Behaviour 13:33-45.

Grumbach, M. M., G. D. Grave & F. E. Mayer (eds.). 1974. The control of the onset of puberty. Wiley, New York.

Hamburg, D. A. & D. T. Lunde. 1966. Sex hormones in the development of sex differences in human behavior. In E. E. Maccoby (ed.), The development of sex differences. Stanford University Press, Stanford, California, pp. 1-23.

Hampson, J. L. 1965. Determinants of psychosexual orientation. In F. A. Beach (ed.), Sex and behavior. Wiley, New York, pp. 108-132.

_______ & J. G. Hampson. 1961. The ontogenesis of sexual behavior in man. In W. C. Young (ed.), Sex and internal secretions. Williams & Wilkins, Baltimore, 2:1401-1432.

Harlow, H. F. 1965. Sexual behavior in the rhesus monkey. In F. A. Beach (ed.), Sex and behavior. Wiley, New York, pp. 234-265.

Heston, L. L. & J. Shields. 1968. Homosexuality in twins. Archives of General Psychiatry 18:149-160.

Hoffman, M. L. 1977. Sex differences in empathy and related behaviors. Psychological Bulletin 84:712-722.

Hutt, C. 1972. Sex differences in human development. Human Development 15:153-170.

Kallmann, F. J. 1952. Comparative twin study on the genetic aspects of male homosexuality. Journal of Nervous and Mental Disease 115:283-298.

_______ . 1960. Discussion of "Homosexuality and heterosexuality in identical twins." Psychosomatic Medicine 22:258-259.

Kleiman, D. 1977. Monogamy in mammals. Quarterly Review of Biology 52:39-69.

Korner, A. F. 1974. Methodological considerations in studying sex differences in the behavioral functioning of newborns. In R. C. Friedman, R. M. Richart & R. L. Vande Wiele (eds.), Sex differences in behavior. Wiley, New York, pp. 197-208.

Lisk, R. D. (ed.). 1974. Neonatal hormone treatment and adult sexual behavior in rodents. MSS Information Corporation, New York.

Luttge, W. G. 1971. The role of gonadal hormones in the sexual behavior of the rhesus monkey and human: A literature survey. Archives of Sexual Behavior 1:61-87.

Maccoby, E. E. & C. N. Jacklin. 1974. The psychology of sex differences. Stanford University Press, Stanford, California.

Martin, M. K. & B. Voorhies. 1975. Female of the species. Columbia University Press, New York.

Masica, D. N., J. Money & A. A. Ehrhardt. 1971. Fetal feminization and female gender identity in the testicular feminizing syndrome of androgen insensitivity. Archives of Sexual Behavior 1:131-142.

Mason, J. W. 1975. Psychologic stress and endocrine function. In E. J. Sachar (ed.), Topics in psychoendocrinology. Grune & Stratton, New York, pp. 1-18.

Mead, M. 1935. Sex and temperament in three primitive societies. Morrow, New York.

Melges, F. T. & D. A. Hamburg. 1976. Psychological effects of hormonal changes in women. In F. A. Beach (ed.), Human sexuality in four perspectives. Johns Hopkins University Press, Baltimore, pp. 269-295.

Meyer-Bahlburg, H. F. L. 1977. Sex hormones and male homosexuality in comparative perspective. Archives of Sexual Behavior 6:297-325.

_______, G. C. Grisanti & A. A. Ehrhardt. 1977. Prenatal effects of sex hormones on human male behavior: Medroxyprogesterone acetate (MPA). Psychoneuroendocrinology 2:383-390.

Money, J. 1973. Pornography in the home: A topic in medical education. In J. Zubin & J. Money (eds.), Contemporary sexual behavior: Critical issues in the 1970s. Johns Hopkins University Press, Baltimore, pp. 409-440.

_______. 1976. Human hermaphroditism. In F. A. Beach (ed.), Human sexuality in four perspectives. Johns Hopkins University, Baltimore, pp. 62-86.

_______ & A. A. Ehrhardt. 1968. Prenatal hormonal exposure: Possible effects on behaviour in man. In R. P. Michael (ed.), Endocrinology and human behaviour. Oxford University Press, London, pp. 32-48.

_______ & A. A. Ehrhardt. 1972. Man and woman, boy and girl. Johns Hopkins University Press, Baltimore.

_______ & V. Lewis. 1966. IQ, genetics, and accelerated growth: Adrenogenital syndrome. Bulletin of the Johns Hopkins Hospital 118:365-373.

_______ & M. Schwartz. 1976. Fetal androgens in the early treated adrenogenital syndrome of 46 XX hermaphroditism: Influence on assertive and aggressive types of behavior. Aggressive Behavior 2:19-30.

_______, A. A. Ehrhardt & D. N. Masica. 1968. Fetal feminization induced by androgen insensitivity in the testicular feminizing syndrome: Effect on marriage and maternalism. Johns Hopkins Medical Journal 123:106-114.

Morrell, J. I., D. B. Kelley & D. W. Pfaff. 1975. Sex steroid binding in the brains of vertebrates. In K. M. Knigge, D. E. Scott, H. Kobayashi & S. Ishii (eds.), Brain-Endocrine interaction II. S. Karger AG., Basel, pp. 230-256.

Moss, H. A. 1974. Early sex differences and mother-infant interaction. In R. C. Friedman, R. M. Richart & R. L. Vande Wiele (eds.), Sex differences in behavior. Wiley, New York, pp. 149-164.

Mountcastle, V. B. 1974. Medical physiology, Vol 1. 13th edition. Mosby, St. Louis.

Nadler, R. D. 1973. Further evidence on the intrahypothalamic locus for androgenization of female rats. Neuroendocrinology 12:110-119.

Pfaff, D. 1966. Morphological changes in the brains of adult male rats after neonatal castration. Journal of Endocrinology 36:415-416.

Phoenix, C. H. 1974. Prenatal testosterone in the nonhuman primate and its consequences for behavior. In R. C. Friedman, R. M. Richart & R. L. Vande Wiele (eds.), Sex differences in behavior. Wiley, New York, pp. 19-32.

_______, R. W. Goy, A. A. Gerall & W. C. Young. 1959. Organizing action of prenatally administered testosterone propionate on the tissues mediating mating behavior in the female guinea pig. Endocrinology 65:369-382.

Pincus, J. H. & G. J. Tucker. 1974. Behavioral neurology. Oxford University Press, New York.

Quadagno, D. M., R. Briscoe & J. S. Quadagno. 1977. Effect of perinatal gonadal hormones on selected nonsexual behavior patterns: A critical assessment of the nonhuman and human literature. Psychological Bulletin 84:62-80.

Raisman, G. & P. M. Field. 1971. Sexual dimorphism in the preoptic area of the rat. Science 173:731-733.

Reinisch, J. M. 1974. Fetal hormones, the brain, and human sex differences: A heuristic, integrative review of the recent literature. Archives of Sexual Behavior 3:51-90.

_______. 1977. Prenatal exposure of human foetuses to synthetic progestin and oestrogen affects personality. Nature 266:561-562.

_______ & W. G. Karow. 1977. Prenatal exposure to synthetic progestins and estrogens: Effects on human development. Archives of Sexual Behavior 6:257-288.

Richards, M. P. M., J. F. Bernal & Y. Brackbill. 1976. Early behavioral differences: Gender or circumcision? Developmental Psychobiology 9:89-95.

Rosenthal, D. 1970. Genetic theory and abnormal behavior. McGraw Hill, New York.

Rossi, A. S. 1973. Maternalism, sexuality, and the new feminism. In J. Zubin & J. Money (eds.), Contemporary sexual behavior: Critical issues in the 1970s. Johns Hopkins University Press, Baltimore, pp. 145-174.

Sackett, G. P. 1974. Sex differences in rhesus monkeys following varied rearing experience. In R. C. Friedman, R. M. Richart & R. L. Vande Wiele (eds.), Sex differences in behavior. Wiley, New York, pp. 99-122.

Schmidt, G. & V. Sigusch. 1973. Women's sexual arousal. In J. Zubin & J. Money (eds.), Contemporary sexual behavior: Critical issues in the 1970s. Johns Hopkins University Press, Baltimore, pp. 117-144.

Sheridan, P. J., M. Sar & W. E. Stumpf. 1974. Autoradiographic localization of ^{3}H-estradiol or its metabolites in the central nervous system of the developing rat. Endocrinology 94:1386-1390.

Thoman, E. B., P. H. Leiderman & J. P. Olson. 1972. Neonate-mother interaction during breast-feeding. Developmental Psychology 6:110-118.

Waber, D. P. 1976. Sex differences in cognition: A function of maturation rate? Science 192:572-574.

Wachtel, S. S. 1977. H-Y antigen and the genetics of sex determination. Science 198:797-799.

Wolfheim, J. H. 1977. Sex differences in behavior in a group of captive juvenile talapoin monkeys (Miopithecus talapoin). Behaviour 63:110-128.

Yalom, I. D., R. Green & N. Fisk. 1973. Prenatal exposure to female hormones. Archives of General Psychiatry 28:554-561.

Young, W. C. 1961. The hormones and mating behavior. In W. C. Young (ed.), Sex and internal secretions. Williams & Wilkins, Baltimore, 2:1173-1239.

_______ . 1967. Prenatal gonadal hormones and behavior in the adult. In J. Zubin & H. F. Hunt (eds.), Comparative psychopathology. Grune & Stratton, New York, pp. 173-183.

Zuger, B. 1970. Gender role determination: A critical review of the evidence from hermaphroditism. Psychosomatic Medicine 32:449-463.

Zussman, J. U., P. P. Zussman & K. Dalton. 1975. Postpubertal effects of prenatal administration of progesterone. Paper presented at the Society for Research in Child Development, Denver.

William Irons

17. Is Yomut Social Behavior Adaptive?

The research reported here is relevant to the general question of whether human social behavior tends to assume forms which are adaptive in the biological sense. An individual's behavior is adaptive in this sense if it makes probable the survival of his or her genes in future gene pools. One form of behavior is more adaptive than another, in a particular environment, if it consistently leads to a higher genetic representation in descending generations for individuals exhibiting the behavior in that particular environment.

There are good theoretical reasons for suspecting that culturally shaped forms of human behavior are frequently adaptive in this sense. This theoretical expectation derives from the proposition that the human capacity and propensity to vary behavior in response to particular local cultural traditions is itself an adaptation (Irons 1979a: 7-8). This adaptation enables human beings to track various features of their environment (including the behavior of conspecifics) and mold their behavior to forms which are biologically optimal given that environment. This theoretical position does not necessarily imply any consciousness on the part of human beings of the biological consequences of their behavior. An explanation of these theoretical considerations can be found in other publications (Alexander 1979; Irons 1979a).

It is important to keep in mind that the theoretical statement that human social behavior tends to assume forms which are biologically adaptive does not imply that such behavior is not malleable in response to environmental influences (Irons 1979a:5-10). It is also important to keep in mind that this theoretical statement is more likely to be correct for populations which have not yet experienced the reduction in fertility by means of contraception which is associated with the demographic transition (Irons in press).

The question of the adaptiveness of human social behavior is addressed here in terms of certain aspects of the social behavior of a single human population, the Yomut Turkmen of Iran. This is a population which has not yet experienced the fertility reduction associated with the demographic transition. The general question of the adaptiveness or nonadaptiveness of human social behavior can only be resolved, in my opinion, by a large number of empirical studies of the sort presented here. If we take as our basic theoretical starting point the proposition that the capacity and propensity of human individuals to vary their behavior in response to local cultural traditions are adaptations (Irons 1979a:7-8), then we must examine behaviors shaped by a large number of local traditions in terms of their possible adaptiveness before we can draw a general conclusion applicable across the entire range of human societies.

Some Alternative Working Hypotheses: Group Versus Individual Selection

The hypothesized adaptive effects of human social behavior are seen as ultimately the result of natural selection even though a large number of intermediate environmental, ontogenetic, and physiological processes can also be seen as causing these behaviors and their effects (Daly & Wilson, 1978:8-13; Wilson 1975:23). This means that the level at which selection is potent in producing adaptations should be reflected in the precise nature of any adaptive effects that can be identified (Williams 1966, 1971). Group selection, that is, selection in the form of the differential extinction and expansion of whole breeding populations, would favor one type of effect of behavior on survival and reproduction, whereas individual selection, that is, selection in the form of the differential reproductive success of individual organisms within a breeding population, would favor different forms of behavior having different demographic effects. It is, therefore, relevant to ask what types of behavior group selection and individual selection would favor and to inquire whether either of these forms of behavior exist.

V. C. Wynne-Edwards (1962) hypothesized that group selection at the level of breeding populations produces behavioral adaptations which homeostatically regulate population density in such a way as to prevent environmental degradation. Environmental degradation for Wynne-

Edwards meant destruction of food resources. He reasoned that if the members of a particular population reproduced as long as food resources were sufficient to allow reproduction, population would continue to grow until food resources became scarce. Scarcity of food resources would lead to more intensive exploitation of the resources which would lead to the destruction of these resources.

For example, a predator once its population became more dense would begin to crop the prey species on which it depended for food more intensively. This would lead to a decline in the number of prey which would set off a vicious cycle of still more intensive cropping of prey and still greater scarcity of prey. The ultimate result would be an ecological crash in which both prey and predator populations would go extinct.

Following such a crash, members of the prey species from other areas which had not recently experienced such a crash would recolonize the area vacated, and this would set the stage for later recolonization by the predator species. If the predator species consisted of a large number of local breeding populations occupying distinct territories which only rarely interbreed, then the process of local-group extinction and later recolonization by different groups could act as a form of natural selection at the level of local breeding populations within a larger metapopulation.

This process of group selection, Wynne-Edwards reasoned, would favor populations which did not continue to reproduce as long as food resources were sufficient to support reproduction. It would favor populations which somehow brought population growth to a halt before food resources became scarce. This, he hypothesized, was frequently accomplished by an evolved tendency to adhere to social conventions which would cause fertility to decline, with increasing population density, to a point of zero population growth before food resources became scarce. These conventions, he suggested, took the form of a conventionalized competition for some token resource--such as a breeding territory larger than needed in terms of food resources, or a high position in a dominance hierarchy--which would become scarce before food resources became scarce. Individuals who failed to acquire the required token would refrain from reproduction even though they could acquire sufficient food resources to do so.

When population density was very low, token resources could easily be acquired and high fertility and population growth would occur. Thus, if below a certain density, the population would grow until reaching its equilibrium density. If, on the other hand, a population should achieve a density greater than its equilibrium (as a result, for example, of contraction of its territory), token resources would become scarce enough to cause a decline in density until the equilibrium density were reached. Hence, such a group-selected population could be described as homeostatically regulating its density in relation to resources.

Local populations which were genetically predisposed to regulate fertility in terms of such conventions would be favored by group selection over those which were predisposed to breed maximally. Such populations would not experience crashes, and could periodically recolonize territory left vacant by maximally reproducing populations which had crashed. During the initial stage of colonization, population density would be especially low, and growth would occur allowing the colonizers to fill the vacant territory up to their equilibrium density. The selective process would thus occur among genetically different local populations within a larger metapopulation.

Wynne-Edwards (1962) emphasized that social limitation of fertility had to bring population growth to a halt before food shortages caused an increase in mortality rates. He reasoned that since animals always tend to react to food shortages threatening mortality by more intensive cropping, populations had to be brought into balance before mortality began to increase owing to food scarcity.

An important theoretical difficulty with the Wynne-Edwards hypothesis lies in the fact that the hypothesized social regulation of fertility would not be favored by individual level selection (Williams 1966, 1971). This can be seen by considering what would happen within a single breeding population if individuals predisposed to socially regulate fertility in the manner hypothesized by Wynne-Edwards were to compete with individuals predisposed to maximize their Darwinian fitness. An individual's Darwinian fitness is the number of offspring he or she produces which survive to become members of the breeding pool of the next generation. This can also be referred to as net reproduction (see below). Individuals genetically predisposed to maximize Darwinian fitness would reproduce if food resources permitted whether or not they had acquired the Wynne-Edwardsian token. As a result they would reproduce at a higher rate than their group-selected competitors, and genes predisposing maximization of Darwinian fitness would increase within the local breeding population at the expense of genes favored by group selection.

Thus, once individuals predisposed to maximize Darwinian fitness enter a group-selected local population, they outreproduce the group-selected members of the breeding population and destroy the population-wide predisposition to limit reproduction in the manner which favors long-term group survival. Once this happens, the group-level adaptation of social limitation of fertility can be maintained in the metapopulation only by the continued extinction of all local breeding populations entered by individuals predisposed to maximize Darwinian fitness. Many evolutionary biologists believe that this requires higher levels of whole breeding population extinctions and lower levels of interpopulation migration than in fact occur in most species (Williams 1971). The theoretical issue here is which level of selection will be potent in producing adaptations when group selection and individual selection are favoring contradictory behaviors. This is a theoretical issue tested in this study.

The Wynne-Edwards hypothesis and the alternative individual selection hypothesis create different expectations concerning the responses of individuals, and of population-wide vital rates to increasing population density. The Wynne-Edwards hypothesis predicts that as density increases social limitation of fertility through competition for token resources should increase causing birth rates to decline to the point of zero population growth before food scarcity causes increases in mortality. The individual selection hypothesis predicts that individuals will not limit fertility before food resources become scarce, and further that as increases in population density cause scarcities limiting reproduction they will compete for these scarce resources and will reproduce and rear offspring to the maximal extent they are able given the resources they acquire through competition.

In fact, individual selection can be shown to favor a maximization of inclusive fitness rather than Darwinian fitness (Hamilton 1964). I believe, however, that in populations in which most adults reproduce, behavioral models assuming a maximization of Darwinian fitness will serve well as good first approximations of the behaviors which will maximize inclusive fitness. (This would, in contrast, not be the case in species in which many adults do not reproduce at all, but instead aid close kin to reproduce, e.g., the social insects.)

Behaviors which are adaptive in terms of group selection are often described as altruistic. Altruism in this sense means an organism's behaving in a way which lowers its own Darwinian fitness and raises that of other individuals. According to the Wynne-Edwards model, organisms behave altruistically in adhering to social conventions which prevent them from reproducing when they are otherwise able. The beneficiaries of this altruism are remote future generations of the altruist's breeding populations which, because of earlier limitation on breeding, enjoy a more secure food supply. Such behaviors--if they exist for the reasons given by Wynne-Edwards--are adaptive in the sense that they increase an organism's genetic representation in remoter generations at the cost of lessening its representation in immediately descending generations. The altruism hypothesized by Wynne-Edwards is different in an important way from that hypothesized in association with kin selection by W. D. Hamilton (1964); the beneficiaries of the latter are close relatives in the same, or close, generations.

Behaviors which are hypothesized by the alternative individual selection model are adaptive in the sense that they tend to increase genetic representation in immediately descending generations, and in the absence of sufficiently potent group selection, tend also to increase genetic representation in remoter generations as well.

The research reported here attempts to determine whether behaviors adaptive in terms of either level of selection can be shown to exist among the Yomut. This, in effect, creates two alternative working hypotheses: (1) Yomut social behavior assumes forms favored by group selection; and (2) Yomut social behavior assumes forms favored by individual selection. These hypotheses are referred to below as the group-selection hypothesis and the individual-selection hypothesis.

Each of these hypotheses were translated into a set of more specific hypothetical statements which are both appropriate to the Yomut ethnographic setting and testable using available data. These statements were then tested empirically. Those derived from the group-selection hypothesis were falsified; those derived from the individual-selection hypothesis were borne out. Potentially the data could have produced the reverse; they also could have falsified both hypotheses. If both had been falsified this would have lent support to the logical null hypothesis, that culturally shaped forms of human social behavior do not tend to be adaptive in any biological sense. Theoretical arguments supporting this hypothesis are also available in various publications (Cloak 1975; Dawkins 1976:203-215; Richerson &

Boyd 1978; Sahlins 1976). The data analyses, however, do not support this third hypothesis.

The results presented here are tentative because the work of analysis is not yet complete. Further data analyses are in progress and the results of these will be published in future publications. It is not clear at this point whether future analyses will also support the individual-selection hypothesis.

The Data

All the above hypotheses are statements about the effect of behavior on survivorship and fertility. They are concerned with both the effect of an individual's behavior on his or her own reproductive performance and its effect on the reproductive performance of related individuals.

The data are records of the economic, social, and demographic history of 566 Yomut households gathered in 1973-1974. They were collected from a sample of households constructed with the aid of a sampling expert, Alan Ross of Johns Hopkins University. The sample was designed to maximize chances of discerning variation within the sample population rather than to maximize the accuracy of estimates of overall population parameters.

The data were collected in the Turkmen language using a questionnaire written by myself and Daniel Bates of Hunter College, CUNY. Before beginning the survey the questionnaire was pretested in two villages. The male interviews were all done by native speakers of Turkmen, and 95% of the interviews were followed up by a second shorter interview controlling for the effectiveness of the initial one. The control was done by myself, Daniel Bates, or a different trained Turkmen interviewer. My wife, Marjorie Rogasner, interviewed the oldest woman in half of the sample households (also in Turkmen) in order to gather additional data from a smaller sample and to provide a further check on the original interviews. Our joint efforts also included a similar survey of the Gokleng Turkmen, but only Yomut data are reported here.

The statistical analyses reported below were designed in consultation with a sociological demographer, Clifford Clogg of Pennsylvania State University. At the beginning of the 1973-1974 survey project I had completed 18 months of participant observation among the Yomut, and the design of the survey project was guided by this earlier experience.

The Population Under Study

The Yomut were, until about 1950, a nomadic population who made their living by a mixture of agriculture and herding, and who had experienced limited government intervention in their affairs. Since that date they have experienced greater government intervention in their affairs, a shift in technology to mechanized agriculture, an increase in economic productivity, and some access to modern medicine. These changes have been carried farther in some Yomut communities than in others. The survey included both communities which have experienced a large measure of modernization and those which have experienced minimal modernization. Differences in the variables reported here do not vary in any important way with the extent of modernization. For an ethnographic description of the Yomut, readers can consult my monograph on the group (Irons 1975). For historical material on the Turkmen, one can refer to Barthold's (1962) history of the Turkmen.

Analyzing a population like that of the Yomut in terms of natural-selection theory provides a test of the hypothesis that natural selection is relevant not only to hunters and gatherers, or simple horticulturalists, but also to populations which use more recent and more sophisticated technologies but are nevertheless pre-industrial.

The Group-Selection Hypothesis

The most reasonable application of the Wynne-Edwards hypothesis to Yomut society is one in which bridewealth is interpreted as the conventionalized token limiting fertility as population density increases. Bridewealth among the Turkmen is fixed by convention at 110 sheep and goats and is not subject to negotiation in terms of the ability of the bridegroom's family to pay. The amount of wealth is large, representing about two to four years' income for a family of median wealth in the community in which I lived in 1966 and 1967. The variable figure two to four is stated because income is highly variable from year to year. A fuller description of the economic factors relevant to this statement and to the conventions governing bridewealth is available in the monograph mentioned above (Irons 1975: 178-192).

The model tested states that, as population becomes denser, the time required for families to gather bridewealth for their sons increases and fewer and fewer men seek brides each year. As a consequence, women must wait longer and longer for husbands. Delays in marriage combined with

Moslem standards of sexual purity would lead to lower fertility until a point of homeostasis is achieved. At this point families which have sufficient resources to support reproduction but lack the additional token resources needed for marriage would be refraining from reproduction. Mortality should remain stable rather than act as one of the factors bringing population into balance.

In the last 30 years, the Yomut have experienced an increase in economic productivity owing to adoption of new technology (Okazaki 1968; Gurgānī 1969). Mechanized agriculture has allowed much previously uncultivated land to be brought under production, and has increased economic productivity per person.

The data collected in 1973-74 allow some measure of the changes in wealth over time. The data on each household include a record of the patrimony which the household received when first established. These patrimonies come in the form of land and livestock and were recorded that way in our survey. Since land of different types (e.g., irrigated versus unirrigated) and in different locations has different values per hectare, and since both livestock of several varieties (sheep, goats, cows, horses, camels, and waterbuffalo) and land were included, comparisons were difficult without deriving a single quantitative value for each patrimony. This was done by substituting for each item in the patrimony, its monetary value in Iranian currency in 1974. By using 1974 values (rather than values current when the patrimony was received), the figures derived are in effect controlled for inflation. In fact, I believe there is good reason to assume that changes in these figures are underestimates of increases in the real value of patrimonies, and hence underestimates of general trends in wealth. These figures reflect only increases in the amount of land and livestock. During this period there have also been increases in the real productivity of land owing to mechanization and integration into world markets (Okazaki 1968; Gurgānī 1969). A shift toward greater emphasis on agriculture has also improved the effective conversion rate when livestock are sold and the money is used to purchase grain or other agricultural produce.

The median value of patrimonies received 20 or more years ago is 2400 tumans. The median for those received 19 or fewer years ago is 4520 tumans. A median test for a difference between these two groups of patrimonies shows that the trend is statistically significant (Table 1).

Table 1. Median test for increase in the value of patrimonies.

Above or below median for total sample	Patrimonies received 0-19 years ago	Patrimonies received 20 or more years ago
Above	179	92
Below	136	133

$\chi^2 = 13.08$ $p<.001$

If the Yomut homeostatically regulate their population density in the manner suggested by Wynne-Edwards, they should respond to an increase in resources by lessening social limitation of fertility. This should be reflected in earlier and earlier marriage as resources per person increase. While this occurs, mortality rates should remain basically constant. Mortality might conceivably fluctuate in response to some density-independent factor during such a period of growth, but it should not act as a density-dependent regulator of rates of population growth.

The data falsify this model. In fact, over the last 30 years mortality has undergone dramatic changes while fertility has increased less sharply. Mortality appears from the data to be acting as the strongest density-dependent factor controlling rates of growth. The increase in fertility is a result of an increase in marital fertility rather than a decline in the age at first marriage (Table 2) or a decline in the average number of years spent married by most women during their fecund years. The results in Table 2 are clear without any tests of significance. Thus, the data indicate that the change in fertility is not a result of lessening the social limitation of fertility as the Wynne-Edwards hypothesis predicts. Rather it appears to reflect a generally healthier population which is physiologically able to reproduce at a faster rate.

Although the data do not indicate any change in the age at first marriage, they do indicate a change in fertility. This can be seen by comparing cohorts of women of different ages (who, therefore, bore their children at different time periods) in terms of the average number of children they had borne by ages 30 and 40 (Tables 3 and 4). The Z scores were calculated by assuming that completed fertility at both ages 30 and 40 has a multinomial distribution with possible outcomes from 0 to 10. Estimates of

Table 2. Variation in age at first marriage among the Yomut women over the past 39 years.

Years ago married	Ave. age at first marriage	Number of women
0-4	15.45	148
5-9	15.73	149
10-14	14.27	110
15-19	13.69	110
20-24	15.06	78
25-29	14.41	74
30-39	14.71	72

Table 3. Variation in completed fertility of Yomut women at age 30 over the past 29 years.

Current age of women	Number of children born by age 30	Number of women in sample	Sample variance in completed fertility	Z scores for differences in adjacent cohorts	P-value
30-39	4.24	173	0.0182	2.470	.01
40-49	3.71	166	0.0271	2.371	.01
50-59	3.06	97	0.0478		

Table 4. Variation in completed fertility of Yomut women at age 40 over the past 30 years.

Current age of women	Number of children born by age 40	Number of women in sample	Sample variance in completed fertility	Z scores for differences in adjacent cohorts	P-value
40-49	6.47	166	0.0530	1.784	.04
50-59	5.77	97	0.1009		

the probability of each outcome for each cohort were made from the data, and these estimates were then used to compute sample variances and Z scores. A fuller description of this and the other statistical tests for variation in demographic parameters will appear in future publications.

There is a possible problem in interpreting the data in Tables 3 and 4. More frequent forgetting of births which are remoter in time could produce an apparent lower fertility at earlier time periods where no differential actually existed. If one assumes that the figures in Tables 3 and 4 are mere products of forgetting and that fertility has not changed over time, the Wynne-Edwards hypothesis would still be falsified.

There is reason, however, to believe the data are accurate for the last 35 years. Forgetting of deceased individuals is more likely than forgetting of living individuals. This trend in forgetting would create an apparent lower death rate at earlier time periods. In fact, however, the temporal trend in mortality (see below) is opposite that which forgetting would create. I think this indicates that the data are accurate. If one assumes that despite this there has been some significant amount of forgetting, then one would be forced to conclude that the earlier death rates were higher than my figures indicate. This would strengthen the inference against the Wynne-Edwards hypothesis.

The fertility records of women interviewed included survivorship data on all children born. Since these data extended over a long time period, they allow an estimate of changes in mortality over time. A large sample of data, however, was available only for the earlier years of life. Thus, a test for changes in death rates was made by comparing survivorship in the age interval zero-19 years during the last five years and during the time period 21-35 years ago. Using the survivorship data the number of individuals reaching each birth day was calculated. Of these, the portion surviving to the next birth day and the proportion dying before the next birth day were then calculated. These proportions were taken as estimates of the probabilities of either surviving the age interval in question or of dying during that interval. For ages five through 19, data for five year intervals were pooled. Assuming a Poisson distribution, the variances in the sample mean for each age interval were then calculated (Tables 5 and 6). An age standardized death rate was calculated by summing the rate for specific age intervals, and a variance in the sample mean for this rate was calculated by summing the variances for

Table 5. Variation in male mortality over the past 35 years.

Age(s) during interval	Survivorship and mortality			
	Last 5 years			
	Chances to die (l_x)	Deaths (D_x)	Estimated mortality	Estimated variance in mortality
Less than 1	512	66	.1289	.000252
1	322	18	.0559	.000174
2	229	4	.0175	.000075
3	153	4	.0261	.000170
4	84	0	.0000	.000000
5-9	871	1	.0011	.000001
10-14	695	4	.0058	.000009
15-19	587	0	.0000	.000000
Age standardized death rate			.2353	
Variance of sample mean of age standardized death rate				.000597

Table 5. (continued)

Age(s) during interval	Survivorship and mortality, 21-35 years ago: Chances to die (l_x)	Deaths (D_x)	Estimated mortality	Estimated variance in mortality
Less than 1	411	67	.1630	.000396
1	344	45	.1308	.000380
2	299	27	.0903	.000302
3	262	12	.0480	.000183
4	260	6	.0230	.000089
5-9	822	12	.0146	.000018
10-14	440	0	.0000	.000000
15-19	278	2	.0072	.000026
Age standardized death			.4759	
Variance of sample mean of age standardized death rate				.001178
		Z=5.27	p<.0001	

Table 6. Variation in female mortality over the past 35 years

Age(s) during interval	Survivorship and mortality — Last 5 years			
	Chances to die (l_x)	Deaths (D_x)	Estimated mortality	Estimated variance in mortality
Less than 1	465	58	.1247	.000268
1	309	10	.0324	.000105
2	248	10	.0403	.000162
3	153	1	.0065	.000043
4	71	0	.0000	.000000
5-9	803	4	.0050	.000005
10-14	637	0	.0000	.000000
15-19	531	4	.0075	.000014
Age standardized death rate			.2154	
Variance of sample mean of age standardized death rate				.000597

Table 6. (continued)

Age(s) during interval	Survivorship and mortality			
	21-35 years ago			
	Chances to die (l_x)	Deaths (D_x)	Estimated mortality	Estimated variance in mortality
Less than 1	357	46	.1288	.000361
1	311	34	.1093	.000352
2	277	16	.0578	.000209
3	251	12	.0478	.000190
4	249	2	.0080	.000032
5-9	676	8	.0118	.000018
10-14	350	2	.0057	.000016
15-19	190	0	.0000	.000000
Age standardized death rate			.3692	
Variance of sample mean of age standardized death rate				.001178
		$Z=3.63$	$p<.0002$	

each age interval. This procedure corresponds to using weightings of one for each age category (see Kitagawa 1964). These age standardized death rates and variances were calculated for two time periods: zero-five years ago and 21-35 years ago. From these statistics Z scores and p-values were computed to determine the probability that the differences resulted from sampling error. The Z scores and p-values reported in Tables 5 and 6 are the results of one-tailed tests of the proposition that death rates were higher in the earlier time period.

The interpretation of variation in death rates over time is complicated by the fact that they could be explained by improvements in medical care and public health rather than increases in economic resources per person. The 35-year time period preceding our survey in 1974 was one in which the quality of medical care available in the nearest urban center and the effectiveness of public health measures have improved. One could infer that the changes in mortality indicated by the data are purely the result of the changes in medical care and public health. However, I believe it is more reasonable to assume the improvement in mortality is the result of many causes: better diet, more adequate clothing and shelter, greater freedom from more stressful and risky forms of labor, as well as improvement in medical care and public health (Cf. also Wrigley 1969 on this issue). As long as increasing wealth per person, i.e., resources per person, improves survivorship through such intermediate variables as diet, the data justify inference against the Wynne-Edwards predictions concerning mortality.

Future data analyses will examine the question of the effects of wealth on vital rates through intermediate variables other than medical care. This can be done because wealth and access to medical care vary independently. In remoter areas, where access to urban medical care is more difficult, there is less tendency to seek such care regardless of wealth. Data on recent use of urban medical care and its cost were recorded for each household, and this I believe will allow tests of the proposition that wealth has a positive effect on health and survivorship through intermediate variables other than the extent and quality of medical care.

The data below on synchronic variation in mortality can aid in deciding what to infer concerning the relative effect of public health versus other factors on mortality. I know of no reason, in the Yomut social context, to assume that wealthier individuals somehow enjoy greater benefits from public health measures than do poorer individuals. Thus, although the effectiveness of public health measures has improved over time, at any one point in time, individuals of differing wealth can be assumed, I believe, to enjoy roughly equal benefits from public health measures. Thus, synchronic variation in mortality--which the data below show to exist--justify the inference, in my opinion, that variation in the effectiveness of public health measures is not the only factor causing differences in survivorship in this population. The other factors appear to be the effect of wealth on diet, clothing, shelter, and types of labor performed, on the one hand, and the effect of wealth in the form of the ability to purchase medical care in nearby urban centers. If the synchronic differences in survivorship can be assumed to be purely a result of the second factor, then it would be possible to infer that diachronic changes in mortality were purely the result of a combination of improvements in public health and medical care, and are not the result of increasing wealth per person. Thus, it could be inferred that in the absence of these novel environmental factors, mortality would have remained constant as predicted by the group-selection hypothesis. In my opinion, this interpretation can be described as possible, but not as probable. The more probable situation, given the data, is that in the absence of improvements in public health and medical care, an increase in resources per person would cause a lowering of mortality.

However, the inference is not as clear-cut as desirable and, therefore, future analyses, such as the one described above, will be carried out in the hope of providing a firmer conclusion.

If one assumes that these difficulties of inference make it impossible to draw any conclusion at all concerning the conformity of Yomut mortality rates to the logic of the Wynne-Edwards hypothesis, one would still, however, be left with the fact that the data on the social regulation of fertility falsify the Wynne-Edwards hypothesis. Thus, despite possible difficulties in interpreting the diachronic data on mortality, it seems to me quite reasonable to conclude that the Yomut probably are not adapted to homeostatic population regulation in the manner hypothesized by Wynne-Edwards.

It may also be relevant at this point to note that there are data indicating that Yomut, in living memory, have generally not been interested in contraception and have generally not made effective use of contraceptives. Rogasner interviewed approximately 350 Turkmen women and part of her inquiries dealt with this issue. She found that, although all of these 350 women knew of contraceptive methods, only seven had ever used any contraceptive and, of this seven, five had done so for only a few months. The two women who did regularly practice contraception were women with several children (five in one case and six in the other) who had been advised by doctors in the nearest urban center that they were unlikely to survive another pregnancy. Given this, it seems to me the only form of social regulation of fertility that could be hypothesized would be ones involving the exclusion of some significant portion of the population's fecund females from marriage. The data, I believe, indicate that this has not been a significant factor affecting fertility among the Yomut.

Another point might be raised in objection to the statement that the above data falsify the group-selection hypothesis. It could be suggested that bridewealth (or perhaps some other Wynne-Edwardsian token that I have failed to identify) would begin to have the predicted effect at a lower level of wealth per person than occurs in the data presented here. It is, of course, difficult to project what would happen under conditions not observed. However, it is worth pointing out that an important testable prediction derived from the Wynne-Edwards hypothesis is that social limitation of fertility will act as a density-dependent damper on fertility and will bring population to a state of zero growth before shortages of resources cause increases in death rates and intensify competition for resources.

The data presented seriously challenge that prediction. Within the observed range of variation in wealth per capita, social limitation of fertility did not change at all and mortality increased sharply. For the above prediction to be borne out at lower levels of wealth per individual than those observed, both of these trends would have to be reversed completely at such lower levels of resources per person. That is unlikely.

The Individual-Selection Hypothesis

The individual-selection hypothesis predicts that net reproduction will increase as resources per individual increase, but makes no clear-cut prediction as to whether this will be reflected primarily in changes in fertility or mortality, or both. It does, however, predict that changes in fertility, if they do occur, will reflect a greater ability to reproduce and rear offspring (owing to greater access to the resources) rather than greater access to Wynne-Edwardsian tokens. The data analyses above already bear out these predictions.

The individual-selection hypothesis also predicts that individuals will compete for scarce resources which enable them to reproduce. A resource is scarce in this sense if greater access to it enables greater reproductive success; conversely, if it is sufficiently abundant that greater access to it does not have this effect, it is not scarce. Competition here is used in the sense common in evolutionary biology (for a useful discussion of this, see: Daly & Wilson 1978:21-23). In this sense, hostile interaction among competitors is not necessarily implied. All that need occur for there to be competition is a striving for something in which different individuals experience different degrees of success.

The following model is a reasonable application, to the Yomut, of the general statement that individuals will compete for scarce resources. The Yomut compete for wealth in the sense that each individual strives to increase his or her own wealth and some individuals are more successful than others in doing this. Higher wealth enables individuals to enjoy a better diet, more adequate clothing and shelter, and greater freedom from the more exhausting and risky forms of labor. For males, greater wealth also means greater ease in accumulating bridewealth and hence earlier marriage, earlier remarriage after the death of a spouse, and more frequent polygyny. Bridewealth is seen, in terms of this individual-selection hypothesis, not as a token designed to limit fertility, but rather as a quid pro quo given by males for a scarce resource necessary for their reproduction: a mate. In a polygynous population, mates are scarce for males, but not for females (Trivers 1972).

The combined effect of the advantages of greater wealth is a higher Darwinian fitness for those who are more successful in accumulating it. In a polygynous society like that of the Yomut, it is also expected that the difference in Darwinian fitness between more and less successful males will be greater than the difference in fitness between more and less successful females (Alexander et al. 1979; Trivers 1972).

These expectations are tested below by analysis designed to determine whether net reproduction increases with wealth, and whether individuals strive to increase their wealth (cf. Irons 1979c). It is important to keep in mind that if either of these predictions were not borne out empirically, the individual-selection hypothesis would be falsified. The general theoretical statement is that individuals will compete for scarce resources that aid in reproductive success. This statement can be falsified either by showing that individuals do not compete for a resource even though greater access to that resource would increase reproductive success, or by showing that individuals invest large amounts of effort in competing for a resource which does not have this effect.

There is also another prediction derived logically from the individual-selection hypothesis which can be tested with the available data. Human social environments vary in terms of the scarcities they present to individuals striving for reproductive success. They also vary in the effectiveness with which male versus female coalitions are effective in gaining access to the scarce resource, or resources. For example, in some societies which depend primarily on gathering wild plant food and which occasionally face food shortages, female coalitions are more effective at overcoming scarcities of food than are male coalitions. In such societies, one would expect household organizations (which are primarily responsible for gathering food) to be built up around groups of closely related females (Irons 1979b). When the opposite is true, that is, male coalitions are more effective at overcoming the most important scarcities, one would expect households to be built up around coalitions of closely related males. This follows from the fact that in a social environment in which coalitions of one sex are more effective in overcoming locally important scarcities, individuals of both sexes gain more in inclusive fitness by the formation of this type of coalition (Irons 1979b).

Applied to a group like the Yomut, who are known in advance to form households around coalitions of closely related males, this theoretical model predicts that male coalitions will be more effective in gaining access to locally scarce resources--in this specific case, more effective than female coalitions at accumulating wealth. This expectation is also tested below, although, as explained, the results are to a degree tentative.

One can restate the above theoretical predictions in more ethnographically concrete terms as follows. Wealth both in the sense of expendable income and accumulated capital is a scarce resource among the Yomut, and greater access to this resource enables greater reproductive success. Economic production is organized by households, and the primary resources for producing income both for consumption and for further capital accumulation are the labor of adult male members of the household and the household's currently accumulated capital. Pastoral and agricultural labor are done by men; woman's work among the Turkmen consists of child care, cooking, sewing, and carpet weaving. Of these, only carpet weaving has any potential for increasing the family's wealth, whereas all male labor has this potential.

Families attempt to increase their capital and to enjoy a high level of consumption. Those domestic units which are most able to do this are those which have a high number of male laborers relative to the number of consumers in the household (cf. Sahlins 1962). The Yomut developmental cycle of domestic groups results from an attempt by Turkmen to create households with two characteristics: a favorable ratio of male producers to consumers and thus an ability to increase their wealth, and a male labor force consisting of closely related males, basically a father and his adult sons, who have a strong interest in one another's reproductive success.

The resulting developmental cycle is one in which men separate from their fathers' households when they have sons of their own approaching adulthood. Such nuclear families become patrilateral extended families as the sons marry and bring their wives into the household, and as daughters leave to join their husbands. Eventually the sons separate off one at a time and repeat the cycle. Fissioning off of sons occurs at a time when both of the new households formed will be economically viable in terms of wealth and labor force and when the male members of the subunits of the earlier households are growing apart in terms of genetic relatedness.

The data analyses designed to test this model are not all complete, but those which have been completed support the model. The first analysis consisted of dividing the sample of households into halves on the basis of their wealth in 1974, and calculating separate age-specific fertility and mortality rates for each half of the population (Tables 7-10). If the wealthier half of the population did not have more favorable vital rates, the prediction that greater wealth enables greater reproductive success would be falsified.

Annual birth rates are ordinarily calculated for a specific age interval by counting the number of women in the age interval and the number of births occurring to these women during a particular year, and then computing births per woman. Since the number of women in the 1973-74 sample was small--roughly 1000--such a procedure is difficult to use as a basis for comparing the wealthier and poorer halves of the population. The number of births in the data for

Table 7. Differences in male fertility between the wealthier and poorer halves of the population.

Age interval	Wealthier half of population			
	Person years in interval (N)	Births per year (B)	Age-specific birth rate (r_i=B/N)	Variance in sample mean of birth rate ($Var(r_i)=r_i(1-r_i)/N$)
15-19	1889	83	.044	.000022
20-24	1468	293	.200	.000109
25-29	1125	345	.307	.000189
30-34	909	297	.327	.000242
35-39	723	257	.355	.000317
40-44	546	178	.326	.000403
45-49	419	105	.252	.000451
50-54	277	58	.209	.000596
55-59	169	38	.225	.001030
60-64	100	17	.170	.001410
65-69	35	5	.143	.003514
70-74	17	2	.118	.006118
Total fertility rate ($5\Sigma r_i$)			13.38	
Variance in sample mean for total fertility rate $25\Sigma Var(r_i)$				.360025

Table 7. (continued)

Age interval	Poorer half of population			
	Person years in interval (N)	Births per year (B)	Age-specific birth rate (r_i=B/N)	Variance in sample mean of birth rate ($Var(r_i)=r_i(1-r_i)/N$)
15-19	2189	49	.022	.000010
20-24	1842	228	.124	.000059
25-29	1516	335	.221	.000114
30-34	1265	337	.226	.000154
35-39	1008	275	.273	.000197
40-44	735	178	.242	.000250
45-49	528	123	.233	.000338
50-54	338	51	.151	.000379
55-59	223	18	.081	.000334
60-64	156	11	.071	.000422
65-69	86	4	.047	.000521
70-74	39	1	.026	.000649
Total fertility rate ($5\Sigma r_i$)			8.795	
Variance in sample mean for total fertility rate $25\Sigma Var(r_i)$				.085675

Z=6.88 p<.0001

Table 8. Differences in female fertility between wealthier and poorer halves of the population.

Age interval	Wealthier half of population			
	Person years in interval (N)	Births per year (B)	Age-specific birth rate (r_i=B/N)	Variance in sample mean of birth rate ($Var(r_i)=r_i(1-r_i)/N$)
15-19	1925	253	.131	.000059
20-24	1476	492	.333	.000150
25-29	1166	391	.335	.000191
30-34	958	301	.314	.000224
35-39	775	213	.275	.000256
40-44	575	95	.165	.000240
45-49	393	17	.043	.000104
50-54	217	2	.009	.000041
Total fertility rate ($5\Sigma r_i$)			8.025	
Variance in sample mean for total fertility rate $25\Sigma Var(r_i)$				.031625

Table 8. (continued)

Age interval	Poorer half of population			
	Person years in interval (N)	Births per year (B)	Age-specific birth rate (r_i=B/N)	Variance in sample mean of birth rate ($Var(r_i)=r_i(1-r_i)/N$)
15-19	2254	292	.130	.000050
20-24	1868	547	.293	.000111
25-29	1366	428	.313	.000157
30-34	1032	303	.294	.000202
35-39	804	218	.271	.000245
40-44	587	92	.157	.000225
45-49	395	16	.041	.000100
50-54	202	0	.000	.000000
Total fertility rate ($5\Sigma r_i$)			7.495	
Variance in sample mean for total fertility rate $25\Sigma Var(r_i)$				.027250
		Z=2.18	p<.015	

Table 9. Differences in male mortality between wealthier and poorer halves of the population.

Age interval	Wealthier half of population			
	Person years in interval (l_i)	Persons dying in interval (D_i)	Age-specific death rate ($r_i=D_i/l_i$)	Variance in sample mean of death rate ($Var(r_i)=r_i/l_i$)
0	981	131	.133	.000136
1	781	43	.055	.000070
2	703	31	.044	.000063
3	634	9	.014	.000022
4	598	9	.015	.000025
5-9	2360	8	.003	.000001
10-14	1695	5	.003	.000002
15-19	1071	1	.001	.000001
Age standardized death rate			.268	
Variance in sample mean for age standardized death rate				.000320

Table 9. (continued)

Age interval	Poorer half of population			
	Person years in interval (l_i)	Persons dying in interval (D_i)	Age-specific death rate ($r_i = D_i/l_i$)	Variance in sample mean of death rate ($Var(r_i) = r_i/l_i$)
0	953	154	.162	.000170
1	744	64	.086	.000116
2	640	29	.045	.000070
3	577	27	.047	.000081
4	512	4	.008	.000016
5-9	2088	23	.011	.000005
10-14	1480	3	.002	.000001
15-19	994	3	.003	.000003
Age standardized death rate			.364	
Variance in sample mean for age standardized death rate				.000462

$Z=3.43$ $p=.0003$

Table 10. Differences in female mortality between wealthier and poorer halves of the population.

	Wealthier half of population			
Age interval	Person years in interval (l_i)	Persons dying in interval (D_i)	Age-specific death rate ($r_i = D_i/l_i$)	Variance in sample mean of death rate ($Var(r_i) = r_i/l_i$)
0	850	117	.138	.000162
1	694	28	.040	.000058
2	639	26	.041	.000064
3	568	15	.026	.000046
4	516	0	.000	.000000
5-9	2116	14	.007	.000003
10-14	1473	1	.001	.000001
15-19	946	2	.002	.000002
Age standardized death rate			.255	
Variance in sample mean for age standardized death rate				.000336

Table 10. (continued)

Age interval	Poorer half of population			
	Person years in interval (l_i)	Persons dying in interval (D_i)	Age-specific death rate ($r_i=D_i/l_i$)	Variance in sample mean of death rate ($Var(r_i)=r_i/l_i$)
0	881	108	.123	.000140
1	714	56	.078	.000109
2	634	35	.055	.000086
3	559	13	.023	.000041
4	502	6	.012	.000024
5-9	2075	18	.009	.000004
10-14	1425	4	.003	.000002
15-19	924	7	.008	.000010
Age standardized death rate			.311	
Variance in sample mean for age standardized death rate				.000416

$Z=2.07$ $p<.02$

any one year are small, and these would have to be subdivided first into two wealth categories and then later into several categories based on mother's age. Attempts to do this did not consistently yield statistically significant results, although they showed trends in the predicted direction which were sometimes significant.

To get around this difficulty, a means of using all births recorded for the last 20 years for estimating variation in fertility by wealth was used. It was assumed that there was an average birth rate for the last twenty years, and that the data for each individual year could be considered a sample allowing an estimate of the average annual birth rate during that time period. The data for each separate year would be the number of women in each age interval during that year and the number of births occurring during that year to those women. The data for each of the 20 years could then be pooled to provide the best estimate of the average rate during the 20-year time period. Variance of the sample mean can be estimated by assuming a binomial distribution. Separate rates and variances in the sample mean were calculated for each half of the population. Summing the annual rates and multiplying by five (each woman spends five years in each age interval) yields a total fertility rate. Variances in the total fertility rates are then the sum of the variances of the annual rate for each age interval multiplied by five squared. These variances were used to calculate the Z scores and p-values reported in Tables 7 and 8. The results are significant in the predicted direction.

Estimating mortality variation by wealth also required using a technique suitable for a small sample. The technique used closely paralleled that used for estimating diachronic changes in death rates (see above). The data on the survivorship of children for the first 20 years of life collected in conjunction with fertility records were used. The population was divided in half by wealth, as in estimating fertility variation, and separate rates of survivorship and mortality were calculated for each half of the population using the same algorithms as were employed above in estimating diachronic variation in death rates. Also the same algorithm was employed for calculating an age standardized death rate and p-values. The results (Tables 9 and 10) are significant in the direction predicted by the individual-selection model.

Irons (1979c) reported similar Z scores and p-values that were calculated using weighting corresponding to a model population structure taken from Coale and Demeny's

(1966) set of model population parameters rather than the weighting of one used here (see Kitagawa 1964). The weightings used were those corresponding to what Coale and Demeny have labeled a South 12 population structure. This is the model structure from the Coale and Demeny models which most closely fits the empirical Yomut data. These results like the ones reported here are significant in the predicted direction.

Estimates of the magnitude of the difference in Darwinian fitness resulting from these differences in vital rates were made by the following method. The empirical survivorship curves up to age 20 were matched to model survivorship curves from Coale and Demeny (1966) using a X^2 test for goodness of fit. The curves showing best fit were then combined with the empirical fertility rates for each half of the population to determine net reproduction. Figures 1 and 2 show the results of these vital rates acting on 100 individuals born in generation one. The abcissa represents the ages of the 100 individuals in generation one, and the ordinate indicates the numbers of individuals born in generation two to the original 100 individuals in generation one. Separate curves are calculated for each sex and each wealth stratum.

The association of vital rates with wealth shown above is a realized prediction from the individual-selection hypothesis. In an interesting way they parallel the variation in vital rates associated with genealogical rank among rhesus monkeys demonstrated by Sade et al. (1977). The data (Figs. 1 & 2) also bear out the individual-selection prediction that variation in male reproductive success will be greater than variation in female reproductive success. The result could have falsified the hypothesis but did not. Further testing, however, is underway. The individual-selection hypothesis claims that individuals strive to increase their wealth and that greater wealth causes more favorable vital rates. Tests of the more specific proposition that higher wealth causes--rather than merely is associated with--a higher Darwinian fitness are underway and will be reported in future publications. One way of testing this is to divide the population in half on the basis of the wealth of households at some time in the past and calculate vital rates using births and deaths occurring after that time.

Although subjecting data to numerous tests is an excellent strategy, the suggestion of future tests not yet conducted should not obscure the fact that the results presented do allow certain inferences. Demographers generally

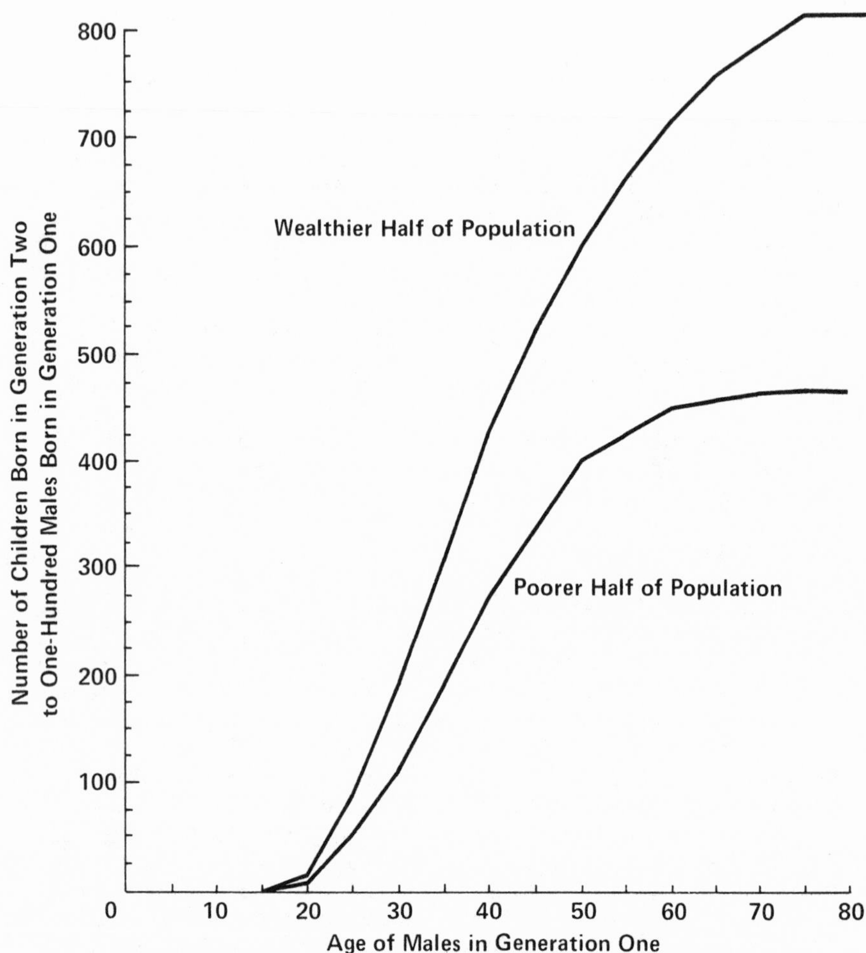

Figure 1. Net reproduction of males in the wealthier and poorer halves of the sample population. From Evolutionary Biology and Human Social Behavior: An Anthropological Perspective by Napoleon A. Chagnon and William Irons. © 1979 by Wadsworth, Inc., Belmont, Ca. 94002. Reprinted by permission of the publisher, Duxbury Press.

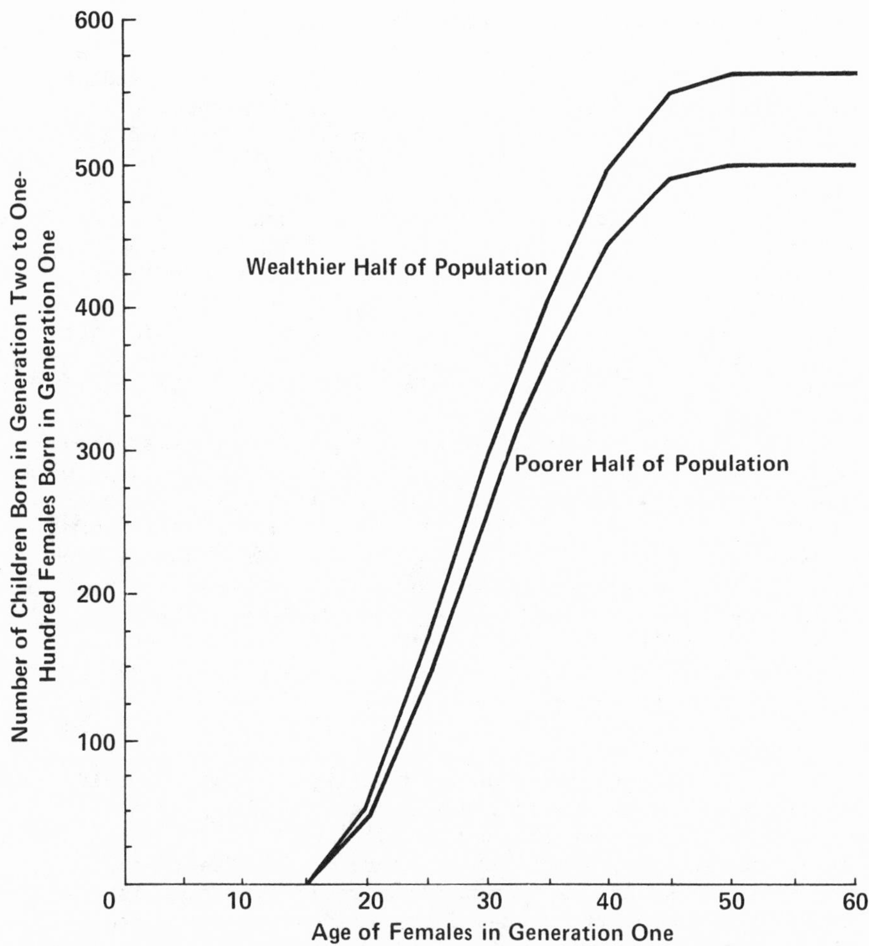

Figure 2. Net reproduction of females in the wealthier and poorer halves of the sample population. From Evolutionary Biology and Human Social Behavior: An Anthropological Perspective by Napoleon A. Chagnon and William Irons. © 1979 by Wadsworth, Inc., Belmont, Ca. 94002. Reprinted by permission of the publisher, Duxbury Press.

assume that greater economic resources do cause higher fertility and higher survivorship in pre-transition populations (Wrigley 1969); I see no reason why this assumption should not apply to the Yomut.

The most reasonable model, it seems to me, is one of two-way causation between wealth and vital rates. In the case of fertility, wealth would appear to have an immediate positive effect on birth rates, while birth rates would appear to have only a delayed and somewhat diluted effect on wealth.

The higher fertility of males is a result of earlier marriage, earlier remarriage after the death of a spouse, and high rates of polygyny. Given the fact that bridewealth is high (Irons 1975:134-136, 163-167) and female labor does not contribute to increases in wealth (see regression equations below), the higher fertility of wealthier males would appear to be primarily an immediate effect of higher wealth.

Higher female fertility, is, I think, most reasonably seen in the light of the data presented here as a result of better health stemming from better nutrition, better medical care, and greater freedom from the more strenuous forms of labor. The reverse effect of fertility on wealth is delayed because child labor does not increase wealth (see regression equations below), and diluted since births of females would not have the delayed effect that births of males would have. Daughters bring in bridewealth, but do not make the greater contribution that adult sons make in labor.

In the case of male adult mortality, causation would appear to be strong in both directions. Higher wealth would seem to improve chances of survivorship. At the same time, mortality by eliminating labor, would affect wealth negatively. Adult female mortality would also diminish wealth by necessitating additional bridewealth. On the other hand, higher rates of infant and child mortality (the data actually used here) would appear to be more an effect of lower wealth than a cause.

Thus, while causation would seem from the available qualitative and quantitative data to be two-way, the strongest effects in fertility and infant and child mortality would appear to be that of a causal arrow flowing from wealth to vital rates with a weaker reverse effect. Future analysis will attempt to test this model as mentioned earlier. However, the association of wealth and favorable vital rates would be spurious as a source of support for the individual-selection model only if wealth had no tendency to cause favorable vital rates, but rather wealth was purely an effect of earlier high fertility and survivorship. This is improbable.

As stated earlier, the individual-selection hypothesis contains three basic statements. They are (1) that higher wealth causes higher reproductive success, (2) that individuals strive to increase their wealth and hence their reproductive success, and (3) that they form those types of kin coalitions which will have the strongest possible positive effect on wealth. Let us next address the question of whether individuals actually strive to increase wealth. (As will be seen below this question becomes inextricably bound up with the question of the formation of kin coalitions; initially, however, the discussion will be addressed only to the question of whether individuals strive to increase wealth.)

Qualitative data from participant observation indicate that Yomut do attempt to increase their wealth (Irons 1975). This would indicate that--whether consciously or unconsciously--their economic activities are directed toward increasing Darwinian fitness. It is also possible to use the available quantitative data to test the proposition that Yomut try to increase their wealth.

Marshall Sahlins (1972) has suggested this can be done by comparing households which are better able to produce wealth in terms of their producer-to-consumer ratio, to households less able to produce wealth in terms of the same measure. If those better able to produce more, do increase their wealth over time more than those less able to produce, that indicates a desire to accumulate capital. If not, that indicates that households produce only enough to meet consumption needs and that they do not wish to produce beyond consumption needs in order to accumulate more capital.

Following Sahlins' suggestion, the proposition that Yomut attempt to increase their wealth was tested by regressing wealth at the time of observation (W_2) onto wealth at the time of founding of the household (W_1), the number of adult male labor years the household has enjoyed from founding to the time of observation (ML), the number of female labor years (FL), and the number of consumer years (CON). The predicted regression equation had the form:

$$W_2 = C_1 + C_2W_1 + C_3ML + C_4FL - C_5CON$$

In this equation C_1, C_2,...C_5 are the constants defined by a linear regression equation. The sign of C_1 was expected to be positive because wealth is generally increasing in the society. The signs of C_2, C_3, and C_4 were expected to be positive because these factors should have a positive effect on wealth. The sign of C_5 was expected to be negative because consumer years should have a negative effect on wealth. It was also expected that $C_4 < C_3$, indicating that female labor would have less of a positive effect on wealth than male labor.

The resulting empirical equation below is a tentative result because not all sample households were included, only those for which the relevant variables could be easily calculated. Work is in progress to calculate these variables for the remaining households, and to compute a regression equation for the entire sample. The tentative result is:

$$W_2 = 103.6 + .7W_1 + .3ML - .06FL - .15CON$$

	Variable	F
N=384	W_1	461.9
r^2=.55	ML	12.1
	FL	0.4
	CON	14.7

In this equation wealth is measured in terms of 1000's of *tumans*, and labor and consumption years are measured in units of ten years.

Only female labor turned out differently than predicted, being preceded by a negative rather than a positive constant, but this value is not significantly different from zero. If anything, this would strengthen the argument to the effect that female labor is less important than male labor, indicating that it has in effect no importance for increasing household wealth. The prediction that male labor would have a positive effect, following Sahlins' reasoning cited above, indicates that Yomut do try to increase wealth, and hence Darwinian fitness.

A more satisfactory form of the equation is the following:

$$W_2 = 62.7 + .91W_1 + .39(ML \times W_1) - .13(CON \times W_1)$$

	Variable	F
N=384	W_1	693.7
r^2=.69	ML x W_1	45.0
	CON x W_1	70.1

This form is a little less straightforward in terms of the brief explanation given above of household formation and economics. It takes into account the interactions of male labor and wealth and the interactions of consumption and wealth. It indicates that the ideal situation for a Yomut family is a combination of a large amount of capital and a large amount of male labor. Since the labor is expended in managing their own capital this is not surprising. It also indicates that wealthy families consume at a higher rate, i.e., enjoy a higher standard of living.

The above empirical findings support the conclusion that the Yomut strive to increase their wealth. They also support the prediction that they form kin coalitions of the type which are most effective in obtaining scarce resources that promote reproductive success.

More refined tests are also in progress concerning the inclusive-fitness effects of the Yomut developmental cycle of domestic groups. The regression equation above indicates in general that a nuclear family with no children over 15 should tend to decline in wealth. A man, wife, and one child would have one producer whose effect is to increase wealth by 39% over ten years, and three consumers whose combined effect would be to decrease the household's wealth by 39% over the same time period. The expected net effect would be no change. But as immature children are added to the household, a net loss would be expected. As sons of the household mature, however, the consumer-producer ratio would become more favorable and gain would be possible. Daughters marry out at about age 15. They do, however, bring into their natal household a bridewealth before leaving. Thus after reaching age 15, they make a positive contribution to their natal household, but a lesser one than do sons.

The Yomut developmental cycle of households makes good sense in terms of the above considerations. Nuclear families during the period in which they are economically weak are usually subparts of larger extended families. The consumer-producer ratio of these extended families is more favorable than that of a nuclear family alone. Nuclear families split off, however, at the point at which their children begin to approach maturity.

The data available will allow estimating the effect of specific cases of household division on inclusive fitness. The wealth, number of consumers, and number of producers for the household before splitting and for the two separate households after the split are known for a number of cases. The probable effect on wealth (or indirectly on reproductive success) can be estimated for all adults involved using the regression equation above and the known effect of wealth on reproductive success. However, estimates for the adult males alone will probably explain most of what is occurring. Since the relationship among household members is known, the effect on each individual's inclusive fitness can also be calculated. This can then be used to test the hypothesis that nuclear families withdrawing from parental extended families, do so at the time at which such a choice becomes advantageous to their member's inclusive fitness. The amount of calculating sounds large, but is manageable with the aid of a computer.

It is also worth pointing out that the projected data analysis will shed light on a number of theoretical predictions dealing with patrilateral inheritance of wealth in polygynous societies (Alexander 1977; Hartung 1976).

The Null Hypothesis

The tests in progress could falsify the individual-selection hypothesis even though the results to date support this hypothesis. If they should falsify it, then the data would support the third alternative hypothesis which I described above as the null hypothesis. This inference would be especially strong if by additional data analyses I should be able to show that greater conformity to Yomut ideology correlates with a lower inclusive fitness. This would suggest that Marshall Sahlins (1976) is correct in stating that human social behavior is shaped by a cultural system of meaning which imposes a calculus of values independent of, and different from, the calculus implied by maximization of inclusive fitness. Tests intended to look for this latter possibility will eventually be designed and carried out as the final stage of the research in progress.

It is important to note that the group-selection and individual-selection hypotheses do not deny that human social behavior is shaped by a cultural system of meaning. Rather, they only deny that this system of meaning leads consistently to forms of behavior which are contrary to what is optimal in terms of natural selection. Thus, they contradict only part of the statement above paraphrased from Sahlins (1976).

Conclusion

The statement has been made that it is possible to fit an "adaptive story" to any set of ethnographic facts (Sahlins 1976:84; Sociobiology Study Group 1977:144-146). This may be true of the type of qualitative data found in most ethnographies. I do not think it holds for the above data which were collected to measure the effect of social behavior on reproductive success. Quantitative data collected with this purpose in mind enable one to distinguish among alternate hypotheses. It would be impossible to fit an "adaptive story" to every conceivable pattern of data of this sort.

Those of the above analyses which are complete do allow some inference to the effect that striving for reproductive success and maximization of inclusive fitness are effects of social behavior in one human population.

It is worth noting at this juncture that a number of recent studies support similar conclusions. Quantitative data analysis allowing similar inferential support for sociobiological models are available for at least two other populations: the Yąnomamö (Chagnon 1975, 1979a, 1979b, this volume; Chagnon & Bugos 1979; Chagnon et al. 1979) and the Ye'kwana (Hames 1979). Support for sociobiological hypotheses dealing with humans is also to be found in various cross-cultural studies (Dickemann 1979; Low 1979) and certain cross-species analyses which include human data (Alexander et al. 1979; Ember & Ember 1979).

The discussion and data above should make it clear that testing the theoretical statement that human social behavior tends to assume forms which are biologically adaptive requires analysis of quantitative data of a variety which are not commonly found in the anthropological literature. Further, it should be clear that the question of whether human social behavior conforms to natural selection theory cannot be definitively resolved without further research designed to collect and analyze such data.

Summary

This paper deals with the relationship between human social behavior and natural selection. Two alternative hypotheses were tested with data drawn from a specific human society, the Yomut Turkmen of northern Iran. The hypotheses are: (1) Yomut social behavior assumes a form which is favored by natural selection at the level of breeding populations (Wynne-Edwards 1962); (2) Yomut social behavior assumes a form which is favored by natural selection at the individual level (Hamilton 1964; Williams 1966). These are referred to as the group-selection and the individual-selection hypotheses. The data potentially could have falsified both hypotheses, in which case the results would have indirectly supported the logical null hypothesis that Yomut social behavior is not optimal in terms of natural selection at any level.

These hypotheses were tested using data on the effects of certain aspects of economic behavior on vital rates. The test supported the individual-selection hypothesis above. But projected future tests, which are described briefly, could reverse the results presented here.

The group-selection hypothesis was tested by examining the expectation that changes in the quantity of resources per individual would be reflected in changes in population growth rates as a result of social regulation of fertility rather than changes in mortality rates. This expectation was tested by examining changes over the last 35 years in resources per capita, age at first marriage, completed fertility of women at ages 30 and 40, and mortality. Contrary to predictions based on the group-selection hypothesis, changes in resources per person are associated with sharp changes in mortality, but no change in social limitation of fertility.

The individual-selection hypothesis predicted that net reproduction (taken here as a measure of Darwinian fitness) would be higher for members of wealthier households, that individuals would attempt to increase their wealth and hence their net reproduction, and that the existing kinship coalitions (patrilateral extended family households) would be those which are most effective at increasing wealth. These predictions were borne out by the tests completed, but future tests could reverse these results.

The null hypothesis would have been supported by a falsification of the first two hypotheses. Up to the present, data analyses have not supported this hypothesis by falsifying both of the natural-selection hypotheses. Analyses specifically designed to test this hypothesis have not yet been conducted, but future ones are discussed briefly.

The types of data and analyses should make the following more general points clear: (a) it is not possible to fit an adaptive "story" to just any conceivable pattern of data when one is examining quantitative data on the effects of social behavior on vital rates, and (b) testing propositions such as the theoretical statement that human beings tend to behave so as to maximize inclusive fitness requires analyses of quantitative data of sorts not generally available in the anthropological literature; thus, the issue of the conformity of human behavior to natural selection theory cannot be definitively resolved without further research.

Acknowledgements

I wish to gratefully acknowledge the support of the research reported here by the Harry Frank Guggenheim Foundation (1976-78), the National Science Foundation (Grant GS-37888, 1973-74; Grant BN576-11904, 1976-78), and the Ford and Rockefeller Foundations' Program in Population Policy (1974-75). Portions of the data discussed here were also presented in faculty colloquia of the Departments of Anthropology at the Pennsylvania State University (1976), Southern Illinois University at Carbondale (1978), and Northwestern University (1978), and in the colloquium on Kin Selection and Kinship Theory organized by Irven DeVore and Robin Fox at the Maison des Sciences de l'Homme, Paris (1978). My appreciation of the implications of the data presented were sharpened by discussions in all of these fora, and I am grateful to the many anthropological and other scholars whose participation in the colloquies assisted me in this way. I also wish to thank Daniel Bates, Clifford Clogg, Marjorie Rogasner, and Alan Ross for the cooperation described above in the text. Further I owe a debt of gratitude to George Barlow and James Silverberg for much assistance in improving earlier drafts of this paper. I alone am responsible for its flaws. My greatest debt of gratitude, however, is that to the many Turkmen who tolerated my lengthy interviews and other forms of inscrutable alien behavior with an admirable patience.

Literature Cited

Alexander, R.D. 1977. Natural selection and the analysis of human sociality. In C.E. Goulden (ed.), Changing scenes in the natural sciences. Academy of Natural Sciences, Special Publication 12, Philadelphia, pp. 283-337.

_______. 1979. Evolution and culture. In N.A. Chagnon & W. Irons (eds.), Evolutionary biology and human social behavior: An anthropological perspective. Duxbury, North Scituate, Massachusetts, pp. 59-78.

_______, J.L. Hoogland, R.D. Howard, K.M. Noonan, & P.W. Sherman. 1979. Sexual dimorphism and breeding systems in pinnipeds, ungulates, primates, and humans. In N.A. Chagnon & W. Irons (eds.), Evolutionary biology and human social behavior: An anthropological perspective. Duxbury, North Scituate, Massachusetts, pp. 402-435.

Barthold, V.V. 1962. A history of the Turkmen people. In V.V. Barthold, Four studies of the history of Central Asia, trans. by V. & T. Minorsky. Brill, Leiden, pp. 75-170.

Chagnon, N.A. 1975. Genealogy, solidarity, and relatedness: Limits to local group size and patterns of fissioning in an expanding population. Yearbook of Physical Anthropology 19:95-110.

_______. 1979a. Mate competition, favoring close kin, and village fissioning among the Yąnomamö Indians. In N.A. Chagnon & W. Irons (eds.), Evolutionary biology and human social behavior: An anthropological perspective. Duxbury, North Scituate, Massachusetts, pp. 86-131.

_______. 1979b. Is reproductive success equal in egalitarian societies? In N.A. Chagnon & W. Irons (eds.), Evolutionary biology and human social behavior: An anthropological perspective. Duxbury, North Scituate, Massachusetts, pp. 374-401.

_______, & P.E. Bugos, Jr. 1979. Kin selection and conflict: An analysis of a Yąnomamö ax fight. In N.A. Chagnon & W. Irons (eds.), Evolutionary biology and human social behavior: An anthropological perspective. Duxbury, North Scituate, Massachusetts, pp. 213-237.

_______, M.V. Flinn, & T.F. Melancon. 1979. Sex ratio variation among the Yąnomamö Indians. In N.A. Chagnon & W. Irons (eds.), Evolutionary biology and human social behavior: An anthropological perspective. Duxbury, North Scituate, Massachusetts, pp. 290-320.

Cloak, F.T., Jr. 1975. Is a cultural ethology possible? Human Ecology 3:161-182.

Coale, A.J. & P. Demeny. 1966. Regional model life tables and stable populations. Princeton University Press, Princeton, New Jersey.

Daly, M. & M. Wilson. 1978. Sex, evolution, and behavior: Adaptations for reproduction. Duxbury, North Scituate, Massachusetts.

Dawkins, R. 1976. The selfish gene. Oxford University Press, Oxford.

Dickemann, M. 1979. Female infanticide, reproductive strategies, and social stratification: A preliminary model. In N.A. Chagnon & W. Irons (eds.), Evolutionary biology and human social behavior: An anthropological perspective. Duxbury, North Scituate, Massachusetts, pp. 321-368.

Ember, M. & C.R. Ember. 1979. Male-female bonding: A cross-species study of mammals and birds. Behavior Science Research 14:37-56.

Gurgānī, M. 1969(1350, Iranian calendar). 'Iqtiṣād-i Gurgān va Gunbad va Dasht. Bungāh-i Maṭbū'ātī-yi Ṣafī 'Alī Shāh, Tehran.

Hames, R.B. 1979. Relatedness and interaction among the Ye'kwana: A preliminary analysis. In N.A. Chagnon & W. Irons (eds.), Evolutionary biology and human social behavior: An anthropological perspective. Duxbury, North Scituate, Massachusetts, pp. 238-250.

Hamilton, W.D. 1964. The genetical evolution of social behavior, Parts I & II. Journal of Theoretical Biology 7:1-52.

Hartung, J. 1976. On natural selection and the inheritance of wealth. Current Anthropology 17:607-622.

Irons, W. 1975. The Yomut Turkmen: A study of social organization among a Central Asian Turkic-speaking population. University of Michigan Museum of Anthropology, Ann Arbor.

_______. 1979a. Natural selection, adaptation, and human social behavior. In N.A. Chagnon & W. Irons (eds.), Evolutionary biology and human social behavior: An anthropological perspective. Duxbury, North Scituate, Massachusetts, pp. 4-39.

_______. 1979b. Investment and primary social dyads. In N.A. Chagnon & W. Irons (eds.), Evolutionary biology and human social behavior: An anthropological perspective. Duxbury, North Scituate, Massachusetts, pp. 181-212.

_______. 1979c. Cultural and biological success. In N.A. Chagnon & W. Irons (eds.), Evolutionary biology and human social behavior: An anthropological perspective. Duxbury, North Scituate, Massachusetts, pp. 257-272.

_______. Evolutionary biology and human fertility. Human Ecology, in press.

Kitagawa, E.M. 1964. Standardized comparisons in population research. Demography 1:296-315.

Low, B.S. 1979. Sexual selection and human ornamentation. In N.A. Chagnon & W. Irons (eds.), Evolutionary biology and human social behavior: An anthropological perspective. Duxbury, North Scituate, Massachusetts, pp. 462-486.

Okazaki, S. 1968. The development of large-scale farming in Iran: The case of the province of Gurgan. Institute of Asian Economic Affairs, Occasional Papers Series 3. The Institute of Asian Economic Affairs, Tokyo.

Richerson, P.J. & R. Boyd. 1978. A dual inheritance model of the human evolutionary process I: Basic postulates and a simple model. Journal of Social Biological Structure 1:127-154.

Sade, D.S., K. Cushing, P. Cushing, J. Dunaif, A. Figueroa, J.R. Kaplan, C. Lauer, D. Rhodes, & J. Schneider. 1976. Population dynamics in relation to social structure on Cayo Santiago. Yearbook of Physical Anthropology 20: 253-262.

Sahlins, M.D. 1972. Stone age economics. Aldine, Chicago.

_______. 1976. The use and abuse of biology: An anthropological critique of sociobiology. University of Michigan Press, Ann Arbor.

Sociobiology Study Group. 1977. Sociobiology: A new biological determinism. In The Ann Arbor Science for the People Editorial Collective (ed.), Biology as a social weapon. Burgess, Minneapolis, pp. 133-149.

Trivers, R.L. 1972. Parental investment and sexual selection. In B.H. Campbell (ed.), Sexual selection and the descent of man, 1871-1971. Aldine, Chicago, pp. 136-179.

Williams, G.C. 1966. Adaptation and natural selection: A critique of some current evolutionary thought. Princeton University Press, Princeton.

_______ (ed.). 1971. Group selection. Aldine Atherton, Chicago.

Wilson, E.O. 1975. Sociobiology: The new synthesis. Harvard University Press, Cambridge.

Wrigley, E.A. 1969. Population and history. Brill, Leiden.

Wynne-Edwards, V.C. 1962. Animal dispersion in relation to social behaviour. Hafner, New York.

Eleanor Leacock

18. Social Behavior, Biology and the Double Standard

I shall make three kinds of points here, the first theoretical, the second empirical, the third sociological. On theory, sociobiology has been criticized, especially by social scientists, as too Darwinian. I shall maintain the reverse--that it is not Darwinian enough. Sociobiological theory as represented by Wilson (1971:458; 1975:4) fails to deal with evolution in its full sense. From an anthropological viewpoint, natural selection not only produces new _forms_, and new social behaviors that are reducible to the same parameters for quantitative analysis, but also produces new _relationships_, so that processes of individual and group behaviors in different phylogenetic lines may be qualitatively distinct.

On empirical matters, I shall indicate the types of anthropological data that are ignored by those researchers who assume Western norms for sex-linked behavior to be universal, and who ascribe them to biologically based drives. As for sociological considerations, I shall stress the responsibility scientists must take for clearly differentiating between conjectures and conclusions, and for avoiding analogical and teleological terminologies that can be confusing. Some ten years of studying the socialization of children in elementary schools have made me painfully aware of the degree to which overly loose speculation about biological bases for human behavior can become presented as accepted findings.

Evolutionary Levels and Sociobiological Theory

Wilson states one function of sociobiology to be the biologizing of the social sciences by reformulating their foundations in such a way as to draw them as far as possible into the "Modern Synthesis" (1975:4). Accordingly, some sociobiologists have already attempted to "cannibalize" (Wilson's term) parts of anthropology. Yet some of what I hear presented as the new synthesis with respect to humanity is what I have long known as the old synthesis of anthropology: the insistence that humans must be studied in their totality, biological and social. The anthropological synthesis was clearly evidenced in the 1959 Darwin Centennial volumes edited by Sol Tax (1960). After all, Lewis Henry Morgan, author of Ancient Society (1974[1877]) and of the first ethnographic report in English on a native American people (1954[1851]), as well as the first anthropologist President of the American Association for the Advancement of Science, wrote a detailed account of beaver and their constructions (1868).

To speak of an anthropological synthesis might seem exaggerated, since anthropologists are engaged in vastly different endeavors. They interpret fossil, archaeological, and primate data in order to reconstruct the processes whereby conscious symbolic behavior and the planned acquisition and sharing of food emerged, and to trace the subsequent interlinked development of human physical form and cultural life. They describe and analyze the myriad sociocultural processes thereby set in motion, with work ranging from such topics as the phonetics of a disappearing language to contemporary problems like unequal schooling or urban labor migration. They study the ongoing processes of human biological evolution and variation in the context of culturally structured relations between humans and their environments.

Despite the wide range of their researches, however, most anthropologists stay cognizant of work in the different subfields of their discipline. And various symposia periodically bring scholars together to focus divergent insights on particular problems or to otherwise demonstrate anthropology's holistic approach. According to the anthropological synthesis, human behavior is a historical phenomenon. It is always understood as having evolved and as continuing to evolve through the interaction of cultural and biological processes.

By contrast with the historical and evolutionary orientation of anthropology, I find much of sociobiology, despite a formal evolutionary stance and the evolutionary bent of Wilson's work on the social insects, to be surprisingly synchronic and nonevolutionary. "A unified science of sociobiology," as defined by Wilson in 1971, would be achieved "when the same parameters and quantitative theory are used to analyze both termite colonies and troops of rhesus macaques" (1971:458).

Wilson has been widely criticized for extending this goal to include humans despite the fact that purposeful production, conscious control of reproduction, and a "unique language and revolutionary capacity for cultural transmission" (Wilson 1971:459) set them apart. Yet qualitative differences in the organization of reproduction had already emerged in the course of organic evolution prior to the emergence of humans. In my view, to use identical parameters for both termites and macaques when analysing relations among reproductive strategies, social interaction patterns, and environmental influences, is as contrary to evolutionary understanding as is the extension of these parameters to humanity. Why should sociobiological writings ignore differences among animals when they implicitly recognize qualitative differences between animals and plants? After all, plants rather more easily than animals can be described as the means DNA uses to replicate itself (Dawkins 1977).

In line with questions raised by Hull (this volume), I would guess that the most telling critique of sociobiology as formulated by its leading practitioners will come from within rather than without the field. It will come from those who begin to apply the methods of ethology, population biology, as well as comparative psychology, in the effort to define the nature of differences among different taxa, and to analyse the processes whereby they emerged. Wilson (1971:459-460) himself has already summarized basic differences in the societies formed by vertebrates and by insects. Personal recognition among vertebrate group members contrasts with the impersonality of large and short-lived insect colonies. Status relationships and role differentiation (in Wilson's terms, "division of labor") are maintained among vertebrates through signalling behavior, instead of being established as genetically and morphologically defined "castes" that include reproductive neuters. Parent-offspring relationships that are "specific to individuals . . . and relatively long in duration" among vertebrates, are absent among insects. Socialization, play and communication through elaborate signalling among vertebrates compare with minimal socialization among insects, the absence of play, and communication through the emission of chemical substances.

It is Wilson's (1971:458) argument that such differences are overridden by broad similarities. To summarize his example of termites and macaques: "both are formed into cooperative groups that occupy territories," and both distinguish between group mates and nonmembers; both are characterized by a "division of labor," and both communicate "hunger, alarm, hostility, caste status or rank, and reproductive status," using some 10 to 100 or so nonsyntactical signals;

kinship is important in group structure and has functioned centrally in the evolution of sociality; and organizational details, the products of evolution, have favored individuals "with cooperative tendencies--at least toward relatives."

The transformation of loosely descriptive generalizations such as these into parameters for defining purportedly universal determinants of social behavior is only made possible by the metaphorical properties of language. Traits that are at best analogous appear to be homologous when grouped in an inappropriately defined category. Theodore Schneirla, the psychologist who was responsible for interpreting the behavior of army ants (Wilson 1975:424) and who also worked with mammals, emphasized the problems posed for theoretical development when analogical thinking becomes embedded in loosely used terms. In 1946 he wrote,

> "Communication" on the insect and human levels appears to be sufficiently different, both in its mechanisms and in the qualitative consequences of its function in social organization, as to require different conceptual terms in the two instances. In view of the very basic psychological differences which exist between the two processes, it seems preferable to use a term such as "social transmission" for interindividual arousal in insects, reserving the term "communication" for higher levels on which a conceptual process of social transmission is demonstrable. The similarity between these processes appears to have only a minimal and an illustrative, descriptive importance for theory (Aronson et al. 1972:424-425).

Similarly, in Schneirla's opinion, "cooperation" should not be used to gloss over fundamental distinctions between what could be called "biosocial facilitation" in insects and "psychosocial cooperativeness" on the primate level, since the latter "involves an ability to anticipate the social consequences of one's own actions and to modify them in relation to attaining group goal" (Aronson et al. 1972:433).

Wilson is critical of "semantic maneuverings" that pass for theory (1975:27), and stresses the need to avoid semantic ambiguities (1975:21), but then allows himself unjustified latitude. For example, he points out that aggression "is a mixture of very different behavior patterns, serving very different functions." He defines the principal recognized forms as associated with territorial defense, dominance, sexual alliance, parental discipline, weaning, moralism, predation, and antipredatory defense (1975:242-243). Having thus demonstrated the variability subsumed under the term aggression, Wilson proceeds to refer to it as an entity, a genetically prescribed "contingency plan" or "set of complex responses . . . programmed to be summoned up in times of stress (1975:248).

With respect to human aggression, Wilson thinks it likely that "aggressive responses vary according to the situation in a genetically programmed manner" (1975:255). However, he clearly defines as "aggression" behaviors that are historically and culturally specific. He writes of "moralistic aggression" that "the evolution of advanced forms of reciprocal altruism carries with it a high probability of the simultaneous emergence of a system of moral sanctions to enforce reciprocation." He gives as examples religious and ideological evangelism, and "enforced conformity to group standards," along with "codes of punishment for transgressors" (1975:243).

However, there is enormous cultural variability in what constitute"group standards," in the degree of their rigidity or flexibility, and in the extent of and reaction to nonconformity with them. This is all sidestepped by Wilson with the statement that it "does not matter whether . . . aggression is wholly innate or is acquired part or wholly by learning," since "we are now sophisticated enough to know that the capacity to learn certain behaviors is itself a genetically controlled and therefore evolved trait" (1975:255). Yet the source of aggression is precisely what does matter. That humans inherit the capacity to learn complex cultural behaviors and attitudes is an insight derived from the anthropological synthesis. This does not mean that the behaviors and attitudes themselves originate from biological, rather than culture-historical, processes.

Sociobiological Conjectures and Ethnographic Data

The program notes for the symposium that led to this volume stated that most social scientists and biologists "find that Wilson took all too much license, in the last chapter of his book ("Man: From Sociobiology to Sociology," 1975), in trying to explain human behavior," and that equating this chapter with sociobiology does a disservice to the field and misrepresents it. However, Wilson's chapter is more restrained than the last chapter of a subsequently written text by David Barash (1977), published with Wilson's foreword. I hope it is also considered unrepresentative.

Barash does not write of behavior-specific genes as Wilson does, but he refers to biologically based "trends" toward cultural behaviors. He draws on the familiar gender roles of Western culture to make species-wide conjectures. "We are going to play 'Let's Pretend,'" Barash writes, "and see where it takes us. . . . If the Central Theorem of Sociobiology holds for humans, and we tend to behave so as to maximize personal, inclusive fitness, then what?" (1977a:277).

Moving back and forth between the subjunctive and declarative modes, Barash speculates: "Men should be . . . sexual aggressors," while women whould be interested in "reproductively relevant resources" controlled by men and marry "up"; women value men who have the "capacity to command respect," while "too much competence and accomplishment by a woman is often threatening to a prospective male partner"; it is more appropriate for an old man to marry a young woman than vice verse; the double standard, greater choosiness by women in mate selection, and pornography aimed at men should follow as biologically based tendencies from the lesser investment by males in possible outcomes of copulation; so too, somehow, does female prostitution (1977a:290-293).

Barash continues, males interact with other adults, since "by competing with other males, [a man] can retain access to his female and also possibly attract additional mates," a line of reasoning that "provides further support for the 'biology of the double standard' argument," and "also suggests why women have almost universally found themselves relegated to the nursery while men derive their greatest satisfaction from their jobs" (1977a:301). Patrilocality is "the most common human living arrangement" since in-laws "can oversee their investment" (1977a:302), (although were Barash not so caught up in Western male-biased norms he might recognize that the "Central Theorem" would just as logically lead to matrilocality so that the woman's parents could oversee their presumably greater investment). Further outcomes of the drive to maximize personal inclusive fitness, according to Barash, are the "ability to identify cheaters" and "our great concern with the evaluation of each other's character, trustworthiness, and motives," as well as sibling rivalry (although sibling unity and kin selection are usually argued from the same basis), and race prejudice (1977a:311, 314).

The anthropologist can catalogue myriad examples of female-male relationships that contradict Barash's expectations. Female sexual "aggression," covertly recognized in our culture by the Shavian saw, he chased her until she caught him, was institutionalized as formal female courtship in many cultures, some of which were noted by Edward Westermarck (1922 I:456-562) many years ago. A recent survey of women's status in a carefully selected sample of 93 cultures ranging from gatherer-hunters to nation states, showed women and men to have had "equal ability to initiate or refuse a match" in over half of them (Whyte 1978:222).

Matrilocality and bilocality (living near either the bride's or groom's parents) were both common among gatherer-hunters and horticulturalists (Leacock 1955, 1977b: 252; Lee & DeVore 1968:8; Murdock 1949:229, 244, 247; Whyte 1978:223). Social rather than biological paternity was the issue in many societies, and to the dismay of early missionaries wives sometimes had full freedom to have lovers. There was no premarital or extramarital double standard, but equal restrictions on males and females with regard to sex, in slightly over half of the societies included in the above-cited survey. Women commonly had extramarital affairs in 33.7% and women's extramarital affairs were openly allowed or very common in another 19.8% (Whyte 1978:220). Women produced as much or more than men in most nonindustrial cultures (Whyte 1978:218), and men sought out competent and accomplished women, on whose labors they in great part depended, a casually noted fact that is sometimes elaborated upon (e.g., Landes 1938:18-19).

Data such as these are apparently irrelevant to those sociobiologists who freely attempt to explain away all contraditions to their assumptions. Barash points out that "the adoption of an unrelated child seems curiously nonadaptive and a potential example of the human tendency to perform true altruism, counter to the predictions of evolutionary theory." However, he argues, adoption is probably a hangover from the past when humanity lived in small groups and orphans were likely to be related to adopters. "Acting to increase their own inclusive fitness," the adopters' "behavior would accordingly have been favored by kin selection"(1977a:312-313).

Data such as the above may also be recast in the form of "cultural overlays" for what are conceived as hidden drives. For example, the Eskimo enjoyment of swapping sex partners would seem contrary to the requirements of male fitness. In this case, Barash writes that "the rigor of the natural environment makes cooperation of greater value than absolute confidence in genetic relatedness" (1977a:296).

In this instance Barash himself undermines his whole structure. All evidence indicates that 99% of human history was spent in groups which, like the Eskimo, do not conform to the "predictions" derived from our society since generosity and sharing are paramount concerns (Sahlins 1972:263-270). The broad sweep of human social evolution has entailed an overall decrease in cooperativeness and an increase in competitiveness (Childe 1939; Fried 1967). Furthermore, the increase of competitiveness has been accompanied by the emergence of the very gender roles that exist in our society but which Barash posits as in large part biologically based. These involve the separation of a superordinate world of "work," defined as masculine, from a subordinate domestic sphere, defined as feminine, and a concomitant male control--or right to control--female sexuality (Leacock 1978; Reiter 1975; Schlegel 1977).

Barash skirts recognition of such evolutionary trends by making an inaccurate citation. He asserts that "whatever the influence of biology upon our behavior, this imprint was established during the previous 99% of our existence as a species" (1977a:311). However, he characterizes the fundamental patterns of human ecology whereby "99% of us made a living, for 99% of our evolutionary history," as "pastoralism, nomadism, hunting-gathering, [and] agriculturalism" (1977a: 226). He refers to Lee and DeVore but what these two anthropologists actually state is that "Cultural Man has been on earth for some 2,000,000 years; for over 99 percent of this period he has lived as a hunter-gatherer" (Lee & Devore 1968: 3). Barash's misrepresentation of this point is critical, because the institutionalization of a subordinate domestic role for women and formalized male control of female sexuality accompanied the development of pastoral and elaborated agricultural economies. These developments only got under way about 10,000 years ago.

Social Behavior in Egalitarian Societies

Contemporary peoples who are categorized as hunter-gatherers--or gatherer-hunters (Teleki 1975)--no longer live in foraging economies. Many of them have not done so for a long time. Their subsistence varies according to their specific histories and to the nature of such lands as they have managed to retain. They may live in part by trading forest products, by government or mission provisioning, by seasonal low-paid wage work, or sometimes, to this day, by enforced labor or virtual slavery. Therefore their lives are far from free and autonomous as they were in the past.

Moreover, our knowledge of the social behavior of gatherer-hunters prior to the period of European colonization is spotty. It was seldom in the interest of settlers, traders, and colonial officials to understand and record the cultural lives of peoples whose labor they were using and whose lands they were moving in on. There were some notable exceptions, especially among missionaries who learned the languages and studied the cultures of aboriginal peoples as part of the effort to convert them to Christianity.

An unusually full account of early relations with a hunting people was written by the 17th century Jesuit, Paul Le Jeune, prefect of the mission at Quebec. He sent detailed reports to his superiors in Paris describing his problems in converting and "civilizing" the Montagnais of the Labrador Peninsula. Le Jeune deplored the independence of Montagnais women. He reported lecturing a converted man "that he was the master and that in France women do not rule their husbands" (Thwaites 1906 V:179). He was offended by the lewd ribaldry the Montagnais enjoyed, and into which the women entered along with the men. "Their language has the foul odor of the sewers," he wrote. A major problem that concerned him was the sexual freedom of the women, and the men's lack of interest in his attempts to curtail it. "I told him that it was not honorable for a woman to love anyone else except her husband," Le Jeune wrote, "and that, this evil being among them, he himself was not sure that his son, who was there present, was his son." Le Jeune was good enough to record the Montagnais' reply: "Thou hast no sense. You French people love only your own children; but we love all the children of our tribe" (Thwaites 1906 VI:255).

The stated Montagnais ideal was matrilocal residence after marriage. In actual practice, however, there was apparently enough flexibility to allow for viable proportions of males and females, old and young, in the groups of up to 20 people who lived together in a lodge (Leacock 1955). Yet the matrilocal preference was so strong that Le Jeune reported it would be necessary to convert and educate girls as well as boys. Otherwise a young man would be lost to the mission upon marriage; according to custom he would, as Le Jeune put it, follow his wife into the woods (Thwaites 1906 V:145).

The Montagnais planned their families, and their norm of three or maybe four children contrasted with the seven or eight of the French. Like the Eskimo, those with more children gave some to be adopted by childless couples. As part of the mission program, French families requested Montagnais children to be adopted and raised as Christians. However, the Montagnais complained that their generosity was not reciprocated: everywhere one saw Montagnais children among the French, but there were no French children among the Montagnais (Thwaites 1906 IX:233).

The egalitarian relations between the sexes among the Montagnais of the Labrador Peninsula were based on a compatibility between the well-being of the group and that of each individual within it (Leacock 1978). By contrast with competitively organized societies, among band societies like the Montagnais, the more able any individual was, the better for other individuals. Since necessities were shared as needed, the more able person did not put the less able out of a job, but made more food available in camp.

All adults participated directly in the acquisition and distribution of necessities; all were primary producers. In warm areas--the climates in which humanity evolved--women as foragers furnished the major proportion of food (Lee & DeVore 1968:43). Contrary to Barash's relegation-to-the-nursery stereotype, women were apparently away from camp as much as men (Draper 1975:85-86; Sahlins 1972:15-24). In cold climates, where the gathering season is short, women fished, snared small game, and hunted when they needed or wanted to, but their most important contribution to group survival was in working leather to make clothing. In both warm and cold climates, women participated in collective hunts which often furnished a major proportion of meat.

The collective hunt of the Mbuti of Zaire as described by Putnam (Turnbull 1965:203) offers an instructive contradiction of the notion that children keep women "housebound." Virtually everyone but the elderly went into the forest and the men set up a row of nets in a large semi-circle. The women left young children with the men, and with infants on their backs, went further into the forest to form a counter semi-circle. They then yelled and beat the brush with sticks, driving animals toward the nets to be speared by the men and grabbing small slow moving game encountered on the way to be thrown into the baskets also slung across their backs.

The inaccuracy of European stereotypes about women's roles was experienced by one Samuel Hearne in the late 18th century. Hearne was enlisting the service of some Chipewyan Indians to guide him from Fort Churchill on Hudson's Bay across northern Canada to the Coppermine River. His first attempt floundered, primarily because the Hudson's Bay post manager decided that the Chipewyan party with whom Hearne was to travel should not include women and children. Without the women's assistance on the trail, the men turned back. Women and men were complementary work teams in the sub-arctic. Among the Chipewyan who had given up communal caribou hunting for the role of "carriers," as Hearne put it, women were essential both as fur workers and as porters who carried up to 150 pounds of furs (Hearne 1911).

Many horticultural societies were also characterized by egalitarian relations between the sexes at the time of European colonial expansion and conquest, as attested to by ethnohistorical materials on the native cultures of colonial North America. Matrilocality was common as both an ideal and an actual pattern of postmarital residence. It still persists among the Hopi and Zuni of the southwestern United States. Women were the farmers among most native North Americans, and were far from housebound. Powell (1880) described how Wyandot Huron women sent their husbands and sons to the forest for meat, and then worked in parties, going from one person's field to another. When the work was finished, all feasted. Mary Jemison, captured as a young girl by the Iroquois, described similar arrangements. The women appointed one of their elders to organize work parties, and they moved together from field to field, getting the work done, enjoying each other's company, and minimizing competitiveness at the same time (Seaver 1977:70).

With regard to control over women's sexuality, the late 19th and early 20th century studies of sexual behavior were usually guilty of unabashed ethnocentrism and occasional exaggeration. Nonetheless, they offered examples of a sexual freedom for women that often no longer obtained, or was not admitted to, later when systematic field work was carried out by professional anthropologists. Even by the mid-19th century, however, practices had already changed. For example, the dormitories where 17th century Iroquois girls were free to receive lovers (Richards 1957:42-43) were either not reported or no longer remembered when Lewis Henry Morgan wrote that Iroquois women could be beaten for adultery (Morgan 1954 [1851] I:322). By that time the female-centered longhouse, from which a husband who did not please could be sent away by his wife, had given way to single family households formally headed by wage-earning men.

Both Westermarck (1922 III:223-266) and Hartland (1910 II:101-248) give extensive examples of patterned extramarital liaisons as well as informal sexual freedom in a variety of cultures, egalitarian and otherwise. Hartland (243-244) comments that in the cultures he reviewed, social paternity was more important to a man than biological paternity. A husband "does not too curiously inquire into the origin of a child who will raise his status and add to his influence in society." Cases of extramarital liaisons by women, both as social or ritual formalities and as informal preferences, were "common enough and distributed widely enough," for Hartland to doubt that "the masculine pattern of jealousy can be as fundamental and primitive as it is sometimes asserted to be."

For those who eschew work prior to the modern period of fieldwork by formally trained anthropologists as unworthy of serious consideration, Ford and Beach (1951:113-116) come to parallel conclusions. They find that in a sample of 139 societies, 39% "approve of some type of extra-mateship liaison" for women as well as men. Their percentage is somewhat higher than Whyte's (1978) finding cited above, since their sample includes a higher proportion of egalitarian cultures and excludes European and Oriental state-organized societies. Ford and Beach (1951:117-118) discuss the reports that American husbands show a greater interest in extramarital intercourse than do American wives:

> Interpretation of this apparent variation . . . must be made with caution. In the light of the cross-cultural evidence which we have presented it seems at least possible that the difference reflects primarily the effects of a lifetime of training under an implicit double standard. It has not been demonstrated that human females are necessarily less inclined toward promiscuity than are males . . . In those societies which have no double standard in sexual matters and in which a variety of liaisons are permitted, the women avail themselves as eagerly of their opportunity as do the men.

Today, given the tenor of changes in the last quarter of a century, Ford and Beach could make their point in less qualified terms.

Male Dominance and the Double Standard

In sum, then, the ethnographic evidence contradicts Barash's simplistic argument for biologically based universal gender roles. What can we say about the emergence of male dominance and the double standard? More work needs to be done both where they are the result of European colonization (Etienne & Leacock, eds., in press) and where they are independent evolutionary developments (Leacock 1978).

The outlines of women's decline in status have been drawn for the Aztecs of Mexico (Nash 1978) and the ancient Mesopotamians (Rohrlick-Leavitt 1977). Nash (p. 350) writes,

> The history of the Aztecs provides an example of the transformation from a kinship-based society with a minimum of status differentiation to a class-structured

empire. By tracing the changes in the aboriginal New World state, we can point to the interrelationships between male specialization in warfare, predatory conquest, a state bureaucracy based on patrilineal nobility supported by an ideology of male dominance, and the differential access to its benefits between men and women.

Parallel developments can be traced in Mesopotamia as the development of trade and the specialization of labor led to politically organized urban societies and systematic warfare for access to trade routes and important resources (Rohrlich-Leavitt 1977). A plaque dating from the 24th century B.C. documents the imposition of a double standard for sexual conduct: "The women of former days used to take two husbands, (but) the women of today (if they attempted this) were stoned with stones (upon which was incribed their evil) intent" (Kramer 1963:322).

New Guinea offers a contemporary instance where the process of men attempting to control women in order to further socialeconomic interests has been observed. Male-female relations have been of considerable interest in highland New Guinea, where openly expressed and often elaborately ritualized hostility between the sexes is common (Brown & Buchbinder 1976). The men do a great deal of posturing, and some serious threatening, as they assert their need and right, as they see it, to dominate women. According to the culture and the situation, women variously accept, defy, or ridicule the male stance, and there may be violence to the point of death on both sides.

Highland New Guinea is an area where the investment of considerable labor on desirable agricultural lands, where specialization and trade, and where an elaborated pattern of warfare related to access to good lands and trade networks are all interrelated (Langness & Weschler 1971). Pigs are of primary importance in all manner of social gift giving, especially in relation to political alliances and negotiations for access (often through marriage) to good lands and trade networks. Women feed the pigs from their gardens, but the pigs are used by men in these negotiations. Hence, as Strathern (1972) has made clear, control of women's labor is enormously important to men.

Men compete fiercely with each other for women, as well as for the service of sometimes landless or at least low status men known as "rubbish" or "garbage" men, but they band together to assert their dominance over women through ritual and other means. I have elsewhere argued (Leacock 1978:254-

255) that the ritualization of sex hostility in highland New Guinea is the acting out on an ideological level of the reality that men are competing with women for control of what women produce. Significantly, in areas where New Guinea women still control their own production, male-female relations are generally amicable and more egalitarian (Goldhamer 1973).

Interestingly, men are usually not macho when it comes to sex. They are taught to be fearful of women and to be wary of too much sexual involvement. Nor are men assured of their superiority; instead, in a typical eastern highland group,

> they recognize . . . that in physiological endowment men are inferior to women, and, characteristically, they have recourse to elaborate artificial means to redress this contradiction and to demonstrate its opposite (Read 1954:26-27).

Seen in its cultural context, then, the New Guinea "battle of the sexes" is anything but the working out of a biological propensity for a double standard of sexual conduct.

The last example I shall offer here of an instance where the emergence of male dominance and a double standard can be studied in detail is from West Africa. Urbanized conquest states and socioeconomic stratification are old in much of West Africa. This plus Moslem influence from the north had adverse effects on the position of women prior to colonial conquest by Europe. Nonetheless, in most sub-Saharan West African cultures, women retained important and publically recognized economic, social, and political roles, and they were not relegated to a "private" household sphere (Mullings 1976; Sudarkasa 1976).

Children were much desired to swell the numbers of one's lineage. In West African societies where descent was patrilineal, social, not biological paternity was the important issue as attested to by many of Westermarck's and Hartland's examples cited above. The bride price was--and often still is--a payment by a man's kin for a right to the wife's children. When a woman of means and ambition wanted to add children to her own lineage in a patrilineal society, she often had the option of becoming a "female husband." This institution enabled her to set up her own household and marry other women, whose children by their lovers belonged to her lineage (Liebowitz 1978:139-142).

Okonjo (1976:45) writes that a number of West African societies traditionally had

> political systems in which the major interest groups are defined and represented by sex . . . within them each sex manages its own affairs, and women's interests are represented at all levels.

Women, as traders, had their organizations to govern market procedures, adjudicate disputes, and protect women's interests.

The most fully documented women's organizations are those among the Igbo of Nigeria, where in 1929, women organized a powerful protest against the colonial policies that were undermining their status. In the "Women's War," or so-called "Aba Riots," thousands of women demonstrated outside the Native Administration centers, ridiculed the British appointed Warrant Chiefs, and burned Native Courts. The British fired on them; between 50 and 60 women were killed and many more wounded. Women were, of course, protesting the loss of their traditional public roles. Of relevance for the present discussion, however, is the fact that in some of these protests their personal sexual freedom was raised along with political and economic issues. In calling for a return to "the customs of olden times," women in one region

> proclaimed that henceforth cultivation of cassava was to be confined to women; that disputes were to be tried by village councils and not by native courts; that brideprices were not to exceed a certain sum and were to be paid in native currency; and that married women were to be allowed sexual intercourse with other men than their husbands (Meek 1937:202).

Sociobiology and Social Considerations

I said at the outset of this paper that my study of children's socialization in elementary school renders me sensitive to the messages that are transmitted to students in the name of scientific truth (Leacock 1969, 1977a). For example, in the film made for high schools, Sociobiology, Doing What Comes Naturally (Document Associates 1976), Robert Trivers and Irven DeVore are presented as ignoring data such as those I have just discussed, and instead as arguing that male competitive aggression and female compliance--sex roles that our society has idealized--are biologically based. The film's alternation of "parallel" scenes showing baboons and humans and the accompanying narration portray male competitive aggression and male dominance as the major biological components of both baboon and human behavior. There is virtually no reference to such essential human traits as communicativeness, cooperativeness, sociality, and restless curiosity.

Today, exciting data are being collected on the complexity, variability, and adaptiveness of animal life that are made possible by the intricacy and power of natural selection, and on the glimmerings of human culture and consciousness that can be seen in primate societies. It is a sorry commentary that these data should be submerged behind an emphasis on competition and aggression. Moreover, the point of the film is not left to the imagination. Trivers states that, "It's time we started viewing ourselves as having biological, genetic, and natural components to our behavior. And that we should start setting up a physical and social world which matches those tendencies."

Scientists have a responsibility to take seriously the ideological messages conveyed by such treatments as this film. With respect to the sociobiological inquiry into the "biological bases of all social behavior" (Wilson 1975:4), the invidious effects of 19th century "social Darwinism" are too well known for researchers to ignore the mandates of scientific rigor and bypass their responsibility to phrase their speculations carefully.

Teleological phrasings that employ terms like "concerned with," "has an interest in," or "wants to," in describing an animal's behavior, are to be regarded as "a convenient shorthand" and not to imply conscious volition (Barash 1977a:51-52). However, such a terminology misleads the lay reader and is open to misuse by the media. It can easily be employed to slough over the complexity and the vast differences in behaviors associated with mating and to reduce them all to a single narrow model of male competitive aggression as an animal "seeks" to improve its inclusive fitness.

The use of terms such as marriage, divorce, and rape to describe behavior of non-human animals also imputes a human kind of volition to them. Worse, it takes behavior from different phylogenetic levels which is merely analogous and derived from varying causes, and implies it to be homologous and derived from the same causes. Irresponsibility is compounded by ignoring the considerable variability in behavior that these terms cover just within the human species as documented by ethnographic data, and by reducing complex, variable human behavior to biologically based "trends."

Barash (1977b:116) might argue that he is merely being humerous when he writes of redwinged blackbirds that "the nicities of domesticity take second place to the selfish realities of evolution," and "females prefer harem membership to cozy monogamy, so long as the harem-master offers enough benefits to compensate for the loss of his undivided attention." Apparently, however, he is quite serious. Since "fitness--the key to sociobiology--is so dependent on reproductive success," Barash (1977:119) writes, "we might expect reproductive behaviors to be especially sensitive to natural selection." Therefore,

> Courtship serves the important function of permitting an individual to assess the characteristics of a prospective mate and to reject those less suitable . . . Among gulls, mated pairs that fail to rear offspring one year are significantly more likely to seek a new mate the following year than pairs that were reproductively successful. (Isn't this equivalent to divorce?) Male hummingbirds permit females to feed on their territories only when the females permit the males to copulate with them. (Equivalent to prostitution?) A male mountain bluebird who discovers a strange male near his mate will aggressively attack the stranger and will attack his own female as well, provided this occurs at the time copulation normally occurs in nature. (Male response to adultery?)

The way in which such terminology can encourage circular reasoning rather than rigorous testing is illustrated by Barash's (1977a:63-66) research on the mountain bluebird. Barash refers to his work as yielding conclusive evidence that male bluebirds respond to potential "adulterers" in a manner strictly compatible with a drive for inclusive fitness. However, Gould (this volume) points out that Barash failed to use control bluebirds in his experiment.

Metaphorical phrasings that focus on individuals apart from their social context obscure both the complexity of interactions among individual behaviors, forms of group organization, and ecological contexts, and the resulting variability of behaviors within a species. Van den Berghe (1977:126) stresses the view that individuals are "mortal conglomerations of billions of cells that evolved as carnal envelopes for the transmission of potentially immortal genes." It is paradoxical that a theoretical statement about sociobiology should reveal such a strong emphasis on adaptation at the level of the individual gene at the very time when geneticists are engaged in strenuous debate over just how important adaptation actually is in the process of evolutionary change (Kimura 1976). Genes of course are not immortal, and never will be. They do make copies of themselves, but these change in response to little understood relations with the organism's environment.

Despite the aura of genetic immutability conferred by statements such as Van den Berghe's, sociobiologists themselves are adding new data to studies of behavioral variability within a species. Barash (1974:419) notes that the yellow-bellied marmot organizes itself differently in different environments. In a synthesis of research on mating patterns among birds, Emlen and Oring (1977:222) report "considerable lability in mating systems" among populations of the same species living in varied ecological settings. In a recent study of crickets Cade (1978) describes variability in male mating behavior in relation to other males. Male crickets may either themselves chirp to attract females, or may wait quietly near another chirping male to intercept a female. These authors each cite parallel data on other species. Perhaps the most dramatic example of social influences on a species is that discovered over a half century ago: the swarming locust is the same species as the solitary grasshopper, but changes its behavior, and after a time its shape, when crowded together (Hemming 1978:12).

These kinds of data raise profound questions about evolution. It is indeed unfortunate that such questions become lost, in the public image of sociobiology, behind oversimplifications about competition, aggression, and an all-consuming drive for personal inclusive fitness by the (usually male) individual. My point is, the media alone are not to blame.

Finally, but most important, it must be pointed out that the histories of particular peoples are sometimes ignored in sociobiologically oriented studies of human groups. The Yąnamamö of Venezuela figure importantly as subjects for sociobiological research on biology and social behavior (Chagnon, this volume). This research has been presented in a widely used film as significant for understanding "primitive man." The Yąnamamö have been tagged "the fierce people" (Chagnon 1968). Accounts of male-female relations among them stress brutality towards women (Harris 1975:399).

However, we should be reminded that the Yąnamamö are on the borders of the Amazon basin, an area in which the estimated 16th century population of 1,500,000 has been reduced by disease, slave raiding, and warfare to just 75,000. In fact, the geographer, William Smole (1976:15), suggests that the Yąnamamö probably first earned their reputation for fierceness in the 18th century when they fought off a Spanish expedition that was supposedly chasing fugitive slaves. Smole himself studied a group living in a more secluded area than that investigated by Chagnon, and more protected from incursions from the outside. He found inter-village relations to be more peaceful and male-female relations more egalitarian (Smole 1976:31-32,70,75).

To ignore these historical and cultural facts in monographs and films means that both students and the general public are reached with an extremely negative message about a people whose lives and culture are at present in serious danger. Valuable deposits of uranium have recently been discovered on Yąnamamö lands and severe conflict has already occurred over their use.

Care in reporting an entire situation cannot wholly safeguard a scientist from irresponsible reportage by others and by the media. But it can help.

Summary

This paper makes three kinds of points, theoretical, empirical, and sociological. On theory, I argue that the anthropological synthesis, whereby humanity is studied in its biological and social totality, is a fuller expression of Darwinism than the sociobiological synthesis that seeks to use the same parameters and quantitative theory to analyze social behavior across all phylogenetic lines. According to the full implications of evolutionary theory, selection not only produces new forms, but also new relationships, and has done so many times prior to the emergence of humanity. Such new relationships require different parameters for their analysis.

Wilson considers it possible to define categories for analysis that override well recognized distinctions between different phyla. I argue that the metaphorical properties of language, which can reduce analogies to homologies, make this appear possible. Based on work on both insects and mammals, Schneirla stressed the pitfalls of analogical thinking. He pointed out that both the mechanisms and the consequences of behavior referred to by a term like communication were so different among insects and mammals that to use the same term for both was misleading. Wilson is of course aware of such problems and writes of the necessity for terminological precision. However, after describing the variability of behaviors covered by a term like aggression, he proceeds to use the term as if he were discussing a single entity. With respect to the biological basis of human behavior, in the end he falls back on the certainty that humans inherit the capacity to learn behaviors--an insight taken for granted within the anthropological synthesis.

With respect to empirical data, I argue that Barash ignores, misrepresents, or attempts to explain away data on the male-female complementarity and sexual freedom that exist in many societies. He does this in the course of arguing that the drive for inclusive fitness, plus the differential investment of males and females in their offspring, lay a biological basis for a double standard for human sexual behavior. I offer several examples of the kinds of evidence ignored by Barash: an account of women's sexual freedom among the 17th century Montagnais of the Labrador Peninsula, Canada, a freedom the missionaries sought to change; anecdotal and quantitative data on the absence of a double standard and on other culture traits that contradict Barash's hypothesis; and brief references to socioeconomic bases for the emergence of male dominance and the double standard in ancient Mesopotamia, among the pre-colonial Aztecs of Mexico and the post-colonial Igbo of Nigeria, and in highland New Guinea.

As for sociological considerations, the media image of sociobiological research, as epitomized by the movie, Sociobiology: Doing What Comes Naturally, purveys to a wide audience a fallacious notion that male aggression and competition over females are major driving forces that underlie human social behavior. Given this problem, and the history of social Darwinism, sociobiologists would do well to avoid teleological and analogical formulations in describing animal behavior, that along with the use of terms like rape, divorce, and adultery for animals, are scientifically misleading, and conducive to reducing causes for complex human behaviors to simplistic formulae of genetic determination. Last, when human populations are studied and the studies are publicized, it is critical that people be considered in the light of their full histories and cultural experiences.

Acknowledgements

I should like to express my gratitude to the editors of this volume, and especially James Silverberg, for detailed and helpful criticisms. I also wish to acknowledge my longterm indebtedness to comparative psychologist Ethel Tobach, whose incisive thinking first introduced me to some of the questions explored in this paper.

Literature Cited

Aronson, L.R., E. Tobach, J.S. Rosenblatt & D.S. Lehrman (eds.). Selected Writings of T.C. Schneirla. Freeman, San Francisco.

Barash, D.P. 1974. The evolution of marmot societies: A general theory. Science 185:415-420.

_______. 1977a. Sociobiology and behavior. Elsevier, Amsterdam.

_______. 1977b. The new synthesis. Wilson Quarterly Summer:108-119.

Brown, P. & G. Buchbinder (eds.). 1976. Man and woman in the New Guinea highlands. American Anthropological Association, Washington, D.C.

Cade, W. 1978. Of cricket song and sex. Natural History 87(1):64-73.

Chagnon, N. 1968. Yąnamamö: The fierce people. Holt, Rhinehart & Winston, New York.

Childe, V.G. 1939. Man makes himself. Oxford University Press, New York.

Dawkins, R. 1977. The selfish gene. Oxford University Press, New York.

Document Associates. 1976. Sociobiology: Doing what comes naturally (film). Hobel-Leiterman Productions, New York.

Draper, P. 1975. !Kung women: Contrasts in sexual egalitarianism in foraging and sedentary contexts. In R.R. Reiter (ed.), Toward an anthropology of women. Monthly Review Press, New York, pp. 77-109.

Emlen, S.T. & L.W. Oring. 1977. Ecology, sexual selection, and the evolution of mating systems. Science 197:215-223.

Etienne, M. & E. Leacock (eds.). In press. Women and colonization: Anthropological perspectives. J.F. Bergin, Brooklyn, New York.

Ford, C.S. & F.A. Beach. 1951. Patterns of sexual behavior. Harper, New York.

Fried, M.H. 1967. The evolution of political society. Random House, New York.

Goldhamer, F.K. 1973. The "misfit" of role and status for the New Guinea highlands woman. Paper read at the 72nd annual meeting of the American Anthropological Association, New Orleans.

Harris, M. 1975. Culture, people, nature. Crowell, New York.

Hartland, E.S. 1910. Primitive paternity. 2 Vols. David Nutt, London.

Hearne, S. 1911. A journey from Prince of Wales's fort in Hudson's Bay to the Northern Ocean. Champlain Society, Toronto.

Hemming, C.F. 1978. A new plague of locusts. Natural History 87(10):6-18.

Kimura, M. 1976. Population genetics and molecular evolution. The Johns Hopkins Medical Journal 138:253-261.

Kramer, S.N. 1963. The Sumerians, their history, culture and character. University of Chicago Press, Chicago.

Landes, R. 1938. The Ojibwa woman. Columbia University Press, New York.

Langness, L.L. & J.C. Weschler (eds.). 1971. Melanesia: Readings on a culture area. Chandler, Scranton.

Leacock, E. 1955. Matrilocality in a simple hunting economy (Montagnais-Naskapi). Southwestern Journal of Anthropology 11:31-47.

______. 1969. Teaching and learning in city schools. Basic Books, New York.

______. 1977a. Race and the "we-they dichotomy" in culture and classroom. Anthropology & Education Quarterly 8:152-159.

______. 1977b. The changing family and Lévi-Strauss, or whatever happened to fathers? Social Research 44:235-259.

______. 1978. Women's status in egalitarian society: Implications for social evolution. Current Anthropology 19:247-275.

Lee, R.B. & I. DeVore (eds.). 1968. Man the hunter. Aldine, Chicago.

Leibowitz, L. 1978. Females, males, families: A biosocial approach. Duxbury, North Scituate, Massachusetts.

Meek, C.K. 1937. Law and authority in a Nigerian tribe. Oxford University Press, London.

Morgan, L.H. 1968. The American beaver and his works. World, Cleveland.

______. 1954 [1851]. League of the Ho-De-No-Sau-Nee or Iroquois. 2 Vols. Human Relations Area Files, New Haven.

______. 1974 [1877]. Ancient society. Peter Smith, Gloucester, Massachusetts.

Mullings, L. 1976. Women and economic change in Africa. In N.J. Hafkin & E.G. Bay (eds.), Women in Africa: Studies in social and economic change. Stanford University Press, Stanford, California, pp. 239-264.

Murdock, G.P. 1949. Social structure. Macmillan, New York.

Nash, J. 1978. The Aztecs and the ideology of male dominance. Signs 4:349-362.

Okonjo, K. 1976. The dual-sex political system in operation: Igbo women and community politics in midwestern Nigeria. In N.J. Hafkin & E.G. Bay (eds.), Women in Africa: Studies in social and economic change. Stanford University Press, Stanford, California, pp. 45-58.

Powell, J.W. 1880. Wyandot government: A short study of tribal society. Annual Reports of the Bureau of American Ethnology 1:59-69.

Read, K.E. 1954. Cultures of the central highlands, New Guinea. Southwestern Journal of Anthropology 10:1-43.

Reiter, R.R. 1975. Toward an anthropology of women. Monthly Review Press, New York.

Richards, C.B. 1957. Matriarchy or mistake: The role of Iroquois women through time. Proceedings of the 1957 Annual Spring Meeting, American Ethnological Society, pp. 36-45.

Rohrlich-Leavitt, R. 1977. Women in transition: Crete and Sumer. In R. Bridenthal & C. Koonz (eds.), Becoming visible: Women in European history. Houghton Mifflin, Boston, pp. 36-59.

Sahlins, M. 1972. Stone age economics. Aldine, Chicago.

Schlegel, A. 1977. Sexual stratification: A cross-cultural view. Columbia University Press, New York.

Seaver, J.E. (ed.). 1977 [1856]. Life of Mary Jemison, Enlarged edition. Narratives of North American Indian captivities, Vol. 41. Garland, New York.

Smole, W.J. 1976. The Yanoama Indians: A cultural geography. University of Texas Press, Austin.

Strathern, M. 1972. Women in between: Female roles in a male world, Mount Hagen, New Guinea. Academic Press, New York.

Sudarkasa, N. 1976. Female employment and family organization in West Africa. In D.G. McGuigan (ed.), New research on women and sex roles. University of Michigan Center for Continuing Education of Women, Ann Arbor, pp. 48-63.

Tax, S. (ed.). 1960. Evolution after Darwin. University of Chicago Press, Chicago.

Teleki, G. 1975. Primate subsistence patterns: Collectors-predators and gatherer-hunters. Journal of Human Evolution 4:124-184.

Thwaites, R.G. (ed.). 1906. The Jesuit relations and allied documents. 71 Vols. Burrows, Cleveland.

Turnbull, C.M. 1965. The Mbuti Pygmies: An ethnographic survey. Anthropological Papers of the American Museum of Natural History, 50(3). New York.

Van den Berghe, P.L. 1977. Sociobiology, dogma, and ethics. Wilson Quarterly Summer:121-126.

Westermarck, E. 1922. The history of human marriage. 3 Vols. Allerton, New York.

Whyte, M.K. 1978. Cross-cultural codes dealing with the relative status of women. Ethnology 17:211-237.

Wilson, E.O. 1971. Insect societies. Harvard University Press, Cambridge, Massachusetts.

_______. 1975. Sociobiology: The new synthesis. Harvard University Press, Cambridge, Massachusetts.

Stephanie A. Shields

19. Nineteenth-Century Evolutionary Theory and Male Scientific Bias

Evidence of the power of science and scientists to effect massive intellectual revolutions can be found throughout history. From Copernicus to Darwin to Einstein, those who challenge prevailing beliefs about the world have endured personal hardship as a result of their efforts. Furthermore, social resistance to scientific progress may be quite strong, is often organized, and not infrequently politically based. As a consequence, the scientist is generally esteemed as an objective, free thinking seeker of truth.

It is simplistic, however, to believe that with the assumption of the scientific role, other well learned social roles and their concomitant values are left behind. Science is objective, but scientists may be subjective, particularly with respect to topics closely associated with their own daily lives. As human beings engaged in science we bring to our work values and attitudes which, though nonconscious, may guide our selection of problems, methodology, and interpretation. This may be of little direct concern when the topic of investigation is far removed from normal human social interaction. It is difficult to imagine, for example, that cultural values could wreak havoc on genetic studies of *Drosophila* without direct government intervention. But the closer the topic to everyday life, the more problematic personal value systems become. The intrusion of cultural values into the conduct of science is nowhere more consistently evident than in the study of human gender differences.

Historically, the study of gender differences has consistently reflected prevailing cultural beliefs regarding the nature of males and females. Early philosophical speculation emphasized the inequality of the sexes on all dimensions of social importance. Sex differences in psyche were accepted as a fact of differences in physiology, thus, investigation of sex differences consisted only of cataloging them. This approach is epitomized in Aristotle's Historia Animalium:

> ...woman is more compassionate than man, more easily moved to tears, at the same time is more jealous, more querulous, more apt to scold and to strike. She is, furthermore, more prone to despondency and less hopeful than the man, more void of shame or self-respect, more false of speech, more deceptive, and of more retentive memory. She is also more wakeful, more shrinking, more difficult to rouse to action, and requires a smaller amount of nutriment (McKeon, 1941:637).

While Aristotle attributed female inferiority to "humors," in later centuries female inferiority was viewed as a function of divine fiat, physiological instability, or defects in the brain. Though the rationale for this belief changed over time, its substance remained the same: Females, in every respect, are lesser beings.

A refinement of the inferiority theme took shape with the development of evolutionary theory in the mid-19th century. Greater emphasis was placed on the complementarity of the sexes. That is, the strengths of each sex were seen as compensating for the deficiencies of the other. Gender differences were viewed as both a product of evolution and a necessary component of further evolution. Complementarity here did not imply co-equality. Rather, those qualities most valued by upper-class Victorian society were those deemed most typically male.

This paper describes the prevailing scientific beliefs regarding gender differences during the latter half of the 19th century. After outlining assumptions regarding general gender differences, beliefs about specific dimensions of female ability and personality will be discussed. I will then consider the unintentional male scientific bias which gave rise to these views and finally discuss the meaning of this social history of views on gender for current sociobiological research.

Assumptions Regarding Gender Differences

The implications of evolutionary theory for the study of human traits were recognized even as the merits of the theory were debated. Darwin himself hewed to the ancient belief in general female inferiority. In The Descent of Man, he noted that:

> The chief distinction in the intellectual powers of the two sexes is shewn [sic] by man's attaining to a higher eminence, in whatever he takes up, than can woman--whether requiring deep thought, reason, or imagination, or merely the use of the senses and hands (1922 [1871]:858).

He, like others, did grant that women had some redeeming qualities, among them "greater tenderness and less selfishness," as well as greater powers of intuition, rapid perception, and imitation. But possession of such traits should not be a source of pride because, as he observed, "some, at least, of these faculties are characteristics of the lower races and therefore, of a past and lower state of civilization" (p. 858).

What had much greater impact than his reiteration of female deficiencies, was his suggestion that males were inherently the more variable sex. His proposal, based on observation of the greater incidence of physical anomaly in males of all species, was intended to account for the fact that males of many species had developed greatly modified secondary sexual characteristics while mature females of the same species retained a resemblance to juveniles.

Once the connection between individual variation and species development was made, it was assumed by many that variation was valuable per se. Without variation, greatness, whether of an individual or a society, could not be achieved. Male deviations thus became legitimized by evolutionary theory and the hypothesis of male superiority through greater variability became a convenient explanation for the facts of social life. By the 1890's it was popularly believed that the female was the conservative and constant element in the species, while the male, being the more variable, was the source of differentiation and thus further species development.

Havelock Ellis, an influential social philosopher and sexologist, extended the concept of male variability from a description of physical traits to all other qualities of character and temperament. He conceded that male variability could explain the fact that there were more men than women in homes for the retarded. But more important, it also explained the fact that genius appeared to be an exclusively male trait. (Genius was defined by achievement of social eminence. Tests of mental ability had not yet been developed.) Variability seemed to be the key to understanding a number of social phenomena as Ellis solemnly observed:

> ...in the greater variational tendency of man we are in the presence of a fact that has a social and practical consequence of the widest significance, a fact which has affected the whole of human civilization (1903:238).

Its "widest significance" was simply the production of men of genius who "have largely created the lines of our progress" (p. 238).

The variability hypothesis enjoyed some degree of popularity until the first World War. Frequently the discussion revolved around the practical social implications of greater male variation. Edward Thorndike, a prominent American psychologist, suggested, for example, that since the narrower range of female ability confined women to "the mediocre grades of ability and achievement," women's education should prepare them for work "where the average level is essential" (1906:213).

The variability hypothesis was periodically met with opposition (Hollingworth 1913, 1914; Pearson 1897; Thompson 1903). Opponents disputed three assumptions. (1) Proponents of the hypothesis assumed that all human traits were normally distributed and so smaller variance would indicate a narrower range. Opponents argued that the assumption of normality was not justified. (2) Proponents of the hypothesis based their conclusions on comparisons of simple variance. Opponents argued that there were many other legitimate ways to compare variability, and that some were more appropriate. (3) Proponents believed that sex differences in social achievement were due to biological differences. Opponents argued that social factors were the more important determinants of success. All of the opponents' arguments had merit, but their objections were largely ignored or buried in rhetoric by the proponents of the variability hypothesis.

While the final cause of female nature was assumed to be the female's role as the conservative element in evolution, the efficient causes of her nature (and thus her place in society) were thought to be her lesser cerebral complexity and her reproductive physiology.

It was common knowledge that women had less opportunity for education and that they were likely to be confined to a life of domesticity. But these social facts were not considered to be modifiable social circumstances. Rather, they were seen as representations of biological necessity. Woman's mental inferiority was an unfortunate consequence of her biological destiny. George Romanes made this observation:

> ...but we may predict with confidence that, even under the most favourable conditions as to culture, and even supposing the mind of man to remain stationary...it must take many centuries for heredity to produce the missing five ounces of the female brain (1887:666).

Channeling women's efforts toward home and family responsibilities was seen as a necessity for the continuation of evolution, not simply as its unfortunate consequence. Women who achieved intellectually were then, as now, less likely to have children. The cause for this, as Herbert Spencer noted, "may be reasonably attributed to the overtaxing of their brains--an overtaxing which produces a serious reaction of the physique" (1873a:486).

The true victim of the childless woman, however, was society. If cheated of its most important product (children), further evolution was impossible. It is therefore not surprising that we find numerous tracts disparaging the higher education of women and glorifying the mother as the angel of the home (e.g., Hall 1918).

Further proof that the exaggerated differentiation of the sexes was a consequence of evolution came from observations of early anthropologists (Fee 1976). "Primitive races" were assumed by these scientists to represent earlier forms of human evolution and they noted that among primitives there were fewer differences between the sexes, physically as well as temperamentally. In primitive races women had flat features and broad bodies like men, in contrast to the wasp-waisted, bosomy Victorian woman. Primitive women also showed less concern with modesty and more concern with sex than the refined Victorian lady. This seemed proof positive that increasing sexual differentiation was an obvious product of evolution.

The Traits of Women

Given the assumptions that women were less variable, physiologically limited, and neurally underdeveloped, and further, that these differences were accentuated with further evolution, it should not be surprising that a number of specific traits were thought to be the simple consequence of being female. Throughout this period, scientific discussion of female behavior and ability emphasized women as a homogenous class of beings. When individual differences among women were acknowledged, departures from those considered typical and appropriate were regarded as aberrations. What then were the attributes of this class? The set of traits ascribed to women did vary from scientist to scientist, but there was almost universal agreement that gentility, perceptiveness, and affectability were uniquely female.

Gentility

One important attribute was morality (today the more accurate term would be gentility). Although biological facts, as interpreted by male scientists, seemed to point to the moral inferiority of the female, it was clear that the Victorian lady was one of great delicacy and refinement. It was, of course, apparent that women lacked the cerebral power to support a sense of justice, yet it appeared that morality was a peculiarly female virtue in higher civilizations. Consistent with the Judeo-Christian tradition scientists concluded that when women were good, they were very, very good. When they were bad they were damnable.

Illustrative of this position is the work of Lombroso and Ferrero, whose book on the female criminal was translated into English in 1899. They argued that true criminality was infrequent among women because they were less variable and thus less prone to exhibit aberration. Furthermore, they claimed the female brain was less active, and so, less likely to produce the irritation that results in criminal degeneration. Nevertheless, they observed that when the female is a criminal, she is much more cruel and violent than her male counterpart. The reason for this? Simply that:

> ...women are big children; their evil tendencies are more numerous and more varied than men's, but generally remain latent. When they are awakened and excited they produce results proportionately greater (Lombroso & Ferrero 1899:151).

In contrast to the relative absence of criminal tendencies in women, there seemed to be a general propensity for lying. Like every other trait, this one, too, seemed to be a natural consequence of physiology and intellectual limitation. Physical weakness, the concealment of menstrual function, the need to win men, and the duties of motherhood all fostered women's predisposition to lie.

Perceptiveness

Another disposition which seemed to be distinctly female was greater perceptual power which was most completely expressed in intuitive ability. Scientists who entertained this sex difference were quick to point out that such superiority did not lead to greater creativity in women because (1) their lesser variability predicted against this and (2) maturation of supportive intellectual powers was lacking.

Cerebral inferiority was often regarded as the cause of perceptual and intuitive superiority in females. But these qualities were not thought to be constituents of the higher mental processes. Proof of this lay in the fact that it was possessed, not only by women, but other creatures of limited mental ability. Among the many who adhered to this view, was a prominent psychologist who noted:

> Some women possess [intuition] in very high degree; young children, whose command of language is very slight, may exhibit it; and even in the higher animals, especially the dog, it is not altogether lacking (McDougall 1923:391).

Emotional Lability

A third trait, affectability, was a purported consequence of woman's mental and physical limitations. Relative deficits in neural development precluded the management of the emotions by the higher brain centers. More importantly, woman's reproductive physiology continually upset her emotional balance.

In the 19th century it was commonly believed that a woman was functionally incapacitated during menstruation. Physicians' descriptions of the typical menstruating woman read like an encyclopedia of mental and physical pathology. Perceptual distortion, physical weakness, even hallucination (Gross 1911) and "slight psychosis" (Icard 1890) were all, at one time or another, thought typical of the woman at menses. It was commonly acknowledged that a woman "...for one quarter of each month, during the best years of life is more or less sick and unfit for hard work" (Maudsley 1884:29).

Emotional lability was a limiting factor for the individual woman, but was thought to have great adaptive value for the species. Affectability subserved two important female instincts: the mating instinct and the maternal instinct.

Affectability made woman dependent on man and also caused her to be irresistibly attractive to him. Her vulnerability had the important function of eliciting the protective instinct in males, which overrode their aggressive and hunting instincts. The coyness which was an important component of her affectability also insured that she would mate only with the most suitable male.

The maternal instinct garnered far more attention than mating instincts, however. The concept of a unique maternal instinct had been accepted by scientists and philosophers long before the development of evolutionary theory. Yet it was within the context of this theory that the concept gained new meaning. Maternal instinct was the perfect vehicle for the 19th century scientist's understanding of female nature. It appeared to explain so much: woman's biological conservatism, her limited intellect, her emotionality.

So ingrained in the culture was the belief in an ideal type of maternal behavior that even those who eschewed the general concept of instinct accepted the instinctive component of maternal behavior. Many echoed Spencer's belief that woman's "...love of the helpless, which in her maternal capacity woman displays in a more special form than man, inevitably affects all her thoughts and sentiments" (1873b:36).

In summary, according to the male scientists of the 19th century woman was: biologically conservative, less variable, neurally underdeveloped, and physiologically vulnerable. She was also genteel, unimaginative, perceptive, modest, emotional, coy, dependent, and, above all, maternal. (See Shields 1975, for further discussion of these issues.)

Values and Science

It is clear that more than simple science was involved in 19th century investigation of sex differences. The "natural" woman, as described by scientists of that time, bears an uncanny resemblance to the "ideal" woman of upper class Victorian society. It is also clear that social reality provided a context for observation and evaluation of gender differences. The implicit values with which scientists approached their work inevitably affected the outcome of that work.

Scientists were the members of a society which they viewed as natural, inevitable, and even progressive. They sought justification for that society and found it in evolutionary theory. This was no conscious conspiracy to keep women in their place. Rather, this was a natural consequence of their attempt at objectivity. However, the need for justifying the prevailing social order and its values was so ingrained that scientists' observations were sometimes quite obviously guided by their expectations.

A striking example of science subserving social values can be found in the 19th century work on cortical localization of function. At mid-century neuroanatomists regarded the frontal lobes of the brain as the center of the higher mental processes, e.g., intelligence and creativity. Many researchers reported that, not only were the frontal lobes comparatively small and less convoluted in human female brains, but also that the parietal lobes (thought to be the center of the lower mental processes such as perception) were comparatively larger than those of male brains (Ellis 1934). Some even reported that these sex differences were visible in the brain of the fetus (Mobius 1901).

At the turn of the century a new theory of cortical function caused a revision of accepted facts concerning sex differences in brain structure. The parietal lobes came to be regarded as the seat of the higher mental processes, while the frontal lobes were credited with less prestigious functions. Once beliefs regarding the importance of these two areas of the brain had shifted, it became critical to reestablish congruence between neuroanatomical observation and accepted sex differences. Now neuroanatomists found that a previous generation had been mistaken in their observations. In 1895, an article in Popular Science Monthly reported these new findings:

> ...the frontal region is not, as has been supposed smaller in woman, but rather larger relatively.... But the parietal lobe is somewhat smaller, [furthermore,] a preponderance of the frontal region does not imply intellectual superiority...the parietal region is really the more important (Patrick 1895:212).

As we now know, the examination of neural tissue tells us nothing of the individual's gender. Nevertheless, structural differences were observed and were claimed to account for many social differences between the sexes.

If I were to sum up 19th century research on gender differences I could find no more accurate appraisal of its quality than one made in 1910 by Helen Woolley:

> There is perhaps no field aspiring to be scientific where flagrant personal bias, logic martyred in the cause of supporting a prejudice, unfounded assertions, and even sentimental rot and drivel, have run riot to such an extent as here (p. 340).

Implications for Sociobiology

It would be comfortable to view the history I have just renewed as an entertaining review of the foibles of science past. Accordingly, it might be claimed that we have progressed to a level of sophistication that precludes the intrusion of social bias into the conduct of objective inquiry. This conclusion, however, would overlook one fundamental fact, a fact as true today as in the 19th century: Science is part of the very fabric of social life which it seeks to investigate.

None of the social, biological, or behavioral sciences have escaped the introjection, however subtle, of cultural beliefs into scientific work. We need not return to the 19th century for specific examples of gender bias. Scientists, from a variety of disciplines, have described the androcentric character of gender difference research: anthropology (e.g., Martin & Voorhies 1975), psychology (e.g., Maccoby & Jacklin 1974), primatology (e.g., Lancaster 1975; Rowell 1972), and biology (e.g., Bleier 1976). The major conclusion one draws from such reviews is this: Science has thus far demonstrated not the adaptiveness of gender differences to biological imperatives, but the adaptiveness of science to cultural imperatives.

Major conceptual differences notwithstanding, sociobiology shares with its parent, evolutionary theory, a number of hereditarian assumptions regarding gender differences. The two assumptions which pose the greatest problem for the conduct of a bias-free investigation of gender differences are:

(1) Observable gender differences, behavioral as well as physiological, are ultimately reducible to genetically determined differences in reproductive role.

(2) Social systems which defy biological imperatives are maladaptive and ultimately doomed to failure.

The merits of these assumptions are currently being investigated by sociobiologists as well as those in opposing theoretical camps. Whatever the ultimate disposition of these assumptions, it is important to recognize their immediate potential for adding an unwanted sexism to research.

The problem is compounded by the apparent simplicity of sociobiology. By purporting to explain so much about behavior, it is attractive to all who would believe in an orderly, if not just, universe. It appears to explain a variety of social, psychological, and cultural events within the "simple" context of personal genetic survival. Though individual behaviors may be maladaptive, for genetic material this is the best of all possible worlds.

The gender-bias problems of science in general are thus even more problematic for sociobiology. It is important to recognize that even the most rigorous attempts to retain objectivity with respect to gender differences will not be completely successful. This is as true for sociobiologists as for nonsociobiologists; for traditionalists as for nontraditionalists. Perhaps the most salient characteristic of those with whom we interact is their gender. We were aware of this classification and socialized to respond to it long before we were socialized as scientists. It would be difficult, indeed, to believe that we leave behind years of earlier training when we enter the laboratory. The question of final importance, then, is this: Are we today any less the products of socialization than our scientific forebears?

Summary

This paper describes the study of gender differences during the latter half of the 19th century. The study of gender was grounded in three assumptions, sometimes explicitly stated, often implicitly accepted. These assumptions were: (1) Without individual variation, further evolution of the species is impossible. The female (of all species) is the conservative and constant element. The male is more variable and is thus the source of further species development. This sex difference obtains not only for physical characteristics, but all qualities of character and temperament, including intelligence. Although the differences between "average" male and female ability may be minimal, the range of male ability is much broader. Therefore, genius is a peculiarly male attribute. (2) Sex differences in ability are accentuated by the female's smaller brain and/or lesser cerebral complexity. (3) Woman's reproductive physiology makes her weaker and more vulnerable.

The nature of the female was believed to produce a number of specific female traits including gentility, emotional lability, and reliance on intuition over cognition.

Examination of the evidence put forth in support of these claims clearly demonstrates that social reality provided a context for observation and evaluation of gender differences. The "natural" woman, as described by 19th century scientists, precisely fits the description of the "ideal" woman of upper class Victorian society. Gender bias was not a conscious conspiracy against women, but a natural manifestation of the well-educated, well-to-do scientist's world view.

Today's social, biological, and behavioral sciences have not escaped the subtle introjection of cultural beliefs into scientific work. Examples of gender bias in contemporary science have been identified in many fields. Sociobiology is, perhaps, most at risk regarding gender bias because of its assumption that social behavior is a direct consequence of genetic imperatives. This assumption suggests a limited set of pertinent research questions regarding gender differences and a limited framework for their interpretation. Scientists of all theoretical persuasions have an important lesson to learn from 19th century evolutionary theory's treatment of gender. Even the most rigorous attempts to retain objectivity with respect to gender will not be completely successful, largely because the scientist is a member of his/her culture as well as a practitioner of objective scientific method.

Literature Cited

Bleier, R. 1976. Myths of the biological inferiority of women: An exploration of the sociology of biological research. _The University of Michigan Papers in Women's Studies_ 2:39-63.

Darwin, C. 1922 (1871). _The descent of man_. Second edition. Murrary, London.

Ellis, H. 1903. Variation in man and woman. _Popular Science Monthly_ 62:237-253.

_____ 1934. _Man and woman, a study of secondary and tertiary sexual characteristics_. Eighth revised edition. Heinemann, London.

Fee, E. 1976. Science and the woman problem: Historical perspectives. In M.S. Teitelbaum (ed.), Sex differences: Social and biological perspectives. Anchor Books, Garden City, New York, pp. 175-223.

Gross, H.G.A. 1911. Criminal psychology. Translated from fourth German edition by H.M. Kallen. Little, Brown & Company, Boston.

Hall, G.S. 1918. Youth, its education, regimen and hygiene. Appleton, New York.

Hollingworth, L.S. 1913. The frequency of amentia as related to sex. Medical Record 84:753-756.

______ 1914. Variability as related to sex differences in achievement. American Journal of Sociology 19:510-530.

Icard, S. 1890. La femme pendant la periode menstruelle. Alcan, Paris.

Lancaster, J.B. 1975. Primate behavior and the emergence of human culture. Holt, Rinehart & Winston, New York.

Lombroso, C. & W. Ferrero. 1899. The female offender. Translated. Appleton, New York.

Maccoby, E.E. & C.N. Jacklin. 1974. The psychology of sex differences. Stanford University Press, Stanford, California.

Martin, M.K. & B. Voorhies. 1975. Female of the species. Columbia University Press, New York.

Maudsley, H. 1884. Sex in mind and in education. Bordeen, Syracuse, New York.

McDougall, W. 1923. Outline of psychology. Scribner's, New York.

McKeon, R. (ed.). 1941. The basic works of Aristotle. Random House, New York.

Mobius, P.J. 1901. The physiological mental weakness of woman (A. McCorn, trans.). Alienist and Neurologist 22:624-642.

Patrick, G.T.W. 1895. The psychology of woman. Popular Science Monthly 47:209-225.

Pearson, K. 1897. The chances of death. Volume 1. Arnold, London.

Romanes, G.J. 1887. Mental differences between men and women. Nineteenth Century 21:666.

Rowell, T.E. 1972. Social behavior of monkeys. Hammondsworth, Penguin, London.

Shields, S.A. 1975. Functionalism, Darwinism, and the psychology of women: A study in social myth. American Psychologist 39:739-754.

Spencer, H. 1873a. The principles of biology. Volume 2. Appleton, New York.

______ 1873b. Psychology of the sexes. Popular Science Monthly 4:30-38.

Thompson, H.B. 1903. The mental traits of sex. University of Chicago Press, Chicago.

Thorndike, E.L. 1906. Sex in education. The Bookman 23:211-214.

Woolley, H.T. 1910. Psychological literature: A review of the recent literature on the psychology of sex. Psychological Bulletin 7:335-342.

Part 6

Nepotism and Conflict

Paul W. Sherman

20. The Limits of Ground Squirrel Nepotism

Introduction

Fifteen years ago Hamilton (1964:19) suggested that "The social behaviour of a species evolves in such a way that in each distinct behaviour-evoking situation the individual will seem to value his neighbours' fitness against his own according to the coefficients of relationship appropriate to that situation" (also Williams & Williams 1957; Williams 1966). Since then, Hamilton's "kin selection" hypothesis (Maynard Smith 1964) has been dissected theoretically (Orlove 1975; Scudo & Ghiselin 1975; Hubbell 1977 ms.) and tested among insects (Wilson 1971; Hamilton 1972; West-Eberhard 1975, this volume; Trivers & Hare 1976; Alexander & Sherman 1977), birds (Brown 1970; Maynard Smith & Ridpath 1972; Woolfenden 1975), nonhuman mammals (Kurland 1977; Massey 1977; Sherman 1977), and humans (Alexander 1977a, 1977b, 1979; Chagnon this volume; Irons this volume; B. Williams this volume). To date, Hamilton's hypothesis has not been falsified (but see Sahlins 1976 vs. Alexander 1977c and Sherman 1978a); indeed field and laboratory data strongly support it (Alexander 1974; Wilson 1975; Barash 1977; Vehrencamp 1978).

Because cooperating with relatives may reduce the genotypic costs (Alexander 1974:336) associated with proximity to conspecifics, kinship may enhance advantages of group-living. However kinship by itself is not an evolutionary cause of sociality (Hoogland & Sherman 1976), and many stable social groups are composed primarily of nonkin (e.g., McCracken & Bradbury 1977). Thus, studies supporting Hamilton's hypothesis do not implicate kinship in the evolution of group-living (Woolfenden & Fitzpatrick 1978; Koenig & Pitelka 1979) or of all social complexity (Brown 1978; Emlen 1978). Rather they suggest that when ecological circumstances favor aggregation (Brown & Orians 1970; Alexander 1974) and cooperation, and when assistance is not usually reciprocated (Trivers 1971), individuals favor close relatives over distant kin or nonkin.

Phenotypically unreciprocated assistance to conspecifics is defined as nepotism when variations in such favoritism are based on kinship, abilities of social donors to assist, and abilities of recipients to benefit from assistance. When potential recipients are equally likely to translate benefits into reproduction (for example they are of the same sex, age, and physical condition), nepotism is reflected in asymmetrical favoritism based on closeness of genetic relationship. While parental solicitude is a frequently observed form of nepotism, in many animals favoritism extends far beyond the immediate family. Further, although nepotism is highly elaborated in eusocial insects, clearly it is not confined to them (Wilson 1975; West-Eberhard this volume). Therefore it is inappropriate to ignore the possible significance of kinship when predicting or interpreting patterns of cooperation and competition (Alexander 1975).

Fifteen different field assistants and I spent four summers observing free-living Belding's ground squirrels, *Spermophilus beldingi* (Rodentia: Sciuridae), with the intent of answering three questions:

(1) Do conspecifics cooperate?
(2) If so, are relatives favored?
(3) What determines the extent of cooperation and competition?

We discovered that males do not behave parentally or cooperate with conspecifics. Females rear young in proximity to and in cooperation with their mothers, daughters, and sisters. Their behavior thus supports Hamilton's (1964) hypothesis. More distantly related females, aunt-niece, cousin-cousin, and grandmother-granddaughter pairs, compete as if unrelated (see Hamilton 1964, 1972 for discussions of degrees of relatedness among near and distant kin). These data suggest that *S. beldingi* nepotism is limited, in contrast to the pattern among some primates, in which slight differences in relationship even among distant kin correlate directly with differences in nepotism (Kurland 1977; Massey 1977).

Following Hamilton (1964), it is usually assumed that patterns of nepotism are predictable from considerations of "inclusive fitness," and that therefore prerequisites are knowledge of (1) genetic relationship among interacting conspecifics, and (2) benefits to recipients of assistance and costs to assisting individuals (West-Eberhard 1975; Bertram

1976). Assessment of benefits and costs must include considerations of intensity of competition (Alexander 1974). Here I suggest that an additional factor, demography, can limit nepotism and therefore must be considered when predicting or interpreting patterns of cooperation and competition. Demography has a spatial component, dispersal, and a temporal component, mortality. Either or both could limit nepotism because favoritism will not extend to relatives whose co-occurrence in space or time is so infrequent that their cooperation has rarely been selected. In other words, the elaboration of nepotism depends on kin accessability and kin availability, which in turn are contingent on the ecological circumstances affecting dispersal and mortality.

It is sometimes argued that an animal's kin recognition abilities limit nepotism. However I suggest that the kin recognition mechanism is of interest not because it limits favoritism, but because it evolves to facilitate nepotism and to prevent its misdirection. Thus "unrecognizable" relatives are those that have not consistently been accessable or available, or else those that it has never been reproductively advantageous (Hamilton 1964) to favor.

In this paper I will show that because female Belding's ground squirrels live in about equal proximity to all categories of kin, asymmetries in their behavior toward close and distant relatives are probably not due to within-matriline differences in dispersal (kin inaccessability). Mortality, on the other hand, may affect the behavioral asymmetries, because various kin are not equally likely to be simultaneously alive. I hypothesize that *S. beldingi* nepotism is limited by historical infrequency of interactions among relatives more distant than sisters (i.e., unavailability of distant kin).

Study Animal and Techniques

Belding's ground squirrels are diurnal, group-living rodents that inhabit the Sierra Nevada and Cascades (Turner 1972). I studied them in a meadow at the summit of Tioga Pass, Mono County, California (119° E, 38° N; elevation 3,040 meters). There they are usually active from May through October, hibernating the rest of the year (Morton, Maxwell, & Wade 1974; Morton, 1975). Females rear one litter of four to six young per summer, are reproductively mature at age one, and live four to six years (Sherman 1976). Males usually live three to four years and are not reproductively mature until they are two (Morton & Gallup 1975).

Exact age and matrilineal (uterine) relationships among

conspecifics are known for most ground squirrels at Tioga Pass. Between 1969 and 1973, M. L. Morton and his students individually toeclipped 731 of them. During 1974-77, my assistants and I eartagged another 1551, including all 651 young from 138 litters. We captured juveniles within three days of their first emergence above ground, and took precautions to ensure that all young were captured and unambiguously assigned to sibling groups.

Behavioral data were gathered during 3817 observation hours over four summers: 16 May-25 August, 1974 (4 observers 916 hours), 17 May-23 September, 1975 (6 observers, 1639 hours), 1 May-18 July, 1976 (6 observers, 527 hours), and 22 April-1 August, 1977 (7 observers, 735 hours). Ground squirrels were observed from platforms in trees or 2-3 m. tall tripods, usually with binoculars.

Animals were live-trapped and weighed at least once a week. All trapping was done during 3000+ non-observation hours. For marking, ground squirrels were hand-held; no anesthetic was used. Animals were permanently marked by attaching a numbered metal "fingerling" tag to each ear (Mohr 1934; Melchior & Iwen 1965). Those losing eartags were toe-clipped. Ground squirrels were also marked with human hair dye, for identification at a distance (Sherman 1976). I looked for but found no differences in behavior of marked and unmarked animals and in behavior of the same animals with different marks.

For each female, the "gestation period" was the 23-26 days between copulation and the precipitous body weight drop that accompanied parturition. The "lactation period" was the 25-28 days between parturition and the first appearance of young above ground. Young ceased attempting to suckle (i.e., were weaned) one to three days after first emergence.

The "natal burrow" was the one from which a juvenile first emerged. "Nest burrows" were those in use about the time young emerged. Burrows were permanently marked with painted rocks, nails, and sticks. Between-burrow distances were measured in the field.

Boundaries of areas defended by females around their burrows were determined by observing where fights occurred, where chases of trespassers stopped, and where scent marks were placed. Comparisons of defended areas were standardized within and between years by mapping boundaries when young first emerged. "Adjacent" females were neighbors that shared a defended boundary or codefended an area. Scale maps of defended areas were drawn in the field.

"Littermate sisters" were female members of the same litter. "Nonlittermate sisters" were female offspring of the same mother, born in different years. Because they frequently had different sires, nonlittermate sisters were usually half-siblings.

Unlike some primates (e.g., Macaca mulatta on Cayo Santiago Island; Missakian 1972), female ground squirrels appeared to be as likely to attack older female relatives that trespassed on their defended areas as older females were to attack younger kin when the latter trespassed. For example, the percent of times mothers chased one-year old daughters (18 of 95 times, 19%) and two-year old daughters (6 of 30 times, 20%) trespassing on their defended areas was the same ($P > .2$) as the percent of times one-year olds (9 of 53 times, 17%) and two-year olds (8 of 44 times, 18%) chased their trespassing mothers. Therefore, in the analyses that follow, mother-daughter chases were combined into a single datum. Similarly, the behavior of older sister-younger sister, aunt-niece, older cousin-younger cousin, grandmother-granddaughter, and older-younger unrelated female pairs were combined.

Unless otherwise indicated, all significance levels are for two-tailed nonparametric statistical tests. Two sample comparisons were made with the Mann-Whitney U statistic. Goodness of fit tests and tests for heterogeneity were usually made with the "G" statistic (Sokal & Rohlf 1969:559), corrected for continuity when there were two samples. Correlations were analyzed with Kendall's Rank test (Hollander & Wolfe 1973:185-199).

Sexual Dimorphism in Dispersal

Female Belding's ground squirrels were significantly more sedentary than males, and they lived in significantly greater proximity to all categories of female relatives than males (Fig. 1). Males permanently dispersed from their birthplaces before their first winter's hibernation (Sherman 1976). Thereafter they lived 5-12 times farther from previous burrows and from kin than females (Fig. 1).

About the time young were born, the most polygamous males left their mates' vicinities and established nest burrows elsewhere. Once settled in the new area, these males were sedentary until after attempting to mate the following spring. The result of such post-mating dispersal was that

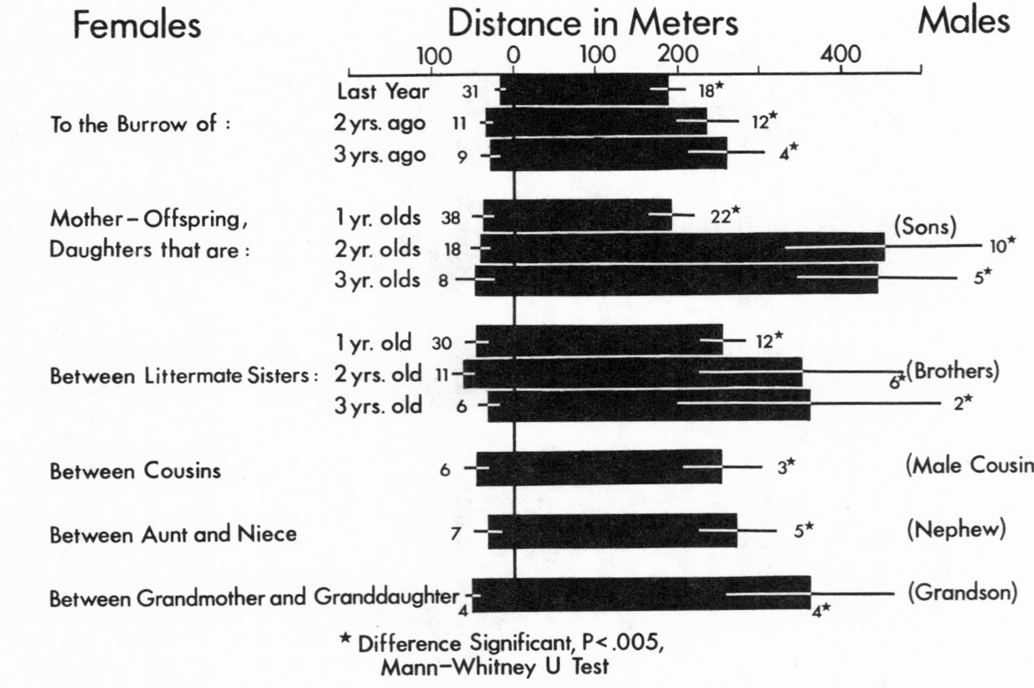

Figure 1. Within-matriline sexual dimorphism in dispersal among Belding's ground squirrels at Tioga Pass, California. Mean distances (thick lines), standard deviations (thin lines), and sample sizes (small numerals) are indicated. All distances were measured in the field. Note that females are more sedentary. These are the most extensive within-family dispersal data ever presented for a rodent.

males did not mate with and seldom even interacted with their previous mates and mates' offspring.

Because daughters nest close to their mothers, a female's genetic relationship to conspecifics might be expected to decrease gradually as distance from her nest burrow increases. That is, nest burrow proximity might be an approximate indicator of relatedness among females. However, probably because of unequal survival within matrilines and local competition for breeding sites, females nested equally close to all categories of female kin (P = 0.14, Analysis of Variance, 5 lowest categories, Fig. 1). Thus, nest burrow proximity does not indicate exact genetic relationship although it suggests common ancestry. In contrast to females, males nested equally far from their female relatives (P = 0.27, ANOVA, Fig. 1). Likewise young males did not associate with brothers or with the male or males that mated with their mothers.

Nepotism Does Not Occur Among Males

Each spring a few males copulate frequently, while the majority seldom or never mate (Sherman 1976, 1977). In 1977, for example, of 13 males, the most successful four (31%) completed 30 of 55 observed copulations (55%). The most successful male mated nine times with seven different females, thus alone accounting for 16% of all copulations. During their four to six hour receptive period, females run along males, thereby inciting fights as the males compete for sexual access to them (see Cox & LeBoeuf 1977, for other examples of female "incitation" of male-male combat). Then females seem to watch male-male fights and chases, and occasionally appear to solicit copulations with consistent fight winners and reject mating attempts by others. Females frequently mate with more than one male. The day after they copulate, females begin behaving agonistically toward their mate(s). By winning the most fights, heavy, old males are able to remain near sexually receptive females and such males mate most frequently. Thus, the mating system of these ground squirrels might be termed "male dominance polygyny" (Emlen & Oring 1977).

About the time their mates' young are born, polygamous males disperse. During the rest of their active seasons, males usually protect only a radius of about five meters or less around their nest burrows. Three of 24 males, however, chased conspecifics from larger areas. These three chased trespassers from the defended areas of the two females nesting nearest them on 54 of 286 occasions (19%) that they and a trespasser were simultaneously present on a female's defended area. If these three males had been polygamous and were living near mates, their occasional chases might be interpreted as paternal care.

Paternal care seems an unlikely explanation for the behavior of these males, however. First, the six females nesting nearest did not allow these three males preferential access to their defended areas. They chased "possibly paternal" males 58 of 72 times the males trespassed (81%), about as often as they chased unrelated adult trespassers (both sexes) or nonmates (256 of 301 times, 85%, and 84 of 114 times, 74%, respectively).

Second, although the mating success of two of the three "possibly paternal" males is unknown, the third did not mate at all in the year of interest (1975). Third, each of the three males hibernated in a burrow within the area he defended, suggesting that each might have been protecting an especially desirable hibernaculum. Finally, none of the three males that copulated most frequently in 1975, 1976, or 1977 nested within 70 meters of a mate nor chased trespassers from the defended areas of females they nested near. These data again suggest that occasional site defense is unrelated to polygamy and that such defense is probably not appropriately viewed as paternal care.

I could not demonstrate that males assist mates or offspring by defending resources or nest burrow locations, protecting nursing young from predatory conspecifics (below), or warning them of approaching interspecific predators. Therefore no behavior of males is nepotistic.

Nepotism Among Females

Alarm Calls and Nest Burrow Defense are Nepotistic

Belding's ground squirrels give alarm calls at the approach of aerial and terrestrial predators (Turner 1973). I investigated the function of the latter call by observing 119 natural interactions between ground squirrels and predatory mammals. On these occasions, alarm callers were usually old (4-7+ years), reproductive, resident females with living mothers, sisters, or offspring, rather than males, nonreproductive, nonresident females, or females without kin. These age, sex, and kinship-related asymmetries in calling tendencies, coupled with the matrilocal population structure (Fig. 1), have led me to suggest (Sherman 1977) that this alarm call alerts relatives and is thus an expression of nepotism (see Dunford 1977a for data on S. tereticaudus).

Reproductive females also exclude most conspecifics from an area surrounding their nest burrows. Each year there are two peaks in nest burrow defense (Fig. 2). The first and higher peak occurs immediately post-mating and reflects female-female competition for burrow locations and suitable defense perimeters. The second and broader peak coincides with lactation.

Nursing young are acceptable prey to conspecific ground squirrels, and intraspecific killing was the largest single mortality source among preweaning juveniles. Of 89 neonatal young that died, 26 (29%) were killed by conspecifics. Of all trespassers, unrelated, nonresident females and unrelated one-year old males were chased by lactating females farthest and most vigorously. These two categories of animals most frequently killed young (Sherman 1976).

Females never killed offspring of close relatives, seldom killed in their area of residence, and seldom ate their victims. When their own neonatal young were preyed on by badgers (Taxidea taxus) or coyotes (Canis latrans), females sometimes dispersed and attempted to kill young in the area to which they immigrated. If successful, they often settled near their victims' nest burrow. It seems likely that female killers were seeking sites safe from interspecific predators for nesting in subsequent years, and that they killed young to reduce future competition for such sites. In contrast to females, one-year old males sometimes killed young near their own nest burrows. Because of juvenile male dispersal (Fig. 1), such killers were never, to my knowledge, closely related to their prey. One-year old males usually ate the young they killed and they occasionally preyed on other small vertebrates and invertebrates. Thus, one-year old males may kill conspecific young to obtain sustenance. A similar suggestion was recently made by Goodall (1977) to explain infant killing by chimpanzees (Pan troglodytes). Female ground squirrels probably defend the area surrounding their nest burrows to thwart both types of killers. Nest burrow defense is thus a part of parental care and an expression of nepotism.

Close Relatives Seldom Fight When Establishing Nest Burrows

Females chase and fight each other to obtain suitable nest burrow locations (Fig. 2). Fighting females snarl and tooth-chatter, then grapple; they kick, scratch, and bite each other. Fights are never fatal outright (N = 427 fights)

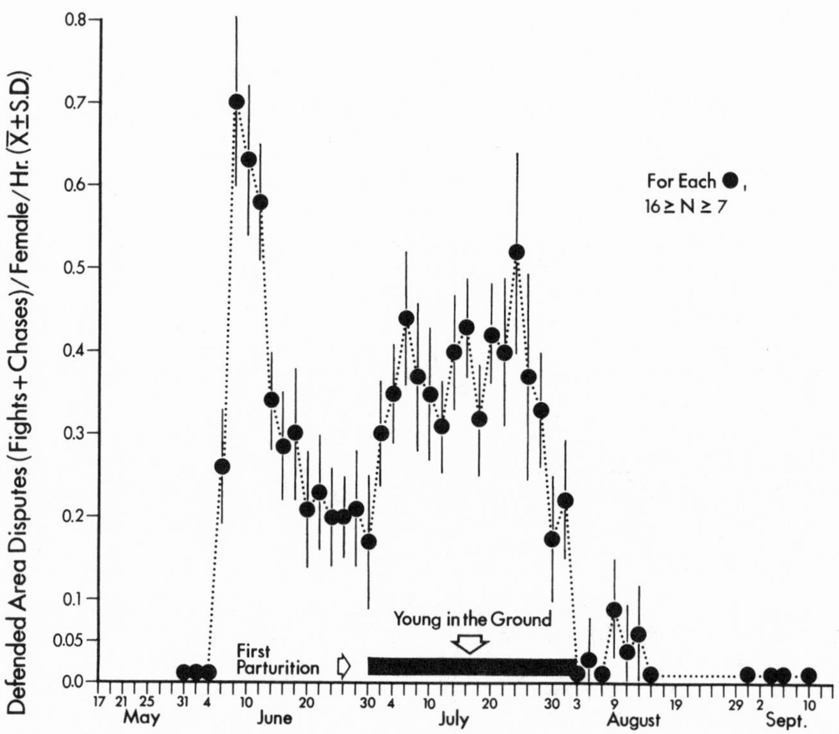

Figure 2. Annual cycle of nest burrow defense, measured in fights plus chases per female per hour, in Belding's ground squirrels. Only females defend nest burrows. Means (solid circles) and standard deviations (thin lines) are shown. For each date, data were obtained from between seven and sixteen different females. Data are from 1975. Note that there are two peaks in defense, the first occurring soon after mating (reflecting competition for nest burrows), and the second coinciding with lactation (reflecting defense of neonatal young against attack by conspecific ground squirrels).

but often result in damage to pelage and skin lacerations; fight wounds occasionally become infected. Thus each year females spend time and energy, and take risks to establish residences.

When female-female fights during gestation were categorized by genetic relationship between combatants (Fig. 3a), it appeared that, as predicted by Hamilton (1970, 1971), close kin fought infrequently. For the analysis of these data, I considered that a fight occurred if females grappled, and I counted each fight as one occurrence, regardless of how many times combatants broke contact. I analyzed the data in two ways. First, I tested for randomness in fight frequency as a function of frequency of proximity. I computed the "expected" number of fights by recording the number of times various relatives and nonrelatives came within one meter of each other during gestation; I then compared the "expected" distribution of fights with observed (Fig. 3a). The result was that expected and observed differed significantly ($P < .001$), suggesting that females avoided fighting with and possibly injuring close relatives. Second, I tested whether or not various relatives and nonrelatives fought each other equally frequently. The result (Fig. 3a) was that significant heterogeneity existed: close and distant relatives did not fight equally often. The heterogeneity was largely due to mother-daughter and littermate sister pairs fighting less often ($P < .01$) than aunt-niece, cousin-cousin, and grandmother-granddaughter pairs. These latter relatives fought as often as did unrelated females ($P = 0.37$, ANOVA, lowest four categories, Fig. 3a). Interestingly, nonlittermate (half) sisters fought more often than did mother-daughter or littermate sister pairs ($P < .05$), but less often than more distant relatives or nonrelatives ($P < .05$).

Close Relatives are Permitted Access to Defended Areas

After their young are born, females chase conspecifics from the area surrounding their nest burrows. Some trespassers, however, are permitted to pass through or stop on a female's defended area without being chased. Should predators suddenly appear, favored trespassers may have temporary access to shelter (i.e., burrows or willow bushes; see Sherman 1977). To see if kinship affects such favoritism, I recorded the frequency with which lactating residents chased variously related trespassers (Fig. 3b). Only behavior occurring when a resident and a trespasser were simultaneously present was analyzed, and trespassers were considered to have been chased if they were pursued across the boundary of a defended area by the resident. Behavior occurring on

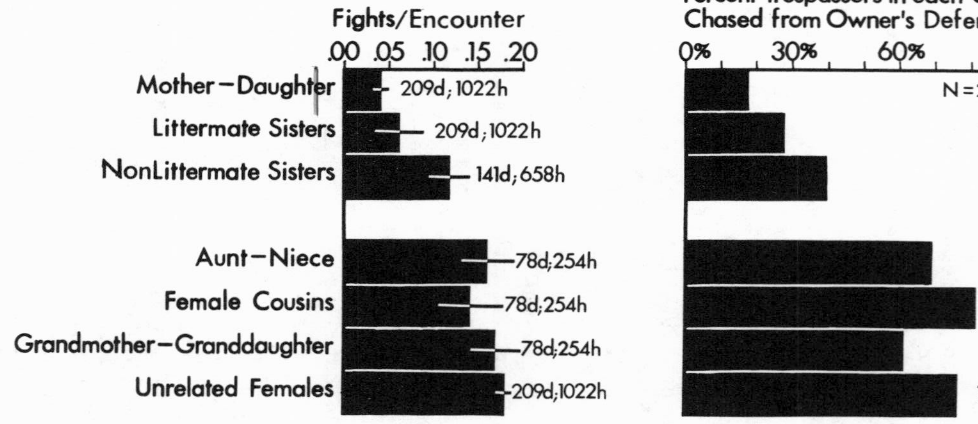

Figure 3. a. Female-female fights during the gestation period, categorized by genetic relationship between combatants. Fights were over nest burrows and defense perimeters around them. An "encounter" occurred when females came within 0.5 m of each other. Between-individual means (thick lines) and s.d. (thin lines) are given, along with days (d) and hours (h) of observation. Note that close relatives fought less frequently than did distant kin or nonkin. b. Chases of variously related trespassers by resident females during the lactation period. "N" is the number of times that trespassers and residents were simultaneously present. Note that close relatives were chased less often than distant relatives or nonrelatives.

portions of defended areas shared between neighboring females (below) was excluded.

There was significant heterogeneity (i.e., a departure from "randomness") in percent of times females chased variously related trespassers (Fig. 3b). Mother-daughter, littermate and nonlittermate sister pairs chased each other equally infrequently ($P \geq .08$, all tests) compared to more distantly related animals. The more distant relatives chased each other equally often and as frequently as did unrelated females ($P > .1$, pairwise tests; $P = .21$, ANOVA, lowest four categories, Fig. 3b).

Even when chases between them eventually occurred mother-daughter and littermate sister pairs permitted each other to remain on defended areas longer than did nonlittermate sisters and more distant relatives (Table 1) ($P < .05$, pairwise tests; $P = 0.41$, ANOVA). Nonlittermate sisters were permitted to remain on defended areas longer than distant relatives or nonrelatives ($P < .01$). Aunt-niece and cousin-cousin pairs chased each other as quickly as did unrelated females ($P > .2$).

Table 1. Length of time in minutes (mean ± s.d.) that relatives were permitted to remain on a female's defended area before being chased. "Time" is from the moment a trespasser crossed the defended area boundary until it was chased. "N" is the number of times animals trespassed when the resident was present and a chase occurred.

Relationship of Trespasser and Defender	Sample Size (N)	Time (Minutes) Before Trespasser Was Chased
Mother-daughter	16	4.8 ± 0.6
Littermate sisters	13	4.5 ± 0.9
Nonlittermate sisters	9	3.1 ± 0.8
Aunt-niece	14	0.8 ± 0.3
Cousin-cousin	19	0.9 ± 0.4
Unrelated females	40	1.0 ± 0.7

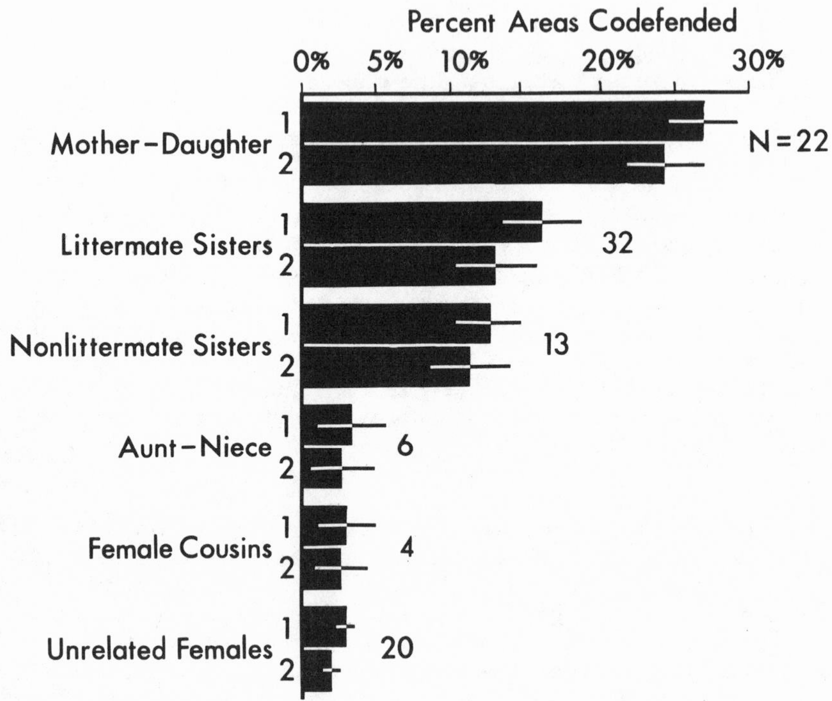

Figure 4. Percent of area surrounding females' nest burrows jointly defended by various relatives and nonrelatives. Number of adjacent females that codefended is indicated. Codefended fractions are presented from the standpoints of both sharing females because defended areas differ in size. The female whose codefended fraction is the larger portion of her total defended area is presented first (i.e., "1"), and the one whose codefended fraction is the smaller portion of her total defended area is given second ("2"). Close relatives codefend larger fractions of the areas defended by each than do distant relatives or nonrelatives. Mean fractions codefended (thick lines) and s.d. (thin lines) are given.

Close Relatives Codefend Areas

Sometimes neighboring females chase trespassers from the same area (Fig. 4). Such "codefended" areas are thus fractions of the areas defended by each female. The size of the fraction varied with the genetic relationship between codefending females ($P < .013$, ANOVA). Mother-daughter pairs codefended the largest portions of their areas ($P < .05$, all tests). Littermate and nonlittermate sisters codefended the second largest fraction. More distant relatives codefended equally little area (1%-6% of their areas), as little as did unrelated females ($P \geq .3$, all tests).

For the preceding analysis (Fig. 4), I considered that areas were codefended if there was overlap in two females' defense perimeters. Additionally, I noted how frequently females defending adjacent areas codefended a portion of those areas. While 22 of 25 (88%) adjacent mother-daughter pairs and 32 of 38 (84%) adjacent littermate sister pairs codefended an area (Fig. 4), only 4 of 9 (44%) adjacent cousins and 20 of 42 (48%) adjacent unrelated females did so. Thus, close relatives are more likely to codefend areas and likely to codefend larger areas than are more distant relatives or nonrelatives.

Close Relatives Cooperate Directly to Defend Their Young

When a trespasser "T", enters the defended area of resident "R_1," and R_1 and "R_2," a resident defending an adjacent area, are simultaneously present, one of three sorts of chases may occur. First, in a sequential chase, R_1 chases T out of R_1's defended area and into R_2's; R_2 then continues to chase T until T is beyond R_2's defense perimeter, etc. Occasionally trespassers are sequentially chased by four or five successive females. Second, in a cooperative chase, R_1 and R_2 converge on T and together chase T from R_1's defended area. Third, in a misdirected chase, R_1 chases T out of R_1's defended area and into R_2's; then R_2 "misdirects" her chase at R_1, leaving T near R_2's nest burrow. A fourth possibility is that no chase occurs and T leaves R_1's defended area unmolested.

The behavior of adjacent, lactating females toward trespassers unrelated to them was observed to see if kinship influences the occurrence of these three types of chases. Sequential chases were most common, and there was no kinship-related heterogeneity (i.e., departure from "randomness") in their occurrence (Fig. 5). There was significant heterogeneity in the occurrence of cooperative and misdirected chases

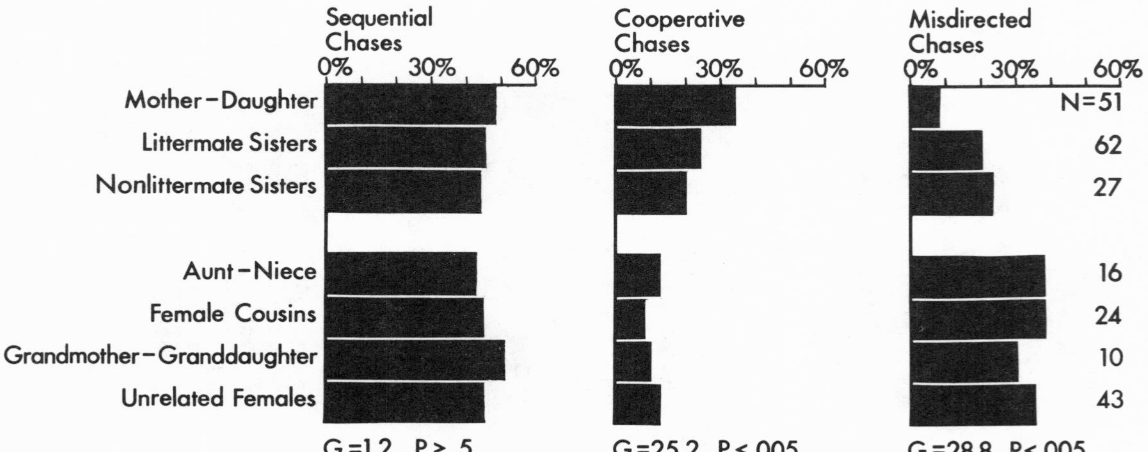

Figure 5. Frequency of occurrence of sequential, cooperative and misdirected chases of trespassers by female Belding's ground squirrels (see text for definitions). "N" is the number of times that adjacent females were present when an unrelated conspecific trespassed. "G" is the goodness-of-fit test statistic. Total percent (added across rows) is less than 100% because sometimes trespassers left unpursued. Note that close relatives cooperatively chased more often and misdirected chases at each other less often than did distant kin or nonkin.

however. Close female relatives cooperatively chased more often and misdirected chases at each other less often than did more distant relatives ($P < .01$; also Fig. 5). Mother-daughter and littermate sister pairs cooperatively chased equally often ($P > .1$) and misdirected chases at each other equally infrequently ($P > .3$). Nonlittermate and littermate sisters behaved similarly ($P > .2$, both tests), but mother-daughter and nonlittermate sister pairs differed ($P < .05$). Relatives more distant than siblings cooperatively chased as infrequently and misdirected chases at each other as often as did unrelated females ($P \geq .09$, pairwise tests; $P \geq .17$, ANOVAs, lowest four categories, Fig. 5).

These data suggest that females' neonatal young may be better protected when close female relatives nest in proximity. I tested this hypothesis by restraining 10 lactating females for four hours or until one of their young was attacked. Five of them lived adjacent to at least one sister, daughter, or their mother, and the other five did not. Females were restrained in live-traps between the tenth and twentieth day after their young were born in 1975, and females with relatives and those without them were tested on alternating days. Of the five test females without close relatives nearby, at least two lost young to conspecific predators. A third might have lost young because an unmarked nonresident entered her nest burrow and emerged with a red substance, probably blood, around its mouth. Fourteen times unrelated trespassers entered these females' defended areas and twice (14%) neighboring females chased them away. By contrast, none of the five females with adjacent close relatives lost young during the four hour tests. Ten times unrelated trespassers entered these females' defended areas, and seven times (70%) they were driven out by a neighboring relative; in the other three cases the trespasser was not chased, but departed without entering the nest burrow. Thus, females' young are apparently better protected when close relatives reside in proximity.

Close Relatives Warn Each Other When Predatory Mammals Approach

Elsewhere (Sherman 1977) I suggested that alerting relatives is the function of the alarm call that Belding's ground squirrels give when predatory mammals approach. Data in my previous publication, from 102 encounters between ground squirrels and predatory mammals (1974-76), are augmented here by observations of 17 more encounters (1976-77): 10 with long-tailed weasels (*Mustela frenata*), four with coyotes, and three with dogs (*Canis familiaris*) unaccompanied by humans

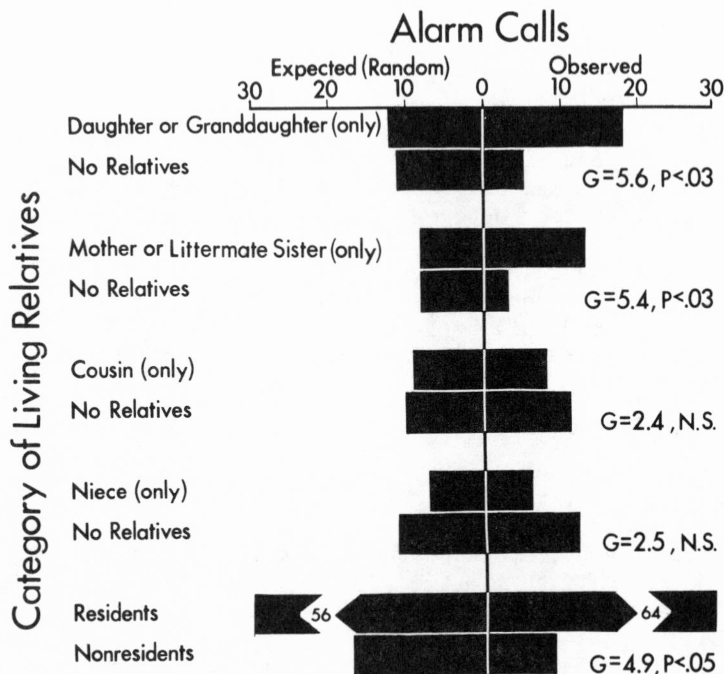

Figure 6. Kinship and asymmetries in tendencies to give alarm calls when predatory mammals approach among female Belding's ground squirrels. Data are from 119 interactions between terrestrial predators and ground squirrels, 1974-77. "Expected" values were computed by assuming that animals call randomly, in proportion to the number of times they are present when a predator appears. Each couplet of thick lines represents occasions when one or more females in each of the two compared categories was present, but when no others were there. The number of calls expected and observed from residents (lowest couplet) is larger than others because at least one and often several "residents" were present on most occasions when predators appeared. Note that nieces and cousins do not appear to affect alarm calling tendencies the way that descendants, mothers, or sisters do.

(Fig. 6, Table 2). These data indicate, in agreement with my previous article, that males seldom call, reproductive females with close relatives call more frequently than females without them, and that reproductive residents are more likely to call than are nonresident females. Additionally, reproductive females with at least one female descendant but without living mothers or sisters are more likely to call than are reproductive females with no living female relatives, and reproductive females whose mother or at least one sister is alive but without female descendants are more likely to call than are reproductive females with no living female relatives. Since my previous publication I have discovered (Fig. 6) that (1) reproductive females whose only living female relatives were nieces (N=3 aunt-niece pairs) were apparently no more likely to call than were reproductive females with no living

Table 2. Frequency with which various categories of Belding's ground squirrels give alarm calls. "N" is the number of times animals in each category were present when a terrestrial predator appeared, 1974-77, regardless of what other categories of ground squirrels were also present (compare with Fig. 6). The number of calls "expected" is computed by assuming that calls are given randomly, in proportion to the number of times animals in each category were present.

Category of Animals	N	"Expected" Number of Callers	Observed Number of Callers[1]
Males, one-year old or older	67	19	12[2]
Reproductive females, one-year old or older, <u>with</u> a living mother, sister, or descendant	190	53	75[3]
Reproductive females, one-year old or older, <u>without</u> a living mother, sister, or descendant	168	46	31[4]

[1]Test of "expected" versus "observed"; $G = 16.6$, $P < .005$
Pairwise Tests [2]N.S.; [3]$P < .01$; [4]$P < .05$

female relatives, and (2) reproductive females whose only living females relatives were cousins (N=4 cousin-cousin pairs) were apparently no more likely to call than were reproductive females with no living female relatives.

Females with at least one daughter and one granddaughter were no more likely to call (P > .3) than were females with at least one daughter but no granddaughter(s), suggesting that living granddaughters did not increase the likelihood that a female would call (c.f. Sherman 1977). I have been unable to test unambiguously the effect of granddaughters on alarm calling, however, because all four females with living granddaughters had at least one living daughter.

The speed with which females respond to predatory mammals also appears to vary with the presence of close female kin. Reproductive females with living mothers or sisters (only) and those with living female descendants (only, Fig. 6) called equally soon (P > .2) after a predator was first noticed by the observing human: 18.7 ± 2.3 seconds (± s.d., N = 16) and 19.1 ± 3.7 seconds (N = 13), respectively. Reproductive females with living nieces or aunts (only) and those with living cousins (only) called equally long (P > .1) after a predator was first noticed by the observer: 40.9 ± 4.2 seconds (N = 9) and 44.7 ± 5.3 seconds (N = 7), respectively. Reproductive females without living female relatives called 43.1 ± 6.7 seconds after a predator was first noticed (N = 11), with about the same speed (P > .08) as females whose only living relatives were aunts (nieces) or cousins. These data suggest that females with close kin are more likely than females without them to be warned of the approach of predatory mammals (Fig. 6), and are likely to be warned more quickly.

Mechanism by Which Close Relatives are Favored

There are at least three mechanisms by which asymmetrical favoritism might be brought about in any species: (1) conspecifics living nearest, whether kin or not, might be favored, (2) those that are most familiar or that have been neighbors longest, whether kin or not, might be favored, or (3) relatives might be recognized, regardless of proximity or prior association. Only if proximity and closeness of kinship are predictably directly related can (1) be the mechanism of nepotism. Likewise, only if degree of familiarity or length of association and closeness of kinship are consistently directly related can (2) be the mechanism of nepotism. If both proximity and prior association correlate poorly with closeness of kinship, (3) will be the mechanism of nepotism.

Several lines of evidence suggest that proximity is not the mechanism of nepotism in Belding's ground squirrels. First, although close and distant female relatives live in equal proximity (Fig. 1), close kin are favored (Figs. 3-6, Tables 1 & 2). Second, while females frequently codefend areas with close kin (Fig. 4) and cooperate with them to chase trespassers (Fig. 5), distantly related or unrelated conspecifics living in the same proximity are treated as competitors. Third, the behavior of six mother-daughter pairs and of seven one-year old littermate sister pairs that did not defend adjacent areas suggests that females do not simply favor conspecifics living closest. Nonadjacent mothers were chased from daughters' defended areas only 3 of 17 times (18%) they trespassed. By contrast, adjacent nonrelatives were chased by the same six daughters 19 of 28 times (68%) they trespassed, and nonadjacent nonrelatives were chased on 27 of 33 (82%) similar occasions. Similarly, one-year old females chased their nonadjacent sisters only 7 of 26 times (27%) they trespassed, while adjacent nonrelatives were chased 21 of 27 times (78%) they trespassed and 16 of 25 (73%) nonadjacent nonrelated trespassers were chased.

Three sorts of information suggest that favoritism based on familiarity or length of association is also unlikely in Belding's ground squirrels. First, for 34 pairs of unrelated females that lived adjacent in year "one" and adjacent or within 60 meters of each other thereafter, there was no inverse correlation between length of their association (one to four years) and fights/hour/gestation period ($P = .21$), percent times/lactation period they chased each other from defended areas ($P = .30$), percent misdirected chases/lactation period ($P = .10$), or percent cooperative chases/lactation period ($P = .13$). Secondly, twenty females shared a defended boundary with unrelated female "A" for two years or more and with nonrelative "B" for one year only. During gestation, the twenty residents fought A and B equally often and during lactation they chased A and B with equal frequency ($P > .1$). Third, twelve 1977 females that had lived next to particular unrelated conspecifics for at least two years favored one-year old daughters, whether or not they lived adjacent, over those longer associates. Mothers fought their daughters less frequently during gestation and chased them less often during lactation than they fought and chased the unrelated neighbors ($P < .05$, all 24 tests).

Thus it appears that in Belding's ground squirrels asymmetrical favoritism (Figs. 3-6) is facilitated by mechanism (3), recognition of close relatives. Indeed, some of the animals' behavior suggests that recognition occurs, probably at close range. When trespassers are detected, residents rush toward them, usually stopping one to two meters away. Then they appear to look at and sniff trespassers, before chasing them or turning away. Sometimes trespassers flee during a resident's first rush, but often they remain and reciprocally look at and sniff the resident, as if trying to identify her.

Recognition of relatives or previous associates, probably based on smell or sight, has been documented in some mice (Bowers & Alexander 1967), primates (Erwin et al. 1974; Erwin & Flett 1974; Wu & Holmes 1979), and at least one other ground squirrel, the only one in which recognition has been investigated under controlled conditions. Studies of Richardson's ground squirrels (*Spermophilus richardsonii*) in the field (Yeaton 1972; Michener 1973; Michener & Michener 1973) and laboratory (Sheppard & Yoshida 1971; Michener & Sheppard 1972; Michener 1974) reveal that mothers and their offspring recognize one another, even when tested in arenas unfamiliar to either. Recognition occurs after up to eight months of separation and after hibernation. Apparently regardless of the length of separation, mothers and their offspring are more "cohesive" and less "agonistic" than the same females and unrelated young (Michener & Sheppard 1972). Siblings are also more "cohesive" than nonsiblings (Sheppard & Yoshida 1971). Because in these experiments mother-offspring and littermate pairs had lived together prior to being isolated and tested, these data suggest that Richardson's ground squirrels recognize either relatives or previous associates (see Erwin et al. 1974). Recent, not yet published, experiments by W. G. Holmes (pers. comm.) suggest that recognition of siblings also occurs in Arctic ground squirrels (*Spermophilus parryii*), and that this recognition may not depend on prior association.

Recognition "Errors" and the Ontogeny of Recognition

Recognition of relatives might occur either through the action of hypothetical "recognition alleles" (Hamilton 1964; Dawkins 1976), or association between kin in social contexts that clarify their relationship (see Hamilton 1971; Alexander 1977a). While I have not investigated the possibility of "recognition alleles" in *S. beldingi*, there are two general theoretical arguments against their existence. First they would have to be fairly complex (Alexander & Borgia 1978), for they must (1) express their presence phenotypically, (2) recognize themselves, their own effects, or assess the population-wide heterozygosity at their loci, and (3) cause their bearers to favor conspecifics carrying copies of them. Second, when "recognition alleles" cause their bearers to favor individuals of less than the mean within-brood or within-population genetic relationship, they might benefit themselves and alleles at loci closely linked to them (Leigh 1977; Partridge & Nunny 1977), but not the rest of the genome. For this reason such hypothetical alleles have been termed "outlaws" (Alexander & Borgia 1978), and mutations at loci unlinked to them might be favored if such mutations cancelled any of the alleles' three required abilities (also Leigh 1977; Kurland 1979).

These theoretical arguments leave open the possibility that phenotypic recognition of genotypically based similarities and differences may occur (Dawkins 1976; Sherman 1979). For example, there are intriguing data suggesting that half-sibling pigtailed macaques (*Macaca nemestrina*), reared in isolation, recognize each other the first time they meet and do so in the absence of social cues (Wu & Holmes 1979). These data indicate the desirability of further studies of genetic mechanisms facilitating recognition of kin.

Belding's ground squirrels apparently erred in recognizing kin under two circumstances involving unusual social situations, suggesting that they are unable to distinguish relatives without prior social cues. Three times in 1974 and three times in 1975 (3% of all closely-observed juveniles, N = 173), a juvenile emerged from its natal burrow and at nightfall on its first day above ground returned to another mother's nest. The second female's young were less developed than the tagged juvenile's own siblings. When members of the second litter appeared above ground a few days later, the larger, older "foster" littermate was among them. Interestingly the mother of the second litter seemed to treat all offspring as her own, suggesting that *S. beldingi*, like *S. richardsonii* (Michener 1974) and some prairie dogs (Hoogland 1978), do not begin to discriminate between their own and foreign young until at least the time juveniles first emerge above ground (25-28 days after parturition in *S. beldingi*) and litters begin to mix. Three of the six "misplaced" juveniles were unrelated to the litters they joined. Two joined cousins in aunt's burrows and one (a male) joined younger aunts and uncles in his grandmother's nest. Four of the six were females and three of these four survived a year. At age one, they "mistakenly" cooperated with unrelated foster sisters (N = 4 foster sibs) and treated genetic sisters (N = 3) as if unrelated (Table 3). These data suggest that the ontogeny of sibling recognition, like that of parent-offspring recognition, may involve association at about the time of weaning.

Table 3. Behavior of 1-year old females toward genetic sisters, with whom they were reared but whose company they left on their first day above ground, and toward (unrelated) "foster" sisters, into whose nest they were naturally displaced and with whom they had lengthy post-emergence associations (see text).

Behavior	"Foster" Sisters	Genetic Sisters	Significance
Fights/hour/day (Gestation period)	0.08 ± 0.02	0.14 ± 0.03	P < .05
Percent times chased from defended area[1]	27% (N=26)	58% (N=19)	P < .01
Sequential Chases[1]	50%	50%	
Cooperative Chases[1]	29%	15%	P < .05
Misdirected Chases[1]	13%[2]	25%[3]	

[1]Lactation period, see Fig. 5.
[2]For the latter three categories, N=32.
[3]For the latter three categories, N=20.

The occurrence of a second sort of apparent recognition error strengthens the hypothesis that social cues facilitate kin recognition in S. beldingi. Twice in 1975 females with living one-year old daughters (two and three of them, respectively) disappeared inexplicably two to three days before their litters first emerged above ground. Because the one-year old daughters had never entered their mother's burrows, the eight surviving juveniles first encountered them, their nonlittermate sisters, in the absence of their mothers. The following summer, four pairs of these nonlittermate sisters lived adjacent. They behaved as if unrelated (Table 4), in contrast to nine pairs of adjacent nonlittermate sisters, also observed in 1976, whose mothers were known to be alive when the nonlittermates first associated. These data suggest that the ontogeny of recognition of at least one category of kin that do not normally associate in the nest burrow may depend on proximity of a conspecific more closely related to each distant relative than they are to each other (here, that conspecific is their mother).

Table 4. Behavior between two-year old females and their one-year old nonlittermate sisters depending on whether or not their mothers were alive during the first contacts between the nonlittermates. (Mean ± s.d. is given.)

Behavior	Mother Present	Mother not Present	Significance
Fights/Hour/Day (Gestation period)	0.10 ± 0.05 (N=31)	0.17 ± 0.03 (N=40)	P < .05
Percent times chased from defended area (Lactation period)	36% (N=28)	68% (N=19)	P < .05

The Limits of Nepotism

Kurland (1977) showed that as putative (see Sherman 1978b) genetic relationship decreases among Japanese macaques (*Macaca fuscata*), frequencies of such cooperative behaviors as allogrooming, defense against conspecifics, and tolerance of proximity decrease simultaneously. Clutton-Brock and Harvey (1976) analyzed Yamada's (1963) *M. fuscata* data and came to the same conclusion about the effect of kinship on tolerance of proximity during feeding. Similarly, Massey (1977) showed that pigtailed macaques (p. 39) ". . . come to the aid of relatives under attack significantly more often than they aid nonrelatives. Not only do they selectively aid related versus nonrelated individuals, but they also discriminate between relatives of varying degrees of relatedness" (see also Bernstein 1972). Massey (1977) then suggested, in agreement with Kurland (1977) and Clutton-Brock and Harvey (1976), that (p. 39) "If such aiding can be viewed as altruistic, then these findings can be used in support of Hamilton's model of kin selection as the mechanism responsible for the evolution of altruism." Consistent with Massey's suggestion is evidence that slight increases in degree of relationship correlate directly with increases in nepotism among rhesus macaques (Sade 1965, 1967), chimpanzees (van Lawick-Goodall 1968, 1971, 1975), and perhaps several other primates (Hrdy 1976), lions (*Panthera leo*; Schaller 1972; Bertram 1976), and possibly humans (Alexander 1977a, 1977b, 1979; Chagnon this volume; Irons this volume).

The behavior of female Belding's ground squirrels also supports Hamilton's (1964) hypothesis, for females live near and assist their closest female kin. However in apparent contrast to some primates, ground squirrel aunt-niece, cousin-cousin, and grandmother-granddaughter pairs do not cooperate (Figs. 3-6). Female ground squirrels also treat some conspecifics that are probably about equally related quite differently (e.g., compare the behavior of aunt-niece pairs with that of nonlittermate sisters). Clearly there are limits of ground squirrel nepotism: relatives more distant than nonlittermate sisters are treated as unrelated. What are the differences between species in which nepotism decreases gradually and those in which it terminates more abruptly, and how do they relate to Hamilton's hypothesis?

To understand any species' pattern of nepotism, two questions about individuals' behavior must be considered: (1) what is reproductively ideal?, and (2) what is socially possible? With his formulation of "inclusive fitness," Hamilton suggested a mathematical way of answering (1). Here I suggest that the answer to (2) depends on <u>demography</u>, particularly its spatial component, <u>dispersal</u>, and its temporal component, <u>mortality</u>. Only when ecological circumstances affecting demography consistently make it socially possible will nepotism be elaborated according to what is reproductively ideal. For example, if dispersing is advantageous and if it usually separates relatives permanently, as in many birds (Nice 1937: 180-189; Gross 1940; Robertson 1969), on the rare occasions when nestmates or other kin live in proximity, they will not preferentially cooperate. Similarly, nepotism will not be elaborated among relatives that have infrequently coexisted in a population's or species' evolutionary history. If an animal's life history characteristics (Stearns 1976; Warner this volume) usually preclude the existence of certain relatives, that is if kin are usually unavailable, the rare coexistence of such kin will not occasion preferential treatment. For example, if reproductives generally die soon after zygotes are formed, as in many temperate zone insects, the unusual individual that survives to interact with its offspring is not expected to behave parentally.

Only among relatives that are consistently likely to be proximate (accessable) and alive (available) will nepotism be elaborated according to what is mathematically ideal. When these two preconditions are met, patterns of nepotism may be predictable with knowledge of genetic relationships among interacting conspecifics and of the ratio of benefits to the recipient of assistance and costs to the assisting individual (Hamilton 1964; West-Eberhard 1975). Analyses of costs and benefits must take competition into account (Alexander 1974), for nepotism will not be elaborated among relatives simultaneously seeking resources that, if diminished, are insufficient to supply either (also Hamilton 1964). Indeed, competing relatives may sometimes kill each other (Ingram 1959; Hamilton 1970, 1971; Eickwort 1973).

Are there then differences between various categories of Belding's ground squirrel kin in probability of living in spatial proximity or being alive simultaneously? Or, if not, are the ratios of benefits and costs of each behavior (Figs. 3-6) so similar that in every case "inclusive fitness" is reduced when kin more distant than sisters are assisted?

Near and distant female relatives live in about equal proximity (Fig. 1) and interact frequently. Nonkin also frequently interact. Therefore differences in behavior among various categories of relatives (Figs. 3-6) cannot be attributed to differences in spatial proximity or dispersal within matrilines. If the 1974-77 dispersal pattern has characterized Belding's ground squirrels over evolutionary time, differences in spatial proximity are not sufficient to explain the observed asymmetries in nepotism.

By contrast, there are apparently differences in the likelihood that near and distant kin will be alive; these differences reflect high infant mortality (below). From yearly live-trapping records I computed probabilities that one-year old females would have at least one living member of various categories of kin (Fig. 7a). There are discontinuities in these probabilities. In particular, relatives more distant than nonlittermate sisters are rarely alive compared to closer female kin.

The ground squirrel kin survivorship pattern (Fig. 7a) differs from that among humans, the only vertebrate other than S. beldingi for which kinship frequency data and demographic information are available (Goodman, Keyfitz, and Pullum 1974). In humans, (expected) frequency of occurrence of various kinship categories increases as genetic relationship decreases.

One possible reason for the apparent difference between humans and Belding's ground squirrels is that in the latter mortality is not constant with age: whereas between 54% and 93% of juveniles perish during their first winter, between

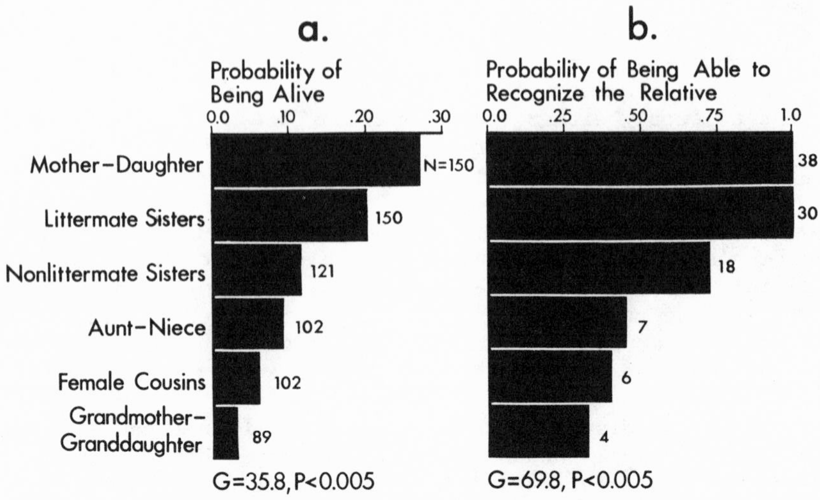

Figure 7. Probabilities of being alive and of being recognized as related (see text) for various Belding's ground squirrel kin. Data are based on yearly mark-release-recapture records at Tioga Pass, California. a. Probabilities of being alive, with "N" defined as follows: For mother-daughter pairs, 150 is the number of juvenile females marked in 1974-76, and "p" is the probability that both they and their mothers survived one year. For littermate sister pairs, 150 is the number of juvenile females marked in 1974-76, and "p" is the probability that both members of each pair survived one year. For nonlittermate sister pairs, 121 is the number of juvenile females marked in 1975-76, whose mothers' litters of the previous year had also been marked; "p" is the probability that one-year-old females had a surviving two-year-old nonlittermate sister. For aunt-niece pairs, 102 is the number of juvenile females marked in 1975-76 that were offspring of one-year-old mothers whose littermates had been marked the previous year; "p" is the probability that one-year-old females had surviving two-year-old aunts. For cousin-cousin pairs, "p" is similar to that described for aunt-niece pairs. For grandmother-granddaughter pairs, 89 is the number of 1976-77 one-year-old females that were direct descendants of females whose litters were marked in 1974-75; "p" is the probability that these females' grandmothers were alive. b. Probabilities of being recognized. "N" is the number of pairs of kin in each category. The probability that they were able to identify each other, which depends on being alive and living in proximity (see text) is graphed.

year mortality among adults is 23%-68% (Sherman 1976). Thus the probability that a one-year old female and her mother are alive is seen to be greater than the probability that a one-year old female and her one-year old cousin are simultaneously alive. For one-year old cousins to be alive, both must have survived the period of maximum mortality, the first six months; for a mother-daughter pair, only the one-year old daughter must have passed through the high mortality period. If the 1974-77 pattern (Fig. 7a) characterized Belding's ground squirrel population demography over evolutionary time, females may behaviorally favor their close relatives because those are the only kin with whom they have predictably interacted, thus the only kin toward which appropriate behaviors have evolved.

In addition, distant relatives that are occasionally available and accessable may be unable to identify each other. In Belding's ground squirrels the ontogeny of recognition seems to involve learning, and depends on interactions in appropriate social contexts, such as being in the nest burrow at weaning. Recognition "errors" are known to occasionally occur between mothers and offspring and littermates, and they may occur more often among distant relatives. At least, distant relatives are treated as if unrelated.

To determine likelihood of recognition errors among near and distant relatives, I computed probabilities that one-year old females had encountered various kin in social contexts that could clarify their relationship. Based on the nature of observed recognition "errors" (Table 4), I considered that females may be unable to identify kin with whom they have not interacted in the presence of a conspecific more closely related to each than they are to each other. For example, cousins that always interact in the absence of the mother of either are probably not identifiable. Even though _S. beldingi_ recognition seems to first occur immediately after weaning (see Michener 1974 for similar data on _S. richardsonii_), because I do not know exactly when they learn to recognize kin, I considered that such learning could occur any time during the two to three months between weaning and hibernation. For this analysis (Fig. 7b), I considered a close relative of a distantly related pair "present" if she was alive, not hibernating, and living in such proximity (less than 60 meters) during the appropriate period (usually July-September) that the three females were likely to simultaneously interact. I chose 60 meters as the maximum distance between females likely to interact because 60 meters is about the farthest distance females travel daily from their nest burrows. There are differences in probabilities that members of various categories of kin will interact in social situations that clarify their relationship (Fig. 7b). One result of these differences might be that relatives more distant than sisters are comparatively rarely able to identify each other. This observation implies that selection has rarely favored nepotism toward distant kin because the recognition mechanism virtually precludes their identification.

Why are the limits of S. beldingi nepotism so similar when they are revealed by studying such different behaviors as fighting, cooperative defense of burrows, and alarm calling (e.g., Figs. 3-6)? Either, as I have suggested, unavailability of kin more distant than sisters and inability to recognize such kin delimit all nepotistic behaviors or else for each behavior I studied "inclusive fitness" is reduced in similar fashions when conspecifics more distantly related than sisters are assisted. For example, costs and benefits of every behavior I studied might be so similar that the same limits of nepotism recur. Although I cannot directly exclude this possibility, it seems unlikely because of the apparent diversity of behaviors under consideration. A second alternative is that intensity of competition might always be greater among distant relatives than among closer kin. Although I have not thoroughly investigated competition, it is unlikely that it always increases as relatedness decreases. Certainly competition for nest burrows and defense perimeters was not restricted to or mainly between distant kin or nonkin. Neither did intensity of competition for food seem to vary with relatedness. When females were feeding off their defended areas, for example, kinship did not affect the distances they allowed other females to approach before they moved away ($P = 0.07$, ANOVA, $N = 83$; categories as in Fig. 5).

Unfortunately too few data exist to permit detailed comparisons of patterns of nepotism among the approximately 20 species of North American ground squirrels (genus Spermophilus). Interestingly however, sexual dimorphisms in dispersal, with females more sedentary, occur in every spermophile studied in this regard: S. armatus (Slade & Balph 1974), S. beecheyi (Evans & Holdenreid 1943; Fitch 1948; Dobson 1978), S. richardsonii (Michener & Michener 1971, 1973, 1977; Yeaton 1972), S. tereticaudus (Dunford 1975, 1977a, 1977b, 1977c), and S. tridecemlineatus (Rongstad 1965; McCarley 1966). Further, in every species at least some females occupy (codefend?) overlapping home ranges.

Nepotism has been explicitly investigated only in

Richardson's ground squirrels and round-tailed ground squirrels. In the latter species, females are more likely than males to give alarm calls, and Dunford (1977a:785) states that "The probability that a round-tailed ground squirrel will emit an alarm call . . . is greatest when the squirrel's neighbors are close kin." Further, adult females are less aggressive toward female kin than toward nonrelatives (Dunford 1977b:892-894), preferentially share nest burrows with kin before young are born (p. 901), and codefend areas surrounding nest burrows with close relatives (p. 899; also Dunford 1977c). In *S. richardsonii*, mother-daughter and sister pairs recognize each other and often nest adjacent; females allow female relatives preferential access to areas defended around nest burrows, and frequently codefend such areas with close kin (Yeaton 1972; Michener 1973, 1974; Michener & Michener 1973, 1977). In addition, Yeaton (1972:142) observed that "More cohesive behavior occurred between related adult females than between unrelated adult females, but the proportion of cohesive interactions observed for related adults is significantly lower ($P < 0.005$) than between related young and related adult and young." Together these data suggest striking similarities among *S. tereticaudus*, *S. richardsonii*, and *S. beldingi* not only in having matrilocal population structures but also in the form and extent of nepotism.

I suggest that nepotism among female Belding's ground squirrels is limited by historical infrequency of interactions with distant relatives in situations favoring cooperation; in other words, distant relatives are ignored because they are evolutionary "oddities." Perhaps only among long-lived animals inhabiting stable, viscous social groups (e.g., some primates, Kurland 1977; humans, Alexander 1977b, 1979), in which distant kin are usually available for social interactions, will it be consistently socially possible for individuals to do what is reproductively ideal (Hamilton 1964; West-Eberhard 1975).

Summary

To see if genetic relationship affects competition and cooperation among Belding's ground squirrels (*Spermophilus beldingi*; Rodentia: Sciuridae), 15 different field assistants and I spent 3817 hours observing them during the summers of 1974-77. At the Tioga Pass California study area, 2282 animals have been permanently marked since 1969, including all 651 young from 138 litters. Thus exact age and matrilineal (uterine) relationships among most study animals are known.

While the highly polygynous males do not live near kin nor behave parentally, females live near and cooperate with their closest female relatives. Mother-daughter and sister-sister pairs (1) fight little, (2) cooperatively protect neonatal young against attacks from predatory conspecifics, (3) allow each other nearly unmolested access to areas defended around nest burrows, and (4) give alarm calls when predatory mammals approach. In contrast, more distantly related females, aunt-niece, (first) cousin-cousin, and grandmother-granddaughter pairs, treat each other the same way they treat unrelated females. Thus Belding's ground squirrel nepotism is limited to offspring and siblings.

Following the suggestion of Hamilton (1964) it is usually assumed that patterns of nepotism are predictable from considerations of "inclusive fitness." That is, prerequisites are knowledge of (1) genetic relatedness among interacting conspecifics, and (2) benefits to a recipient and costs to the assisting individual (including intensity of competition between them; Alexander 1974; West-Eberhard 1975). In this paper I suggest that an additional factor, demography, merits consideration. Demography has a spatial component, dispersal, and a temporal component, mortality. Either or both could limit nepotism because favoritism will not extend to relatives whose co-occurrence in space or time is so infrequent that their cooperation has seldom been selected. Only when the ecological factors affecting dispersal and mortality (Stearns 1976) consistently make it socially possible will nepotism be elaborated according to what Hamilton (1964) has suggested is reproductively ideal.

Between various categories of female Belding's ground squirrel kin there appear to be sharp discontinuities in survival probabilities. The result is that relatives more distant than sisters are seldom alive or available for social interactions; they are evolutionary "oddities." I suggest therefore that ground squirrel nepotism is limited by infrequency of interactions among relatives more distant than sisters. The mechanism of kin recognition supports this hypothesis, for distant relatives are essentially unidentifiable. Probably only among long-lived animals that inhabit stable, viscous social groups (e.g., some primates) will the pattern of change in nepotism coincide closely with differences in genetic relationship.

Acknowledgements

I thank my field assistants: L. Blumer, K. Dunny, M. Flinn, S. Flinn, S. Gurkewitz, C. Kagarise, J. Kenrick, D.

Knapp, D. Kuchapsky, B. Mulder, J. Odenheimer, M. Roth, B. Schultz, D. Weber, and C. Wood. M. Morton's encouragement was invaluable. For other assistance I thank R. Alexander, D. Barash, G. Barlow, J. Blick, E. Charnov, W. Holmes, J. Hoogland, C. Kagarise, J. Kurland, F. Pitelka, T. Rowell, J. Silverberg, K. Taft, and D. Wilson. The Southern California Edison Company provided housing and the Clairol Company donated hair dye. B. Phillips typed the final manuscript. My work was financially supported by the National Science Foundation (grant GB-43851), the Theodore Roosevelt Memorial Fund, the American Philosophical Society, the Museum of Zoology at Michigan, and the Museum of Vertebrate Zoology and the Miller Institute at Berkeley. The American Association for the Advancement of Science made possible my participation in the symposium "Sociobiology: Beyond Nature-Nurture" where these ideas were first presented.

Literature Cited

Alexander, R.D. 1974. The evolution of social behavior. Annual Review of Ecology & Systematics 5:325-383.

_______. 1975. The search for a general theory of behavior. Behavioral Science 20:77-100.

_______. 1977a. Evolution, human behavior, and determinism. Philosophy of Science Association Symposium 2:3-21.

_______. 1977b. Natural selection and the analysis of human sociality. In C.E. Goulden (ed.), The changing scenes in natural sciences, 1776-1976. Philadelphia Academy of Natural Sciences Special Publication 12:283-337.

_______. 1977c. Review of: The use and abuse of biology (M. Sahlins). American Anthropologist 79:917-920.

_______. 1979. Evolution and culture. In N.A. Chagnon & W. Irons (eds.), Evolutionary biology and human social behavior. Duxbury Press, North Scituate, Massachusetts, pp. 59-78.

_______ & G. Borgia. 1978. Group selection, altruism, and the levels of organization of life. Annual Review of Ecology & Systematics 9:449-474.

_______ & P.W. Sherman. 1977. Local mate competition and parental investment in social insects. Science 196:494-500.

Barash, D.P. 1977. Sociobiology and behavior. Elsevier, New York.

Bernstein, I.S. 1972. Daily activity cycles and weather influences on a pigtail monkey group. Folia Primatologica 18:390-415.

Bertram, B.C.R. 1976. Kin selection in lions and in evolution. In P.P.G. Bateson and R.A. Hinde (eds.), Growing points in ethology. Cambridge University Press, Cambridge, pp. 281-301.

Bowers, J.M. & B.K. Alexander. 1967. Mice: Individual recognition by olfactory cues. Science 158:1208-1210.

Brown, J.L. 1970. Cooperative breeding and altruistic behavior in the Mexican jay, *Aphelocoma ultramarina*. Animal Behaviour 18:366-378.

______. 1978. Avian communal breeding systems. Annual Review of Ecology & Systematics 9:123-155.

______ & G.H. Orians. 1970. Spacing patterns in mobile animals. Annual Review of Ecology & Systematics 1:239-262.

Clutton-Brock, T.H. & P.H. Harvey. 1976. Evolutionary rules and primate societies. In P.P.G. Bateson and R.A. Hinde (eds.), Growing points in ethology. Cambridge University Press, Cambridge, pp. 195-237.

Cox, C.R. & B.J. Le Boeuf. 1977. Female incitation of male competition: A mechanism in sexual selection. American Naturalist 111:317-335.

Dawkins, R. 1976. The selfish gene. Oxford University Press, Oxford.

Dobson, F.S. 1978. An experimental study of dispersal in the California ground squirrel, *Spermophilus beecheyi*. Masters Thesis, University of California, Santa Barbara.

Dunford, C.J. 1975. Density limitation and the social system of round-tailed ground squirrels. Ph.D. Thesis, University of Arizona, Tucson.

______. 1977a. Kin selection for ground squirrel alarm calls. American Naturalist 111:782-785.

______. 1977b. Social system of round-tailed ground squirrels. Animal Behaviour 25:885-906.

_______. 1977c. Behavioral limitation of round-tailed ground squirrel density. Ecology 58:1254-1268.

Eickwort, K.R. 1973. Cannibalism and kin selection in *Labidomera clivicollis* (Coleoptera: Chrysomelidae). American Naturalist 107:452-453.

Emlen, S.T. 1978. The evolution of cooperative breeding in birds. *In* J.R. Krebs and N.B. Davies (eds.), Behavioural ecology: An evolutionary approach. Sinauer Associates, pp. 245-281.

_______ & L.W. Oring. 1977. Ecology, sexual selection, and the evolution of mating systems. Science 197:215-223.

Erwin, J. & M. Flett. 1974. Responses of rhesus monkeys to reunion after long-term separation: Cross-sexed pairings. Psychological Reports 35:171-174.

_______, T. Maple, J. Willott, & G. Mitchell. 1974. Persistent peer attachments of rhesus monkeys: Responses to reunion after two years of separation. Psychological Reports 34:1179-1183.

Evans, F.C. & R. Holdenreid. 1943. A population study of the beechey ground squirrel in central California. Journal of Mammalogy 24:231-260.

Fitch, H.S. 1948. Ecology of the California ground squirrel on grazing lands. American Midland Naturalist 39:513-596.

Goodall, J. 1977. Infant killing and cannibalism in free-living chimpanzees. Folia Primatologica 28:259-282.

Goodman, L.A., N. Keyfitz, & T.W. Pullum. 1974. Family formation and the frequency of various kinship relationships. Theoretical Population Biology 5:1-27.

Gross, A.O. 1940. The migration of Kent Island herring gulls. Bird Banding 11:129-155.

Hamilton, W.D. 1964. The genetical evolution of social behaviour, I & II. Journal of Theoretical Biology 7:1-52.

_______. 1970. Selfish and spiteful behavior in an evolutionary model. Nature 228:1218-1220.

_______. 1971. Selection of selfish and altruistic behaviour in some extreme models. In J.F. Eisenberg and W.S. Dillon (eds.), Man and beast: Comparative social behavior. Smithsonian Institution Press, Washington, D.C., pp. 59-91.

_______. 1972. Altruism and related phenomena, mainly in social insects. Annual Review of Ecology & Systematics 3:193-232.

Hollander, M. & D.A. Wolfe. 1973. Nonparametric statistical methods. Wiley, New York.

Hoogland, J.L. 1978. Costs of prairie dog (Sciuridae: Cynomys spp.) coloniality. Behaviour (in press).

_______ & P.W. Sherman. 1976. Advantages and disadvantages of bank swallow (Riparia riparia) coloniality. Ecological Monographs 46:33-58.

Hrdy, S.B. 1976. The care and exploitation of nonhuman primate infants by conspecifics other than the mother. Advances in the Study of Behavior 6:101-156.

Hubbell, S.P. 1977. A critique of the genetic foundations of kin selection theory. Manuscript. Zoology Department, University of Iowa, Iowa City.

Ingram, C. 1959. The importance of juvenile cannibalism in the breeding biology of certain birds of prey. Auk 76:218-226.

Koenig, W.D. & F.A. Pitelka. 1979. Ecological factors and the role of kin selection in the evolution of communal breeding in birds. In R.D. Alexander and D.W. Tinkle (eds.), Natural Selection and Social Behavior. Chiron Press, New York (in press).

Kurland, J.A. 1977. Kin selection in the Japanese monkey. Contributions to Primatology 12:1-145.

_______. 1979. Can sociality have a favorite sex chromosome? American Naturalist (in press).

Lawick-Goodall, J. van. 1968. The behaviour of free-living chimpanzees in the Gombe Stream reserve. Animal Behaviour Monographs 1:161-311.

_______. 1971. In the shadow of man. Houghton Mifflin, Boston.

_______. 1975. The behavior of the chimpanzee. In G. Kurth & I. Eibl-Eibesfeldt (eds.), Hominisation und Verhalten. Rishcer Verlag, Stuttgart, pp. 74-136.

Leigh, E.G., Jr. 1977. How does selection reconcile individual advantage with the good of the group? Proceedings of the National Academy of Sciences 74:4542-4546.

Massey, A. 1977. Agonistic aids and kinship in a group of pigtail macaques. Behavioral Ecology & Sociobiology 2:31-40.

Maynard Smith, J. 1964. Kin selection and group selection. Nature 201:1145-1147.

_______ & M.G. Ridpath. 1972. Wife sharing in the Tasmanian native hen, Tribonyx motierii: A case of kin selection? American Naturalist 106:447-452.

McCarley, H. 1966. Annual cycle, population dynamics, and adaptive behavior of Citellus tridecemlineatus. Journal of Mammalogy 47:294-316.

McCracken, G.F. & J.W. Bradbury. 1977. Paternity and genetic heterogeneity in the polygynous bat, Phyllostomus hastatus. Science 198:303-306.

Melchior, H.R. & F.A. Iwen. 1965. Trapping, restraining, and marking Arctic ground squirrels for behavioral observations. Journal of Wildlife Management 29:671-678.

Michener, D.R. & G.R. Michener. 1971. Sex ratio and interyear residence in a population of Spermophilus richardsonii. Journal of Mammalogy 52:853.

Michener, G.R. 1973. Field observations on the social relationships between adult female and juvenile Richardson's ground squirrels. Canadian Journal of Zoology 51:33-38.

_______. 1974. Development of adult-young identification in Richardson's ground squirrel. Developmental Psychobiology 7:375-384.

_______ & D.R. Michener. 1973. Spatial distribution of yearlings in a Richardson's ground squirrel population. Ecology 54:1138-1142.

_______ & D.R. Michener. 1977. Population structure and dispersal in Richardson's ground squirrels. Ecology 58:359-368.

______ & D.H. Sheppard. 1972. Social behavior between adult female Richardson's ground squirrels (*Spermophilus richardsonii*) and their own and alien young. *Canadian Journal of Zoology* 50:1343-1349.

Missakian, E.A. 1972. Genalogical and cross-genealogical dominance relations in a group of free-ranging rhesus monkeys (*Macaca mulatta*) on Cayo Santiago. *Primates* 13:169-180.

Mohr, C.E. 1934. Marking bats for later recognition. *Proceedings of the Pennsylvania Academy of Sciences* 8:26-30.

Morton, M.L. 1975. Seasonal cycles of body weights and lipids in Belding ground squirrels. *Bulletin of the Southern California Academy of Sciences* 74:128-143.

______, C.S. Maxwell, & C.E. Wade. 1974. Body size, body composition, and behavior of juvenile Belding ground squirrels. *Great Basin Naturalist* 34:121-134.

______ & J.S. Gallup. 1972. Reproductive cycle of the Belding ground squirrel (*Spermophilus beldingi beldingi*): Seasonal and age differences. *Great Basin Naturalist* 35:427-433.

Nice, M.M. 1937. Studies in the life history of the song sparrow. I. A population study of the song sparrow. *Transactions of the Linnean Society of New York* 4:1-247.

Orlove, M.J. 1975. A model of kin selection not invoking coefficients of relationship. *Journal of Theoretical Biology* 49:289-310.

Partridge, L. & L. Nunney. 1977. Three-generation family conflict. *Animal Behaviour* 25:785-786.

Robertson, W.B. 1969. Transatlantic migration of juvenile sooty terns. *Nature* 222:632-634.

Rongstad, O.J. 1965. A life history study of thirteen-lined ground squirrels in southern Wisconsin. *Journal of Mammalogy* 46:76-87.

Sade, D.S. 1965. Some aspects of parent-offspring and sibling relations in a group of rhesus monkeys, with a discussion of grooming. *American Journal of Physical Anthropology* 23:1-18.

______. 1967. Determinants of dominance in a group of free-ranging rhesus monkeys. In S.A. Altmann (ed.), Social communication among primates. University of Chicago Press, Chicago, pp. 99-114.

Sahlins, M. 1976. The use and abuse of biology. University of Michigan Press, Ann Arbor.

Schaller, G.B. 1972. The Serengeti lion. University of Chicago Press, Chicago.

Scudo, F.M. & M.T. Ghiselin. 1975. Familial selection and the evolution of social behavior. Journal of Genetics 62:1-31.

Sheppard, D.H. & S.M. Yoshida. 1971. Social behavior in captive Richardson's ground squirrels. Journal of Mammalogy 52:793-799.

Sherman, P.W. 1976. Natural selection among some group-living organisms. Ph.D. Thesis, University of Michigan, Ann Arbor.

______. 1977. Nepotism and the evolution of alarm calls. Science 197:1246-1253.

______. 1978a. Why are people? A comparative review of The Selfish Gene (R. Dawkins) and The Use and Abuse of Biology (M. Sahlins). Human Biology 50:87-95.

______. 1978b. A comparative review of The Langurs of Abu (S.B. Hrdy) and Kin Selection in the Japanese Monkey (J.A. Kurland). Quarterly Review of Biology 53:491-492.

______. 1979. Insect chromosome numbers and eusociality. American Naturalist, (in press).

Slade, N.A. & D.F. Balph. 1974. Population ecology of Uinta ground squirrels. Ecology 55:989-1003.

Sokal, R.R. & F.J. Rohlf. 1969. Biometry. W.H. Freeman, San Francisco.

Stearns, S.C. 1976. Life-history tactics: A review of the ideas. Quarterly Review of Biology 51:3-47.

Trivers, R.L. 1971. The evolution of reciprocal altruism. Quarterly Review of Biology 46:35-57.

_______ & H. Hare. 1976. Haplodiploidy and the evolution of the social insects. Science 191:249-263.

Turner, L.W. 1972. Autecology of the Belding ground squirrel in Oregon. Ph.D. Thesis, University of Arizona, Tucson.

_______. 1973. Vocal and escape responses of Spermophilus beldingi to predators. Journal of Mammalogy 54:990-993.

Vehrencamp, S.L. 1978. The roles of individual, kin, and group selection in the evolution of sociality. In P. Marler (ed.), Handbook of behavior. McGraw-Hill, New York (in press).

West-Eberhard, M.J. 1975. The evolution of social behavior by kin selection. Quarterly Review of Biology 50:1-33.

Williams, G.C. 1966. Adaptation and natural selection. Princeton University Press, Princeton.

_______ & D.C. Williams. 1957. Natural selection of individually harmful social adaptations among sibs with special reference to social insects. Evolution 11:32-39.

Wilson, E.O. 1971. The insect societies. Harvard University Press, Cambridge, Massachusetts.

_______. 1975. Sociobiology: The new synthesis. Harvard University Press, Cambridge, Massachusetts.

Woolfenden, G.E. 1975. Florida scrub jay helpers at the nest. Auk 92:1-15.

_______ & J.W. Fitzpatrick. 1978. The inheritance of territory in group-breeding birds. BioScience 28:104-108.

Wu, H.M.H. & W.G. Holmes. 1979. Kin preference in infant Macaca nemestrina. Manuscript (submitted).

Yamada, M. 1963. A study of blood-relationship in the natural society of the Japanese macaque. Primates 4:43-66.

Yeaton, R.I. 1972. Social behavior and social organization in Richardson's ground squirrel (Spermophilus richardsonii) in Saskatchewan. Journal of Mammalogy 53:139-147.

Napoleon A. Chagnon

21. Kin-Selection Theory, Kinship, Marriage and Fitness Among the Yąnomamö Indians

Introduction

The applicability of theory from evolutionary biology to human social behavior, particularly the theories of kin selection (Hamilton 1964; Maynard Smith 1964) and reciprocal altruism (Trivers 1971) is a question that can only be answered by translating those theories into testable hypotheses and subjecting the hypotheses to rigorous quantitative tests. By the same token, denials that these theories apply to human social behavior (Sahlins 1976) must be predicated on the same kind of rigor, not on appeals to a 'received wisdom' whose recipients appear also to be its purveyors. The issues, simply, are testable ones and the tests must necessarily follow scientifically well understood relationships between theoretical propositions, analytical methods and well documented evidence.

The field research I conducted among the Yąnomamö Indians (Chagnon 1968, 1974, 1977) of southern Venezuela (Fig. 1) between 1964 and the present, entailed some 41 months of residence in various villages of the tribe. That research was conducted in ignorance of the theories of kin selection and reciprocal altruism, but some of the data I collected are relevant to those theories. A major motivation behind that field research had to do with reconciling the facts of demography with the ideology of kinship and marriage (Chagnon 1966). I wanted to show that observed patterns of marriage constituted a system that was comprehensible in terms of both ideology and demographic data. Demonstrating that proposition necessarily required the collection of meticulously documented genealogies that linked the residents of numerous villages in time and space (Chagnon 1974) as well as data on age and sex distribution, mortality patterns, village fissioning and settlement redistribution, kinship classification and reproductive histories.

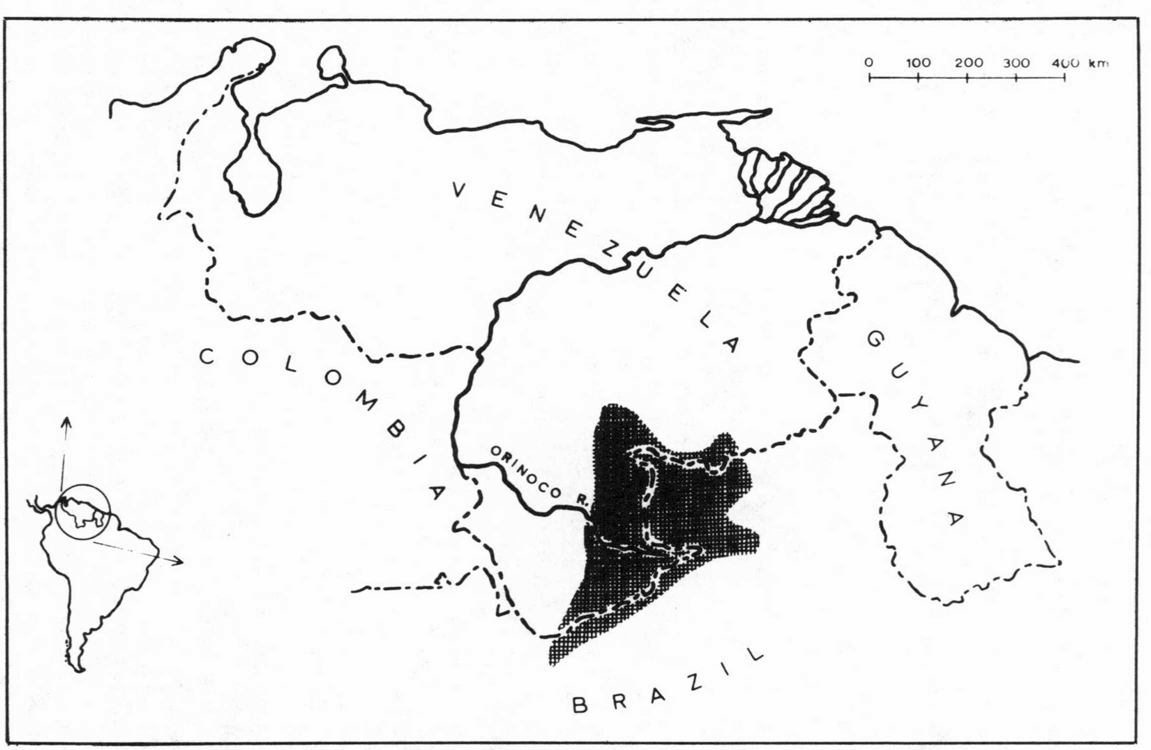

Figure 1. Location of the Yąnomamö Indians in South America.

This work brought me to some 50 or 60 different Yąnomamö villages whose several thousand collective residents subsequently appeared, genealogized, in my field notes. But the lion's share of my field effort was spent in some dozen villages that comprise two historically distinct population blocs each containing seven or more villages. Those two populations consist of approximately 1,400 living individuals and, with the approximately 2,100 deceased ancestors and relatives, constitute a data base of 3,500 individuals. While none of the field research was inspired by the general theory of evolutionary biology, the resulting data are sufficiently detailed and comprehensive that they can be examined from the vantage of this body of theory. The historical connections among the several villages in the two population blocs is reflected in Figure 2, which schematically illustrates the political history and fissions of the populations during the past 125 odd years.

Tests of kin-selection theory require demonstrating that (1) individuals favor kin over nonkin, and among kin, favor more closely related individuals over less closely related individuals, and (2) differences in inclusive fitness (Hamilton 1964) have something to do with patterns of preference for kin over nonkin or close kin over distant kin.

To carry out these tests and demonstrations, one must begin with a detailed data base of the sort just described, one that includes data on reproductive success and kinship among the constituent individuals. Moreover, kinship must be verified (Chagnon 1974), measurable and quantified.

I have codified all 3,500 individuals in such a way that the data can be analyzed by computer (ibid.). Each individual in the sample, with approximately 20 discrete variables such as age, sex, birthplace, parents, spouses, etc., has been put on computer tape.

Through the use of programs developed specifically for kinship analyses, all relationships between any given individual and all others can be calculated using a variant of Wright's Inbreeding Coefficient (Wright 1922). Each individual has been systematically compared to all others in the sample to establish all demonstrable genealogical connections, the associated coefficients of relationship calculated for each connection, and the results stored on magnetic tapes. The kinship data amount to approximately 1,300,000 pieces of information and can be correlated to variations in reproduction by individuals. Results of serological studies conducted with medical colleagues at the Department of Human Genetics, The University of Michigan Medical School, indicate that

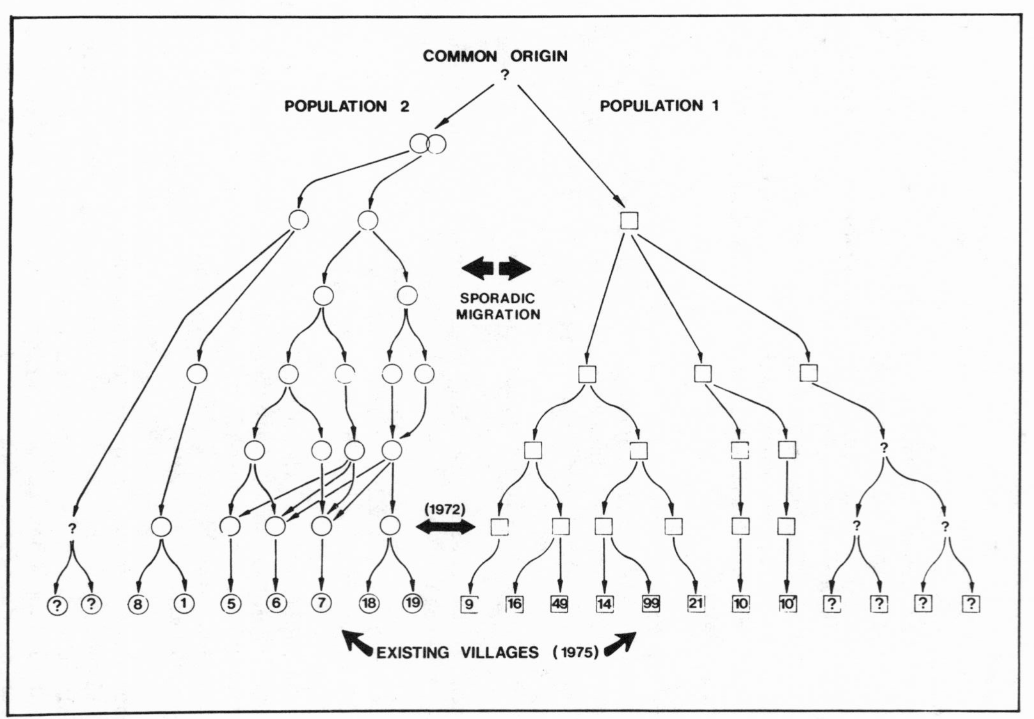

Figure 2. Schematic diagram of village fissioning in two Yąnomamö populations. Present-day villages (bottom row) are connected by common history and common ancestors.

reported paternity is close to actual biological paternity among the Yąnomamö.

Analyses completed to date indicate that the social behavior of the Yąnomamö conforms to predictions from the theory of evolutionary biology. I will briefly review some of these results and then introduce additional new information that will illustrate the scientific merit of examining human social behavior from the general argument that much of it is adaptive in biological terms. The new data analyses refer to the practice of cross-cousin marriage, widespread in the tribal world, and it's potentially adaptive features in the Yąnomamö population. Since this work is still in preliminary form, the conclusions at this juncture must be considered tentative and subject to modification as the projected analyses are carried out in the months to come. For the moment, I am excited by the possibilities that are now revealing themselves, for if they hold up on further testing, the widespread occurrence of bilateral cross-cousin marriage will take on new meaning, one that makes sense in terms of the general theory of natural selection.

Favoring Kin

Despite the fact that human kinship has symbolic and fictive dimensions, important in their own right, human kinship behavior can be demonstrated to have biological dimensions as well. A number of examples from Yąnomamö kinship behavior, drawn from earlier work, illustrate this.

The fissioning of larger villages into smaller ones is a primary example, showing that close kin favor each other by preferring to remain together. I have documented this in previous publications (Chagnon 1974, 1975) by taking each individual in the pre-fission village, calculating his/her coefficient of relationship to all other coresidents and then, after the village fissions into two new groups, calculating the coefficients of relationship between each individual and all others who constitute the newly formed fission villages. Invariably, the average coefficient of relationship between all individuals in the pre-fission larger village is lower than it is in the newly-constituted fission groups. Village fissioning results in close kin remaining together and separating from more remotely related kin and nonkin---irrespective of how they classify themselves by kinship terms (Chagnon, 1979c). It is likely that this pattern results from attempts on the part of adult males, who compete for marriageable females, to maximize their reproductive opportunities and those of their close agnates (relatives through the male line of descent) by separating from less closely related coalitions of male competitors (Chagnon, 1979a).

Another, and somewhat dramatic, illustration that individuals choose to aid close relatives over more distant ones stems from an analysis of an ax-fight that took place in one of the larger Yąnomamö villages. The conflict was filmed, permitting a detailed analysis of the individuals involved in the conflict and their interrelatedness. The contesting factions were led by specific individuals, around whom numbers of supporters rallied to offer aid and to fight.

I calculated the coefficients of relationship among all the members of each faction, the average coefficients of relationship between the factions and the village at large, and, finally, the average coefficients of relationship between leaders and their factions and opposite factions. The results all indicate that in this high-risk conflict---individuals could have been killed---people aided close kin: Individuals in each faction were more closely related among themselves than they were to the village at large, more closely related among themselves than they were to members of the opposing faction and more closely related to their respective champions than they were to the opponents' champion (Asch & Chagnon [16 mm film] 1975; Chagnon & Bugos 1979). In brief, the participants in the fight behaved as if they 'evaluated' the coefficients of relationship among their neighbors before tendering their support, and elected to support those individuals who were more closely related to them.

I have also tested the relative merits of fictive kinship and kinship classification with respect to coefficients of relationship to determine if the symbolic dimensions of Yąnomamö kinship override the demonstrable genealogical aspects of kinship. For example, the term applied to an actual brother is extended outward and includes many individuals who are demonstrably <u>not</u> actual brothers: They may be half brothers, half parallel cousins, full parallel cousins---even people who are totally unrelated. But they do not treat all 'brothers' in the same fashion or favor them equally.

In one large village I collected the kinship term used by each of six informants for all 278 other coresidents and then compared their kinship classification to coefficients of relationship to the same individuals. The village fissioned into three new groups afterwards, scattering 'brothers' among the newly formed groups. The distribution showed that genealogically close relatives remained together and that the coefficients of relationship were better predictors of the distribution than the terminological system of 'salutations' (Chagnon 1979c).

Differences in Reproductive Success

Bateman's classic study of sexual selection in Drosophila (1948) and Trivers' equally classic extension of that work (1972) in the formulation of his theory of parental investment make it clear that variation in reproductive success by males is of signal importance in understanding mating systems and their behavioral correlates. Natural selection, by definition, entails the differential reproduction and survival of individuals (or genes) from one generation to the next, and variation in reproductive success by males can contribute significantly to this process. Among the Yąnomamö, it can be shown that marked differences occur in the reproductive accomplishments of individuals, i.e., some individuals succeed in getting disproportionate representation in succeeding generations. While there is some variation in reproductive success among females, there is much more variability in male reproductive success (Chagnon 1974, 1979b). That stems in large measure from the differing abilities of males to acquire multiple spouses and, because of polygyny, to leave relatively larger numbers of offspring than their monogamous peers. The strategies developed by Yąnomamö males to acquire multiple spouses puts the mating system itself in the theoretical context of sexual selection and kin selection, since polygyny can be demonstrated to be achieved by cooperation among coalitions of closely related males who compete with other males for the available females. The more successful are 'chosen' more often as mates by the females: It must be understood that 'choice' here includes the strategic decisions made by the female's kin to cede them to men in particular kin groups (Chagnon 1979a, 1979b).

While it cannot be assumed that <u>all</u> headmen in this society achieve high fertility and reproductive success, the general picture is that, on average, headmen have higher reproductive success than nonheadmen of comparable age (Tables 1 & 2). The higher reproductive success of headmen stems primarily from their ability to acquire multiple spouses rather than from greater fertility per spouse (Chagnon, Flinn & Melancon 1979).

The differential reproductive success of some males has a remarkable effect on the reproductive potentials of their offspring and other descendants. Many of the sons of particularly successful men, in turn, achieve high reproductive success. In addition, there appears to be some correlation between a woman's reproductive success and the 'significance' of either her own lineal descent group or that of her husband, 'significance' here being defined in terms of relative representation, numerically, of that descent group in the village

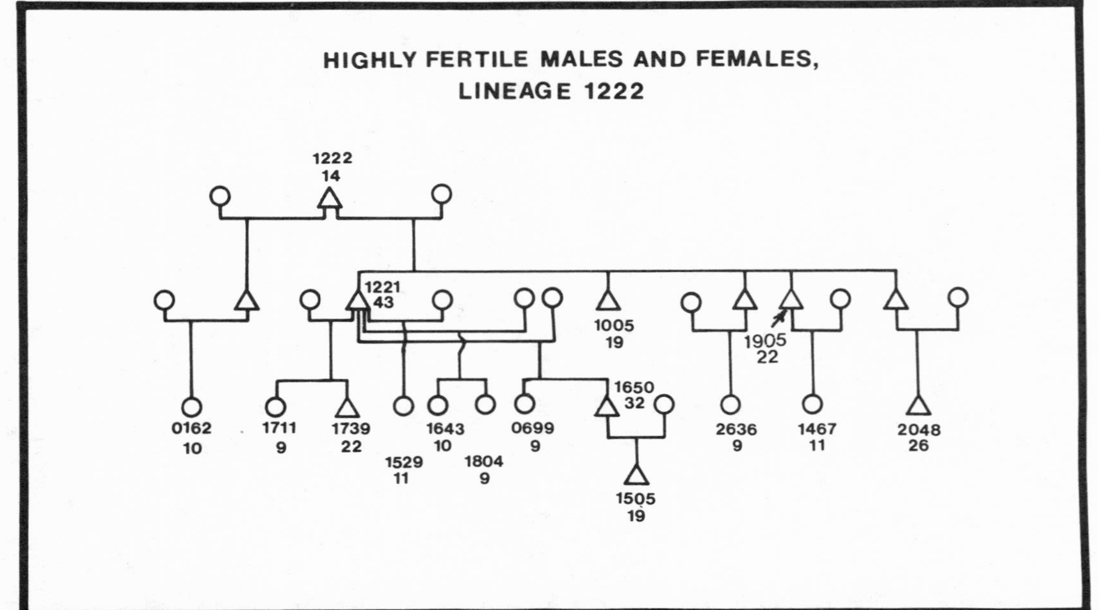

Figure 3. Genealogical connections among the more fertile offspring and descendants of 'founder' 1222. Four-digit numbers are computer identification numbers; the second number gives the number of children for that individual. From Evolutionary Biology and Human Social Behavior: An Anthropological Perspective, by Napoleon A. Chagnon and William Irons, ©1979 by Wadsworth, Inc., Belmont, Ca. 94002. Reprinted by permission of the publisher, Duxbury Press.

Table 1. Marital performance of headmen compared to other males 35 years old or older.

Status of Male	Number	Wives	Average Number of Wives	Offspring per Wife
Headmen	20	71	3.6 ± 1.9	2.4 ± 2.5
Nonheadmen	108	258	2.4 ± 1.4	1.7 ± 2.0
			p = .007	p = .238

and in the population (Chagnon 1979b; Chagnon, Flinn & Melancon 1979).

If we identify the 20 most fertile males and females in the entire population (ibid.) and then examine the kinship relationships among these individuals, we find that a surprisingly large number of them are related through male kinship or descent ties to the same common ancestor. Figure 3 illustrates this graphically.

One of the intriguing features of the correlation of a female's fertility with that of her agnates (Fig. 3) and her spouses (not shown in Fig. 3 but documented in Chagnon 1979b) is the possibility that females receive investments from both agnatic kin and spouses that affect their reproductive potential. That suggests that the study of the economic aspects of reproduction in future field research should lead to valuable new insights and perhaps demonstrate the nature of the relationship between production and reproduction (cf. Goody 1976).

Table 2. Reproductive performance of headmen compared to other males 35 years old or older.

Status of Male	Number	Sons	Daughters	Sex Ratio	Mean number of Offspring
Headmen	20	90	82	110	8.6 ± 4.6
Nonheadmen	108	246	203	121	4.2 ± 3.4
					p > .001

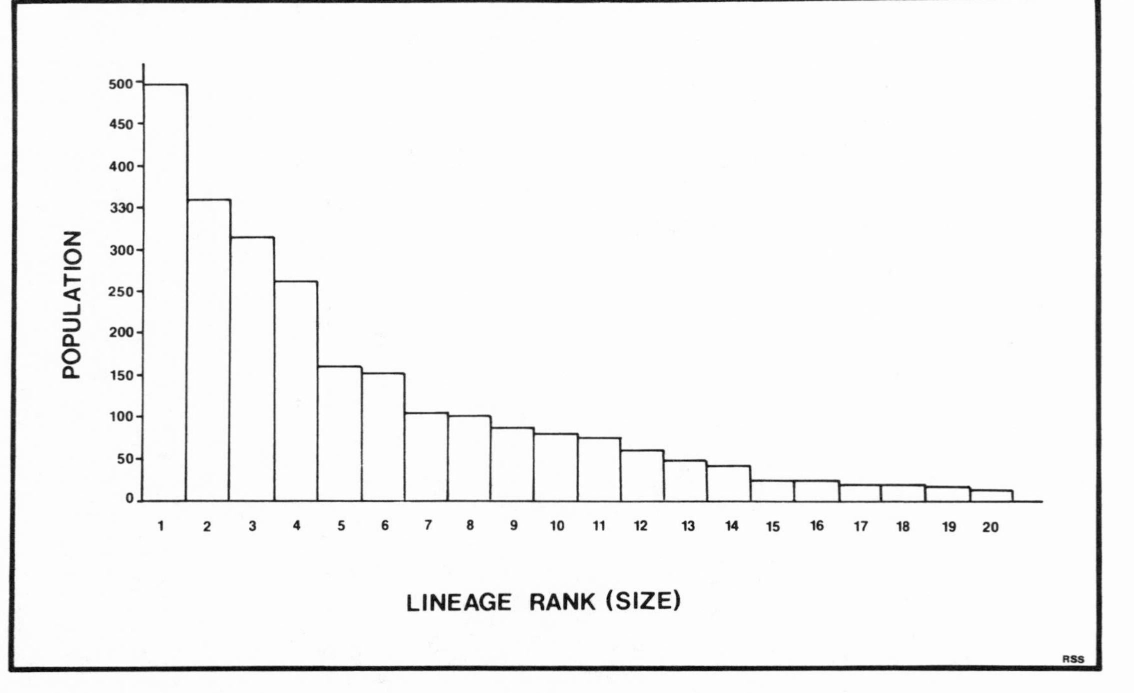

Figure 4. Comparative sizes of larger Yąnomamö patrilineal descent groups in the two populations discussed in this paper. Approximately 20% of the population (living and deceased) falls into a single lineage and approximately half the population falls into the four largest descent groups. From _Evolutionary Biology and Human Social Behavior: An Anthropological Perspective_, by Napoleon A. Chagnon and William Irons, © 1979 by Wadsworth, Inc., Belmont, Ca. 94002. Reprinted by permission of the publisher, Duxbury Press.

The data (Fig. 3) also suggest that differential growth of patrilineal descent groups occurs and that there will be marked differences in the sizes of lineages in the population. A small number of patrilineal descent groups embraces a large fraction of the members of most Yąnomamö sub-populations (Fig. 4): For the populations shown, approximately 50% of the population of 1,400 (living) individuals belong to only four patrilineal descent groups (Chagnon 1979b).

The relative size and distribution of the lineal descent groups in the population is crucial in understanding the politics of mate competition, since descent groups are exogamic. Most villages contain representatives of several such groups and most marriages are village endogamous. That is, individuals must marry outside of their descent group, but may marry into another descent group <u>within</u> their own village. There is a marked tendency for the members of particular descent groups to preferentially give their sisters and daughters to <u>one</u> other descent group, receiving <u>its</u> sisters and daughters in exchange. Reciprocal exchange of marriageable females between such 'matrimonially bound' segments of descent groups continues over several generations in most cases and, expectably, individuals often marry people to whom they are related <u>cognatically</u>, and related in complex ways.

When behavior follows the 'ideal' Yąnomamö model (Fig. 5) patrilineal descent and prescriptive bilateral cross-cousin marriage are seen to operate as an overall system. Thus, beyond the first generation, all males of, for example, Lineage 'Y' marry women of Lineage 'X' who are simultaneously their Mother's Brother's Daughters (MBD) <u>and</u> Father's Sister's Daughters. Figure 5 provides an ideal model showing how a village might be comprised of just two descent groups (members of Lineages X and Y) and therefore have a 'dual organization', but the model also suggests how other lineages (Lineage W) might 'penetrate' the dual organization. While no village conforms precisely to the ideal patterns given in Figure 5 because of the vagaries of demography, differences in age at marriage between males and females, and manipulators who break the rules, there is a general tendency for marriage practices to approximate this model in most Yąnomamö villages. I will examine the possible adaptive features of this system at the end of this paper.

The 'ideal' system (Fig. 5) and the actual practices suggest that the population should be characterized in such a way that many people will be related to large fractions of their covillagers (Chagnon 1979a) in various ways, i.e., that a large fraction of the population will be descended from relatively few ancestors. A few particularly successful lineage

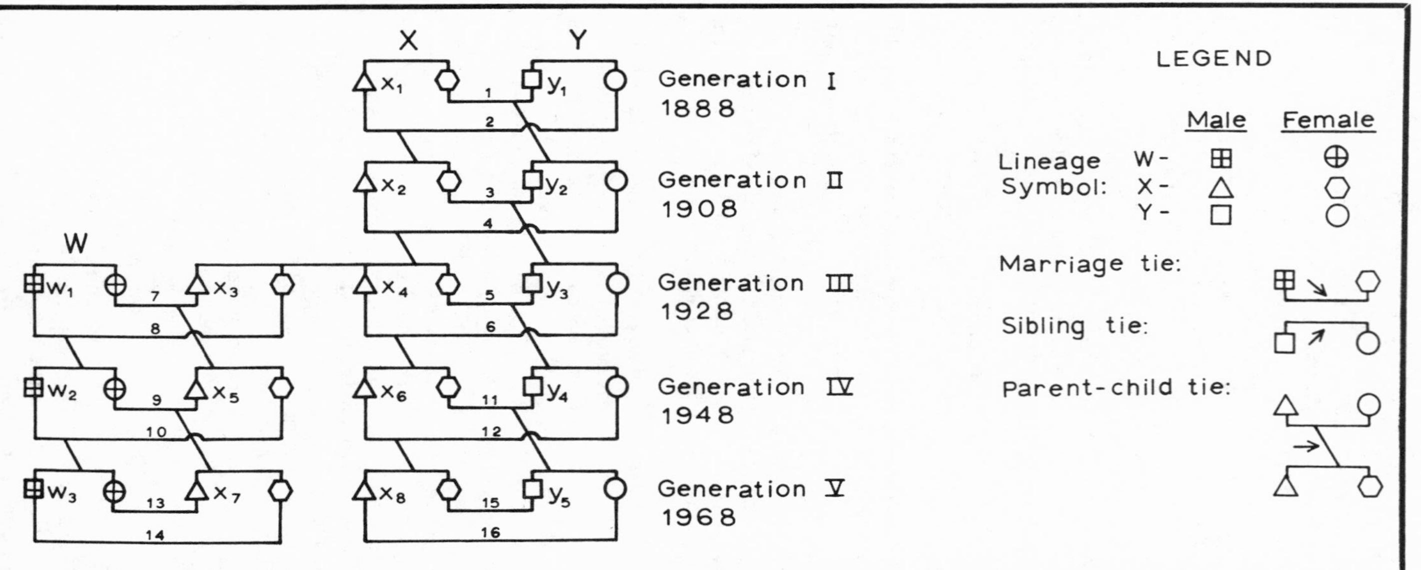

Figure 5. The 'ideal' structure of Yąnomamö villages as determined by their rule of reciprocal cross-cousin marriage and patrilineal descent. Ideally, if everyone followed the rules and everyone had one son and one daughter, the village would have a dual organization, i.e., it would be comprised of two intermarrying descent groups such as 'X' and 'Y'. In actual practice, villages are comprised of more than two descent groups (such as 'W') and violations of the marriage rules occur for a number of reasons. From Yąnomamö: The Fierce People, Second Edition, by Napoleon A. Chagnon.

Table 3. Descendants in six Yąnomamö villages from three founders, showing the number and percent of descendants in each village through the male line (lineal) and through both the male and female line combined (cognatic).

Village	Size	Founder 1222				Founder 2936				Founder 2967			
		Lineal	%	Cognatic	%	Lineal	%	Cognatic	%	Lineal	%	Cognatic	%
09	97	48	49%	92	95%	7	7%	52	54%	11	11%	52	54%
14	119	20	17%	91	77%	35	29%	97	82%	27	23%	93	78%
16	116	56	48%	107	92%	2	2%	39	34%	5	4%	50	43%
21	95	4	4%	92	98%	7	7%	80	84%	74	78%	89	94%
49	77	23	30%	52	68%	20	26%	38	49%	26	34%	58	75%
99	37	5	14%	18	49%	5	14%	33	89%	1	3%	21	57%

'founders' have had a large impact on the populations in blocs of villages (Table 3) through their descendants. Thus, founder '1222' has left few lineal descendants in Village 21 (only 4% of the village members are his lineal descendants). But when descent through both sons and daughters (cognatic descent) is considered, 98% of the members of that village can trace ancestry back to him. Similarly, 94% of the individuals in the same village can trace ancestry back to founder 2967, and 84% back to founder 2936. Needless to say, the descendants of these founders have intermarried with each other over a number of generations (Chagnon 1979a).

Possible Adaptiveness of Yąnomamö Marriages

With this hurried overview, we are now in a position to examine the possible adaptive features of the Yąnomamö marriage system. Cross-cousin marriage, as a system of mating, appears to solve many of the mate competition problems characteristic of this population. In so doing, it binds the inclusive fitness interests of brothers and sisters together. It is worth pointing out at this juncture that preliminary analyses of reproductive success in terms of kinship between spouses indicates that on a per-marriage basis, it is adaptive---it pays in reproductive terms---to marry a relative (Table 4). All marriages by all males to females who were 31 years old or older were examined. Those in which the spouses were known to be related were segregated from those in which the spouses were not demonstrably related. The per-marriage reproductive accomplishments were then examined in each group, with the conclusion that the fertility of related spouses was appreciably higher than the fertility of the pairs of unrelated spouses.

Table 4. Comparison of fertility on a per-marriage basis where spouses were (1) related or (2) unrelated.

Spouses	Number	Children	Average
Unrelated	113	217	1.92
Related	146	330	2.26

A further segregation of the data was then established to determine if particular types of relatedness, such as cross-cousins of various degrees and laterality, were associated with high fertility. That meant subdividing the 146 marriages of Table 4 into a large number of categories, categories that contained relatively few numbers. Nevertheless, two categories emerged from the analysis having markedly higher average reproductive success associated with them: marriages by males with Father's Sister's Daughter (FZD type) and Mother's Brother's Daughter (MBD type). These statistics (Table 5) are based on an analysis of the entire set of marriages in the population as a whole, i.e., the two population blocs considered in this paper.

Table 5. Preliminary findings on per-marriage fertility by type of (actual) cross-cousin marriage.

Marriage Type	Number	Children	Average
FZD	16	35	2.19
MBD	17	55	3.24

I then identified the 20 most fertile males of the population and examined their reproductive success on a per-marriage basis and compared the fertility of the 'related' spouses category to the 'unrelated' spouses category (Table 6).

Table 6. Preliminary findings on fertility on a per-marriage basis among the 20 most fertile males, where their spouses were: (1) related and (2) unrelated.

Spouses	Number	Children	Average
Related	33	117	3.54
Unrelated	46	120	2.61

The pattern among the most fertile males is similar to that of the population as a whole in that males produce more offspring by spouses to whom they are related than they do with spouses to whom they are not related. I then examined the fertility of marriages within this group of marriages that involved just (actual) cross-cousins (Table 7).

These findings are, in their present form, merely suggestive. They imply that marriages with (actual) MBDs and FZDs are somewhat more productive than alternative types of consanguineal marriages. That finding stimulated me to consider the practice of cross-cousin marriage among the descendants of particularly successful founders, rather than look at this marriage practice across the population as a whole,

Table 7. Preliminary findings on fertility among the 20 most fertile males on a per-marriage basis where their related spouses were: (1) MBD type and (2) FZD type.

Marriage Type	Number	Children	Average
MBD	6	27	4.50
FZD	7	31	4.43

or in the marriages of particularly fertile individuals who may or may not be members of descent groups founded by particularly successful individuals. My suspicion at this point in the data analysis is that cross-cousin marriages represent an adaptive strategy for only a fraction of the Yąnomamö population, i.e., for those individuals who were fortunate enough to have a highly successful grandfather---someone who, through polygyny, produced large numbers of sons and daughters and whose sons and daughters built on their 'kinship fortunes' through reciprocal marriage alliance by giving <u>their</u> children in marriage to each other as implied in the 'ideal model' (Fig. 5). This 'building on kinship fortune' is, in effect, comprehendible in terms of fitness-maximizing strategies, in this case, strategies that pursue the reproductive possibilities of bilateral cross-cousin marriage.

I have just recently initiated the analysis of this problem and will now report on some of my initial findings. The present effort has been confined, as a feasability study, to the marriages and fertility patterns among the descendants of a single successful individual, but the projected research will cover all major descent groups and their founders to determine the extent to which cross-cousin marriage is a general reproductive- and fitness-maximizing strategy among members of the <u>larger</u> descent groups that are found in the two subpopulations under consideration.

Fitness and Cross-Cousin Marriage in One Descent Group

The largest single descent group in the Yąnomamö populations that I have concentrated my field research on was initiated by a man, long since deceased, whose lineal and cognatic descendants are heavily represented in the population as a whole, but, in particular, in the villages listed in Table 3 above (and as 'Shamatari' or Population 1 in my publications; Chagnon 1974, 1979a, 1979b). This individual was designated as '1222' (Table 3) and is the founder of the group shown in

Figure 3. Much of his inclusive fitness was due to the remarkable reproductive achievements of one of his eleven children, a son called Matakuwä, and, in turn, the reproductive achievements of many of Matakuwä's descendants (Fig. 3). The following discussion will focus on the marriage and reproductive accomplishments of Matakuwä (ID 1221) and his lineal and cognatic descendants.

Figure 6 summarizes Matakuwä's descendants by 'type' and by reproductive success according to 'type'. He had 20 sons and 23 daughters; his 20 sons then produced a total of 62 sons and 58 daughters, etc. (Fig. 6). Matakuwä's grandchildren, counting only cognatic ties back to him (i.e., not to other common ancestors they might also have), would be related among each other as siblings, half-siblings, full parallel cousins, half parallel cousins, full cross-cousins and half cross-cousins. Since descent is patrilineal and the male descent line exogamic, a number of logically possible marriage patterns can occur among his grandchildren. They could marry nonrelatives, or, they could marry among themselves---either according to the positive (prescriptive) rules of cross-cousin marriage, or by marrying individuals in prohibited categories (parallel cousins, for example), which, by Yąnomamö definition, is 'incest'.

Figure 7 summarizes the possibilities of marriage just listed, giving the logical expected components of his inclusive fitness for his great-grandchildren's generation. Technically, this represents only a fraction of Matakuwä's inclusive fitness, since the reproductive accomplishments of <u>his</u> siblings and their descendants are not considered in Figure 7, or in the discussion that follows.

How the actual distribution of the components of Matakuwä's inclusive fitness (Fig. 7) will appear in the respecive categories will depend on the strategies of marriage/mating followed by his sons and daughters after they are adults and have children of their own. He may be influential in arranging marriages for his sons and daughters, but they are more influential in arranging the marriages of <u>their</u> sons and daughters. Since it takes females (sisters and daughters) to acquire other females (wives and daughters-in-law), the relationships between adult males and their adult sisters (and the husbands of these sisters) are central to understanding the marriage arrangements in Matakuwä's grandchildren's generation. Because of mate competition, the sons of Matakuwä could optimize, or perhaps even maximize, <u>their own</u> sons' mating opportunities by giving daughters to the sons of their sisters <u>if</u> these sisters (and their husbands) reciprocated by giving

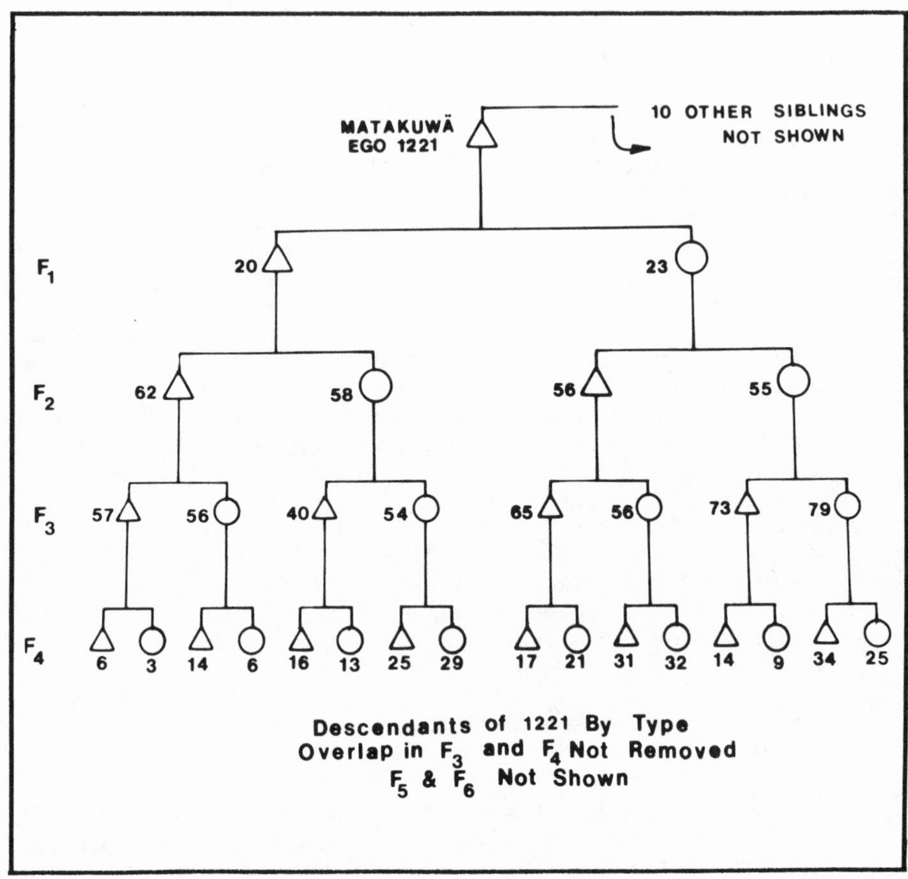

Figure 6. Distribution by generation, number and sex of the descendants of Matakuwä (Ego 1221). In the F_1 generation, he had 20 sons and 23 daughters. The 20 sons had 62 sons and 58 daughters, etc. In the F_2 generation, male descendants of the F_1 sons can marry the female descendants of the F_1 daughters and, in turn, the male descendants of the F_1 daughters can marry the female descendants of the F_1 sons---they are cross-cousins to each other.

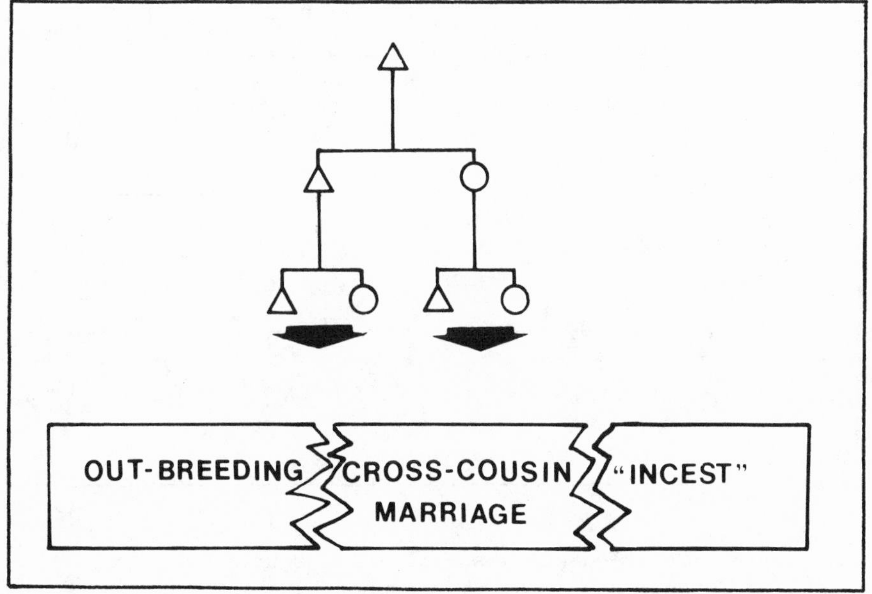

Figure 7. Components of inclusive fitness in a bilateral cross-cousin marriage system with reciprocal marriage exchange. A fraction of the inclusive fitness of a founder will be the result of cross-cousin marriage among the grandchildren. Another fraction of inclusive fitness will be due to marriages by grandchildren to non-relatives (outbreeding), and a third fraction will be due to violation of the marriage rules which, by Yąnomamö definition, is incest.

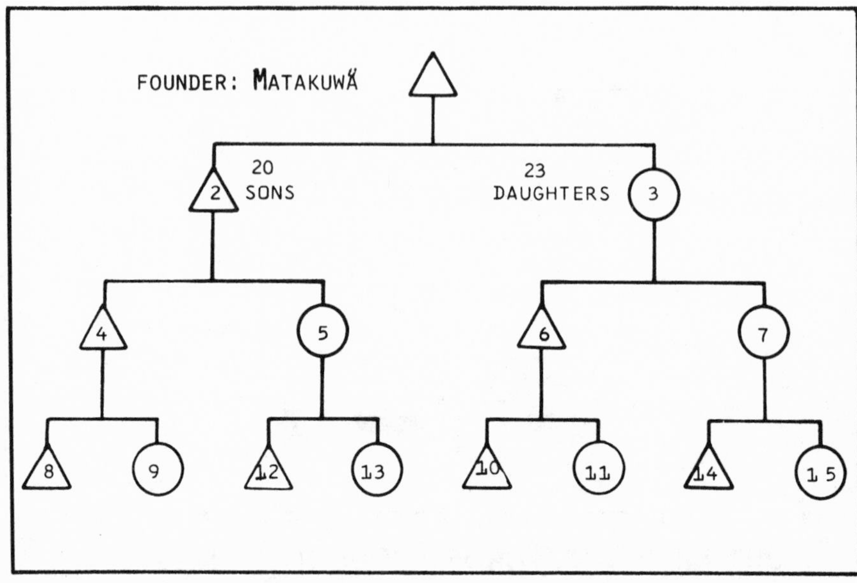

Figure 8. Genealogically-specified categories of descendants of Founder Matakuwä. The numbers within the circles and triangles are genealogical categories; for actual counts of individuals in each category, see Fig. 6. If some of the males in Category 4 married cross-cousins (father's sister's daughter) in Category 7, then some of the sons of these men (who would be in Category 8) would also be sons of the women in Category 7, i.e., would also occur in Category 14. Table 8 shows that 29 of the sons of women of Category 7 also occur in Category 8 as sons of the men in Category 4.

their daughters back as mates for their sons. Should this be a valid hypothesis, then we should find that there would be a significant fraction of Matakuwä's great-grandchildren who can trace ancestry back to him through both their fathers and their mothers, a consequence of the fact that they are the issue of cross-cousin marriages.

To investigate this hypothesis, I searched for identities among the eight categories of Matakuwä's great-grandchildren that descend through his four genealogically distinct types of grandchildren: Sons' sons, sons' daughters, daughters' sons and daughters' daughters.

Figure 8 illustrates the procedure as it was developed for computer analysis. If cross-cousin marriages occurred in the grandchild generation, then the individuals who belong to the genealogically specified categories numbered 8, 9, 10, 11, 12, 13, 14 and 15 on Figure 8 will occur in at least two categories of this generation. Thus, if some males of Category 4 married father's sister's daughters (in Category 7), then some of their sons (in Category 8) should also appear in Category 14, and some of their daughters (in Category 9) should, for the same reason, appear also in Category 15. Table 8 gives the results of the search for correlations between great-grandchild categories, and brings out the remarkable degree to which the practice of cross-cousin marriage within this (cognatically considered) group has characterized the mating strategies of many of its members, or, rather, the machinations of their parents and older agnates.

Table 8. Correlation of Matakuwä's great-grandchildren by genealogically specified types that result from cross-cousin marriage in the grandchild generation, giving sex and number of great-grandchildren for each category.

	Female Categories and Number of Individuals					Male Categories and Number of Individuals			
	9	11	13	15		8	10	12	14
9	56	--	--	38	8	57	--	--	29
11	--	56	26	--	10	--	65	20	--
13	--	26	54	--	12	--	20	40	--
15	38	3	--	79	14	29	1	--	73

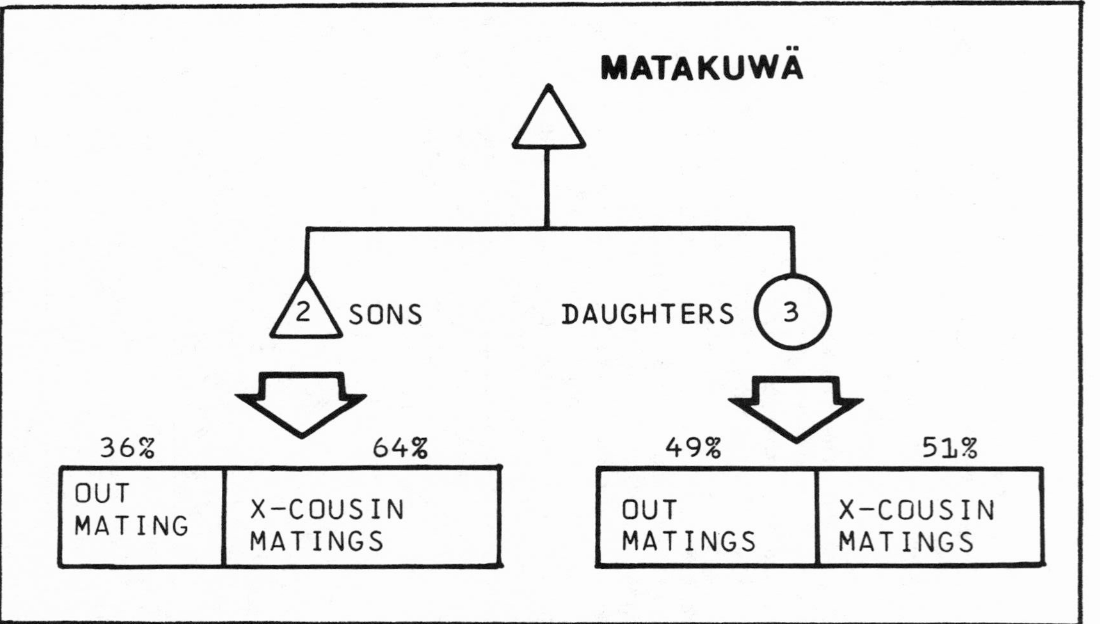

Figure 9. Components of inclusive fitness of the sons and daughters of Founder Matakuwä due to (1) out mating and (2) marriages with cross-cousins. The inclusive fitness of the founder's sons is more dependent on the marriage practices of the founder's daughters than vice-versa, suggesting that males would be expected to try to control the marriages of their sisters.

While the individuals in the great-grandchild generation contribute to the inclusive fitness of the founder, Matakuwä, the more important feature of the pattern has to do with the reproductive strategies of Matakuwä's sons and the degree to which <u>their</u> inclusive fitness hinges on their ability to acquire the daughters of their sisters as mates for their sons. The disadvantages for males in having their sisters marry outside the village are obvious.

If we focus on the sons and daughters of Matakuwä (Categories 2 and 3, Fig. 8) and calculate their inclusive fitness, some remarkable conclusions emerge. Figure 9 summarizes these findings, calculated by using coefficients of relatedness between members of Categories 2 and 3 to descendants in Categories 8, 9, 10, 11, 12, 13, 14 and 15 (Fig. 8). The inclusive fitness of Matakuwä's sons (in their grandchildren's generation) is strongly affected by the degree to which their sons married cross-cousins within this (cognatically considered) group of relatives: 64% of their inclusive fitness results from such marriages, whereas only 36% is the result of their sons marrying outside this (cognatically considered) group.

The degree to which Matakuwä's daughters' inclusive fitness depends on cross-cousin marriages is less, but nevertheless remarkable: About half of their inclusive fitness (51%) in their grandchildren's generation is a function of cross-cousin marriages by their children.

While I have yet to explore the details of average fertility for the marriages just described and compare them to the fertility in other types of marriages, it is clear that males, by 'favoring' close kin (sisters), increase their inclusive fitness by so doing. Males attempt to keep sisters (and other close relatives) with them when a village fissions, but are variably successful at doing so (Chagnon in preparation).

The above analysis is probably an underestimate of the degree to which a male's inclusive fitness is a function of favoring sisters. Recall from Figure 7 that there will also be a component of inclusive fitness attributable to marriages that are illegitimate ('incestuous'). This fraction of the inclusive fitness of Matakuwä's sons and daughters has not been calculated or considered here, and remains to be demonstrated in the projected future analyses. Its potential significance will be due, in part, to the fact that generation length for females is shorter than that for males. Because of this, opportunities will arise for individuals of the appropriate ages to marry individuals who are in the 'wrong' genealogically-defined generation. The foregoing analysis considered only those marriages between individuals of the same genealogically-defined generation.

In addition, the shorter generation length of females must be examined and analyzed from the implications that this has for possible differences in investment patterns by males in both sisters and spouses on the one hand, and daughters and daughters-in-law on the other. While an occasional son of a fertile founder may in turn be highly fertile, most of the sons do poorly by comparison. The cumulative effects of modest but predictable reproduction by all females, coupled with the fact that they have shorter generation lengths, eventually begins to show in the inclusive fitness returns in subsequent generations (Fig. 6).

Summary

The applicability of the theories of kin selection and reciprocal altruism to human social behavior can be determined through scientific procedures commonly understood in the academic community. Research in this area should attempt to determine if individuals favor kin over nonkin and the degree to which differences in inclusive fitness are associated with these behavioral patterns. My previous publications indicate that among the Yąnomamö Indians of Venezuela, individuals prefer to remain with kin when villages fission, choose to take risks to aid kin during fights and assort themselves after a fission in ways that are more predictable from the theory of kin selection than from a knowledge of their kinship classification and kinship term usages.

There is marked variability in reproductive success by males, due largely to the ability of some males to acquire multiple wives. The ability to acquire multiple wives is, in turn, a function of the kinds of coalitions that males enter into with other, related, males. Such coalitions operate in the context of mate competition, and allied males reciprocally give their sisters and daughters to each other.

Preliminary analysis of fertility patterns indicate that related spouses produce more offspring on a per-marriage basis than unrelated spouses. The data also suggest that cross-cousin marriages are somewhat more fertile than other types of marriages, a finding that must be tested further, but one that suggests that a close examination of marriage patterns among members of large descent groups will lead to an appreciation of the adaptive features of cross-cousin marriage.

An initial examination of marriages and inclusive fitness among the members of one large descent group suggests strongly that the inclusive fitness of males is more a function of their sisters' reproductive abilities and marriage practices than a woman's is of her brother's marriage practices. This underscores the crucial importance of understanding the nature of social rules about marriage in human societies, often ignored by biologists, but also reveals that such rules make good sense in terms of predictions from theoretical biology, often denied by anthropologists.

Acknowledgements

The research on which this paper is based was provided by the Harry Frank Guggenheim Foundation, the National Science Foundation and the National Institute of Mental Health. I am grateful for the comments and criticisms of earlier drafts of this paper made by William Irons, Thomas F. Melacon and Mark V. Flinn. The shortcomings and flaws that remain are my own responsibility. Finally, I am indebted to George W. Barlow and James Silverberg for numerous editorial suggestions that greatly improved the final draft.

Literature Cited

Asch, T. & N. Chagnon. 1975. The ax fight. 16mm film. Documentary Educational Resources, Watertown, Massachusetts.

Bateman, A. J. 1948. Intrasexual selection in Drosophila. Heredity 2:349-368.

Chagnon, N. A. 1966. Yąnomamö warfare, social organization and marriage alliances. Ph.D. Dissertation. University Microfilms, Ann Arbor, Michigan.

_______. 1968. Yąnomamö: The fierce people. Holt, Rinehart and Winston, New York.

_______. 1974. Studying the Yąnomamö. Holt, Rinehart and Winston, New York.

_______. 1975. Genealogy, solidarity and relatedness: Limits to local group size and patterns of fissioning in an expanding population. Yearbook of Physical Anthropology 19:95-110.

_______. 1977. Yąnomamö: The fierce people. 2nd edition. Holt, Rinehart and Winston, New York.

_______. 1979a. Mate competition, favoring close kin, and village fissioning among the Yąnomamö Indians. In N. A. Chagnon & W. Irons (eds.), Evolutionary biology and human social behavior: An anthropological perspective. Duxbury Press, North Scituate, Massachusetts, pp. 86-132.

_______. 1979b. Is reproductive success equal in egalitarian societies? In N. A. Chagnon & W. Irons (eds.), Evolutionary biology and human social behavior: An anthropological perspective. Duxbury Press, North Scituate, Massachusetts, pp. 374-401.

_______. 1979c. Terminological kinship, geneaological relatedness and village fissioning among the Yąnomamö Indians. In R. D. Alexander & D. Tinke (eds.), Natural selection and social behavior. Chiron Press, New York (in press).

_______. In preparation. Genealogical specifications of social allies and competitors in Yąnomamö mate competition.

_______ & P. E. Bugos. 1979. Kin selection and conflict: An analysis of a Yąnomamö ax fight. In N. A. Chagnon & W. Irons (eds.), Evolutionary biology and human social behavior: An anthropological perspective. Duxbury Press, North Scituate, Massachusetts, pp. 213-238.

_______, M. Flinn & T. F. Melancon. 1979. Sex-ratio variation among the Yąnomamö Indians. In N. A. Chagnon & W. Irons (eds.), Evolutionary biology and human social behavior: An anthropological perspective. Duxbury Press, North Scituate, Massachusetts, pp. 290-320.

Goody, J. 1976. Production and reproduction: A comparative study of the domestic domain. Cambridge Studies in Social Anthropology 17. Cambridge University Press, Cambridge.

Hamilton, W. D. 1964. The genetical evolution of social behaviour, I & II. Journal of Theoretical Biology 7:1-52.

Maynard Smith, J. 1964. Kin selection and group selection: A rejoinder. Nature 201:1145-1147.

Sahlins, M. 1976. The use and abuse of biology: An anthropological critique of sociobiology. Univeristy of Michigan Press, Ann Arbor, Michigan.

Trivers, R. L. 1971. The evolution of reciprocal altruism. Quarterly Review of Biology 46:35-57.

______. 1972. Parental investment and sexual selection. In B. H. Campbell (ed.), Sexual selection and the descent of man, 1871-1971. Aldine, Chicago, pp. 136-179.

Wright, S. 1922. Coefficients of inbreeding and relationship. American Naturalist 56:330-338.

B. J. Williams

22. Kin Selection, Fitness and Cultural Evolution

The two major modes of evolutionary change that are not based on differences in individual fitness have been termed group selection and kin selection (Maynard Smith 1964; 1976). Both have been of interest primarily as providing explanations for the evolution of apparent "fitness altruism" among individuals of certain species. Group selection, now that it has been given a specific mechanistic basis in different models, appears to be feasible only under highly restrictive conditions (Levin and Kilmer 1974). Because of this the concensus seems to be that group selection is unlikely to occur in animal populations while the conditions for kin selection are much more likely to be found.

This presentation reviews some arguments and some data which indicate that the opposite is true in our species; that the conditions found in our species are not very favorable for the operation of kin selection and that, on the other hand, a form of group selection is not only likely but accounts for much of the gene frequency change in our species today. The data presented will be drawn from my own work among the Birhor (Williams 1974), a hunting group of India, and Lorna Marshall's published data on the !Kung Bushmen of Southwest Africa (Marshall 1976).

Kin Selection

I will first consider kin selection, particularly in human hunting-gathering populations. Recent hunter-gatherer groups can be taken as the best analog we have to the form of society in which much of human evolution occurred (Bicchieri 1972; Coon 1976; Damas 1969; Lee and DeVore 1968; Service 1962).

The kin selection model proposed by Hamilton (1963;

1964) for explaining fitness altruism spoke primarily of a single recipient of an altruistic act although Hamilton did not limit the applicability of the model to these situations. The fitness gain of a single recipient might have to be large to compensate for the fitness loss of the altruist. The importance of a group of recipients, whose mean coefficient of relationship was $\bar{r}$, was stressed by Emlen (1973) and, especially, West Eberhard (1975). This renders kin selection more feasible as each recipient need enjoy a proportionately smaller increase in fitness to maintain or increase the allele.

The first question to be addressed is, how many close relatives will be available as recipients of an altruistic act? Such an estimate provides an index of how easily kin selection is achieved and, consequently, how likely it is to occur. Whether or not lineal descendants are to be included along with collateral relatives in a kin selection system is not clear. Most proponents of kin selection have included both of these categories of relationship as kin selection. This, however, seems to introduce a covariance term between fitness due to individual selection and fitness due to kinship effects. With such a covariance term, and with offspring (of further lineal descendants) as major beneficiaries of parental behavior, it is impossible to have a critical test of individual versus kin selection effects on fitness. Therefore this discussion is confined to collateral relatives, under the assumption that it is the collateral relatives who are critical in the differentiation of kin selection from individual selection.

First we note that, quite aside from actual data, the assumption of a stable population size for human groups imposes strong restraints on the expected number of relatives of different degrees available as recipients. The expected sibship size is 2, which means the expected number of sibling recipients is 1. Similarly, the expected number of first cousins as recipients is 4, and so forth, to more distant degrees of relationship.

It is also important to note that, when considering expected numbers, the expected number of recipients available, n, increases with more distant degrees of kinship but the expected value of the product, nr, decreases. This is important in the relationship

$$\frac{\Delta\bar{W}_R}{\Delta\bar{W}_A} > \frac{1}{nr}$$

which is the statement of the condition under which there

will be an increase in a recessive allele affecting whatever behavior is involved. $\Delta\bar{W}_R$ is the increment in fitness of the recipient; $\Delta\bar{W}_A$ the decrease in fitness of the altruist; r is the coefficient of relationship as defined by Wright (1922). So, as the product nr gets smaller, kin selection is less feasible as a mechanism for increasing such an allele.

That the product nr decreases as the expected value of n increases can easily be shown. We can write both r and n as functions of g, the number of generations of descent from a common ancestor.

$$r = (\tfrac{1}{2})^{(2g - 1)}$$

$$n = 2^g - 1$$

It is immediately obvious that the product, nr, decreases as g increases. This means that chances for the operation of kin selection are optimal for siblings and drop off rapidly for more distant kin. We shall look, then, primarily at the distribution of siblings.

In considering human hunting-gathering groups two generalizations, which seem to hold true, affect the possibility of significant aid between individuals. The first generalization is that these are kinship based societies and aid is sought and given along kinship lines. But, as usual, we must note that the sociological kinship categories of a society contain individuals of differing degrees of genetic relatedness. The mean coefficient of relationship is something to be determined for each category in a given society.

The second generalization which holds for hunting-gathering groups is that aid is always limited to individuals who are physically proximate to one another. Hunters show little or no accumulation of goods and no way of communicating aid except in the presence of one another. If an individual seeks aid he or she must reside in the same group as the individuals from whom aid is sought.

The two residential groupings found among all hunters and which are significant in rendering aid are the household and the band (Service 1962). A household is a little larger than a simple nuclear family. The band is a small group of related households. The 25 Birhor bands which I censused averaged 26.8 persons per band. This represented 6 households per band. Lorna Marshall (1976) gives exact data on 13 bands of !Kung Bushmen; these average 22.9 individuals per band. Including these with some bands on which Marshall has a less exact estimate of size we get an average of 24.8 persons per band among 19 bands of !Kung. It is within such a grouping that we must consider kin selection to be workable or not.

It is usually difficult to get genealogical data having any time depth for hunting groups. Inheritance presents no problems to such people and genealogical data have little intrinsic interest to members of such societies beyond the assignment of living individuals to kinship categories. True siblings can be reliably ascertained and, as shown earlier, this is the category which is optimal for the operation of kin selection.

I have genealogical data on four Birhor bands; Marshall presents data on ten !Kung bands. For the Birhor, if we consider all ages from infancy to old age, the average individual has 1.65 siblings co-resident in the band. This includes a large number of children who cannot be considered effective aid givers. If we consider only adult siblings of adults the average is 0.87 possible recipients. For the !Kung the mean number of siblings of an individual, for all ages is 0.98; and considering adults only the mean is 0.67 adult siblings per adult.

Table 1. Number of siblings per band present as potential recipients.

Society	Mean Band Size	Mean No. Siblings All Ages	Range	Mean No. Adult Siblings	Range
Birhor	27.3	1.65	1.00-2.00	0.87	0.25-1.25
!Kung	20.5	0.98	0.50-1.28	0.67	0.09-1.12

To make my data comparable to Marshall's data I have included as adult (which includes "young adult") everyone from approximately 16 to 50 years of age. Since these are small sample sizes the differences between the adult populations of Birhor and !Kung Bushmen (0.87 vs. 0.67) could easily be sampling error. The larger difference found when considering all ages, in part, represents a broad-base population pyramid among the Birhor.

In both cases we must conclude that, among the reproductive populations, the mean number of siblings of a given individual is less than one. This is what we would expect in a stable population where not all siblings remain coresident in a band.

We can look at similar figures for first cousins. These data are not given in Marshall's publication. But for the

Birhor, considering only adults, there are 1.26 cousins per adult resident within the band. Compared to an expected n of four for an ideal stable population this means that first cousins are even more dispersed than are siblings. This is as we would expect. Hunting bands of this size are exogamous. One spouse must leave his or her natal band and live in the band of the other. This provides a diffusion process which guarantees that categories of relatives who are generationally further removed from one another will be geographically more dispersed.

There are other degrees of relationship within the band. There is also "distant consanguinity" not accounted for in data based on shallow genealogical information. But the number of recipients, n, cannot rise greatly because of the limited size of the band and the mean $\bar{r}$ rises very little, or drops, in taking the mean of a group of recipients which includes more than one degree of relationship. For example, the weighted $\bar{r}$ for adults among the Birhor, when grouping siblings and cousins is $\bar{r} = 0.59$. This corresponds to an $n = 2.13$. As more of the adult generation are added $\bar{r}$ drops rapidly. Members of the adult generation average about eight persons per band or seven adult recipients of a band-wide altruistic act. We have accounted for 2.13 of these seven. Approximately four of the remaining 4.87 individuals are "outsiders" with respect to the altruist, having r approximately zero. So $\bar{r}$ drops rapidly once r is averaged over more than siblings and first cousins.

Distant consanguinity, that which is unknown to participants, increases the degree of relationship, to an indeterminant amount, of both "outsiders" (out of the altruist's natal band but within the breeding population) and close relatives. But such distant consanguinity must be viewed as a characteristic of the breeding population. And as the breeding population is taken as the sampling unit for computing the coefficient of relationship (a correlation) distant consanguinity does not increase the r between individuals.

To summarize the points above, in a low fecundity species such as _Homo sapiens_ the "index of potential selection" (Crow 1958) cannot achieve the levels possible in a high fecundity species such as salmon or the social insects. This means that the potential for benefit from being a recipient can never be as great, per individual, in the low fecundity species. This makes kin selection less feasible in the low fecundity species. An alternative is to have a large number of recipients benefiting from the act of fitness altruism. Our data indicate that large numbers of recipients are not available in the demographic and social structures which typify human prehistory.

Now let us turn to another point which seems to be a more severe restriction on the workability of kin selection in human populations. It appears that the Hamilton model of kin selection is premised on a particular kind of population growth and decline which is extremely unlikely for humans. To explain this I must present some quantitative description of the kin selection model.

Hamilton (1964) used what I would term a biometrician's approach to modelling kin selection and the proof, in this case, became very involved. J. Merritt Emlen (1973) has derived Hamilton's result using a much simpler approach of a kind once referred to as "bean bag genetics." I shall use Emlen's symbols and approach to demonstrate the point I wish to make.

Emlen showed quite simply that, in a breeding population of stable size, the rate of change in the frequency of a recessive allele affecting altruistic behavior will be

$$\Delta p = \frac{\theta(1 - p)(n\Delta\bar{W}_R r - \Delta\bar{W}_A)}{n + 1 + \theta(n\Delta\bar{W}_R - \Delta\bar{W}_A) - (1 - \theta)\Delta\bar{W}(n + 1)}$$

where

p = the allele frequency
Δp = the rate of change of allele frequency
θ = the proportion of kin groups with an altruist
n = the number of recipients of altruistic behavior
r = the coefficient of relationship between altruist and recipient
$\Delta\bar{W}_R$ = the average gain in fitness per generation on the part of recipients
$\Delta\bar{W}_A$ = the average loss in fitness per generation among altruists
$\Delta\bar{W}$ = the loss in fitness in kin groups not having an altruist present

Whether the numerator is negative or positive provides the standard result for the gene decreasing or increasing in frequency. But where it is the case that

$$\frac{n\Delta\bar{W}_R}{\Delta\bar{W}_A} > \frac{1}{r}$$

it is also the case that the kin groups containing an altruist are expanding rapidly. This growth is paid for by negative growth in the kin groups having no altruist. Since $\Delta\bar{W}$ has a lower bound of unity there is only so much negative growth these subgroups can achieve. The premise of the model is that it is always the case that

$$\theta(n\Delta\bar{W}_R - \Delta\bar{W}_A) = (1 - \theta)(n + 1)\Delta\bar{W}$$

therefore,

$$\Delta\bar{W} = \frac{\theta(n\Delta\bar{W}_R - \Delta\bar{W}_A)}{(1 - \theta)(n + 1)}$$

But since $\Delta\bar{W}$ can decrease to a maximum of one, θ itself must be limited. For example, if $\Delta\bar{W}_A = 1$, $\Delta\bar{W}_R = 2$, $r = 0.5$ (no change in gene frequency), θ cannot exceed 2/3 even when $\Delta\bar{W}$ is maximal. Beyond this the logic of the model breaks down, or it is not a stable population model. But more important is the premise which implies that, regardless of demographic and ecological considerations, kin groups with an altruist grow without interfering with the growth of one another. But the growth of kin groups not having an altruist is always adversely affected -- again regardless of spatial relationship or ecological setting.

Let me propose another simple model which achieves population stability in a different way. Each kin group is stable in size and the only trade-off is in the fitness differential between altruist and recipient within a kin group. Within kin groups having an altruist the situation is always one in which a homozygous individual has decreased fitness and the fitness of those with a lower mean frequency of the allele is enhanced. Obviously the frequency of the allele decreases within altruist-containing kin groups as a result of altruism. If all kin groups are stable in size then the frequency of the allele for altruism decreases in the population overall. In this case kin selection cannot increase the frequency of the allele regardless of the magnitude of fitness differential between altruist and recipient.

This model is also unrealistice with respect to human populations. Differences in the growth of kin groups are quite marked. In the kind of populations studied by anthropologists the variance in sibship size is found to be best approximated by a negative binomial distribution; this means there is a larger variance than in the usually assumed Poisson distribution. Small kin groups are anything but stable in size (Weiss and Smouse 1976).

This model of kin selection and the usual model of kin selection are unrealistic in opposite directions. In one kin selection works, in the other it doesn't. The real situation is somewhere in between these extremes. Whether kin selection will work, even in theory, in a more realistic model of human populations is unknown. Such a model does not seem to be amenable to treatment with simple differential equations. It may be that numerical simulation techniques similar to that used by Levin and Kilmer (1974) for group selection will provide an adequate approach. But for the moment we must conclude that the conditions for the operation of kin selection are somewhat more stringent than has been supposed, with kin selection correspondingly less likely as an evolutionary mechanism in human populations.

Group Selection and Cultural Evolution

As my second major point I wish to show that group selection, in contrast to kin selection, occurs rather easily in human populations, is common, and probably accounts for most systematic change in gene frequency in the human species today.

Although the term group selection has been widely used there is disagreement on the definition of the term. This is being vigorously debated in the literature at the present (cf. Maynard Smith 1976). To clarify what I am going to discuss I will give a definition of group selection which I believe to be unambiguous and to cover most of the cases which people want to discuss as group selection.

I use group, in this context, in the restricted sense of a breeding population. Therefore a "kin group" as discussed in the preceding section would not be included; interdemic selection would be included -- as a synonym. Lewontin has noted that a necessary condition for evolution by natural selection is that "there is a correlation between parents and offspring in the contribution of each to future generations (Lewontin 1970:1)." Using this we can say that group selection occurs whenever the correlation between parents and offspring in the contribution of each to future generations arises as a result of mean differences in growth rates between breeding populations. As I have said, this definition of group selection is general and unambiguous. With it we can discuss the relationship between cultural evolution and group selection.

Cultural evolution occurs whenever the frequency of particular learned behaviors change within a society. Biological evolution, as we understand it today, implies intergenerational changes and applies only to traits transmitted through descent relationships. Therefore the old phrase "descent with modification" is still apt. The changes in cultural evolution, on the other hand, can be transmitted not only to descendants but can diffuse "laterally" to collateral relatives or to non-relatives.

Natural selection maximizes the fitness of a breeding population. This is not an empirical observation; it is a theorem derived from the basic premises of the population genetic model of evolution and presented in Fisher's "fundamental theorem of natural selection" (Fisher 1958). But there is no comparable set of premises and deductions which permit us to say that cultural change will increase biological fitness in the population concerned.

This means there is no necessary connection between cultural evolution and the biological or Darwinian fitness of a population. Specifically -- and quite importantly -- cultural evolution does not necessarily maximize biological fitness.

A particular cultural trait or learned behavior may increase in frequency while lowering the Darwinian fitness of carriers. For this to occur it need only be necessary that the rate of diffusion of the trait be more than enough to compensate for the reduced reproductive contribution of carriers. The most dramatic recent example of a trait spreading while reducing fertility is the spread of contraceptive devices in Western societies.

Fertility differences are only one component of overall fitness differences. It might be supposed that reduced fertility is accompanied by reduced mortality to an extent that overall fitness, measured by the intrinsic rate of growth of the populations in question, increases. Such has not been the case in most Western societies whose birthrate has fallen in recent decades (Hauser 1969; Freedman 1964).

Culture can be regarded as environment with respect to genes. So cultural evolution is the evolution of the environment. Although there is no necessary connection between cultural evolution and biological evolution the evolution of environment can bring about marked Darwinian fitness differences between populations. If there are genetic differences between these breeding populations, as there are between all human breeding populations, this leads to a correlation in fitness between parental and offspring genotypes. This, then, fits our definition of group selection. Group selection, viewed in this light, does not require fitness altruism.

Many biologists will take exception to the preceding conditions as representing group selection. There seem to be two major bases for this; the first somewhat less valid than the second. First, group selection as presented above, will seem somewhat insignificant to biologists who concentrate on "adaptations" rather than gene frequency change. Adaptations in this sense, strongly advocated by G. C. Williams (1966), are structures having a function or goal. Although Williams tried to avoid the implication there seems to be a strong element of teleology in this concept of adaptation.

Group selection, as described above, does not lead to or result from adaptations in the sense used by G. C. Williams. But adaptations, however they may be defined, must be considered to result from fitness differentials. Between-group fitness differentials are definitely equivalent to group selection whether or not they result in, or result from, an adaptation however defined.

The second basis for objecting to the preceding view of group selection is that it does not correspond to the conventional model of fitness differentials. We normally consider fitness differentials to be established when differential mortality or differential fertility is shown to exist given that environments are randomized with respect to genotypes. This establishes that the fitness difference is due to genetic differences. In the situation envisioned as group selection due to cultural differences the environments are definitely non-random with respect to genotype. But the result is deterministic gene frequency change which seems best regarded as a form of selection, group selection.

It is undeniable that many cultural and environmental changes affect the growth rate of human populations. In fact, the most realistic assumption about human populations, one for which we have much evidence, is that environments -- that is, the cultural aspects of environments -- can and usually do become differentiated between populations fairly rapidly.

Demographers have amassed a great deal of data documenting marked changes in fertility and mortality in Western societies (Hauser 1969). The cultural-environmental correlates of mortality rate changes are easily documented (Freedman 1964). Long term changes in fertility rates prior to the recent spread of contraceptive devices is less easily related to direct cultural-environmental factors.

Fisher estimated the heritability of fertility among the British to be approximately 40% (Fisher 1958). With such within-population genetic differences fertility trends might be, in part, genetic. Williams and Williams (1974) have shown that Fisher's estimate, based on data of Karl Pearson, was based on spurious correlations between parents and offspring due to secular decline in fertility during the time period the data were gathered. The heritability of fertility in humans is not far from zero as has been found the case in all other species that have been investigated in this respect (Falconer 1960:167). This means that historic fertility changes are environmental even though the connection with specific environmental variables is not as dramatic or direct as is usually the case with mortality changes.

Demographic data on hunting-gathering populations is scant and inadequate compared to national populations. But model life tables for such populations have been developed (Weiss 1973) and these give a reasonably good fit to archaeologically known paleolithic populations (Acsádi and Nemeskéri 1970). Although the average growth rate of such populations is near zero there are cases where, under unusually favorable circumstances, small groups have doubled their size within a generation (Birdsell 1957). This means that the potential for growth differentials was as great in paleolithic societies of man as that found in modern populations.

What are the magnitudes of genetic effects which can be achieved by differential growth rates having a cultural-environmental basis? This can be conveyed by a numerical illustration. Suppose we have two populations which differ in the frequency of an allele recessive with respect to fitness and which also differ in growth rates. Population One has a growth rate of zero and a recessive allele frequency, $\bar{d}$ = 0.38. Population Two has a growth rate of 1.5% per annum and a recessive allele frequency of $\bar{d}$ = 0.02. These are reasonable figures for human populations.

If both populations start with equal sizes the frequency of the recessive allele for the total region is $\bar{d}$ = 0.20. After one generation of population growth the mean frequency of the allele is $\bar{d}$ = 0.16. This drop from 0.20 to 0.16 would be totally due to more rapid growth in the population with the lower allele frequency.

What is the magnitude of selection required to achieve this rate of change with individual selection? It would require heavy selection indeed; the coefficient of selection against the homozygous recessive would have to be 80% in both populations.

The same thing can happen at hundreds of loci simultaneously -- at all of the loci exhibiting gene frequency differences between the populations. With individual selection a human population could not support the selection necessary for this rate of change in as many as 65 independently assorting loci of this type.

Similar considerations compel us to the view that the frequency of most genes can change little over a few tens of generations due to individual selection. But we know of a great deal of genetic diversity between human populations today which differ in growth rates. Therefore we must conclude the most systematic gene frequency change in human populations is due to this kind of group selection.

This kind of evolutionary change has been of little interest to investigators up to the present. The genes which increase or decrease in frequency are only fortuitously associated with growth or decline of populations. They are not functionally related to such growth. Perhaps this is the reason for lack of interest in the phenomenon. But as a mechanism of evolutionary change this is obviously the dominant mechanism in the human species. And group selection, without the problem of altruism and without extinctions, is extremely important in the human species.

Summary

Data are presented on two hunting-gathering groups, the Birhor of India and the !Kung Bushmen of Africa. These data indicate that only a few kin are available as potential recipients of fitness altruism. This means that the benefit derived, per recipient, must be large to offset the decrement in fitness to the donor or altruist. Such a demographic picture makes kin selection less likely than in high fecundity species (social insects, salmon, and so forth) where a large number of siblings or other relatives may be present in a local group.

Hamilton's model of inclusive fitness, referred to by most as kin selection, implicitly assumes that kindreds containing altruists grow without density dependent regulation of numbers. Presumably, in a breeding population that is neither growing nor decreasing in overall numbers, the kindreds without altruists "pay for" the growth of the altruist containing kindreds by a decrease in size. This does not seem, a priori, a likely model of human populaticn growth regulation. It is not clear that kin selection will work under more realistic assumptions about population growth and density dependent inhibition of growth in segments of the populations.

Finally, it is shown that it is not a logical deduction

that cultural evolution maximizes biological fitness. Conversely, some cultural changes can be shown to have lowered the fitness of populations. However, cultural changes which increase or decrease population growth can account for important changes in gene frequency in the species as a whole or within a geographic region. It is argued that such cultural evolution represents evolution of the environment and second, that this can be regarded as a form of group selection.

Acknowledgements

I would like to thank Bruce Levin and Jon Goguen for their critical comments on the first draft of this paper, and for assistance in presentation of the paper.

Literature Cited

Acsádi, Gy. & J. Nemeskéri. 1970. History of Human Life Span and Mortality. Adadémiai kiado, Budapest.

Bicchieri, M.G. (ed.). 1972. Hunters and Gatherers Today. Holt, Rinehart and Winston, New York.

Birdsell, J.B. 1957. Some population problems involving Pleistocene man. Population Studies: Animal Ecology and Demography. Cold Spring Harbor Symposia on Quantitative Biology 22:47-69.

Coon, C.S. 1976. The Hunting Peoples. Penguin Books, New York.

Crow, J.F. 1958. Some possibilities for measuring selection intensities in man. Human Biology 30:1-13.

Damas, D. (ed.). 1969. Contributions to Anthropology: Band Societies. National Museums of Canada Bulletin No. 228. National Museums of Canada, Ottawa.

Emlen, J.M. 1973. Ecology: An Evolutionary Approach. Addison-Wesley, Reading, Mass.

Falconer, D.S. 1960. Introduction to Quantitative Genetics. Ronald Press, New York.

Fisher, R.A. 1958. The Genetical Theory of Natural Selection, 2nd revised edition. Dover, New York.

Freedman, R. 1964. Population: The Vital Revolution. Anchor Books, Garden City, New York.

Hamilton, W.D. 1963. The evolution of altruistic behavior. American Naturalist 74:354-356.

________ 1964. The genetical evolution of social behavior. I. Journal of Theoretical Biology 7:1-16.

Hauser, P.M. 1969. World population growth. In P.M. Hauser (ed.), The Population Dilemma. Prentice-Hall, Englewood Cliffs, N. J., pp. 12-33.

Lee, R.B. & I. DeVore (eds.). 1968. Man the Hunter. Aldine, Chicago.

Levin, B.R. & W.L. Kilmer. 1974. Interdemic selection and the evolution of altruism: A computer simulation study. Evolution 28:527-545.

Lewontin, R.C. 1970. The units of selection. Annual Review of Ecology and Systematics 1:1-18.

Marshall, L. 1976. The !Kung of Nyae Nyae. Harvard University Press, Cambridge, Mass.

Maynard Smith, J. 1964. Group selection and kin selection. Nature 201:1145-1147.

________ 1976. Group selection. Quarterly Review of Biology 51:277-283.

Service, E.R. 1962. Primitive Social Organization. An Evolutionary Perspective. Random House, New York.

Weiss, K.M. 1973. Demographic Models for Anthropology. Memoirs of the Society for American Archaeology, Number 27. Issued as American Antiquity, V. 38, No. 2, Pt. 2.

________ & P.E. Smouse. 1976. The demographic stability of small human populations. In R.H. Ward and K.M. Weiss (eds.)., The Demographic Evolution of Human Populations. Academic Press, New York, pp. 59-73.

West-Eberhard, M.J. 1975. The evolution of social behavior by kin selection. Quarterly Review of Biology 50:1-33.

Williams, B.J. 1974. A Model of Band Society. Memoirs of the Society for American Archaeology, Number 29. Issued as American Antiquity, V. 39, No. 4, Pt. 2.

Williams, G.C. 1966. Adaptation and Natural Selection. Princeton University Press, Princeton, New Jersey.

Williams, L. & B.J. Williams. 1974. A reexamination of the heritability of fertility in the British peerage. Social Biology 21:225-231.

Wright, S. 1922. Coefficients of inbreeding and relationship. American Naturalist 56:330-338.

Judy A. Stamps, Robert A. Metcalf

23. Parent-Offspring Conflict

The history of the study of antagonistic behavior between animals is long and encompasses many types of interactions. Usually these behaviors are interpreted as the result of natural selection operating on competing individuals, each acting so as to maximize its own fitness. Somewhat surprising, then, have been the scattered reports of apparently antagonistic behavior between parents and their offspring, the most obvious example being weaning conflict in mammals. It is easier to explain cooperation and alliance between parents and offspring by invoking natural selection, since the individual fitness of the parent depends on the successful raising of offspring, and the offspring's fitness depends on care received from the parent. More difficult to explain are instances where the community of interest breaks down, i.e., when selection seems to favor one strategy in the offspring and an opposing one in the parent.

Trivers (1974) presented a model of parent and offspring interactions that suggested that antagonism between them might be a result of natural selection. His discussion is analogous to that of Hamilton on the spread of altruistic traits via kin selection (Hamilton 1972). Just as Hamilton's work generated intense interest in kinship theory and altruism, Trivers' model has resulted in a series of papers on the theoretical and empirical aspects of parent-offspring interactions. But as a subject of inquiry parent-offspring conflict is younger than altruism, so that most of the recent work has concentrated on theoretical aspects of the model; empirical field tests of parent-offspring conflict are just beginning.

Theoretical Models of Parent-Offspring Conflict

Parent-Offspring Conflict and Reproductive Success

Trivers (1974) argued that parents and offspring have large areas of common interest in terms of individual fitness because they are highly related to each other (i.e., share substantial portions of their genomes). However, in any sexually reproducing species which is not completely inbred, parents and offspring are not genetically identical. Therefore the optimal strategies for maximizing the fitness of parent and offspring, respectively, may not be identical.

More specifically, Trivers argued that a parent is related equally to each of its offspring ($r = 1/2$, where r is the probability of an allele in the parent being identical by descent). However, an offspring is related to itself by $r = 1$ and to a full sibling by $r = 1/2$. In terms of fitness, therefore, an offspring values itself twice as much as a full sibling. Thus, Trivers suggested that selection on an offspring should favor the spread of alleles that skew parental investment (PI) toward itself at the expense of the parent's other offspring. From this analysis, selfish alleles would be expected to spread as long as the ratio of cost for full siblings to benefit for the selfish offspring was less than 2 to 1.

Alexander (1974) raised serious objections to the concept of parent-offspring conflict. He argued that alleles causing selfish behavior of the type described by Trivers cannot spread because they would lower the reproductive success of the selfish individuals carrying them. The main point is contained in the following quotation from Alexander (1974):

> Suppose that a juvenile ... cause(s) an uneven distribution of parental benefits in its own favor, thereby reducing the mother's own overall reproduction. A gene which in this fashion improves an individual's fitness when it is a juvenile cannot fail to lower its fitness more when it is an adult, for such mutant genes will be present in an increased proportion of the mutant individual's offspring.

To paraphrase Alexander, selfish genes cannot spread because a selfish individual would have a lower reproductive success than would a nonselfish individual. The gain in extra parental resources going to a selfish animal as a juvenile would be insufficient to outweigh the net loss in reproductive success when it became a parent and had selfish offspring.

No less than three models have been independently developed to resolve the question raised by Alexander as to whether selfish genes could ever spread (Blick 1977; Parker & MacNair 1978; and Stamps et al. 1978). All three analyses are in agreement that alleles responsible for selfish behavior can spread to fixation. Blick and Stamps et al. make the further point that selfish alleles can spread despite the fact that they decrease the reproductive success of the selfish individual. This is because in mixed families of selfish and nonselfish individuals, the nonselfish offspring is always hurt more than the selfish offspring.

More specifically, consider a species in which offspring are produced sequentially, such that the first offspring is independent before the next is produced (Stamps et al. 1978). A parent with all nonselfish offspring distributes parental investment so as to maximize the total number of offspring surviving to maturity. If the first offspring is nonselfish, then it asks for and receives a certain amount of parental investment and has a survivorship x. The second offspring also has a survivorship x. But if the first offspring is selfish, it asks for and receives extra parental investment which results in extra survivorship, b. The second offspring, whether selfish or nonselfish, has a survivorship reduced by some amount, c.

Assume that selfish behavior is determined by a dominant allele A, nonselfish behavior by a recessive allele, a. A cross between a selfish parent Aa and a nonselfish parent aa would result in families of two offspring in the proportions shown in Table 1. Note that in this cross, nonselfish individuals sometimes absorb cost (c) but never absorb any benefit (b) while selfish individuals absorb twice as much benefit as they absorb cost. In any cross which produces a mixture of selfish and nonselfish offspring, the selfish offspring will have a higher average survivorship than will a nonselfish offspring.

Table 1. Families resulting from a cross between Aa and aa. Survivorship given in parentheses.

Birth order	Family 1	Family 2	Family 3	Family 4
1st offspring	aa (x)	aa (x)	Aa (x + b)	Aa (x + b)
2nd offspring	aa (x)	Aa (x)	aa (x − c)	Aa (x − c)
Total expected survivorship	2x	2x	2x + b − c	2x + b − c

Returning to Table 1, consider the reproductive success of an individual with selfish or nonselfish offspring. If $c > b$, then the parent with two nonselfish offspring will have a higher reproductive success (2x) than a parent with a selfish first offspring (2x + b - c). The reproductive success of a selfish offspring mating at random with selfish and nonselfish individuals will also be reduced. The reproductive success of an offspring depends on the ratio of c to b and on the frequency of the selfish trait in the population (p). Mathematical analyses show that unless p is very small and c is small relative to b, the reproductive success of a selfish individual is lower than that of a nonselfish individual (Stamps et al. 1978).

Blick (1977) arrived at similar conclusions by analyzing a model based on species with simultaneously produced offspring which interact with each other in a litter. He assumed that nonselfish offspring absorbed all of the cost resulting from selfish behavior. He found that by adjusting the survivorship values in families with selfish offspring, selfish alleles could spread even though they decreased the reproductive success of selfish individuals.

Both Blick and Stamps et al. point out that individual fitness as measured by reproductive success is not conceptually appropriate to analysis of genetic systems such as parent-offspring conflict. A better measure is the relative success of one allele versus others at the same locus. The models show that a selfish allele could spread with respect to a nonselfish allele despite the fact that a selfish individual would have a decrease in the number of descendents relative to a nonselfish individual. The important point is that with each generation the frequency of nonselfish alleles would decrease more than that of selfish alleles.

At the same time, the allele causing selfish offspring behavior and hence reduced reproductive success would be in conflict with alleles at other loci in the same individual. For any alleles randomly distributed among an individual's offspring, a maximal reproductive success would be the optimal strategy. Thus, the strategy maximizing individual fitness is not always the same as the one maximizing the fitness of a single allele contained within that organism (Blick 1977; Stamps et al. 1978).

Recently Dawkins (1976) in his book <u>The Selfish Gene</u> has argued that genes rather than individuals produce copies of themselves in future generations. Though there is a temporary alliance between genes which are tied together in an individual, any individual gene is expected to be "selfish" about its own future success as measured by its frequency relative to other alleles at the same locus. The hypothetical alleles for selfish behavior would represent ideal examples of "selfish genes," sensu Dawkins, since they theoretically spread at the expense of fitness of all of the other loci in the individual.

The deduction that selfish alleles which decrease individual reproductive success can spread is tantamount to a statement that selection can favor alleles which lower r (the intrinsic rate of increase) and K (the carrying capacity) as defined by the logistic growth equation (Stamps et al. 1978). The intrinsic rate of increase, r, would be reduced because fewer total offspring would survive when offspring were selfish than when they were nonselfish.

The carrying capacity, K, should also decrease as selfish alleles spread in a population. Consider a parent with a certain limited amount of resources to be distributed among the young. These resources could support a certain number of nonselfish offspring to maturity (e.g., 2x). If some of the offspring were selfish, then the same resources would support fewer total offspring (e.g., 2x + b - c). In essence, selfish offspring are less efficient at using parental resources than their siblings would have been. That is, an extra amount of parental investment taken by a selfish offspring would give it less benefit in terms of fitness than the cost to its sibling's fitness.

The conditions for the spread of altruistic traits by kin selection represents an exactly converse case. Selection for altruism theoretically occurs when the cost to the actor is less than the benefit to the recipient(s) devalued by their relatedness to the actor ($c < br$) (Hamilton 1964). When $c < br$, there should be an increased efficiency of resource conversion into individuals, i.e., an increased r and K (Stamps et al. 1978).

A number of models of evolutionary processes assume that r and K will always increase as a result of natural selection (Fisher 1958; MacArthur 1962; Gadgil & Bossert 1970). The discrepancy between the conflict models and their results arises because these workers have assumed that fitness is always equivalent to reproductive success, and that the interests of an individual are always the same as those of an allele at any one of its loci.

Conditions for the Spread of Selfish Alleles

Conclusions about the conditions necessary for the spread of selfish behavior depend on the nature of the model one is

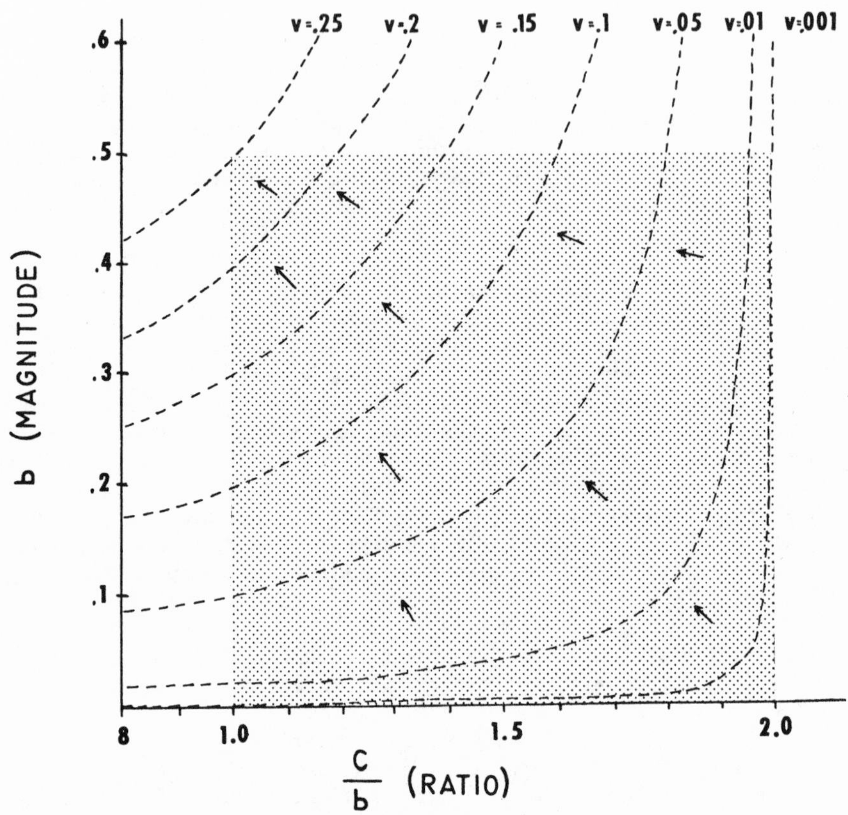

Figure 1. Selfish alleles in the offspring can be plotted on the ratio of cost to benefit c/b and the magnitude of the benefit, b. Selfish alleles will spread if $1 < c/b < 2$, and $b < .5$ (stippled area). The allele with the higher value of v, where $v = b - .5c$, will spread in the population relative to all alleles with lower v's. Offspring alleles will replace each other in the direction indicated by the arrows.

using. Several different approaches have been made to modeling parent-offspring conflict. Trivers (1974) used cost-benefit analysis; Parker and MacNair (1978) and MacNair and Parker (1978) relied on maximum fitness functions, and Stamps et al. (1978) and Metcalf et al. (1979) constructed genetic models. The models of Parker and MacNair and of Stamps et al. dealt with offspring that are produced sequentially and have no interaction with each other. Metcalf et al. have considered the case where multiple offspring are raised simultaneously and do have an opportunity to interact with each other. Stamps et al. and Metcalf et al. have considered cases in which performance of the selfish act has a significant cost to the actor. In this section the results and problems of these various modeling approaches will be examined.

The cost-benefit model of Trivers has already been discussed. Its major conclusion is that selfish alleles will spread if $1 < c/b < 1/r$, where r is the coefficient of relationship of the offspring absorbing the cost of the selfish behavior. Stamps et al. have produced a genetic model of simultaneous offspring intended to approximate the case discussed by Trivers. One example of a model from Stamps et al. is that given in Table 1.

In this model selfish behavior results in a decrease in parental investment (PI) and hence the survivorship, of future offspring regardless of phenotype. Genetic models for variable numbers of offspring were constructed for recessive, codominant and dominant alleles, and all gave the same result: as predicted by Trivers selfish alleles spread if $1 < c/b < 1/r$.

If one considers not only the ratio of cost to benefit but also the amount (or magnitude) of the benefit, then one can specify which selfish alleles may spread with respect to other selfish alleles. Specifically, the allele with the higher value of v (where $v = b - rc$) will replace any allele with a lower value of v. When the ratio of cost to benefit (c/b) for an allele is plotted against the magnitude of b, one obtains equipotential lines for different selfish alleles (Fig. 1).

The ratio of c/b represents the relative efficiency of the transfer of survivorship to the selfish offspring from its siblings, while the magnitude of b represents the amount of extra survivorship obtained as a result of selfish behavior. Hence the fittest selfish allele from the viewpoint of the selfish offspring is the one with the most efficient transfer (c/b near 1) and the largest possible magnitude of transfer (b near .5).

Parker and MacNair have constructed another type of model of parent-offspring conflict based on species with sequentially produced, nonoverlapping young. However, in their models selfish behavior performed by an early offspring decreases the total number (not the survivorship) of later siblings. All selfish offspring regardless of birth order receive extra PI from the parent and hence have a higher probability of surviving than do nonselfish offspring.

There are two difficulties in applying these models to Trivers' predictions. First, Parker and MacNair define the conditions for gene spread in terms of the (1) probability of survivorship of a selfish relative to a nonselfish individual (= f(m)) and (2) the PI given to a selfish relative to a nonselfish offspring (= m). These variables are not shown to be equivalent to b and c in Trivers' formulation, and hence they cannot be used to test Trivers' predictions.

A second problem involves the amount of PI available to be given to the last offspring. If total PI is finite and each selfish or nonselfish offspring receives the PI requested, then at some point in the sequence of offspring a remainder of PI insufficient to produce an offspring is expected. Yet by the definition of the model, selfish offspring, whatever their birth order, always obtain the same amount of PI and have the same probability of surviving. Hence we must conclude that any leftover PI will be wasted, and no offspring produced whenever the amount of PI left at the end of a sequence of offspring is less than that requested by the last offspring. The impact of this unused remainder of PI is not considered in the models of Parker and MacNair. The problem is negligible only if very large numbers of offspring are produced. When small numbers of young are expected this model would underestimate the cost absorbed by selfish offspring.

The models of Trivers and of Parker and MacNair assume that there is no cost to the actor as a result of performing a selfish behavior. This may be true of certain types of offspring behavior (for example, a higher pitch of begging cries) but it is unlikely to be the case for energetically expensive behaviors like "tantrums" or "pestering" behavior (Goodall 1973; Russell 1973). The cost of performing selfish behavior can be thought of as the portion of resources gained by the offspring that does not increase its survival, but is expended by that offspring in the contest over the control of allocation of parental investment. Stamps et al. show in a sequential model that the inequality $1 < c/b < 1/r$ does not define the ratios of c/b at which alleles for selfish behavior are expected to spread when there is a cost involved in performing selfish behavior (θ). As the cost of performing selfish behavior increases, only alleles with a high value of v (v = b - rc) can spread. That is, if selfish behavior costs more to perform, the benefit must be larger and the efficiency of the transfer of PI greater than if the act is less costly to perform.

Models defining the conditions for the spread of selfish alleles in cases where offspring are produced simultaneously have been considered by Metcalf et al. (1979). They find that interactions with siblings in the litter or nest can lead to fundamentally different results than conflict involving siblings that have not yet been produced. The relative amount of PI and hence survivorship of each offspring will depend on the relative number of its nestmates which are also selfish. If selfish individuals take more from nonselfish littermates than they do from selfish littermates, then selfish alleles can theoretically spread even if the c/b ratio is greater than 1/r (Metcalf et al. 1979). For example, assume that a parent assigns food on the basis of the relative volume of a begging cry and selfish offspring cry more than nonselfish ones. In a brood in which all offspring are nonselfish, each offspring receives the same amount of PI and has an equal probability of survivorship (x). If all are selfish the parent again divides the available PI equally among them and the survivorship of each is x. But if selfish and nonselfish occur in the same brood, the selfish obtain extra PI and survivorship to the detriment of their nonselfish nestmates. In this case selfish individuals never suffer from the selfishness of siblings, and a selfish allele could theoretically spread even if c/b were infinite (Table 2). If there is a cost to performing selfish behavior (θ) (for example, louder cries might attract predators to the nest) then the spread of selfish alleles can still occur when c/b > 2, and depends on the relative cost to selfish animals of performing the behavior versus the cost to nonselfish animals in mixed broods (Metcalf et al. 1979).

The simultaneous models reinforce the idea that the spread of selfish alleles is determined by the probability that the animal bearing the cost of the selfish behavior also

Table 2. A model of conflict when offspring are produced simultaneously. N = nonselfish phenotype; S = selfish phenotype. Survivorship in parentheses. If the cost θ = 0, then selfish offspring always benefit at the expense of nonselfish siblings.

Family 1		Family 2		Family 3	
N (x)	N (x)	N (x - c)	S (x + b)	S (x - θ)	S (x - θ)

has the selfish allele. The coefficient of relationship is only important insofar as it allows the best possible estimate of the chances that a relative shares a given gene. For example, in the sequential case discussed by Trivers and modeled by Stamps et al., the younger siblings of a selfish offspring (the siblings that would bear the cost of the selfish act) are not yet conceived when the selfish act is performed. The best estimate of the chance that a future sibling would share a given allele would be made on the basis of the coefficient of relationship between the two offspring. But when offspring are contemporaries, mechanisms may exist whereby cost falls disproportionately on nonselfish offspring. Then the coefficient of relationship no longer determines the conditions for the spread of the allele. A selfish offspring could eliminate many full siblings for meager benefit as long as none of them share the genes for selfish behavior.

Coefficient of Relationship and Parent-Offspring Conflict

Throughout this review we have relied on a single definition of coefficient of relationship, that r is the probability that a gene present in one organism will be present in a relative, through descent from a common ancestor. An alternate definition of r has been followed in several studies of parent-offspring conflict. This interpretation states that r is the proportion of genes that are shared between two relatives as a result of common descent (Fagen 1976; Barash et al. 1978). As a first approximation the two definitions are similar, and the early models of parent-offspring conflict (Trivers 1974; Trivers & Hare 1976) would have yielded the same conclusions regardless of the definition used. But the conclusions of more recent studies do depend on the interpretation of r.

For example, both Fagen (1976) and Barash et al. (1978) pointed out that r by the second definition is usually an estimate of the proportion of genes shared by a relative. Some full siblings will actually have more than 50% of their genes in common, some less; r = .5 is merely a mean of the proportion of genes shared among full siblings. An individual might be expected to be more selfish to a sibling with which it shared fewer genes, less selfish to a sibling with whom it shared more genes. Both Fagen and Barash suggested that the amount of physical resemblance could be used by an animal as a measure of the proportion of shared genes: an animal should be more altruistic (less selfish) to relatives that look like itself, because these relatives would be more apt to have more genes in common with the actor.

On the other hand, if r is defined as the chance that a relative has a particular <u>allele</u>, such as the selfish allele in recent studies of parent-offspring conflict, then the total proportion of shared genes is immaterial to the spread of selfish traits. In this case physical resemblance could influence selfish behavior only if physical resemblance and the performance of selfish behavior were determined by the same or closely linked genes. Dawkins (1976) discussed this problem in detail, and persuasively argued that it is unlikely that genes governing a behavioral trait (e.g. propensity to cry more loudly) would be necessarily linked to those governing a conspicuous physical marker (e.g. a green beard). Arguing from this definition of r, physical resemblance between relatives should have no effect on the distribution and intensity of selfish behavior.

Resolution of this problem depends on which of the two definitions of r best predicts which types of selfish alleles can spread through a population. What is required is a model of parent-offspring conflict derived independently of r, which can pinpoint the factor (proportion of genes in common, or probability of having the selfish gene) which governs the spread of selfish genes among related animals. Several models which fulfill these criteria indicate that the proportion of genes shared between relatives is irrelevant to the spread of a selfish trait in a population (Stamps et al. 1978; Metcalf et al. 1979).

Consider the simultaneous-offspring model outlined in Table 2. In this case, the offspring in a family are full sibs, hence selfish offspring have an average of half their genes in common with their nestmates. If the proportion of genes held in common determines the spread of selfish behavior, then traits should spread only if $c/b < 1/r$. Yet mathematical proofs and simulations of this model both show that selfish alleles spread even if c/b is infinitely large. The selfish allele spreads despite huge c/b ratios because all of the cost is absorbed by individuals lacking the selfish trait. That is, under these conditions the probability that a selfish offspring will absorb the cost of a selfish act is zero.

Clearly, the proportion of genes shared between the siblings in this case cannot predict whether selfish alleles would spread. Instead, the crucial factor is the probability that a given allele occurs in the animal absorbing the cost. This and similar analyses (Charnov 1978; Stamps et al. 1978) indicate that coefficient of relationship is probably best interpreted as the probability that the recipient of an act bears the same gene as the actor through common descent. Hence, in relation to parent-offspring conflict, Fagen and Barash's contention that selfish behavior and conflict will be influenced by physical resemblance is probably incorrect.

Empirical Tests of Parent-Offspring Conflict

Does Conflict Exist in Nature?

A second point raised by Alexander is difficult to answer theoretically. Alexander (1974) noted that even if selfish alleles could theoretically spread, parental alleles counteracting them should also quickly spread. Parents are larger, stronger, and more experienced than their offspring. Hence it is unlikely that offspring would be able to gain extra PI for long before parental alleles restoring the original distribution of PI would spread.

The question of whether alleles to counteract selfish behavior could spread in the parents has been answered in the affirmative (Stamps et al. 1978; Parker & MacNair 1978). However, parental counteracting alleles spread at different rates than do offspring selfish alleles. If a selfish allele has a low c/b ratio ($1 < c/b < 1.5$), then the selfish allele will spread more rapidly than will a counteracting allele in the parent. The reverse is true when the c/b ratio is high ($1.5 < c/b < 2$) (Stamps et al. 1978). As the cost-benefit ratio approaches 1, offspring selfish alleles spread infinitely faster than do parental counteracting alleles. Hence theory predicts that when a selfish allele is relatively efficient (low c/b), offspring will tend to win (i.e. obtain extra PI) for a relatively long time before parental alleles can spread and restore the original distribution of PI.

Theoretical models can provide a framework for the study of parent-offspring conflict, but ultimately the question of whether it exists can only be answered by empirical tests. If offspring ever win parent-offspring conflict, then we expect that selfish offspring would gain extra PI at the expense of their siblings, thereby decreasing the reproductive success of their parents. Observations cannot differentiate between two other alternatives: if parent-offspring conflict doesn't exist or if parents always win, then offspring will not gain more PI than the parent is selected to give.

Despite widespread interest in field tests of parent-offspring conflict, few data are forthcoming. The problem is the extreme difficulty in measuring the variables of conflict, including the amount of PI given to offspring, the benefit and cost of selfish actions, or the reproductive success of parents. Parental investment, for example, is defined in a way that makes it inconvenient to test: "parental investment is anything done by the parent which increases the offspring's chance of surviving while decreasing the parent's ability to invest in other offspring" (Trivers 1974). It is not sufficient to measure the amount of parental time, energy or risk going into one offspring (even if this were feasible) but the resulting decrease in the survivorship of all other siblings must also be measured to calculate PI. No one has shown a simple direct way to do this for any species, so tests of parent-offspring conflict must rely on indirect methods of measuring the distribution of PI and the reproductive success of parents.

Control of Egg Laying in Social Hymenoptera

Trivers and Hare (1976) have used analysis of haplodiploid societies (bees, wasps, and ants) to provide the first set of readily quantifiable predictions for testing the validity of parent-offspring conflict theory. Their analysis and conclusions have been supported by two independent mathematical models (Oster et al. 1977; Charnov 1978).

Haplodiploid societies are made up of one or more mated females (queens), unmated female workers and male and female reproductive forms. In general, the workers help their mother raise the colony's reproductive forms, which are brothers and sisters to the workers. Because of the haplodiploid sex determination system in which fertilized eggs develop into females and nonfertilized eggs develop into males, unmated workers which are capable of laying eggs can only produce males.

As a result of haplodiploidy the relatedness of family members may differ from that occurring in diploid species. For example, for haplodiploids the relatedness of full sisters is .75 and of sisters to brothers is .25. However, as in diploid species a haplodiploid mother is related by .5 to both her sons and daughters (Hamilton 1972).

Consideration of these relatedness values lead Trivers and Hare (1976) to predict that parent-offspring conflict exists between queens, on the one hand, who are selected to rear sons and daughters ($r = .5$) and workers capable of egg-laying, on the other hand, who are selected by try and rear sisters ($r = .75$) and sons ($r = .5$).

In colonies with many workers, another type of worker, incapable of laying eggs, is also common. Nonfertile workers are expected to prefer to rear sisters ($r = .75$) and nephews ($r = .375$) and are thus in agreement with laying workers.

These simple relationships are complicated by two phenomena that occasionally occur among haplodiploid insects: multiple matings and multiple queens. If a queen mates with more than one male, then the coefficient of relatedness between the workers will be less than .75. In the extreme case, with a different father for each worker, the relatedness between workers would be .25. Similar arguments can be made for species in which several queens found a nest together.

Many of the predictions from the Trivers and Hare model can only be tested if information on relatedness between workers is available. For example, they suggest 1) that non-laying workers should be selected to raise nephews over brothers as long as the relatedness between workers is greater than .5, and 2) that if the relatedness between laying workers is less than .5 they should be selected to raise their own offspring rather than their sisters. Only one prediction related to egg-laying does not depend on worker relatedness: 3) laying workers should always prefer to raise their own sons rather than brothers or nephews.

Tests of the Trivers and Hare model currently rely on social, colonial Hymenoptera. The literature suggests that a variety of reproductive patterns occur, ranging from species with workers incapable of egg-laying through species where workers produce a substantial proportion of the colony's unfertilized (male) eggs (Wilson 1971). However, data on relatedness between workers (r_{ww}) is scanty. Information on the number of males mating with the queen is insufficient to establish paternity, because some females (such as honeybees) use sperm from multiple matings in a semisequential fashion (Taber 1955), while others (*Polistes metricus*) use sperm from multiple matings unequally when fertilized young (Metcalf & Whitt 1977).

Genetic analysis is required to establish paternity, but as yet these data are too meager to allow generalizations on relatedness. For example, with regard to multiple matings, Johnson et al. (1969) indicated that *Pogonomyrex barbatus* queens use sperm from multiple matings ($r_{ww} < .75$) while Crozier's (1973) data indicate a single mating for the ant *Aphaenogaster rudis* ($r_{ww} = .75$). Metcalf and Whitt (1977) showed for the wasp *Polistes metricus* that sperm from two matings are used simultaneously in a 9:1 ratio ($r_{ww} = 0.66$). Finally, honeybees *Apis mellifera* use sperm from numerous matings sequentially with some undetermined amount of mixing between sperm pockets ($r \simeq 0.5$) (Taber 1955).

In the honeybee, workers can lay infertile male eggs but normally refrain from doing so in the presence of the queen (Taber 1955). Hence workers raise brothers rather than sons and nephews. This might occur because the queen "wins" parent-offspring conflict by dominating the workers or because the conflict hypothesis of Trivers and Hare is incorrect.

More data are available from another species, the social wasp *Polistes metricus* (Metcalf 1975; Metcalf & Whitt 1977). They found 1) r_{ww} = .63, 2) workers are able to lay eggs, and 3) only 0.2% of the mature males on a nest with a living queen were the offspring of workers. Again, these results are consistent with the hypotheses that the queen is "winning" or that there is some flaw in the analysis of Trivers and Hare. The first hypothesis is more reasonable because of the evidence that the queen does manipulate the workers in various ways. The colonies are small (on average 6.6 workers in *P. metricus*) and these are physically dominated by the queen. The importance of dominance is underlined by the interactions between workers if a queen dies. Two workers take over all of the egg-laying of the nest, with the most dominant individual producing an average of 19 offspring for each one produced by the second most dominant individual (Metcalf & Whitt 1977).

Control Over Sex Ratios in Social Hymenoptera

Trivers and Hare (1976) have also analyzed the action of selection on sex ratios in haplodiploid societies in terms of parent-offspring conflict. Specifically, they predicted the conditions in which the workers will be selected to produce a higher ratio of female to male reproductives than will the queen.

This prediction is based on an extension of Fisher's sex-ratio theory for diploid species. Fisher (1930) argued that in large, panmictic populations selection favors an equal parental investment in the population's males and the population's females. Hamilton (1972) has extended Fisher's argument to cover haplodiploid species.

Trivers and Hare argued that since the workers in a haplodiploid society are more related to sisters than to brothers, they should be selected to value sisters more than brothers. For example, if the queen is monogynous and lays all of the eggs, workers are .75 related to sisters and .25 related to brothers, hence they should value sisters three times as much as they value brothers. In this case the workers are expected to skew the colony's PI towards a 3:1 (♀/♂) sex ratio. Since the queen is equally related to all offspring, she should prefer the 1:1 investment ratio suggested by Fisher's and Hamilton's analysis. Hence parent-offspring conflict is expected to exist over the colony's allocation of PI.

One simple test of this prediction is that, in general, social *Hymenoptera* should have a higher average ratio of PI (female = male) than should solitary, nonsocial *Hymenoptera*.

In solitary Hymenoptera all PI is distributed to the reproductives by their mother (1:1 ratio expected); in social species the workers might be able to skew the ratio in favor of females. Trivers and Hare (1976) obtained sex ratios from reports in the literature and used dry weights of museum specimens to estimate relative male and female PI. Their results supported the prediction of higher ratios of PI (♀:♂) in social hymenoptera. Alexander and Sherman (1977) reexamined the data and came to the same conclusion. These preliminary results tend to support the concept of parent-offspring conflict, but the high variance in the observed investment patterns indicates the need for further investigation.

Several workers (Trivers & Hare 1976; Alexander & Sherman 1977) have indicated a number of factors that can reduce the ratio of PI that workers are selected to prefer. Most important of these is the frequency of worker-produced males. As the proportion of worker-produced males increases, the PI ratio preferred by the workers decreases; in the extreme case if all males are worker-derived then laying workers are predicted to prefer a 1:1 ratio of PI. Other factors which can decrease the worker's preferred ratio are the frequency of multiple matings by the queen, and the number of queens in the nest. Hence the lack of a female-biased investment ratio in a social hymenoptera is not necessarily proof against parent-offspring conflict theory. Genetic data on workers' relatedness are necessary to interpret any studies showing equal investment ratios among social insects.

On the other hand, a high investment ratio, skewed in favor of females, is not necessarily proof of the theory. Recently Alexander and Sherman (1977) have noted that the phenomenon of local mate competition, first analyzed by Hamilton (1967), can also lead to female-biased sex ratios in haplodiploid species. Interpretation of a female-biased sex ratio is complicated by the fact that it is predicted by two competing theories (parent-offspring conflict and local mate competition).

For local mate competition to be responsible for the female-biased investment ratios collected by Trivers and Hare (1976), there must be on average more local mate competition among the social haplodiploids (with female biased investment ratios) than among the solitary haplodiploids (with 1:1 investment ratios). Unfortunately, there is currently no information on local mate competition for either group.

Another less global approach to the problem is to focus on an individual species, and try to determine whether its pattern of reproduction supports either theory. All studies to date have concentrated on one genus of social wasps, Polistes. The most detailed work is available on Polistes metricus (Metcalf 1975, MS; Metcalf & Whitt 1977). Through analysis of isozymes, it was determined that virtually no males were produced by the workers and that the average relatedness of sisters was 0.63 and of workers to males was 0.24. Thus the queen(s) are selected to prefer a 1:1 ratio of PI and the workers a 0.63/0.24 = 2.63 (female:male) ratio of PI. The observed ratio of PI was 1.07, which is not significantly different from 1.0 (fraction of female investment = 0.52, SE.=0.0140). PI was assumed to be proportional to adult dry weight (Trivers & Hare 1976). Female P. metricus were observed to nest near their parents' nest and no significant inbreeding was found. These data make it unlikely that local mate competition was occurring because it would have required related males to emigrate together for an appreciable distance, there to compete with each other for unrelated females. The observed ratio of PI is consistent with either no parent-offspring conflict or the queen's winning. Noonan (1978) has reported a 1:1 ratio of PI for the social wasp, Polistes fuscatas. She observed mixing of males from multiple nests at mating sites which would tend to reduce local mate competition. Metcalf (MS) has found for the social wasp, Polistes variatus, a sex ratio (female:male) 1.01 (x=0.503 SE.=0.0072). As with P. metricus the workers do not produce males and there is evidence against local mate competition.

Although the studies on P. variatus and P. fuscatus are incomplete they tend to agree with the observations for P. metricus and are thus consistent with either parental "winning" or a lack of parent-offspring conflict. However, in a recent study Metcalf and Finer (personal communication) have found a 2.5 (female:male) PI ratio (x=0.71 SE.=0.0046) for Polistes apachus. Data indicate that local mate competition is not occurring, leaving no existing theory other than parent-offspring conflict to explain this sex ratio.

Brood Reduction in Birds

A second promising method of testing parent-offspring conflict has just been suggested by O'Connor (1978). He has analyzed brood reduction in birds in terms of kin selection and coefficients of relationship. Several predictions from his model should eventually be testable using data from the field.

Traditionally brood reduction has been viewed as an adaptive response of the parents to adjust their brood size to the food levels prevailing during the nesting period (Lack 1954).

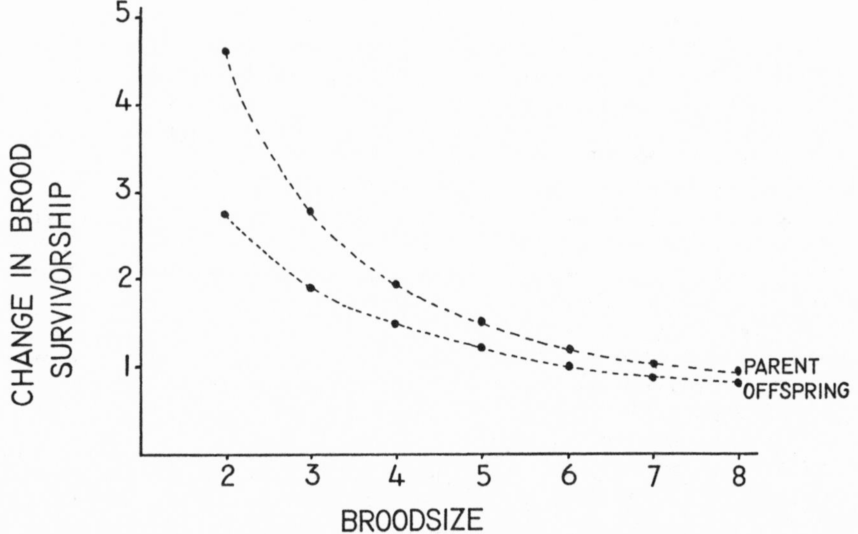

Figure 2. Taken from O'Connor (1978), Figure 2. If one offspring is eliminated, there is a change in brood survivorship. The threshold values of change of brood survivorship at which a parent or selfish offspring would favor eliminating an offspring are shown for different brood sizes. When brood sizes are large, parents and offspring approximately agree on the amount of change in brood survivorship necessary to justify eliminating another offspring. When brood sizes are small, parents and offspring tend to disagree about the sacrifice of the other offspring. © (Reprinted with permission of the publisher.)

When food is plentiful all of the offspring are raised; when food is scarce one nestling is selectively starved and dies, so that sufficient food is available for the survival of the remaining young. Hence brood reduction may be viewed as a strategy which increases parental reproductive success during periods of food shortage. The phenomenon of brood reduction has recently been discussed and analyzed by many authors (Ricklefs 1965; Hussell 1972; O'Connor 1973; Procter 1975). However, O'Connor's is the first analysis to suggest that brood reduction may be a result of parent-offspring conflict, and that selfish offspring may cause brood reduction to the detriment of their parent's reproductive success.

O'Connor's analysis assumes that the sacrifice of one offspring will reduce the food-related mortality of the surviving offspring. Since the parent is related equally to all of its offspring it will selectively starve one sibling only if the total number of surviving offspring is increased by this strategy. An offspring will value itself more than it will value a full sibling. Hence, in general, it will be more apt than the parent to sacrifice its sibling in times of moderate food shortage. In particular, O'Connor assumes that an offspring will sacrifice a sibling whenever its total inclusive fitness is increased, where its inclusive fitness is measured by the increase in the survivorship of the selfish offspring, plus the increased survivorship of the other surviving siblings multiplied by their coefficient of relationship to the selfish sibling, minus the loss in survivorship to the sacrificed sibling multiplied by its coefficient of relationship to the selfish sibling.

The critical point of this approach is that the parent's or offspring's assessment of when to sacrifice an offspring should depend on the typical brood size for the species. O'Connor generates a series of equations based on coefficients of relationship, and shows that both parents and offspring should be more apt to sacrifice one sibling when average brood sizes are large than when they are small. More important, when brood sizes are large, parents and offspring should approximately agree on when to sacrifice a sibling, but when brood sizes are small they are apt to disagree (Fig. 2). These conclusions have been verified using a genetic one-locus, two-allele model similar to those previously discussed for sequential and simultaneous offspring (Stamps, data). One advantage of the genetic model is that it offers an intuitive explanation of why parent and offspring interests diverge with small broods and converge with large broods.

Assume that the last offspring (the "victim") in a clutch of full siblings is smaller than the rest and may be

Table 3. In a clutch of nestlings, one individual (selfish) sacrifices its youngest sibling (victim). Distribution of benefit (b) and cost (c) for clutches of two different sizes are shown.

	Pariorder	Genotype	Survivorship
Clutch Size = 2	1st offspring (selfish)	Selfish	x + b
	2nd offspring (victim)	Selfish or nonselfish	x − c
Clutch Size = 4	1st offspring (selfish)	Selfish	x + b/3
	2nd offspring	Selfish or nonselfish	x + b/3
	3rd offspring	Selfish or nonselfish	x + b/3
	4th offspring (victim)	Selfish or nonselfish	x − c

killed by one of its siblings. If the clutch size is two, the selfish offspring that sacrifices the victim will obtain the benefit (b) and the cost (c) will be absorbed by the victim (Table 3). However, if the brood size is large, the benefit of sacrificing the victim will be distributed among <u>all</u> of the surviving offspring in the nest, the cost again being absorbed by the victim. The more offspring in the nest, the less benefit obtained by the selfish offspring as a result of its selfish act. The rest of the benefit is absorbed by the other surviving offspring, but each of these has only a .5 probability of sharing the selfish trait. The model shows that with more offspring, the ratio of benefit to cost must be higher if a selfish allele is to spread. At the limit, when there are an infinite number of offspring, one offspring will sacrifice its sibling only if $b > c$. At this point both parent and offspring are in total agreement, and there is no conflict.

These results lead to a number of interesting empirical tests of parent-offspring conflict based on brood size. In general, more manifestations of conflict are expected in species with small broods, where parent and offspring interests differ, than in species with large broods, where parent and offspring strategies substantially agree. For example, sibling rivalry and fratricide should be most apparent in species with small broods, while the death of selected offspring by parental neglect (e.g. by starvation) should be most apparent in species with large broods.

O'Connor's study is a distinct advance over previous theoretical literature, because he is careful to outline the field conditions under which conflict might be expected, and to provide specific predictions of the type of data needed to support the conflict theory. However, his paper glosses over two problems which should be kept in mind when designing empirical tests in the field. First, he tends to neglect the implications of parental counterstrategies on the expression of parent-offspring conflict. Second, he provides few tests to discriminate between the conflict model and alternate hypotheses which give the same predictions. Both problems are illustrated in the following example.

A number of species lay two eggs but raise only one offspring. Brood reduction occurs by fratricide, with one offspring killing the other, usually within a few days of hatching (e.g., hawks (Meyberg 1974; Skutch 1976; Steyn 1977), skuas (Doward 1962; Young 1963), cranes (Miller 1973)). O'Connor interprets this as an example of parent-offpring conflict: the fratricide has a higher inclusive fitness by eliminating its sibling than if it allowed it to survive, whereas the parent would have preferred to attempt to raise both offspring to adulthood.

One problem with this approach is that O'Connor stops short of considering parental counterstrategies when parents have fratricidal offspring. If early fratricide is the rule in a species and parents are unable to prevent it (often the attacks occur when the parents are absent), then one obvious parental strategy would be to lay a single egg instead of two. Parents would then save both the investment wasted on the second egg and the investment expended by the fratricidal offspring when dispatching its sibling. Yet even in species in which early fratricide has always been observed to occur, parents continue to lay two eggs (Doward 1962; Young 1963; Meyberg 1974; Steyn 1977). It is possible that the cost of laying and incubating an egg is negligible, or that these birds cannot readily change their clutch size, but neither explanation seems to fit previous data or theory (Lack 1954, 1968; Ricklefs 1965, 1968; Hussell 1972). Another possibility is that parents continue to lay an extra egg as insurance against inviability, loss, or damage. In any event, it is clear that conflict theory alone cannot explain why parents continue to lay two eggs when one offspring always seems to kill the other.

On the other hand, several workers have suggested that the insurance hypothesis can explain this phenomenon without invoking parent-offspring conflict (Doward 1962; Miller 1973; Meyberg 1974; Skutch 1976). They have proposed that brood reduction by fratricide actually works to increase parental fitness and reproductive success. The idea is that parents can only raise one offspring, but lay two eggs as insurance. If both eggs hatch then the parent leaves it up to the most vigorous offspring to kill its sibling. Skutch (1976) noted that fratricide is most prevalent among predatory species, the offspring of which possess both the weapons and the behavior patterns necessary to make a quick and efficient kill.

O'Connor suggests no way to discriminate between two hypotheses for fratricide. The insurance hypothesis and the parent-offspring conflict hypothesis differ chiefly in the matter of parental reproductive success, which will be reduced if fratricide occurs because of offspring selfishness, but increased if fratricide is a parental strategy to reduce the brood size to one. Hence one might discriminate between the two hypotheses by experimental manipulation of broods among species with fratricidal young. For example, it might be possible to prevent young from interacting by dividing the offspring with nest partitions. The number and weight of fledglings could be compared for normal nests (fratricidal young), nests with a reduced clutch (one egg) and nests with two nonconflicting young (separated siblings). This type of test would require large sample sizes and careful techniques (see Rice & Kenyon 1962; Nelson 1964), but would be necessary if parent-offspring models are to be adequately tested against alternate hypotheses.

While O'Connor emphasized conflict in avian species, a similar approach might prove rewarding in mammals. Simultaneous sibling aggression and rivalry have been reported in several species, the most notable example being pigs, which fight for preferred teats and wound each other with their sharp teeth (McBride 1973; Fraser 1975). The production of a "runt of the litter" is a well-known phenomenon in mammals; Dawkins (1976) suggested that it might represent a parental strategy to channel offspring competition onto one, less viable, victim.

The general impression from the literature is that brood reduction by starvation or fratricide is less frequent in mammals than in birds, but this may be due to sampling error. Most mammals with multiple simultaneous offspring keep their litters sequestered in protected locations not easily found or monitored by observers. Species with easily observed offspring often have only one offspring at a time (e.g., bats, seals, primates or ungulates). In contrast, birds' nests are easily accessible and the progress of nestlings can be readily followed from egg-laying to fledging. There are numerous captive studies of mammalian parental behavior, but usually mammals are provided with food ad libidum, so that the effects of food shortage on offspring conflict with starvation are unknown.

Small mammals, especially rodents, are more conveniently studied in captivity than birds. The available literature suggests that litter reduction, starvation, and sibling rivalry as a function of food shortage and litter size would be relatively simple to measure by appropriate laboratory experiments using rodents (Priestnall 1972; Grota 1973; Smith & McManus 1975). The variables and assumptions of O'Connor's model could be more precisely measured in the laboratory than in the field. If the conflict models are to have general applicability they should also apply to mammals. Appropriate, well controlled experiments with mammals should provide valuable evidence on the existence or nature of parent-offspring conflict among the vertebrates.

Parent-Offspring Conflict Versus Altruism

Parent-offspring conflict is the "flip side" of altruism. Instead of accounting for the evolution of traits for helping relatives at the expense of the actor, the theory of parent-offspring conflict attempts to account for the evolution of traits in the offspring for hurting close relatives (parents and siblings). However, the history of the study of parent-offspring conflict differs from that of altruism in several important respects.

Hamilton's ideas on altruism (e.g. Hamilton 1964, 1972) were at least partly stimulated by the extensive discussion of altruistic behavior in the early sixties (see Wynne-Edwards 1962, for another approach to the problem). In contrast, there was much less information available on parent-offspring antagonism when Trivers (1974) presented his model. The two animal systems discussed here to test conflict in the field (social insects, brood reduction in birds) were both presented subsequent to and in response to Trivers' paper.

Another point of difference is the extent of the controversy over the implications of the theories. The critical point is that whereas altruism would increase the reproductive success of the altruistic individual, a selfish act perpetrated on a parent or a sibling would decrease the reproductive success of the selfish individual. There was no theoretical objection to the possibility that altruistic alleles might spread in a population. But as long as individuals were considered the unit of natural selection then the spread of selfish alleles remained problematical. The theoretical models of conflict, however, have indicated that alleles for selfish behavior can spread to fixation despite the fact that they would decrease the reproductive success of the selfish individuals, and hence r and K for the population as a whole. These results have implications far beyond the study of parent-offspring conflict, since they suggest that selection may operate on the level of genes or gene complexes rather than individuals.

The subject of parent-offspring conflict was raised ten years after Hamilton's discussion of altruism, so it is natural that there should be less empirical evidence for the former theory. Yet it has been five years since Trivers' paper, and there is still no compelling evidence on the subject. In part this is due to difficulties with the theory. As we have mentioned, the parameters of conflict are extremely difficult to measure in the field (e.g., PI or reproductive success). It may also have been unreasonable to expect field biologists to design empirical experiments when there was still serious controversy over whether conflict could ever occur in nature. A final point is that it was not until recently that the distinction between sequential and simultaneous conflict was appreciated; it should be much easier to test conflict when the affected siblings are contemporaries than when they are unborn offspring expected sometime in the parent's reproductive future.

There is one final difference between theories of altruism and those of parent-offspring conflict, one which may have influenced the course and tenor of research in the area. Altruism is, in human terms, more ethically acceptable than selfish behavior. It may be morally abhorrent to some that natural selection could favor behavior in which an offspring hurts a parent or hurts its sibling. Certainly, there has not been the furor over a kin-selection interpretation of the many examples of offspring helping their parents raise siblings (Skutch 1961, 1976; Brown 1974) as there has over a kin-selection interpretation of offspring sometimes hurting their parents and siblings.

While it is by no means clear that parent-offspring conflict does exist in nature, research on the problem should not be biased by the palatability of the theory of parent-offspring conflict. Conversely, empirical studies on altruistic behavior cannot afford to be biased by the moral implications of that theory. In particular, one would hope to find the same high standard of empirical proof required for either theory, and an open mind from both investigators and critics until the empirical studies have been completed.

Summary

Trivers (1974) presented a model of parent-offspring conflict based on the concepts of inclusive fitness and coefficients of relationship. Alexander (1974) raised serious theoretical objections to this model, suggesting that parent-offspring conflict could not exist because selfish offspring would have a decreased reproductive success as compared to nonselfish offspring. This problem was addressed by a series of independently derived mathematical models, which indicate that genes favoring selfish behavior in offspring could spread in populations, despite the fact that the spread of selfish traits would decrease the reproductive success of both parents and offspring. These results have general significance because they suggest that selection and evolution of social behavior may operate at the level of the gene rather than the level of the individual organism. With respect to parent-offspring conflict, the mathematical models remove the theoretical objections raised by Alexander, and indicate that parent-offspring conflict of the type envisioned by Trivers could exist in nature.

The mathematical models also indicate that the evolution of parent-offspring conflict may be a more complex process than was originally supposed. Many factors strongly influence the nature and extent of such conflict. These include the pattern of offspring production (offspring produced sequentially or simultaneously), the cost of performing a selfish behavior, and the efficiency of parental strategies to counteract the demands of offspring.

Disagreement between the predictions of several theories can be traced to differences in the interpretation of the meaning of coefficient of relationship (r). Genetic models suggest that r is best defined as the probability that a certain gene is shared with a relative through common descent, rather than as the proportion of genes shared between relatives through common descent.

Empirical testing of parent-offspring conflict is still in it infancy. One group of animals, the social insects, have attracted interest because their haplodiploid sex determination system leads to a number of nonintuitive predictions about parent-offspring conflict. Trivers and Hare (1976) analyzed conflict between workers and queens in the social _Hymenoptera_ and outlined two series of tests of the theory, one based on the frequency of eggs laid by workers and queens, and the second on the ratio of parental investment given to the male and female reproductives produced within a nest. Methods to test these predictions in the field have only recently been developed and, while suggestive, the empirical data are insufficient to state unequivocally that parent-offspring conflict exists in the social insects.

Interest in application of the theory to vertebrates is particularly acute, but only recently has a practical framework for empirical tests with this group been devised. O'Connor (1973, 1978) has presented a set of predictions based on the idea that brood reduction in birds is an example of parent-offspring conflict. His analysis suggests that conflict over the sacrifice of one offspring (a victim) in times of food shortage should occur between the parent and the other offspring in the nest. In particular, he predicts that more conflict will be seen in species that have small brood sizes than in those with large brood sizes. While there are several conceptual and methodological problems with this approach, it should eventually prove useful in testing parent-offspring conflict in vertebrates that demonstrate parental care.

Literature Cited

Alexander, R.D. 1974. The evolution of social behavior. Annual Review of Ecology and Systematics 5:325-383.

_______ & P.W. Sherman. 1977. Local mate competition and parental investment in social insects. Science 196:494-500.

Barash, D.P., W.G. Holmes & P.J. Green. 1978. Exact versus probabilistic coefficients of relationship: Some implications for sociobiology. American Naturalist 112:355-363.

Blick, J. 1977. Selection for traits which lower individual reproduction. Journal of Theoretical Biology 67:597-601.

Brown, J.L. 1974. Alternate routes of sociality in jays -- with a theory for the evolution of altruism and communal breeding. American Zoologist 14:63-80.

Charnov, E.L. 1978. Sex-ratio selection in eusocial hymenoptera. American Naturalist 112:317-326.

Crozier, R.H. 1973. Genetic differentiation between populations of the ant Aphaenogaster 'rudis' in the southeastern United States. Genetics 47:17-36.

Dawkins, R. 1976. The selfish gene. Oxford University Press, Oxford.

Doward, D.F. 1962. Comparative biology of the white booby and the brown booby Sula spp. at Ascension. Ibis 103b: 174-200.

Fagen, R.M. 1976. Three generation family conflict. Animal Behaviour 24:874-880.

Fisher, R.A. 1930. The genetical theory of natural selection. Clarendon Press, Oxford.

_______. 1958. The genetical theory of natural selection. 2nd revised edition. Dover, New York.

Fraser, D. 1975. The "teat order" of suckling pigs. II. Fighting during suckling and the effects of clipping the eye teeth. Journal of Agricultural Science 84:393-399.

Gadgil, M. & W.H. Bossert. 1970. Life historical consequences of natural selection. American Naturalist 104: 1-24.

Goodall, J. Van Lawick. 1973. The behavior of chimpanzees in their natural habitat. American Journal of Psychiatry 130:1-12.

Grota, L.J. 1973. Effects of litter size, age of young and parity on foster mother behavior in Rattus norvegicus. Animal Behaviour 21:78-82.

Hamilton, W.D. 1964. The genetical theory of social behavior (I and II). Journal of Theoretical Biology 7:1-16, 17-32.

_______. 1967. Extraordinary sex ratios. Science 156:477-488.

_______. 1972. Altruism and related phenomena, mainly in social insects. Annual Review of Ecology and Systematics 3:193-232.

Hussell, D.J. 1972. Factors affecting clutch size in Arctic passerines. Ecological Monographs 42:317-364.

Johnson, F.M., H.E. Schaffer, J.E. Gillespy & E.S. Rockwood. 1969. Isozyme genotype -- environmental relationships in natural populations of the harvester ant, Pogonomyrmex barbatus, from Texas. Biochemical Genetics 3:429-450.

Lack, D. 1954. The natural regulation of animal numbers. Oxford University Press, London.

_______. 1968. Ecological adaptations for breeding in birds. Methuen, London.

MacArthur, R.H. 1962. Some generalized theorems of natural selection. Proceedings of the National Academy of Science U.S.A. 48:1893-1897.

MacNair, M.R. & G.A. Parker. 1978. Models of parent-offspring conflict. II. Promiscuity. Animal Behaviour 26:111-123.

McBride, G. 1963. The "teat order" and communication in young pigs. Animal Behaviour 11:53-56.

Metcalf, R.A. 1975. The microevolution of social behavior in the social wasp Polistes fuscatus. Ph.D. Thesis, Harvard University, Cambridge, Massachusetts.

_______. MS. Sex ratios, ratios of parental investment and foundress-worker conflict for the social wasps Polistes metricus and Polistes variatus. Submitted.

_______ & G.S. Whitt. 1977. Intra-nest relatedness in the social wasp Polistes metricus — a genetic analysis. Journal of Behavioral Ecology and Sociobiology 2:339-352.

_______, J.A. Stamps & V.V. Krishnan. 1979. Parent-offspring conflict which is not limited by degree of kinship. Journal of Theoretical Biology 76:99-107.

Meyberg, B. 1974. Sibling aggression and mortality among nestling eagles. Ibis 116:224-228.

Miller, R.S. 1973. The brood size of cranes. Wilson Bulletin 85:436-441.

Nelson, J.B. 1964. Factors influencing clutch-size and chick growth in the North Atlantic gannett (Sula bassana). Ibis 106:63-77.

Noonan, M. 1978. Sex ratio of parental investment in colonies of the social wasp, Polistes fuscatus. Science 199:1354-1356.

O'Connor, R.J. 1973. Growth and metabolism in some insectivorous birds compared with a granivorous species. D. Phil. thesis, University of Oxford, Oxford.

______. 1978. Brood reduction in birds: Selection for fratricide, infanticide and suicide? Animal Behaviour 26:79-96.

Oster, G., I. Eshel & D. Cohen. 1977. Worker-queen conflict and the evolution of social insects. Theoretical Population Biology 12:114-136.

Parker, G.A. & M.R. MacNair. 1978. Models of parent-offspring conflict. I. Monogamy. Animal Behaviour 26:97-111.

Priestnall, R. 1972. Effects of litter size on the behavior of lactating female mice (Mus musculus). Animal Behaviour. 20:386-394.

Procter, D.L.C. 1975. The problem of chick loss in the South Polar skua Cataharacta maccormicki. Ibis 117:452-459.

Rice, D.W. & K.W. Kenyon. 1962. Breeding cycles and behavior of laysan and black-footed albatrosses. Auk 79:517-567.

Ricklefs, R.E. 1965. Brood reduction in the curve-billed thrasher. Condor 67:505-510.

______. 1968. On the limitation of brood size in passerine birds by the ability of adults to nourish their young. Proceedings of the National Academy of Science U.S.A. 61:847-851.

Russell, E.M. 1973. Mother-young relations and early behavioral development in the marsupials Macropus eugenii and Megaleia sufa. Zeitschrift für Tierpsychologie 33: 163-203.

Skutch, A.F. 1961. Helpers among birds. Condor 63:198-226.

______. 1976. Parent birds and their young. University of Texas Press, Austin.

Smith, B.W. & J.J. McManus. 1975. The effects of litter size on the bioenergetics and water requirements of lactating Mus musculus. Comparative Biochemistry and Physiology (A) 51:111-115.

Stamps, J.A., R.A. Metcalf & V.V. Krishnan. 1978. A genetic analysis of parent-offspring conflict. Journal of Behavioral Ecology and Sociobiology 3:369-392.

Steyn, P. 1977. The tawny eagle in South Africa. Ostrich 44:1-22.

Taber III, S. 1955. Sperm distribution in the spermathecae of multiple-mated queen honeybees. Journal of Economic Entomology 48:522-525.

Trivers, R.L. 1974. Parent-offspring conflict. American Zoologist 14:249-264.

_______ & G.H. Hare. 1976. Haplodiploidy and the evolution of the social insects. Science 191:249-262.

Wilson, E.O. 1971. The insect societies. Harvard University Press, Cambridge, Massachusetts.

Wynne-Edwards, V. 1962. Animal dispersion in relation to social behaviour. Oliver & Boyd, Edinburgh.

Young, E.C. 1963. The breeding behavior of the South Polar skua Catharacta maccormicki. Ibis 105:203-233.

Index

activity level
  heritability in mice, 275, 277, 279, 290-291
  sex-linked in humans, 387, 394
adaptation
  adaptiveness, 10, 11, 14-16, 26, 30, 34, 44-50, 108-111, 140, 153-155, 167-171, 338, 387, 405, 558-560, 582
  social behavior, 35, 59-60, 62, 63, 127, 210, 235, 308, 331, 417-459, 549, 567
andrenogenital syndrome, 391-399
aggression, 12, 51, 54, 59, 60, 213, 218, 260, 261, 262, 281, 332, 335, 348, 388, 396, 400, 468, 479, 483-484, 494, 509, 515, 520
alarm call, 221, 339, 512-513, 521-524
albinism, 227-281
alcoholism, 313-315
altruism, 127, 319, 339, 372, 421-422, 471, 529, 589, 611-613
  reciprocal, 5, 6, 80, 92, 198-199, 350, 469, 545, 568
analogy, 10, 14, 51, 105-108, 175, 177, 260, 465, 480, 483
anisogamy, 6, 377-380
anthropology, 25-35, 137-139
  biological/physical, 26, 27, 30, 35, 62
  sociocultural, 26-27, 35, 45, 62, 308, 388, 405
  synthesis in, 33, 34, 62, 63, 325, 466, 469, 483
antiphonal singing, 231
assortative mating, 234-235, 287-288, 376, 381

behavior
  actual, 28, 52, 54, 56-57, 63, 310, 568-569
  adaptiveness, 137, 227, 308
  animal, 62-65, 104, 129, 467, 480, 482
  biological basis of, 12, 36, 80, 308
  diversity in, 50-57, 60, 62, 65, 137, 310, 338, 351-352, 405-406, 417
  economic, 423, 438, 453, 455, 471, 474-478
  genetic, 13, 40-41, 42, 44, 212, 262, 273, 290, 311, 417
  idealized, 29, 56-57, 65, 79, 104, 331, 332, 555-556, 560, 569
  intraspecies, 32-33, 63, 217, 509
  putative, 28-29, 54, 63
  selfish, 590, 596-598, 600

species-specific, 57, 83, 316
systems of, 10, 63
See also aggression; fitness; humans, behavior of; socialization
Birhor, 573, 576-577
brood reduction, 162, 169, 605-611

causal models, 103-104, 308
See also models
Centris pallida, 344
cognitive abilities, specific, 273, 287, 387, 397, 497
consanguinity, 318
distant, 547, 577
conspiracy of doves, 335
cost/benefit ratio, 8, 48, 55, 129, 131, 140, 381, 534, 590, 608
courtship, 212, 471
culture, 13-14, 26, 227, 243, 299
adaptation, 31, 43, 44, 137, 308, 417-418
disruption, 30
evolution of, 25, 27, 31, 308, 355-356
group selection and, 579-584
values, 48, 142, 263, 456, 489, 496-498
See also determinism; ecology, human; social transmission

damselfishes, 213-219
Darwinism, 4, 48, 49, 78, 83, 257, 358, 465, 484, 490-491
defense, *see* predators
demography, 8, 26, 35, 40, 62, 177, 323, 417-418, 422, 423, 429, 448-449, 530, 533, 536, 545, 555, 575, 579, 582-583
determinism, 98-99, 127, 139, 141, 143-144
cultural/social, 35, 81, 137, 545
ecological, 26-27, 29-32, 33-35, 36, 38-39, 40, 44-47, 52-53, 60, 62-63, 64-65, 127, 129
genetic, 3, 12-14, 33, 36, 38-39, 43, 78, 81, 261, 301-303, 331
See also culture; ecology, human; social transmission
developmental topography, 302
dialects, 231, 241, 244
digger wasp, 334-335, 337, 338, 342-344, 350, 352
discovery, *see* innovation
dispersal, 161, 197, 308, 351, 509-511, 530-531, 536
dominance, 12, 15, 51, 61, 81, 125, 263, 275, 281, 283, 285, 355, 387, 398
dungfly, 334, 340-341, 353, 357

ecology, 8-10, 53, 351, 372, 417-420, 438
feedback, 9-11, 15, 141
human, 11, 142
manipulation, 133, 141, 142
pressure, 308-309
See also culture, determinism
egalitarian society, 472-475
emballonurid bats, 191-196
epigenesis, 12, 14, 39, 41, 42, 64, 405
epomophorine bats, 199-203
Epomops franqueti, 200-203
essentialism, 83-90, 92
ethics, 16, 111-113, 141, 143, 144, 500
science and, 17, 62, 78, 480, 489, 496-498
sociobiology and, 97, 127, 141, 262, 479-482
ethnography, 28, 61, 422, 453, 457

actonic, 28-29
ethology, 11, 25, 26, 28-29, 209, 218, 406, 467-468
evolution, 25
biological, 29, 34, 258, 421, 466, 549
change in, 16, 42, 47, 50, 308
conceptual, 85-87
genetic, 8, 11, 308
models of, 308, 325
ongoing, 322
social, 87, 472
sociobiology and, 151, 308
synthetic, 325
theory of, 4, 8, 10, 12, 100-101, 308, 482, 490, 497, 500, 545
variability and, 491
See also genes
exclusivity, *see* range

female
defense, 165, 189, 193, 195, 196, 219, 513, 519
emotionality, 495-496
gentility, 494
inferiority, 490
perceptiveness, 495
traits, 387, 397, 490, 493-496, 499
fertility rates, 49, 161, 170, 324, 417-459
fetal hormones, 391-399, 403
fitness, 4, 8, 45-46, 283, 379, 545-569, 573-585
determinants, 110, 153, 309, 325
exemplar for, 9
inclusive, 5, 40, 47, 49, 55, 57-58, 260, 336, 417, 438, 455-459, 506, 534, 547, 556, 558, 560-569, 593
foraging, 343, 357, 358
See also hunter-gatherers
fratricide, 609-610

game theory, 8, 47-48, 332
scorpion game, 336
See also models
gender
differences, 489-493, 497-499
identity, 38, 391-393, 402
social bias, 81, 498, 499-500
See also sex
genes, 49-50, 102
changes in, 38, 42, 308, 325, 583
correlation, 4, 10, 12, 54, 277, 279, 311
intelligent, 47-49, 65, 312
population, 26, 35-36, 49, 62-63, 303
twin studies, 42, 290, 300, 311, 405
See also determinism; evolution
geographical determinism, 29
ground squirrel, 40, 52, 61, 505-537
groups
intimate, 52
size of, 51-53, 65, 163, 176, 178, 190, 195, 574
See also selection

handedness, 302
haplodiploidy, 5, 262, 601
health, 35, 45, 426, 434, 435
heredity, 38, 41, 42, 64, 273
heritability, 13, 262, 279, 300, 310-311
fertility, 288, 582
hermaphroditism, 151, 162, 170, 174, 178
heterosis, 283, 287, 291
home range, 165, 190, 195, 201-202. *See also* territoriality
homology, 10, 15, 51, 105-108, 260, 297, 399-400, 468
homosexuality, 401-403
humans
behavior of, 14, 25, 27-32,

41, 137, 229, 307, 469-470
comparisons with, 14-16, 33, 177, 243, 399
genetics of, 13, 288-289, 299, 312
social behavior of, 480
sociobiology and, 11, 267, 307, 322, 490, 498-499
uniqueness, 33, 40, 51, 62, 467
See also culture
hunter-gatherers, 60, 319, 471-474, 573. *See also* foraging
Hymenoptera, 5, 6, 601-605
hypothesis testing, 45, 61, 174-177, 179, 418, 421-459
Hypsignathus monstrosus, 200

ideas, exploitation of, 17, 97
ideology, of kinship, 545
See also kinship
imitation, 229-245
imprinting, 228, 230, 235
inbred strain, 275, 277, 283-287
inbreeding, 7, 318
coefficient of, 318, 547, 555, 558
incest taboo, 54, 57, 59, 298, 316-319, 563
infanticide, 54, 300, 323, 513, 521
innovation, 30-32, 34-35, 38, 41-42, 57, 60, 63, 83, 229, 230, 232
intelligence
population differences in, 42-43, 312
sex differences in, 393, 397, 491, 497, 499
invention, *see* innovation
investment, 48, 373-374
non-parent, 378, 553, 568
ratio, 378
See also parents, investment; paternal investment

isogamy, 377-380
iteroparity, 8, 169

just-so-story, 45, 64, 174, 258, 259, 260-264

kinship
classification, 56, 545, 550, 568
hunting groups, 575-576
matrilineal, 506, 507
recognition, 507, 524-526, 532-534, 536, 575
selection, 5, 6, 49, 55, 197, 351, 371, 438, 471, 505, 529, 545-569, 573-585
terms, 550
See also relatedness; selection
!Kung, 323, 573, 576-577

labeling, interpretation by, 60-61, 65
lactase deficiency, 314
language, 27, 33, 321, 468, 483
learning, 11, 16, 26, 155
observational, 238
prepared, 303
social, 38, 42-43, 131, 227-245, 315, 528
See also social transmission
lek, 190, 351
exploded, 135, 199-203
life histories, 151, 153, 159-163, 177, 178, 353, 507, 530-531
local enhancement, 229, 232, 235, 241

marriage rules
cross-cousin, 44, 46, 56, 58-59, 549, 555, 559, 563, 565
general, 57, 545
parallel-cousin, 46, 58-59
maternal instinct, 495-496
mating
behavior, 52, 165, 166, 389, 399

competition, 549-551, 555, 561, 567-569
selection, 58, 125, 135, 213-219
systems, 127, 135-136, 151, 163, 177, 178, 189-190, 317-319, 511, 555, 561
matrilocal population structure, 471, 509-511, 535
meiosis, 7, 371, 372-375, 378-381
menstruation, 391, 395, 495
mental evolution, 321, 493
mental retardation, 299, 491
methodology, 33-35
difficulties, 79, 174-177, 179, 388, 394-395
mice, 233, 241, 242, 273, 283, 285, 385, 387
models, 15, 47, 49, 135, 210, 308, 358, 591, 593-594, 597. *See also* causal models; game theory; strategies
monogamy, 6, 52, 135, 193, 195
Montagnais, 474
mortality rates, 57, 153, 157, 160, 161, 173, 309, 323, 417-459, 531, 533

natural selection, 4, 9, 48, 296, 308, 549, 589
challenges to, 257-267, 458
consistency as criterion, 419
optimization, 356-358, 456
See also kinship; selection
nature/nurture, 12, 38, 41, 100, 141, 307, 403
nepotism, 40, 438, 453, 455-456, 458, 505-537, 547, 550, 567-569

oogamy, 378
open-field behavior, 273-281, 290-291, 385, 399
optimal foraging, *see* foraging
outbreeding, 283, 285, 372-375, 381, 563, 566

parents
care, 135, 166, 167, 170-171, 173, 176, 213, 219, 229, 236, 243, 513, 521
investment, 7, 125, 161, 372, 373, 376, 378, 590-591, 593-595, 600
parent-offspring conflict, 7, 82, 125, 240, 350, 589-614
See also investment; paternal investment
parthenogenesis, 162, 372, 375, 376, 380-381
paternal investment, 165-166, 171, 173, 178, 213, 373, 378, 380-381, 470, 475, 483, 512. *See also* parents; investment
paternity, 283, 471, 549
Phyllostomus hastatus, 198-199
phylogenetic constraints, 53, 137, 172-174, 178-179, 259, 297
phylogenetic relationships, 10, 33, 40, 50-51, 63, 65, 297
Planck's principle, 86
plants, 40-51, 371, 467
play, 229, 238, 243, 297, 394
rough-and-tumble, 388, 400
political factors, *see* ethics
polyandry, 53, 54-55, 61, 171
polygamy, 135, 165, 166, 170
polygenic characters, 50, 277, 279, 290, 300, 312
polygyny, 6, 44, 52, 61, 65, 160, 165-167, 172, 173, 176, 178, 191, 511, 536, 551-552
population
control, 322-325
regulation, 6, 322, 325, 334, 418, 420, 422, 424, 435, 458

structure, 308, 547
predators, defense against, 130, 135, 213, 219, 221, 519
primates, 32-33
  nonhuman, 32-33, 50-51, 63, 233, 317, 403
  old world, 50-51, 296
protozoan perspective, 50
psychosexual differentiation, 385-407

range, exclusivity of, 165
  See also home range
reciprocity exchange, 555, 558, 568
recognition errors, 231, 526-528, 533
reductionism, 36-38, 63-65, 78-79, 91, 264-266
relatedness
  coefficient, 55, 56, 58, 373, 378, 549-550, 595, 598-600
  degree, 439, 506, 515-516, 518, 520-521, 530, 536, 547, 550, 577
  See also kinship
reproduction
  asexual, 377
  effort, 9, 159-161, 167, 169, 172, 174, 176, 178
  maximization, 323-325, 549, 560
  success, 9, 34, 38, 45-46, 55, 60, 167, 283, 422, 437-439, 449-453, 457, 547, 551-559, 561, 590-592, 600, 607, 610
  variation, 49, 324, 436, 547, 551, 552, 554
  woman's role in, 493, 498
resource, 9, 189
  acquisition and division, 127, 130, 133, 139, 156
  defense, 130-131, 133, 189, 192, 199
  limiting, 130
retaliator, 48, 337
rhesus monkeys, 317, 400
Rhynchonycteris naso, 194
rules, *see* behavior, idealized

Saccopteryx bilineata, 191-193, 194, 196
Saccopteryx leptura, 194, 195
science
  communities as invisible colleges, 80, 82-83, 92
  histories of, 89
  hypocrisy, 78, 90
  paradigms, 86, 490
  patron saints, 87-88, 92
  questions appropriate for, 77
  social bias and, 498-500
  socioeconomic factors, 81
  sociology of, 48, 62, 79-80, 82-83, 112, 257
selection, 33-34, 44-50, 49-50, 219
  group, 6, 34, 46, 64, 322, 338, 352-354, 418, 422, 424, 435, 456, 573, 579-584
  index of potential, 577
  individual, 6, 46, 49, 64, 125, 354, 420-422, 436-456, 573
  K-, 8, 159, 593
  kin, 49, 55, 125, 260, 372-375, 459, 550, 573, 589
  r-, 8, 159, 593
  replicator as unit, 353-354
  sexual, 135, 170, 172, 176, 244, 349, 437, 551
  See also groups; kinship; natural selection
semelparity, 9, 159, 169
sex
  allocation, 162-163, 170, 172, 174, 178, 347-348
  asymmetry, 12, 15
  behavior, 298, 299, 340, 389, 465, 482
  chromosomes, 59, 390, 391, 406
  cross-culturally, 471, 475-476, 484

differences, 385-407, 490-493, 496-497
dimorphism, 15, 52, 386, 400, 493, 509-511
ratio, 4, 161-162, 169-170, 172, 174, 178, 347-348, 374, 553, 603-605
roles, 470-479
See also gender
sexism, 263, 498
sibling rivalry, 7, 48, 609, 611
social facilitation, 130, 131, 229
social spacing patterns, 127
social transmission, 26, 30, 34, 37, 40, 46, 53, 62-64, 227-245, 315. *See also* culture; determinism; ethics; learning; teaching
socialization, 26, 32, 297, 479, 499-500. *See also* behavior
sociobiology, 3, 10, 11, 15-17, 25, 35-36, 142, 209, 262, 307, 322, 371, 465, 469
defined, 295
exemplars, 5, 93
Spermophilus beldingi, 506, 535
standardized social living units, 283, 285
strategies, 34
conditional, 4, 40, 341, 344-345
culturally stable (CSS), 40, 355-356
developmentally stable (DSS), 6, 40, 354-355
evolutionarily stable (ESS), 8, 40, 155, 219, 331-361
mixed, 40, 335, 341-344
survivorship, 46, 49, 420, 421, 429, 430-435, 448, 452, 531-532, 591, 595

teaching, 229, 237, 244
teleology, 104, 465, 480, 484, 582
territoriality, 59, 61, 77, 127, 131, 165, 190, 191, 193, 199-200, 213-215, 230, 233, 235, 317, 352, 513, 515
testicular-feminizing syndrome, 390-391
tool use, 232, 239-240
trade, 479
tradition, 13-14, 26, 33, 38, 43-44, 227, 231, 232, 240, 417-418
triads, *see* standardized social living units
Turner's syndrome, 299, 391-393, 395-396
type specimens, 36, 86, 87

values, *see* ethics
variability, 83-84, 154, 156-157, 308, 338, 492
vegetative reproduction, 377
village fissioning, 547-550, 568
vital rates, 418, 434, 439, 449, 452-453, 459

war of attrition, 340-342
wealth, 423, 425, 434-459
white-crowned sparrows, 219-224
Wynne-Edwards hypothesis, 322, 418-422, 424, 426, 429, 434, 458

Yąnamamö, 46, 56, 58, 298, 318, 457, 482-483, 545-569
Yomut Turkmen, 422-428, 435, 438, 452-453, 456, 459